Superbrands

AN INSIGHT INTO 100 OF BRITAIN'S STRONGEST BRANDS

This book is dedicated to Zoe, Talia, Jonah and Issy
– constant reminders of what life is really about.

Australia • Denmark • Holland • Ireland • Japan • Philippines • United Kingdom • USA

EDITOR-IN-CHIEF
Marcel Knobil

AUTHORS
Alex Benady
Greg Brooks
Simon Creasey
James Curtis
Jane Simms
Jennifer Whitehead
Bruce Whitehall
Victoria Young

SUB-EDITORS
Martin Benedyk
Paul Nolan

MANAGING EDITOR
Blair Hamilford

EDITOR
Angela Pumphrey

ART DIRECTOR
Adam Selwyn - Creative & Commercial

DESIGNER
Maya Twersky - Creative & Commercial

Special thanks to:
Bill Colegrave, Director; Richard Thomas, Director;
Annie Richardson, Brand Liaison Director and the
Superbrands organisation.

And Mintel for providing a considerable amount of
market research material.

For Superbrands publications dedicated to: Australia,
Denmark, Holland, Ireland, Philippines and USA email:
brands@superbrands.org or telephone 020 7267 8899.

For Superbrands publications dedicated to Business-to-
Business brands and to internet dedicated brands email:
brands@superbrands.org or telephone 020 7267 8899.

Printed in Italy

ISBN 0-9528153-6-2

Contents

Marcel Knobil

Chairperson, Superbrands Council
Founder, Superbrands organisation
Chairperson, Creative & Commercial

The Superbrands book is published by the Superbrands organisation – the independent arbiter and authority on branding. The organisation promotes the discipline of branding and pays tribute to exceptional brands.

The Superbrands organisation has previously published three books addressing consumer Superbrands in Britain and one dedicated to business-to-business brands. The organisation is also present in Australia, Denmark, Holland, Ireland, Philippines and the USA.

In the following pages of this book you will gain an insight into the majority of Britain's most admired brands.

The brands have been awarded Superbrand status by the Superbrands Council. The Council is made up of eminent figures from the world of branding. Each member has a deep appreciation of what makes a great brand and keeps the following definition top-of-mind:

'A Superbrand offers consumers significant emotional and/or physical advantages over its competitors which (consciously or sub-consciously) consumers want, recognise, and are willing to pay a premium for.'

Superbrands explores the history of these brands, observing how they have developed over the years and highlights their marketing, advertising and design achievements.

The Superbrands organisation has featured analysis of over 350 brands in its publications. It is no accident that by far the majority of these brands have: been built upon a high quality product or service; lived up to their promises; stood for something distinctive; generated considerable awareness; defined a clear personality and set of values; and consistently remained faithful to their brand principles.

There is, however, no simple formula for becoming and remaining a Superbrand. But, through evaluating many of the greatest Superbrands in Britain, numerous lessons can be learned.

The Superbrand Recipe

How to become a Superbrand
according to members of the Superbrands Council

John Ballington

Corporate & Consumer Affairs Director
Lever Brothers Ltd

Ask any aspiring Brand Manager to define a Superbrand and you will get a range of measures – scale, share of market, longevity, awareness, repeat purchase – even 'share of stomach' as consumers eat and graze on the run. Ask the same manager how to become a Superbrand and you will generate a sharp intake of breath and a request for a massive budget!

The simple truth is you cannot build a Superbrand just on big bucks. Without the sound foundations of basic brand husbandry, familiar to all marketeers, and some real creativity in motivating consumers to try and buy again and again, you can be a spectacular failure.

This year's crop of Superbrands illustrate the full spectrum of product, services and household brands that have passed the most critical test of consumer choice.

How did they become Superbrands? Because they have clarity of purpose in their relentless pursuit of satisfying their consumers, and the businesses behind them have invested their talent year after year in continuous improvement.

Quentin Bell

Founder
The Quentin Bell Foundation

I recently appeared on CNBC TV's 'The Entrepreneurs' in the august company of Venture Capitalists. What better way to assess Superbrands of the future, than from those able to judge which start-up to back? I said, sagely, that it is people, pure and simple, that determine the growth of Superbrands.

Yet:
– Having myself sat in on countless presentations, my judgement is that most people haven't thought through their offering, and have no unassailable proposition.
– Most have no flair. They lack the 'corporate charisma' that will differentiate them to ensure that staff queue up to work for them, shareholders invest – and consumers buy their brands to elevate them into Superbrands.
– Most don't demonstrate the personal courage 'to be famous', to create PR issues and beliefs that relate to their brands – and stand up for them in the media.

These three things will catapult you on the way.

David Mercer

Head of Design
BT

Brands if they are about anything are about people and how people use them to relate themselves as individuals to others and the world around them. In today's complex and interdependent world, brands are an ever more vital means by which people can find their place in society. Brands have in a sense evolved to become an extension of our egos, consumed to express an impression of who we are and what we stand for and thence convince our inner selves that we truly are who we would really like to be.

Superbrands therefore need to be like people; they need to be individual and unique, they need to be held in affection, they need to evolve, but retain their essential DNA, and they need to reach out and communicate. Superbrands fundamentally need to engage people's emotions and consciousness and evoke a feeling that they are indispensable or at least difficult to do without.

Easy really.

Michael Peters OBE

Managing Partner & Executive Creative Director
The Identica Partnership

When one thinks of the most successful brands, names like Coca-Cola, Virgin and Nike – icons of the twentieth century – automatically spring to mind. But what unites them all? They are all great ideas – unique, inspirational and innovative. Coca-Cola and Nike are both all-pervasive, consumed globally from Manchester to Melbourne, while Virgin continues to break new ground, conquering a multitude of sectors from airlines to financial services. However, Branson's empire must monitor its image carefully, as scrutiny grows.

Emotionally, creating inspiration and trust are also vital characteristics that must transcend any Superbrand. These attributes are reflected in the appeal to a variety of age segments and types of customers who buy into the experience and attitude of such brands each time.

Coca-Cola's dominance over the past century has much to do with evolution, and in today's multimedia age, the ability to evolve physically and digitally and be more dynamic will be a vital quality for any new Superbrand, such as Manchester United and Tiger Woods, along with unique, inspirational and attitudinal values.

Drayton Bird

Managing Director
The Drayton Bird Partnership

The man who built up one of the greatest brands (though not one of my favourite products) of the last century – McDonald's – had a favourite quotation. It was taken from something US president Calvin Coolidge said, and ended with the words "Persistence alone is omnipotent."
I believe great brands are built by those who persist most – and are most consistent. Fixity of purpose and determination are the keys. This will, incidentally, also apply to e-commerce, where the naive either believe, or have been conned into believing, either that a brand can be built quickly, or that they don't matter any more.
It takes years, not months; and they will always matter.

Stephen Factor

Chief Executive
NFO WorldGroup UK

Successful brands are invariably the product of 10% inspiration and 90% perspiration. Managing brands successfully is like running the marathon. Brand guardians need in-depth understanding of consumer needs, and must constantly manage and monitor all the dimensions of the brand to meet them. When it comes to Superbrands, the balance is probably more towards inspiration. Brands have personalities and Superbrands have huge personalities. Understanding the implicit, irrational aspects of brand personality is the key. Ensuring that all aspects of brand development are in harmony with its personality is perhaps the most important element of creating and maintaining a Superbrand.

Marcel Knobil

Chairperson, Superbrands Council
Founder, Superbrands organisation

Building tools: a fine product; exceptional design; powerful advertising; skilful public relations; and the right corporate culture.
Rules: stand for something distinctive; have a well defined personality; achieve high awareness amongst target audience; deliver against promises; and be consistent and enduring.
The additional magic: huge investment; the vision to identify, anticipate and capitalise upon a market trend; and inspiration.
These final two factors require a brave and talented brand guardian.
Flora spotted a future health trend to lower fat consumption. Perrier anticipated the coming of a designer style alternative to alcohol. Henry Ford spotted the potential of affordable cars. All saw a dynamic in their markets, went in early and defined the soon to be sector to their great enrichment.
Whether inspiration is in the form of a radical departure from traditional strategy or an exceptional creative manifestation of it – this can result in the 'catapulting' of the status of a brand. It takes a brave brand guardian, but the rewards are tremendous.

Chris Powell

Chief Executive
BMP DDB

Start with an insight and pursue it with tenacity.
Your insight must deliver a strong customer preference.
Your tenacity must be unreasonable enough to drive you through great obstacles.
If you succeed in this, your brand will be the template against which all other brands in the category are measured.

Tim Sutton

Chief Executive
Charles Barker BSMG Worldwide

The secret is to charm. When we meet someone at a party or any other social encounter what is it that makes us think they are charming? Certainly not because they talk tediously and endlessly about their wonderful achievements. No, rather it's because they end up, somehow, making us feel that we are more interesting than we thought we were. Good brands do the same: they make us feel that an aspect of our lives, however tiny or trivial it may be, is somehow more valuable, worthwhile and interesting than we thought it was. Something both tangible and intangible is added to us and to our self-perception.
And what is the difference between a 'good brand' and a 'Superbrand'? Longevity: the old charmers are the best. They understand that to impress is not about japes, tricks and gimmicks. It's about the consistent delivery of added worth.

Will Whitehorn

Corporate Affairs Director
Virgin Group

Brands come and go for a whole variety of reasons. BSB were bought by Sky and the de Lorean car company went bankrupt, the Nimslo camera did not work properly and Sinclair never got the financial backing that they deserved to become a Superbrand.
All that said, some brands transcend all the difficulties of entrepreneurship, corporate politics and fickle consumers to become real Superbrands that can stand the test of time. No one really knows why – catchy names are good but no guarantee of success. In the year 2000 Virgin looks like a natural but it didn't feel that way twenty years ago! On the other hand, Hoover and Biro were just people's names, which half a century later became the name of the whole product category.
If a catchy name alone won't work, some combination of the following will: good products, great marketing, superb customer service, healthy financial business plans, entrepreneurial vision and most of all determination in some of all the above going array at some point.

ABBEY NATIONAL®

Because life's complicated enough.

Market

The UK financial services market is a very fragmented one. There are 540 different banks, six of which are major clearing banks. These are Abbey National, Halifax, National Westminster, HSBC, Barclays and the merged Lloyds TSB. There is now also a number of former building societies in the sector including Halifax, Woolwich and Northern Rock.

Achievements

In 1989 Abbey National became the first building society to convert to banking status with the intention of becoming the outstanding financial services provider in the UK. In terms of assets, it has already become the fifth largest banking group in the UK and is ranked within the top 50 of the world's largest banks. Abbey National is currently the second largest mortgage lender in the country, helping more than two million people to buy their own homes, and has a relationship with one in three UK households.

Since it was founded in 1944, Abbey National has enabled thousands of families in the UK to own their own homes and save for the future. One of Abbey National's chief achievements has been to combine the best of its building society heritage with its banking status.

Ian Harley, the Chief Executive of Abbey National plc, says: "Abbey National exists to help millions of people achieve financial security. Since conversion we have diversified away from our original role as a provider of mortgages and savings, to the extent that nearly 50% of income comes from non-traditional businesses such as life assurance, general insurance, unsecured lending and wholesale banking."

Since conversion in 1989, the Abbey National Group has acquired major operations in life assurance, personal finance and point of sale finance businesses among others, and has developed a strong wholesale banking arm.

The Abbey National Group also has a broad base of international operations, with subsidiary companies in Jersey, Gibraltar, Italy and France.

Abbey National's traditional businesses of mortgages and savings are still important and this area of the business has been enhanced through the development of telemarketing and e-banking, which offers retail customers access to their accounts via the internet and on digital television through Open..... Abbey National's e-banking service is the fruition of its 'bricks & clicks' strategy, which is designed to give customers choice about how they deal with the bank, whether over the telephone, at a cash machine, in a branch, or via e-commerce channels.

The Abbey National Group's separately branded e-bank cahoot went live in 2000, offering a competitively priced credit card and current account. cahoot has also forged links with a number of non-financial retail and service partners such as Blackstar (video), Boxman (CDs), Thomas Cook (travel) and Dell (computers) to offer its customers a range of lifestyle products and services.

Chairman Lord Tugendhat says: "We continue to use the Abbey National brand to develop personal financial services as well as to grow our other brands rapidly. This means we are far less dependent on our traditional mortgages and savings businesses than most of our competitors and better placed in other more rapidly expanding and higher margin sectors." He continues: "We also place a strong emphasis on retaining customers and on building their relationships with the company. Currently, over 2.7 million customers hold three or more accounts with us."

History

Abbey National was formed in 1944 following a merger between the London-based Abbey Road Building Society, founded in 1874, and the National Building Society, established in 1849. There was large scale public demand for housing in post-war Britain which Abbey National helped to meet with the provision of mortgages.

At first, Abbey National focused on savings accounts and mortgages, but during the 1960s and 1970s a wider range of financial services was gradually introduced. By 1989, when Abbey National was officially recognised as a bank by the Bank of England, it had 681 branches nationwide – a huge leap from 1960 when the building society had just 60 branches. By 2000 the bank had over 740 branches.

Abbey National's transition to plc status in 1989 was strongly supported by its members. Up to five million voted their approval in a secret ballot. Almost overnight, the total number of private shareholders in the UK rose from six million to 9.5 million. Today, the Abbey National Group has just over two million shareholders, of whom a large number have held shares since 1989. Abbey National's change to bank status also resulted in the formation of its wholesale banking arm, Abbey National Treasury Services plc.

Every leading brand has its legend and Abbey National is no exception – it enjoys a strong association with the fictional detective Sherlock Holmes. The company's London headquarters occupy 221b Baker Street – the home of Sherlock Holmes. Abbey House, as the head office is known, has received thousands of letters over the years from fans all over the world, addressed to Sherlock Holmes.

Abbey National employs a secretary on behalf of the great detective, informing interested parties that Sherlock Holmes has retired from the strains of detective work and now keeps bees in Surrey.

Product

Abbey National Retail offers a whole range of financial services, from banking services and mortgages to insurance and financial planning and acts as a 'one-stop-shop' for all its customers' financial needs through its network of branches, telephones, cash machines and e-banking.

Mortgages have always been the backbone of Abbey National's business. It is the second largest mortgage lender in the UK, assisting more than two million people to buy their homes. It offers an extensive range of different mortgages including fixed, capped and now Flexible Mortgages, which enable customers to stop, start and vary their payments. Advice on mortgages is available face to face in the branch or over the phone from Abbey National's financial planning advisors, who

www.abbeynational.co.uk

Bank Account subject to status.

are on hand to guide customers through a lifetime of financial needs.

Abbey National acquired Scottish Mutual in 1992. Although it continues to operate independently, it has helped Abbey National set up its own life assurance operation, Abbey National Life plc, which provides protection products, mortgage related products, savings and investments and pension plans using the Abbey National brand.

Abbey National Retail also offers a full range of banking services, including a bank account, credit card, savings accounts and a variety of loans to reflect different needs. Abbey National's bank account is user-friendly and pays out interest on accounts with balances of as little as £1.

The account also comes with an overdraft facility – an ideal way to bridge a gap or cover unexpected expenses. Other features include a 24-hour telephone banking service and AbbeyLink automated teller machines (ATMs) linked to over 28,000 cash machines and now e-banking.

Abbey National has added to its range of saving and investment accounts for people with anything from £1 to £2 million to invest. These accounts range from instant access through a range of fixed rate bonds to ISAs and other stockmarket-linked products.

Recent Developments

In 2000 Abbey National Retail entered the e-commerce world with the launch of its e-banking service. This offers customers access to their accounts via the internet and digital television through Open...., making Abbey National the first bank in the world to offer interactive e-banking services on both the internet and digital television. During 2000 e-banking through digital television was further expanded to encompass NTL, ONdigital and Telewest and is also available through WAP mobile phones.

Promotion

Abbey National repositioned its brand in December 1997 following extensive consumer and staff research. The vision is 'to make our customers lives easier', by delivering products and services in a straightforward, unstuffy, astute, friendly and 'can-do' manner that suits individual needs. This is encapsulated in the strapline 'because life's complicated enough'. The tangible demonstrations of this are fair banking, flexible products, use of jargon-free, plain English and a choice of channels to suit the individual – branch, telephone, cash machines or e-banking.

Since the brand repositioning, a successful television advertising campaign featuring comedian Alan Davies in a number of humorous situations has been used. The television advertising is complemented with press, radio and cinema activity supporting specific initiatives.

1997 saw the launch of AbbeyVison, a satellite television station, in larger branches as well as a new look across all the bank's marketing material including press ads, posters, literature and direct mail. An additional satellite channel was also launched to improve

communications with branch staff.

In 1996, Abbey National was one of the first banks to establish an internet site (www.abbeynational.co.uk) and this is now one of the main distribution channels for retail e-banking.

Abbey National supports charitable organisations and projects focusing on housing issues, families in crisis and equal opportunities for disabled members of the community through the Abbey National Charitable Trust. Donations and community support now total in excess of £2.5 million annually.

Brand Values

Abbey National's positioning in the financial services market is typified by its mission statement which reflects the company's desire to blend the old with the new. Its intention is to "achieve above average growth in shareholder value over the long term, which can be achieved only if we meet the needs of our customers, our staff, and all the other stakeholders in the business."

This approach, combined with listening to and understanding its customers and staff is what 'because life's complicated enough' is all about.

Things you didn't know about
Abbey National

About one in seven mortgages in Britain is provided by Abbey National, making it the second largest mortgage lender in the UK.

Branch staff carry out around 98 million transactions for customers every year.

Abbey National owns several Eurostar trains, satellites and over thirty planes through its Wholesale Banking arm.

In November 1984, Abbey National became the first building society to offer a £100 cheque guarantee card.

In 1989, Abbey National became the first UK company to sell mortgages over the telephone.

During the 1989 ballot to decide Abbey National's conversion to plc status, there were three flights a day to Germany to pick up ballot boxes billeted at the British army bases.

For the past ten years Abbey National Treasury Services plc has been one of the largest issuers in the international bond markets and in July 2000 extended its lead in the securitised bond market with a £2.25 billion bond backed by mortgages – Europe's largest issue in this market.

Market

During the 1990s the UK sporting goods industry enjoyed a period of sustained growth. The market continues to be driven by two or three main brands plus a number of niche players although there continues to be market penetration by 'traditional' fashion brands into the field of sport.

SERGIO GARCIA

Within the UK, estimates show the sporting goods market commanded annual retail sales of £2.8 billion during 2000. It is anticipated that these levels will be maintained, albeit in a rapidly consolidating retail sector, during 2001 and 2002.

Another legacy from the 1990s is the interest shown in sports brands by the nations youth, where apparel and footwear are as likely to be worn in everyday life as on the sports field.

Achievements

After the 1980s, when the brand experienced several years of declining sales, adidas embarked on a strategy of improving the brand's image in the eyes of consumers. Robert Louis-Dreyfus, who became the owner of adidas in 1992, oversaw the development of this strategy, along with a review of all operating procedures.

With the newly rejuvenated image, improvements in production efficiency, turnover and market share followed to establish adidas as the market leader in sportswear apparel and the clear number two in sports footwear.

More recently, as the competition became increasingly fierce, it was necessary to defend this strong position through a sustained and significant marketing and communications programme. This investment placed adidas among the top spending brands in the consumer marketplace in the late 1990s.

This period also presented a different set of challenges. It became increasingly necessary to navigate a rapidly changing sports consuming market by targeting the wider youth segment

(along with the sports participants) through a number of tailored marketing initiatives. This allowed adidas to move into the new millennium in a position of strength relative to both sports competitors and emerging 'youth' brands.

The brand continues to focus on and believe in a 'performance' philosophy. Practically, this means supporting the best athletes, teams and competitions across the globe. With this in mind there are currently partnerships being built with the likes of David Beckham (football), Zinedine Zidane (football), Sergio Garcia (golf), Ato Bolden (athletics), The New Zealand All Blacks (rugby), Real Madrid (football) and the reigning World and European football champions, France.

The brand has, and will continue to have a long association with a number of sporting events. The 2000 Olympics in Sydney is the latest chapter in a rich history. This event also saw adidas supply sportswear to the British Olympic Association for the fifth time (since the event was held in Los Angeles 1984).

Football has been an important part of the adidas sporting calendar. 1998 saw adidas as an official sponsor of the World Cup in France and in June and July 2000 the brand was an official supplier to the European Football Championships that took place in the Benelux.

History

Adi Dassler, a cobbler from the village of Herzogenaurach, Bavaria, created the very first adidas sports shoe in 1920. From humble beginnings the adidas corporation expanded into a global company that has become synonymous with world sport. Many of the fundamental principles that the first shoes were built upon remain firmly rooted in the company philosophy today.

Dassler was an athlete as well as a shoemaker and applied his understanding to producing products for athletes that helped improve performance at the highest level of sports.

Dassler's efforts in the service of sport earned him more than 700 patents and other industrial property rights, many of them for

DWAIN CHAMBERS

revolutionary new products.

The company was, and remains today, committed to acting on athletes' requirements and learning from them to develop better performance footwear and apparel.

Today, the phrase 'listen, test, modify' which was first used by Dassler himself, remains the key to the company's research and development operation.

DAVID BECKHAM

Technical innovations included the world's first soccer shoe with screw-in spikes for track and field shoes. Since adidas equipped the first athletes at the Olympic Games in Amsterdam in 1928, over 800 world records and medals have been won by athletes using adidas footwear and apparel at Olympic Games and World Championships.

The company's obsession for making the best performance products for athletes remains central to the brand's philosophy today.

Product

Since the introduction of Dassler's first sports shoe in the 1920s, the adidas brand has expanded to such an extent that products are now available for almost every sport.

adidas designs both its apparel and footwear ranges with athletes' functional needs in mind. Design concepts begin with the athlete and as a result top competitors past and present confirm that adidas equipment always takes into account the latest developments in modern technology.

In preparation for the 2000 Sydney Olympics, adidas put its apparel and footwear through eighteen months of athlete track and laboratory testing to ensure the best possible performance under extremes of heat and humidity. This process paid rich dividends during the 1996 Atlanta Olympics when, after a similar development period, adidas athletes such as Steve Redgrave and Haile Gebreslassie (Ethiopia) achieved record breaking performances.

Recent Developments

The adidas Olympic range is the product of four years of research and testing using some of the world's best athletes. Energy maintenance is the aim with the resulting footwear and apparel being the most technologically advanced to date.

Swimming is at the forefront of the new technology in the form of the Equipment Bodysuit, originally pioneered with top swimmers Paul Palmer and Sue Rolph (Great Britain). The bodysuit was further refined during 2000 with the help of world beating swimmer Ian Thorpe (Australia). There are now stroke-specific Equipment Bodysuits to ensure maximum comfort and fit for those competing in all swimming disciplines.

Track & Field footwear has also been given the Equipment treatment. The Z-spike is a revolutionary new running spike. Shaped in a 'Z' form the spike grips the track rather than sinking into it. This reduces the drag effect of extracting the spike from the track, thereby saving valuable energy.

Other technological Track & Field advances include the Performance Plate. This feature, which lies in the soles of shoes helps replicate the speed benefits of metatarsal joint stiffness as found in cheetahs.

At Euro 2000 the world was introduced to the latest Predator football boot, Precision, as worn by David Beckham, Alessandro Del Piero, top scorer Patrick Kluivert and player of the tournament Zinedine Zidane. Once again, adidas worked with these top players to ensure that the next incarnation of the Predator boot fully enhanced their natural ability.

The new strategic placing of the Predator rubber zones on the metatarsal and medial areas of the boot give greater accuracy and power to passes and shots and can impart over 20% more swerve on a ball than a standard leather boot. The introduction of Exchangeable Traxion studs allows a player to customise the sole of the boot to differing pitch conditions.

As with its predecessors, the new boot is designed to fit the exact shape of the foot for exceptional comfort. This, coupled with the new technology, produces a product delivering even greater swerve, power and control.

The official ball used during the Euro Championships was also supplied by adidas. It is called the Equipment Silverstream.

TIM HENMAN

Promotion

adidas is continuing to acknowledge communication's pivotal role in the ongoing success of the brand. Furthermore, adidas is now committed to a totally integrated approach to all its marketing activity. This alignment will allow the brand to defend and grow its equity with confidence.

The most significant and public side to the set of activities is the high profile brand advertising (pictured below). Recently, a number of key

ADIDAS MAKES YOU BETTER

symbols and teams have featured in media rich campaigns targeted at both the sports and wider 'youth' audiences. adidas is committed to incorporating new and developing media into the mix, a strategy that has seen everything from giant 80 foot high billboards to the internet being utilised to connect with the adidas target audience.

Continuing sponsorship and support of some of the world's top athletes and teams has also helped adidas successfully position itself as the brand of choice in sport.

Finally, there is an extensive 'grassroots' sport program where adidas, along with some of the nation's best coaches, help athletes of all ages get the most they can from their sport.

The brand mission is quite simply to become the 'best sports brand in the world' and the leading performance brand in all competing sporting goods categories.

This is achieved by producing the highest quality performance products at marketplace prices. Products will continue to be designed and developed to enhance the performance of all sports participants, irrespective of their age, gender or ability.

Brand Values

The adidas brand positioning is clear and distinct. adidas has a genuine respect for sport and this is manifested in its obsession for making the best performance products for athletes.

EURO 2000 CHAMPIONS FRANCE

Market

Although the UK car market has remained largely static over the past few years, the prestige sector has expanded by over 50% since 1995, and now totals some 250,000 units. The prestige marques provide more discerning drivers with cars that measure up to their high expectations in terms of performance, luxury and status. The Alfa Romeo range competes in these sectors and, thanks to innovative, award-winning products, strong brand image and astute marketing activities, it has in recent years tripled sales to over 10,000 units a year. Alfa Romeo sales and market share are still on an upward trend, with further growth expected through new models.

Achievements

Translated into English, Alfa Romeo's slogan 'Cuore Sportivo' means 'The Sporting Heart.' While this goes some way to communicating the marque's motor racing credentials and love of performance cars, in Italian these two words mean much more – they encapsulate a philosophy and whole way of life that sum up the company's dedication to achieving excellence in all aspects of automotive manufacturing.

With a pedigree that goes back over 90 years to the dawn of the automobile, Alfa Romeo's list of achievements could fill several volumes of motoring history. In motor racing alone Alfa Romeo has won 86 Grand Prix, eleven Mille Miglias, five Le Mans 24-hour races, nine Targa Florios, two Formula One World Championships and two World Sportscar Championships. Plus, the British, German, Spanish and Italian Touring Car Championships in the 1990s.

Recently, Alfa Romeo's main achievements have been product-based, reflecting its pre-eminence in design and engineering. The current range has received numerous awards, among them: Autocar magazine naming the Alfa GTV 'Best Car' in 1995, Car magazine naming the Alfa Spider and GTV 'Best Designed Car', while its design engineer, Bruno Cena, was voted 'Engineer of the Year'.

Following on from these press accolades, when the Alfa 156 was launched it picked up over 30 major international awards, including the prestigious European 'Car of the Year' title in 1998. Sales of the Alfa 156 have exceeded all expectations and it is now one of Alfa Romeo's all-time best sellers. Excellence in engine design was also recognised with Alfa Romeo's all-alloy, 190 bhp 2.5 V6 unit being voted 'Engine of the Year 2000'.

History

At the turn of the last century, the horseless carriage obsessed many a young Italian engineer, and no more so than Giuseppe Merosi, who built the first ever Alfa in 1910 – a 24 horsepower model that could achieve a staggering – for those days – 62mph. An instant success with the Italians with their craving for fast cars, the 'Anonima Lombarda Fabbrica Automobili', or A.L.F.A. for short, entered the Targa Florio road race for the first time in 1911 and then began to compete in events all over Italy.

In those days, success in races meant successful sales figures too, so much so that by 1914 the company was producing over 350 hand-built cars a year. Even then it was clear that sales success was directly linked to technological innovation and engineering excellence – a philosophy that has guided the company ever since.

In 1915, industrialist and visionary Nicola Romeo took over A.L.F.A. and in 1918 added his name to the company title, thus creating 'Alfa Romeo.' In the 1920s he brought together engineering genius Vittorio Jano and motorsport maestro Enzo Ferrari to establish an unbeatable racing team. After many Grand Prix wins, plus carrying off the first ever World Championship in 1925, Alfa Romeo entered the Mille Miglia – the perfect event to show off a car's abilities on ordinary public roads. With eleven first and eleven second places, its Mille Miglia record stands unbeaten today. Alfa Romeo then went on to win more than 118 major events over the next six years, using just two basic cars, the P3 and the 8C 2300. Nearly all the motor racing superstars of the day drove for the Alfa team under the expert guidance of Enzo Ferrari; names like Antonio Ascari, Achille Varzi, and Tazio Nuvolari, whose exploits are legendary.

Over these decades, Alfa Romeo's engineering expertise and technological superiority on the racetrack were also being put to good use in its road-going cars. Working with the great coachbuilders and styling houses of the day like Touring, Zagato and Pininfarina, it forged a unique reputation for supercars with great performance, handling and luxury for affluent clients.

After the war, Alfa Romeo again turned its attention to Grand Prix racing, and in 1950 it won the first modern Formula One World Championship with Nino Farina behind the wheel of a Tipo 158. The next year, Juan Manuel Fangio achieved the double for Alfa Romeo in his Tipo 159. The 1960s and 1970s then saw a change of direction towards World GT and Sports Prototype Championships, with victories in 1975 and 1977. In the 1990s, Alfa Romeo concentrated on European touring car racing, where it met with great success.

Alfa Romeo's history is an integral part of motor racing history in the twentieth century: this is a company with a unique racing heritage and the reputation for building some of the finest cars ever created with flair, elegance and inimitable Italian 'brio.'

Part of the Fiat Group today, Alfa Romeo no longer targets the super-rich customer, but neither is it a mass-market brand. Today's models, like their predecessors, continue to inspire, excite and stir the spirit in the very best traditions of its 'Cuore Sportivo' philosophy.

Product

Throughout its 90 year existence, Alfa Romeo has not only been at the very front of engineering and technological development, but it has also been one of the world leaders of car design thanks to the team of accomplished designers at Alfa Romeo's Centro Stile design studio.

Take any current model and the marque's sporting heritage is immediately obvious. Starting with the badge at the front, located in its famous triangular shield, a V-shaped design theme flows backwards, producing a dynamic, forward thrusting image. Graceful lines, elegant contours and perfect proportions make a unique style statement about Alfa Romeo as a brand – warm, welcoming and passionate. Tradition is not just bodyskin deep though: it is also acknowledged inside, with the driver treated to a proper 'cockpit-like' feel. In the Alfa Spider, GTV, 156 and Sportwagon this is enhanced further with the main instruments being recessed in hooded binnacles and the secondary gauges angled in towards the driver, evoking the golden age of Alfa Romeo sports cars.

The current Alfa Romeo line-up comprises the Alfa 147 three and five-door hatchbacks, the mid-range Alfa 156 saloon, the Alfa 156 Sportwagon and its flagship, the luxurious Alfa 166, along with the Alfa GTV and Spider

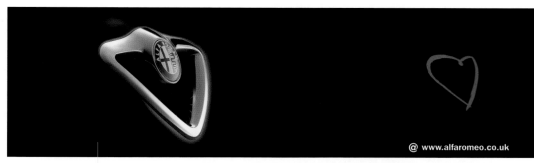

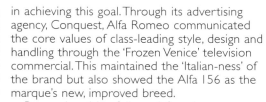

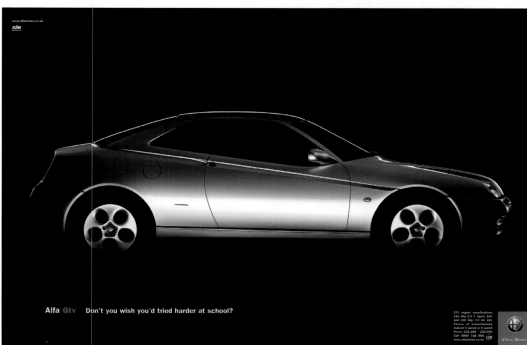

Alfa Gtv Don't you wish you'd tried harder at school?

in achieving this goal. Through its advertising agency, Conquest, Alfa Romeo communicated the core values of class-leading style, design and handling through the 'Frozen Venice' television commercial. This maintained the 'Italian-ness' of the brand but also showed the Alfa 156 as the marque's new, improved breed.

Press advertising followed, focusing on upmarket newspapers and magazines using premium site double-page colour spreads and outside back covers. The photographic images and text were used to underpin quality, build and safety. The executive-class Alfa 166 was launched in 1999 on television and in the press using the slogan 'It's all about confidence' – positioning it as an alternative choice for the discerning driver. The Alfa Romeo brand image has also been enhanced by poster and press advertising for the stunning Alfa GTV Coupé and Alfa Spider Convertible models.

During 2000, the famous Alfa Romeo grille shape was likened to a heart and used on posters to great effect. This campaign typifies a simple yet stylish, confident and impactful advertising style which has become an Alfa Romeo hallmark.

Brand Values

The year 2000 marked Alfa Romeo's 90th anniversary and with those nine decades of history comes a proud heritage of sporting performance, leading edge design, style, passion and inimitable Italian 'brio' – the values that shape the brand.

Alfa Romeo has established itself as one of the major prestige car manufacturers in the UK and has created an attraction for the marque by re-affirming its traditional core strengths. These strengths are original and distinctive design, a unique and rewarding driving experience through charismatic, high performance engine and superb handling dynamics, and levels of comfort, quality and reliability to match the market leaders.

Alfa Romeo is also committed to both active and passive safety features, which enable it to deliver the performance expectations of Alfa Romeo drivers, but in a safe, responsible way.

Alfa Romeo offers a range of cars which provide an exciting alternative to the established players in the prestige car market. An Alfa Romeo represents an independence of mind and a desire to challenge convention.

sportscars. Powered by state-of-the-art Twin Spark, V6 or Common Rail turbo diesel engines, their performance capabilities are highly developed and finely tuned suspension set-ups ensure excellent roadholding and handling.

Recent Developments

The significant increase in Alfa Romeo sales in recent years can be largely attributed to strategic decisions taken back in the mid 1990s to bring to the market the most stylish, desirable and uncompromising range of sporting saloons and hatchbacks – with the emphasis on 'sporting.' A highly successful product development programme has resulted in a model line-up that benefits from innovative and radical features. There is the super-quick steering rack found on most models – just 2.2 turns from lock to lock makes it the fastest steering rack of any production car. Unique Twin Spark engines deliver exceptional power plus incredible fuel economy thanks to the two spark plugs in each cylinder that burn fuel vapour more efficiently, while the revolutionary Common Rail JTD engine sets new standards for diesel engines in

power and smoothness. The Alfa 156 and Alfa 147 can be ordered with Selespeed push-button sequential transmission while the Alfa 156 is also available with the Q-system gearbox that offers the driver the choice of an automatic operation or clutchless manual changing. On top of that, all Alfa Romeos feature the latest in active and passive safety equipment.

Promotion

The renaissance of the Alfa Romeo brand in Great Britain has come about not only due to new and exciting models but also because of its effective and consistent marketing communications. For many years Alfa Romeo has been cherished by a devoted but relatively small band of enthusiasts. These 'Alfisti' love the cars for their sporting heritage, performance, handling – and distinctive engine noise.

However, to establish Alfa Romeo as a serious competitor amongst the prestige brands required more than just the cultivation of its Italian sporting heritage – it required mainstream credibility and appeal. The advertising campaign launch of the Alfa 156 in 1998 marked the first step

AmericanAirlines®

Market

The transatlantic airline market is the most competitive in the world. As well as two British contenders, British Airways and Virgin Atlantic, there are seven major US airlines operating flights between the US and the UK. In such a cluttered arena, it is difficult to create a brand that stands out from the crowd. American Airlines has achieved it by first defining and then focussing on its core attributes – the best loved aspects of American culture in terms of service, hospitality, quality and innovation.

Achievements

American Airlines operates the world's largest commercial airline fleet with more than 700 aircraft carrying around 85 million passengers a year. American Airlines has always been at the cutting edge of the airline industry setting new standards in customer service and product development. It is responsible for many industry firsts including the design of the DC-3 aircraft, the introduction of the first airline loyalty scheme – AADVANTAGE – and most recently has pushed back the boundaries of in-flight comfort for all classes on the aircraft.

The airline's achievements have been recognised in a number of prestigious awards. In 1999, American Airlines was awarded first prize as North America's leading airline at the sixth annual World Travel Awards ceremony. It has retained its number one position and won this accolade every year since the awards began in 1994. American Airlines' AA.com award-winning website was the first airline to qualify for the Better Business Bureaus' BBB OnLine privacy seal in 1999, a symbol identified by consumers as safeguarding online customer information and transactions.

History

American Airlines can trace its roots back more than 75 years. On April 15, 1926, the first regular scheduled flight of what would later become American Airlines took off with pioneer aviator Charles Lindbergh at the controls. Lindbergh, then chief pilot for Robertson Aircraft Corporation in Missouri, flew three planeloads of mail in a DH-4 biplane from St Louis to Chicago. It was one of the scores of companies that eventually consolidated to form the modern-day American Airlines. The consolidation began in 1929 when the Aviation Corporation was formed to acquire young aviation companies, including Robertson. In 1930, the Aviation Corporation's airline subsidiaries were incorporated into American Airways Inc and in 1934, American Airways became American Airlines Inc.

American Airlines' first transatlantic venture was through a subsidiary called American Overseas Airlines (AOA) who were heavily involved in the Berlin Airlift after the Second World War. American Airlines then went on to sell AOA to Pan American Airlines in 1950.

More than thirty years later American Airlines stepped into the void when Braniff International Airlines abruptly suspended service between London Gatwick and Dallas/Fort Worth.

On May 19, just five days after Braniff had shut down, an American Airlines Boeing 747 took off on schedule from Dallas carrying passengers and a supply of Texan cowboy hats to pass out to English VIPs on arrival at Gatwick, the first-ever transatlantic flight operated by American Airlines.

Since then American has spread its wings across Europe and now flies to thirteen European cities in eight countries including London Heathrow & Gatwick, Paris Charles De Gaulle, Frankfurt, Milan and Rome.

Product

The airline has built its success on the tradition of providing great service to all its passengers both in-flight and on the ground. It has constantly been at the forefront of innovation, setting new industry standards by introducing improvements to its product and service.

The most recent innovation is the Flagship Suite on its Boeing 777 aircraft. This unique first-class seat has completely revolutionised air travel. The seats swivel so companions can turn towards each other for meetings or to dine together. Two drop-down armrests allow easier access and a more spacious sleeping area, as the 21.5 inches wide seat becoming 30.5 inches wide when both armrests are dropped, and reclines 180 degrees to fully-flat six foot six inches bed.

American Airlines has also set a new standard in comfort for economy passengers. More Room In Economy is an extensive programme giving all passengers

travelling in American Airlines' economy cabins significantly more space. The airline has removed thousands of economy seats across its entire fleet of more than 700 jet aircraft creating more space for customers. In total, American Airlines removed more than 7,200 seats. Living space in economy has been expanded from the present industry standard of 31-32 inches to a level of 34-35 inches of space per seat.

Space between business class seats is also being expanded by approximately 20% to 60 inches, meaning a 10-12 inches increase in legroom. Complemented by a nearly flat recline of 150 degrees, the conversion offers business class passengers an exceptional level of comfort.

As well as space and comfort, American Airlines has also introduced advanced measures for the safety of passengers' health. All of American Airlines' aircraft carry automatic external defibrillators and enhanced medical kits to help deal with medical emergencies on board and was the first airline to install equipment of this type across its whole fleet.

American Airlines believes in being something special on the ground as well as in the air. It was the first airline to introduce a VIP lounge when it opened the first Admirals Club at New York's LaGuardia airport in 1939. Today the Admirals Clubs form a network of 51 airport lounges. Open to first and business class transatlantic travellers they offer a comfortable, quiet retreat

When American Airlines planned its business travel advertising campaign, executed through television ads and posters, it wanted to find out what British travellers loved most about America. The qualities chosen were 'their can-do attitude, wide open spaces, flexibility, technology and dedication to customer service'. The aim of this exercise was to incoporate these qualities into the American Airlines offer. The idea of the company being an ideal state was born – a state that flies at 35,000 feet.

away from the bustling airport terminal. Passengers benefit from office facilities, showers, and refreshments. American Airlines was also the first US carrier to introduce an arrivals lounge for passengers to use after a flight. American Airlines operates purpose-built arrivals lounges at London Heathrow and Paris Charles de Gaulle where passengers can grab a snack, shower, use the conference area or business facilities and even work out in a fully-equipped gym.

the main terminal. A team of dedicated Park Avenue agents are on hand to ensure a quick, calm and exclusive check-in.

Another recent airport development at London Heathrow is American Airlines' Flagship Lounge. One of four throughout American Airlines' worldwide network, the dedicated first class lounge provides first class travellers with an exclusive lounge equipped with telephones, fax machines, massage chairs, showers, televisions and refreshments.

The campaign line was developed and emerged as 'American Airlines. The American state at 35,000ft.' It comes from the airline that is committed to providing the very best of American service, hospitality, comfort and cuisine both in the air and on the ground.

As well as television and posters, the campaign line and proposition has reached the target market through multi-media. Posters, sponsorship of a London Underground passenger tunnel, radio competitions and even a game has been used to relay this message.

As well as a successful corporate brand campaign supported through an on-going public relations campaign, the individual routes are supported with targeted press ads. Direct mail works to promote the evolving offering that the AADVANTAGE presents to its millions of members, as well as bringing them up-to-date information on new routes, new technology and service.

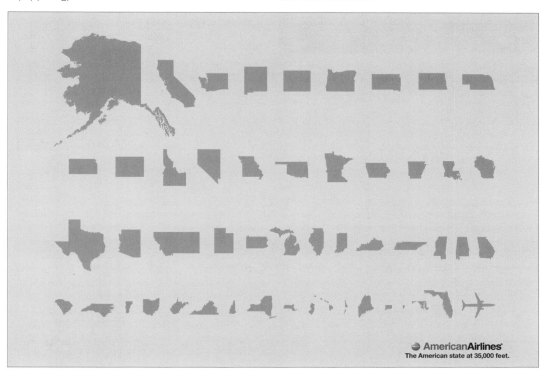

AmericanAirlines
The American state at 35,000 feet.

Brand Values

American Airlines is known for its commitment to all passengers – first, business and economy. Great service, excellent quality and comfort are key values to the airline and it is constantly striving to find new ways of making flying a pleasurable experience.

American Airlines set another industry first with the introduction of the AADVANTAGE travel awards programme. It is the largest of its kind and was designed to reward frequent flyers of American Airlines. Launched in 1981 with 283,000 members, it has now grown to more than 35 million members worldwide, claiming more than three million awards in 1999. AADVANTAGE members can earn mileage credit by flying with American Airlines, American Eagle and other airline participants. Members can also earn mileage credit from other AADVANTAGE programme participants including hotels and car hire companies.

The airline also operates one of the most successful industry websites. Its award winning website AA.Com, was launched in 1995 and is recognised as one of the largest e-commerce sites with more than five million hits each month. The website's ability to provide news, information and travel specials that are personalised to the user sets it apart from other online booking services.

Recent Developments

Park Avenue is a new concept in premium check-in facilities at London Heathrow. This purpose-built, drive-up check-in facility with its own car lane is situated opposite the existing Terminal 3 departures building at Heathrow and offers premium passengers a private, relaxed alternative check-in area, completely bypassing

American Airlines is also a pioneer of in-flight amenities and is the only airline to provide first and business class passengers with the exclusive acoustic noise-cancelling headset from Bose. Not only providing superior sound quality when watching films or listening to music, the headset also blocks out ambient noise on the plane. In addition, the airline is the first and only carrier in the industry to introduce personal DVD players to premium customers. Other inflight innovations include non-static blankets and inflight amenity Spa kits from Origins.

American Airlines was the first US airline to recognise the importance of offering daily transatlantic flights from UK regional airports such as Manchester, Birmingham and Glasgow.

American Airlines is the only airline to give more room to all its passengers with expanded seat pitch throughout the plane including an expansive 34-35" in the economy cabin.

American Airlines introduced the world's first airline loyalty programme in 1981 with AADVANTAGE.

American Airlines' engineers drew up the specifications for a new aircraft in the 1930s, the DC-3. It became one of the most famous commercial airplanes in history and American Airlines was the first airline to fly it on a commercial service.

American Airlines developed Sabre in 1964, the first computerised reservations system in airline history.

On an average day American Airlines 113,000 employees will receive more than 338,000 reservation calls, handle more than 293,000 pieces of luggage, serve more than 200,000 meals and snacks, fly more than 2,400 flights and change.

Market

To millions the world over, the words 'American Express' are synonymous with 'plastic money' or with Travellers Cheques, and, whilst it is true that many other financial institutions issue credit cards, American Express undoubtedly boasts one of the most prestigious brands.

Both credit cards and charge cards are fast replacing hard cash as increasing numbers of consumers recognise the convenience of carrying a card rather than large amounts of cash. In fact, American Express has over 46 million Cards in circulation worldwide. In 1999 alone $254.1 billion was spent using American Express plastic.

American Express now provides a full range of financial and travel products and services, to its customers around the world – ranging from its Credit Cards to Travellers Cheques, banking, financial planning and investment advice.

Achievements

American Express celebrated its 150th anniversary in 2000. American Express operates financial services businesses all around the globe and, as the world's largest travel company, it has continued to re-define the experience of international travel for both the leisure and business traveller.

American Express is a truly global brand, offering products and services in over 200 countries and employing some 88,000 staff worldwide. The classic Green American Express Card, first launched in 1958 and introduced to the UK in 1963, remains the most widely recognised charge card in the world. Over the decades the Card has evolved, and in 2000 the Green Card was given a fresh, contemporary, new look with new added benefits, to reflect its Cardmembers' changing aspirations and lifestyle requirements. It is American Express's commitment to constantly drive the brand forward over time to ensure it maintains its position as the world's leading provider of charge cards.

In 1999, American Express reported record net income of $2.48 billion, up 16% on the previous year. The UK credit card market is booming, and with an increasing number of players in the market offering cards, well known brands such as American Express are increasingly important in a crowded marketplace.

In 2000 American Express launched an innovative scheme to donate funds to the Arts with its Culture Card. Created in conjunction with Arts and Business, the card offers staff a discount at over fifteen cultural venues in the areas where American Express employees are based. It also provides financial support to participating venues through the American Express Foundation.

History

Founded by Henry G Wells, William G Fargo and John Butterfield in 1850, the business originally began life as an express freight company. Its origins date back to the opening up of the American Wild West when business

was driven by the need for safe and speedy transportation of goods, valuables, bullion and bank remittances.

During the 1860s as the US moved towards civil war, American Express transported vital supplies to Union army depots and undertook the high risk task of delivering election ballots to troops in the field. As a safer alternative to shipping large amounts of cash, the 'Money Order' was created in 1882.

In 1886, American Express established relationships with banks across Europe to allow immigrants to the US to transfer money to their families back home. Offices and agents were set up in Europe to collect accounts, sell consignments and deliver goods for merchants. The company also started to pay money by telegraph and sell small drafts or money orders which could be cashed at over 15,000 locations.

In 1891, American Express introduced the American Express Travellers Cheque – the first of its kind and automatically refundable if lost or stolen – which guaranteed that dollar cheques could be converted into a variety of currencies. In addition, American Express freight offices in England, Germany and France also began selling tickets for railroads and transatlantic ships and offering travel information and itineraries.

During World War I the American Express European offices helped 150,000 American Express tourists who were trapped in Europe to get home safely. At one of the company's most famous offices in Paris, people queued six deep to get funds, and in the areas worst affected by the war, locals traded with American Express cheques rather than their own currency.

After the war, American Express expanded its travel organisation and extended its international

financial operations to Latin America, Europe and the Far East. The business continued to grow after World War II, with the expansion of the international tourism business.

In 1963, American Express launched its first Green Charge Card in the UK and proved to be an immediate success. The Card not only provided Cardmembers with a flexible means of payment in outlets throughout the world, but conferred an immediate status on its holders – a mark of exclusivity that continues today. In 1970, the company launched the Corporate Card in response to growing demand from business executives who needed a tool that would allow ease of payment for business expenses worldwide. Today, American Express provides expense management tools to over 70% of Fortune Magazine's top 100 companies. Since the 1970s Amex has broadened both its financial and travel services, and in 1996 American Express introduced its first Credit Card in the UK.

Product

Operating in three core areas – travel, finance and consultancy – the company's main businesses are American Express Travel Related Services, American Express Financial Advisors and American Express Bank.

American Express Travel Related Services is by far the largest of the three and generates around half of all American Express profits. It operates American Express Card products as well as a worldwide network of American Express Travel Service and Representative Offices.

American Express Financial Advisors offer financial planning and investment advisory services to individuals and businesses in the US. The banking division has three parts – correspondent, commercial and private banking and consumer financial services.

Perhaps most famous for its Charge Card – which has no pre-set spending limit, and is available in Green, Gold, Platinum and 'by invitation only' Centurion, American Express offers a broad range of products, including Credit Cards, Insurance and Travellers Cheques. Charge Cardmembers can benefit from the award winning American Express Membership Rewards Programme.

Recent Developments

In 1999, American Express announced the launch of the world's most exclusive Charge Card – the Centurion Card. Designed for a select group of American Express's very best customers, the Centurion Card offers the ultimate in personal service, combined with a unique package of benefits unmatched by any other card in the world.

With the launch of the Centurion Card, American Express took personal service to a new level by giving its Cardmembers access to dedicated teams of experts in travel, entertainment and finance 24 hours, seven days a week, 365 days a year. The Card with the 'do anything personal service' has been well received by both Cardmembers and the

New **green** can get you tickets to selected shows.

To apply for the card, call 0800 700 767.

live entertained
live green

media as a unique offering.

American Express continues to lead the market by being a constant innovator, offering consumers tailored products designed to suit their individual needs. In 2000, the Green Charge Card, the cornerstone of the American Express brand, was given a fresh contemporary look. The new 'Live Green' strapline reflects the new travel and
entertainment benefits
which include: a £99
companion ticket when
Cardmembers purchase
an economy, business or first
class ticket to anywhere
in the Americas as well
as bump insurance, which
offers Cardmembers
immediate compensation
if they are denied boarding access due to their flight being overbooked. The Card's new entertainment advantage package offers exclusive ticket allocations, two for one offers and reductions on concert, theatre and sporting events.

Building on the success of its Charge Cards, American Express now also leads the credit card sector with its Blue, Green and Gold Credit Cards. In 2000, American Express launched version two of its successful Blue Card in the UK, which included several cutting edge benefits, comprising an Online Fraud Guarantee,
Refund Protection and
an Online Wallet.
The Online Fraud
Guarantee ensures that
Cardmembers will not
be held responsible
for any unauthorised
charges made with their
Card. American Express
Blue Cardmembers
were the first in the UK
to benefit from a Refund
Protection Promise
which covers them for
any goods they wish to
return within 90 days of
purchase, should any UK
retailer online or offline
refuse to do so.

The UK Blue Card which offers Cardmembers MoneyBack of 1% on all purchases has proved extremely successful and has contributed significantly to the growth of Card numbers in the UK. The Blue Card has attracted a younger group of consumers to the American Express franchise, broadening consumer perceptions and usage of the American Express brand beyond its core travel and entertainment expenditure.

Promotion

In 2000, an extensive television and print advertising campaign accompanied the launch of the new look Blue Card in the UK market. The television campaign centred around the
new card design, comprising
four hi-tech treatments set
to music ranging from Gary
Numan's 'Cars' to classical
pieces. Each execution used
a different modern image
– such as robotic arms – and
short, snappy straplines to
communicate the various
product benefits: MoneyBack;
Online Fraud Guarantee;
Refund Protection; Online Services and Payment Flexibility. The campaign continued to re-inforce the 'must-have' style credentials of the brand.

Over a number of years the company has been involved in a number of sponsorship deals. Since 1997, it has been the sole sponsor of the Alexander McQueen catwalk show at London Fashion Week and has collaborated with him on a number of projects including the launch of the American Express Gold Credit Card and the limited edition Blue Card – first designer credit card – one of which is now on permanent display at the Design
Museum in London.

In 2000, American Express extended its involvement and support for the fashion industry by pioneering a new award at the Graduate Fashion Week. Creating the first ever American Express Innovation Award, American Express extended its partnership with McQueen who judged the award and presented the prize to the winner.

Also in 2000, American Express announced the launch of a major integrated marketing campaign to support the evolution of its Green Charge Card. The 'contemporary feel' campaign used the strapline 'Live Green'

and combined a series of striking visuals by renowned photographer David Stewart and wordboards, to communicate the new travel, entertainment and security benefits. The campaign broadened the appeal of the card by highlighting its lifestyle advantages, demonstrating that it is more than just a payment tool.

Brand Values

American Express continues to enjoy an international reputation for prestige and excellence as a result of its commitment to constant innovation with a view to driving the brand forward over time. This innovative spirit that pioneered the original Charge Card in 1963, has seen American Express consistently develop ground-breaking products to suit consumer spending needs. Despite many imitators, American Express distinguishes itself in a competitive marketplace by combining first class products with superior customer service.

Market

Dairy products are an essential part of our everyday diet with ANCHOR providing great tasting butter, cheese and cream products.

ANCHOR was first launched in the UK in 1925 and by the late 1960s ANCHOR was the biggest selling butter brand in Britain – a position it has held for over 30 years with one in three households now using it. One reason for its long-standing success is that it is made with milk from free range cows.

With continuous growth and segmentation, the yellow fats market is currently valued at over £760 million, with butter and blends holding the largest value share (approximately 40%). ANCHOR butters have over a quarter (26.8%) share (£80 million per annum) within the butter-blends sector.

Achievements

ANCHOR is synonymous with innovation, being a leader in new product development and pioneering the development of major new segments. 1991 witnessed a groundbreaking launch with the introduction of the first ever spreadable butter, ANCHOR Spreadable. Using the latest butter blending techniques, ANCHOR was able to meet the increasing consumer demand but with all the taste of 100% pure butter. In 1998 ANCHOR took the dairy spread sector head on with ANCHOR SoSoft, the only dairy spread to contain real ANCHOR butter.

ANCHOR was also the first to introduce innovative added value promotions offering high quality premium items such as toast racks and mugs, and linking with a blockbuster family film 'Chicken Run' to offer branded merchandise on-pack. These promotions were designed to build loyalty, drive category value and reduce reliance on price promotion.

Last year witnessed the launch of ANCHOR Organic, the first major brand to enter the organic yellow fats sector, capitalising on the growing trend towards purchasing 'natural' products.

New Zealand Milk, manufacturer of the ANCHOR brand, has led the way in other key dairy sectors including cheddar cheese and aerosol cream categories. In 1982 ANCHOR launched the first branded aerosol cream and 1985 heralded the arrival of an award winning cheese – ANCHOR Cheddar, the first branded cheddar in the pre-pack cheese sector.

History

In 1886, Henry Reynolds, a Cornishman, emigrated to New Zealand and started butter-making. He built New Zealand's first butter factory and in the same year made the first churning.

At the Melbourne Exhibition in 1886, ANCHOR butter was awarded first prize encouraging Reynolds to extend the business further. Ten years later he sold his company and the brand name to the New Zealand Dairy Association. In succeeding years, other amalgamations took place and eventually the New Zealand Dairy Company was formed in 1919.

Still Britain's favourite butter.

In 1924 ANCHOR was launched in the UK, appearing as retail packet butter at the Empire Dairies Exhibition in Wembley. The first promotional activity took place on the stand where one pound butter cartons were sold with a free ANCHOR butter knife. This was followed in 1934 with the creation of the first ANCHOR brand loyalty scheme, the 'ANCHOR Club' – offering badges to members in exchange for wrappers, a monthly magazine and 'Uncle ANCHOR' birthday cards sent to members on their birthdays.

In 1936, success of the ANCHOR brand was growing, with turnover reaching over £5 million. That same year its first print and poster advertising appeared. The year also heralded the ANCHOR cow as brand ambassador with model cows utilised at point of sale.

In the post-war years, the ANCHOR brand grew extensively, with tonnage sales increasing by 52% year on year. In 1959 the ANCHOR logo was redesigned and for the first time a Consumer Guarantee was included on butter, offering a replacement pack to dissatisfied customers.

The 1960s were butter's Golden Age. Increased

national and personal financial security made butter accessible. Children of the 1960s were reared on butter, providing a powerful nostalgia base for the ANCHOR brand. The advent of commercial television offered a huge opportunity and in 1962 ANCHOR launched its first television advertising. In 1969, ANCHOR was crowned 'Britain's best selling butter'.

The 1970s saw the ANCHOR brand diversify into other areas with the launch of ANCHOR butter portion packs and ANCHOR cheddar.

In 1979 the New Zealand Dairy Board invested in a new packing plant in Swindon to handle the 75,000 tons of butter used by the UK annually, demonstrating a firm commitment to the local market. That same year the ANCHOR brand history dramatically changed with Empire Dairies changing its name to ANCHOR Foods Ltd – a sign of the intention to expand the business – and in 1979 the first packets of ANCHOR butter were produced.

In 1982, ANCHOR broadened its business beyond butter by launching ANCHOR Real Dairy Aerosol Cream. It was the first of its kind and still remains brand leader today. In 1983 Mature Cheddar, Vintage Cheddar and cheese catering portions joined the brand-leading and award winning ANCHOR Cheddar Cheese portfolio.

1980s consumers were driven by a national obsession with health. The yellow fats market was crowded by numerous brands claiming a variety of health benefits. ANCHOR Half Fat Butter was launched in packet form, providing the quality reassurance but answering the consumer need for a lower fat product.

In the 1990s butter fought back. As consumers became better informed and increasingly independently minded, they grew to believe a balanced approach to a diet was more beneficial to health and wellbeing. Aggressive Butter Council generic advertising was driven by ANCHOR and helped reintroduce butter back to the nation's diet.

In 1997, the ANCHOR brand relaunched focusing on its unique 'Free Range' proposition – producing the finest ANCHOR butter made from milk from free range cows reared on fresh green grass all year round.

In June 1999 ANCHOR Foods changed its name to New Zealand Milk (UK) Ltd to better reflect the global consumer business. The term 'New Zealand Milk' reflects the company's competitive advantage – the New Zealand climate provides possibly the best environment in the world for dairy products via year round grazing, and 'Milk', the basis of all its products.

Product

At the heart of the ANCHOR brand is a brand philosophy – The ANCHOR Way – which captures the belief that ANCHOR food tastes better because it is made the right way, not the cheapest, not the fastest, but the right way. With its universally recognisable logo and packaging, ANCHOR provides the best quality products, making the brand accessible and relevant to the breadth of consumer needs and lifestages.

Recent Developments

Millennium consumers are seeking authenticity, quality and natural food products and therefore butter, and specifically the purity of the way ANCHOR Butter is made, is enjoying a comeback. In the last ten years, New Zealand Milk has undertaken a huge investment in the ANCHOR brand, with aggressive communication support and added value drives, new product innovation and brand repositionings. The aim of which is to meet differing consumer needs, build effective relationships, and leverage the values of one of the UK's top grocery brands.

In the last five years the butter market has increased by more than £20 million, 45% of this increase being attributable to ANCHOR Packet Butter. 1999 witnessed the 75th anniversary of the nation's favourite butter with celebratory promotional support securing over 100% sales uplifts in key retailers.

That same year – capitalising on the growth in the organic food market – ANCHOR launched ANCHOR Organic. Available in a spreadable format, it is the only leading brand to date to enter the organic yellow fats sector.

In 1999 ANCHOR also increased its health credentials by reformulating ANCHOR Half Fat Spread with Low Cholesterol butter, broadening its appeal among 'butter mourners'. But it is not just about butter: in the UK Cheddar market, ANCHOR Cheddar is the clear market leader and this year a brand relaunch stimulated interest in the category and ensured that

ANCHOR Cheddars maintain their number one position.

The year 2000 saw significant developments for the ANCHOR aerosol cream range. The ANCHOR Swirls Real Dairy Cream launched two new flavoured variants, Chocolate and Strawberry followed by a groundbreaking new product launch – ANCHOR Tia Maria® Chocolate Cream: an entirely new brand partnership that clearly demonstrates ANCHOR's role as the driving force in the Aerosol Cream market.

2000 saw the £10 million ANCHOR relaunch, comprising a totally fresh communication strategy including new advertising and brand identities, providing recognition for the need to continuously build and keep pace with consumer and retailer demands. The new strapline campaign, 'ANCHOR – It's Second Nature', captures the essence of making food the best way – the right way – which comes naturally to ANCHOR. The new ANCHOR logo retains the strong brand association, while the 'ribbon' has evolved into the most striking visual of the ANCHOR equity – a rolling green field and nature scene featuring the ANCHOR cows.

Promotion

Television advertising has always been a major strength for the ANCHOR brand and over the decades consumers have responded to and enjoyed ANCHOR's quirky yet effective advertising – from hippies to dancing cows.

First introduced in 1936, the ANCHOR cows are one of the most instantly recognisable brand icons in the grocery trade and have gone through many transformations always seeking to symbolise the 'Free Range' message intrinsic to ANCHOR.

Building on the years of impactful and creative advertising, summer 2000 saw the launch of a new campaign incorporated within the strategy – ANCHOR – It's Second Nature. The campaign aims to capture ANCHOR's conviction that the best tasting food is made in a certain way, working with the best that nature has to offer.

COWS SHOULD EAT FRESH GRASS ALL YEAR ROUND

ANCHOR believe that the best tasting butter comes from cows that are fed on fresh green grass all year round.

COWS SHOULD EAT GRASS ALL YEAR ROUND

The television campaign, supported by press, posters and radio, communicates that ANCHOR tastes better because ANCHOR cows are free range and eat fresh grass in the open air all year round.

Brand Values

The ANCHOR brand equity embodies the current consumer agenda – ANCHOR is an authentic, warm and trusted brand with a strong heritage prided on its use of natural ingredients and flavour. Extensive research has identified that consumers believe in and actively seek out products that communicate that food tastes better when it is made the right way.

Market

Toilet tissue may not seem a particularly glamorous product but it is undoubtedly an essential household purchase, with penetration more or less static across all ages, socio-economic grade and household size in the UK. Consumers spend £767 million on toilet tissue each year, much more than any other North European country (Source: ACNielsen 2000). It is often used for 'secondary' functions such as make-up removal and nose-blowing due to the UK tissue being generally softer than anywhere else. As all products have improved, becoming softer, more absorbent and offering better wet strength, toilet tissue has become more universally suitable and less restricted to the main purpose for which it is purchased. This has heightened competition in both the toilet tissue and facial tissue markets in addition to the increasing number of players in these markets.

Some 99% of the UK market favours soft toilet tissue, with 46% of the market favouring coloured toilet tissue, as consumers still find it important to match their toilet tissue with the décor of their bathroom. This use of coloured toilet tissue shows a huge increase on 1957 when it accounted for just 25% of the total market. In the 1950s the product was sold mainly through chemists; today however it achieves nearly 90% of its sales through major grocery multiples (Source: ACNielsen 2000).

When consumers were asked to what they would be most likely to look for in a toilet tissue, softness emerged the most important factor, followed by strength and value for money.

Achievements

Andrex® has been the market leader in the toilet tissue market for over 39 years and has consequently become a household name due mainly to high-profile advertising. The Andrex® puppy has won the hearts of the nation since 1972 and is famous for being the longest-running consistent television advertising campaign in the UK. The puppy has appeared in over 100 commercials and celebrated its 25th anniversary in 1997.

Andrex® achieved the number five position in Checkout Magazine's top 100 UK grocery brand list in December 1999. In this feature Andrex® was ahead of such brands as Ariel, Pampers and Robinsons and was valued at £219.8 million, a figure which was beaten only by Coca-Cola, Walkers Snack Foods, Nescafé and Persil (Source: ACNielsen August 1999). In Interbrand's The Biggest Brands 2000 report, Andrex® was rated as the seventh biggest UK brand of 2000.

In 1992, Andrex® successfully launched a moist toilet tissue variant which contributed to a 45% growth in the moist category during its launch year. Andrex® Moist toilet tissue has been brand leader since 1993 and enjoys a 57% value share within the moist category (Source: ACNielsen June 2000).

History

Andrex® was developed from a design for gentlemen's disposable handkerchiefs that were sold exclusively in Harrods, London's famous department store. The tissue took its name, however from St Andrew's Mill in Walthamstow where it was first produced in 1942. Before soft toilet tissue such as Andrex® was introduced, the market consisted of much harsher products often known as 'shinies', which were sold mainly through chemists – famous brands included Bronco and Izal. Andrex® was endorsed by Hollywood film stars of the day who demanded that studios stock softer toilet tissue rather than the ubiquitous 'shinies'. By 1961 the brand achieved market leadership, a position it has retained ever since.

The Andrex® range has been greatly extended in recent years. It can be purchased in a range of colours and pack sizes which have been continuously developed since 1957 when Andrex® launched its first colour variant, Magnolia. In 1966 a full range of coloured variants were introduced.

The famous Andrex® puppy commercials

were first screened in 1972. The original concept included a little girl running through her house trailing a roll of Andrex®. However, this was blocked by television regulators who believed it would encourage children to be wasteful. So the little girl was replaced by a playful Labrador puppy and the campaign went on to become one of the best-known commercials throughout the country.

In 1978 the manufacturers of Andrex® were awarded Royal Warrants of Appointment.

By 1991 over 81% of Andrex® sales were generated through multiple grocery outlets. A growing concern at this point was the increase in 'green' products made from recycled paper which then accounted for 20% of the market. Andrex® responded by informing consumers through its advertising that it was an environmentally aware brand and took part in a programme of planting new trees. In addition Andrex® mass production facilities converted to non-chlorine gas bleached pulps.

Product

Kimberly-Clark Ltd, the manufacturers of Andrex® toilet tissue is committed to maintaining its number one position in the marketplace. Development is continuously underway to improve product quality which is a priority due to the rising competition from retailers' own brand and other named brands. Andrex® was strengthened considerably by the 'New Feel' relaunch in 1996 when over 1.5 million consumers were re-introduced to the product, resulting in a rise in value of 7% (Source: ACNielsen 1996). This relaunch was then followed by the 'Softest Ever' relaunch in January 1999, driving a further 7% growth by the end of the year (Source: ACNielsen 1999).

Andrex® has maintained its reputation as one of the highest quality products on the market. There are six colours in the range and three standard pack sizes – two-roll, four-roll and nine-roll.

Andrex® Moist toilet tissues also share the key attributes of softness and strength which have made the parent brand so successful. They are enriched with natural aloe, are lightly moistened to cleanse and refresh, and are available in both tub and refill formats.

Recent Developments

In January 2000, an additional twenty sheets were added on to rolls of the toilet tissue to give consumers even better value for money. Every roll of Andrex® now has 300 sheets making it up to 50% longer than some of its competitors' rolls.

After 25 years of successful puppy advertising it was felt that a new approach was needed in order to re-establish the well-known brand icon. In 1999, Andrex® offered consumers the chance to apply for an exclusive Andrex® Bean Puppy.

More than one million buyers responded to the offer, helping to raise over £110,000 for the National Canine Defence League. It also reaffirmed amongst customers the popularity of the puppy. The promotion was awarded the ISP Grand Prix Award for the most successful promotion of 1999 and helped reassert the position of Andrex® as the UK's favourite toilet tissue brand .

The Andrex® puppy has also now found a kennel on the internet. Consumers can meet the puppy and play online games and collect tokens for merchandise at www.andrexpuppy.co.uk. The site has the younger visitor in mind and, in addition to the other activities available, gives visitors the opportunity to email comments in the 'bark back' section of the site.

www.andrexpuppy.co.uk

Promotion

The Andrex® puppy has become inextricably linked with the brand itself, symbolising the qualities of softness and strength that are at the core of the Andrex® brand.

The puppy has featured in 117 commercials to date, generally appearing in the family home but also with various other animals including an elephant and a giraffe. During filming, each puppy is used for only 10-15 minutes at a time. On average 12-18 puppies are used to shoot each commercial, with each puppy being between six and eight weeks old.

It was not until 1991 that the product was actually shown in the bathroom. The 'Little Boy' execution was one of the most successful in the history of Andrex® advertising and was voted as the favourite commercial of 1991 by the public. It is still recalled by consumers, despite the fact it has not been televised for over eight years.

As a brand icon the puppy is also used in a variety of other marketing and promotional devices. This has included calendars as well as a joint activity with Disney's 101 Dalmatians, and several soft toy promotions. In 1999 the Andrex® Puppy Appeal raised £110,000 for the National Canine Defence League which helped them care for over 11,000 dogs. To celebrate the 25th year of puppy advertising, Andrex® sponsored an appeal for the Guide Dogs for the Blind Association, raising £270,000 for the charity.

Market

This is the internet century and the industry is one of the most competitive, fast growing and fast-paced in the world. A few years ago, relatively few people had heard of the internet, let alone ISPs (Internet Service Providers), the companies that provide you with access to it. Yet today it's a very different story. The internet is big news and plays an important part in people's everyday lives. Indeed, when America Online Inc announced it was to join forces with the giant publisher Time Warner, it wasn't just something to read about on the business pages, it made front page news.

The industry is extremely fast-moving and

many ISPs have come and gone. Currently in the UK there are approximately 320 ISPs – but only the strongest will survive. The industry leaders will be those who focus on the consumer providing them with quality, convenient, easy-to-use services that are safe and reliable.

Achievements

From its first service launch in 1996, AOL UK, a division of AOL Europe, Europe's multinational leader in internet, online and e-commerce services, rapidly became the UK's leading interactive services company. AOL in the UK now has over one million members, while worldwide it enjoys a membership of more than 25 million.

AOL UK's unique and pioneering Social Inclusion Policy team – believed to be the only one of its type in Europe – focuses on extending the benefits of the online medium to those who would most benefit from access but are least likely to obtain this through traditional means. It is responsible for liaison with UK and European policymakers addressing 'Digital Divide' issues, and for the AOL UK Community

Investment programme, which supports a range of charities working with children at risk, people with disabilities and others. The AOL Schools programme which enables thousands of UK schools to get online, for the first time, with AOL.

Members of the AOL service in the UK are very loyal, and spend a lot of time within the content areas of the service, rather than on the internet at large. In fact, research has shown that for a six month period, AOL members spent an average of 162 minutes per month online (Source: Media Metrix, Jan-June 2000).

History

AOL UK was formed in late 1995 as a joint venture between America Online Inc, and Bertalsmann AG as a division of AOL Europe, the service first launched in 1996. AOL UK is committed to the same multiple-brand strategy successfully developed by AOL in the US through which it operates the leading AOL, CompuServe and Netscape Online services, as well as AOL Instant Messenger plus AOL and CompuServe portals, across the UK.

AOL is the service for the whole family, providing its members with interactive education, entertainment, financial and informative content while giving access to a global online community. CompuServe is aimed at the 'new professional' user offering specialised information, large scale databases, matchless forums and professional communication tools. Netscape Online, AOL UK's subscription-free online service, is targeted at the UK 'value' sector and provides pure, high performance internet access.

In early 1999 AOL UK began drawing public attention to a serious flaw at the heart of the emerging UK internet revolution. It was clear

that metered internet telephone rates, charged on a minute by minute basis by telecoms providers, unjustly penalised UK consumers and severely jeopardised the UK's future economic potential.

Local telephone call charges of up to £2.40 an hour at peak rates meant that average UK internet usage levels – time spent online – were just one-quarter of those in the US, where consumers pay a monthly flat-rate fee for unmetered internet access. AOL UK's dialogue with its members revealed serious concern about these per-minute costs. In an online poll of 11,000 members, 92% said that metered phone rates were the only barrier preventing them from spending more time online.

If UK consumers were to enjoy, without restriction, the most powerful medium yet invented – and if UK policymakers' e-commerce aspirations were to be realised – the organisation at the root of this charging structure, BT, needed to be persuaded to respond to calls for reform.

In November 1999, the first cracks in BT's position appeared. Having always insisted that unmetered internet access was not viable in the UK, BT announced its intention to launch what was to be the first variant of its proprietary 'Surftime' product. This offered unmetered internet access – but at a price twice that paid by

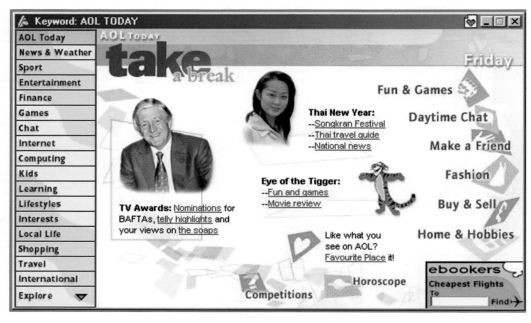

consumers in the US. The proposed offering by BT proved to be unworkable and was subsequently abandoned. AOL UK prepared to escalate its campaign.

In December 1999 the regulatory process was initiated by asking Oftel to require BT to provide unmetered services. As Oftel began to consider this complaint, other ISPs – including those who had initially refused to join AOL UK's campaign – attempted to launch unmetered offerings in the interim. However, these carried unsustainable levels of financial risk, as those companies were still obliged to pay per-minute charges to BT in order to provide connections for their customers.

The complaint before Oftel therefore became an issue of great urgency for the entire UK internet industry. Without a positive outcome, truly unmetered internet access would remain the preserve of consumers across the Atlantic.

The outcome was a complete vindication of all that AOL UK had fought for and signalled a victory for consumers, competition and common sense. In May 2000 the regulator forced BT to offer wholesale unmetered internet tariffs to its telecoms competitors – at a stroke creating the conditions for some of the most affordable flat-rate internet telephone access rates in the world.

Product

AOL is the largest subscription-based ISP in the UK and is looked upon as the ideal first step onto the internet for all the family. With unmatched value, ease-of-use and convenience the service features world-class content, a global community and family-friendly parental controls to ensure your children can go online in safety. Its leading edge infrastructure, AOL Instant Message to chat online in real-time, its own search engine AOL Search and unlimited freephone member support, all aim to ensure that AOL members enjoy their online experience. An AOL account provides up to seven screen names giving every member of the family access to seventeen channels of exclusive content, promotions, chatrooms and much more.

The typical AOL user is a family member who uses the internet for a range of reasons. Research has shown that over 50% of users connected to AOL for the fun and entertainment element of the net and a high percentage believed the net would help with family education.

www.aol.co.uk is the web portal for non-AOL subscribers. The site reaches a wide audience of internet users and gives the world a taste of the AOL service and what they can receive as an AOL member.

As part of its AOL Anywhere strategy, AOL Europe has announced a number of alliances with technology manufacturers and mobile network operators, to extend its world class content, community and hallmark ease of use to the mobile platform.

Recent Developments

In September 2000 AOL UK announced the rollout of AOL FLAT RATE, the UK's first genuine US-style flat-rate unmetered internet access service. Initially available to members only, by November it was to open to all UK consumers. Following the earlier failure of many other ISPs to provide such a service, AOL FLAT RATE was offered through a staged rollout to ensure a quality, reliable unmetered online experience to all users.

AOL FLAT RATE gives the consumer a world class service at a market-setting price that includes all access and telephone internet charges, providing true peace of mind for members who are now free from the tyranny of the online clock.

Promotion

In 1998 AOL UK maximised its consumer reach through the first mainstream television advertising campaign by an internet provider. The pioneering ads launched 'Connie the online genie,' who has become an instantly recognisable, interactive icon for the service and its members.

This advertising campaign has continued to promote AOL's image as a safe, family-oriented service, as well as offering specific packages and deals. Summer 2000 proved to be a pivotal time in AOL's marketing history, with the brand launching a number of innovative promotional efforts.

At the Live 2000 exhibition, AOL welcomed thousands of visitors to the 'AOL House', an exhibition covering 367 square metres. It comprised a kitchen, study, living room and kid's playroom, featuring four giant plasma screens

complete with 45 PCs, allowing visitors to discover why AOL is the world's leading interactive service. This followed soon after the redesign of the www.aol.co.uk portal, to ensure it was more convenient and easy for members to use.

Several joint initiatives were announced with leading UK 'bricks and mortar' retailers. The first of these was a strategic alliance with Carphone Warehouse in Mviva, the independent mobile internet portal. This saw AOL Europe take a 15% stake in Mviva, and its PC-based service promoted in more than 800 Carphone Warehouse and Phone House retail outlets across six European countries.

A joint marketing initiative was announced between AOL and Domino's Pizza, one of the UK's leading pizza delivery companies. It ensured that with every Domino's Pizza food order – either delivered or collected – customers would receive co-branded AOL software, offering a free 24 hour trial.

AOL Europe also linked-up with Wal-Mart Europe to cross-market services and brands and Wal-Mart's 240-strong chain of ASDA stores to become the first retailer to distribute the AOL FLAT RATE with completely free 50 hour trial software discs. Accompanied by AOL UK's achievements in successfully lobbying Oftel, these advertising and marketing activities have ensured the brands' consumer presence.

Brand Values

AOL is the UK's quality service for all the family offering up to seven email addresses. It is designed to be simple for anyone to use, whatever their age and whatever their level of technical (or non-technical) knowledge and prides itself on being convenient, easy to use and offering something for everyone.

All new version 5.0 for Windows & Mac
One month's Free Membership   Plus No Internet phone bill
AOL'S NEW INTERNET TRIAL
24 HOURS
COMPLETELY FREE!
*Your 24 free hours must be used within your first month online

Market

As the internet continues to explode, it is becoming harder for people to find useful, objective, information online. As a result, some of the strongest and best-known internet brands are those, which help people find what they are looking for – classically known as search engines.

Many of these search engines rely on a technology called Boolean logic, a system that allows commands to be mapped into bits and bytes, to match keywords with web addresses. But in itself, Boolean logic can be a complicated and frustrating experience for many users, particularly if they are new to the web, because it requires a skill to use the right combination of key words, mathematical symbols and punctuation marks to find things, and then there is no guarantee they will even be relevant.

Ask Jeeves UK (www.ask.co.uk), overcomes these problems because it allows users of any online skill level to ask questions in plain, natural English and they are directed to a web page with the relevant answer. The whole look and feel of the service is designed to be friendly and easy to use, literally humanising the internet experience.

Achievements

Since its launch on February 24th 2000, Ask Jeeves UK has achieved phenomenal success. By April, the service was among the top ten UK favourite websites and its name was among the best known on the web. Ask Jeeves UK now has a reputation as being one of the first places new users come to find what they want on the web, answering over 850,000 questions each day. This was borne out in September 2000 when readers of the UK's most widely read internet

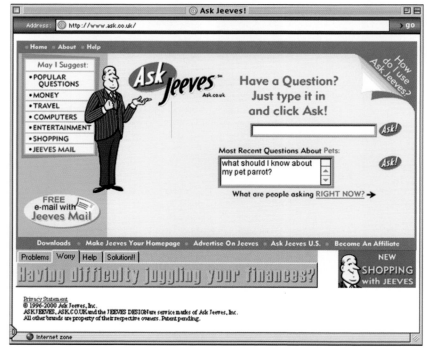

magazines voted Ask Jeeves as 'Best Portal' in the Future Publishing Internet Awards.

The brand's use of innovative, patented technology to facilitate searching for information on the web is another important achievement. Its unique natural-language question and answer approach to web searching is one of the most sophisticated internet technologies on the market, yet it is easy to use and is constantly helping to open up the net to new and inexperienced users.

History

Founded in 1996 in Emeryville, California, Ask Jeeves was the brainchild of Garrett Gruener, a venture capitalist and David Warthen, the creator of the Ask Jeeves natural language technology. In April 1997, www.askjeeves.com was launched, fast becoming the leading provider of question and answer services on the web. In 1998, it launched Ask Jeeves for Kids (www.ajkids.com) – a fun and child-friendly version of the original that allows kids to use the same natural-language approach but with added safety features.

Quickly, Ask Jeeves grew from a small enterprise to an international organisation. In February 2000, Ask Jeeves UK was launched (www.ask.co.uk) as a joint venture between Ask Jeeves International, Carlton Communications plc and Granada Media Group. Both these media giants became involved in Ask Jeeves UK to reinforce their commitment to exploring opportunities in new media and the company has become an important addition to their respective portfolios.

Ask Jeeves has since become the default search facility for users

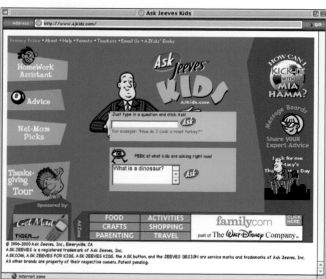

of ONnet, the interactive web service from ONdigital.

Product

Ask Jeeves is a question answering site for web users. It uses proprietary, award-winning, 'natural language' software that actually understands the questions people ask and directs them to the most relevant sites on the web to help them find an answer. Jeeves can answer questions as simple as 'Where can I find rail timetables?' and 'Where can I buy CDs online?', or he can really show off his knowledge with more complicated requests such as 'What was the biggest earthquake to ever hit the UK?' and 'Am I in love?'.

In order to find the most relevant answer in the most efficient way, Ask.co.uk uses a combination of web navigation methods. Firstly, sites are selected by a team of UK editors who apply strict quality controls to pick out only the best sites on the web to answer a user's question.

The second method involves Ask Jeeves' unique popularity-based technology, which automatically searches the web and tracks the most popular sites as defined by other users of these sites.

Finally Ask Jeeves also uses a 'meta-search' facility to see what relevant sites other search engines such as Lycos, Yahoo! and Alta Vista find to give the user the 'best of the rest' in one go.

Qualitative research regularly undertaken by Ask Jeeves has led to constant refinement of the site, such as introducing a 'new user guide' for first time users which takes people through the ask.co.uk site step by step, and making the 'Ask a question' box a central part of the site.

There are also other elements to the Ask

Jeeves product, such as Jeeves Mail. Launched in August 2000, this is a free e-mail and calendar service. Fast, easy to use, friendly interface and accessible anywhere in the world, Jeeves Mail is one of many services being introduced to support and add value to the Ask Jeeves brand and experience.

Another extension to the service is the Ask Jeeves Shopping Channel, launched in October 2000. Helpful, friendly and again very easy to use, the shopping channel offers twelve product categories to help users find just what they are looking for. If you want to do your grocery shopping online, just click on the Food and Drink section and Jeeves will take you to the best places to fill your virtual shopping trolley. If you are looking for an outfit for a special party or an accessory to wear to the office, simply click on Clothing and Fashion and Jeeves will take you to the best boutiques.

Ask Jeeves has signed up a number of exclusive partners including eBay, QM4 and DealTime, to provide users with more advanced shopping services such as an online auction, as well as requests for quote and price comparisons. For added reassurance, all sites selected in any

how to convert potential buyers into customers and encourage them to keep returning to the site. The reason most people fail to buy online is due to the fact that they cannot find what they are looking for and help is not immediately available. With Ask Jeeves for Business, large companies can now offer online visitors a similar helpful, friendly and welcoming experience to the one they have on the Ask.co.uk site. So in the same way, people can ask a question in plain, natural language to search a corporate website for the information they need to make a purchasing decision.

The benefits to companies that have deployed Humanise™ software on their corporate websites are many-fold. Firstly they can maximise sales by removing the barriers to purchase, making it easier for people to find what they want and buy online. Through self-help, they can automatically provide answers to people's questions there and then, thus reducing support costs and allowing service agents to focus on more complicated enquiries and upsell opportunities. And because the whole user experience has been vastly improved, companies can build their customer satisfaction and loyalty.

Promotion

With an initial marketing investment of £10 million, Ask Jeeves had a high profile launch in the UK across television, radio, press and online. This was executed through advertising and PR, including nationwide 'Butler Blasts' where actors dressed as butlers went out onto the streets, at train stations and at events such as Wimbledon to raise awareness of the brand and its associated values.

In October 2000, Ask Jeeves ran a week-long promotion with The Express newspaper to win a life of luxury worth £100,000.

Brand Values

The personality of the brand, embodied by the character Jeeves, has achieved fame across all media. Now almost a celebrity figure in his own right, Jeeves is the world's first internet butler and is instantly recognisable. Forever at your service, Jeeves is efficient, easy to use, reliable, friendly, intelligent, trustworthy and has become synonymous with helping you find what you are looking for on the web. In the world of e-business, Ask Jeeves stands for profitability and great customer service.

of the sections of the channel will have undergone a strict selection process to make sure that they offer the best possible shopping experience. For instance, Ask Jeeves editors check each site against criteria such as ease of use, security and customer care before allowing that site to be part of the Ask Jeeves Shopping Channel. For those users who are more concerned about security on the web, the channel also has a step-by-step guide with hints and tips to buying safely over the internet.

Recent Developments

In July 2000 Ask Jeeves announced a new division – Ask Jeeves for Business – with a proposition to take the Ask Jeeves software suite called Humanise™ to corporate website owners in the UK.

The challenge facing e-businesses today is

In another commercial development, Ask Jeeves introduced in September 2000 a revolutionary new advertising model that helps advertisers target their customers more accurately on the Ask.co.uk site. Dynamic Response Anchor Tenancies (DRATs) allows advertisers to effectively 'own' key words, so that their ad appears every time their keyword is included in a question. This delivers information about products and services directly to users who have already expressed an interest in that particular area. Not only has this proved to be a success with advertisers, but qualitative research also shows that Ask Jeeves users have recognised anchor tenancy as something that adds value to their overall experience of the site – by making it more relevant to the user. This is also borne out with the increased click-through rates that DRAT advertising attracts.

AVIS

Market

Avis is synonymous with vehicle rental. Alongside Hertz, Budget, Europcar and Sixt, it dominates the sector.

As the top rental company in Europe with 2,700 locations, Avis is the only one of the majors to rent cars in every European country. Overall, the European car rental market is worth nearly £3.3 billion annually.

Worldwide, Avis has 4,200 rental locations and a fleet of 370,000 vehicles in over 160 countries. Annually, it completes around sixteen million rental transactions, generating an annual gross revenue of approximately £1.7 billion.

This network helped to make Avis the brand that 75% of Europe's top 500 companies do business with. The company is constantly expanding its network to further improve service, mostly by granting licences to local franchises. This is a flexible and safe route for it to expand into more diverse territories, such as Africa, Asia and the Middle East.

Achievements

From humble beginnings at Detroit Airport, Avis has built itself into a world-leading brand. It is not only an instantly recognisable name to consumers and business users all over the world, but also market leader in Europe, Africa and the Middle East, with the largest fleet and widest choice.

The company has successfully pioneered car rental in several international markets, including Central and Eastern Europe, where it subsequently expanded its operations. It was the first car rental company to open an office in East Germany after the fall of the Berlin Wall – a move that helped it springboard into neighbouring former eastern bloc territories, such as the Czech Republic and Romania. It has achieved a similar goal in the former Soviet Union and, when it opened an office in the Ukraine in 1997, became the first and only car rental company to have an office in every European country. This gives it an unrivalled European network – including a presence at all 75 major European airports.

The company has been similarly pioneering in Africa, where it now has representation in over 85% of the region. Again, this has given it greater coverage than any of its competitors. In the Middle East it is represented in 90% of the region, and in Asia is licensed to operate in 27 territories.

Avis has been equally committed to high customer service levels since the mid 1960s and the introduction of the first computerised reservation system, Wizard, in 1972. It has also built one of the best partnership structures in the business, with 50 airline partners.

History

Warren Avis opened the first Avis office at Willow Run airport, Detroit, in 1946. At that time, he had a grand total of three cars, but it was the world's first ever car rental operation at an airport.

By 1953, Avis was the second largest car rental company in the US and already expanding overseas, opening franchised operations in Mexico, Canada and Europe. By 1963 it was struggling with a 10% US market share, compared to 75% for Hertz. It launched an advertising campaign that proved crucial in turning its fortunes around. The slogan 'We're only No.2. We try harder' emphasised its commitment to customer service and remains at the core of its brand today. The slogan has subsequently been recognised as one of the ten best of all time.

In 1965, Avis officially launched Avis Europe to look after its growing operations in Europe, Africa and the Middle East. By 1973, it was market leader in these areas – a position it still holds today.

In 1979, Avis entered worldwide advertising and marketing agreements with General Motors and began featuring GM cars in its fleet

The idea behind Avis Preferred service.

No queues, no paperwork, no problem. More time for your business trip.

Ask at the desk for details.

AVIS We try harder.

Avis recommends Vauxhall cars

worldwide. In 1986, Avis Europe legally separated from its owner, Avis Inc, and became the first ever car rental company to float on the London Stock Exchange. In three years, it tripled its market value before reverting to private ownership again in 1989.

In 1987, Avis Inc became employee-owned, with a £1.2 billion Employee Stock Ownership Plan – making it the largest employee owned company in the US and a role model for other companies to follow.

In 1996, the company's impressive technological track record continued, when it became the first car rental company to launch a website – www.avis.com. The following year, Avis Europe re-floated on the London Stock Exchange to fund expansion of the business. In the same year, Avis Europe licensed its name for use in 27 new Asian markets and signed a partnership deal in the Ukraine.

Product

Avis was an early leader in technical support systems with the introduction of its Wizard computerised reservation system in 1972. This is still in operation today and is the most extensive online, real time reservation, rental and management information system in the industry. Wizard controls the fleet, knowing where every car can be found, to whom they are rented and when they will be returned. Wizard is also invaluable when it comes to managing company fleet costs and travel policy. Reports can be customised for corporate customers so they can optimise the management of their rental costs.

Thanks to partnerships with major airlines, Avis offers streamlined services at airports. This includes a British Airways check in desk at the Avis Heathrow location, allowing customers to return their car and check-in for an onward BA flight all at the same desk. Avis Preferred offers customers some of the quickest car rental

Avis is only No.2 in rent a cars. So why go with us?

We try harder.

(When you're not the biggest, you have to.)

We just can't afford dirty ashtrays. Or half-empty gas tanks. Or worn wipers. Or unwashed cars. Or low tires. Or anything less than seat-adjusters that adjust. Heaters that heat. Defrosters that defrost.

Obviously, the thing we try hardest for is just to be nice. To start you out right with a new car, like a lively, super-torque Ford, and a pleasant smile. To know, say, where you get a good pastrami sandwich in Duluth. Why?

Because we can't afford to take you for granted.

Go with us next time.

The line at our counter is shorter.

service in the industry. Having completed a personal profile just once, customers can call ahead and then arrive at a Preferred desk to find a car pre-assigned with all the paperwork completed. Returning a car is just as quick – the Rapid Return Service allows the vehicle details to be entered into a hand-held terminal, which automatically calculates the bill and issues a receipt before the customer even reaches the desk.

Avis has special arrangements for corporate clients packed into its Corporate Contract service. Corporate accounts are given priority and each client is assigned a Corporate Account Manager to tailor services to a company's needs.

Avis also offers services tailored for smaller businesses, like Avis Advance, and Maxi-Rent – a flexible programme for long-term rentals designed to facilitate fleet management.

Recent Developments

Avis has recently launched its online rental booking service – www.avis.co.uk – allowing customers to use the online booking facility wherever they are in the world.

In March 2000, an all-new central reservations centre, based at Salford Quays in Manchester, went live. Staffed by 300 agents, the centre is designed to take over two million calls and make over 400,000 outbound calls in its first year. Agents can speak English, French, and German, and also handle fax, post and email reservations.

Avis is also working to safeguard the environment, promoting responsible car usage through a variety of schemes. A core element of this is the partnership with Future Forests, an environmental task force planting trees to offset carbon emissions. Avis is the only car rental company working with Future Forests. Since 1999 Avis UK has been 'carbon neutral' planting

sufficient trees to offset the carbon emissions of the head office operations. Avis has also pioneered a car-sharing club in Oxford called Carvenience. This allows members, who pay an annual membership fee, to pick up cars from specially allocated points as and when they need them. It is designed to be a cost-effective alternative to car ownership or long term rental.

Promotion

Avis is one of the most promotionally active of the major car rental brands. During 2000, major promotions included 'Jet, Set, Go!', 'Get around the Easy Way' and a summer national promotion.

Through this pan-European promotion 'Jet, Set Go!' provided British Midland passengers with the opportunity to win a Vauxhall VX220/Opel Speedster as a top prize together with ten test-drive weekends in Cannes for runners-up. In addition, all British Midland passengers, enjoyed money off their Avis rentals during the promotional period.

'Get Around Easy Way' targeted British Airways passengers offering the chance to win a VIP trip around the world as well as receive up to 10% discount off British Airways rental rates on every rental worldwide. This was a worldwide promotion with supporting literature distributed in all four corners of the globe.

The summer national promotion targeted leisure customers looking for straightforward value for money. The promotion was a price-led offer supported by a range of discounts at key leisure attractions around the UK, including the

London Aquarium, Manchester United Museum and Blackpool Pleasure Beach.

Brand Values

The company is driven by a singular vision – established in 1965 – 'to be the best and fastest growing company with the highest profit margins in the car rental business'. These values are enshrined in the 'We Try Harder' slogan. From

the 1960s, when Avis made a virtue of being second biggest but the best in terms of service, it has put the customer at the centre of the business. Empathy (understanding customer needs), Honesty (value for money and integrity) and Humanity (putting the customer first) underpin the We Try Harder philosophy. These values have contributed to Avis having one of the strongest and most consistent corporate cultures in the world.

Things you didn't know about Avis

Over 40% of Avis's licensee partners have been associated with the group for twenty years or more.

The Heathrow Avis station is the largest car rental location in Europe.

Avis planted up to 26,000 trees in the UK in 1999 to offset carbon emissions made by head office operations, plus one tree for every car in the fleet.

Avis Europe offers 60 models from twenty manufacturers.

Avis has 57 travel partners worldwide and more airline partners than any other car rental company.

Avis was the first car rental company to operate a 100% lead-free fleet.

Market

The UK broadcasting industry has changed beyond all recognition since the BBC was first launched in 1922. The twenty first century technological revolution is dramatically changing the broadcasting and media environments, as telecommunications, IT and broadcast media converge and revolutionise traditional communications.

Digital broadcasting has led to the launch of hundreds of new niche and broad-based entertainment and educational channels and established broadcasters now face unprecedented competition, given the dramatic increase in the number of multi-channel homes.

The internet has been a catalyst for radical change, spearheading the convergence of traditional broadcasting and communications media and leading to the creation of global giants, such as the merger between AOL and Time Warner.

Audiences can now access entertainment and information in whatever media format they want, whenever they want. Interactive and digital television, EPGs (electronic programme guides), WAP phone technology and digitally enhanced video recorders are providing audiences with more choice than ever before.

The challenge for established and new broadcasters and service providers alike is to ensure brand presence and standout across a broad range of multi-media. The need for relevant, focused and clearly positioned brands and marketing strategies has never been greater.

Achievements

The BBC has been the most significant British broadcaster for over 78 years and has become a world-renowned trademark for quality, professionalism and innovation. For almost a century the corporation has delivered the corporate challenge laid down by its first Director General, John Reith, 'to educate, entertain and inform'.

Throughout history the BBC has not only been responsible for groundbreaking programming but also for pioneering technological and broadcasting innovation. From its inception as a radio broadcaster in 1922 to the launch of colour television in 1967, Ceefax in 1974, NICAM stereo in the 1980s and enhanced digital services in the 1990s, the

BBC has continued to set the benchmark for quality broadcasting.

The BBC remains the most trusted broadcaster audiences turn to at times of national significance. Over twelve million people chose to welcome in the new millennium with the BBC at midnight on December 31st 1999, representing a 60% share of viewers, versus four million (20%) for ITV.

The BBC's acclaim is worldwide and BBC World Service now reaches over 150 million homes. Its global presence is enhanced by BBC America and BBC World channels, ensuring there is a major British voice in an increasingly global media market.

The BBC has become a national institution, universally recognised for the depth, breadth and quality of its award-winning news, drama, comedy, natural history, music and factual programming and content. Walking with Dinosaurs was the most popular factual television programme ever and was nominated for a record number of six Prime Time Emmys in America. It is just one of the many quality programmes that helped BBC Television in 1999 to win 21 BAFTAs, nineteen Royal Television Society Awards and five Montreux

International Television Awards, including the Golden Rose. BBC Radio also received 21 Sony Awards, including Station of the Year for BBC Radio 2.

History

Formed in October 1922, the British Broadcasting Corporation was originally launched as a commercial radio broadcaster. Five years later, in 1927, it received its Royal Charter, establishing it as the UK's public service broadcaster.

The BBC has developed into a national institution, offering a range of multi-media broadcast services providing access to high quality, distinctive programming and content to all its licence fee payers. Innovations from its early years have become enduring institutions, such as the time 'pips' which have been used on the hour, every hour since 1924. The Week in Westminster, launched in 1930, is still broadcast weekly on BBC Radio 4.

1932 saw the launch of the Empire Service (a forerunner to today's BBC World Service) and the BBC's first major live outside broadcast was of George VI's coronation in 1937.

During World War II the BBC established itself as the voice of the nation in the UK and of resistance in Europe, marking key historical moments, including the declaration of war by Prime Minister Neville Chamberlain, as well as King George VI's and Winston Churchill's speeches to the nation.

BBC Television began broadcasting with the launch of its first channel in 1939. Transmissions were closed down during the war, but resumed in 1946 and continued to capture moments of national and historical significance with the transmission of live pictures of Queen Elizabeth II's coronation from Westminster in 1953 and man's first steps on the moon in 1966.

The BBC's second television channel, BBC Two, was launched in 1964. Full colour television transmissions, again pioneered by the BBC, began in 1967, together with the launch of BBC Radio 1 and local radio. Other major developments included Ceefax (1974), breakfast television (1983), Nicam Stereo (1980s) and the introduction of BBC World Service television in 1991.

In September 1955, the launch of ITV, a national advertiser-supported channel made up of regional franchises, provided the BBC's first commercial broadcasting rival. This duopoly lasted until the launch of Channel 4 in 1982 and domestic competition increased further in 1997 with the launch of Channel 5, the latest terrestrial player.

The most significant development in the industry, however, has been the explosion of cable and satellite channels, dominated in the UK by BSkyB, launched in 1989.

Product

The BBC is the most valued provider of broadcast services in the UK, reaching 95% of all households every week. Its service comprises two national television channels, BBC One

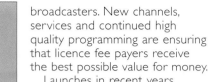

and BBC Two, five national radio stations, BBC Radio 1, 2, 3, 4, 5 Live, 39 local radio stations and dedicated services for listeners in Scotland, Wales, and Northern Ireland. It has also launched, during 1997-2000, four public service digital television channels – BBC News 24, BBC Choice, BBC Knowledge and BBC Parliament.

BBC World Service radio broadcasts in 44 languages to over 140 million homes and BBC Online is the most popular content-based website outside of Europe, achieving more than 150 million page visits a month.

News remains at the heart of the BBC's public service purpose. It has the largest news gathering operation in the world with over 2000 journalists in 55 bureaux and has built an unrivalled reputation for delivering high quality impartial in-depth reporting. BBC News 24, launched in 1997, provides 24 hour rolling news.

The BBC is the world-leading provider of education and learning for a multi-media environment and transmits more general and specialised programming than any other broadcaster.

The BBC's public services are funded by an annual licence fee. As part of its public service remit the BBC is committed to providing an innovative and dynamic mix of national and regional programming, some of which would be commercially unattractive to independent channels, to meet the requirements of a diverse range of licence fee paying audiences.

BBC publicly funded services carry no advertising or sponsorship. The BBC does, however, make use of its archive and brand portfolio on a commercial basis to supplement the licence fee. This is achieved though programme and publishing sales and commercial joint ventures from which the profit is reinvested into the core licence fee service.

BBC Worldwide is the BBC's wholly-owned commercial subsidiary. It is responsible for selling BBC magazines, videos, books, audio and visual materials worldwide and in 1999 generated an additional £81 million revenue for the BBC. In the UK, it has launched five subscription channels under the UKTV brand in a joint venture with Flextech. A joint venture with the Discovery Channel is leading to the establishment of a worldwide network of factual channels. BBC America has been successfully launched in the US; and BBC World, a global continuous television news service, is in 167 million homes and hotels worldwide.

Recent Developments

The BBC has a duty to fulfil its public service remit to satisfy its audiences in the UK with 'services that inform, educate, entertain and enrich their lives in a way that the market alone will not'. Because of the unique way it is funded, the BBC is able to provide to audiences a diverse range of services, which may not prove attractive to commercial

broadcasters. New channels, services and continued high quality programming are ensuring that licence fee payers receive the best possible value for money.

Launches in recent years include a rolling 24 hour new channel, BBC News 24. BBC News now reaches approximately 360 million people a week

through its television, radio and online services. A new digital channel, BBC Knowledge, has been successfully launched, together with a new digital text service, BBC Text, the first of its kind on digital terrestrial television. Wimbledon 2000 was supported by a new enhanced interactive text service, providing a comprehensive results and information service, and technological advances have led to the launch of new online and WAP phone listing services, providing detailed BBC programme and content information.

Original and inspiring content and programming are key to the delivery of the BBC's public service remit and it has continued to provide a rich variety of exceptional factual, drama and comedy content. Walking with Dinosaurs, The Planets, MacIntyre Undercover and Castaway 2000 are just some of the factual series produced. Outstanding drama included Wives and Daughters, Gormenghast, Great Expectations and BBC Radio 4's Nicholas Nickleby. The winning line of comedy was headed by The Royle Family and included The League of Gentlemen and Goodness Gracious Me.

Other initiatives include the GCSE Bitesize campaign, which was used by more than 65% of all GCSE students, and successful social campaigns such as Get Your Kit On, Kick The Habit and History 2000.

BBC Music Live 2000, a five day national music event, culminated with a global audience of 100 million coming together for the BBC's 'Perfect Day' which was transmitted simultaneously across BBC One, BBC Two, BBC World Service, BBC News 24, BBC local, national and regional radio networks and BBC Online.

Promotion

The BBC is recognised as one of the world's leading media brands and is respected and trusted for its creativity, integrity, and impartiality. The letters B, B, C have become instantly recognisable to audiences worldwide as a trademark of quality broadcast services. In 1997 the BBC relaunched its corporate identity to take it into the twenty first century and the digital age of broadcasting. A simpler logo was devised and implemented across all brands, services and channels, to ensure consistency of communication and to strengthen and protect the core BBC Brand, one of the corporation's most valuable assets.

The BBC's logo is one of its most effective promotional devices and it is used extensively and creatively across television and radio channels, online services, microphones, merchandising, cameras, books, CDs and videos around the world.

The BBC uses a variety of on and off air media to support its channels, services and programmes. Television trails are commonly used as appointments to view, providing details of forthcoming programmes and features. Both of the BBC's terrestrial analogue channels, BBC One and BBC Two, have their own individual identities, which enable them to communicate their own specific personalities and style under the core BBC Brand.

Corporate trails have been used historically to communicate the range of diverse and unique services available from the BBC in its role as public service provider, such as its unrivalled news coverage, children's and natural history programming and online services.

Brand Values

Since it received the Royal Charter in 1927, the BBC has remained true to its core purpose of being educational, informative and entertaining. Through the explosion of new technology, the BBC has ensured it has delivered its public service remit, as generations of audiences have grown up to be replaced by new audiences with their own specific needs. The BBC has consistently delivered original, inspiring programme content and production values and achieved an unrivalled reputation for quality, impartiality and integrity that has helped make it one of the world's leading media brands.

Market

Today's twenty-somethings and thirty-somethings are probably the most food-literate generation the UK has ever known. For proof, just look at the television schedules or scan the newspapers. Cookbooks and cookery programmes regularly top the best-seller lists and television ratings, and chefs are now counted among the best known celebrities in the country. In fact, never before has a generation taken so much interest in food, known so much about food – and yet known so little about cooking it.

This is almost entirely because of the stunning growth in the market of convenience meals which doubled in the UK over the space of the five years from 1992 to 1997. And it continues to grow strongly. Increased working hours, higher numbers of working women and less free time has led to a revolution in the UK's eating habits. The once-universal household ritual of gathering ingredients and cooking a meal from scratch has declined sharply, as has the concept of the formal meal occasion. In their place has come widespread reliance on convenience foods, and an informal approach to meals. For the vast majority of the UK population, the staple meal solution is now frozen food, sales of which rose a further 3.4% year on year to May 2000.

If food is now fashion – which judging by the media, it most certainly has become – then Birds Eye is a timeless classic. Despite the phenomenal changes which have taken place in eating habits over the last few years, Birds Eye remains as popular as ever and is the brand leader with a 16.9% value share (worth £640 million) of the frozen food sector which in total is worth £3.8 billion. And the trends would seem to indicate further success in the future. As lifestyles continue to become ever more demanding and as smaller-size households increasingly become the norm, the Birds Eye brand is more relevant than ever to the UK consumer.

Achievements

Having established itself as the first company in the UK to manufacture and market frozen foods back in the late 1930s, Birds Eye has maintained its leadership of the industry ever since. Today Birds Eye remains the leading brand in grocery stores across the country, and of the top-selling frozen food lines in Britain in 1999, no fewer than five belonged to Birds Eye.

The reasons are plain to see. The Birds Eye range has something for everyone. It has

kept pace with the latest market developments, such as the growth in importance of foreign-influenced foods, sustainability and environmental issues. This has helped to ensure that Birds Eye remains the UK's best and most popular food brand.

Today the company is made up of two parts, one being Birds Eye, and the other Wall's, Britain's oldest and best-known ice cream brand. Together, Birds Eye Wall's now employs more than 5,000 people and operates four manufacturing sites. These are in Gloucester, producing ice cream and frozen desserts; Lowestoft, producing meat and vegetable products; Grimsby, making ready meals; and Hull, which makes all Birds Eye fish products.

History

If Captain Birds Eye had not existed, they might well have had to invent him. But there was no need. The image of Captain Birds Eye, one of the most enduring and powerful advertising icons of the past century, is based on the man who founded the business after World War I.

The original Clarence Birdseye, an American scientist and explorer, conceived the notion of commercially frozen food whilst on an expedition in Labrador, Canada, in the 1920s. The idea came to him after eating with the Inuit,

or Eskimos, in Canada's Arctic region. He realised that fish and meat, once thawed, still retained its freshness after months of freezing.

On his return to the US, Birdseye patented a freezing device known as the Birdseye Plate Froster. By 1930 the brand was up and running. A group of Massachussetts shopkeepers started selling 'Birds Eye' branded frozen fish, meat and vegetables. Throughout the 1930s Clarence Birdseye continued to pioneer his quick-freezing business under the auspices of the General Foods Corporation.

In 1938 the brand crossed the Atlantic and was launched in the UK by Frosted Foods Ltd, part of General Foods. The outbreak of World War II temporarily halted production, but in 1945, by then under the ownership of Unilever, Birds Eye resumed operations with added urgency, determined to help ease the post-war food shortages.

Today the company continues to uphold the heritage of its past, whilst developing the business to ensure that it retains market leadership now and in the future.

Product

Birds Eye's mission is to be the UK's most trusted and preferred food brand. This is to be achieved by offering the consumer nutritious, tasty and exciting meal ideas. Family favourites such as beefburgers, fish fingers and peas are still the best sellers, but changing eating habits and constant innovation have resulted in a wide and varied product range. These include products such as Chicken Chargrills, Hungry Joes, Alphabites, Simply Fish, Homestyle Burgers, Freshly Frozen Herbs, speciality breads and, of course, a host of recipe meal ideas.

Recent Developments

Birds Eye has refined and developed its marketing strategy in recent years. There has been a move away from sub-brands and a much greater focus on the core Birds Eye house brand. The result is that Birds Eye is now the biggest food brand in the UK and all activity is focused on building the brand's status for the future. There have been innovations in fish, meals, burgers and herbs, with ground-breaking new products such as Simply Fish, Homestyle, 95% Fat Free meals and a range of freshly frozen herbs.

The entire range of packaging has been redesigned, with a greater emphasis on food and appetite appeal. Captain Birds Eye has been given a new modern look, and an interactive Captain Birds Eye website for children has been launched. The website –

www.captainbirdseye.co.uk – offers youngsters the opportunity to go online and become a member of the Captain's crew. This opens the way to take part in a variety of exciting and educational adventures, from exploring the Arctic, to battling the evil Piranha Gang in a bid to defend the world's oceans.

the bearded sea-dog figure of the past into a younger, clean-cut captain, the emphasis has changed. The campaign has been subtly adjusted so as to appeal to the main consumers of the product – the children themselves – who increasingly hold the balance of influence on the choice of mealtime favourites.

A strong mix of media has always been a key strength of Birds Eye's promotional success, with magazines, posters, and radio among the channels supporting and complementing television. Today the company is widening its ability to engage the consumer in dialogue. The selection of channels used is growing. In relationship marketing, Birds Eye makes full use of the Jigsaw Consortium database run by the alliance of Unilever, Cadbury and Kimberly Clarke, and also benefits from the successful consumer magazine, Voila, published by the consortium and mailed direct to one million customers.

On the internet, the European website for Captain Birds Eye provides children with the opportunity to sign on as crew members and participate in interactive adventures and promotional opportunities. Hugely popular, this site has received accolades from the web industry for its imaginative construction and stylish design. On interactive television, Birds Eye is participating in leading-edge experiments by Unilever companies developed by the British Interactive Broadcasting consortium. All this

demonstrates that the promotion of the Birds Eye brand, well established on a sound history of successful communication, is continuing to lead now, just as it did with that first move into colour television more than 30 years ago.

Promotion

The strength of the Birds Eye brand today draws on a long and distinguished history of advertising. As with most major brands, television has played a starring role in building the public's trust and affection for Birds Eye. In fact, Birds Eye has played a direct role in the development of the medium as an advertising vehicle. When the UK made its long-awaited move from black and white to colour broadcasting in the late 1960s, it was a 30-second spot for Birds Eye Peas that marked the country's first-ever colour television commercial.

Birds Eye has enjoyed many successes over the years across its entire product range but it is the Birds Eye fish fingers promotion, spanning 25 years of lively and loveable ads, which stands out as one of the most sustained and popular long-term campaigns in the history of marketing. The campaign has reassured generations of mothers that Birds Eye is a product of superior quality.

Now, with the transformation of Captain Birdseye from

Brand Values

Consumers are at the heart of Birds Eye's business. Indeed, it is the Birds Eye brand ambition to be the top-of-mind brand in the total food market, and to make the life of the food provider simpler and better by making great-tasting food, preferred because it is safe, natural and simply fresh-frozen. In order to achieve this goal, Birds Eye places a huge emphasis on food and production quality, customer research and customer relations, social and environmental responsibility, and on Birds Eye's biggest asset – its own employees. The essence of the company's brand values is conveyed in the phrase: 'Only the best passes the Birds Eye test'. The phrase is as true now as it was when it was coined some years ago.

Things you didn't know about
Birds Eye

The good old fish finger was invented by Birds Eye in 1955, and remains the top favourite with children to this day.

The famous Birds Eye brand is Britain's top grocery brand with a retail sales value of £700 million each year.

Birds Eye makes 515 million fish fingers every year. Placed end to end, they would stretch around the Equator.

Each year Birds Eye makes enough burgers to stretch from London to Moscow and back.

Birds Eye grew its first peas in the UK in 1946. In 1999 it sold 36 million packets.

Every pea is harvested at the peak of perfection, with no more than two and a half hours from vine to freezing.

BLACK&DECKER®

Market

The increasingly competitive DIY industry is now enjoying a boom period after suffering badly in the uncertain economic climate of the late 1980s.

Throughout the early 1990s the industry struggled to find its feet due to the scarcity of new homeowners and a subsequential slump in the home improvement market.

This situation was further exacerbated by an influx of brands from the Far East. However, the mid 1990s saw early signs of recovery in the market place and since then the industry has gone from strength to strength.

Gardening and DIY are now amongst the nation's favourite pastimes and with the healthy UK economy and the strengthened housing market the power tool industry continues to enjoy growth.

This upsurge in fortunes has been aided by media programmes and lifestyle magazine coverage of DIY such as the BBC programme Changing Rooms. This has helped to introduce new users to the market with a 'do it now' attitude to style and decoration. DIY is now being perceived as being more of a pastime than a chore.

Women now represent 14% of main users compared with 9% in 1996 (Source: Home Audit) with 37% considering themselves active or very active in DIY activities (Source: Hometrak). In addition, 39% of power tools are purchased by women – 48% of these are gifts (Source: Home Audit). This is reflected in the great upsurge in sales at Christmas with 60% of trade being in the fourth quarter compared to 22% in quarters 1-3 (Source: GFK Home Audit Q4).

Achievements

Black & Decker is the biggest manufacturer of power tools in the world and one of the leading manufacturers of lawn and garden power tools and power tool accessories. This is reflected in eight out of ten households in the UK owning a minimum of one Black & Decker product.

Moving into the new millennium Black & Decker continues to place emphasis on the importance of design, research and development. This has led to Black & Decker receiving numerous awards with special recognition for the Mouse and the Quattro – two of its best selling tools. In 1999

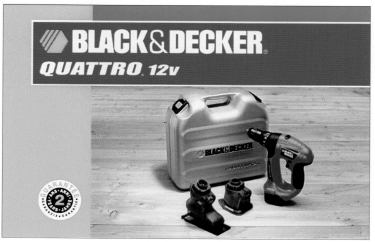

The Mouse was awarded Millennium Product status by the Design Council.

As well as introducing new tools to the market place, old favourites from its range are updated to meet ever-increasing consumer demands. Black & Decker was the first company to develop cordless tools and the classic Workmate.

History

Black & Decker began life in 1910, when two young Americans, Duncan Black and Alonzo Decker formed their own manufacturing company. To raise the initial capital needed for their fledgling enterprise, Duncan Black sold his treasured Maxewell-Briscoe car, whilst Alonzo Decker borrowed an equal sum.

With their $1200 investment they leased premises in Baltimore, and began contract machine work.

The early Black & Decker products ranged from equipment for the US mint, to bottle capping machinery. In 1914 the first hand-held power drill was patented with its pistol grip, trigger switch and universal motor. Black & Decker had now begun to produce the goods for which it would subsequently become world-renowned. Early successes such as this, and the Lectroflator – an electric air compressor used to inflate tyres – pushed sales to above $1million, which enabled the company to expand. Service centres were opened in Boston and New York and a new factory was built in Towson, Maryland, to cope with the phenomenal growth. In 1922 another milestone was reached when the first subsidiary outside the US was formed in Canada, and in 1928 the first factory was built in the UK, in Slough. This factory produced a range of heavy-duty tools including tappers, screwdrivers and grinders. The outbreak of World War II proved a testing time for the new UK business, though it aided the general war effort by manufacturing armaments from its factories. The scarcity of metals at the time forced a rethink in the design of its tools. Tools were soon being manufactured with plastic housings.

In 1946, it came to Black

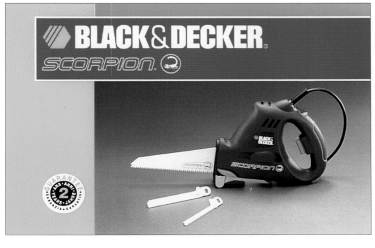

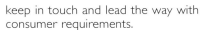

a massive three-year research and development programme, which saw the company spend £500,000 on end-user research alone.

Since its conception Black & Decker has continued to introduce stylish, effective, and easy-to-use equipment, to the marketplace with constant design and product development playing a key role.

& Decker's attention that industrial tools were going missing – often ending up in workers' homes. This alerted Black & Decker to the possibility of a thriving home tools market. So, the company decided to make tools specifically aimed at the DIY market – a major decision that was to change the face of the company, and form its core business for the next 50 years.

The extraordinary growth in sales that this decision prompted, ensured continuous expansion. By 1957, sales had exceeded £25 million.

The 1960s saw further expansion, with the opening of new branches in Scandinavia as well as in the UK, and the opening of new headquarters in Maidenhead.

At the end of the 1960s, Black & Decker turned its hand to 'space development' in association with the National Aeronautical and Space Agency (NASA). Black & Decker devised a cordless zero-torque space tool, used on the Gemini project, and in the early 1970s, a Black & Decker moon drill was used to remove core samples from the lunar surface.

Product

Black & Decker produces a wide range of tools and products for the home and the garden. In its garden range it supplies a range of equipment including mowers, trimmers, shredders, chainsaws and the multi purpose 'Mastervac'. Black & Decker's power tools range includes cordless drills, jigsaws and sanders.

For the home, Black & Decker produces a range of 'Dustbusters', a hand held vacuum cleaner for quick spills and tidy ups. 50 million Dustbusters are sold wordwide each year, and with the range being constantly improved with more power, attachments and colour, it continues to find new audiences.

The Workmate, is a classic piece of equipment that needs no introduction. It is still the ultimate accessory for all serious DIY-ers.

In the latter half of the 1990s Black & Decker relaunched under the 'New Generation' banner, with new packaging and a new advertising strategy. The move was instigated following

Recent Developments

Black & Decker has launched a variety of innovative new products over recent years, including one of the best selling home improvement products of the last few years, the Mouse. The Mouse is a compact decorating and sanding tool which will sand down a variety of surfaces including paint and varnish, and will clean and polish metal and plastic surfaces as well as be used for rust removal.

Spring and summer 2000, saw the launch of the 12V Quattro and Scorpion powered hand saw. The 12V Quattro, an updated version of the highly popular 7.2V Quattro, is an all-in-one answer to the four key DIY tasks – drilling, sanding, screwdriving and jigsawing, achieved with its interchangeable heads. With its soft grip handle and powerful battery pack, the Quattro is one of the most successful and easy to use power tools on the DIY market.

The addition of the Scorpion powered hand saw, to the Black & Decker sawing range, makes a traditionally hard working tool, into a safe and efficient one with three blades for different sawing needs.

The arrival of the 4x4 lawnmower, after four years of research and development, to the Black & Decker lawn and garden range, also made the brand a force to be reckoned with beyond its core power tool market. The revolutionary 4x4 offers the benefits of both a hover and a rotary mower in one.

Promotion

One of Black & Decker's earliest examples of television advertising was in 1928, when a specially fitted out six-person monoplane was used as a flying showroom to demonstrate how Black & Decker power tools could be used in the reconditioning of aircraft engines.

The company's first network television advert came in 1955 with a series of advertisements for its power tool range. Since then Black & Decker has used a combination of television advertising, in-store promotions and publicity campaigns to keep in touch and lead the way with consumer requirements.

Current television adverts show DIY tasks being undertaken with successful end results that can be easily achieved by using Black & Decker tools. These advertisements illustrate that even DIY novices can achieve professional results.

To assist first time buyers, Black & Decker launched a number of in-store promotional catalogues which explain the benefits of the tools in layman's terms with easy-to-understand dialogue that avoids clumsy and confusing technical dialogue. This user-friendly approach is reinforced by a series of detailed illustrations and graphics.

In the UK the promotion of Black & Decker products also relies on in-store demonstrations, videos and direct marketing campaigns. This is backed up with give-aways and 'tried and tested' features in consumer and national media.

Black & Decker is also a regular attendee at home interest shows to help enhance the brand's association with the DIY market and to reinforce relationships between consumers and retailers.

Brand Values

Black & Decker prides itself on being able to offer innovative and value for money products. It offers a product for every job and increasingly is offering one product for a variety of jobs.

With the improvement in imported products, Black & Decker has managed to keep one step ahead through the emergence of multi-functional tools in the range, which has increased its strong hold over the rest of the market. As well as offering quality and innovative tools, Black & Decker offers guarantees to give reassurance to the most nervous customers.

Being a visionary, customer focused brand, Black & Decker aims to ensure that its products are both exciting and challenging, but remain the best tool for the job.

Things you didn't know about Black & Decker

Black & Decker's tool production plant at Spennymoor is the biggest of its kind in the world.

The Black & Decker Workmate – the multi-purpose workbench – was invented by Ron Hickman, designer of the Lotus Elan sports car, in 1961.

Black & Decker employs over 30,000 people across 100 countries worldwide, and makes an annual turnover of around $5 billion.

Seven out of ten households own a Black & Decker drill and five out of ten households own two or more Black & Decker products.

Bostik
BLU-TACK

Market

The adhesives industry as a whole is currently characterised by the presence of a small number of multi-national companies, many of which are chemical-based, whose ownership includes UK operations.

The industry has shown signs of becoming increasingly concentrated in recent years. Characteristically, companies within this market often supply a wide range of products with a relatively low level of specialisation. In addition, a number of smaller, more specialised adhesive manufacturers exist which concentrate on specific end use markets.

Blu-Tack dominates the 're-usable tack' sector. It is manufactured by Bostik, which is a large producer of adhesives, mainly for the industrial and construction markets.

One of the key elements of the consumer product Blu-Tack is that it is manufactured to the same standard, with the same advanced technology as other more heavy duty adhesives.

Achievements

In view of the fluctuating economic climate facing many countries throughout the 1970s, Bostik UK focused on research and promotion to counteract this. Blu-Tack is one of Bostik UK's 2000 product formulations. Since its launch in 1970, it has held the position of market leader. Blu-Tack now commands a 94% brand share of the office adhesives re-usable tack market.

History

Bostik UK was founded in 1898 as the Boston Blacking Company. In 1935 the first industrial Bostik product was launched and the brand was born. In 1937 the company renamed itself BB Chemical Company Ltd to reflect its ongoing work in other fields of adhesives away from the footwear industry. World War II brought contracts from the military and Bostik products were utilised on many military vehicles, most notably they were used to waterproof amphibious vehicles used in the landings of the Allied forces. During the 1950s boom after the war and due to the advancement in technology Bostik products really began to succeed. In 1952 the first consumer product was launched. By the end of the 1950s Bostik had become the number one market leader in adhesives and sealants. The American company which set up UK offices in Leicester specialising in supplies to the footwear industry came to be Bostik UK in 1962. Bostik launched Blu-Tack in 1970 into a market with no existing knowledge of removable or re-usable 'putty-like' adhesives.

The product was discovered during the development of a Bostik industrial adhesive. Blu-Tack was originally white during the concept stage, but fears raised in consumer research about the new tack being mistaken by children for sweets led to the tack being coloured blue, as there were no sweets on the market at the time that were this colour.

In addition to this strong position within the office market, Blu-Tack is bought by consumers for use in the home across a wide range of markets and also from a wide range of outlets. Blu-Tack has the advantage of being usable to complete a wide diversity of tasks. Examples of usage include the obvious, such as attaching posters to a wall without damage, to less obvious uses including putting chunks under each corner of stereo speakers to make them adhere with their stands; applying it to surfaces that need a little vibration damping, and sticking it on the end of a stick to retrieve that little item that fell behind the sofa.

In 1990 Bostik UK became part of the French-owned Total Oil Group. This allowed the company to meet the challenges of the decade by investing heavily in all areas of the operation to capitalise on new product development and modernise manufacturing processes. Administration and distribution facilities have been further improved and ambitious sales and marketing initiatives have been implemented.

Product

Blu-Tack is composed mainly of synthetic rubber and selected mineral fillers. The ingredients are carefully chosen to give a formulation with a good balance of properties so it is clean to use, tacky and strong enough to give good adhesion, yet still have the ability to be re-used as and when required. There are five main stages in the production of Blu-Tack: mixing, blending, discharge, final extrusion and packaging. During mixing, a heavy duty Banbury mixer is used to masticate rubber and mix it with fillers to form an intermediate compound. In the blending process further rubbers, fillers, pigments and oils are added to the compound and thoroughly blended in a Sigma Blade Mixer. Then the product is screw-discharged in large irregular shaped tubes of Blu-Tack. At this stage the product is formed into its final shape, covered in waxed sterilized paper and cut to size. Finally the Blu-Tack is packed into wallets and display boxes which are shrink wrapped ready for transit. Blu-Tack is available in two pack sizes – Handy and Economy.

Recent Developments

1997 saw the redevelopment of Blu-Tack packaging, with the new style showing the possible uses of the product and has helped to strengthen brand share in the stationery market.

Recently the packaging of Blu-Tack has become an automated process: up until a new packaging line was devised, all Blu-Tack was hand packaged. This innovation will ensure consistency of supply in the future.

Recently Bostik has targeted the children's market by launching Oodles, a fun product that offers creative play. The new product includes a pack of Blu-Tack, a 'craft sheet' with ideas of what to make and a game with lots of bits and pieces to play with.

Promotion

When Blu-Tack was first launched onto the consumer market the initial reaction to what was then a completely new concept was fairly poor. This was mainly due to the lack of knowledge about the product so Bostik turned to advertising to educate the UK population about the uses and advantages of Blu-Tack.

Through television advertising and word of mouth, Blu-Tack quickly entered the growth phase of its life cycle. Early television campaigns included a hippo called 'Tubby Tacker' who introduced the public to the versatility of

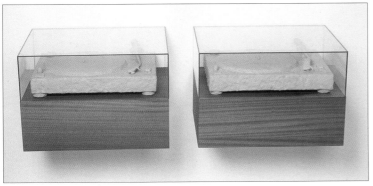

Blu-Tack. Within ten years of the launch of the product, Blu-Tack had become a household name.

The strategy for Blu-Tack is to grow the business through promotion which reflects the versatility of the product and encourages consumers to use Blu-Tack in situations that may not have occurred to them before.

A big part of promotion for Blu-Tack is its support of many animal related charities through on-pack promotion. The largest of these promotions was the 'Seal Appeal' in conjunction with the RSPCA, supported by then World Snooker Champion Stephen Hendry and also by Dennis Taylor. This campaign helped to raise funds to build a seal sanctuary on the east coast of England. Blu-Tack has also supported a walk by RSPCA inspectors from Lands End to John O'Groats.

Another animal oriented campaign was the 'Endangered Species Project', an on-pack promotion that raised funds to pay for the first re-flotation unit, based in the West Country for whales in the northern hemisphere. It was also able to send a team from the UK to New Zealand for training purposes. The appeal raised awareness of the importance of whale and dolphin conservation, by offering a wall chart to schools, as well as to the general public, giving facts and locations of all the endangered whale and dolphin species in the world.

Blu-Tack has also worked closely with the RSPB. Schools were given the opportunity to send their ideas for plans to build bird boxes during CDT classes. In addition, households could send off for a wall chart showing four endangered bird species in the UK, and also received a badge of the bird of their choice. The money raised from the promotion went towards protecting the key habitats of endangered bird species in the UK. Each of these promotions was used by Blu-Tack to promote the brand to schools, parents and children through its close association with these well known charities.

Significant national press attention has been gained for Blu-Tack through its use in art. In 2000 artists James White and Tim Sherward created three two foot tall sculptures entitled Cowboy

Cardealer, Squid and Ian that were displayed in Walsall's new art gallery as part of an exhibition to show how the colour blue has influenced twentieth century art. Other sculptures, again by White and Sherward, displayed at the Modern Art Inc in London included a palm tree a microphone and an alien doll. They were described as reflecting 'the raw clay of the artist's soul'.

Brand Values

Blu-Tack is the original re-usable adhesive. The unique formula makes Blu-Tack distinct from all the imitations that have attempted to challenge its market dominance. Blu-Tack offers a clean, safe and simple alternative to tapes and pins. It also benefits from a customer loyalty that has been built up over the last 30 years.

Things you didn't know about Blu-Tack

If you laid back to back all packs of Blu-Tack which are sold in the UK each year they would reach from Lands End to John O'Groats and back.

A yachtsman sailing around the world was able to stop his boat from sinking only by plugging a hole with Blu-Tack.

Blu-Tack was used by artists to create 3D models at the opening of a new gallery in Walsall.

Applications for Blu-Tack the company has received over the years have included: preventing doors from banging on walls, sticking down moveable objects in caravans and boats, making moldable fishing weights, cleaning fluff from typewriters and keyboards, ear plugs for swimmers and even holding in false teeth.

A concerned psychiatric hospital nurse telephoned Bostik regarding patients in her care. They had been stealing Blu-Tack from behind posters, drying it out in the airing cupboard, rolling it into a cigarette and smoking it. Bostik UK obviously doesn't recommend this more unusual use of its product.

Market

13.5 million kilograms of sweet pickle were sold in 1999 resulting in a market worth £24 million (Source: ACNielsen 2000). This is equivalent to 2.7 billion teaspoons of sweet pickle spooned onto a whole host of foods.

One in every two households purchases at least one jar of sweet pickle every year and more than one in three of those buys the market leader, Branston. Only a small minority of consumers, 8.4%, according to TGI, now makes its own chutney or practises the art of pickling fruits and vegetables. Therefore the convenience offered by off-the-shelf ready-made products is a considerable advantage.

Almost 70% of sweet pickle is used in sandwiches, with cheese being the most popular filling. With 28 billion sandwiches a year being made in the home and rising, this provides a strong platform for continued brand sales.

Sweet pickle is one of the most popular condiments in home prepared sandwiches. In fact, as part of the nation's daily diet, lunchbox occasions have grown steadily over the last seven years by 21% with the majority of those lunchboxes featuring sandwiches.

Current changes affecting the pickles, chutney and relish market include the growth of chilled ready meals, where condiments are occasionally incorporated in complete meals. Another factor is the significant growth in the retail sandwich market, either sold pre-packed (in most grocery outlets), ready-made or cut to order in sandwich bars (Source: Mintel 1999).

Achievements

Branston is the number one brand in the £24 million sweet pickle market with a 76% value share (Source: ACNielsen). The brand has successfully introduced a number of variations to the Original Pickle recipe. In 1988, the launch of Branston Sandwich led to a 10% category growth (Source: Nestlé). Branston's continued success has been as a result of its all year round appeal and is testament to its enduring popularity.

In 1999 the brand was voted one of the top 50 brands of the twentieth century in The Grocer's 'Brands of the Millennium' survey conducted amongst leading figures from the manufacturing, retailing and marketing communications fields.

History

The Branston name comes from a village two miles south of Burton-on-Trent in Staffordshire. It was there in 1922 that Crosse & Blackwell owned the factory where the famous pickle was first produced. At that time it was the largest and best equipped food-preserving plant in the British Empire.

Production switched in the mid twenties from Branston village, on the river Trent, to Crosse & Blackwell at Crimscott Street in Bermondsey, South London and then to the Silvertown factory in London's Docklands and subsequently to Peterhead on the North East coast of Scotland. Finally, in 1998 it moved to the Hadfield factory, near Glossop, Derbyshire where it is manufactured today. It was in 1960 that Branston, under the Crosse & Blackwell brand, joined the Nestlé business and enjoyed further success with the support of the world's largest food company. Nestlé has a total workforce of approximately 230,000 people in some 500 factories worldwide.

The Branston brand now looks different from how it did in the early days but it is still as relevant to spicing up food today as it was when it was first made. As food fads come and go, the Branston brand has maintained its reputation as a classic, trusted British brand, bought by generations of families.

Branston Pickle is made to the same unique recipe now as when it was first produced and it is still prepared with the same care, in the traditional manner, using only the finest quality ingredients. Nestlé maintain that it is the distinctive tangy taste and crisp crunchy vegetable bite that makes Branston the most popular sweet pickle in the supermarket.

Product

Throughout the past 80 years Branston has been a firm family favourite. Despite changes in

The Ten-o'clock Test makes BRANSTON the most popular sweet pickle in the world

CROSSE & BLACKWELL

consumer shopping habits and more cosmopolitan, sophisticated tastes, sweet pickle is still enjoyed in millions of homes around Britain and indeed the world.

There is a significant peak in sales around Christmas, when thoughts turn to all things family and traditional, as Branston Pickle plays a key role in livening up the turkey leftovers.

At the same time, usage is very much in line with current trends in eating as it increasingly accompanies cold meats, salads, vegetables, fish and baked potatoes as well as its famous partner, cheese.

Sweet pickle has been unaffected by the fads and fashions of the years and is one of the best loved British food icons relevant to the needs of British consumers today.

Back in 1988 Nestlé identified a trend towards increasing sandwich consumption – a trend which continues today – and recognised that there would be a tremendous opportunity for a Branston Pickle variant specifically developed for this eating occasion. Branston Sandwich Pickle was launched, with a finer diced recipe.

campaign strapline has not been used since 1985, it is still widely recognised and remembered today.

Following on from the hugely successful 'Bring out the Branston' campaign, new television campaigns were produced to support the introduction of new Branston variants. In the late 1980s the Antique Roadshow commercial supported the launch of Branston Sandwich Pickle and in the 1990s, as international food trends slowly began influencing people's tastes, UK food trends evolved from traditional English fare to more

Branston also continues to be strongly supported with in-store displays and promotions. The brand has developed a series of themed-linked promotions using relevant host foods – the Christmas promotion paired Branston with turkeys purchased for Christmas. This theme has also been extended to other relevant host foods, including cheese.

Brand Values

Branston is the classic recipe for sweet pickle. With its unique combination of ingredients, distinctive tangy taste and blend of crisp, crunchy vegetables, it delivers an extra bite.

Quintessentially a British brand with a classic food heritage, the Branston brand is very much a British brand trusted and recognised by generations, evoking a sense of nostalgia.

This resulted in significant brand growth as heavy sandwich users saw the benefit of an easier-to-spread product.

Recent Developments

A further variant – Branston Chilli with a hotter, spicier flavour – was launched into the market in 1991 to meet the needs of more adventurous meal accompaniments and to extend beyond the sweet pickle market into hot food.

Mintel research found that more people are preparing curries in the home, as the thriving ethnic cooking sauce market shows, and this in turn is beneficial to sales of related chutneys and pickles.

Branston Tomato, targeted at the younger consumer, was launched as an extension into relishes reflecting the increasing popularity of American style burgers and the greater number of meals eaten outdoors, such as barbecues. Indeed, it is estimated that half of all annual relish sales are made in the period of May to August and the popularity of holding or attending a barbecue is increasing (Source: Mintel 1999).

Promotion

In 1992 the brand celebrated its 70th anniversary and the pack sported commemorative labels to reinforce heritage and quality. Promotions have played a key role in maintaining strong brand sales and loyalty. The anniversary celebrated the brand's heritage by offering Special Edition replica 1920s vans, in full Branston livery.

1972 saw the introduction of the highly memorable 'Bring out the Branston' television advertising campaign. This quickly became an iconic advertising slogan, which prompted consumers to bring Branston out from the back of the kitchen cupboard. And although the

experimental and spicier foods. The advertising to support the launch of Branston Chilli Pickle continued to prompt usage in the home. However, rather than support traditional English serving suggestions such as cheese and ham, it focused on more exotic foods such as kebabs and curries.

During the mid 1990s, a Crosse & Blackwell Megabrand support campaign broke with the 'Now there's a thought' idea which continued to talk about serving suggestions for specific variants in the range. This evolved to a campaign further supporting Sandwich Pickle with a student making and indulging in a huge, thickly sliced white bread, doorstep sandwich. Tomato Pickle followed in the summer of 1998 with a radio and regional sampling campaign. This catered for the increasing popularity of American foods such as barbecues, hot dogs, burgers, ribs, nachos and chicken wings.

The Christmas 1999 campaign saw Branston

prompting usage at Christmas in order to help consumers enjoy their turkey leftovers. The advertising was primarily targeted towards light users who needed to be reminded to buy Branston at this festive time of year.

Market

The telecommunications industry is probably the fastest growing and the most competitive in the world. In 1999 BT led a sector estimated by Keynote Research to be worth £23.5 billion in the UK, a sum that has grown by 58% since 1994.

This rate of growth is due to telecommunications moving beyond the realms of traditional voice telephony and into the rapidly expanding worlds of mobile communications and the internet. In the UK there is a new internet user every ten seconds and a new mobile phone user every three seconds.

The world of communications is changing. In order to keep up with the rapidity of this change it is vital for any telecommunications company to evolve and grow at the same pace. The industry is expanding from narrowband to broadband, from fixed to mobile and from voice dominated communication to a data and internet dominated environment. In 1994, 49% of the world's major telecom companies' income came from fixed lines; a figure that shrank to 36% in 1999 (Source: Keynote). Meanwhile revenue in the cellular sector increased from 16% to over 28% in the same time period.

In 1998/99 a third of BT's income came from the high growth new-wave areas of the internet, mobility and data solutions; a figure that is continuing to grow and expected to reach three quarters by 2004.

Previously separate technologies are also converging – broadband and mobile, internet and mobile, broadband and internet. And at the same time the industry is consolidating; merger and acquisition activity is rife as major companies join forces in order to compete on what is an ever-larger stage. As markets are liberalised and technology ismaking boundaries and time zones increasingly irrelevant, the communications industry is a truly international business.

E-business has the potential to change everything about the way companies work. For example it can enable companies to slash the costs of dealing with customers and suppliers by up to 90% and will change the way in which companies market, sell and communicate.

Achievements

BT is one of the best known, most powerful brands in the UK. It is one of the world's leading providers of telecommunications services to residential and business customers and is currently focused on becoming the most successful communications group in the world.

In research, the BT brand scores highly in terms of awareness. It has been one of the most consistently strong performers in Marketing magazine's long running Adwatch survey.

Operationally, BT has made important strides towards transforming itself into a new wave communications company. It is building global strength by expanding its activities outside the UK. It is also transferring its focus towards the five high growth areas of mobility, the internet, multimedia, data and solutions – investing heavily in building new, high bandwidth networks in order to do so.

The result of all of this is that BT now boasts a worldwide operation, which includes some 30 equity-based ventures and nearly 50 distributors as well as having its own operations in key markets. Directly or indirectly, BT has gained access to 85% of the European and 100% of the Asia-Pacific region's addressable markets.

BT was the first company with a mobile ISP (Genie Internet) and the first to launch WAP email and the first company to reach half a million mobile ISP registrations (Source: CEO Technology Forum June 2000).

BT has created backbone networks which are capable of carrying massive volumes of internet traffic as well as voice calls. In the UK, BT has spearheaded the move towards the provision of broadband services, with major investments in creating a broadband internet protocol network.

BT Internet's customer base continues to grow at an extremely rapid rate, illustrating its success in keeping up with the demands of the market. For example, between just May and June 2000, BT Internet customer base grew from 405,000 to 421,000.

History

British Telecommunications did not exist until 1969 when the General Post Office, which until then had provided the UK's telephone service, became a state public corporation. The Post Office was then split into two separate entities and the corporation responsible for telecommunications given the trading name of British Telecommunications.

In 1984, the company – by now called British Telecom – became the first European state-owned Telecommunications Company to be privatised. In 1991, British Telecom was restructured and re-launched as BT with new branding and a new logo.

BT rapidly became a leader in the field of many other communications technologies including the internet and corporate intranet markets. The launch of BT's Intranet Builder portfolio in 1997, enabling customers to build their own intranets, followed the announcement in late 1996 of an alliance with Microsoft to jointly develop and market a range of intranet services to meet growing demand.

On January 1st 1998, the European telecommunications market opened to competition. BT was poised to exploit the new opportunities this represented. The company already had a number of 'distributorships' – joint venture and alliances in France, Germany, Gibraltar, Ireland, Italy, the Netherlands, Portugal, Spain, Sweden and Switzerland.

Product

BT is one of the world's leading providers of telecommunications services. Its main business has grown to provide local, long distance and international telephone services, private networks, and the supply of mobile communications services. However, as technology develops at an ever increasing pace, voice calls do still form an important part of BT's business, but an increasingly large proportion of revenue now comes from new wave areas. BT's products and services are now suitable for a huge range of applications.

BT services include national and international directory services, public payphones and maritime services. BT provides customers on digital exchanges with a range of Select Services including Call Waiting, Call Diversion, Caller Display and Ring Back When Free. Its most popular digital service is the 1471 service, which allows customers to know which telephone number last called.

BT provides a range of services for customers with special needs including a free priority fault repair service for customers whose telephone is a vital lifeline, free directory assistance for

visually-impaired people and telephone bills in Braille or large print. BT also operates Typetalk which allows deaf and speech-impaired customers to use textphones to make or receive calls from hearing people. Typetalk is run by the Royal National Institute for the Deaf with substantial funding from BT.

Mobile services are becoming an increasingly important part of BT's offering. The BT Internet phone was the first commercially available Wireless Access Protocol (WAP) service in the UK and offers a wide range of services. This includes BT's own Genie Internet – already a leading mobile information service – sending information, such as sports scores, share prices, and e-mails to users' phones.

Recent Developments

In 1999 BT made major acquisitions in Japan, Canada, the Republic of Ireland and the Netherlands, largely in the new wave areas of mobility and the internet. It has also invested significant amounts in new high bandwidth networks, primarily in the UK and throughout continental Europe.

BT has acquired a licence from the UK government to operate so-called third generation mobile data services. These allow BT to offer broadband data transmission to mobile users, enabling them to access the internet with the kind of download speeds and data capacities previously only available on powerful personal computers.

BT has also introduced various new products designed to reduce prices and to simplify its price structure as well as new options to give customers greater choice and control over how they are charged. For example, the BT Together range of pricing plans provides residential and smaller business customers with competitive prices, inclusive call allowances and other value features for a single monthly fee. BT has also introduced a commitment to deliver competitive prices to the corporate business customer.

Building on the momentum created by BT Together, BT introduced BT SurfTime. This offers unlimited internet calls for a fixed fee and means that accessing the internet in the UK is cheaper.

In April 2000, BT announced another radical restructuring, dividing the company into a number of new international businesses: BT Ignite, BTopenworld, BTWireless, Yell.com and Concert. Each business has its own character and priorities and focuses on a particular sector of the industry. However, they work together to meet customers' needs.

BT Ignite is an international broadband network business, focused primarily on corporate and wholesale customers and is responsible for UK and continental Europe Internet Protocol (IP) networks.

BTopenworld is an international mass market broadband internet business that includes all of the company's Internet Service Providers (ISPs) in the UK and elsewhere, as well as Open.... (a digital interactive television joint venture) and Genie Internet (BT's pioneering mobile internet service).

BTWireless combines BT's worldwide mobile assets with a particular emphasis on mobile data. As new technology makes mobile data and internet services possible, mobile services are one of the fastest growing parts of the international communications business. BTWireless has extensive interests in Europe and the Asia Pacific regions and has, in particular, been building its presence in Japan, the second largest mobile market in the world. BT's strategic alliance with AT&T – Advance – gives BTWireless global scale and reach with the ability to reach more than 55 million subscribers around the world.

Yell.com is BT's international directories and associated e-commerce business and offers, in addition to traditional printed directories, a range of web-based services in the US as well as the UK.

Concert, BT's global joint venture with AT&T, offers high-speed network services to mainland Europe's largest international multinational companies, internet carriers and ISP's. Concert has the world's largest global public network, carrying twice as much international traffic as any other carrier and reaching 237 countries.

As a result of these strategic changes, BT is increasing the proportion of revenue that comes from outside the UK with operations in more than 50 countries.

Promotion

For some time BT's overall marketing strategy has been to stimulate overall communication, be it by phone or the internet. The long-running 'it's good to talk' television advertising campaign was a classic example of this approach, as is the more recent 'Stay in touch' campaign, featuring ET. Aimed at increasing call usage and the penetration of the internet, the campaign has addressed many communications issues, including the launch of a special website designed for people who work from home.

BT's website, www.bt.com, is increasingly used for marketing and promotion. It is also a means of communication

between BT and its customers which has resulted in a steady increase in orders, particularly for additional exchange lines.

For businesses, the 'You Can' campaign has highlighted the role that BT can play in helping customers find solutions to their communications needs as well as the potential improvements to efficiency and effectiveness that telecommunications can offer.

BT also enforces brand awareness through sponsorship of events like the BT Global Challenge, the 30,000 mile yacht race which started in September 2000.

Brand Values

Until 1991, traditional voice telephony was BT's core brand position. This was redefined in 1999 in order to keep pace with the massive changes occurring in the company and in the world of telecommunications.

The new BT brand proposition is founded on presenting the company as a guide to the potentially bewildering range of new technologies on offer. The overall BT brand consists of three key attributes: trust, potential and freedom.

Within that there are three categories, each with brand values of their own: BT operates in an expert, progressive and trustworthy way. In communications with customers, BT is empathetic, imaginative and pro-active. The personality associated with BT is friendly, helpful and enthusiastic.

Building for the net generation.
bt.com
BT Stay in touch
0800 800 845

The essence of the BT brand is rooted in the basic human need to connect with people, places, information, experiences and ideas. Connected to the familiar and to the new and to the world in general, the brand encapsulates connection in every sense of the word.

Millions are better off with BT Together.
0800 055 555
www.bt.com   BT Stay in touch

Market

In the old days, the UK television market used to be very simple – three terrestrial channels corresponding to the 1, 2 and 3 buttons on your set. When Channel 4 came along in 1982 it was the most radical shake-up the television market had seen since ITV was launched in the 1950s. Those days seem long gone now. Not only has Channel 5 added another terrestrial option, but the advent of cable and satellite has created an environment in which viewers have literally hundreds of channels to choose from. Digital television is growing the number all the time, as well as adding new services which radically change the role and use of the television. No longer a passive viewing medium, television is now interactive – a portal for a host of activities, from shopping and banking to choosing camera angles when watching a football match.

In all, 20% of the UK's 21 million television households have digital television, a figure which is projected to reach 53% by 2003 and 75% by 2008. By 2010, the government hopes for all UK homes to have digital television so that it can switch off the analogue television signal for good.

These factors create a complex and challenging environment for broadcasters like Channel 4. There are great opportunities to explore with digital subscription channels, but also much to protect in trying not to lose viewers to the new breed of multi-channel brands. Also, as traditional television increasingly vies for viewers' attention with the internet and video games, broadcasters have to adapt their programming to keep it relevant in the fast changing world of home entertainment.

Achievements

Channel 4 is one of the success stories of British broadcasting. With a public service programming remit and a reliance on commercial funding system, Channel 4 is in a unique position. This formula, combined with the strength and compelling personality of its brand, have helped Channel 4 steadily increase its audience share at a time when other terrestrial channels are in decline. Currently, its share of the UK television audience stands at 10.6% – a figure it has achieved with the help of highly innovative and award-winning programming.

Its output won Channel 4 one International Emmy and over 260 other television and film awards in 2000 alone. Too numerous to list them all, the channel's achievements can be encapsulated in some recent high-profile successes. Big Brother – a show that was rejected by rival channels – was one of the most popular television programmes in living memory. Attracting phenomenal ratings, an

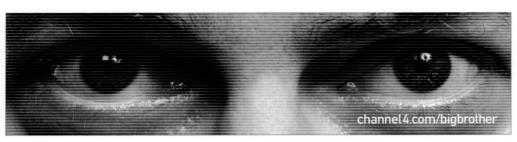

channel4.com/bigbrother

incredible 70% of the UK population watched at least one episode of Big Brother. Some ten million tuned in to its dramatic final instalment and 80% of all 18-34 year olds watched Big Brother at least once.

The programme also took television into new territory, encouraging viewer interaction via the telephone and the internet. The Big Brother website was the most popular in western Europe, attracting 200 million page impressions over nine weeks. Some 7.5 million voted in the final phone poll, making it the UK's biggest ever

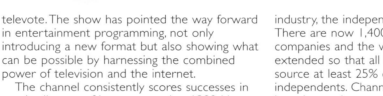

CARIBBEAN SUMMER — A SEASON OF PROGRAMMES, MUSIC AND LIVE CRICKET. FROM JULY 29.

televote. The show has pointed the way forward in entertainment programming, not only introducing a new format but also showing what can be possible by harnessing the combined power of television and the internet.

The channel consistently scores successes in nearly all areas of its programming. 1900 House was a hit in the field of 'edutainment', Queer as Folk pushed the boundaries as the first drama series about gay sex, and in sport, Channel 4 has revolutionised television coverage of test cricket. This has won numerous awards, including a BAFTA for Best Sports Coverage, and two prizes from the Royal Television Society – the RTS Television Sports Award and the RTS Live Outside Broadcast Coverage of the Year Award.

However, not all of Channel 4's achievements lie in its programming. It is also a tour de force in the film industry, investing £220 million in film production since 1982. Thanks to investment by FilmFour Productions, British cinema is producing box office hits like East is East and She's all That.

FilmFour was launched in 1998 as a subscription film channel and attracted 250,000 subscribers in its first year.

In all, Channel 4 is helping to make the UK a hotbed of creative talent in the television and film industries. In 1999 it invested £316 million in original British film and television.

History

Channel 4 was established after the 1981 Broadcasting Act which paved the way for a second commercial channel alongside ITV. When it began broadcasting in 1982, Channel 4 was required by law to cater for tastes, interests and audiences not served by existing broadcasters. It caused a sensation by giving airtime to people and social groups who had rarely been represented on television up to that point. It also created a new blueprint in UK broadcasting: commissioning or buying in almost its entire schedule. This revolutionary way of working has given rise to a whole new industry, the independent production sector. There are now 1,400 independent production companies and the working method has been extended so that all terrestrial channels have to source at least 25% of their programmes from independents. Channel 4's role as a publisher/broadcaster has attracted worldwide interest as a business model other television companies have sought to adopt.

Up until 1992, Channel 4 was tied financially to ITV, which sold its advertising space and funded programme budgets. In 1993 a change in legislation allowed Channel 4 to become self-funding and truly independent. Release from its financial ties with ITV means that Channel 4 is able to invest all of its income in programmes and new ventures, such as FilmFour.

Product

As well as the terrestrial television channel, Channel 4 operates other divisions offering subscription services, international programme and film sales, studio and post-production facilities and educational support material for schools and colleges.

Channel 4 is dedicated to offering an alternative to the mainstream on other channels and places a high premium on innovation, originality and diversity. Channel 4's identity as the channel of innovation is exemplified by a number of ground-breaking programmes, ranging from the entertainment of Big Brother to the harrowing and revealing documentary Staying Lost, which exposed the abandonment of British children lost on our streets.

FilmFour Ltd is one of the UK's pre-eminent

film companies, producing, distributing, financing and marketing films around the world. In 1999, FilmFour Productions invested in 26 feature films, including the hit, She's all That, which took £6 million at the UK box office. FilmFour International sells and markets the company's productions around the world, while FilmFour Distributors is responsible for UK distribution. Some of its successes include East is East, which generated £10 million – the largest ever UK box office receipt for FilmFour Distributors. Amongst the numerous awards won by East is East, is the Alexander Korda Award for Outstanding British Film at the 1999 BAFTAs. As a whole FilmFour's cinematic output has won numerous awards, including 32 BAFTA nominations.

The FilmFour subscription film channel is a great success and now a major brand in the Channel 4 stable. Placing a strong emphasis on British film, the channel has established a strong position in the UK's pay TV homes, helping to raise Channel 4's profile on digital satellite and digital terrestrial platforms. It shows over 120 films per month, transmitting nightly from 6pm to 6am. Offering titles like Human Traffic, Buena Vista Social Club and LA Confidential, FilmFour is dedicated to showing the best in modern independent cinema.

Other areas of Channel 4's product include Channel 4 International, which is responsible for selling and distributing programming overseas. This can either be homegrown brands like Dispatches, or programmes that Channel 4 buys exclusive international rights for, such as The Monica Lewinsky Interview, which it sold to over 30 territories. Channel 4 International also invests in co-productions with overseas partners, such as The History Channel.

Another important department is Commercial Development, which grows revenue streams in areas such as programme sponsorship as well as book and video sales. In addition to arranging deals such as Nescafe's sponsorship of Friends, Commercial Development oversaw the release of 'Ali G Innit', the best-selling video of 1999.

4Learning is responsible for the channel's educational programming which amounted to some 419 hours in 1999. This output is supported by educational material for schools, such as booklets and videos to sophisticated online projects.

Recent Developments

As well as the recent runaway success of Big Brother, the reinvention of UK cricket coverage has been another significant development for the Channel 4 brand. Not only has the channel managed to introduce more viewers to television coverage of cricket but it has also taken a highly innovative approach to scheduling programmes around it. The Caribbean Summer season of programmes was a prime example, aggregating programmes about Caribbean culture throughout the summer tour of the West Indies cricket team.

Channel 4 backed this up with investment which not only increased the entertainment value of cricket, but also supported the game itself. For example, over 26,000 children

from around the UK took part in a Channel 4 Grass Roots coaching programme, which involved coaching by West Indies Test players. Other events included a party and concert on Clapham Common, where Channel 4 provided live match coverage via giant screens, and a concert by the Wailers at the London Astoria.

Other important developments at Channel 4 include the launch of E4 – a new digital entertainment network. E4 consists of a pay TV channel screening top-drawer entertainment shows from around the world, and E4.com, a network of interactive comedy, games, music and entertainment channels. Launched in January 2001, E4 is representative of Channel 4's investment in digital and interactive media.

Another sign of this strategy to embrace opportunities offered by new media is Channel 4 Interactive. Created in 1999 as a new division, it is responsible for expanding and enhancing the services offered to the Channel 4 audience via digital and interactive channels. Channel4.com – the main website – lies at the core of this. It also aims to build filmfour.com into a definitive film website. In education, new media initiatives include homeworkhigh.com – a site designed to help 11-16 year olds with their homework. Homeworkhigh.com regularly receives two million hits per week. This will be followed by more exciting interactive learning aids which support Channel 4's schools programming. The division is also exploring opportunities in the mobile internet and enhanced services for digital television viewers.

Promotion

With one of the strongest brands in broadcasting, Channel 4 is an active marketeer, choosing communication channels and executions that reflect its innovative brand values.

It thinks about marketing in the same way as it approaches its output – as a platform to engage and entertain. Examples of this approach include the Caribbean Summer campaign of 2000, which was centred on the West Indies test cricket tour. Music events, featuring reggae artists flown in from the Caribbean, were staged at cricket grounds and other venues around the country, raising awareness for the channel's cricket coverage in an entertaining and innovative way. Channel 4 also stages outdoor film screenings to promote FilmFour. These are both examples of what Channel 4 calls 'experiental marketing'. Other promotional tools include outdoor advertising promoting individual shows which are chosen to reflect the values of the Channel 4 brand. Channel 4

owns its own 96-sheet billboard sites around the UK. It also makes extensive use of press advertising, again promoting selected broadcasted programmes.

'Idents' – short promotional previews for forthcoming attractions – are an invaluable tool. Worth an equivalent of £70 million in commercial airtime, idents are created and monitored with all the attention of a normal advertising campaign.

Channel 4 also makes extensive use of sponsorship, backing events which reflect the values of its brand. Examples include The Turner Prize, which it has sponsored for the last ten years, the Edinburgh International Film Festival and the Sheffield International Documentary Festival.

Brand Values

Channel 4's aim is to make 'television that matters' and to be a relevant and compelling channel for modern society. It aims to play an enlivening role in contemporary culture.

It also aims to be 'smart' – to be insightful, intelligent and ahead of the mainstream.

Innovation and creativity are at the heart of its brand and programme making, and it strives to embrace risk and be adventurous.

Libertarianism is another core value. It is not didactic, but strives to be a platform for free expression and a range of opinions. It wants to provide new perspectives on ideas, challenging accepted thinking.

CLASSIC fM

CLASSIC fM

Relax...

Market

Radio took an important step forward when the UK's leading commercial radio company, GWR Group plc, launched Classic FM in 1992. For years, publicly funded networks had dominated the market place. The advent of Classic FM broke that monopoly and challenged the notion that only the BBC could create a radio station that successfully broadcast classical music.

At the time of its launch, Classic FM was the first and only national commercial FM network. Since then two more national services and 131 new local radio licences have been awarded, bringing the current number of independent radio services to 246 in addition to the BBC's five national and 46 local and regional services.

New technology has revolutionised the radio broadcast market even further. The advent of digital radio is already delivering its promise of up to 200 new services broadcasting via DAB, cable and satellite, whilst the internet has fuelled a global explosion of some 9,000 online radio services.

Achievements

As the new Millennium gets underway, Classic FM can claim that access for a broad based mass audience to classical music has at last been created. The fact that this unique situation has been brought about by a commercial radio station makes this achievement all the more remarkable.

Eight years after transmitters were first switched on, Classic FM has achieved its ambition to become a respected, high quality international broadcaster. Bright, unpretentious and professional, it is one of the decade's broadcasting success stories. Despite an increasingly competitive market place, audiences have grown significantly. Within four months of its launch Classic FM had 4.2 million listeners. Today there are 6.3 million adults a week tuning in, as well as half a million children aged between four and thirteen years old.

The station's policy of allowing only six minutes of advertising per hour when the rest of the industry was broadcasting around twice that amount, was a bold and necessary part of developing and nurturing a discerning ABC1 audience. It was also important to persuade advertisers to produce commercials that fitted in with the station sound.

Classic FM introduced a completely new national ABC1 audience to advertisers for the first time. Commercial radio is now able to reach ABC1 adults on a national scale and in significant numbers.

The station has clearly shown how creativity can thrive in a commercial environment. Enthusiasm for new initiatives such as 'Music Teacher of the Year', 'Music of the Millennium' and 'Classic FM Families' has inspired many projects both on and off air under the umbrella title 'Do More with Music'. Strategic alliances with partners such as the London Symphony Orchestra, Save & Prosper and British Reserve Insurance are encouraging a whole new generation of music lovers.

Classic FM's pioneering approach to its programming, advertising and marketing has won the station many accolades, including more than ten Sony Awards. Classic FM has been voted UK Sony Station of the Year three times in just seven years, and has been nominated for the award on four occasions. It has two Gold Sony Awards for On Air Station Sound. Classic FM has won the Charles Grove Award from the National Federations of Music Societies for outstanding contribution to classical music

GRACE

POWER

EXHILARATION

CLASSIC fM

UK STATION OF THE YEAR

and was voted Campaign Medium of the Year in 1995.

History

Classic FM was awarded the first Independent National Radio Licence on September 30th 1991 and officially launched on Monday, September 7th 1992 at 6am, serving 95% of the UK population.

The sound of the station is a careful mix, balancing the personality of the presenters with a carefully selected repertoire, the music knowledge and skill of the producers and a range and variety of programmes. Presenting the music were a host of well known, talented broadcasters who successfully set a tone of intelligent irreverence for which Classic FM is now renowned.

From the start it has been a consistent policy to treat Classic FM not simply as a radio station but as a brand in its own right. This philosophy has driven forward a number of new and successful ventures over the years.

In 1994, Classic FM launched its own record label of compilation albums which regularly reach the top of the classical charts. Albums reflect programme strands such as the Hall of Fame, Smooth Classics and Relax, a spin off of the station's award-winning on air sound. A brand new range of Full Works recordings was introduced in 1997 in a successful joint venture with BMG Conifer.

1994 also saw the launch of the Classic FM Music Store, now called the Music Shop, a busy information call centre for listeners who want to know more about the music

and buy from a comprehensive range of CDs which can be ordered and delivered direct to listeners' doors. The development of online home shopping has seen a steady increase in sales.

Classic FM marked its second birthday by launching the Classic FM Listener Club. The club gives listeners a chance to interface with the station and experience all areas of the arts from concerts and exhibitions to film previews, wine tastings and exhibitions.

Further developments in 1995 saw the arrival of Classic FM Magazine which has since developed as the genre's UK news stand market leader. In July 1999, Classic FM launched its Live

Concerts division to develop concerts and events in association with partners such as Rover and United Airlines.

Classic FM has continued to develop its overseas market, which started in 1994, and which saw the launch of Classic FM Holland as well as a network of licences in Finland. In December 1996, Classic FM UK went on air via cable in Japan, reaching a potential audience of more than five million. Classic FM South Africa launched in Johannesburg on September 1st 1997.

In 1999, Classic FM launched 'Music Teacher of the Year', a brand new initiative to celebrate the work of music teachers in schools and raise the profile of music education. Other developments followed to enhance the music and programming schedule, including the introduction of 'Tonight at 11', a nightly series of stimulating music-led feature programmes.

In August 1999 Classic FM relaunched its website, recording six million hits within just fifteen hours. With unique users of the site rising by an average of 35% per month, classicfm.com is fast becoming the world's number one classical music portal, attracting online listeners from all over the world, in particular the US and Australia.

Throughout the 1990s, Classic FM has followed a clear strategy to meet the challenges of the changing media landscape. In November 1999 it was the first national broadcaster to launch digitally on the Digital One network and via digital television in the UK.

Product

The global development of Classic FM is based on three simple facts. Firstly that the music is as close as one can get to an international language. Secondly, the audience attracted by classical music tends to be one which is demographically very appealing to advertisers. Thirdly, Classic FM has developed a unique programming format and station sound which have proved extremely popular with a large audience.

Classical music is enjoyed throughout most of the developed world, but it is the way in which it is delivered that is crucial to Classic FM. Time poverty is rapidly increasing the need to find environments that help cope with the stress and pace of modern life. Classic FM creates the environment which makes classical music a relevant part of modern living. Programmes such as 'Smooth Classics at Seven' and 'Relaxing Classics at Two' reflect this mood driven philosophy.

The music is carefully programmed to match the listening requirements of a discerning audience which is often on the move. In the mornings and late afternoons when people are travelling, shorter pieces of music and individual movements are played. In the evenings, a complete concert of works takes listeners on a deeper musical adventure.

Classic FM is designed to appeal to a range of listeners, from those with considerable knowledge of classical music to those who have more recently come to enjoy it. In addition to the mainstream

programming are specialist programmes which range from current affairs and new technology to music discussion and exploration. Live music is an important part of Classic FM, with live concerts from venues and halls all over the world.

The other key value of the brand is involvement in bringing the music to the people. On air this is achieved through programmes such as 'Lunchtime Requests', 'Access All Areas' and the 'Fantasy Evening Concert' in which listeners get to choose the music.

Off air, Classic FM encourages a wider community of participation through special schemes such as 'Classic FM Families' which gives selected families the chance to go to live concerts for the very first time.

Recent Developments

Classic FM is not funded by a public licence fee so all of its activities rely on the development of partnerships with brands which share common aims and objectives. However, the absence of public cash funding has not prevented Classic FM from making a major contribution to the cultural life of the UK.

Year on year, the radio station has built up its audience across all ages and those who are tuning in are listening for longer. In 2000, Classic FM recorded a record set of listening figures, which include best ever reach, market share and total listening hours.

The station has revitalised the classical music CD market with two recent releases. Relax and Hall of Fame 2000 both turned Gold, reaching not only the top of the classical compilation charts but also entering the pop album charts.

Live concert production continues with a successful series of City Classics in London's Broadgate Centre. In the spring of 2000 the very first Classic FM Live! concert took place at London's Royal Albert Hall in aid of the Classic FM Charitable Trust. The event was so successful that Classic FM now regularly promotes its own concerts at this prestigious London venue.

Promotion

'Relax.......It's Classic FM', Classic FM's highly distinctive on-air promotional campaign has come to signify

quality, accessibility – and the unexpected.

In 1996 posters ran on billboards across the country using unusual shots of musical instruments to evoke the power, grace and glory of music. Since then promotion has concentrated on a mix of high profile alliances and sponsorships which gives leverage to the Classic FM brand with other partners to achieve maximum impact.

In the run-up to the release of Disney's animated extravaganza Fantasia 2000, Classic FM formed a cross promotional alliance which combined airtime and newspaper advertising with Listener Club interaction. A live performance of the film's London premiere formed the centrepiece of the promotion.

The launch of the new Rover 75 enabled Classic FM to stage three outdoor concerts featuring Kennedy, Lesley Garrett and the Medieval Baebes. And a close co-promotional relationship with Channel 4 saw the advent of 'Music of the Millennium', the country's biggest ever poll of music tastes, and more recently a live simulcast from Paris of Verdi's La Traviata.

Classic FM promoted its Easier Breakfast show and Full Works CDs in an on-pack promotion with Nestlé's Fruitful cereal brand which included a free front-mounted Breakfast Choice CD and discount tokens for the Full Works CDs. Other joint promotions have linked Classic FM with House and Garden magazine and Woman and Home magazine.

On air, the Relax proposition is successfully supported with a series of on-air trailers voiced by the actor Stephen Fry and created by Classic FM's award winning producer Tim Lihoreau. The recent album release 'Relax More' has been supported with a national press and television campaign.

Brand Values

Classic FM remains committed to its aim to present classical music to an ever increasing audience though its unique proposition as the accessible classical music choice which puts a contemporary face on classical music. In a crowded market place, Classic FM retains its relevance as the antidote both to the stresses and strains of everyday life and to all other radio stations. It encourages involvement through interaction and brand extensions and most importantly, has finally diminished the perception that classical music is elitist.

Club Med

Market

With the advent of mass market travel and the ease and frequency with which time zones are crossed, horizons within the holiday market have been significantly widened. Previously undiscovered corners of the globe are being brought to more people than ever before. The recent explosion of television travel programmes and websites also aid the traveller in becoming more aware of possible holiday destinations, previously out of the ordinary holidaymaker's grasp.

Such factors have led to consumers becoming more demanding. They want value for money, new experiences, the finest surroundings and good quality food and accommodation. As more people have greater experience of travelling abroad they are well aware of the standards that can be expected. Their time is limited and they want the best possible quality from their holiday.

It is an extremely competitive market with cut throat price promotions, all-in deals for families, special arrangements for single-parent travellers as well as an increase in more flexible package holidays becoming available. In addition, the trend towards last-minute booking and increased use of the internet to search for the best deals possible have also added to the plethora of choices open to consumers. Holiday companies must therefore be more adaptable in order to cope with the changes in this sector.

Achievements

Club Med is a global organisation, dedicated to giving consumers not only an escape from reality but also an opportunity for regeneration. Its unique philosophy makes it different from other operators in the travel business. It offers more than just a holiday – it proposes a way of life. It is the largest most comprehensive, all-inclusive holiday organisation in the world, annually organising over 1.6 million holidays, over

250,000 of which are for children. The 50th anniversary in 2000 was a momentous milestone, marked with celebrations throughout the Club Med organisation.

History

In June 1950, 300 people inaugurated a new leisure organisation, the dream of Gérard Blitz, a Belgian diamond cutter who was also a water polo champion and ex-resistance fighter. His vision was to create an escape for the general public from the drudgery of everyday life in post-war Europe.

His inspiration was the result of a camping holiday that he had shared with a group of friends. He decided to place a small advert in newspapers offering the first ever all-inclusive holiday. Over 2000 people responded and Club Méditerranée was born. Blitz was soon joined by Gilbert Trigano whose vision and commercial acumen drove subsequent development of the Club Med business.

The first Club Med village was opened on a deserted beach at Alcudia on the Balearic island of Majorca in 1954 and consisted of army surplus tents. In the same year, the first of Club Med's straw hut villages was opened on the island of Corfu. It was modelled on a Polynesian village and used beads as currency at the bar. The village at Ipsos still features strongly in Club Med's programme today. Not much has changed since the early days, although huts now have concrete floors and electric lighting.

A mountain village in Switzerland opened next in 1956 and the first Club Med village-hotel opened in Agadir, Morocco, nine years later. As Club Med's vision proved to be a popular formula, resorts opened all over the world, in no fewer than 120 destinations in 30 countries across five continents, with further additions in 2000 and 2001 including Crested Butte, Colorado, Kani in The Maldives and Beldi in Turkey.

Club Med became a limited company in 1957 and in 1966 its shares were first traded on the French Bourse. Club Med was rated on the New York stock exchange in 1984 and in 1994 it celebrated its twenty millionth customer. In 1999 the business was expanded again through the acquisition of Jet Tours Company.

For those with a penchant for cruising and the open sea, Club Med's first sailing cruiser was launched in 1990 followed by the second largest

sailing cruiser in the world, Club Med 2, in 1991. Since 1997, with Philippe Bourguignon at the helm, Club Med has regained its leadership position in the holiday market and started claiming a new position in the leisure industry.

Product

The beads, huts and lotus-eaters are still part of the Club Med image, but today they exist alongside smart-cards, luxury accommodation and a clientele varying in age from infants to pensioners. The average Club Med member is aged between 35 and 40, with 65% of guests travelling as part of a family. A high proportion of club members, as many as 60%, return year after year to soak up the sun, meet like-minded people, and enjoy the ever-increasing range of activities on offer.

In order to go on a Club Med holiday, you have to become a 'Gentil Membre' (otherwise known as a 'GM' or 'kind member'), and pay a minimal joining fee and annual subscription. Holidays are then all-inclusive and the price covers return flights and transfers, full-board (including wine and beer with lunch and dinner), sports facilities, qualified instruction, children's clubs, evening entertainment and comprehensive travel insurance. Extras, over and above this basic package, are also available and include activities such as scuba diving, excursions, health and beauty treatments.

Another main feature of Club Med is its 'GO' system. 'GOs' are multi-lingual, multi-talented, multi-national hosts and hostesses who are responsible for everything in the village from food to accommodation, sport to entertainment. Teams of 'GOs' are headed by a 'Chef de Village' (resort manager). They participate in all aspects of village life, as instructors by day, table companions at meal times and entertainers at evening events.

In addition to the Club Med villages that offer sun, sea and sand, Club Med is also one of the world's oldest ski-tour operators. Its first such village was launched in Leysin, Switzerland, in 1956. Today, the company features 29 winter sports destinations including centres in France, Japan and the US. The winter sports holidays include area lift passes and optional ski or snowboard lessons.

Recent Developments

In 1997, Club Med's President Philippe Bourguigon set up a five-key initiative to strengthen and update the original company foundation values. Among the improvements were the renovation of all village resorts, completed in 2000, and a refocusing of business services and their marketing. The implementation of a fair-price strategy and the streamlining of all pricing policies were also put under review. This up-dated approach sought to attract and retain a broader range of customers and to reinforce the brand's youth and strength.

Club Med has also been enlarging its leisure and recreational services as a means of turning the company, whose sole asset is the management of resorts, into one whose primary asset is its brand. Club Med's unique image expressed by its name will be applied to other activities and products with a high growth potential. The latest development in this area is the launch of Club Med World at Bercy in Paris. This offers a new Club Med concept, being situated in an exciting urban arena right in the heart of Paris. The resort offers a host of leisure activities, special events and creative ideas. Here you can discover the world of travel, gastronomy and a variety of arts and adventure activities in the centre of Paris.

Promotion

As part of Club Med's globalisation strategy, its brochure is translated into ten languages, with a circulation in Europe of around three million. In addition, it is available on CD Rom and at the website, www.clubmed.com, which also has a French version, www.clubmed.fr. The sites include virtual visits, where the customer can pan around the facilities available at various villages, giving customers a chance to become familiar with the company and its values before visiting a holiday village in person. After a Club Med holiday, the website which can also be used by holidaymakers to keep in touch with friends and Club Med staff, includes online promotions, contests and advice in the form of a discussion forum.

In June 2000, as the result of a £50 million investment, Club Med went online for sales and reservations offering a 24-hour, seven day a week secure payment system, together with a printout registration form. Club Med aims to become the world's leading virtual community for leisure activities and to develop sales or products and services that complement its core activities.

Throughout 2000 and into 2001, Club Med's celebration of its 50th anniversary took on a carnival atmosphere, using specific logos with the strap lines 'Happy Birthday Club Med' and 'Happy Club Med to you' appearing on related promotional material. All Club Med villages throughout the world devoted one day every week to its birthday celebrations. The celebrations have also been used to restablish Club Med's positive attributes and brand values in customers' minds, the message of trusted, solid, value-for-money holidays being a continuous theme.

Numerous events were also planned to create a lasting memory for guests of the celebrations, including exhibitions promoting 50 symbolic photographs of the history of Club Med. The 'GOs' in each village wore special 50th birthday outfits and organised a variety of special sports and games events. The restaurants in every resort had birthday themes, which ran throughout Club Med bars and boutiques.

Special events have been held, such as Trivial Pursuit nights on the history of the Club, interactive shows, and children's drawing competitions with a giant party including songs such as the Stevie Wonder musical hit 'Happy Birthday', remodelled and adapted to become 'Happy Club Med to you'. A CD entitled 'Crazy Signs' amalgamating eighteen tunes that 'Gentils Membres' and 'Gentils Organisateurs' have always danced to was also produced.

The celebrations finale was the launch of the state of the art catamaran 'Club Med' which took part in the prestigious around-the-world sailing event, 'The Race'. Measuring 33.5 metre long with a 40 metre high mast, the catamaran is one of ten boats especially designed for this race and symbolises Club Med's values of maintained momentum and a capacity to create and innovate beyond conventional limits. 'The Race' was created by the famous French sailor Bruno Peyron, and is the first ever 'non-stop', 'no-rules', 'no-limits' round the world sailing event. The event began when the boats left Barcelona on New Year's Eve 2000. The course circles the earth keeping the three great Capes to port, with a prize of two million US dollars. "We had to be part of The Race. We both share the same pioneering spirit," says Philippe Bourguignon, who also described 'The Race' as "a planetary challenge for a global brand".

Brand Values

Club Med is committed to providing trusted, solid value-for-money holidays and ensuring its customers' experience of a Club Med resort as happy, relaxing and enriching. This pledge goes right to the core of Club Med's philosophy. In addition Club Med is committed to maintaining the youthfulness and fun-loving nature of their global brand.

Things you didn't know about
Club Med

Club Med has over 30 village resorts featuring golf facilities in sixteen different time zones. It is the largest Golf Club in the world, using 9000 golf clubs, 84,000 golf balls and over 150 golf professionals.

The largest Tennis Club in the world is run by Club Med where 800 courts play host to 8,000 rackets, using 44,000 balls with the help of 300 qualified tennis instructors.

Similarly impressive is the largest water-sport club in the world run by Club Med, where 1,600 windsurfers are making use of 1,500 sailing boats, 85 waterski boats, 250 kayaks, 1,200 diving tanks and 2,000 pairs of flippers.

Continuing the water theme, Club Med employs a team of underwater gardeners to keep the lagoons and coral reefs clean in and around the Polynesian village at Bora Bora. They are also responsible for re-planting using plants from the underwater nursery.

Club Med opened its first ecology reserve in Rio das Pedros, Brazil, in 1994.

As part of the company's interest in survival and preservation of world species, Club Med jointly operates a Giant Turtle egg hatchery program at Cherishing in Malaysia. The program increases the turtle's chances of survival to maturity and a weight of up to 900 kilos.

Staff at Club Med speak up to 30 different languages are of 80 nationalities and can offer 70 different trades. There are 1800 sports instructors, 600 cooks and 2,000 child minders. The company serves 27 million meals every year.

Market

While the five established terrestrial players continue to dominate the UK broadcasting market, the 100 plus channels now available by cable, satellite and digital terrestrial continue to fragment the marketplace in a dramatic change of the broadcasting landscape that is being mirrored throughout the developed world.

At the same time, the opportunities afforded by the move from analogue to digital for even more channels and the ongoing competition for carriage in a limited cable universe, coupled with the proliferation of online services offering PC-based alternatives to television viewing, has seen broadcasters rush to provide branded services across as many of the new platforms as possible.

This explosion in viewer choice has also seen an accompanying debate about whether the broadcasting industry is sacrificing quality for quantity.

In the year that CNN marks twenty years since it first created the concept of 24-hour rolling news, the UK has seen ITN enter the 24-hour news business with the launch of the ITN News Channel alongside other UK players Sky News and BBC News 24.

On the pan-European front, there are five players: CNN, BBC World, Euronews, and business news services CNBC and Bloomberg.

More than ever, this has resulted in an increased need for strong marketing and branding so that channels can stand out from the competition with a clearly defined communications strategy to enable them to reach their target audience.

Achievements

When CNN launched in 1980 it was a single US network available to 1.7 million homes. Twenty years later the brand comprises fourteen television networks, fifteen websites, two radio networks and a mobile phone news service, and is available to a billion people worldwide.

Since it first launched, CNN has become synonymous around the globe with breaking news that is fast, accurate and impartial. Since the first story about a shooting in Indiana, the network has become a visual history book for the world, providing images from as wide a canvas as the Challenger Space Shuttle disaster, the Gulf War, Tiananmen Square, the Bosnian War, the Hong Kong handover, and the turn of the millennium.

In CNN's early years it offered a comprehensive, highly acclaimed American news service. In recent years, it has evolved to offer those same core brand values for regional audiences around the world. In 1997, CNN launched a regionalisation strategy and CNN International now comprises five separately scheduled networks for Europe/Africa/Middle East, Asia-Pacific, Latin-America, South Asia and the US, as well as a number of local-language joint venture television and online services.

CNN's pioneering approach to news broadcasting and its commitment to speed, integrity and credibility has earned it recognition from partners and competitors alike.

As the CNN brand enters the twenty first century, it is continuing to evolve to meet the needs of today's news consumers – not only through the traditional media of television and radio, but also through new media such as the internet and mobile telephony.

History

CNN first went on air on 1st June 1980, the brainchild of media entrepreneur Ted Turner, and the first round-the-clock news channel.

The fledgling cable channel, initially dismissed by sceptics as the Chicken Noodle Network, is now one of the world's most recognised brands.

It is a commonly held misconception that it was with its ground breaking coverage of the Gulf War that CNN's reputation of being first on the scene began. In fact, five years earlier CNN was the only network to provide live television coverage of the Challenger Space Shuttle disaster. This was followed by a string of events in which CNN attained critical acclaim for providing live coverage of issues of global concern: Tiananmen Square, the Bosnian War, the Olympic Park bombing, the OJ Simpson trial, the Hong Kong handover, the Clinton/Lewinsky scandal, the bombing of the American embassies in Africa, the tragic earthquakes in Turkey and Taiwan and the turn of the millennium. With this track record, CNN has established itself as the news channel of choice for world leaders, captains of industry and even its media peers, as well as millions of viewers worldwide.

In 1985 Ted Turner launched CNN International and beamed his news network into homes and hotels around the globe. The 24-hour network then became a defining part of the burgeoning

JUANITA PHILLIPS
CNN THIS MORNING

cable and satellite industry in Europe, the Middle East, Africa, Latin America and Asia, proving that CNN was an international channel that happened to be based in America – not an American channel that just happened to broadcast internationally. CNN International is now available in more than 151 million households worldwide, 230 million including its US distribution.

CNN continues to lead the way in

broadcasting and in 1997 introduced a strategy of 'regionalisation'. The biggest change was the introduction of five separately scheduled international CNN networks enabling the European and Asian channels to produce and broadcast programming targeted to their specific regions. This has meant more 'regionalised' feature programming, offering audiences a tailored and relevant service.

Internationally, London, Berlin and Hong Kong are now major production centres with nearly 50 hours of programming a week produced

CNN NEWS

from Europe and 30 hours a week from Asia. Additional staff and newsgathering bureaux in major cities enable CNN International to broadcast more than 90% of its programmes exclusively for international viewers.

Product

With the resources of its worldwide network of 39 bureaux and 850 broadcast affiliates, CNN is

committed to providing objective, accurate and relevant coverage of the most compelling stories for its viewers worldwide.

There is no substitute for first hand reporting and CNN International continues to strive for the highest level of access and presence in all parts of the world. While many news organisations reduce their bureau operations, CNN continues to expand, with new bureaux in 2000 in Islamabad and Belgrade, and there are still more countries on the list.

While the network's commitment to breaking news remains its trademark, CNN's range of regionalised programming means it is not purely a network to turn to when there is a major breaking story. With news programmes on style, business, arts, the environment, technology, travel and music, this is an evolving network that tailors its programming for its audience. Over 90% of the output is now generated specifically for an international audience and the network has come a long way from its early days as a pure

American export.

CNN London, CNN's largest bureau outside of the US, is a prime resource of output for the European feed. It currently produces three hours of live morning news and financial programming, and two live daytime shows as well as evening news broadcasts.

In autumn 2000, CNN opened a new digital state-of-the-art production centre in Hong Kong, CNN's first fully integrated television and internet newsroom.

CNN news is also available online at the award-winning CNN.com and on mobile telephony services through CNN Mobile.

Recent Developments

CNN's regional strategy continues apace through local-language joint venture partnerships both in television and online to make CNN content available to as many audiences as possible worldwide.

The years 1999/2000 saw the launch of television services CNN Turk and CNN+ in Spain, and a European edition of CNN.com, CNN.com Europe, as well as local language websites CNNItalia, CNN.co.jp in Japan and CNN.de in Germany, with more in the pipeline. These join existing local language websites CNNenEspanol.com, CNNBrasil.com, CNN Sverige, CNN Norge, and CNN Danmark.

CNN continues to aggressively pursue new media opportunities, including broadband and interactive television platforms, to fulfil its position as the pre-eminent provider of news content. The CNN brand values of fast, accurate news are now available in more than thirteen languages around the world and CNN is well placed to maximise its presence across all platforms as the digital age unfolds.

Promotion

The CNN logo is one of the world's most

instantly recognised brands. CNN's core message of being the world's news leader has remained unchanged over the years, and the logo has retained its consistent look since launch.

In January of 1999, CNN unveiled a series of new 'timelapse' on-air idents for its international networks. Shot on 35mm film to provide a cinematic quality, these included a diverse range of country landmarks from around

Europe, Asia, Latin America and Africa to give the brand a contemporary personality that would connect both geographically and emotionally with CNN viewers in 212 countries around the globe.

The brand was broken down into the following categories: the network trailers – with the CNN logo animated over a series of energetic backgrounds to convey the energy and technology of the network; the global identities – time-lapsed images to convey that the CNN brand is truly worldwide; the current ongoing introduction of regional identities – same time-lapsed concept, only with a more intimate feel by showing the faces up close and personal of specific people in their regions; and the house brand – the animation that runs prior to individual programming, using images, textures, colours and music that relate to the feel, content and time of day that the different programmes air, from the relatively light context of a travel show to the more serious tone of a current affairs discussion show.

The trailers for CNN programming have also incorporated the new logo treatments to provide a more elegant feel to the network identity without corrupting the logo itself. In October 1997, CNN London opened its first Creative Services unit, allowing for the bulk of the European network's promos to be made for Europe from Europe. The unit also supplies off-air support for the channel, through sales tapes and marketing show reels.

Brand Values

CNN continues to stand by the values of accuracy, impartiality, integrity, credibility and speed. Despite the increase in competition, it remains the breaking news service against which others continue to be measured. It also stands for entrepreneurialism and ubiquity – CNN is the global village broadcaster.

Things you didn't know about
CNN

CNN Chairman and CEO Tom Johnson lent Mikhail Gorbachev his pen to sign the papers officially dissolving the Soviet Union.

Actor James Earl Jones celebrates twenty years of being the voice that announces: 'This is CNN.'

CNN's worldwide audience of nearly one billion on the night that the Gulf War began in 1991 was the largest for a non-sporting event in television history.

CNN International's distribution outside the US has grown 1,700% in less than ten years – from 8.5 million to 151 million.

To project CNN network signals to satellites 23,600 miles above the Earth requires 300-400 watts of energy – half that of the average microwave oven.

Market

Coca-Cola is a truly global brand. Not only is it at the top of Interbrand's global brand league, beating off mammoths which include Microsoft, IBM, Ford and McDonald's. It also leads the £7 billion UK soft drinks category (Source: Keynote Research) and is the biggest Fast Moving Consumer Goods (FMCG) brand in the UK. Diet Coke is a powerful brand in its own right. It is the UK's second biggest soft drink brand and fourth biggest brand (Source: ACNielsen 1999).

Coca-Cola aims to serve consumers their choice of non alcoholic ready-to-drink beverages and has a broad portfolio of drink brands to meet consumers needs. Coca-Cola's products continue to perform well, displaying steady long term growth and are consumed over one billion times a day in over 200 countries.

In Great Britain carbonated soft drink (CSD) per capita consumption stand at 87 litres well below many of our European counterparts for example Norway (117) and the US (195) (Source: Canadean & The Coca-Cola Company estimates 1999).

Achievements

As a brand which attracts superlatives the achievements of Coca-Cola are manifest. For example, 'Coca-Cola' is the most recognised trademark in the world, with 94% global recognition. Incredibly, it is the second most widely understood word in the world, after 'OK'.

All of this makes Coca-Cola the most powerful and valuable brand on the planet, worth an estimated $72.5 billion in Interbrand's global brand league. The strength of this global success lies in the local connections that Coca-Cola builds with its consumers every day.

All of this has been achieved through a stunningly successful combination of global distribution and persuasive local marketing. The drink is distributed to more than 200 countries and its strategy is based on the aim that nobody should be more than a few minutes away from an opportunity to buy a Coke. Supporting this is one of the biggest and most widespread bottling and distribution networks in the world, sending Coke to all corners of the globe.

Its marketing is legendary, investing in one of the first-ever global advertising campaigns with the 1979 'I'd like to buy the world a Coke' strapline. It has also ensured its name remains in the world's consciousness by sponsoring global events like The Olympic Games and The World Cup. Coke's marketing strategy is based on a

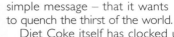

simple message – that it wants to quench the thirst of the world.

Diet Coke itself has clocked up some impressive achievements and is now the most popular diet soft drink in the world and has a bigger category share in GB than Pepsi, Pepsi Max and Diet Pepsi combined.

History

Coca-Cola was invented in 1886 by John Styth Pemberton, a pharmacist in Atlanta, Georgia. He brewed the syrup that would eventually become the world's favourite drink in a brass pot in his backyard. When the syrup was mixed with carbonated water, Pemberton knew he had created a delicious and refreshing drink and began selling it at 5 cents per glass.

Even at this early stage, the power of branding was important, with Pemberton's partner, Frank M Robinson, naming the dark brown liquid 'Coca-Cola' because he thought the two Cs would work well in advertising. Their earliest slogan read simply, 'Drink Coca-Cola'. Despite laying the foundations for the product and the brand, the two failed to realise its full potential and sold their interests to an Atlanta businessman, Asa G Candler, shortly before Pemberton's death in 1888.

The famous signature 'flourish' of Coca-Cola was registered in 1893. The word 'Coke' was trademarked in 1945. The Coca-Cola bottle was registered as a trademark by the US Patent Office in 1977.

Candler was a marketing genius and ensured that the Coca-Cola trademark appeared on countless products, from clocks to glass chandeliers. He created coupons which could be redeemed for a free Coca-Cola glass and put the brand's name in lights on trolley cars and in shop windows. By 1895, Candler's skill had made Coca-Cola available in every US state.

The design for the famous Coke glass bottle was created in the early 1900s. It was created to protect the brand from a growing army of imitators, determined to cash in on the success of the new Superbrand. The company wanted

to communicate to consumers that there was only one, genuine, Coca-Cola. Designers were given the brief to create a bottle 'which a person will recognise as a Coca-Cola bottle, even if felt in the dark'. The bottle should be shaped that, even if broken, a person could tell at a glance what it was'.

In 1900, Charles Candler, son of Asa, bought a gallon jug of the famous syrup to London. He introduced the new drink to James Spence, owner of James Spence & Company, at 76-79 St Paul's Churchyard, who served the first glass of Coca-Cola in Great Britain on August 31st 1900. Between 1900 and 1920 Coca-Cola could be found in soda fountains at Selfridges, the London Coliseum and other top department stores.

In 1919 the Candler family sold The Coca-Cola Company to Atlanta banker Ernest Woodruff and a group of businessmen. In 1923 Ernest's son Robert Woodruff, elected president of the Company, decreed "Coca-Cola should always be within an arm's reach of desire", setting down a principle which remains central to the company's distribution strategy today.

Coke's distribution skill has been built on the backbone of its bottling operations. The first bottling device was set up by a shopkeeper in 1894, allowing him to trade crates of Coke up and down the Mississippi river. The first major bottling plant was inaugurated soon after and, from 1926 bottling operations spread abroad. In 1932 the first GB plant opened in Brighton and, by 1939, had a further eight in operation.

By the outbreak of World War II, the drink was being bottled in over 44 countries. The war helped boost the brand's international distribution and profile, as US soldiers posted abroad demanded Coke in vast quantities. Robert Woodruff decreed that: "Every man in uniform get a bottle of Coca-Cola for 5 cents, wherever he is and whatever it costs the company."

Coke was first canned in 1955 and in 1982 it launched Diet Coke. This was the first brand extension of the Coca-Cola trademark and was an instant success. Within one year of its launch, Diet Coke was the largest selling low calorie soft drink in the US, and, by 1984, it was the third biggest soft drink in the US.

Product

The Coca-Cola phenomenon is built on a

Parental consent under 16's. Terms and conditions - see pack. No purchase necessary

Parental consent under 16's. Terms and conditions - see pack. No purchase necessary

remarkably simple brand portfolio. Coca-Cola and Diet Coke are the twin pillars of the brand, supported by extensions such as Cherry Coke and caffeine-free Diet Coke.

As for the formula, there's very little to say. It is one of the most closely guarded secrets in the world.

Recent Developments

The 100th anniversary of Coke's arrival in GB in 2000 was a huge landmark for the brand and celebrated by a frenzy of activity. This included support for the Millennium Festival, over 15,000 local events featuring artistic and cultural exhibitions, pageants and sporting activities, organised by local people for local people across the country.

On a corporate level, The Coca-Cola Company recently acquired Cadbury Schweppes' beverage brands in 155 countries. This adds popular brands such as Schweppes, Malvern and Dr Pepper to Coke's strong brand portfolio in GB.

Promotion

The first-ever Coca-Cola advertisement was an oil cloth sign, bearing the phrase 'Delicious and Refreshing'. Since then the brand's slogans have developed from 'Things go better with Coke' in 1963 to 'It's the real thing' in 1942 and used again in 1969. Then there's been 'Coke adds life' (1976), 'Have a Coke and a smile' (1979), 'Coke is it!' (1982) and 'Always Coca-Cola', introduced in 1993.

In 2000 Coca-Cola launched a new television campaign 'Coca-Cola Enjoy', the first new campaign since 1992, which featured two executions, both of which communicate what it's like to drink an ice cold Coca-Cola. 'Waterfall', shot in Hawaii, features a pouring Coke bottle which transforms into a waterfall. 'Parrot' brings to life some of the anticipation of opening a bottle of Coke. The new advertising was backed by huge sampling campaigns and localised PR activity. The 'Coca-Cola Enjoy tour' travelled around GB in 2000 giving out one million glass bottles of Coca-Cola.

Coca-Cola is one of the country's biggest advertisers for which it has received many accolades, especially for its Diet Coke ads. Highly successful television advertising has helped strengthen the popularity of Diet Coke with national favourites based around the 'Diet Coke Break' theme. The 'Appointment' ad in this series was voted Britain's Best Loved ad at the 1998 National TV Awards. The commercial features a posse of female workers who 'check in' for an

'11.30' appointment to feast their eyes on a hunky office window cleaner who takes a break at the same time to drink a Diet Coke.

A new campaign has recently been created in GB for Diet Coke, centred around an office Diet Coke vending machine. With three different executions, the ads are based around the relationships of four office workers, Jennifer, Brenda, Linda and Matthew and the theme of Diet Coke's advertising taps into the ritual of office staff taking refreshment breaks during the day.

As leading marketers, Coke continues to innovate. Launched in GB in 2000, Coke Auction was designed to give consumers the opportunity to bid for goods with credit accumulated from Coke ring pulls through a dedicated website. This activity was supported by extensive television advertising.

As well as broadcast media, Coke invests billions in additional promotional activities. Coke's connection with sport is essential as there is an irresistible link between the way that the world comes together in sport and also in its enjoyment of Coca-Cola. On the global arena Coca-Cola has sponsored every World Cup tournament since 1978 and has maintained an unbroken presence

at every Olympic Games since 1928.

It also invests in national level deals. Coca-Cola is the Official Soft Drink of the Football Association and the Official Soft Drink of Team England. It is an Official Sponsor of the Football League's Charter For Excellence and title sponsor of the Scottish Schools Football Association 'Coca-Cola Sevens' – Scottish Schools' U12s 7-a-side football tournament.

It is the official soft drink of the Welsh Rugby Union Team Wales and the Dragons Rugby Trust. Coca-Cola is also title sponsor of the Coca-Cola Netball Skills Award Scheme.

Brand Values

The Coca-Cola brand is all about making everyday moments more special through its optimistic spirit, authentic enjoyment, leadership and sociability. Coca-Cola is special because it inspires and energises consumers to get the most out of every day experiences bringing confidence and openness that helps consumers connect with others. The unique taste of Coca-Cola provides energy and exuberance through thirst-quenching, ice cold refreshment.

Things you didn't know about Coca-Cola

Coca-Cola is committed to making a positive contribution to local societies, particularly by helping young people to achieve their full potential.

In 1995 Coca-Cola established The Coca-Cola Youth Foundation. The initial focus of the charity is to provide a positive contribution to the development of youngsters. Current beneficiaries include Second City, Second Chance which implements The Coca-Cola Valued Youth Programme, a pupil tutoring scheme to meet the needs of secondary school students who need help to keep them in school.

Coca-Cola has also supported Special Olympics UK since 1978, which, through a programme of sports training and competition, enables people with a learning disability to acquire the confidence and social and life skills that will help their inclusion in society.

Since 1988, Coca-Cola has been an active member of Business in the Community and is also a member of the PerCent Club, which is the most widely recognised benchmark of a company's commitment to community investment.

Coca-Cola is also committed to conducting its business in ways that protect, preserve and enhance the environment. Coca-Cola was a founder member of Tidy Britain Group, established in 1965 and has a long association with three key programmes including National Spring Clean and People & Places.

Market

Over 300 years looking after the financial affairs of some of Britain's richest individuals has made Coutts a name that people automatically associate with wealth and success.

Its market is international private banking, serving 'high net worth' clients with a range of tailored services. Its traditional target market is older and more conservative. This, however, is changing – Coutts' client base is becoming younger and more financially sophisticated, with the company's target market being compiled of people from all walks of life with over £500,000 of investable assets.

Not surprisingly, this top end of the banking market – known as 'wealth management' – is highly competitive and attracting the attention of a wide range of financial service providers. As well as traditional private banks like Hoare & Co, Coutts competes with investment companies like Schroders, Flemings and Merrill Lynch, global banks such as UBS and Citibank, stockbrokers such as Cazenove & Co and, of course, the high street banking giants such as Barclays and Lloyds TSB who have private banking divisions. Internationally, there are even more competitors, all trying to zero in on the most affluent end of the market.

The private banking market is characterised by strong growth, both the number of high net worth clients and the wealth they hold grew by 18% in 1999 (Source: Merrill Lynch/Gemini Consulting World Wealth Report 2000). But, as well as growing, the sector is changing as clients are now younger and more sophisticated in their expectations of a private bank's performance and services. They demand not only personalised service but also a range of innovative investment and other financial products.

Achievements

With 20% of the UK's wealthiest individuals on its books, Coutts is the UK's leading private bank. Captains of industry, business professionals, sports and music stars are all among its exclusive clientele. Thanks to its reputation, heritage and service, Coutts has an international client base of 70,000, for which it manages assets worth over US$45 billion.

Given the increasingly pressurised nature of its market, Coutts has done well to remain competitive, combining its traditional strengths of personal service and confidentiality with the development of innovative products to suit the changing conditions of the modern wealth management industry. An example is its unique approach to investment management.

History

Coutts was founded in 1692 by John Campbell, who developed the banking side of his goldsmith business, primarily serving Scotland's aristocracy. He opened for business in London's Strand under the 'sign of the Three Crowns', which still features in Coutts' brand today.

Following Campbell's death in 1712, George Middleton and subsequent partners steered the thriving family business through a boom period and the financial chaos of 1720 into new premises at 59 Strand.

James Coutts, a Scottish banker, married Campbell's granddaughter in 1755. Six years later, as the widowed solitary partner, he took his brother Thomas into the business.

Widely credited with laying down the core values which still drive Coutts today, Thomas successfully nurtured enduring relationships with the rich and powerful including William Pitt, the Duke of Wellington, Sir Joshua Reynolds and even King George III.

His widow and heir, Harriot, selected Thomas's youngest granddaughter, Angela Burdett, to inherit. A noted philanthropist, Angela was a close friend of Wellington and Dickens and was created Baroness Burdett-Coutts by Queen Victoria. Her inheritance passed to her sister, Clara Money, who added the surname Coutts to her own.

A period of growth and consolidation ensued including moving to 440 Strand, the current Head Office, in 1904. In 1920 Coutts affiliated with National Provincial Union Bank of England but retained its identity and own board of directors. During the 1920s, the bank began to expand, opening more branches in London – in locations such as Cavendish Square and Park Lane – and, in 1961, its first branch outside the capital, in Eton.

In the 1920s, Coutts was one of the first UK banks to introduce machine posted ledgers. It continued to innovate with technology and, in 1961, installed its first computer. By 1963, Coutts was the first British private bank to have a fully computerised accounting system.

In 1969, Coutts affiliated with National Westminster Bank which had been formed from the union of the National Provincial & District Bank and Westminster Bank. This allowed Coutts to retain both its separate identity and to benefit from being part of a large and strong financial institution. In 1978, the Queen opened a new, modern, headquarters for Coutts, built on the same site at 440 Strand.

In March 2000 The Royal Bank of Scotland took over National Westminster Bank. As a result of this, Coutts continues to operate independently, as the international private banking arm of The Royal Bank of Scotland Group, one of the largest financial institutions in Europe.

Product

Worldwide, Coutts looks after clients in Europe, the Middle East, Latin America and Asia. Coutts specialise in providing expert wealth management services – including investment management, financial planning, trust and fiduciary services – and banking services to high net worth clients.

As well as exclusive banking services, Coutts offers a range of investment services, including discretionary and advisory investment management, alternative investments, liquidity management and customised investments. It is one of the leading providers of bespoke trusts and other structures, both on and offshore, providing tax and financial experts to design tailored wealth protection services. Coutts offers a wide range of tax advice and assists clients in their tax and estate planning needs.

Coutts is pleased to sponsor
Welsh National Opera's
production of

Orphée et Eurydice

Coutts is the UK's
leading private bank.
We provide expert
wealth management
for private individuals.

www.coutts.com

In order to create a 'consultancy' feel, a new office design was implemented. The design embodies the discretion and personal service that Coutts' reputation has been built upon, whilst creating a more exclusive business environment.

Recent Developments

To remain competitive and relevant in today's banking market, Coutts has developed a new range of innovative products which allow it to meet the changing needs of its clients.

The new range of investment products is one example of how Coutts is constantly adapting its service to keep up with the competition. Giving investors access to world-leading fund managers, these programmes, launched in January 1999, have already attracted over $5 billion in assets.

Another example is a new series of leading edge alternative investment programmes, available exclusively to Coutts clients. These products, which are offered in dollar, sterling and euro-denominated investment programmes, have assets under management of over $1.5 billion. This makes Coutts one of the largest fund of hedge fund managers in Europe.

The bank also recently opened its first Middle East office, in Dubai. Looking after clients in the Gulf States and the Indian sub-continent, the office is the latest international expansion for the brand. It is also expanding in Europe, with four further offices planned to open in 2001.

As with other companies that want to excel in the financial services industry, Coutts has been investing heavily in technology to improve its service standards and product offering. In September 1999 it was the first UK private bank to launch an internet banking service and plans to continue to harness the best of new technology to introduce innovations in the field of investment management.

Promotion

Over the years, Coutts has advertised less than other financial brands – even other private banks. Its central brand value of highly personalised, discreet service is often better served by word of mouth and personal introductions than 'noisy' marketing. Datamonitor recognised this in a 1998 report on private banking. It said:"As most private banks' services are broadly similar, campaigns tend to focus on brand name and image. However, the main source of new business in this sector is still personal recommendations."

However, that is not to say that Coutts does not invest in appropriate advertising to communicate its core brand message. 2001 sees Coutts rolling out a new campaign called

'In your world', starting with a new range of brochures. The campaign positions Coutts as understanding the exclusive world in which each of its clients live. Featuring photography using a fish eye lens and 360 degree panoramic shots, the design of the advertisements blend the bank's old values with contemporary style. Coutts also invests in sponsorship, especially in the arts. In 2000, it invested in a sponsorship programme with the Royal Shakespeare Company and Welsh National Opera.

Brand Values

The essence of the Coutts brand is quality and personal service. It is built on a tradition of service dating back to the seventeenth century, but Coutts is also a modern brand, representing a world-class private banking organisation.

The brand is supported by four core values which Coutts believes today's financially successful individuals expect from a private bank of its stature. They are: professionalism; performance; personal service and security.

Historically the Coutts brand has combined understated traditional values with cultural awareness and discretion. Going forward, Coutts wants to be seen as individual, stylish, objective and innovative.

The brand is positioned around its proposition – to offer expert wealth management to private clients by providing access to innovative, world-class expertise, delivered through the outstanding personal service of its experienced private bankers.

With the key aim of protecting and growing its client's wealth, this premier British private bank will continue to blend its traditional values with a state-of-the-art approach to wealth management.

DIRECT LINE™

Market

There are thirty five million private motorists in the UK, all of which are obliged by law to have insurance covering themselves, other members of the public, their car and other people's property against injury and damage.

Most motorists prefer the security of comprehensive cover, and to date two thirds of the £8 billion spent annually in the UK on motor insurance is for policies offering comprehensive insurance.

The price war of the 1990s helped to push premiums down for many motorists but it resulted in a battle for supremacy among the growing number of companies in an overcrowded market. The introduction of direct selling, cutting out the middleman, helped to change the face of the insurance market in addition to increased use of the internet, with an estimated 12.3 million internet users in 1999 (Source: National Opinion Poll1999). The success of this approach was pioneered by Direct Line, the UK's largest direct motor insurance company. The simplicity of its selling methods modernised the world of motor insurance and revolutionised the insurance market in all sectors from motoring to mortgages, pet cover to life assurance. In addition it raised the expectations of millions of consumers in terms of value for money and customer service.

Achievements

When Direct Line was launched in 1985, it was the first insurance company to use the telephone as its only method of selling its policies. By dealing directly with the public and cutting out middlemen and their commissions, the company was able to use the advantages afforded by its technological efficiency to reduce premiums for millions of UK drivers.

Having begun with motor insurance by phone, it followed with home insurance as its second core product. More recently it has become a provider of financial services including mortgages, pensions and travel insurance.

Direct Line has three million customers. It is the UK's largest direct private motor insurer and the sixth largest insurer of homes and their contents. It employs over 7000 people in six cities and has total assets of more than £2.7 billion.

Direct Line recorded a profit by its third full year of trading despite offering premiums which were typically 20% lower than those of its competitors. In the following three years after launch, Direct Line achieved 500% growth and signed up its one millionth customer less than a decade since its arrival in the marketplace.

Direct Line can lay many 'firsts' at

its door. It was the first insurance company to extend its opening hours from 8am to 8pm on weekdays and from 9am to 5pm on Saturdays. It was also the first motor insurer to enable customers to register their claims by telephone and the first again to provide 24-hour emergency helplines.

History

Since it was established in 1984, Direct Line has remained a wholly owned subsidiary of The Royal Bank of Scotland Group. The company's first television advertisements appeared during

the late 1980's but its branding breakthrough came in 1990 when the first television commercial featuring the distinctive Direct Line red phone on wheels appeared on UK screens.

Within three years of its launch, the business extended its product range into home insurance, adopting the same tactics of keen pricing, a straightforward product and a challenge to the status quo which – in the case of home insurance – involved challenging the grip on the market exercised by the mortgage lenders of the time.

By 1993, with the company's two flagship products the fastest growing in their sectors, Direct Line decided to enter the broader financial services market with the introduction of unsecured personal loans for existing customers. This was followed by a mortgage product in 1994 and then a series of further financial services including life insurance in 1995, a tracker PEP and a savings account in 1996, followed by travel and pet insurance in 1997. In addition Direct Line Rescue, a service to challenge traditional motor breakdown companies, was launched in 1998. This made an

immediate impact on the roadside assistance and breakdown recovery market. Its unique approach enabled Direct Line to price 20% lower on average than the AA and RAC.

Green Flag, the UK's third largest roadside recovery service, became part of the Direct Line Group when it was purchased in 1999 from Cendant for £220 million. The business has 2.5 million customers which represents 12% of the UK breakdown market. This acquisition established Direct Line Rescue as the UK's third largest breakdown recovery provider.

Product

Each of Direct Line's products is designed with the same basic philosophy – to offer consumers a clear, straightforward, good value alternative to products which are sold through traditional distribution channels, especially where those channels involve a middleman who can be cut out to reduce costs further. For all its products Direct Line aims to continuously provide products that can be adapted to meet the individual customer's needs. As the company carries out a vast majority of its business using the telephone, customer service is at the core of the Direct Line proposition. To ensure that standards are maintained, the company provides all staff with customer care training and re-engineers sales processes to cut out complicated forms and jargon. One of its first revolutionary moves was the removal of the need for 'cover notes' by arranging for all documents such as policy schedules and insurance certificates to be laser-printed immediately and forwarded by first class post to customers, usually for delivery the following day.

Innovative technology helps Direct Line keep down costs which in turn helps to reduce premiums. For example, most Direct Line products are paid for using credit cards or Direct Debits so that all payments are processed electronically. This keeps staffing levels and overheads to a minimum.

Automated call handling systems also ensure that the company's fifteen million customer calls each year are quickly and effortlessly re-routed between its six call centres located in various cities across the UK. This ensures the length of time that customers have to wait to speak to an operator is kept to a minimum.

Recent Developments

Following the success of Linea Directa in Spain, which is now Spain's largest direct provider of motor insurance with almost 300,000

Take an extra 5% off this summer.

.com
www.directline.com

Get 5% off your travel insurance when you buy online.

Direct Line Insurance, Direct Line House, 3 Edridge Rd, Croydon, CR9 1AG.
Calls maybe monitored or recorded to improve service.

Take an extra 5% off this summer.

.com
www.directline.com

Get 5% off your travel insurance when you buy online.

Direct Line Insurance, Direct Line House, 3 Edridge Rd, Croydon, CR9 1AG.
Calls maybe monitored or recorded to improve service.

internet. Jamjar.com also offers an online part exchange facility.

In 2000 Direct Line launched the world's first online life assurance policy which offers immediate cover. Traditional rating was based on age, sex and smoker status, which resulted in 90% of customers being offered the same rate. Direct Line's system assesses specific factors to provide a more accurate prediction of life expectancy on which the rates are based. It has seven underwriting categories – three smoker classes and four non-smoker classes.

Promotion

The famous red phone continues to appear in all advertising and marketing communications and is a constant 'cheeky but likeable' symbol of Direct Line's brand personality. It evokes feelings of friendliness, fun, innovation and the arrival of a rescuer – emotions that are rarely associated with the dry world of insurance.

This icon, with its associated jingle, rapidly established high levels of recall among consumers helping to push the company's awareness ratings to levels normally associated with high profile consumer brands.

In line with the company's continuing business online, the red telephone is used in the logo for the website www.directline.com. It is also included in all the company's extensive advertising campaigns. The 2000 campaign incorporated three months of television advertising in London, Scotland and other satellite regions which focused on the two minutes it takes to get a motor insurance quote online. Other media used included advertising on sandwich bags, London Underground posters, national newspapers and online banners. The diversity of the campaign reflected the need to target internet users according to their lifestyle and location.

Sponsorship continues to be high on its list of promotion essentials. Previous recipients have included the International Ladies Tennis Championships at Eastbourne, a preparatory event for Wimbledon, and the Cliff Richard Tennis Trail which introduces tennis to youngsters who might not otherwise get the chance to play. In Autumn 2000 Direct Line became the sponsor of the ITV Movie Premiere season.

customers, Direct Line announced a joint venture with the Japanese life insurer Yasuda Mutual Life Insurance in 1999 to sell motor insurance in the world's single largest motor market.

Direct Line is the UK's leading online insurer. Since its launch in 1999 www.directline.com has commanded a 30% share of the online general insurance market and carries out upwards of 250 thousand quotes per month. The company's aim is to sell 15% of its motor insurance business online by 2003.

The online 'quote and buy' process is simple: customers complete a few personal details, type in their registration number for a car insurance or breakdown recovery quote, or house details for a home insurance quote, and instant cover can then be taken out. The system is integrated with the call centre operation so that during opening hours customers can call up to complete the transaction.

Brand Values

Direct Line has set itself a mission to succeed. The company as a whole and the individuals it comprises strive to treat customers in a way that is always trustworthy, straightforward, human and challenging. It is customer-focused, innovative and pioneering. Its level of consumer awareness in the UK is high, reflecting the success of the red phone icon.

Direct Line's new online motoring site, www.jamjar.com was launched in July 2000. www.jamjar.com sources UK cars at up to 30% off the manufacturer's list price and passes on the saving to the customer in its 24-hour showroom. Each car comes with a warranty and a customer friendly returns policy and can be delivered to the customer's door months earlier than competitor imports. Direct Line estimates that by 2005, 15% of cars will be sold via the

Things you didn't know about Direct Line

Direct Line's first office opened in 1985 in Croydon with just 63 staff.

Direct Line sells a motor insurance policy every six seconds of every working day.

The voice-over on Direct Line's television commercials from 1990-1997 was actor John Alderton.

Since it was launched in September 1999 www.directline.com has averaged over 250 thousand quotes per month.

Direct Line operates a pet bereavement helpline.

Market

'These boots were made for walking' went the song. But boots and shoes aren't what they used to be. These days they are made for walking in, working in, dancing in, and playing sport in. Current fashion trends are blurring the boundaries between work and leisure, and shoes, as well as clothes, are crossing the functional divides. In industry jargon traditional footwear is called 'brown shoes' and trainers 'white shoes'. The new trendy hybrid is the 'athleisure' shoe, a blend of the two. There are trainer details in formal shoes and vice versa. Though athleisure tends to be a mid-market shoe, even top-end brands such as Prada and Gucci have an athleisure twist. The traditional brown shoe is now targeted at traditional 'businessmen' rather than being a mainstream fashion item.

So footwear which used to compete in one segment of the market now competes across the entire market.

There have been some equally major changes in distribution since the mid 1990s. The break-up of the British Shoe Corporation, which owned over a third of high street shoe shops began in 1996, and sent the market into a state of flux. With many of the traditional outlets gone, distribution has become more difficult. The problem has been compounded by the rise of own brand shoes from the likes of Next, George (for Asda) and Matalan, which offer consumers a similar look at lower prices than the branded products.

Achievements

Dr. Martens – or Doc Martens, Docs or DMs as the footwear is familiarly known – have achieved global cult status, winning allegiance from a diverse array of subcultures since they were launched in 1960. What started off as a worker's boot rapidly became a mainstream fashion item. With each shift in youth fashion and thinking, new generations have moulded the shoe and recycled it for their own ends. It has been adopted by tribes, from mods and skinheads to punks. The original 1460 style is a design icon, in the same league as the Volkswagen Beetle, Levi's and Marlboro cigarettes. What was once a bulbous and plain workwear boot has become an attractive essential, a perfect blend of form and fashion. Like the subcultures that created them, Docs are scruffy, smart, sexy, macho, fashionable, fashionless, classy, classless, uniform and unique.

People develop an emotional attachment to the Dr. Martens brand. They are 'worn in' rather than 'wearing out', and wearers see them as 'old friends' which often catalogue whole periods of their lives. As such, though wearers may buy new styles, they are loath to throw the old ones away.

Doc Martens have revolutionised shoe fashion for women. A sixteen-year-old girl is more likely to buy a pair of DMs as her first solo purchase than a teetering pair of stilettos.

In 2000 Dr. Martens celebrated the fortieth anniversary of the traditional black boot and mounted an exhibition on the brand at the Design Museum in London.

History

In post-war Germany a 25 year old German soldier, Doctor Klaus Maertens, broke his foot in a skiing accident in the Bavarian Alps while on leave. He teamed up with a friend, Dr Herbert Funck, a mechanical engineer, to devise a shoe sole that would be easier on his damaged foot when walking. They invented a sole filled with air, made with ex-Luftwaffe plane tyres, and attached a crude leather upper to it made out of the leather leggings of ex-officers' uniforms.

So comfortable was this boot, that the pair tried it on their friends, and it became so popular that they began hand-made production of it in Germany in 1947. The boot was extremely popular, particularly with elderly women and in 1952 Maertens and Funck opened a factory in Munich. By 1959 they decided to advertise for overseas manufacturers of their patented air cushion sole in overseas trade magazines.

In the UK, R. Griggs & Company Limited, bootmakers since 1901, were anxiously scouting for new products. Griggs made the best-selling Bulldog boot which marched its way on British soldiers' feet through two world wars, but now that the War was over competition was intense, not least from the Tuf boot. They saw Maertens and Funck's advert in Shoe & Leather News, contacted them, and acquired the exclusive licence to produce the air-cushioned sole in the UK.

Griggs made a few key changes before launching the boot. The elongated German heel was altered to a more rotund and orthodox shape and because they intended to market the boot as workwear, a strong leather upper with a bulbous shape was attached, with a distinctive yellow welt stitch. Griggs also designed a two toned grooved sole edge and unique sole pattern. They called their brand of Dr. Martens footwear AirWair.

On April 1st 1960 the first Dr. Martens boot rolled off the production line in the small village of Wollaston in the UK. Taking its name from the date of its birth, the eight hole 1460 boot had arrived. During the first few years of the 1960s sales of DMs were almost exclusively to postmen, factory workers, builders, policemen, medics, London Underground staff and other workers. Costing just £2 when they launched, the boots were soon complemented by the three hole plain Derby shoe, known as the 1461, which proved particularly popular with the Post Office.

The boot has always been popular with the police and became standard uniform in the late 1970s. The soles were resistant to oil, fat, acid, petrol and alkali and proved particularly useful with leaking car fuel at traffic accidents. Some policemen also reckoned that the soft soles proved invaluable for sneaking up on criminals.

Labour MP Tony Benn, champion of workers' rights, was the first public figure to consistently wear Doc Martens, and other figures from across the political spectrum followed suit. Trotskyist lecturers and Socialist Worker students often wore Docs, possibly as a sign of political alignment with the workers they campaigned for, who trudged to work every day in the very same boots.

When the skinheads picked up on Dr. Martens, the boots' place in modern sub-culture began.

1977.

1999...

We make the boots.
You make the history.

You made the history.
We wrote the book.

Their simple utilitarian style was both an anti-fashion statement and a nod to their working class roots, a badge of both power and pride.

Pete Townshend of 'The Who' was one of the first celebrities to be seen wearing Dr. Martens, and the movie version of the album Quadrophenia provoked a scooter and Mod revival, which led to Docs being worn by a new generation.

Doc's were later adopted by punks. Tribes came and went and cultures changed, but Doc Martens stayed.

One of the traditional manufacturing methods used to make Dr. Martens footwear – Goodyear Welted Construction – hasn't much altered since 1960, but the designs have developed in leaps and bounds, never more so than in the mid 1980s when women adopted Docs as an emblem of 'proletarian chic'. The burgeoning women's market led to a flurry of fantastic styles, colours and patterns, and by 1994 half of Dr. Martens wearers were women.

In the 1990s Dr. Martens began exporting to the US, and, as it had grown in the UK through the underground movement, it began life across the Atlantic among small independent retailers, before quickly exploding into the mainstream.

The brand remains strong as a result of consumer loyalty and product development.

Product

The Dr. Martens brand has a series of product categories including the Classics along with Open AirWair sandals and more formal footwear.

Dr. Martens makes products for eight key markets. The traditional classic products – including the eight-eyelet black boot and the three-eyelet

Gibson. A range of fashion shoes are aimed at 15-25 year old women. There's a 'street fashion' unisex range, an 'urban outdoor' range, a children's range, and a youth range. There is also a men's shoe range, from suit shoes to jeans shoes, and Open AirWair sandals for both men and women.

Each category covers a broad range of product. There are about 275 styles in total, which are updated twice a year.

Dr. Martens footwear is sold in over 78 countries round the world. The US is the biggest market, representing 60% of sales, followed by the UK and then France.

Recent Developments

In the mid 1990s Griggs opened the Dr. Martens Department Store in London's Covent Garden, stocking a wide range of footwear plus Dr. Martens clothing and licensed merchandise.

Dr. Martens operates in the fashion business and launches new products every six months. As well as keeping up with fashion trends, the shoes feature innovations such as new sole and upper shapes and unique fastening systems. Materials for uppers have included neoprene, which is used in wetsuits, lightweight mesh and moulded rubbers and plastics.

Promotion

The Dr. Martens brand has always been associated with sub-cultures, be they social or musical. However this following was never sought: it happened spontaneously from a grass roots level. So it was inevitable that by the 1980s the brand was becoming increasingly involved in music sponsorship and promotion, and this strategy saw it through a decade.

Its involvement in the music scene ranged from sponsorship of breaking and emerging bands, through financial aid for small bands to allow them to tour, to sponsorship of large music festivals across the world, be it Reading, Glastonbury or Phoenix in the UK, or one of many regional concerts in the US.

However, over recent years the brand's active tie to music has become less of a feature of its advertising and promotion. One reason is its global promotional strategy of 'one brand, one image'. Dr. Martens is at different stages of its

development in different regions of the world, and international music genres are very disparate. As such it is difficult for the brand to have one voice when it is promoting itself to different youth cultures around the world who are not united by any strong tribal ties.

The Dr. Martens book, published in 1999, was a celebration of 40 years of the Dr. Martens brand. There have been four above-the-line advertising campaigns, the first international ad campaigns the brand has ever run. Dr. Martens has also launched a website which facilitates two-way interaction with consumers and showcases all the products - www.drmartens.com. In addition, the brand publishes a Dr. Martens lifestyle magazine and sponsors West Ham football club.

The current promotional strategy focuses on the brand's authentic and quirky heritage while stressing its evolution and relevance to modern customers. Dr. Martens used to say, 'Fashion came to us', but it is now 'taking the brand to fashion'. Thus it is advertising in fashion magazines, including Maxim, FHM and Marie Claire, as well as music magazines. A new global campaign across press, cinema, television and outdoor, is highly visual, showing rather than telling people, what it can do.

Brand Values

The Dr. Martens brand values focus primarily around authenticity and youth culture, with durability, fashion and quality also being important.

Things you didn't know about
Dr. Martens

Legend has it that the original boot was intended to have an oily finish, suitable for use in the fish markets of east London. But a rogue batch slipped through uncoated and proved to be equally durable and more appealing to the eye.

Dr. Martens has an entry in the Oxford English Dictionary.

Dr. Martens has its own tartan, the MacMartens Tartan.

Thousands of pairs of fake Doc's have been seized by AirWair internationally and redistributed to homeless and war charities around the world.

Crack SAS troops wore Dr. Martens in the Falklands War.

The prototypes for the Open AirWair range were made for a Polaris submarine crew.

Market

DIY has never been more popular. The DIY market was estimated as being worth £8.12 billion in 1999 (Source: Mintel). Decorating has now become a fashion statement. The way a person decorates their house says as much about them as the way they dress. The huge increase in the market is a product of the large number of television programmes and magazines influencing decorating tastes. In the past ten years the total circulation of home-interest magazines has increased by 84% with more than 40 major titles on the news stands including Dulux's own Colour Magazine which is sold in newsagents and DIY stores. BBC Changing Rooms, one of the most popular DIY programmes has a viewership of over twelve million, a figure comparable to an episode of Eastenders.

Research shows that traditional home decorating roles have also changed. Women are now taking an increasing interest in DIY making 57% of DIY purchases and more than a half do their DIY single handed. The average female DIY enthusiast is 25-35 years old and likes colours and styles that are contemporary and individual. Women are also buying brighter and bolder colours. This demand for stronger, individual colour is reflected by sales of the In-Store Mixing System paints which have more than doubled since 1998. Colour trends for the Ethnic themes using Oriental and African colours are also dominating the market.

The housing market also reflects the amount of paint sold in the UK. At the moment one in ten adults moves each year which equates to 4.5 million home owners who need to redecorate every twelve months.

Achievements

Dulux is a brand leader in both the decorative and retail paint markets. For 30 years it has had a consistent share of at least 36% of the UK paint market.

Part of Dulux's success has to be laid at the feet of the advertising campaign that created the Dulux Dog. This unforgettable furry friend has made the brand both accessible and instantly recognisable over the past 40 years.

The continuing success of the Dulux brand today is due to fresh PR and advertising campaigns that aim to capture the essence of new trends, and

the attention of younger professional consumers.

History

ICI was first formed in the 1920s however, it wasn't until after World War II that the DIY market was properly established. The DIY market came into being in response to an increasing consumer demand for cheaper ways to decorate and a shortage in labour. From 1955 onwards ICI began to recognise the demand for more DIY products and soon became a market leader.

As decorative paint was, and still is, the main product sold to DIY customers, ICI focused most of its attention on producing a range of glosses and emulsions called Dulite. It was not until the early 1960s that the brand was re-named Dulux.

The Dulux Dog marked a momentous moment in the brand's history. It signified a new era of dominance in the paint markets for Dulux, establishing it as one of the UK's most distinctive brands.

By the 1970s the market had grown so much that the Dulux brand had to be split in two, to supply the needs of retail and trade sectors. Since then there

have been several brand extensions such as wall coverings and carpet tiles. However in the 1980s the Dulux brand was rationalised focusing on its core business – paint.

Throughout the 1990s Dulux continued to bring colour to life with new ranges such as Heritage and Inspirations and the revolutionary In-Store-Mixing System which can tint paint to consumers specifications on request.

Product

The Dulux range now consists of ready-to-use ranges including Weathershield, Dulux Discovery and ONCE. The In-Store Mixing System is a pioneer in its field providing over 4000 colours on demand in a variety of finishes at most local DIY outlets. Thanks to the increase in paint effects used by celebrities in DIY television programmes, consumers are now much more aware of the decorative effects that paint can achieve. In response to demand, Dulux produced the Special Effects range which includes paint, transfer stencils, colour wash, wood wash and metallic finishes. In September 1999 Dulux launched KidZone, a range of paints designed especially for children. The colours in the range are grouped into six themes and have transfers, stencils, novelty glitter and luminous paint finishes to go with them.

Specialist paint emulsions include the Kitchens and Bathrooms range which is designed to cover hairline cracks and combat damp and moisture. Dulux ONCE (interior paint) and Weathershield ONCE (exterior paint) are ready-to-use paint ranges that cut decorating time in half by producing perfect coverage in one coat.

The gloss range comprises paints in Brilliant White and a range of colours in water-based, non-drip and gloss finishes. There is also a specialist exterior wood gloss system under the Weathershield range. All glosses are supported by a range of undercoats and primers.

The garden is now perceived as an extension of the home in terms of décor. In response to demand for colour in the garden ICI paints has produced the Cuprinol Garden Shades range for wooden fences, sheds and furniture and a range of bright colours for brick or rendered walls.

Recent Developments

Dulux has developed a new paint range called Dulux Discovery. Inspiration has been taken from all over the world to bring the consumer three contemporary themed collections, Oriental Discovery, African Discovery and Urban Discovery. The consumer simply chooses one of the themed collections and selects any combination of colours and special effects to achieve the desired 'look'. The Discovery range also comes with Match Patch Paint Testers – the first ever mess-free peelable paint swatches. All the consumer has to do is apply a patch to the wall and 'match' it with another colour or paint effect from the same collection.

The KidZone collection from Dulux is a simple and effective solution to every parent's problem of decorating their child's bedroom in an easy, but exciting way that appeals to the imagination. Parents and children can choose from six popular themes. Space – with starships, planets and stars and glow-in-the-dark paint; Underwater – with exotic fish, tropical colours and shimmering paint effects; Action Adventure – with bright fluorescent colours, fast cars and aircraft; Dreamworld – with ballerinas, fairytale castles, magical unicorns and pretty glitter paint; Football Crazy – which creates a fantasy football game in the room and Really Cool! – with Party Pink and Groovy Green flowers, hearts and bright fluorescent paints.

Promotion

Advertising and PR initiatives over the last few years have given the Dulux brand a contemporary, aspirational edge.

In 1997 Shandwick International, Dulux's Public Relations company of 28 years, launched what became known as 'The Dulux House'. The house was a large property on the banks of the River Thames in Hammersmith, featuring a variety of aspirational, spacious room styles. The house was launched to 60 key journalists in January 1998 through an imaginative press event hosted by television's Changing Rooms celebrities Carol Smilie and Lawrence Llewellyn Bowen.

At the event the Dulux House was offered as a free shoot location to home interest journalists in exchange for features exclusively illustrating Dulux products. A simple but effective idea, the Dulux House was used by the top consumer magazines of the day such as Vogue, Good Housekeeping, Ideal Home and Homes and Ideas.

The 1999 consumer campaign was known as Crazy for Colour and was supported by an advertising campaign that was a landmark shift in style for Dulux.

Three commercials showed a woman painstakingly seeking inspiration for the perfect colour to paint her room. Inspiration finally comes to her in each commercial as she sees the colours she needs on a neighbour's washing line, on a baby's dummy and the yellow hood of the person in front of her on the bus. The woman removes lilac knickers from the washing line, steals the dummy and snips a piece off the yellow hood so that she can have the exact colours mixed for her by Dulux.

During the campaign, Dulux painted and branded the lamp posts along the route of London's famous Notting Hill Carnival. A series of one-off celebrity paint cans were also produced to match the personality of the chosen celebrities. Celebrities, Chris Evans, Zoë Ball, and Chris Tarrant were all presented with their paint live on air.

The year 2000 saw the launch of Dulux ONCE. A 40 second commercial added a striking edge to the Dulux brand. The commercial revolved around a young couple re-decorating their new flat which had previously been used as a strip bar. ONCE shades are shown effortlessly covering deep red illustrated walls, in the ultimate demonstration of the products one coat performance, summed up by the strapline – ONCE covers up a multitude of sins in just one coat.

Brand Values

Over the past couple of years Dulux has shifted its' tone and key messages to appeal to a younger audience. The tone of the brand has moved towards creating a bold and cheeky image that symbolises harmless fun and

the essence of naughty but nice. Dulux's key messages for the millennium are that it is a brand that is innovative in its approach, empathetic to the needs and desires of its consumers and individual in its ability to cater for everyone's taste.

DURACELL®

Market

The new millennium arrived with a high tech bang, our increasingly modern world utterly dependent on batteries to power our everyday items, without which life would be a lot harder. The average household now has sixteen battery-operated appliances including remote controls, alarm clocks, radios, smoke alarms, cameras, personal stereos and CD players. Not to mention, of course, the piles of toys and handheld games scattered around most modern homes.

Today's gimmick is tomorrow's commonplace object – and they all need batteries too.

When mobile phones first arrived on the scene, only a privileged few had them while the rest of the population moaned that they were antisocial. Now, well over half of all UK adults have mobile phones and people wonder how the populace got by without them. New technology enjoys an initial flurry of excitement and uniqueness before becoming a 'must have'. As consumers need these appliances, so these appliances need batteries.

A quiet lifestyle revolution is therefore taking place, made entirely possible by innumerable battery-operated appliances used every day. Although subtle, this is seeing people increasingly reliant on these small packets of power.

As times have changed so of course have batteries, in addition to the 'good old' zinc carbon batteries, there is a vast choice of long-lasting super batteries including alkaline, high-tech, lithium, lithium ion and nickel metal hydride.

The true turning point in batteries – alkaline technology pioneered and promoted by Duracell – resulted in long-lasting batteries which did not leak and were supremely reliable. Suddenly batteries were a truly viable portable power source and now, in the twenty-first century, batteries are even more fundamental to life, powering a wide range of appliances that are almost essential to today's lifestyles.

Achievements

In the 1970s when Duracell made its UK debut, many people thought that alkaline batteries would not catch on. However, today 75.8% of all batteries sold are alkaline while zinc batteries continue to decline.

By the late 1980s Duracell had achieved the successful elimination of virtually all mercury from its batteries and in the same and subsequent periods made dramatic improvements to the performance of its products. In the three decades of Duracell batteries the life expectancy of an AA cell has increased by nearly 100% though the battery is the same size and is much the same design. Unlike some other brands which have stood the test of time by changing shape, size and even livery, today's Duracell battery is outwardly little different from the one that arrived in the country 30 years ago. But inside, its advanced technology has changed almost beyond recognition.

In 1992, Duracell gained the British Standards Kitemark for product excellence and 1995 saw

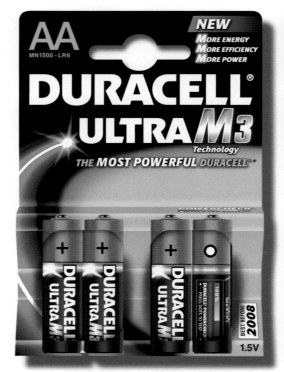

the introduction of titanium dioxide to its batteries which acted as a catalyst to make the other ingredients work harder and give more power. In 1996 the company went a long way to answering the previously almost unanswerable question of when the battery was going to run out by introducing its Powercheck battery tester – firstly on packs, then on the batteries themselves. Having answered the question of when the battery should be taken out of an appliance, Duracell then set out to answer the other question of by when the battery needs to go into an appliance by printing 'best before' dates on all packs and batteries.

The last decade has seen the most rapid developments and achievements – prompted by more discerning consumers and their ever-more demanding lifestyles. The number of new portable appliances for both leisure and work use has been unprecedented, with the arrival of mobile phones, powerbook computers and minidisc players etc.

History

The millennium marks the 200th birthday of the battery which was invented in 1800 by Alessandro Volta, who described it as 'a construction of an apparatus of unfailing charge, of perpetual power'. This discovery is now an 'essential' of modern living.

Early batteries, however were hardly the neat cylinders such as are slipped into today's personal stereos – the Voltaic Pile battery, based on Volta's design and constructed in 1813 by Sir Humphrey Davy at the Royal Institution in London, covered 889 square feet.

The first portable batteries were seen at the turn of the nineteenth century where they were used in conjunction with flashlights – so called as the battery power could sustain only an intermittent light. By World War I, batteries were being used extensively in communication equipment and from there technology moved fast, simultaneously reducing the cell size and increasing capacity. The arrival of battery –

Battery innovation meets changing devices...

70's radio

80's radio & personal stereo

90's boom-box & personal CD

2000 MP3

powered radio brought further demand.

The leading developer of battery technology was Samuel Ruben. He carried out research in conjunction with Philip Mallory, founder of PR Mallory and Co. which went on to become the world's leading alkaline battery company, Duracell.

Product

Duracell is well-established as a world leading battery brand – and a name that is simply synonymous with batteries. However, Duracell has been in the UK market for just about 30 years. Until the product arrived, everyone appeared content with their zinc batteries – then they tried Duracell, which really did last longer than zinc batteries. Now consumers had a choice, and they increasingly chose alkaline batteries.

Duracell battery sales achieved a meteoric growth which ran hand-in-hand with the development of more complex appliances that operated better on alkaline power than zinc. The developement of the personal stereo also ensured that sales of AA Alkaline batteries continued to escalate.

However, Duracell does not manufacture just alkaline batteries – the brand was at the forefront of lithium technology – used primarily for photographic applications and allowing the surges of instant power required to operate several features simultaneously. Today, over half of all new battery-operated cameras use lithium power.

Recent Developments

The most significant development is the recently launched Duracell Ultra M3 alkaline range.

Designed specifically with power-hungry high-tech appliances in mind, Duracell Ultra M3 is the third generation of Duracell Ultra batteries – a range that is

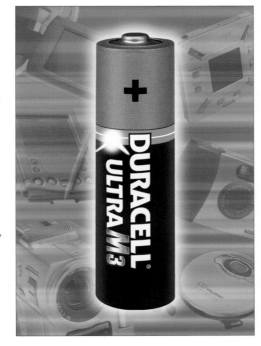

recognised as one of the best for applications including palmtop computers, minidisk players, LCD televisions, digital cameras and portable CD players – all of which demand greater, faster and more sustained battery power.

These applications represent a burgeoning marketplace, and Duracell Ultra already commands over 10% of alkaline battery market sales (a significant market gain in just two years). Duracell Ultra M3 meets the needs

of the ever- increasing numbers of appliances that require its impressive power capability – setting the future trend for Duracell.

At the same time as the development of the Duracell Ultra M3, primarily for the growing high-tech market, Duracell has also launched Duracell Plus – a battery designed to provide long-lasting dependable power and quality across a wide range of everyday appliances.

The launch of Duracell Plus alongside Duracell Ultra M3 provides consumers with the choice of the best battery for all types of devices – Duracell Ultra M3 for the new generation of 'power-hungry' appliances and Duracell Plus for everyday appliances.

Promotion

Duracell has consistently promoted itself as a long-lasting battery brand. The line 'No ordinary battery looks like it or lasts like it' was a long-running statement in which consumers had great confidence. Now Duracell simply states 'Duracell Power. More Life.' Whatever the advertising line, the overall message remains constant and it is this single-minded proposition used across all advertising which,

despite the varied treatments of its campaigns, remains unchanged. That message is clearly getting through – Millward Brown research shows that 79% of people consider Duracell to be the longest-lasting battery on the market.

Besides the instantly recognisable battery, the brand has had more than a little help from its ever-lovable Duracell bunny 'mascot'. First seen back in the 1980s drumming, then boxing, canoeing, jetting into space and footballing (in celebration of Duracell's involvement with the 1998 World Cup) his latest pursuit is globetrotting complete with rucksack and heavy duty walking boots.

The Duracell bunny has become a very successful marketing icon which sees 85% recall among consumers who immediately link it to Duracell batteries.

Brand Values

Duracell is the number one battery brand in the world. It is a pioneer of new battery technology and has many ground-breaking technology launches to its name. The brand's reputation has been built on making batteries that are high quality, long-lasting and good value for money for consumers.

Things you didn't know about
Duracell

The smallest Duracell battery is the 317 watch battery weighing in at 0.19g and measuring just 5.5mm x 1.6mm.

The biggest Duracell 'battery' ever seen is 25 feet long and has travelled the length and breadth of the country on several occasions, first promoting Powercheck and then Duracell Ultra.

In the UK around £428 million was spent on batteries in 1999 – over one third of sales being at Christmas time.

Despite the hundreds of battery sizes available, just five account for 95% of all batteries sold. They are AA, AAA, C, D and 9V.

The Duracell Bunny has been seen playing football on Waterloo station waiting for the Eurostar to arrive to take fans to the 1998 World Cup, as well as cheering on cyclists in the annual London to Brighton Bike Ride when 100 toy bunnies were strapped to the Duracell team's bikes and drummed all the way to the seaside – for all 56 miles.

One in three batteries sold in the UK is a Duracell.

Duracell was the first company ever completely to take over a London Underground station when the bunny went to Warren Street station (where else?). He appeared on posters, stickers, tickets, and even on the overhead platform sign.

easyJet.com
the web's favourite airline

Market

easyJet operates in one of the world's most competitive air travel markets, the European short haul sector. Before 1987 European air travel was effectively carved up by the national flag-carriers which considered air routes between the major European cities to be their own permanent kingdom. Under the old regime flying schedules, fares and even the amount of passengers that each national airline could carry were negotiated between governments in hugely uncompetitive 'bilateral' agreements. Competition from other airlines was almost unheard of. That was all changed when the European Commission, in the face of huge opposition from a number of EU States wanting to protect their own airlines from competition, introduced its three phase, ten year reform process in 1987.

Today any airline holding a valid Air Operators Certificate in the EU cannot be prevented from operating on any route within the European Union, including wholly within another country. Since this ruling European air travel has been flooded with an influx of low cost airlines. Having been one of the only budget carriers when it launched in 1995, easyJet now has several direct competitors, including Ryanair, Virgin Express and the off shoots of a couple of the flag carriers, British Airways with Go and KLM with Buzz. Together they fly to around 80 European destinations, carrying over fifteen million passengers per year. The effect of price cutting on European routes has hit some of the major carriers hard and the cut-price concept is beginning to find favour in the business market too. easyJet now competes with established names including Lufthansa, United Airlines and American Airlines. easyJet will continue to target the business traveller as it rapidly expands its European flight network.

Achievements

The airline's biggest achievement to date has been to survive and prosper in a market which is highly competitive. While other operators have gone bust or have made heavy losses, easyJet has constantly expanded its operations. Founder Stelios Haji-Ioannou put easyJet into profit in its third financial year, and reported

profits of £22 million in the year to 30th September 2000. As well as building a network of 28 European routes served by 150 flights a day, easyJet has won plaudits for operating one of the youngest fleets in the airline industry. Every one of its fleet of 737's is now bought direct from Boeing in Seattle. When the airline began in 1995, it had two leased Boeing 737s – this has risen to 21 and by 2004 the airline will have 44. Awards won by the airline are numerous and include Best Low Cost Airline (Business Traveller Magazine) 1999 and 2000, Best Interactive Campaign (Media Awards) 1999, Best on-board Service Concept (International Flight Catering Association Awards) and was also rated as one of the best airlines in the world by a Guardian and Observer readership survey.

History

Ioannou, son of a Greek shipping tycoon, launched easyJet in 1995. With an initial £5 million, the company began with a headline grabbing fare of £29 from Luton to Glasgow. Then as now, all marketing, design and PR is done in-house. This included work on the brand name, the familiar orange colour and logo design. Ioannou played a major part in designing the look and feel of the brand, as well as contributing heavily to the on-going brand values. Ioannou got the idea for easyJet from Southwest Airlines in the US, which also prospered by introducing a no frills, low price service on short haul routes.

easyJet caught the imagination of customers in the late 1990s. It had the feel of a new economy company, low cost, bright and energetic. Additionally, its use of the internet marks it out as one of the most dynamic companies in its sector.

At first easyJet operated without too much competition from other budget carriers, who stuck to different routes, or from the major airlines. However, after only a year of business British Airways made an attempt to buy the airline. This initially friendly approach soon turned sour when the global giant launched its own budget carrier, Go, in 1998. easyJet accused British Airways of unfairly cross-subsidising Go and took its case to the High Court in February 1998.

easyJet began to fight the airline, initially in the media and then in the air as its rival launched a service to Edinburgh, one of easyJet's most important routes.

However, since Go's launch, easyJet has had to deal with competition on other fronts. Ryanair has rapidly expanded its fleet and KLM has launched Buzz as yet another budget brand in an increasingly crowded market.

Product

easyJet offers low cost airline travel within Europe. It currently serves 28 routes to eighteen airports in sixteen cities. The airline is based in a bright orange building adjacent to the main taxiway at Luton Airport from which it serves fifteen destinations. From its Liverpool base it serves nine more destinations and a further seven airports from its European base in Geneva. easyJet does not use travel agents or other middlemen to sell its seats, which was one of the key differences in its initial product offering. Tickets can only be bought directly from the airline, either through its website or over the telephone. Each easyJet aircraft has 149 seats, all in a single class. There are no free meals on board and the company issues no tickets. Eliminating free catering on-board cuts out cost and unnecessary bureaucracy and management, everybody always jokes about airline food, so easyJet take the stance 'why provide it if people do not want it?'.

The internet plays a vital role in the easyJet

business plan and is critical to its ongoing success. As a low cost operation, controlling the cost of doing business is crucial to the airline's ability to offer low fares. The internet provides the most cost effective distribution channel, so easyJet has aggressively pursued its strategy of encouraging passengers to book their seats online.

Since easyJet started selling seats via the internet in April 1998, the airline has enjoyed dramatic growth in its online sales. The airline reached the one million seat mark in October 1999 and celebrated this important landmark by giving that lucky passenger unlimited free flights for a whole year. Five months later in March 2000, easyJet reached two million seats – it only took another three months after that to reach the three million mark, indicating a huge acceleration in the growth of online sales.

easyJet now sells over 75% of its seats online every week which is a higher percentage than any other airline, reinforcing its position as the 'Web's favourite airline', a slogan approved for usage by the Advertising Standards Authority.

As businesses seek to cut down on their travel budgets, easyJet is winning a bigger slice of the business traveller market. As such, the network of destinations and timetables are designed to suit business and leisure customers' needs. easyJet calculates that companies could save up to 89% on their travel budgets by using low cost airlines.

easyJet employs a yield management strategy, meaning that prices are closely linked to demand and the amount of time in advance that the ticket is booked. A ticket booked three months in advance will be significantly cheaper than one booked a week before the flight.

Equally, peak time tickets, like 6pm on a Friday, will cost more than one at a less busy time. The idea behind this strategy is to maximise seat sales for every flight.

easyJet's product relies not only on cost effectiveness, but also punctuality. Central to this is the ability to turn the aircraft around quickly on the ground. Compared to the hour and a half that it takes on average to turn a 737 around at Heathrow, easyJet's target time on the ground between flights is just twenty minutes.

All tickets are booked direct, either on the internet or the telephone. Buying a ticket involves being given a reference number, which is used in place of a ticket. The direct sales approach is a prime example of how easyJet seeks to simplify business processes to maximise efficiency and reduce costs to itself and its customers.

Recent Developments

easyJet continues to add to its existing routes. There have been five new routes added in 2000 and new routes are constantly being planned for launch over the next few years. The airline is also planning to launch new bases and services to new countries.

On 22nd November 2000, after just five years of trading, easyJet shares were admitted to the London Stock Exchange. The IPO (initial public offering) valued the company at approximately £777 million, further strengthening its potential for growth by funding the planned acquisition of 32 Boeing 737-700 aircraft.

Promotion

easyJet does not use television advertising. Instead it relies heavily on press, outdoor and radio advertising. All advertising is intended to reinforce the easyJet brand values. easyJet has developed its brand values of 'consumer champion' and 'up against the big boys' with its campaigns, which the airline has initiated on behalf of consumers to defend their right to affordable air travel, and vigorously opposes any activities that might jeopardise this.

All easyJet sales promotions are exclusive to the internet, so customers must get online if they wish to take advantage of special fares. If customers wish to book seats more than two months in advance of the departure date of the flight, they can only do so by booking online. As fares generally increase as the departure dates get closer, this means that the best fares are first available to those who book via the internet.

In summer 1999 Ioannou launched easyEverything, a chain of the world's largest internet cafés and in March 2000 he launched easyRentacar.com, the group's new car rental brand, which has added value for the airline's customers. A fleet of Mercedes A-Class cars is available for rental at all easyJet destinations for as little as £9 per day.

Brand Values

As the name suggests, the company's mission is to take the complexity and hidden costs out of every sector it enters. easyJet balances its cost cutting image with an emphasis on safety,

security, punctuality and in-flight service.

In the beginning the principal brand values were 'cheap' and 'fun'. All the advertising sought to reinforce this message, taken for granted to a certain extent now, but a huge advantage in the mid 1990s when most airlines promoted themselves on quality of service, rather than sense of fun. In the intervening years, other values have been added to the brand. Today, most people would consider the airline to be 'challenging the established order' and a 'consumer champion'. These values have been imparted by a series of high profile campaigns over the past five years.

As Richard Branson has done with Virgin, Stelios Haji-Ioannou has made himself the personification of the easyJet brand. He appears in many of the advertisements and conducts numerous PR stunts.

ERICSSON

Market

The introduction of mobile phones in 1988 created a booming industry that continues to evolve at a rapid pace. Initially a 'yuppie' accessory the size of a brick, the mobile has come a long way: in 2000 over half of the UK population owned a mobile phone with the projection that by 2002 the number of mobile phones in existence will exceed the number of land lines.

Mobile phones are now used by all ages and have become so streamlined in appearance that they can slip unnoticed into a pocket. The market is extremely competitive and dominated by three companies worldwide: Ericsson, Nokia and Motorola, which make up almost 80% of sales.

Despite the progress already made, there is still great scope for evolution. As technologies converge, mobile phones are becoming capable of rapid internet access as well as downloading and sending of images and locations based information.

Ericsson has been involved in the infrastructure side of telephony for over 120 years, leaving it well placed to keep up with these future demands of the market. It is now a world-leading supplier in the fast growing and dynamic telecommunications and data communications industry, offering advanced communications solutions for mobile and fixed networks, as well as consumer products and service providers.

Achievements

Ericsson is at the forefront of this rapid-paced industry. It has been one of the key pioneers of WAP technology, responding in a timely fashion to the phenomenal increase in internet usage and was responsible for the first ever commercially available WAP product – the MC218 – launched in 1999.

June 2000 saw the long anticipated arrival of the Ericsson-innovated wireless technology known as 'Bluetooth'.

The company has won numerous awards for its products including Best Design, Mobile Phone of the Year and Service to Customers at the Cellnet Awards for Excellence, Service and Reliability, known as CAESAR. Ericsson also won the Manufacturer of the Year award at the Mobile News Awards in 1998.

In 1999 Ericsson founded The Ericsson Internet Community Awards (ERICA) which is a yearly awards program. It aims to help recognise the community-building power of the internet and provide technological resources to organisations with undeveloped ideas for websites that benefit a range of social causes.

In 2000 Ericsson launched RESPONSE, a project for disaster preparation and response to disaster prone countries. The unit will establish relationships with the UN and local governments to ensure rapid development of communication solutions should disaster strike.

History

Ericsson was founded in 1876 by Lars Magnus Ericsson in Sweden. Called Telefonaktiebolaget LM Ericsson, the company designed and manufactured telephones, switchboards and networks. A British subsidiary of the company, Ericsson Telephones Ltd (ETL) was then founded. In 1928 the two companies diverged for twenty years, for financial, technical and international reasons.

ETL quickly developed a reputation for excellence and, despite the economic upheavals of the 1930s, the company flourished as a result of the combination of financial caution, technical product excellence and continuous development of modern design that still exists today. The UK plant quickly became the company's most important plant, accounting for 8.9% of group sales outside Sweden in 1931.

In 1948 Ericsson withdrew from the UK, signing an agreement with ETL not to manufacture or compete in the UK telephone market for twenty years. All shares in ETL were sold to a British finance consortium and it became an independent UK company until Plessey purchased all the shares in 1961. Through the 1950s and 1960s, Ericsson maintained a trading presence in the UK through the Swedish Ericsson Company Ltd.

The 1964 Labour government brought with it a minister for technology and an emphasis on modernising industry and opening the UK market. In 1968 Swedish Ericsson Telecommunications Ltd was formed and the twenty year agreement to avoid the UK market had expired just in time for the nationalising of the Post Office. In 1972, the company won the £14 million Post Office contract

to create an ARM crossbar exchange capable of connecting 800,000 calls a day.

In 1974 Ericsson and Thorn Electrical Industries formed Thorn-Ericsson Telecommunications Ltd (TEL) and although restricted mainly to the UK market, the company rapidly grew. The Conservative government gained power in 1979 and established British Telecom as a separate public corporation which resulted in TEL completing the UK's first digital international telephone exchange in 1984: the first of a series of major Ericsson contracts advancing the state of UK telecommunications.

In 1988 Thorn sold its 51% share of the company back to LM Ericsson and from then on Ericsson Ltd (ETL) continued to grow.

Although mobile phones were not on the market until 1988, they were in development from the late 1940s when the first specifications for a digital mobile telephone system were complete and the development of Global System for Mobile Communications products began. Ericsson was one of the driving forces behind the development of cellular radio technology for the new networks.

Until this point Ericsson had been largely invisible to the public despite being such a major supplier of equipment for the fixed network. Now it became a supplier to UK operators of systems for mobile communications and through an increasing promotion of mobile phones, the company began to make a public name for itself.

Ericsson began to treat subscribers as customers, focusing on adding value to its products and services in order to gain market advantage.

The deregulation and liberalisation of the UK telecommunications markets enabled Ericsson to

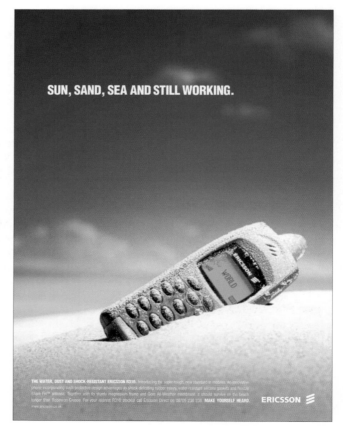

strengthen its position in all major areas of UK telecommunications. The company recognised that future success in public networks would depend on the development and introduction of new products, more efficient networks, a greater range of services, and customer communications.

With the introduction of the Ericsson range of cellular mobile telephones in the UK the company expanded its activities very successfully into mass-market telecoms products. In 1992 Ericsson launched its first mobile handset in the UK: the EH97, otherwise known as the 'Hotline'. The GH337 was launched in 1994 and went on to become the world's best selling and smallest GSM phone.

Today, Ericsson is the leading communications supplier, involved in fixed and mobile telephony, data as well as voice communication and, increasingly, internet and multimedia services. The company has also put research investment into the next generation of wireless technology and is investing heavily in new key technologies.

Product

Ericsson has developed a reputation for pioneering excellence and reliability within the mobile phone industry. The company has expertly identified and targeted different groups of mobile phone users with different needs and has launched a number of products that have been developed specifically to suit them.

In a market where mobile phones are increasingly small and fragile, the extremely rugged R250, launched in 1999, bucked the trend. Water, dust and shock resistant, it was an industry first and marketed by Ericsson to those in professions such as the building industry. A huge success, it was closely followed by the R310 – its consumer counterpart with the same 'rugged' qualities that was targeted towards groups such as rugby players, mountain bikers, outdoor sports enthusiasts and those with an active lifestyle.

Another example of targeted product flexibility is the A2618, a small GSM dual band phone that is fun and flexible. Aimed mainly at the 17-20 year old youth market, the phone can be personalised with colourful, exchangeable snap-on covers for both the front and back, voice activation, a choice of ring tones and a snap-on mini QWERTY keyboard for easier messaging. Accompanied by a bold and visible advertising campaign, it was Ericsson's biggest volume selling phone in 2000.

Recent Developments

In April 2000 Ericsson launched the Ericsson R320, its second WAP enabled product after the MC218 personal digital assistant. The slimmest, lightest WAP enabled mobile phone yet, it is a high-end WAP business phone with an impressive range of technologically-advanced features. The phone is only 15mm wide and yet has a five line graphic display, built-in modem, calendar function and WAP technology. Infra-red technology enables users to send and receive electronic business cards, phone melodies and phone book entries between two phones.

The R520, is a Bluetooth phone and the world's first GPRS mobile phone to be combined with Bluetooth. These new technologies ease the whole communication process for consumers, offering a cable free world of connectivity between devices.

Also in early 2000 the company announced a range of accessories that can be attached to a mobile phone. For example, Ericsson's MP3 player, with an accompanying multimedia card, allows users to store up to 30 minutes of music and then listen to it on near CD quality audio through a stereo earpiece that is automatically muted with the arrival of an incoming call.

Promotion

Ericsson began advertising to a broad audience in 1994, focusing on the EH237 phone. Until this point, general awareness of Ericsson was limited to the telecommunications industry and so this was consumers' first exposure to the brand.

The company focuses most of its advertising spend on launching new products. In 1998 the 'Make yourself heard' brand campaign hit Europe's television screens and is still one of the brand's best recalled advertisements.

Advertising for the R250 was focused on press, targeted mostly at the construction industry, using titles like Construction News. Ads showed the phone covered in mud, or with a brick smashed over it with the headline 'can also take an ear bashing'. A dramatic 30m x 14m poster was hung from scaffolding in Cromwell Road, London to publicise the launch.

In order to exploit the huge public interest in WAP at the time, it was decided to focus promotion of the R320 on the phone's WAP services. The result was a highly visible campaign brought to life by the media environments in which it was placed. For example, the front page of some newspapers ran with the headline 'Why are you reading yesterday's news?' to highlight the fact that up-to-the-minute news reports are available via WAP. This was accompanied by a prominent poster campaign that greatly increased awareness of Ericsson's innovative new product.

As well as television and print advertising Ericsson has focused on increasing brand awareness laterally, capturing target audiences through means such as sponsorship. Ericsson sponsored 'Frasier', the hugely successful Channel 4 series aired on Friday nights. This created links between Ericsson and Channel 4 at the same time as increasing awareness of Ericsson amongst Friday night viewers.

Other sponsorship includes QPR football club and major sponsorship of London Wasps RFC where Ericsson encourages fans to 'make themselves heard' at games, at the same time as using the players for joint promotions.

Ericsson is also heavily involved with music and is the title sponsor of ericsson@homelands, the Ericsson Muzik Dance awards and sponsored the MTV European Music Awards in 1999 and 2000. To coincide with the awards,

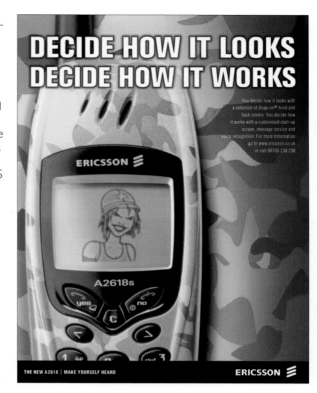

Ericsson launched a limited edition of its A2618 phone to celebrate the festivities and also enabled consumers to vote for the nominees via their mobile phones on a special WAP-site.

Again, Ericsson encourages musicians, DJ's and singers to 'make themselves heard' and the new music based accessories, such as MP3 players and radio 'handsfree' kits make the link closer still.

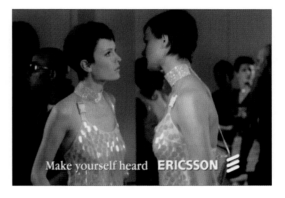

Make yourself heard ERICSSON

Brand Values

Ericsson's brand is still based on the vision of the company's founder, Lars Magnus Ericsson: that technology is communication for all. Ericsson harnesses all its resources to provide people with a full range of communications.

The Ericsson brand stands for being open, optimistic and inspiring, exemplified by the slogan 'make yourself heard'. The Ericsson brand also seeks to empower and encourage. Ericsson believes that people should be able to communicate anywhere, anytime without having to wait to be connected.

Things you didn't know about Ericsson

Ericsson's annual turnover increased from £430,000 in 1920 to £22 billion in 1999.

Ericsson has more than 100,000 employees in 140 countries.

The prize for The Ericsson Internet Community Awards (ERICA) in 2000 was $100,000 worth of web development services for each of the five winners.

Ericsson invests 15% of sales in research and development and has 23,000 employees in 23 countries working in this area.

eurostar

Market

Eurostar can justly claim to have revolutionised links between three of the most exciting capitals in Europe – London, Paris and Brussels. The high speed passenger trains provide frequent connections between London and Paris and London and Brussels. Eurostar also provides direct trains from London to Disneyland Paris and during the winter ski season, to Bourg St Maurice in the French Alps. Some trains stop en route at Ashford (Kent), Calais and Lille in northern France.

Competition in this market mainly comes from airlines and Eurostar competes with them head to head, both with the established carriers and the growing number of low-cost alternatives. For the business traveller, Eurostar promotes its product benefits of the seamless journey from city centre to city centre with time on board to work and relax. In the case of leisure travellers, Eurostar competes in an altogether broader area, faced with the competing attractions of other destinations or, indeed, with other leisure activities.

Achievements

Eurostar's claim to have revolutionised travel between London and the continent is without exaggeration. Before its launch in November 1994 about five million passengers per year were carried by air between London and Paris and London and Brussels, but now Eurostar on its own carries over seven million passengers annually and has a market share in excess of 60% on the Paris route and around 45% on the Brussels route. Indeed, Eurostar has doubled the overall market in its first five years of operation.

Eurostar has achieved this leadership by a combination of convenience, speed, comfort, reliability and frequency of service, while striving to provide the best levels of customer service in the industry. It is used by business travellers who value the uninterrupted time on board to work or relax, and leisure travellers who are now finding the continent so much more accessible and affordable. Eurostar has been

responsible for developing the short break market in this area, to the benefit of the tourism industry in all three countries, while opening up more travel opportunities for the public.

With a wide appeal, Eurostar is used by people from all walks of life, from royalty and senior politicians to stars of stage and screen to families, to the student backpacker. Its passengers come from every country in the world and it is an important link in European tours for visitors from such regions as North America and the Far East.

Eurostar has received a long list of awards from a range of organisations including the Royal Institute of British Architects, National Heritage Arts Sponsorship, the Civic Trust, English Tourist Board, Queen Elizabeth's Foundation (for disabled access), French Chamber of Commerce and numerous awards from trade and national press for the quality of the service provided.

History

Eurostar traces its origins back to 1981, when the British and French governments announced the studies for a fixed link under the English Channel. By 1986 the decision in favour of a rail tunnel was taken and planning started on linking the three capitals of London, Paris and Brussels by what was then known as the 'Trans-Manche Super Train'. This was based on the successful French TGV (train à grande vitesse or high speed train) which by then was starting to capture the imagination of travellers on the continent and in Britain.

Following construction of the Channel Tunnel, the first train arrived in England for tests in June 1993 and commercial service started on November 14th 1994 with just two trains per day each way on each route. However, the timetable was soon expanded; the millionth customer travelled in May 1995, after six months service and within twelve months Eurostar had carried three million passengers. Subsequent enhancements to the service included: the opening of Ashford International station, Kent in January 1996; the inauguration of direct trains to Disneyland Paris in June 1996; the introduction of business lounges at terminals; and the frequent traveller programme in November 1996. The following year saw the opening of high speed line in Belgium, reducing London-Brussels journey time from three hours fifteen minutes to two hours 40 minutes, and the start of a through service from London and Ashford to the French Alps.

The UK arm was privatised in 1996 and in 1999 the three operators created Eurostar Group, a centralised company

responsible for determining the commercial direction and development of the Eurostar service.

Product

The product for Eurostar spans all points at which the customer makes contact with the service from the initial phone call, to the check in, to the experience on board, to arrival at the destination. Usually the first contact will be at Eurostar's busy call centre which takes the majority of bookings direct from the public. Travellers also have the option of booking through travel agents or direct-selling tour operators, while increasingly, the internet is assuming greater importance.

The passenger arriving at any of Eurostar's modern terminals will find Eurostar's service is much more 'hassle-free' than airlines. Passengers need check in only twenty minutes before departure, or, in the case of passengers travelling on fully flexible tickets, just ten minutes.

On board, Eurostar offers two classes of accommodation, First and Standard. On the London-Paris route within First Class, a Premium First service offers a range of additional benefits. All passengers benefit from air conditioned coaches and the articulated design gives an exceptionally smooth ride even at maximum speed. The benefits of First Class include wide reclining seats, complimentary newspapers on board, aperitifs, and a meal appropriate

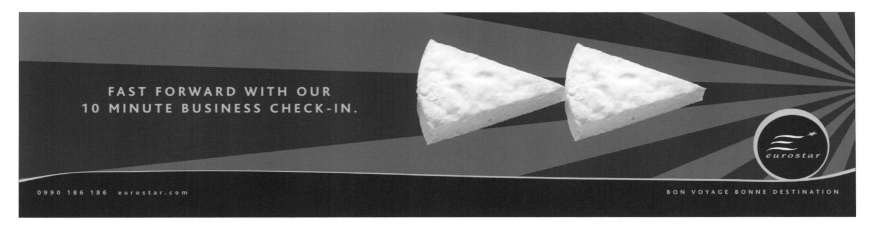

to the time of day served at the passengers' seats. Premium First includes automatic access to lounges at Waterloo or Paris Nord, a superior on board meal service with four courses and fine wines, and the benefit of a complimentary car to take customers to their final destination.

Eurostar's sales and customer service staff are a very visible part of the product. Those in contact with customers speak both English and French and those working on the Brussels route also speak Dutch. On-board there are two train managers to look after the needs of customers and a catering crew to meet and greet first class passengers, provide the meal service and staff the two buffet cars which are available to standard class passengers. Staff are available at all terminals to help passengers with enquiries and particularly to attend to the needs of special needs passengers. Eurostar is highly accessible to those passengers with disabilities, and assistance can be given to wheelchair, blind or elderly passengers and those with children.

Finally, there is the hardware itself. Eurostar trains can be distinguished from other trains by their eye-catching, award winning design and sheer size. Each one is almost 400 metres long (approximately 1/4 mile), travels smoothly at speeds of up to 186 mph (300 kph), and seats up to 766 passengers – almost the equivalent of two fully loaded Boeing 747 'Jumbo' jet aircraft. Each Eurostar train is a fixed unit, with two power cars and eighteen coaches, formed in two nine-car half sets. Eurostar trains are at the forefront of railway technology. Derived from the basic mechanical features of the highly successful French TGV trains, Eurostar trains have many additional systems and attributes, including the ability to operate from three different electrical supply systems in Britain, France and Belgium, and four different signalling systems.

Recent Developments

Currently, construction work is under way on the UK section of the high speed line which will open in two stages, the first section in 2003 and the second stage to a new London terminal at St Pancras in 2007. When it is completed, the transit times between London St Pancras and Brussels will be just two hours, and two hours twenty minutes between London St Pancras and Paris.

Promotion

In its advertising, Eurostar aims to drive awareness, create desire to travel by Eurostar and build on its brand values. When targeting business customers directly, product benefits tend to be stressed (eg city centre to city centre, time on

board to work and relax), while to leisure customers the emphasis is more on destination marketing, offering potential customers added value reasons to travel to Paris, Brussels or Lille.

Communications therefore embraces both the on-board experience and the destination experience. Destination marketing is founded on a unique 'insider' view of destinations. Many partnerships with key influencers are being developed so that Eurostar will become an acknowledged 'expert' on the destinations it serves. So not only is the journey easy, seamless and enables quality time, but the whole experience of the trip will be memorable and satisfying.

Eurostar uses all available communication channels – television, press, radio, outdoor, and direct marketing, including use of the frequent traveller loyalty scheme. Eurostar's internet site is also increasingly used as a marketing tool.

Eurostar has a high public relations profile and is regularly featured in print and broadcast media, whether as part of a travel feature or within completely unrelated subjects. Eurostar is frequently used as a unique and tangible visual symbol of the links between Britain and Europe.

Brand Values

Eurostar's brand encompasses both functional and emotional values. Among the former would be included reliable, safe, comfortable and consistent. Emotional descriptions include cosmopolitan, culturally aware, forward looking and stylish. In its short history, Eurostar has succeeded in appealing to a wide range of people and has established itself as an aspirational brand without being exclusive.

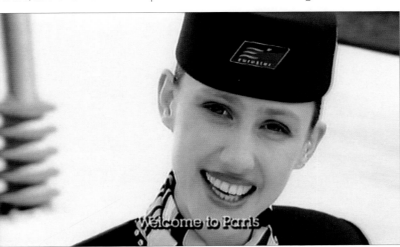

Welcome to Paris

Things you didn't know about
Eurostar

Eurostar's power cars generate 16,408 bhp – the equivalent of twenty formula one racing cars.

Last year Eurostar served 1.2 million meals on board its trains. Each day it washes up 84,000 pieces of cutlery, 14,000 cups and saucers and 36,000 items of glassware.

A couple arrived at Waterloo from Paris and made for the exit. They entered what they thought was a lift and after a few minutes wondering which buttons to push they realised it wasn't a lift at all, but the train's disabled toilet.

Fashion glitterati on their way to the Paris shows were taken aback to find themselves being asked questions by stray passengers about railway timetables and tickets. It turned out that the latest trendy pussy-bow scarves which they were sporting made them look uncannily like Eurostar staff, who wear a smart Pierre Balmain number.

Market

The future of the bottled water market in the UK is immense. It has grown five-fold in just twelve years and has now burst through the billion litre milestone to reach 1,402 million litres.

Now after a decade of strong growth, still bottled water is the key driver of the total soft drinks market, with Evian being one of the fastest growing soft drink brands in 1999. Consumers now perceive bottled water as a credible, more natural and healthier alternative to traditional soft drinks.

Si pure ! Si légère !

Evian is the best selling bottled water brand in the world and the overall number one bottled water brand in Britain with a 23% value share. In addition, it is the nineteenth best selling soft drink brand in the UK. Evian's dominant position in the bottled water sector is largely responsible for driving innovation and market growth.

Achievements

Evian helped to create the UK bottled water market back in the 1980s and has become an increasingly dominant brand leader despite the plethora of competitive brands and own-label offerings that have entered the market over the past five years.

Evian leads the sector in terms of

marketing investment, which has driven growth of the brand and raised spontaneous brand awareness in the category.

Evian has the highest market penetration of any bottled water brand and its consumers are increasingly drinking Evian on a daily basis, demonstrating that the brand has become part of their lives (Source: TGI 2000). In 1999 Evian became the first still water brand to sell 100 million litres.

History

From the spring's formation tens of thousands of years ago, to its discovery during the French Revolution and its current status as the world's most popular natural mineral water, Evian's history is as unique as the water itself.

The aquifer in the French Alps through which Evian travels was formed thousands of years ago in 30,000 BC. These glacial sands are what give Evian its unique taste and mineral composition.

Evian's protected source in the foothills of the French Alps, in the small town of Evian-les-Bains, was first discovered by the Marquis De Lessert during the French Revolution in 1789. Suffering from tiny kidney stones, he drank water from the fountain of Sainte-Catherine, which flowed free from a spring in a certain Monsieur Cachat's garden. This water was Evian. The French nobleman swore that the spring's pure, refreshing water cured his ailments and word of the benefits of Evian spread.

BUVEZ TOUS

EVIAN · CACHAT

The first Spas opened in 1824 in Evian-les-Bains to accommodate those seeking to benefit from the spring. Following this, in 1826 the Dukes of Savoy granted the first official authorisation to bottle Evian.

Recognising the health benefits of Evian, the Government first registered water from the Cachat Spring in 1878, after it had been consumed for over 200 years.

Due to increasing demand, the present pump room was opened

at the source in 1956 and a new state-of-the-art bottling facility opened in 1965. The bottling facility is continuously updated and modernised with the world's leading bottling technology. Four million litres of Evian are bottled here each day.

In 1969, 'Evian Major' was launched – the first bottle produced in PVC. Innovations in packaging continued with the launch of the first compactable bottle in 1995.

A hotel at source, L'Espace Thermal Evian, opened in 1984 and has added a certain charm to the benefits of Evian water and the surrounding mountains. The hotel offers thermal treatments and body conditioning.

Evian's first foray into television advertising was in 1994. Developing an educational stance and showing the generic health benefits of water, the advertising message was: 'Evian. Every day for everybody's wellbeing'.

The late 1990s saw a change in consumer attitudes. Previously sceptical about mineral waters, consumers, unhappy with the taste and quality of tap water, turned to the purity and premium quality of bottled water.

The resulting advertising campaign, which repositioned the bottled water market as more humorous and approachable, was conveyed initially through posters and then through the hugely successful 'Sugar Daddy' television commercial – featuring well known actor Anthony Zerbe and former boxer Gary Stretch. Both the posters and television advertisements featured the line: 'Purity. Not just for the innocent'.

Purity. Not just for the innocent.

evian

Filtered by the French Alps.

Product

The name Evian comes from the Celtic word 'Evna' which means water.

Evian natural mineral water comes from rain and snow which falls on the Chablais foothills, north of the French Alps. Evian water is filtered

It's not what you put on
It's what you put in

for many years through a vast aquifer deep within the mountains before emerging at the source, Cachat, in the town of Evian-Les-Bains on the banks of Lake Geneva.

The aquifer, a geological phenomenon formed over several millennia, is what makes Evian natural mineral water so remarkably pure and drinkable.

Evian acquires its essential minerals by filtering through the glacial sand compacted between two plates of waterproof clay. These plates are several tens of metres thick, and were created by the most recent glaciers on the Northern French Alps.

Gets drunk and collapses.

The compactable bottle from **evian**

Evian is naturally pure and well balanced in calcium and magnesium. It is low in nitrates, sodium and sulphates and is suitable for salt-free diets, pregnant women and people of all ages.

For decades now, a very extensive series of hydro-geological studies have been carried out at the source of Evian. The studies confirmed the composition of Evian natural mineral water. They also investigated the physical characteristics of the water in the glacial sands, the minerals in the source compared to the local soil and the underground flow rate of Evian. Using the laws of hydrodynamics, the flow rate is estimated at between 100 and 300 metres per year.

This confirms that Evian water takes over fifteen years to travel through the mineral filter, leading to an extremely stable composition and complete absence of chemical or microbiological contamination.

To preserve the water's

purity, Evian is bottled at source in packaging made exclusively for Evian mineral water.

In answer to the growing trend for bulk packs, Evian has launched multi packs of its successful 50cl, 1.5 litre and 2 litre bottles.

Today, Evian is the number one brand in the world and is available in more than 120 countries around the globe.

Recent Developments

Brand appeal was broadened in 1995 with the innovative launch of the world's first compactable bottle. The bottle was designed to collapse when empty, to encourage recycling. This unique concept cemented Evian's number one brand status and was supported with a witty advertising campaign with the line 'gets drunk and collapses.'

New for the Millennium, Evian Action has again brought totally new packaging innovations to the market. Evian Action is in an innovative 75cl squeezable bottle that offers superior water flow via a unique dispensing system and a highly distinctive cap. The patented cap is revolutionary – allowing for easy handling, and carrying. As well as being a technical innovation, the bottle is very attractive and has a strong visual appeal. Evian Action meets the needs of the growing market of consumers who want to drink water on the go.

Promotion

In summer 2000, Evian launched the biggest poster and press campaign ever undertaken in the water category. Each of the three treatments showed models making abstract fashion statements and carried the strapline: 'It's not what you put on. It's what you put in.' The end line of 'Ultimate Purity' supports the idea of the brand's superior product quality.

In addition, Evian has supported its Action format with an advertising campaign featuring stylish models with holes in their clothing or about their person with the end line 'for those who prefer holes'. The line makes specific reference to the 'Ring Cap' and is delivered with an edge that strikes a chord with consumers.

In 1997 Evian embarked on a hugely successful 'Pure Style' on-pack promotion. Appearing on more than 32 million bottles, the promotion offered new and exciting Evian branded merchandise such as t-shirts, bags etc. The promotion was so successful that it was updated and ran for a further two years, including more off the wall items such as shower curtains, lamps, and inflatable armchairs.

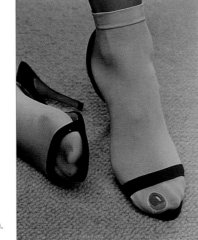

For those who prefer holes.

Evian also developed a youth marketing strategy in 1997, which has included targeted sampling to students, sponsorship of music and dance festivals, including the MTV Tour, London Fashion Week and clubs and bar installations. This has allowed the brand to become more credible within the youth market and become the water of choice for young people.

Evian is the official mineral water for numerous sporting events and associations including the Stella Artois Tennis Championship and the Lawn Tennis Association of Great Britain. Evian also is a sponsor of the 'Evian Masters' women's golf open tournament, and now headline sponsor of the Ladies European Golf Tour.

Brand Values

Evian is the UK's and the world's leading premium natural mineral water. It is a quality brand of water that has been long favoured by young, fashion conscious and discerning consumers. Its heritage is very important to consumers who recognise Evian as being the expert in water, and as such remains the referent of the market.

As the bottled water market becomes more mainstream, Evian will continue to operate at the top end, where reassurance of product quality and a forward thinking image will continue to attract consumers who want the best quality.

Things you didn't know about **Evian**

It takes fifteen years for Evian to filter through the glacial sands of the French Alps.

Evian's spring is fed by rain water and melted snow.

Evian is completely untouched by man from the time it flows from the source until it reaches your lips.

Evian is available in over 120 countries worldwide.

Evian bottles over 1.4 billion litres per year.

You can holiday in Evian, staying at the Royal Club Evian Spa Resort.

Legend has it that Kim Basinger and Nicole Kidman wash their hair in Evian.

Market

Traditional branch banking has shown a marked decline over recent years, as more and more people take advantage of financial services based on new technology. Telephone banking is commonplace, internet banking is growing daily and the advent of wireless application protocol (WAP) and interactive digital television offer even more opportunities and options.

Today, the market has a very different look from when First Direct launched its 24 hour telephone banking service in 1989. The UK's 38 million banking customers are grasping 'direct' banking more and more and joining a revolution started by First Direct.

First Direct is embracing all these new technologies, while recognising the telephone's continued importance in serving present and future customers. It is becoming a 'multi-channel' bank, offering great service wherever, whenever and however its customers wish.

As far as brands are concerned, the real winners in this technological revolution will be those who offer their customers both excellent customer service and value. While the new

their bank to others, too. Since 1991 it has been the UK's most recommended bank. 94% of its' customers have recommended it since joining, compared to only 51% of High Street banks being recommended by their customers (Source: NOP Q4 1999).

This has been achieved in a climate where customers are increasingly demanding. They expect individual attention, high quality and 24-hour accessibility, through more and more channels.

In recent years, First Direct credentials have been strengthened further, by illustrating an overt link, through its logo, to its parent organisation HSBC (The Hongkong and Shanghai Banking Corporation). Since Midland Bank evolved to become HSBC in 1999, the parent bank has quickly grown a reputation for

other banks.' (Source: NOP Q4 1999) Crucially, three quarters feel First Direct is personal and friendly, emphasising the fact that a telephone service can be more individualised than branch banking.

Product

First Direct has always offered a full range of banking services, including current accounts, savings, loans, mortgages and investments. A key difference in its product proposition is free banking, which means no charges for normal banking transactions within the UK, irrespective of whether the customer is in credit or overdrawn. In addition, all customers can also have access to an automatic fee-free overdraft of £500.

First Direct offers excellent rates to all customers, irrespective of how they choose to do their banking, whether by telephone, internet, WAP or interactive digital television.

However, the real 'product' and point of difference for First Direct is in the level of service delivered through its Customer Representatives over the telephone. While fee-free day to day banking and fee-free overdrafts of £500 are important components, the care and understanding provided by Customer Representatives is crucial. First Direct personnel have always been chosen on the basis of their interpersonal skills and trained to treat customers as individuals rather than account numbers.

Recent Developments

Over 200,000 customers, a fifth of First Direct's entire base, are now using PC Banking as a complementary channel to the telephone.

Summer 2000 saw the introduction of a full internet banking service, with extremely competitive pricing across banking products. Customers will be able to use WAP technology to bank via their mobile phone. This is a logical extension of First Direct's Short Messaging Service (SMS), a text messaging service already used by more than 10,000 people and growing at the rate of 500 new customers per week.

The SMS service already offers balances on up to three accounts and can warn customers if they are about to go overdrawn or if a certain amount is about to be credited to or debited from their account.

breed of Internet banks may offer competitive pricing, it is difficult to see how they will be able to sustain these prices, operate a profit focused model and provide excellent customer service. All the recent market research points to the fact that personal contact will remain highly valued by banking customers.

Achievements

Since launch, First Direct has acquired one million customers – an average of around 100,000 a year. Ironically, while the UK is currently witnessing a programme of branch closures nationwide, if First Direct had branches, around 125 would appear on our high streets tomorrow.

First Direct has also consistently had the most satisfied personal banking customers in the UK. Year on year, more than 80% of its customers are very satisfied with the service they receive, against a current level of around 47% satisfaction among customers of the traditional high street banks (Source: NOP Q4 1999).

First Direct customers actually recommend

excellent service, innovation and reliability. The brand link between HSBC and First Direct has meant that both brands are benefiting from each other's strength and the net result is a stronger, more competitive group position.

History

First Direct was the UK's first 24-hour person to person bank, taking its first calls on October 1st 1989. There were no branches, no managers, no closing times and no queues. The traditional banks (with, of course, the notable exception of Midland Bank), ridiculed the whole concept, saying people would always want branch contact and face-to-face dialogue. Yet traditional banks were disliked by customers, who believed they were getting a poor deal, both in terms of being treated like a human being and getting value for money.

From the very start, a new type of dialogue was opened up. First Direct emphasised what it could do for customers, rather than what it couldn't do. 'To this day, 80% of customers feel the service they are getting is better than at

In addition to WAP, which was introduced in December 2000, First Direct interactive digital television banking will be launched in the future, offering yet another banking option to its customers.

The goal is a fully integrated multi-channel banking service, where each channel complements the others. Customers are offered a wide choice of options that allow them to bank wherever, whenever and however they wish, without any hidden charges or conditions.

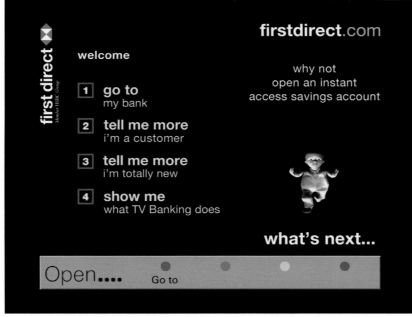

Promotion

The First Direct brand has never been about mass targeting and huge media spend. It has focused advertising and marketing around the ABC1 21-54 market, – specifically those who are looking to switch banks and are relatively up to speed with technology. More importantly, the target market is attitudinally, rather than demographically based. First Direct customers tend to be busy professional people who are looking for ways to simplify their lives, particularly with regard to rather mundane matters like banking. They are smart but not smug, 'switched on' but not vocal about it, and are attracted to First Direct's common sense, modern approach to banking, something still viewed as radical in financial services. Between April and December 1999, First Direct's television spend was approximately £2 million, while Barclays spent £5.5 million, Halifax £12.1 million, Abbey National £6.9 million and NatWest £15.6 million (Source: Millward Brown).

Despite this, First Direct still attracted almost 120,000 customers in 1999. As MORI calculated the 'switcher' market (those moving their main bank account from one bank to another), to be approximately 575,000 people in 1999, more than 20% of all 'switchers' changed to First Direct that year. (Source: MORI/First Direct Management Information, 1999).

First Direct's television advertising has always attracted a great deal of attention, both within the marketing world and among the public. The brand has won a number of awards in the

industry for its effectiveness, including a Gold award from the British Television Advertising Awards for the 'Little Fella' campaign during early 2000.

As well as 'Little Fella', recent years have seen the 'Tell me one good thing about your Bank' campaign, followed by comedian Bob Mortimer's – both of which have been particularly striking and attention grabbing. 'Tell me one good thing' was an extremely effective and probing question, causing people to think long and hard about their relationship with their existing bank. During the time of the campaign between January and July 1996, advertising awareness of First Direct rose from 10% to 40% and more than 95,000 new customers were acquired.

The initiative was followed by a television campaign, again devised by London agency WCRS, featuring the comedian Bob Mortimer. This focused on the absurdities of traditional banking, highlighting the anti-customer stance of banks closing early, forcing people to queue, imposing unfair charges and so on. Different television ads focused on different First Direct propositions, such as 'no queuing' and 'no closing'. Assorted media extended this television theme with more specific and targeted direct mail and 'ambient' media, including branded car park barriers.

First Direct's fruitful association with the advertising agency WCRS continued during 2000. The creation of the iconoclastic character 'Little Fella' has attracted a great deal of attention, as the brand icon swept onto television, the internet and into print. 'Little Fella' is designed not only to highlight problems in banking, but also to show the irritations of everyday life. He helps convey the message that First Direct can help to eradicate some of these problems, allowing customers to get on with what's next in their lives.

First Direct positions itself as the 'independently minded bank for independently minded people'. While peoples' lives become more complex, banking with First Direct can at least sort out one area of life quickly, easily, without fuss and with personality and friendliness.

First Direct is now promoting a whole range of new services, including new internet accounts with excellent prices, WAP banking, digital television and more SMS services. These are all within the context of being the most recommended bank in the UK.

Brand Values

First Direct has always maintained the same set of values, based around offering its customers an unrivalled level of service through 'direct' channels.

As far as customers are concerned, this is all about convenience, availability, efficiency and peace of mind, coupled with an attitude which embraces personality, friendliness, co-operation and advice.

In an age when it sometimes seems that technology is being used for technology's sake rather than for the benefit of customers, First Direct is re-emphasising its commitment to customer service.

While First Direct will offer service across different channels, banking customers will come to expect this whoever they bank with. The real advantage will be a communications experience that benefits the customer, whether they choose telephone, internet, e-mail or in the future an online service that combines both telephone dialogue and on-screen vision.

Things you didn't know about First Direct

Over a third of all customers join First Direct as a result of word-of-mouth.

During the early years of First Direct, 60% of customers were male, 40% female. The ratio is now 50:50.

First Direct has had the most satisfied banking customers in the UK since 1991; it has been Britain's most recommended bank for the same time period.

Each day, 266 people start using First Direct's PC banking service.

71% of First Direct customers have a PC, compared to 44% of the population as a whole.

First Direct's second operational site at Stourton, Leeds uses 329 miles of voice and data cabling in order to function.

Market

The UK butter and margarine market is huge – equal to 391,000 tonnes and valued at £802 million (Source: ACNeilsen 1999).

Butter has been around for centuries and was first mentioned in the Bible's Book of Genesis. Margarine made its debut when Napoleon requested a wholesome butter alternative to be produced. Mege Mouries, a French scientist, addressed Napoleon's request and the first margarine was made in 1869.

As traditional market sectors have become increasingly segmented over the years, the butter and margarine market has become ever more complex and consumer demand for more sophisticated products has grown.

The product has remained versatile with 76% of all butter and margarine used for spreading, 10% for baking and the remaining 14% for other uses.

Almost the entire population of Great Britain buys butter and margarine at least once a year (Source: Taylor Melson Sofres 2000). An average household purchases 13.8 kilograms of butter and margarine a year, buying it around once every two weeks.

In an average lifetime a male will consume 439 kilograms of butter and margarine, while a woman will consume 473 kilograms.

Achievements

Flora was the first polyunsaturated spread to be launched in the UK and is the market leader. The brand has a heritage of trust that occupies a special place in the hearts of UK consumers.

By 1987 Flora had overtaken Anchor Butter to become the top brand in the butter and margarine market.

Since 1996, sponsorship of The London Marathon has underlined Flora's commitment to a healthier Britain. More than 35,000 people

You know why you buy Flora.

take part in the run each year and the event raises around £20 million for charitable causes.

Flora is still the leading brand with around a 16% volume share of the butter and margarine and spread market. The company sells around 140 million packs of Flora each year.

History

Flora was launched in 1964 when Van den Bergh and Jurgens recognised the health benefits and market potential of producing a margarine that was high in polyunsaturates and low in saturates. The advantages of polyunsaturates were first acknowledged in the late 1950s and medical evidence soon made fat types in diet a growing issue.

By 1968 Flora margarine had been rolled out from its test areas, which included Bolton and Brighton, to become a fully national brand. It also made its first national television appearance at this time.

Very specific legal restrictions, unseen in most other European countries, prevented Flora from making clear heart health claims and forced the brand to develop a more general health positioning.

Previous margarines had a reputation as inferior replicas of butter but Flora steered itself away from this old fashioned image and was marketed as a product in its own right.

The first commercials featured Rupert Davies, who played the French television detective Maigret and a well respected gourmet, eating Flora. With its light delicate taste, Flora was used to offset the other rich foods he enjoyed. The food values of taste and performance were important to Flora then and are today the most important choice criteria used by consumers when evaluating food products.

By 1973 Flora's volume share stood at around 2% of the margarine and low fat spread market. Four years later this had increased to 6%.

In the 1970s the 'Margarine for Men' campaign was highly appropriate when men were considered to be most at risk from coronary heart disease. In 1976 the Royal College of Physicians and the British Cardiac Society report recommended an increase in polyunsaturated fat and Flora saw a virtually instant boost in sales. The brand grew by a phenomenal 89% that year.

The Committee on Medical Aspects of

Food Policy wrote a new report in 1984 that recommended reduced consumption of saturated fat. It achieved widespread media attention and helped to increase consumer awareness of the health issues involved. During this phase of Flora's history the brand increased sevenfold and by the end of 1985 had reached a share of almost 6% of the yellow fats market.

The later realisation that women were also affected by heart disease influenced the 1986 black and white press campaign. This featured young women and the copyline, 'There's a good reason to eat Flora. The reason is you.' Flora then became 'The Margarine for You' and this helped increase awareness of the problem of coronary heart disease amongst women. The credibility of Flora's health message was reinforced by the first promotional link with the British Heart Foundation. Advertising was further broadened to include all of the family.

In 1989 market share stood at 19.9% in a very overcrowded and segmented market. At this time Flora was purchased by nearly half of all households in the country.

In 1991 the volume peaked at 98,000 tonnes, equal to a 23.6% share.

It was recognised early on that Flora's association with health meant the brand had a responsibility to educate the consumer and an information service was created. First created in 1970, the Flora Project for Heart Disease Prevention remains a source of consumer information and support today.

Product

Flora has undergone numerous product changes throughout its history. In 1989 Flora Low Salt was launched in support of dietary recommendations to reduce salt intake. Flora Light was also introduced that year and in 1991 Vitamin E was added to the whole Flora range.

The fat content of Flora changed from 80% to 70% in 1993. A product must contain at least 80% fat to be classified as a margarine. The reformulation meant that Flora was from then on legally classed as a spread. After a further change in formulation Flora could claim in 1994 to be virtually free of trans fatty acids.

In 2000 the Unique Flora Balance was introduced to reinforce the brand's health credentials. The logo is featured on each Flora pack, on which are listed the Flora ingredients vitamins A and D, antioxidant vitamin E and polyunsaturates.

Flora pro.activ is a recent addition to the Flora family. A spread with a healthy balance of essential fats plus added plant sterols, it dramatically reduces LDL cholesterol by 10-15% in three weeks

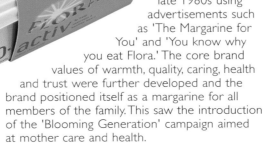

when eaten as part of a healthy diet. Flora pro.activ was the first spread to go through European Union Novel Foods approval.

Recent Developments

In 1994 Flora Buttery was launched, which is aimed at the consumer's move into the 'taste' sector. The Flora advertising focused on 'Living life to the full today and in the future.'

When Flora became sponsor of The London Marathon in 1995, the brand achieved huge awareness through the company's involvement in one of the biggest events in the UK. In 1998 the Flora Women's Light Challenge was created. This three mile fun run around Hyde Park in London aims to encourage more women to take part in sporting activity and charity fundraising.

New packaging design has increased product standout on shelves, emphasised different varieties and given the brand a more contemporary feel.

Promotion

The butter and margarine market is very competitive. To keep ahead of its competitors, Flora relies on product quality and effective advertising. Flora's first television campaign was in 1965, following its national launch. This featured the use of a television presenter as a food expert to convey the idea that 'Flora puts natural goodness into good eating.' It described Flora as a pure blend of vegetable oils, 'a good mix with richer foods' and 'a light alternative to butter'. The same presenter was retained as brand spokesman for the remainder of that decade.

In the 1970s an extensive medical public relations programme took place and towards the end of the decade the 'Margarine for Men' campaign was aired. This emphasised Flora had a taste men liked and that 'a Flora man knows what's good for him'.

A new campaign targeting women was developed in the late 1980s using advertisements such as 'The Margarine for You' and 'You know why you eat Flora.' The core brand values of warmth, quality, caring, health and trust were further developed and the brand positioned itself as a margarine for all members of the family. This saw the introduction of the 'Blooming Generation' campaign aimed at mother care and health.

In 1996 the comedian Richard Wilson was introduced in the campaign 'Flora, for Everybody' which focused more on the health benefits of Flora.

Strong packaging design has also played an important role in Flora's marketing strategy and contributed to a distinctive brand identity. Flora packaging is well known for its familiar green and white livery.

Brand Values

Flora enjoys a strong brand heritage and reputation as a quality, healthy product for all the family. It is seen as a trusted brand, committed to excellence and is associated with a relaxed and enjoyable approach to life.

Things you didn't know about
Flora

When Flora was launched in 1964 the first regional tests took place in Bolton and Brighton.

In 1989 almost half of all British households purchased Flora.

Flora is spread on 25 million slices of bread a day.

Half a million packs of Flora are sold every week and around 140 million a year.

The Government's 'Health of the Nation' White Paper proposed a 35% reduction in saturated fat intake by the year 2005.

Market

The UK car market is one of Europe's largest and most competitive. Over two million new cars are sold every year, and there is a total of 24.5 million privately owned cars on the UK's roads.

We are a nation of serious car-lovers, with car ownership growing at a faster rate than the population itself. While the UK population remains almost static in its growth, car ownership is growing by around 3% per year. Sales of new cars grew faster than used cars between 1995 and 2000.

With models in every segment of the car market, Ford is well positioned to see how demand is shifting. The biggest sector, accounting for 33% of the market, are 'lower medium' cars, such as the Ford Focus and Ford Escort. Next biggest are 'mini and supermini' models, such as the Ford Fiesta and Ford Ka. Increasingly popular are sports utility vehicles like the Ford Explorer and multi-purpose vehicles such as the Ford Galaxy. These segments are two of the success stories for the car industry during the 1990s.

Achievements

The Model T Ford was the world's first mass produced car, marking the beginning of the long love affair between man and his four-wheeled friend.

Ford has kept its 'cars for the people' mantle throughout its long history, making some of the most widely owned and best-loved cars in the world. In fact in 2001, Ford marks its 25th year of leadership in the UK new car market. The Ford Escort, first manufactured in 1968, became a legend in its own life time selling over twenty million worldwide in 33 years, evolving through four different model shapes before finally being discontinued in July 2000. With UK sales of 4.6 million, the Escort is the UK's best-selling car of all time. It remained in either first or second place of the UK sales chart right up until 1998, only to be overtaken by its successor, the Ford Focus, which is now the UK's (and the world's) best-selling car. The car also helped Ford make its name in motorsport, claiming victory in 31 World Championship rallies.

It is not just the Escort that has kept Ford at the top of the new car market. It has an outstanding record as Britain's best-selling brand

for the past 23 years. For example, Fiesta has been the UK's most popular small car for the past fifteen years. The Ford Transit has been Britain's best selling commercial vehicle for over twenty years, truly earning the 'Backbone of Britain' accolade used in its advertising.

Ford has made great strides in car safety and innovative design. When it launched in 1993, the Ford Mondeo was the first car in its segment to offer a driver's airbag as standard. The innovative and mould-breaking Ford Focus has won a string of awards since its launch in 1998, including European Car of the Year 1999 and was awarded 'Millennium Product' status by the UK Design Council, which honours the best of British innovation and design.

Ford's latest offering, the new Ford Mondeo, heralds a new era in safety, customer value and driving quality. It is the first car in its class to offer an intelligent protection system; comprising occupant sensitive dual stage driver and passenger airbags, side airbags and side curtain airbags for total passenger protection.

History

The Ford Motor Company was created on June 17th 1903 when Henry Ford started business in a converted Detroit wagon shop, staffed by ten people. Just ten years later, the company was making half the cars in the US.

Between 1903 and 1908 Ford and his engineers used the first nineteen letters of the alphabet to designate their creations. Henry Ford was convinced the future lay in making affordable motor cars for the masses and, in 1908, launched the legendary Model T. Famously 'available in any colour, as long as it's black', the Model T sold fifteen million units in nineteen years, not only transporting millions of people, but transforming Ford into an industrial giant spanning the globe.

In 1927 the Model T was succeeded by another highly successful Ford, the Model A (available in a variety of colours) which proved to be another massive seller. During World War I civilian car production ground to a halt as Ford poured its resources into the war effort, making B-24 bombers, aircraft engines and jeeps.

Ford has been an international company almost from day one, exporting cars to Europe within a year of its foundation. The Model T was the first Ford to be built in the UK at

Trafford Park in Manchester starting in 1911. Construction of its Dagenham manufacturing facility began in 1929, with the first vehicle, a Model A truck, rolling off the line in 1931.

In the years that followed Ford built a long line of British classics, such as the Zephyr, Zodiac, Consul and, in 1962, the Cortina. By 1980, four million Cortinas had been sold, making it one of the UK's most popular cars. In 1965, Ford launched the Transit van.

In 1982, Ford launched the Sierra to replace the Cortina. It invested £250 million in manufacturing facilities to build the new car, which, with its aerodynamic body shape, broke new ground in the saloon sector. By 1988, Ford had built two million Sierras at Dagenham.

Ford redefined the class again with the launch of the Mondeo in 1993. It was the company's first 'world car', selling across multiple markets. A year later, the Mondeo had won over twenty European motor industry awards, including European Car of the Year 1994. Since it launched, the Mondeo has sold over 2.5 million units in 60 markets around the world.

In 1994, the company announced Ford 2000, a global re-organisation aimed at making it the world's leading automotive company. The Ford Engineering Centre at Dunton, Essex, teamed up with its counterpart in Merkenich, Germany, to design and develop all of Ford's small and medium-sized cars around the world. Nearly £300 million in R&D investment was matched by £235 million for additional manufacturing facilities.

In 1996, Ford launched the Ka, one of its most daring and innovative designs yet. The move marked the beginning of Ford's 'new edge' design, a concept that has now been extended across the entire product range.

Product

Ford manufactures leading models in all segments of the car market. In the 'supermini' and 'mini' class, it has the Ford Ka and the Ford Fiesta. In the 'medium' segment, it has the UK's best-selling car, the Ford Focus, while the Ford Mondeo is a leader in the 'saloon' sector. In the popular sports coupe market, it offers the Ford Puma, while the Ford Galaxy is the best-selling model in the multi-purpose vehicle (MPV) market, claiming over 25% of the segment's sales. The off-road sports utility vehicle (SUV)

market is growing fast, and in this area Ford has the Ranger and the Explorer. Finally, in the commercial vehicle sector, Ford makes the market-leading Transit and small van versions of the Fiesta and Escort.

Ford manufactures from several facilities in the UK, including Dagenham and Southampton.

Recent Developments

Ford has recently enhanced its product range with the introduction of all-new Mondeo and Galaxy models. These are the first of a new aggressive five-year launch campaign that will see Ford of Europe triple the pace of its new model introductions. They also mark the application of Ford's 'new edge' design strategy across the entire range. This striking new look, featuring sleeker angles and a more daring approach to design, began with the launch of the Ford Ka and has been gradually rolled out to encompass all models in the Ford family.

The new Mondeo, manufactured at Ford's Genk, Belgium, assembly plant, boasts a raft of new safety and design features which build on the enormous success of the original model. It is the first Ford to be digitally created, using a new computer engineering tool called C3P. This enables Ford to develop new vehicles more quickly and achieve even higher levels of quality. Using C3P shaved thirteen months from Mondeo's development process.

The new Galaxy, which went on sale in August 2000, features fresh interior and exterior styling and a host of other improvements, such as the introduction of an optional on-board multi media system, allowing passengers to watch movies or play console games. Other options include satellite navigation.

Ford recently announced a highly competitive package of prices for the majority of its new models. Recommended retail prices have been reduced, bringing the cost of a new Ford Puma, for example, down by over 13%. In addition, the company launched a new three year 60,000 mile warranty on all new Fords.

Another important recent development is Ford's new online sales channel, allowing customers to purchase new Ford cars over the internet. Called Ford Journey, the service was launched at the British International Motor Show in October 2000.

Promotion

In terms of its annual spend, Ford is the UK's 9th biggest advertiser (Source: ACNielsen MMS) and spent a giant £57.3 million on advertising in 1999. The bulk of this spend – some 70% – goes on television advertising. However, it also uses a broad range of other media, like radio, press, new media, direct mail and outdoor.

Some of Ford's best known campaigns of late include the Galaxy 'Travel First Class', which compare the luxury of riding in a Galaxy to first class air or rail travel. The ads positioned the brand as being aspirational and stylish and helped Galaxy achieve market leadership within a year of launching.

The Ford Focus launched in the UK with the positioning of 'Expect More'. This not only reflected an attitude to life, but also highlighted that consumers in this segment no longer had to compromise between performance, economy and design.

One of Ford's most ambitious ad campaigns launched the Puma. Positioning the car as a 'driver's dream' the ads innovatively crafted Steve McQueen driving a Puma around San Francisco, recreating a famous scene from the 1960s classic film 'Bullitt'. Ford has also invested significantly in the launch of its new Transit, featuring the 'Backbone of Britain' campaign.

Ford is involved in a wide range of sponsorship activities, placing a particular emphasis on sport. It was a founding partner of the UEFA Champion's League and is into its eighth year as an official sponsor of the prestigious competition. It also sponsors Sky's Premiership football coverage and was a broadcast sponsor of the 1999 Rugby World Cup.

Ford also supports Breakthrough Breast Cancer which is a charity committed to fighting breast cancer through research and awareness. Ford offers an internal breast screening programme for its female employees and helps with fundraising activities.

Ford also sponsored the Journey Zone in the Millennium Dome, which takes a historical and future-gazing look at the contribution of transport to society.

Brand Values

As long ago as 1907 Ford's brand was defined as 'the hallmark for reliability and efficiency'. Like the famous 'script in oval' design of Ford's logo – which was first used in 1911 – these values have remained consistent ever since.

Nowadays, the Ford Primary Brand stands for 'Maintaining Brand Excellence and Consistency.' Supporting this over-arching mission are three brand pillars – dependable, contemporary and driving quality.

Ford's central offering is to provide attractive and accessible products in the heartland of the vehicle market. The Focus and the Transit act as the car and commercial vehicle 'centres of gravity'.

www.ford.co.uk/cv

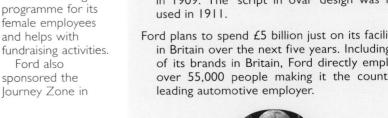

Gillette®

Market

The male blades and razors category is now worth £187 million in the UK alone, an increase of 35% since 1995, making it one of the fastest growing sectors within the toiletries market. Furthermore, the male grooming market is predicted to experience even higher growth over the next five years.

The main catalyst for spectacular growth has been a fundamental change in men's attitudes to the grooming process over the last decade. The rise in popularity of 'lads' mags' and influential sportsmen evolving into 'model-esque' icons, has made it acceptable for men to care about their appearance. Today 69% of men use aftershaves and out of the 82% of men who wet shave, 92% are using shaving preps.

This trend has resulted in a massive influx of male grooming products on to store shelves, dramatically increasing choice for the male grooming regime. Moving into the new millennium, the male bathroom cabinet now rivals the female's, both in size and choice.

Female grooming is also maturing into a very important part of the health and beauty category. It now equates to 15% of the total blades and razors sector and delivers retail sales of more than £38 million – up 42% since 1995.

Women view the process of hair removal as very important in their beauty routine, with more than 46% removing hair at the slightest re-growth (twice a week or more). Wet shaving continues to be by far the most popular amongst 83% of women – an increase of four million women since 1991.

Achievements

The Millenneum heralded Gillette's centenary year. Much has changed over this 100 year period. However the passing of time has not changed the number one position that Gillette holds in both the male and female grooming markets. While Gillette is synonymous with shaving, it is a global leader in nearly a dozen major consumer product categories. Grooming undoubtedly remains the principal business unit, but the company is also a major supplier of toothbrushes and oral care applications under its Oral B and Braun brands, and the number one source of portable power with the Duracell brand.

The core element of the wet shaving category remains blades and razors, of which Gillette has a 78% value (74% unit) share of the male and a 71% value (70% unit) share of the female market. Gillette has a long established position as the most popular brand and is market leader in the two principal wet shaving categories – blades & razors and shave preps.

For men, shave preps go hand-in-hand with shaving. While this is secondary to blades and razors in the wet shaving market as a whole, the category is becoming a very significant player. The male shave prep market is worth more than £68 million (up from £53 million in 1995) of which Gillette holds a 58% share. With the growing success of 'own brand' labels and an increase in competition from other brands, Gillette has also aggressively attacked market trends with the launch of a new fragrance line for its series range – Arctic Ice.

The company's strong focus on technological advancement has created new market opportunities. Many of Gillette's pioneering innovations have become patented inventions accepted as industry standards: from adjustable razors, fully contained cartridges, pivoting heads, lubrastrips, flexible microfins spring-mounted twin blades to the first razor designed specifically for the unique shaving needs of women.

The success of the Sensor for Women razor helped establish Gillette for Women as a worldwide leader in the female shaving market. Since the razor's launch in 1993, female shaving has become the fastest growing part of the Gillette Grooming portfolio, attaining annual growth of 27%. The razor, 'designed by a woman, for a woman, to address the shaving needs of a woman', revolutionised the female market.

This achievement saw the Gillette for Women Sensor shaving system receive the Gold award in the 'Design of the Decade: Best in Business 1990-1999' award competition.

In the early 1990s, just under 70% of women removed hair, but with the introduction of the Sensor for Women and the SensorExcel for Women, eight out of ten women now do so.

Gillette for Women also holds the number one position in the other two areas of the female shaving category: Satin Care holds a 61% value share of the £8.1 million female shave prep market and Agilite has a 46% value share of the £9.2 million female disposables sector.

History

100 years ago, US travelling salesman King C Gillette had the idea of developing a safe and easy to use razor – an idea which was to revolutionise the shaving market. His frustration with traditional cut-throat shaving led him to start work on a model razor, and so the Gillette Company was founded in Boston in 1901.

Gillette's early success was built on strong technological foundations.

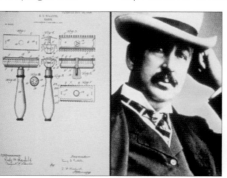

The 'wafer thin' metal needed to make the razor blade was even dubbed by Thomas Edison to be a 'technical impossibility'. However, Gillette broke new ground with the development of new processes for tempering and hardening mass produced steel. In 1903 the Gillette Safety Razor was finally launched.

In spite of a slow start (only 51 razors and 168 blades sold in the first year) more than 90,000 Americans possessed a safety razor by the end of Gillette's second year of trading. The safety razor had already become a hit. It was deemed to have changed the face of a nation. In 1905 the rapidly growing company established a factory in South Boston under the new name of the Gillette Safety Razor Company.

Strong domestic growth prompted international expansion. Overseas operations commenced in 1905, with a manufacturing plant just outside Paris and a sales office in London. Annual blade sales had risen to more than 40 million units before the outbreak of World War I.

The Great War saw Gillette become the first supplier of razors to the US Army when, in 1918, the US Government decided to issue each of its servicemen with their own shaving equipment. 3.5 million Safety Razors and 36 million blades were duly supplied.

The company has come a long way since its first patent in 1904. Techmatic, the first system razor, was introduced in 1967. Its 'continuous band' meant that consumers would no longer have to touch the blade. This was followed in 1971 by the GII, the world's first twin-bladed system. The first twin bladed disposable razor followed in 1976 and Contour, the first razor with a pivoting head, arrived in 1977.

While developments in the 1960s and 1970s focused mainly on blades, the 1980s and 1990s saw improved features for a smoother, more comfortable shave. The Contour Plus in 1985 heralded the first lubrastrip and 1990 saw the company's first ever Pan-Atlantic launch with the introduction of Sensor in sixteen countries. This razor featured the first spring mounted blades and shell-bearing pivot. Then, three years later, the SensorExcel was launched with soft, flexible microfins. Mach3 finally arrived in 1998, introducing the revolutionary triple bladed shaving system.

There had been little development in the female shaving market before the 1990s. Gillette introduced the first ever razor for women called 'Milady Decollete' in 1915 and the first disposable for women called Gillette Daisy in 1975. The ground-breaking Gillette for Women Sensor arrived in 1992, which was then surpassed by the new and very much improved SensorExcel for women.

Product

The company's biggest technological breakthrough in recent years has also been Gillette's biggest success

The toiletries business, driven by the Series range, has experienced accelerated product development over the past five years in order to maximise incremental demand in an ever-expanding market. The Series Range of premium quality shaving preparations offers a wide selection of shave foams, shave gels, shaving concentrate, body sprays, antiperspirants, shower gels and aftershave (gels, balms and lotions). These all complement the shaving process.

Recent Developments
The pioneering launch of Mach3 in 1998 added over £27 million to the value of the wet shaving market in its first year alone, securing Mach3 a 32% share of male system blade sales.

Another success story has been Arctic Ice. The Gillette Series Range was introduced in 1993 as a response to the ever expanding market. Cool Wave was the first fragrance, followed by Wild Rain and Pacific Light. Arctic Ice was launched in February 2000, quickly becoming the number one Series fragrance in body sprays, clear gels, splash and shave gel.

Gillette for Women has introduced a funky new collection of products aimed at appealing to a wider female audience. The range combines fashionable colours and fragrances with Gillette's most advanced shaving technology available for women. The SensorExcel for Women is now available in three new shades – pink, blue and silver. Two new Satin Care Moisture Rich Shave Gels have also been developed with light and subtle new fragrances, Wild Berry and Flower Twist and packaged in fashionable techno-silver cans to complement the razors. These new gels, as with all Satin Care gels, include moisturisers and skin conditioners, keeping legs feeling smooth and smelling great.

Promotion
Everyone still remembers the 'Gillette, The Best a Man Can Get' advertising campaign of the 1980s and 1990s. The creative imagery of Mach3's advertising has focused on breaking the performance barrier and draws parallels between the high-tech, high speed, high performance and aerodynamic nature of jet planes/test pilots and the razor. Media spend in the first four months of the Mach3 launch amounted to £5 million and totaled £11 million in its first year.

Sponsorship has also played a large part in the promotion of Mach3. In 1998 Mach3 sponsored Richard 'Rocketman' Brown in his world record breaking attempt at the land speed record. The Maximum Impulse team was successful in breaking the British motorcycle land speed record in the Gillette Mach3 Challenger and on their second attempt in September 1999 unofficially broke the world record. Cutting edge technology, highly innovative style, breaking performance barriers and the consistent theme of three (the bike had three wheels) all form strong synergies with the values of Mach3. The story attracted strong media interest, culminating

in a prime time BBC television documentary.

In 1998 Gillette sponsored the World Cup Championships in France, backed by a fully integrated marketing campaign.

This football association continues with both Mach3 and Gillette Series sponsoring premiership football on Sky Sports' 'Gillette Soccer Saturday'. Historically, Gillette has used sport as a major promotional vehicle and embarked on its first sponsorship deal with a radio broadcast of the US Baseball World Series back in 1939. There remains a strong association due to the performance focused and highly aspirational nature of sport.

Brand Values
Gillette is dedicated to driving superior technology that will develop and produce hair removal products which can deliver a superior shave with superior performance.

Its male image is sporty, masculine, clean and immaculately groomed. The female image is modern, energising and understanding of women's needs. Gillette's success has been its ability to make men and women look and feel their very best by continuously developing technologically superior grooming products.

In essence, the Gillette Company celebrates world class products, world class brands and world class people. It is committed to growth through innovation in order to maintain the company's position as a world leader in the consumer products marketplace.

story to date – the Mach3 shaving system.

Mach3 is a revolutionary triple-blade shaving system designed to give 'the closest shave ever, in fewer strokes – with less irritation.' Special alignment and positioning of the three blades enables a progressively closer shave, removing the need to re-shave and reducing irritation.

Mach3 has also seen a fundamental re-engineering of blades, the first major blade innovation since the 1960s. The patented DLC comfort edges are the thinnest produced by Gillette, cutting hair more easily and ensuring less drag and pull.

The creation of Mach3 involved more than a decade of research and development, the involvement of hundreds of Gillette scientists and engineers and financial investment of over £449 million.

Things you didn't know about Gillette

In the Stone Age, women used sharpened rocks and shells to scrape off unwanted hair.

On average, men's beards have the same number of hairs as a woman's legs and underarms combined. However, women shave an area that is approximately nine times larger than men's.

Beard hair, when dry, is the same strength as copper wire.

On average, a man's beard grows 15/1,000 of an inch a day and 5.5 inches a year.

During his lifetime, a man will spend approximately 3,350 hours removing 27.5 feet of whiskers from his face.

Goldfish™

Market

In about 500 BC, the quasi-existentialist Greek philosopher Heraclitus wrote 'You cannot step twice into the same river, for other waters are continually flowing in.' From the mid 1990s onwards the previously calm waters of financial services markets in the UK began to flow much more quickly, thanks to several factors. The markets are being liberalised such that competition is increasing and becoming more open. In parallel, the regulatory infrastructure is being strengthened, so that both traditional players and new entrants have to operate within consumer orientated regulatory frameworks.

Encouraged by the opening of the markets, new players have entered across a range of personal financial services. Fragmentation has occurred due to the growth in the number of providers, which has blurred consumer perceptions, bringing about a degree of confusion. Increasing competition has led to aggressive price based promotion, encouraging brand promiscuity and the general commoditisation of products.

An increasing emphasis on retaining customers is now reflected in improvements in customer service quality and the extensive use of loyalty and reward programmes.

The UK credit card market is still dominated by a clear market leader in Barclaycard Visa. More generally, the market can be broken down into three categories. Firstly, traditional players such as the clearing banks. Secondly, new entrants such as MBNA and Capital One from the US and affinity offerings such as those from grocery retailers like Tesco and Sainsbury's. Thirdly, more recent online providers including Egg, Smile and Marbles.

The Goldfish

The Frontosa Fish

The Pufferfish

Achievements

In just four years, Goldfish has grown to become the UK's seventh largest credit card and this growth is continuing (Source: HPI Research credit card tracking study 1996-2000). The rate of growth from zero to over 1,000,000 cardholders was extraordinary and unprecedented in the UK. Market studies have shown that since launch, the Goldfish share of 'new cards' has at times reached 15%.

Awareness levels, both spontaneous and prompted, have also been unusually high. Against benchmarks of 20%, Goldfish consistently achieves spontaneous awareness amongst cardholders of 40%-60% correlating with bursts of advertising. During such campaigns, Goldfish has achieved peak prompted awareness of 83%. In relative terms, this makes Goldfish the third to fifth most well known credit card in the UK (Source: HPI Research credit card tracking study 1996-2000).

Advertising recognition and brand attribution support these high awareness levels, bearing testament both to the strength of the brand identity and to the strength of the advertising messages.

Wolff Olins originally engineered this strong brand identity. Since the launch of the brand, great effort has been invested in staying true to the original vision, through carefully managed branded communications regardless of marketing discipline and medium.

TBWA GGT Simons Palmer have been retained as the Goldfish advertising agency since launch; similarly DP&A have been the retained agency for direct communications. Both agencies have delivered strong, award winning branded communication, whilst also adding value through contributing thought as participants in the development of the brand.

Research also highlights the degree to which the brand engages customers, reflected in the strength of Goldfish's relationship with its customer. In commercial terms this leads to comparatively high customer retention rates. Another measure of customer engagement is the level of take-up of the Goldfish points loyalty programme, with over 200,000 of the one million plus cardholders redeeming Goldfish points each year.

Goldfish regularly wins plaudits for customer service quality. Although this has been built into the brand experience since launch, maintaining service levels takes a continuing investment in time and resource.

A further sign of the health of the brand is the mythical 'armour plated' status given to Goldfish in research studies. For example, in Goldfish 'brand personification' exercises, customers struggle to offer negatives when probed to characterise the brand (Source: Directions Research Brand Audit March 2000).

History

The story of the Goldfish brand is short but action packed. Launched in 1996 by the then British Gas plc in partnership with HFC Bank Limited, the original positioning was as a credit card, which saved you money on your British Gas gas bill. This was closely followed by potential savings on other household essentials.

A blaze of publicity and advertising contributed to a high profile launch which was seen to 'shake up' the traditionally staid and lifeless UK credit card market. This high profile was followed up with high volume and strongly branded direct marketing activity.

The success of the launch highlighted the opportunity for Goldfish to become a significant player in credit cards, so a repositioning of the brand supported the broader long term development. Through expanding the range of partners through which Goldfish points could be redeemed, Goldfish could be repositioned as the surprisingly practical credit card that saves money on a range of household essentials.

Progressively, the basic credit card and points programme offering was extended, as well as added to with a range of cardholder services, with the objective of adding value to the customer relationship.

Product

The Goldfish launch positioning stood out at the time – a credit card that gave something back. For every pound spent on the card, the cardholder earned a Goldfish point, which could

What other credit card has so many desirable features?

The more you look at a Goldfish, the more **attractive** it gets

have used similarly distinctive style and humour, whilst moving away from the celebrity connection.

Press advertising has been direct response oriented and backed up with advertorial endorsement as well as local field marketing through agencies. Customer word of mouth has been particularly effective and encouraged through regular member-get-member (MGM) communications offering incentives to current customers to introduce others to Goldfish. Similarly, regular credit card statement enclosures and volume personalised direct mail have strengthened the customer relationship. Direct communications have consistently attracted new customers at market leading promotional costs of sale.

The brand is always carefully communicated to customers, especially through Goldfish's increasing online presence. Goldfish credit card online can be accessed at www.goldfish.com. New functionality means that you can apply for a Goldfish card live and receive a real-time response to your application within 60 seconds. Goldfish credit card customers can check their balance, their statements and their Goldfish points total online, as well as carry out various transactions.

then be redeemed as a saving on everyday household essentials. It quickly became clear that the concept of customer rewards delivered through the simple mechanic of Goldfish points was a winning element of the Goldfish proposition.

The Goldfish points programme was soon extended to other points redemption partners including household names such as Marks & Spencer and Boots.

In addition, Goldfish entered the market with a highly competitive interest rate, and with no annual fee. Competitively, the major credit card providers were experiencing widespread criticism for their lack of consumer orientation reflected in the charging of an annual fee for a credit card, and in the rates of interest (APR) charged on uncleared balances.

Other popularly received Goldfish card product elements included a choice of Goldfish card design; regular proactive contact from Goldfish through customer direct mail and statement inserts; ongoing developments of attractive value added services for cardholders; new product launches and a high quality of customer service.

Recent Developments

Developments since launch have drawn heavily upon regular market research studies. Due to the popularity of the choice of card designs available to customers, a programme of new card designs are carefully managed.

Value added services for cardholders have been invested in significantly, through a dedicated management resource. A number of other services are now in place including a direct wine service, a discounted telephone service, travel insurance, a travel service, personal accident insurance, home insurance, personal loans and mobile telephones as part of the Goldfish points redemption programme.

New product launches have taken place on average every six months, keeping the brand fresh and dynamic. Although some products have been more successful in take-up than others, the levels of take-up have consistently out-performed expectations.

Promotion

Goldfish advertises on a regular basis using national television. Advertising campaigns have maintained the high profile of the brand since launch, with the use of initial teasers heightening anticipation before launch. The style that was adopted was distinctive and quirky, with subtle humour, fronted by the Scottish comedian Billy Connolly.

The 'Everywhere' commercials built upon the initial success by communicating the popularity and worldwide acceptance of the Goldfish card. These commercials still achieve high recognition despite not having been aired since 1998. Subsequent television advertising bursts

Brand Values

At launch, the values engineered into the Goldfish brand were: Simple, Honest, Challenging, Inclusive, Engaging and Unique.

The Goldfish tone of voice is particularly important in supporting these brand values. The brand values and tone of voice are primary elements of detailed brand identity guidelines that are updated annually.

Great value wines and beers delivered **free** to your door

Redeem your Goldfish points for even greater value

The Goldfish Card Wine Service offers fine wines and beers at competitive prices – but did you know that you can exchange your Goldfish points for even greater value? Simply call **08705 133 000** to redeem your Goldfish points in part or in full.

And, when you consider that every purchase you make with your Goldfish card earns you further points, buying direct from the Goldfish Card Wine Service makes perfect sense.

Expert advice, free delivery and our no-quibble guarantee

As you would expect from Goldfish, our wine and beer service offers so much more. In addition to free delivery* within 4-10 days, we also offer complimentary advice from our team of experts. Whatever the occasion, whatever you wish to know, simply call us on **0870 783 0066** and we'll be happy to help (you don't have to be placing an order to call).

Finally there's the reassurance of our no-quibble guarantee*: if for any reason you're not completely satisfied with your wine or beer, we'll replace it for you free of charge.

To place your order, call **0800 783 0066**

Cool and crisp whites

Fresh and dry wines that make ideal summer drinking. Our case comprises two bottles of each of the following. Case price £50. **Call and quote reference 100411. Complimentary bottle of wine with every two cases of wine purchased.**

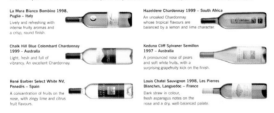

The International Beer Selection

Premium strength and full-flavoured - a fine international collection. Our case comprises four bottles of each of the following. Case price £28. **Call and quote reference 100412. Save £4 when you buy two cases of our International Beer Selection.**

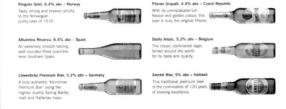

The Classic British Beer Selection

Traditional beers with a distinctively British flavour. Our case comprises three bottles of each of the following. Case price £22. **Call and quote reference 100413. Receive four extra bottles with every two cases of Classic British Beer.**

Gordon's ®

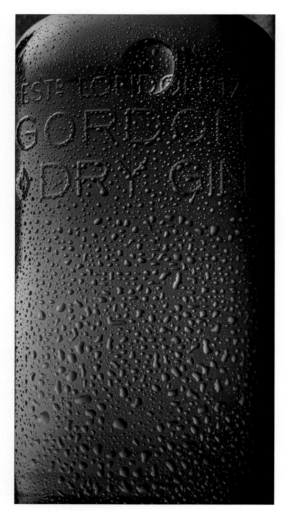

Market

The gin market has grown steadily since commercial production began some 200 years ago. By the early twentieth century worldwide consumption was established and Gordon's Gin enjoyed leading brand status in many markets, particularly in the UK.

Throughout the 1980s and early 1990s gin manufacturers battled against declining gin consumption. In 1980 10.3% of UK adults regularly drank gin, however by 1995 that figure had fallen to 8.6%. Volume consumption similarly declined – from 144,000 h/ltrs pure alcohol to 100,000 h/ltrs over the same period. The problem was an ageing customer base as younger drinkers found the drink uninspiring in comparison to a host of newer alcoholic drink brands offered as an alternative choice, encroaching on the occasions when gin was traditionally consumed.

Today Gordon's is leading the renaissance in gin consumption, which is being achieved through aggressive marketing and a dedicated brand building programme, a programme that has seen UDV invest some £20 million per annum in the Gordon's brand.

Gordon's strategy for the new millennium is to broaden its appeal but to do so in a balanced way. The strategy focuses on making the brand more contemporary, thus appealing to a new category of drinker, but at the same time maintaining its core brand values, values that

will build upon the loyalty of its existing customer base. A simple, attractive and lively brand proposition, supported by an integrated marketing campaign of advertising, one to one marketing and public relations is further enhanced by a fresh look at innovative in-store promotions for Gordon's. The cumulative effect is an invigorated brand that is broadening its relevance and appeal considerably.

Achievements

Gordon's Gin has long been brand leader in many markets and today accounts for seven out of every ten gins sold in UK pubs and bars. In the off licence sector, Gordon's again dominates – accounting for 31.7% of sales, although own label collectively accounts for a greater proportion at 47.8%.

The Gordon's brand enjoys two Royal Warrants (one from the Queen and one from the Queen Mother) and has won many awards including a Bronze in the 1996 International Wine & Spirit Awards and a Gold at the same event in 1995. The brand has also won Gold, Grand Gold and Gold (Trophy) at the Monde Selection.

History

The first spirits flavoured with juniper and produced on any significant scale were developed in Holland in the sixteenth century and brought home by English soldiers and merchants. Within two centuries gin was the English national drink holding the position whisky had in Scotland.

In the late eighteenth century, much of the gin produced in Britain was poor in quality and made by distillers of dubious reputation. A handful however became known for the quality of the product and most of these have survived in business until the present day. Gordon's Gin was one of these.

The brand was founded by Scotsman Alexander Gordon 200 years ago. He established a distillery in Goswell Road, Finsbury in 1796. By 1800 Gordon's Gin had made its name both at home and abroad, thanks to the sailors of the British Navy who carried it to all corners of the world. By the late nineteenth century, Gordon's was established as a truly international brand.

The early twentieth century saw gin gain popularity throughout the US. Expansion in markets closer to home, notably continental Europe, has come more recently as people switched from other drinks. Today Gordon's Gin, now owned by UDV, occupies the leading position in almost every European market, and is exported to some 150 countries around the world.

Product

Gordon's Gin is the world's most famous and highest selling London Dry Gin. Recognisable by its distinctive green bottle and logo, it is consumed at the rate of two bottles a second, day and night. The recipe for Gordon's Gin has remained pretty much unchanged for years.

London Dry Gin is essentially a rectified or redistilled grain alcohol flavoured with juniper berries, coriander seeds and various other aromatic herbs. The production of an authentic dry gin comprises three important and distinct processes: the distillation of the basic spirit; the rectification or redistillation which gives it the required degree of purity and, finally, a new redistillation with the flavouring ingredients. (The exact recipe for which is a closely guarded secret known only by twelve people in the world.)

Unlike whisky or cognac, there is no maturing or ageing process required. On the day London Dry Gin is produced it can be drunk, it is one of the most adaptable of drinks and mixes well with fruit juices, soft drinks and colas. In many countries however, the most popular accompaniment for Gordon's is tonic which,

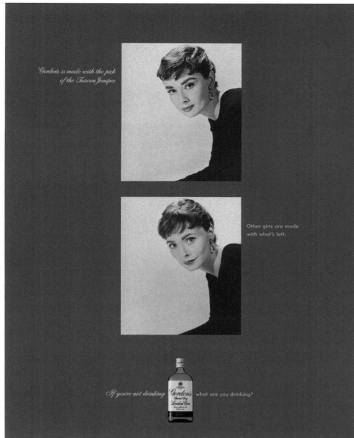

Gordon's as being more approachable, humorous and clever than its rivals in an attempt to ditch any perception of the brand as stuffy and traditional. This worked well for Gordon's with younger consumers reassessing how they felt about the brand. However, as the only media used were cinema and print, the campaign was not exposed to the mass market and did not seem to make the audience it reached want to choose gin over other spirits.

This all changed in 1995, when Gordon's unveiled its national advertising campaign on television, ending the voluntary television ban on spirits advertising in the UK. This new campaign adopted a fresh theme – 'innervigoration' – which focused on the physical, emotional and spiritual refreshment offered by a Gordon's Gin and Tonic. These activities were designed to strengthen the brand and appeal to two groups – upmarket gin drinkers aged 45 and over and 25 to 34 year olds – with the message of quality and relevance.

In one commercial, created by Leo Burnett, that was shown in cinemas, Gordon's demonstrated how to make the perfect gin and tonic accompanied by the smell of juniper berries which was pumped amongst the audience.

At the same time, Gordon's focused on staff training to improve the general presentation of Gordon's in pubs and bars. It developed a 'Perfect Serve' programme which focuses on presenting the perfect Gordon's and Tonic in bars; fill a tall, clean chilled glass with ice, pour Gordon's over the ice, top up with a chilled bottle of premium tonic, add a wedge of lime or lemon and stir. The 'Perfect Serve' programme goes from strength to strength and is today reporting an average uplift of 40% in participating outlets.

Brand Values
Gordon's core values are style, stature and invigoration. At its heart is a recipe, which has remained unchanged since 1769. As a product, Gordon's Gin has always been known for its refreshing aromatic, clean, crisp and reviving qualities.

when mixed together, transform into an invigorating and uplifting drink.

Recent Developments
Today Gordon's are pioneering a relationship marketing programme to increase consumption of Gordon's and build loyalty amongst heavy gin drinkers. Over 500,000 consumers joined in the first year of the campaign and research has shown significant increases in Gordon's consumption. In addition, Gordon's has developed a number of innovations to extend the Gordon's franchise. These include Gordon's & Schweppes Tonic premixed as a ready to drink pack designed to appeal to new and current users of the brand, and sold in grocers and specialist off-licence channels. This allows the definitive gin and tonic to be enjoyed at a number of outdoor events and locations from Glyndebourne to Henley.

Promotion
Gordon's advertising has developed significantly since the still remembered slogan of the 1970s and 1980s – 'It's got to be Gordon's' – and the versatility of the early 1980s encouraging the use of several mixers.

In the late 1980s, Gordon's set about presenting a more contemporary image to attract new users with the launch of the 'Green' campaign (1989). This was designed to present

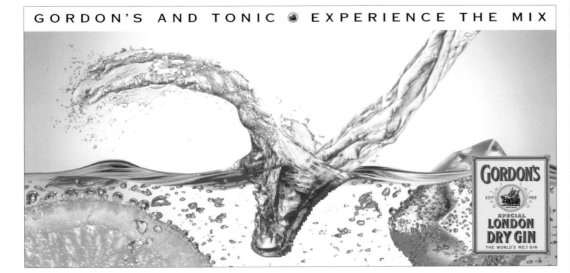

GORDON'S AND TONIC ⚓ EXPERIENCE THE MIX

GORDON'S
SPECIAL LONDON DRY GIN
THE WORLD'S NO.1 GIN

Market

Ice cream was once viewed as merely a treat for children. Not any more. Since the launch of Häagen-Dazs in the UK in 1988, luxury, premium quality ice cream has become a sophisticated and stylish indulgence for adults.

Over the past twelve months Häagen-Dazs has performed very strongly in the premium ice cream market, claiming a 21% market share in value terms with a total brand growth of 11.1%. A highly successful advertising campaign throughout the summer of 1999 was partially responsible for a 25% increase in Häagen-Dazs penetration. (Source: ACNielsen July 2000).

Achievements

Häagen-Dazs is the brand leader in the 'super premium' ice cream market. It virtually created the premium ice-cream market in the UK, which had previously consisted of one or two regional brands. In its first year alone it took 8% of the market, proving popular with gourmets and the style-conscious alike. Häagen-Dazs is now a global brand, and enjoys strong sales in Singapore, Japan, France, Germany, Canada, North America and a host of other countries. The Häagen-Dazs brand is no longer alone in the super premium sector and greatly increased level of competition has seen the overall category enjoying a tremendous growth rate over the past twelve months.

History

From humble beginnings in the USA back in the 1920s, the Häagen-Dazs brand has grown and developed to become the global mega-brand we know today. Häagen-Dazs was registered as a company in 1961 and still it remains a mystery as to where the Scandinavian sounding name originated. In the same year, the first three

Häagen-Dazs flavours – vanilla, chocolate and coffee – were sold in New York delis. News of its irresistible quality soon spread by word of mouth until there was nationwide demand for the product, all without the help of advertising. By the mid 1970s, 'dipping stores' in Brooklyn were opening, paving the way for what have now become approximately 650 Häagen-Dazs Cafés around the world.

In response to global demand for the product, international distribution of Häagen-Dazs took off in 1982 when it first became available in Canada. Shortly afterwards, the Häagen-Dazs brand was sold to the Pillsbury Company Limited. Just one year later, it signed an agreement with Japanese companies Suntory and Takanaski to produce Häagen-Dazs in Japan where it quickly became the best selling premium ice cream brand in the country.

Since 1987, Häagen-Dazs has made in-roads into European countries including Britain, France and Germany. In January 1989, Pillsbury was acquired by Grand Metropolitan plc and latterly became one of the food divisions of Diageo, which was formed by the merger of Grand Metropolitan and Guinness plc.

Product

Häagen-Dazs ice cream is made with the highest quality natural ingredients – fresh cream and milk, sugar, eggs and natural flavourings, with no artificial flavours or colourings. The rich, creamy texture is created by ensuring that the ratio of cream to air is extremely high, unlike cheaper brands in which substantial quantities of air are pumped back into the ice cream. This explains why, once removed from the freezer, it needs to be left to temper – or melt a little – before it can be eaten.

Nowadays, the pint size tub comes in a grand total of fifteen flavours. Consumers have the tricky decision of which flavour to choose to indulge in. Top sellers in the UK include Vanilla, Pralines & Cream and Belgian Chocolate, although the recent arrival of new flavour Cookie Dough Chip is proving especially popular with younger consumers.

For those wanting to ensure that they don't allow themselves to over-indulge, seven of the fifteen flavours are available in a mini-cup size (50ml). These include favourites such as Bailey's, Toffee Crème, Cookies and Cream and Choc Choc Chip, as well as classics such as Strawberry, Vanilla and Belgian Chocolate.

In addition, there is also a range of Häagen-Dazs sorbets in three flavours to stimulate the senses: Mango Tropicale, Raspberry Classic and

Peach & Strawberry. Just to ensure that true fans of Häagen-Dazs are able to fulfil their desires even when they are on the hop, there are also stick bars especially designed for those impulse moments when only Häagen-Dazs will do.

Häagen-Dazs is created in three high-tech plants, located in northern France, Japan and the USA.

Recent Developments

In March 2000 Häagen-Dazs introduced four new ice cream flavours: Lemon Passion Pie, Cookie Dough Chip, Chocolate Fudge Swirl and Caramel Cone.

In June 2000, Häagen-Dazs opened its doors to a whole new experience of ice cream indulgence with the launch in London's Leicester Square of the new-style flagship Häagen-Dazs Café. Burgundy sofas and cosy booths add a feeling of comfort, cocooning and intimacy throughout the café. Other unique features include an improved scooping and serving area where customers can experiment with flavours. The Café has been luring Häagen-Dazs devotees with the promise of an experience of pure pleasure whilst out and about in town.

Hazel Dunlop / Eyecatchers

Investment in the brand continues to break boundaries and August 2000 saw the launch of www.haagendazs.co.uk, the UK-specific website. The brand has demonstrated its commitment to the art of indulgence through the site – the aim of www.haagendazs.co.uk is to deliver to consumers all they would expect from their favourite indulgence brand.

The website offers a chance for consumers to take a step back from their busy day and dream about indulging themselves or someone special. For example, the website provides recipes for an indulgent meal at home, tips for indulgent nights in and even a database of indulgent events.

The website is an integral part of Häagen-Dazs's continuing marketing plan. The site aims to go way beyond being just another fast-moving consumer goods brochure site. It is designed to appeal to the lifestyle of the Häagen-Dazs consumer and at the same time strengthen the brand's indulgent positioning.

Dedicated to Pleasure.

Fall head over heels in Häagen~Dazs.

Fall deeply in Häagen~Dazs.

Promotion

The marketing campaigns behind Häagen-Dazs have been instrumental in the success of the brand. The company started stealthily and did not advertise; instead it made sure that the product was distributed in upmarket outlets such as Harrods and began a 'whispering campaign' about this new, incredibly creamy ice cream from the US. The campaign then went one step further with PR activity and sampling of the 'Häagen-Dazs experience' in stores, at college freshers' balls, at celebrity parties and film premieres.

Full scale press advertising began in 1991 and presented the brand as an adult pleasure through images of couples enjoying the product together. At a time when ice cream was seen as something for children, Häagen-Dazs attempted to challenge this notion by presenting ice cream as sensual and seductive.

In spring 1988 Häagen-Dazs launched a $30 million European marketing package to take the strategy one step further. The 'Dedicated to Pleasure.' campaign led the way for food adverts to feature in lifestyle magazines. Erotic pictures of couples in provocative embraces adorned the glossy magazines of Vogue and Harpers & Queen.

This marketing blitz was followed with the 'temperature-rising' advertising campaigns. The year 1995 saw the launch of 'Heat' – at the time the ultimate in risqué advertising that appeared on television and in cinemas. Viewers were just able to see the bodies of a man and a woman, who were sensuously covering one another with Häagen-Dazs.

While Häagen-Dazs advertising remains renowned for its controversial approach, 1998 saw a more light-hearted take on the idea of perfection with the '100% Perfect' creative. Memorable moments - such as the old man with a beautiful young wife, unable to remember where he lives – are served up to remind everyone that only Häagen-Dazs is 100%

perfect. Häagen-Dazs, through its unique positioning and advertising campaigns, created a whole new product category – 'a grown-up, luxury ice cream indulgence' which other brands have since tried to replicate.

At the end of June 2000 Häagen-Dazs launched an advertising campaign in response to extensive consumer research conducted around the brand. The research revealed that Häagen-Dazs has an intrinsic link with sensuality and indulgence in the minds of consumers.

It was Häagen~Dazs at first sight.

Fall deeply in Häagen~Dazs.

I've never had Häagen~Dazs like that before.

New Lemon Passion Pie.
Fall deeply in Häagen~Dazs.

The resulting advertising campaign included a series of stylish portrait shots of couples and women alone enjoying Häagen-Dazs and places a new twist on well-known phrases connected with passion and sensual experience. The word 'love' is replaced by 'Häagen-Dazs' in, for example; 'It was Häagen-Dazs at first sight', and: 'Fall head over heels in Häagen-Dazs.' The television advertisement features a loving couple sharing Häagen-Dazs against the backdrop of a stylish city apartment with elements of the room responding subtly to the passionate mood.

Brand Values

Häagen-Dazs is recognised as a brand dedicated to indulgence, providing its consumers with moments of pure pleasure. The sensual and emotional experience of eating Häagen-Dazs is a key feature in the brand's positioning and has transformed the way ice cream is viewed by adult consumers. Quality is at the core of the brand – a fact which is demonstrated by its use of only the finest ingredients.

Market

Heinz is a leading global food brand with over 400 branded products available in the UK alone. One of the oldest and best loved of these varieties is Heinz Salad Cream, created by Charles Hellen in 1914. It took eight years for Hellen to perfect the recipe that has enhanced salads and other dishes for more than 85 years.

The total salad dressings category is currently worth £129 million, and is growing at around 9% per annum. This growth has been fuelled by healthy eating trends, with the traditional host foods of salad vegetables and breads also increasing consistently over the last four years. Heinz is synonymous with salad cream and has consistently held over 50% of the market. At the end of 1998 Heinz held a 59% value share – the only major competitor being private label with around 20% of the market. The remainder is made up of smaller brands such as Waistline and budget brands.

However, by the late 1990s the salad cream sector was in long-term decline due to competition from mayonnaise and pourable dressings and under-investment by the major players. Heinz was faced with the fact that Salad Cream had an uncertain future and undertook a strategic review of the brand. The company had two choices: one option was to discontinue the product altogether; the other was to invest significantly in Salad Cream, giving it a new lease of life.

Consumer research confirmed the brand's popularity and Heinz took the decision to invest £10 million to relaunch this long-standing family favourite. This decision heralded one of the biggest relaunch programmes in Heinz's history.

In other markets, Heinz dominates the sauces sector with its Tomato Ketchup. Although this product is loved by all the family, Heinz is keen to make its Ketchup the definitive brand for kids and has therefore launched its Sq-easy Ketchup in a squeezable bottle which will allow children to create works of art with their food.

Heinz also has a strong presence in the soup market, having recently diversified into the pouch soups market and introduced new concepts with its Fridge Door and Microwaveable soups. These innovations aim to position soup as a core product within the fast-growing snacks market. Heinz continues to dominate the canned soup market, with one in every seven cans bought in the UK being Heinz Cream of Tomato.

Achievements

With sales of over $9 billion, the H J Heinz Company is one of the world's leading food processors and purveyors of nutritional services. Its 50 affiliates operate in 200 countries offering more than 5,700 varieties. Among the company's famous brands are Heinz, Farley's, Weight Watchers, Linda McCartney meat free foods and John West.

Heinz is well known for its product innovation. It has pioneered many technological developments, from the introduction of the ground breaking Simplifeed three way feeding system for the Farley's brand, to its move into the frozen pizzas market.

History

In 1860, sixteen year old Henry J Heinz began bottling dried and grated horseradish from his family's garden in Pennsylvania. Unlike others, he packed his product in clear glass bottles so that his customers could see he was only selling horseradish without cheap fillers. By 1869, he had transformed the company, and Heinz pickles and other bottled products appeared in many local shops. The product positioning was clear: no artificial preservatives, no impurities and no colouring. He also offered a money back guarantee if his product failed to please. Business prospered and in 1886 Heinz sailed to the UK. He brought with him five cases of products and called first at Fortnum & Mason who bought the lot. In 1905 business was sufficient to merit the opening of the first Heinz factory in Peckham. Twenty years later, Heinz's first custom-built factory opened in Harlesden, west London.

With the end of World War II, it soon became clear that additional manufacturing capacity was needed. A temporary factory was opened and remained in production for the next 30 years. In addition a factory was built in Kitt Green, Wigan, which has enjoyed substantial investment over the years to ensure it is a state-of-the-art operation.

Product

Heinz's products are extremely well known and feature in almost every larder or fridge in the UK. Some, such as Tomato Ketchup, Soup, Baked Beans and Salad Cream are national institutions. They have their own fan clubs and celebrities often include Heinz products in their 'desert island hampers'.

As well as its established product range, Heinz is constantly looking to launch new products – for example, the favourite Heinz Spaghetti has been joined by a wide variety of tasty pasta shapes which appeal to young and old alike, from Tweenies and Pokémon Pasta to Manchester United Pasta Shapes.

Classic Heinz Baked Beans are a family favourite, but consumers' insatiable appetites for new products, has led Heinz to develop a range of Baked Bean meals. The company has also launched Cheezy Beans, an ideal combination of favourite flavours for a lunchtime treat or tasty snack.

Heinz's innovation also extends to frozen products, with the recent launch of Heinz's All Day Breakfast, a full English breakfast which can be microwaved in just a few minutes.

In addition, Heinz has recently launched a range of organic products in order to extend consumer choice. The new Organic range includes an organic version of Heinz Tomato Ketchup, Heinz Baked Beans and Heinz Spaghetti.

Heinz not only launched a number of new products – it has also repackaged a number of its famous varieties.

The '57' stamp of quality is positioned prominently across all packaging, bringing with it all the reassurance of Heinz. The Heinz keystone acts as an umbrella across the icon brands – Baked Beans, Tomato Ketchup, Spaghetti and Tomato Soup. Each of these varieties has its own personality, its own proposition and its own set of values. Their appeal goes far beyond immediate brand imagery into a more emotional realm that operates at a predominantly subconscious level, offering consumers familiarity and reassurance, securing them as firm favourites. The Heinz keystone is more than that too – it is also one of the world's most famous packaging symbols.

The keystone stands for simplicity, continuity and security. For Heinz, it is a focal point – reassurance of the underlying quality of everything that bears its mark.

Recent Developments

In 1999, Heinz acquired UB Frozen & Chilled Foods from United Biscuits (holdings) plc. The transaction was valued at $317 million. UB Frozen & Chilled Foods was one of the leading companies in the UK and Ireland producing frozen desserts, meat-free products, frozen pizzas and added value potato products, as well as fresh sandwiches. The company markets and licenses San Marco pizza, Go Ahead!, Jane Asher desserts, Linda McCartney meat-free products and value added potato products under the Ross, Hula Hoops and Harry Ramsden trade names. Heinz is using the acquisition to build on its profitable Europe-wide frozen and chilled food business.

In March 2000 Heinz unveiled the biggest relaunch programme in its history, putting a £10 million campaign behind Salad Cream. This unprecedented, major investment in the famous icon brand aimed to double the size of the salad cream market, and make Heinz Salad Cream the number one table sauce in the UK.

The restage programme has brought Heinz Salad Cream up to date, with the aim of making it a 'must-have' accompaniment to any food. The fully integrated campaign has re-introduced people to its unique, quirky, tangy and individual taste. It included television, poster and radio commercials aimed at the young and young at heart, the sponsorship of a comedy tour and a dedicated website at www.saladcream.com. The relaunch of Heinz Salad Cream has reinvigorated interest not only in the brand but in the salad cream sector overall.

ready in two minutes.

Promotion

Heinz has been responsible for some of the most famous advertising campaigns such as the 'Joy of Living' campaign in the 1920s, 'Beanz Meanz Heinz' campaign in the 1960s, and the highly popular 'Toast to Life' campaign of the late 1990s.

Heinz's marketing campaigns are highly targeted and include the classic disciplines of sales promotion, advertising and PR, as well as new media such as the internet.

It is not just food that has changed since Henry J Heinz bought his first horse and cart. The world is unrecognisable from the one that the twelve year old knew. These days, we live in an instant world of global communications. Information, entertainment, communications – they're all there at the touch of a hot key or the click of a mouse. Heinz is part of the new world and recognises the powerful impact of the internet and uses it to provide customer service and communication.

Heinz's website at www.heinz.co.uk provides

a wealth of historical, nutritional and general information on Heinz products. Plus, for those people who live abroad and miss the unique taste of Heinz, a dedicated website, www.heinzdirect.co.uk, has been set up.

A new advertising campaign, 'There's a bit of Heinz in all of us', delivers Heinz's key messages to a wide consumer audience. In addition, targeted campaigns have been developed to promote products to discrete audiences. These include the 'Eddie Spaghetti' advertising aimed at kids and the Salad Cream campaign targeted at twenty-somethings.

Most recently, Heinz television campaign for microwaveable soups has created humorous stories around events that happen in just two minutes.

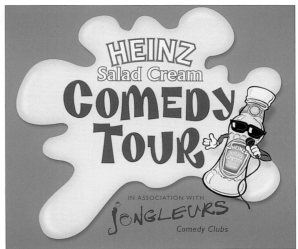

Brand Values

Undoubtedly Heinz is a brand icon. It is a heritage brand familiar to generations of British consumers and widely appreciated for product quality and consistency. Heinz is committed to constantly improving that quality and ensuring that both its icon products and newer varieties meet the stringent demands of twenty first century consumers. Heinz is one of the most potent global brands.

Any food tastes supreme with

www.saladcream.com

HMV

Market

The market for pre-recorded music in the UK is now worth an estimated £2 billion (Source: BPI). Of that, 12% is accounted for by sales of singles, with albums responsible for the remaining 88% of all sales. Compact disc is now the dominant format, accounting for 90% of all sales, while 9% of customers buy their music on cassette, with just 1% buying traditional vinyl.

After a particularly buoyant period in the mid-1990s, when sales were boosted by Brit Pop and Girl Power, annual rates of growth levelled off in the late 1990s. However, stimulated by new artists, strong releases and a re-emerging US market, sales are again showing signs of growth.

Music retail is becoming increasingly polarised, with specialist stores such as HMV offering range, knowledge and service at one end, and supermarkets and convenience retailers carrying limited, discounted chart titles at the other. Although still only accounting for less than 1% of all music sales, the internet is creating downward pressure on prices, whilst also prompting debate over the future delivery of pre-recorded music. In HMV's other major markets, UK video sales – boosted by the arrival of DVD – are now worth in excess of £1 billon, while the launch of PlayStation 2 is expected to push UK computer games sales above the £1 billion mark for the first time.

Achievements

HMV is the UK's leading specialist retailer of music, video and computer games with a 20% share of UK music sales, and around 10% of the video and computer games markets respectively. With 120 stores nationwide, the chain operates in all major population centres around the country with flagship stores in London's Oxford Street and regional superstores in Glasgow, Edinburgh, Newcastle, Leeds, Liverpool, Manchester, Birmingham, Reading and Southampton.

In 1996 HMV celebrated its seventy-fifth anniversary, and another landmark was achieved a year later with the opening, by Robbie Williams, of its 100th store at Birmingham's Fort Shopping Park. Since then the company has continued to grow rapidly, both in the UK and internationally where it now operates some 300 stores across nine countries, including the USA,

Canada, Australia and Japan.

Since its very first store was opened in 1921, HMV has always sought to offer the widest possible access to music, and to play a pioneering role in the way music is sold and promoted. Appropriately, in 1997, HMV was among the first retailers to launch a website, which became transactional just one year later to offer the best online selection in the UK. In May 2000 HMV's new 'internet friendly' Oxford Street store generated considerable interest as the first UK record outlet to offer a CD burning facility.

The new Oxford Street store takes on the mantle of the original HMV at 363 Oxford Street, which was universally recognised as 'The World's Most Famous Music Store', and was officially closed by Sir George Martin in April 2000.

History

On 20th July 1921 Sir Edward Elgar, the celebrated British composer, opened a new record store in London's Oxford Street and it was to prove a transforming moment in popular culture, as HMV's new store was the first to tap the burgeoning demand for recorded music and effectively established a template for record retailing as we know it today.

The store's many innovations, including listening booths and self-service record counters, combined with its range of titles, dedicated customer service and striking interiors, were all key factors in laying the foundation of HMV's rich heritage.

Such brand values were to become symbolised in one of the world's most enduring and compelling images: the picture of a Jack Russell fox terrier, head slightly cocked, ears pricked up, listening to an old gramophone with a brass horn – instantly recognisable as the trademark of 'His Master's Voice'. The dog's name was Nipper and the artist was Francis Barraud, who painted the famous image back in 1898. The painting initially featured a phonograph, but a year later this was replaced by a gramophone after The Gramophone Company, later to become EMI, paid the princely sum of £100 to acquire the painting and copyright. Today the Nipper trademark still adorns the modern face of HMV stores.

From the company's earliest days, EMI had franchised HMV products exclusively to just one store in major towns around the UK but this system was abandoned in the mid 1950s when HMV goods were made available to all dealers.

HMV Oxford Street was now free to stock the products of EMI's rivals – thus paving the way for real high street competition.

The move came just in time for the rock 'n' roll explosion. Indeed, one meeting, in February 1962, played a decisive role in shaping the very direction of popular music. At that time the store had a small recording studio, and a Liverpool entrepreneur, Brian Epstein, paid a visit to cut demo discs in his bid to secure a record deal for a band he was managing called The Beatles. The store loved what they heard and, through publishers Ardmore & Beechwood, who were based in the building, put him in touch with Parlophone's George Martin; just four months later the band were recording at Abbey Road studios.

In the years that followed, HMV took advantage of a buoyant market to expand from its Oxford Street base. Initially taking sites around London, by the 1970s HMV had opened stores in Manchester, Glasgow, Birmingham, Leeds and Bristol. By 1976 the number had risen to 25, and HMV could stake its claim as the UK's first chain of specialist record stores. With the 1980s came Live Aid, a new wave of recording artists and, most crucially, the compact disc – all of which helped maintain HMV's momentum. In October 1986 it opened the world's largest record store, again located in Oxford Street, and a year later the Midlands-based Revolver Records was acquired to boost the overall store number to fifty.

Expansion continued throughout the 1990s, significantly raising HMV brand awareness and also underlining HMV's position as the UK's dominant specialist retailer of music, video and games. During this time HMV opened its 100th store, launched a transactional website and celebrated its 75th anniversary. In March 1998 HMV and its sister company, Dillons, were acquired along with the Waterstone's book chain to form a new company – the HMV Media Group.

Product

Through its range, knowledge and customer service, HMV aims to provide the widest possible access to music, video and games. Although high street stores remain at its core, HMV's website (www.hmv.co.uk) and digital technology is likely to play an increased role in the future.

HMV stores carry the widest selection of music and, unique among music retailers, they also stock three own label series: HMV Classics, HMV Jazz and HMV Easy. The chain is also a committed specialist retailer of video and DVD and computer games software, including PC, PlayStation, Sega and Nintendo, while all stores carry an extensive selection of related products, including t-shirts, books and accessories.

In addition to chart releases, HMV constantly seeks to give added-value to its customers through monthly sales campaigns, which often follow the 'multi-buy' format i.e. 'Buy 2 CDs for £22 or 'Buy 3 Videos for £15'.

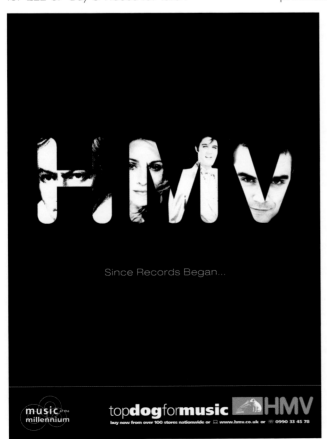

Recent Developments

To mark the new millennium HMV looked to its original brand values to create a new legacy. In April 2000 the HMV store at 363 Oxford Street was closed to make way for a much larger replacement at 360 Oxford Street, which was officially opened by Ronan Keating in May 2000. The store reflects the heritage of its predecessor while also embracing new technology to offer a glimpse of the future. It features a 'Virtual Music Store' CD-burning facility, a DVD cinema area, scan-activated listening posts and catalogue information points.

HMV's website, www.hmv.co.uk, launched in 1997 and fully transactional since 1998, is now one of the UK's leading online music stores, generating both sales and increased brand awareness.

In 1998 HMV re-launched the HMV Classics own label series, adding HMV Jazz and HMV Easy just one year later to offer a wide range of budget priced titles, beautifully presented and drawn from the finest EMI repertoire. During this time HMV also launched its own free, consumer publication, HMV Choice, to further support its specialist music credentials.

Promotion

HMV at 363 Oxford Street virtually invented the idea of record store promotion. As early as the 1920s and 1930s it staged personal appearances by leading artists of the day, and this still remains a fundamental part of today's public relations strategy. Around 200 are staged each year, both to launch new stores and promote new releases. In recent years, those making special appearances at HMV have included Sir Paul McCartney, The Spice Girls, Blur, Robbie Williams, Prince, Tony Bennett and Jose Carreras. HMV stores also regularly stage midnight openings and other events to launch cult releases such as Star Wars and X-Files, or new products like PlayStation. Capitalizing on the appeal of its brand, HMV has held nationwide searches, often in conjunction with a media partner, to find a real life Nipper look-a-like to attend events and perform other promotional duties. In recent years major coverage has been secured in The Mirror newspaper and on the That's Life and This Morning television programmes. Taken as a whole, HMV's promotional activity seeks not only to create media opportunities, but also to support HMV brand values of range and authority in order to raise corporate profile and differentiate it from its rivals.

Marketing activity is fundamental in reaching the core youth market HMV operates in, and this is usually achieved in partnership with music, video and games suppliers. This generally involves co-operatively funded advertisements across a range of media – most commonly press and posters, but also television and radio during key trading periods. These are often tied to in-store merchandising and window campaigns, while customer listening posts, radio broadcasts and video screens provide further means of in-store support.

Promotions play a key role in attracting customers to stores and in raising their spend levels. HMV therefore run numerous third party promotions each year in partnership with other leading brands with the basic aim of raising brand profile and generating increased sales.

Brand Values

Famously symbolised by its 'dog & trumpet' trademark, HMV's core brand values are based firmly on key customer service requirements of outstanding product range and staff knowledge. Such values help underline HMV's authority as a specialist retailer, and also support its trading ethos of giving customers the widest possible access to music, video or games.

HMV's authority and position as the UK's leading specialist retailer is further reinforced by the company's current advertising strapline 'Top Dog'. This play on a popular expression is simple but direct, and is used by HMV in a versatile way, i.e. Top Dog for Music, Video and Games, Top Dog for Jazz and Top Dog for Christmas etc.

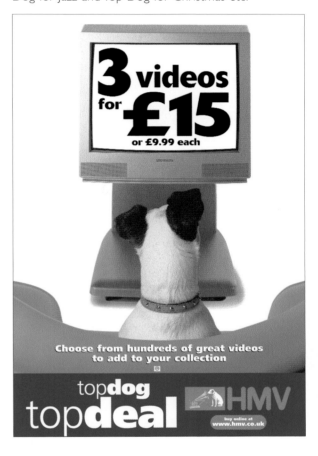

msn™ Hotmail®

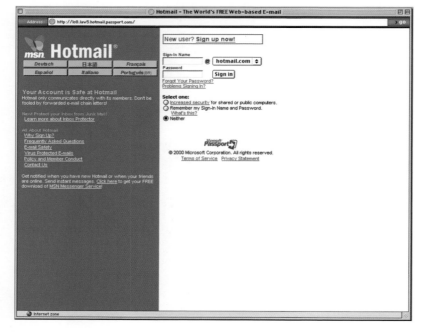

Market

Free web-based email services have become one of the most important internet innovations. Email is one of the core drivers for internet adoption because people can quickly see the benefits and it is very easy to use. The ability to check email from any internet connected PC offers obvious benefits to many different groups: transient students moving from schools to colleges and then jobs; travellers who want to keep in touch with friends and family on the move; and workers who require a personal account independent of that provided and administered by their employer.

Most well known online brands including AltaVista, AOL, BT, Excite, Freeserve, Lycos, Netscape and Yahoo! – and many more lesser known ones – offer free email services. In fact competitors offering a similar set of features and the promise of free, reliable service crop up almost every day. Many of these services have had success, others have been a flash in the pan, but none has generated the popularity of MSN Hotmail.

Achievements

Hotmail has become an indelible part of the internet and one of its most recognisable brands. Just four years after it first appeared on the web, Hotmail became the world's largest free web-based email service provider with over 70 million members, claiming its place in the Guinness Book of Records.

It is rapidly approaching the enviable position of being a brand name which is synonymous with the service it offers – just like Hoover, Sellotape and Walkman have become in their respective market sectors. The world over, and particularly in South East Asian countries popular with foreign travellers, internet cafés have sprung up advertising Hotmail as their core offering.

Rapid growth from zero to over 70 million members in just four years – including one year in which the service tripled in size – has been

challenging, and not without growing pains. Hotmail has navigated this astounding growth well. The initial software architecture put in place by the founders has proved extraordinarily scalable: as capacity grows, Hotmail engineers are easily able to implement additional hardware. While Hotmail has experienced slowdowns and occasional outages – something many sites of its size have had to deal with in the past – Hotmail's problems are usually short lived and affect only a small percentage of its users.

Hotmail's recipe for success is relatively simple: its growth is driven largely by the ability of MSN to deliver the features its members find most important – reliability, speed, overall ease of use, features, and integration with other communications services such as MSN Messenger Service.

History

It is said anecdotally that an 'internet year' is roughly the equivalent of a dog year. In one calendar year, the new economy companies experience seven times the life cycle experiences of old economy industries. Nevertheless, for such a well known product, Hotmail has one of the shortest brand histories of any in the world.

On 4th July 1996, when the Macarena dance craze was sweeping the planet and Independence Day was packing cinemas, Sabeer Bhatia and Jack Smith quietly changed the web for ever: casually flicking some switches in their tiny Silicon Valley office, they brought Hotmail online for the first time.

Hotmail pioneered the use of the web as a platform for email, winning the support of both internet users and the technology media for its simplicity. Less than eighteen months after the launch Hotmail was acquired by the Microsoft Corporation the world's largest software company, for $400 million, becoming

MSN Hotmail, part of Microsoft's consumer internet service MSN. The success of Hotmail speaks volumes about how email has become a critical communications tool in people's everyday lives.

When Bhatia and Smith approached venture capital firm Draper Fisher Jurvetson with their idea for a free email service the year before, the firm praised the idea but wondered how they would attract members and build a company around it.

Product

Hotmail is a free email service based on the world wide web, which means you can access your email from any internet connection, anywhere in the world. You can have as many accounts as you want, for work or personal use, and it doesn't matter if you change jobs, swap internet service provider, buy a new computer, move house or go travelling – your Hotmail account is yours for life as long as you use it at least once every 60 days. Hotmail offers the WebCourier service, which delivers news, entertainment listings, jobs, shopping and travel information of your choice direct to your inbox.

In the UK Hotmail has over four million registered users, and it is a fully integrated part of MSN.co.uk, the UK's most visited website (Source: MMXI Europe At Home panel September 2000). MSN.co.uk's Communication Centre tells you how many new messages are in your Hotmail Inbox, and you can log in retrieve and send emails direct from the MSN.co.uk homepage.

Hotmail is available in over ten languages worldwide – English, French, German, Japanese, Italian, Spanish, Brazilian Portuguese, Korean, Chinese, and the Nordic tongues.

Recent Developments

In 2000 MSN continued the integration of Hotmail with some of its other services, and introduced several new features, which helped to strengthen Hotmail's position as the world's

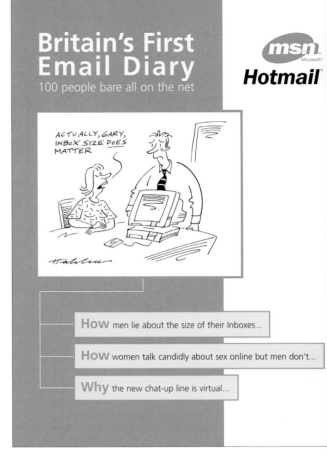

leading email service.

The integration of Hotmail with MSN Messenger Service offers free instant text and voice chats, and lets users know instantly when new messages arrive in their Hotmail Inbox. Microsoft's Outlook Express email software has Hotmail integration so that users can download their messages to their PC, enabling them to read and write emails while not connected to the internet, saving money on internet connection charges. MSN Calendar enables users to manage their diary online from any computer with internet access and is now easily accessible via a link on the Hotmail navigation bar.

Because privacy and security are paramount, Hotmail became the first web-based service to introduce anti-virus software. Free virus checking for attachments is done through McAfee's popular VirusScan software, which uses an array of scanning features to determine if attachments are safe before being downloaded to the PC.

And the Inbox Protector can help deal with unsolicited email, currently one of the most controversial by-products of the internet. Junk mail messages — commonly called 'spam' — can be automatically re-directed to a special folder using a filter that captures all messages sent to large distribution lists or as blind copies to the recipient.

Promotion

Hotmail has traditionally not been heavily marketed. There are two historic reasons for this. Firstly, as with many online brands and products, Hotmail's early promotion and adoption occurred almost naturally by word of mouth. In technology, perhaps more than any other sector, the advocacy of 'early adopters' plays a critical role in raising the awareness of

a product or service. By the very nature of the internet and email, word spreads quickly. The fact that users themselves sing the praises of the product is perhaps one of the most powerful factors in the success of Hotmail.

Secondly, in the days when internet penetration in UK households and businesses was still very low, internet brands had little to gain from embarking on expensive mass media advertising campaigns. Hotmail's marketing strategy was focused heavily around online advertising and below-the-line activities such as public relations and direct marketing.

As understanding and awareness of the internet — and the size of the online audience — took off in the late 1990s, so Hotmail's promotional activity began to move above-the-line. In 1998 an integrated campaign was launched encouraging people to 'be who you want to be with MSN Hotmail'. A national press and outdoor poster advertising campaign was launched, including executions entitled 'Lurve God', featuring a cheesy medallion man who was anything but, and 'Posh & Becks', which showed an aristocrat drinking a bottle of lager.

The following year email became a genuine mass market phenomenon. This was due to factors ranging from its widespread introduction in the workplace to featuring in popular films and books; notably You've Got Mail and Bridget Jones' Diary. A successful PR campaign tapped into both the nations' consciousness and the media's appetite for information surrounding this new form of communication. 'Britain's First Email Diary' was a report published following the analysis of 38,000 messages sent over one month by 100 people. The unique and revealing insight into the online lives of everyday Britons received widespread media coverage for Hotmail.

Hotmail continued its almost grass roots promotional approach as the internet and dotcom phenomenon reached a frenzy in early 2000. Brands, products and services launched mass media marketing campaigns and were the subjects of hugely over-subscribed stock market flotations. When several high profile operations failed on their promise to deliver — either to customers or to investors — the inevitable backlash began. Hotmail was one of the few true online great brands to ride out the storm.

Towards the end of 2000, promotional activity targeted two specific core user groups — job seekers and students. An online campaign to promote a Hotmail account as the perfect tool for protecting privacy while searching for a new job effectively targeted the growing number of internet recruitment sites. Hotmail went on the road to university freshers' fairs the length and breadth of the country with an integrated online, direct marketing and sampling campaign, encouraging students

— an extraordinarily transient group — to sign up for a Hotmail account which would enable them to have a single email address for the rest of their lives.

Brand Values

Hotmail's core brand values are providing a free, high-quality email service that lets its members access a permanent email address from any computer with an internet connection anywhere in the world. These sit within MSN's 'everyday web' strategy, and Microsoft's vision of offering a wide range of products and services designed to empower people through great software — anytime, any place and on any device.

Things you didn't know about Hotmail

Hotmail's name is derived from HTML, the programming language used to build web pages. Just take HTML, add some vowels, and you've got Hotmail.

Hotmail has members in every one of the world's 227 countries. If Hotmail itself were a country, its population of over 70 million in September 2000 would rank it as the fifteenth largest in the world.

On a peak day, 270,000 new members sign up to Hotmail — which surpasses the number of people (2,216,741) who travelled through London's Heathrow airport — the world's busiest airport, on its busiest day, 1st August 1999 (Source: Heathrow Airport).

In 1998, Wired magazine reported that the Hotmail user base grew faster than any media company in history — faster than CNN, faster than AOL, and even faster than the television audience of Seinfeld.

The average delivery time it takes to sign up for a Hotmail account is less than one minute. The average delivery time of a message sent from one Hotmail account to another is less than one second.

HOVIS

Market

Bread is the staple item in the British diet, with virtually every household consuming some type of bread. Approximately 80% of bread is wrapped and sliced – for convenience and keeping qualities.

Bread remains a traditional and versatile part of our diet and its modest price means consumers recognise it as being good value for money. In addition, bread is an excellent source of carbohydrate, energy, vitamins (especially B vitamins), protein and calcium, as well as being the nation's main source of fibre.

The total market for bread and bakery snacks was valued at around £2.8 billion in 1999. The great success story of recent years has been the introduction of branded sliced premium loaves. Between 1995 and 1998 this sector grew from a 3.8% share of the domestic bread market to 19.6%. Hovis has been a pioneer in premium sliced bread and remains the driving force behind this market sector.

The fact that Hovis products are all of premium quality and that the brand is widely recognised by shoppers has helped the value of Hovis sales to increase from £20 million in 1980 to £165 million in 2000.

Achievements

The Hovis brand has an illustrious history as one of the UK's oldest bread brands and it has consistently been the market leader. Throughout its existence, Hovis has been synonymous with high quality and has developed many different products in line with a changing society.

Keeping abreast of changing consumer demands, Hovis has produced bread for most sectors of the market, most famously its soft and tasty white and brown loaves. Hovis has also recently introduced Hovis Crusty bread (which maintains its crusty outside and soft inside for up to four days), new pre-packaged, substantial sandwiches and organic loaves, all of which have maintained the Hovis reputation of being a leader in innovation.

History

For most of the nineteenth century, brown bread was considered the basic food of the lower classes. This all changed towards the end of the century, however, when Richard 'Stoney' Smith, a flour miller from Stone in Staffordshire, decided to put into practice his belief that wheatgerm was a healthy component of any diet. His aim was to preserve the goodness of the wheatgerm while ensuring that the bread was longer lasting, and so he devised a flour which he felt matched his requirements. He took this to a milling company in Macclesfield called S. Fitton & Son. Together, they registered 'Smith's Patent Germ Flour' in 1887.

Yet 'Smith's Patent Germ Flour' wasn't deemed a particularly inspirational name. In 1890, both Richard Smith and Thomas Fitton, a descendant of the mill-owner who had first bought Smith's brown flour, launched a competition to decide on a suitable name for their product.

After some deliberation, one potential name, 'Yum Yum', was soon discarded.

Hovis is the slice of life

Eventually a student from London, Herbert Grime, claimed the £25 prize money with his Latinate idea of 'hominis vis', meaning 'the strength of man' – which was soon abbreviated to the simpler sounding Hovis.

With a good name and a good marketing tale to tell, sales of Hovis bread flour became one of the success stories of Victorian British enterprise. In 1896, Thomas Fitton bought Imperial Mills on the Embankment by the House of Lords. There has been a mill on the site for many years, and that is why Millbank is so called.

As the business grew, so the Hovis Bread-Flour Company Limited was formed. 'Stoney' Smith died in 1900 and is buried in Highgate cemetery in London.

In 1928, Cecil Gorden Wood joined the board of Hovis and the company began a rapid expansion. Hovis soon became a name with a string of mills, and domestic and overseas milling establishments. Intelligent advertising, plus the dissemination of Hovis teashops across the land, had certainly served to popularise the Hovis brand name. However, the Hovis company underwent particular strain during Word War II, including the destruction of its Manchester Mill in 1940. Under the terms of the national emergency, the government took complete control of all Hovis's proceedings, but Hovis ensured that Britain never went short of bread. In addition, it also helped on the front line, providing a Spitfire, to the Royal Air Force appropriately named 'Hominis Vis'.

The succeeding post-war years saw the fortunes of Hovis thrive through a merger with the McDougall Trust in 1957, to form Hovis-McDougalls Limited and the formation of Rank Hovis McDougall Limited in 1962. The company went from strength to strength until 1979, when control of Hovis Limited was vested in Rank Hovis Limited. The Rank connection had started with Joseph Rank in 1875, when he started his own chain of flourmills in Hull, London, Barry and Birkenhead.

Together, the Rank Hovis partnership was formidable, leading the way in UK flour-making for many years to come.

The Hovis millers at Rank Hovis celebrated their centenary in 1986, and have continued to provide top quality flours for its bakers ever since, consolidating the brand's leading position in the UK market as the best flour for the most popular branded bread.

Product

In recent years, innovation and new product development, driven by changing consumer demands, have generated an enormous range of high quality products for consumers to choose from. Hovis has consistently driven the bread market forward, with the 1990s proving to be a period of extensive new product development.

In 1994, Hovis entered the bread rolls market with Hovis Cobble, a very successful flagship roll with a cobblestone shape, which lends itself particularly well to lunchbox usage. Hovis Hoolies followed in 1997. Their name means 'a good old-fashioned knees up' in Celtic, and these cheeky, rustic-looking, long, split rolls are ideal for adult lunchtime occasions. The most recent addition to the Hovis rolls range is Hovis Bolders, launched in 1999 – chunky, dusted soft white rolls available in packs of six which are ideal for both kids' and adults' lunchboxes. Hovis is continuing to develop this range.

In 1995, the Half 800g Hovis loaf was introduced. As the name implies, this is not in fact a 400g loaf, which has smaller slices than an average 800g loaf, but is a half size loaf with full size

slices. This loaf is available in white, brown, or Granary©, and was developed to reflect the growing number of one and two-person households in the UK.

In 1996 Hovis expanded into the 'treats' market with the launch of Hovis Scones, and is continuing its development in this area. Latest new products include Hovis Crusty Bread and Hovis Ready-Made Sandwiches.

With all of these developments, Hovis has been able to build upon its implicit commitment to natural goodness.

Recent Developments

In 1999, British Bakeries launched Hovis Crusty White and Hovis Crusty Golden Brown, two innovative premium loaves that have revolutionised the pre-packed bread market. This is because the bread maintains its crusty outside and soft inside for longer, filling a gap in the market for a more convenient crusty product that does not need to be eaten on the day of purchase. Hovis Crusty is made without the use of preservatives – its secret being attributed to an innovative and award-winning process for baking and packaging the product. The loaves were an immediate success with consumers. The sandwich market has grown by 50% in just three years. Sandwiches are the most frequently consumed snack food and have a wider range of distribution outlets than other bread products. It was therefore a natural progression for a brand that has always been used for making sandwiches to enter into the pre-packed sandwich market. The first Hovis sandwiches were launched in October 1999. Consumers are demanding high quality sandwiches that are not only full of natural goodness, but are also excellent-tasting – attributes with which Hovis has always been synonymous.

Promotion

Hovis has been a distinguished advertiser for the whole of its 110 year history and has been inventive in its approach. At the turn of the century, as cycling became popular, thousands of Hovis Cycle Road Maps and Guides were published to promote the bread and to indicate those cafeterias where it might be enjoyed on the road. In the 1920s, Britain's strongest man, Thomas Inch, was called upon to tour the country boasting of the bodybuilding qualities of Hovis flour.

Hovis was among the first exhibitors at the Daily Mail Ideal Home Exhibition and the Hovis bakery remained a memorable feature of that event for many years. In the early years of the twentieth century, bakers' shop fronts were adorned with a Hovis gold-lettered 'V' sign, teashops advertised 'Tea with Hovis', and tea tricycles carrying this slogan were introduced to serve seaside promenades.

Many famous artists were commissioned throughout the years to create Hovis advertisements, including Mabel Lucie Attwell, Heath Robinson, and Tom Eckersley.

One of Hovis's most memorable advertising slogans, 'Don't say Brown, say Hovis' was first used in 1924 and was given greater visual emphasis with the advent of commercial television in the 1950s. Hovis was among the first to use the new medium and its short, black and white advertisements featuring George Benson and Kenneth Connors were notably humorous.

A much-praised series of Hovis commercials with a nostalgia theme followed in the 1970s, and the images of the baker's boy pushing his bike up cobbled Gold Hill to the sound of Dvorak's New World Symphony, and the Coronation street party

Take me home and smother me in strawberry jam.

HOVIS' Hoolies

The roll that's open to suggestions.

(directed by celebrated film directors Ridley Scott and brother Tony) remain forever in the memory. They won more than 36 international awards, and parodies of the Gold Hill commercial entered the repertoires of many comedians.

After twenty years of the famous 'sepia tinted' television advertising campaign, Hovis introduced a major creative development in 1994 called 'Raised the Hovis Way' which featured voice-overs by the popular actress Julie Walters.

Hovis Crusty has been supported by a huge £7 million above and below the line support programme that included a brand new television advertising campaign. The new television advertisement, written by Roger Holdsworth and art directed by Phil Chitty at D'Arcy, is entitled 'Richard's Wasted Years' and stars Dr Richard Roberts,

DNA biologist and Nobel Prize winner. The advertisement features Dr Roberts eating a piece of Hovis Crusty bread and lamenting that of all British discoveries in his lifetime – the jet engine, the web and DNA – he wishes he could have come up with something as good as Hovis Crusty bread.

Brand Values

For decades Hovis has been a bread brand consumers can trust and a name that generations of British families have relied on for 'natural goodness'. Over the years, while the advertising campaign may have changed, the message that Hovis is the best loaf you can buy for your family has remained.

Hovis has kept pace with changes in consumer lifestyles by undertaking extensive consumer research programmes to ensure they understand the key factors that influence consumers when making a purchase, and in order to provide consumers with the healthy, tasty and convenient products they demand.

As a result of its long line of innovative products and the ability to consistently meet today's consumer demands, Hovis has become an icon among British buyers and continues to be the toast of the town.

Things you didn't know about
Hovis

In 2000 Hovis was voted as one of the nation's favourite advertisements in a poll by the Sunday Times and Channel 4.

The founder, Richard Smith, died in 1900, and is now buried in Highgate cemetery. His grave is marked by a special headstone in remembrance of this particular contribution to the British diet.

During World War II, Hovis donated a spitfire to the RAF, called 'Hominis Vis', Latin for 'the strength of man', which in its shortened form became the brand name Hovis.

The first Hovis advert appeared in 1888, in the form of an analyst's report on the nutritional value of bread baked from germ flour. Professor William Jago said, "The prepared germ meal and flour yield a bread far superior in nutritive value, flavour and texture."

Hovis television advertising has won over 36 international awards, including a prestigious Gold Clio in 1974.

Dvorak's New World Symphony has become synonymous with Hovis advertising.

110 years after Hovis flour was first introduced, Hovis is still the number one bread brand in the UK.

HSBC

Market

In recent years, the financial services sector has been transformed. Developments such as changing working patterns and the burden of welfare shifting from the State to the individual have greatly changed the market. People need to be able to access and manage financial products, taking responsibility for their finances from a young age into their increasingly late years.

Financial services companies have responded by designing wider product ranges, ensuring that they have something to suit consumers' many different needs. This expanding market has made financial products into consumer brands, attracting entrants from outside the traditional banking sector. Now, as well as its established industry rivals, HSBC competes against brands like Sainsbury's, Tesco and Virgin.

Modern technology has had a big impact on the financial services industry. In the past, the only way to interact with your bank was to visit a branch. Today it can be reached via the internet, television and telephone.

This 'remote banking' revolution has attracted even more new competitors for the high street banks – a new breed of 'virtual' brands offering branchless banking over the internet. Without the costs of a 'bricks and mortar' network to support, brands such as Egg and Smile are competing fiercely on price and cherry-picking business. The internet is also underlining the fact that modern banking is a borderless, international business. As HSBC is now unifying most of its global businesses under one single brand, the Group is well positioned to be a powerful player.

The London-based HSBC Group provides a comprehensive range of financial services: personal, commercial, corporate, investment and private banking; trade services; cash management; treasury and capital markets services; insurance; consumer and business finance; pension and investment fund management; trustee services; and securities and custody services.

HSBC is a truly international brand, with some 6,000 offices in 81 countries and territories in Europe, the Asia-Pacific region, the Americas, the Middle East and Africa. In the UK, the parent company HSBC Holdings plc owns HSBC Bank plc, while in continental Europe, Crédit Commercial de France has recently become a member of the Group. In Asia it owns The Hongkong and Shanghai Banking Corporation Limited and has a 62.14% equity interest in Hang Seng Bank Limited. In the US, it owns HSBC Bank USA and operates a joint venture

trade bank with Wells Fargo Bank. In Brazil it owns HSBC Bank Brasil S.A.-Banco Múltiplo.

With some 170,000 staff and assets of over US$580 billion, it is one of the world's largest banking and financial services organisations.

Achievements

Key to its many achievements in the financial marketplace is HSBC's commitment to building one of the banking world's most recognisable international brands. In November 1998, it announced a plan to create a universal brand for the entire organisation, uniting most of its businesses under a single identity. As a result, it replaced corporate signatures and names of companies around the world with the distinctive HSBC and hexagon symbol. This decision demonstrates the Group's realisation that it needs a strong, internationally recognisable brand in a worldwide market.

The Group is also making headway in its aim to be the world's leading financial services company. It was recently rated the 'world's strongest bank' by The Banker magazine and the 'best bank in Asia' by Euromoney. Forbes rated HSBC second in its 'Super 50' league of international companies.

History

Although HSBC's holding company, HSBC Holdings plc, was formed only in 1991, most of the principal companies under its banner have been in operation for over a century. For example, The Hongkong and Shanghai Banking Corporation Limited opened for business in 1865 and the UK's HSBC Bank plc (formerly Midland Bank) dates back to 1836.

The Hongkong and Shanghai Banking Corporation Limited is the founding member of the modern group and is the company from which HSBC derives its name. It was founded by Thomas Sutherland, then the Hong Kong superintendent of the P&O Company, who saw the need for a local bank to handle the increasing amount of trade occurring around the China coast in the 1860s.

Initially, HSBC expanded by establishing new offices in its name. However, this changed in the 1950s when it began to create and acquire subsidiaries. In 1992, HSBC made one of the biggest cross-border acquisitions in banking history at that time when it took over Midland Bank, firmly placing the HSBC name on the map in the UK.

Midland's origins were in Birmingham where it opened its first office in 1836. Here, in the homeland of the Industrial Revolution, the bank started life in a thriving local economy. Over the years, it expanded and acquired other banks, eventually moving to London in 1891.

In 1967, Midland moved into merchant banking, buying a share in Montagu Trust. Samuel Montagu & Co Limited became a wholly owned

subsidiary in 1974 and in 1993 was transferred to HSBC Investment Bank plc.

In 1980, HSBC acquired a 51% share of New York State's Marine Midland Bank, which became wholly owned in 1987. By now, HSBC had also established a prominent presence in the Middle East, acquiring The British Bank of the Middle East in 1959 (now called HSBC Bank Middle East), taking a 40% shareholding in The Saudi British Bank in 1978, and a 40% interest in Egyptian British Bank S.A.E. in 1982, which increased to approximately 90% in October 2000.

In 1986, it further extended its merchant banking operations, buying James Capel & Co Limited, a leading London-based securities company. Following the purchase of Midland Bank in 1992, HSBC moved its Group head office to London in 1993.

In 1994 The Hongkong and Shanghai Banking Corporation Limited was the first foreign bank to incorporate locally in Malaysia, forming Hongkong Bank Malaysia Berhad – now HSBC Bank Malaysia Berhad. In 1997, Banco HSBC Bamerindus S.A. was established in Brazil and the acquisition of Roberts S.A. de Inversiones was completed. The banks were subsequently renamed HSBC Bank Brasil S.A.-Banco Múltiplo and HSBC Argentina Holdings S.A., respectively.

Product

HSBC aims to become one of the world's leading providers of financial services through its international network of personal, commercial, corporate and investment banking and insurance businesses.

Its personal banking arm offers a range of products and services to suit customers' needs. From financing education to retirement, and from day-to-day transactional requirements to

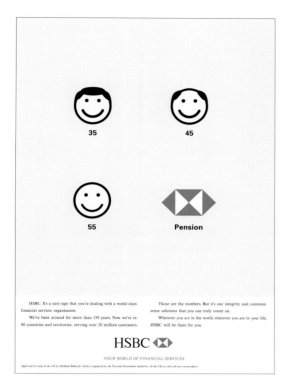

sophisticated investment and insurance planning, HSBC has a product or service to cater for every aspects of personal financial services.

HSBC's automatic teller machine (ATM) network allows customers to access their accounts through more than 500,000 machines worldwide.

HSBC Premier is an international service for personal customers built around local market requirements. HSBC Premier customers benefit from a dedicated relationship manager, personal financial advice and enhanced banking facilities such as commission-free currency exchange and 24-hour telephone banking.

HSBC's remote banking services allow customers to manage their finances when and how they want. So, as well as its extensive branch network and call centres – which offer person-to-person contact – HSBC has introduced banking services via the internet, interactive television and mobile phone. Using technology that enables these channels to talk to each other, rather than working in isolation, allows HSBC to offer a consistent service however customers choose to access their accounts.

Trade finance and related services, are long-standing core businesses of the HSBC Group, whose office network is well placed to facilitate and finance the world's primary trade flows. As its customers make increasing use of the

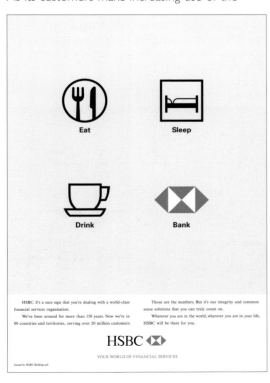

internet for trading, the Group is well placed to support this vital market.

Securities Services is a leading player in international securities and custody markets, offering services to domestic and cross-border investors in eighteen Asia Pacific centres and thirteen in Europe. Custody and Clearing is the largest custodian in Asia-Pacific and the Middle East and Global Investor Services is one of the largest UK-based international custodians.

Investment Banking and Markets brings together the advisory, financing, equity securities, asset management, private banking and trustee, private equity, and treasury and capital markets activities of the HSBC Group. Operating through dedicated offices and via the Group's network of commercial banks, this division employs over 13,000 staff around the world.

Recent Developments

HSBC already maintains one of the world's largest private data communication networks and is reconfiguring its business for the e-business age. It has a growing e-commerce capability, including the UK's first banking service available on interactive television, through Open.....

Other recent deals reflect HSBC's commitment to this area. For example, in April 2000, it joined forces with Merrill Lynch to invest US$1 billion in a new online banking and investment services company targeting private investors. The service will have research, equity dealing, planning and profiling tools, serving customers with between US$100,000 and US$500,000 in assets.

HSBC's acquisition of the French bank Crédit Commercial de France (CCF) in July 2000 gives it a sizeable foothold in the euro zone. The deal allows HSBC to build up its asset management portfolio, with CCF adding significantly to HSBC's US$93 billion in assets under management. HSBC also hopes to build even stronger internet banking capabilities with CCF.

Promotion

To raise awareness of its brand, HSBC is investing heavily in a range of promotional activity. Following the announcement of its single brand, HSBC undertook a phased approach to advertising. The first phase built brand awareness recognition for the new brand and focused on who HSBC is and what it can offer. The second phase, launched in 2000, focused on promoting HSBC's core values, such as trust, integrity and excellent customer service. The second phase is running in selected international markets and continues to run in 2001.

As well as television advertising, HSBC is also an active sponsor. Investment in community and educational initiatives by Group members is an important element of all the Group's marketing activities. It announced a £40 million sponsorship deal in London, partnering the British Airports Authority, the London Tourist Board and the City of Westminster. The four-year deal is part of a wider scheme called Partners for London, which is the world's first commercial capital city sponsorship programme.

The initiative sees HSBC's brand appearing on street furniture in the City of Westminster – including lampposts, signposts and hanging baskets – as well as on 201 passenger jetties at Heathrow, Gatwick and Stansted Airports. The deal will help market the brand to some 100 million people per year, building awareness among Londoners and international travellers. The revenue will be invested in enhancing customer services at the airports and, in Westminster, it will be used to 'clean and green' the borough's streets, thereby raising awareness of HSBC's community activities.

HSBC's other major sponsorships include a £3 million deal backing Drama Premieres on ITV

and a £25 million, five-year sponsorship of the Jaguar Formula One motor racing team. HSBC also sponsors the UK's top tennis player, Tim Henman.

Brand Values

HSBC's 'cultural values' are those of a responsible, prudent, cost-conscious, ethically-grounded, conservative, trustworthy, international builder of long-term customer relationships. The Group aspires to be highly productive, team-oriented, creative and customer driven. Its vision is to be the world's leading financial services company. In essence, its brand is built on integrity, trust and excellent customer service.

The diversity of the 81 countries and territories in which HSBC operates means that its operations can vary according to the regulatory and market requirements of different jurisdictions. However, HSBC aims to ensure that its brand's principles apply consistently to all of its activities. These are to treat customers as individuals, recognise their value, leave them in control, anticipate their needs, provide easy to understand products and accessible expertise.

Things you didn't know about HSBC

HSBC Bank was the first major UK bank, in 1905, to have a foreign exchange department.

It was also the first UK bank to advertise on television, in 1955.

HSBC Bank is responsible for many banking innovations. These include personal loans (1958); personal cheque and cheque cards (1958). In 1988, it was a leader in the introduction of the 'Switch' paperless cheque and, in 1989, it launched the UK's first telephone bank, First Direct.

HSBC printed Thailand's first ever banknotes, in 1888.

HSBC's head office in the Hong Kong Special Administrative Region is one of the territory's most famous buildings, designed by Sir Norman Foster and officially opened in 1986.

HSBC Bank was the first UK bank to offer personal banking via interactive television.

HSBC's new Group headquarters, opening in London's Canary Wharf in 2002, will be 44 floors high.

Market

The furniture and furnishings market in the UK is tough. While the picture of total retail sales throughout the 1990s is one of modest annual growth, furniture retailing has shown an erratic pattern with deep troughs and some peaks in a generally uncertain market.

There was a small boom in 1996 and 1997, in large part as a result of building society windfalls, but this was not sustained. The following year saw many furniture retailers experience financial difficulty in an oversupplied marketplace, and mergers, acquisitions and closures began to characterise the industry.

Though worth a total of around £7 billion a year, the UK furniture and furnishings sector is highly fragmented with only a handful of multiples claiming a share of more than a couple of percent. MFI is the biggest player with 11% of sales, with IKEA holding the second largest share at 7% (Source: Mintel 1999). What is remarkable, however, is that IKEA has achieved this share with only ten stores in the UK, compared to MFI's 225 outlets.

Achievements

IKEA is most proud of being the retailer that brought stylish, functional and affordable furniture to the majority of people and is now commonly regarded as the world's largest furniture retailer with 158 stores in 29 countries.

It has achieved this by following a strong and living corporate culture. The culture has its origins in Småland, southern Sweden, where the founder of IKEA, Ingvar Kamprad, was born and where the IKEA concept first saw the light of day more than 50 years ago.

Values, norms and informal rules are strong and ever-present elements that create identity, togetherness and strength among IKEA co-workers worldwide. In 1976 Ingvar Kamprad described these elements in what later became known as The Testament of a Furniture Dealer. Everybody working with the IKEA concept knows and understands this document and, according to Ingvar Kamprad, maintaining a strong IKEA culture is one of the most crucial factors behind the group's continued success.

IKEA believes in leadership by example and the willingness to try unconventional solutions without reinventing the wheel over and over again. In order to stay close to reality the store strives to maintain practical connections with daily activities. This leads on to another key concept, the importance of being constantly 'on the way' – that is, being more stimulated by finding ways of achieving the goal than by the goal itself.

History

IKEA has its roots in Småland, historically one of Sweden's poorest regions, where the harsh countryside demands thrift, inventiveness and hard work. Here many small businesses, craftsmen and traders are to be found, and it is here that Ingvar Kamprad was born in 1926 on a farm called Elmtaryd in the village of Agunnaryd, a few miles outside Älmhult, the heart of IKEA to this day.

The entrepreneurial Ingvar started his career by selling matches, fish and ballpoint pens to the local villagers and in 1943 he registered the IKEA name – made up of his initials and the first letters of his family farm and village.

When IKEA added furniture to its range and started to sell it at factory prices by mail order in 1950 it was met by firm resistance from the established furniture trade. Suppliers were threatened with boycotts and IKEA was literally thrown out of the big furniture trade fair in Stockholm. But customers poured in and a year later the first IKEA catalogue was issued followed by the first permanent showroom in Älmhult in 1953.

By the mid 1960s the IKEA experience as we know it today was pretty much established – a large warehouse-style store selling furniture and home accessories, where the customers serve themselves and the goods are available to take home that day. What characterised these early years of IKEA was a lateral approach to problem solving, a disregard for convention and an obsessive cost-consciousness. All of which contributed to the vision: to create a better everyday life for the many by providing stylish, functional items for the home at an affordable price.

With its own product development in close co-operation with manufacturers, its own catalogue, its own stores, enthusiastic employees, suppliers all over the world, self-assembly furniture in flat packages and motivated customers who can save themselves money through their own efforts, IKEA had found its niche.

Product

IKEA primarily sells furniture – for every room in the house. But it also offers everything else for the home in the form of soft furnishings and accessories. The foundation behind all these products is the unique IKEA style – furniture that is simple, practical and easy to live with, using natural materials, light woods and cotton and linen fabrics.

The product range is unique to IKEA. Its vision of offering well-designed, functional furnishings at prices that as many people as possible can afford is reflected in everything that enters its range.

IKEA achieves this through following the principles of what it refers to as Democratic Design. Any item that enters the IKEA range must meet criteria set under the following three headings: Form, Function and Price. Is it pleasing to the eye? Does it serve the purpose for which it was intended? Is it good value for money? If the answer is no to any of these questions then it has no place in the IKEA range.

IKEA designs all its products itself in Älmhult. New products often emerge from close co-operation with suppliers. By adapting customer demands to suppliers' resources, it reduces its production costs. Suppliers know their job. They know what can be done and what puts the price up. IKEA's task is to know its suppliers and to understand production technology. The company's designers do this by spending more time on the shop floor than at their drawing boards, pushing for new solutions and new methods.

Recent Developments

IKEA in the UK is moving ahead with its ambitious expansion strategy – twenty new stores, two distribution centres and 10,000 new jobs. All this at a time when traditional retailers are feeling the pinch.

The UK expansion is driven by a concern not to exclude any section of the UK population from access to good design at affordable prices. In order to widen this access IKEA needs to reduce average journey times to its stores and champion even lower prices. From 1997 to 2000, IKEA UK prices have dropped on average by 9% in a period where the retail index went up by over 7%.

August 2000 saw the introduction of longer opening hours in the UK to reflect the changes in shopping behaviour and ease the pressure on the ever-popular existing stores.

The most interesting international expansion of the recent period has been into the new markets of Russia and China.

Promotion

IKEA meets its customers in three very different areas of its marketing mix: in the store, with the catalogue and through its advertising.

The stores are the outward image of IKEA. It is here that the customers meet the products from the catalogue or advertisements in reality. IKEA stores are designed to be inspiring and stimulating as well as functional. The stores are often located out of town, where land is comparatively cheap. This is important as they have sales and storage in the same location as well as free parking. IKEA is a destination visit and often becomes a day out for the whole family, with play areas for children and restaurants to add fun to the shopping experience. Most products are in stock and can be taken home straight away.

The catalogue is IKEA's best sales tool and is more than a presentation of its range. It is a source book, full of information about prices, materials, colours and care. Customers can plan

their purchases in the peace and quiet of their own home and then arrive at the stores armed with the information they need. The catalogue, produced in Älmhult, is an obligatory part of the IKEA concept and is based on a uniform model,

the main catalogue being largely the same in all markets but adapted to the local language and currency. The catalogue is free and is distributed en masse in the stores' catchment areas every year.

Whereas the store and catalogue concepts are fairly standardised, the advertising strategy for IKEA varies considerably from country to country to enable the company to address

specific market needs. For example, in the UK IKEA was faced with the bleak reality that its offering simply did not match the UK consumer's tastes. Therefore rather than softening the concept or the product range it embarked on a mission to change the tastes of the British nation with a campaign called 'Chuck out your Chintz'. Subsequent campaigns continued the offensive on traditional tastes and style in the form of 'Furniture Findings' and 'Stop Being So English', both executed in a tone which has since become described as the friendly rebel, with an ability to generate debate and controversy in the media. This strategy has successfully amplified IKEA's message in an extremely noisy category where it is significantly outspent by their competitors.

Brand Values

IKEA stands for partnership. The role played by the consumer in this partnership is an extremely important one. By choosing the furniture themselves, collecting it off the shelves themselves, taking it home and assembling it themselves, IKEA is allowed to fulfil its side of the partnership – keeping the prices down. IKEA calls this partnership 'prosumerism', and the end result is clearly beneficial to both parties.

It is this honest and progressive approach to the retail sector that has made IKEA the world's largest furniture company. But probably the most important value IKEA stands for is fun.

Interflora®

Market

Sales of flowers and houseplants have risen rapidly since 1995. Even allowing for the effect of the additional boost of an estimated £10 million extra sales in 1997 following the death of Diana, Princess of Wales, the growth has been exceptional.

Purchasing of flowers in the UK stands at around £25 per head with the most frequent buyers of flowers and plants being women, aged 35-54 (Source: Mintel 1999). The choice of flowers available is becoming increasingly influenced by the style of home décor. The growing number of television programmes, books, magazines and newspaper pages devoted to interior design and home styling encourages more frequent makeovers of rooms. Houseplants and flowers are often portrayed as the simplest way to introduce change.

Demand for flowers still has great seasonal bias. Mother's Day is the single most important occasion for giving flowers, with 39% of all adults purchasing, fairly equally divided between men and women. Valentine's Day ensures another peak in sales, with 90% of the day's flowers being bought by men and over seven million red roses given (Source: Mintel 2000). Christmas also represents a peak purchasing time.

from Dublin to Western Samoa. Interflora can deliver just about anywhere within 24 hours. This special service has even gone beyond this world – British astronaut Helen Sharman sent a message to Interflora from space, requesting a bouquet to be sent to her mother.

Each member florist has an in-store terminal linked to the main computer which processes orders from one place to another. Each year over half a billion orders are sent through the Interflora network worldwide.

Interflora has played an important part in so many of the key occasions in customers' lives from births to funerals. For over 70 years it has handled sensitive situations with tact and sincerity.

Interflora also goes to great lengths to meet the needs of its customers ensuring that deliveries are on time and that the flowers selected are appropriate. Interflora florists are renowned for their ingenuity and often have to sculpt very complicated designs in flowers, such as motorbikes, footballs, military coats of arms and the poignant family tributes that help to convey messages of sympathy, love and respect.

History

Interflora originated in the US where two florists, frustrated that it took up to four days for their bouquets to journey by train across the country, agreed to telegraph requests to each other and settle up later. The idea spread and the Florists Telegraph Delivery Service was set up. The idea reached the UK in 1920 when a florist in Glasgow and a nurseryman in Essex applied to become 'foreign members' of the Telegraph Delivery Service, allowing flowers ordered in the US to be delivered by hand in the UK. By 1923 there were seventeen 'foreign members' – enough for them to form a British unit.

In 1935 the British Unit ceased to be part of the American operation and eleven years later initiated the concept of floral relay. The name changed in 1953 and the famous symbol featuring Mercury, the messenger of the gods, was adopted. Since then,

the Interflora network has grown enormously, allowing deliveries worldwide.

Today, the sending of flowers worldwide has become, a way of life. There are now 2,300 member florists conveniently located throughout the UK and Republic of Ireland. Same day delivery can be guaranteed in most of the UK and Republic of Ireland and in many other countries, depending on time zones. It is this level of service that brings consumers back to Interflora.

Product

The principle behind Interflora is that the customer can choose a product in one location confident that it will be delivered in another. To help the selection of the most appropriate gift, Interflora produces its Collection Guide. This is a catalogue promoting a range of products, featuring traditional bouquets, hand-tieds, basket arrangements and plants. In addition, a range of 'finishing touch' products are available including balloons, various soft toys and Thornton's chocolates to complement any floral gift.

In addition to the core range of products, Interflora also develops specific ranges for key times of the year, such as Christmas, Valentine's Day and Mother's Day.

Seasonal products for special summer or autumn promotions are also designed, in order to offer greater choice with the flowers available at the time of year. All Interflora products are individually developed by an award winning team of Interflora floristry designers. Drawn from all parts of the country, the new product development process results in the innovative products that are show cased in the media and

Great balls of fire 0500 43 43 43

This year's Valentine's range from Interflora delivers passionate ideas for explosive results. Prices from £18.50 to £50. Order from your local Interflora florist, freecall 0500 43 43 43 or visit our website at www.interflora.co.uk
Prices include VAT and standard local delivery. Relay charge £3.50 extra. In some areas, extra charges may apply. For deliveries on Monday 14th February, orders must be placed by 5pm Saturday 12th February 2000. Promotion ends 18th February 2000.
www.interflora.co.uk

Interflora DELIVERING PASSION

Naturally occurring, seasonally available flowers stimulate additional purchases, such as daffodils and tulips in spring and cornflowers and sunflowers in summer.

Achievements

Interflora is a unique organisation. It is not a franchise but a democratically run network of 60,000 independent florists able to deliver flowers to 165 countries worldwide. A heartfelt message can be relayed from America to Russia,

...Interflora... the worldwide flower delivery service was founded in 1923 by a group of florists who met in London to discuss the best possible utilization of an invention which was growing in popularity – the telephone.

The idea was quite simple and soon caught on.

By telephoning orders to other members of their newly formed association, they could arrange to send fresh flowers to other parts of the country.

available in the high street branches of Interflora.

In June 2000, Interflora launched its long-awaited New Baby products. Divided into two distinct ranges, these gifts are designed to please new mothers everywhere, as well as offering a special keepsake for the new baby.

The traditional 'Round and Round the Garden' baby range features the well known nursery rhyme theme. The floral gifts are presented in gentle hues, carefully packaged with matching sundries. Each gift comes with the option of a uniquely designed teddy bear as an accompaniment. Rose Bear and Sweet William Bear were specially designed for Interflora by Pete Bowman, the famous illustrator of children's books. The two bears are manufactured and supplied by Russ Berrie, as part of their ongoing business partnership with Interflora.

Russ Berrie have also produced a cheeky set of toweling 'Sea Life Creatures', to complement the contemporary and vibrant Baby products known as 'The Sea Life Range'. Impactful funky floristry in primary colours along a seaside theme gives this innovative range a very different look from more traditional arrangements.

Recent Developments

As business patterns change, the place of the florist on the high street is constantly being challenged. In order to keep abreast of such changes in the retail environment, Interflora has increased access points to its service. As well as visiting the local Interflora florist shop, customers can also place orders using a freephone number, or via the Interflora website, www.interflora.co.uk. The website, which was set up in 1998, is extremely popular and highly regarded, gaining media exposure for Interflora and positioning the brand as a dynamic player in the floristry industry. Interflora also has a presence on a number of other online services such as CompuServe, LineOne, AOL and Zoom and is accessible through virtual shopping malls such as ShoppersUniverse and the WAMworld interactive kiosks at Heathrow airport. In addition, Interflora has a presence on interactive digital television services, such as Cable & Wireless, Open.... and Telewest. Using either keypad or remote control, customers are able to view, select and pay for product in the comfort of their living rooms.

Interflora also features on a major international airline's seatback monitors. Travelers are able to send orders whilst in-flight, with the possibility of deliveries being made before the plane reaches its destination.

Promotion

In 1997 Interflora sponsored the GMTV weather slot. Since then, it has been involved in one-off small scale sponsorship deals involving ice hockey, skating and motor racing.

Interflora is the most significant and consistent advertiser in the florist category. During 1998, the company ran product based advertising campaigns in June and July, utilising weekend magazine supplements and women's monthlies. This was followed up in October with a black and white national campaign in the dailies focusing on the emotional values of sending flowers, utilising the strapline 'If you feel it, we can express it'.

This campaign was adapted for television and ran in a small number of regions in the lead up to Valentine's Day and Mother's Day in 1999.

A further product-led campaign was launched in Summer 1999 across the daily press, weekend supplements, women's magazines and lifestyle magazines.

Throughout 2000 Interflora ran press advertisements both in national newspapers and women's magazines.

In July 2000 Interflora launched its own style show. 'On Show with Interflora' ran from 28-30 July at the Business Design Centre in Islington, London. This lifestyle event, featured a bridal and fashion show, cookery, decorating and floristry demonstrations.

Brand Values

Interflora members have to meet strict criteria to join the organisation's network. Interflora demands optimum standards of professionalism and operates a strict quality assurance programme. Research studies of consumer trends play a vital part in the future planning for the association. The Interflora service signifies quality, professionalism and a dedication to meeting the needs of its customers.

Kellogg's CORN FLAKES

Market

Many people view breakfast as the most important meal of the day. Research shows that 96% of the UK population eat or drink something for breakfast and 49% start the day with ready-to-eat cereals.

This signifies a huge change in UK breakfast eating habits over the last twenty years. In 1968 approximately half the population tucked into a cooked breakfast on a regular basis, but, by 1990 this had dropped to an estimated 10%.

This change can be attributed to increasingly busy lifestyles and an awareness of the importance of healthy eating. However, hectic lifestyles can mean breakfast is often sacrificed to keeping to a tight timetable. The major challenge facing cereal companies today is to persuade consumers that eating cereals is both convenient and beneficial at breakfast time or at any time of the day.

In terms of volume, the UK is the largest consumer of cereals in Europe. In 1999, the market was valued at £944 million. Per capita consumption has risen in the last decade by almost 10% and currently stands at 5.9 kilos, with the over 35s being the greatest consumers.

Achievements

Kellogg's Corn Flakes is the UK's and Europe's number one breakfast cereal. In 1999 alone, more than 100 million packets of Kellogg's Corn Flakes were consumed, while over 40% of all UK households are likely to have Kellogg's Corn Flakes in their home.

Kellogg's Corn Flakes is the biggest brand in the UK ready-to-eat cereal market. With sales for 2000 valued at around £110 million in the UK, Kellogg's Corn Flakes holds an 11% volume share of the market. Its closest contender, Weetabix, has a 9% market share. Within the UK cereal market as a whole, the Kellogg Company has eleven out of the top twenty brands and holds a 39% volume market share. Kellogg's now enjoys international renown and Kellogg's Corn Flakes can be bought in more than 100 countries.

History

Kellogg's Corn Flakes were discovered by a quirk of fate. Back in 1884, Dr John Harvey Kellogg, superintendent of the internationally famous Battle Creek sanitarium, in collaboration with his business manager brother, Will Keith (WK) Kellogg, developed a nutritious cereal food for his patients.

However, a freak laboratory accident exposed cooked wheat to the open air for over a day. The Kellogg brothers then processed the wheat through rollers, ensuring an even distribution of moisture – resulting in wheat flakes.

The patients loved this new flaky cereal product and demanded supplies even after leaving the sanitarium.

Building upon this opportunity, the Kellogg brothers formed a company in partnership with The Sanitas Nut Company, with WK Kellogg as general manager.

From wheat flakes to corn flakes was a simple process. WK added malt to his

flake product and used only the heart of the corn in manufacture. He was so impressed with his corn flakes that he started up his own company to market them.

However, his business plans were put on hold when a fire swept through his brother's sanitarium, which WK volunteered to help reconstruct and re-establish. It took until 1906 to kickstart his business activities. The company he formed was called The Battle Creek Toasted Corn Flake Company.

By now, the sanitarium's success with its flake products had spawned up to 42 imitations from local rivals. To counter this, WK had his name and signature scripted on each individual package of Kellogg's Corn Flakes.

WK quickly realised the benefits of advertising and demand was soon exceeding expectations. By 1909, more than a million cases of Kellogg's Corn Flakes had been sold across the US. A variant, Kellogg's Bran Flakes, was introduced in 1915. Coco Pops, Frosties and Special K are amongst many others that have been added to Kellogg's repertoire in subsequent years.

With the introduction of other brands, international expansion became inevitable. Kellogg's Corn Flakes was first introduced into the UK in 1924 and in 1938 a new factory was opened in Trafford Park, Manchester.

Manufacturing plants were also built in Canada and Australia. Today, Kellogg's operates plants around the globe, marketing its products in more than 160 countries worldwide.

Product

Nutritionists recommend that a good breakfast should supply about one quarter to a third of our daily nutritional needs and Kellogg's Corn Flakes do just that, providing up to 25% of the recommended daily allowance (RDA) of essential vitamins such as thiamin, riboflavin and iron. Added to this, they are 99% fat free.

The size of the brand is reflected in the variety of pack sizes and formats which are available. This ranges from 1kg to 35g serving size packs, as well as special ambient

'To Go' formats that come complete with their own serving of milk, designed to be eaten at work or on the move.

Consistent quality checks and testing ensure Kellogg's Corn Flakes are always in top condition. Since 1914, Kellogg's has used a sealed inner liner as well as an outer carton to ensure fresh and high quality products.

Recent Developments

For Kellogg's Corn Flakes, there has been a need to deliver to consumers a clear and relevant message, that not only drives reappraisal of the brand but also encourages consumption. The launch of the 'Wake Up' campaign in 1999 has done just that. Initiated in early 1999 it has used a deep understanding of morning habits as well as the brand's strengths to communicate a meaningful and salient message.

Extending beyond television, the brand's traditional medium, to morning radio and press, the campaign has maximised its impact at the most relevant time of day.

The performance of Kellogg's Corn Flakes since the campaign's inception is testament to its success.

Promotion

Kellogg's Corn Flakes has always been a well-supported brand. Even from the outset, WK Kellogg realised that promotion was vital to growing his first brand. In 1906, he invested in a full-page advertisement in The Ladies Home Journal with astounding results. Sales grew from just 33 cases a day to 2,900.

Spurred on by this success, WK Kellogg's embarked on a series of sales promotions offering free samples of 'The Original and Best' Kellogg's Corn Flakes, including the 'Give the Grocer a Wink' campaign and a book in 1910, 'The Jungleland Funny Moving Pictures'. One of Kellogg's early promotions in 1938 was a realistic gliding model aeroplane offered free to Kellogg's customers.

By 1911, Kellogg's had spent $1 million on advertising – a huge sum in those days. This was capped by a 160ft wide and 80ft tall electric sign, bearing a 60ft 'K', positioned on the roof of the Mecca building in Times Square, New York.

The support for Kellogg's Corn Flakes has continued year on year, including the remarkably effective reminder campaign – 'Have you forgotten how good they taste?'– from the late 1980s. The campaign was designed to drive retrial of the brand and people who

had strayed to new cereals returned to the 'original and best' in droves.

Launched in 1999, the 'Wake Up' campaign for Kellogg's Corn Flakes established the product as the best way to wake up. It is based on the universal truth that many people find it hard to get started in the morning. Research has highlighted that this clear brand benefit is reinforcing the relevance of the brand in people's lives.

The campaign has not, however, remained solely in the realms of advertising. Given the brand's substantial consumer loyalty, the Kellogg's Corn Flakes Wake Up Collection was launched in 1999: an on-pack collector scheme for branded breakfast and early morning items such as crockery, radios and alarm clocks. This on-pack promotion has been remarkably effective and the collection offer has now been added to the Kellogg's corporate website to reach the growing number of e-consumers.

Brand Values

Kellogg's Corn Flakes have enjoyed a long history of popularity based on offering a quality product with appetising taste and high nutritional value. The brand has been driven by a belief first perpetuated by its founder, WK Kellogg, that cereals can provide an integral part of our diet as a high carbohydrate, low fat food. This approach holds special appeal for today's increasingly health-conscious consumer.

Kellogg's Corn Flakes continue to be the original and best, a position they have held for 80 years, bringing 'sunshine' to breakfast time and helping people 'wake up' in the morning.

Things you didn't know about
Kellogg's Corn Flakes

A Nottinghamshire housewife, Mrs Florence Millward, opened Kellogg's Trafford Park factory, home of Kellogg's Corn Flakes, in 1938. She attended all subsequent Kellogg's events.

It takes 140 days of sunshine to grow the corn that makes Kellogg's Corn Flakes.

The official mascot is Cornelius Cockerel, who features on the front of all packaging.

An early advertising campaign for Kellogg's Corn Flakes coined the slogan 'the sweetheart of the corn' to describe the corn grit main ingredient used in the product's manufacture.

The Kellogg Company founder, WK Kellogg, was an interesting character whose destiny appears to have been linked with the number seven. He was the seventh son of John Preston and Ann Janette Kellogg, born on the seventh day of the month. His father was also a seventh child and the family surname Kellogg, has, of course, seven letters. WK Kellogg first started work at the age of seven. He spent the rest of his life indulging a superstitious liking for the number – opting for seventh floor hotel rooms with numbers always ending in seven.

Market

Total confectionery sales reached record levels in 1999 with around £5.5 million spent on it – an average of £1.81 per person in the UK, a figure that makes the total market worth more to retailers than newspapers, bread and breakfast cereals put together. Nestlé Rowntree continues to vie with Cadbury for overall market leadership, both manufaturers securing 19% of sales.

Chocolate fulfils most of the important criteria for a snack product – it provides an instant energy boost, is highly portable and can be eaten anywhere requiring no preparation and is quick to eat, yet satisfying. UK consumption of chocolate is one of the highest in the world ahead of the US, France and Japan and chocolate confectionery accounts for almost half the sweet sector.

Kit Kat is estimated to be worth over £220 million and is sold in more than 100 countries around the world from Iceland to the Far East.

Achievements

In 1999 Kit Kat chalked up its 14th consecutive year as the UK's best-selling confectionery brand with sales of over £225 million and volume sales of four-finger Kit Kat up by 7% compared with the previous year.

Kit Kat's popularity has increased steadily, with the quantity of Kit Kat made at Nestlé Rowntree's York factory almost doubling in the last 20 years. A total of 23 basic pack formats for Kit Kats are made at York.

Kit Kat has won numerous awards for advertising creativity and marketing effectiveness including Silver awards at the Cannes International Advertising Festival in 1991 and 1992; Gold in the 1993 Epica awards and Grand Prix in the 1990 Eurobest competition. In 1995, Kit Kat won

Gold with its Burger King promotion in the ISP Promotional Awards.

Kit Kat is the top selling impulse brand (ACNielsen 1999). Figures covering the twelve weeks up to August 7 1999 show Kit Kat impulse sales to be in excess of 3,300 tonnes, which is nearly a quarter as much again as second-placed Mars.

Kit Kat was the best selling confectionery brand of the 1990s with sales pushing through the £0.25 billion mark for the first time (helped by the launch of Kit Kat ChunKy).

History

Kit Kat was launched in 1935 under the name Rowntree's Chocolate Crisp. Launched first in London and the south east, its success had spread throughout the UK within a year and by 1937 Kit Kat was established as Rowntree's leading product, a position it has maintained ever since.

The name Kit Kat, which was coined after World War II, was almost certainly influenced by the infamous Whig meeting house where writers and politicians of the gentry met in the 1920s. The Kit Kat Club took its name from mutton pies called Kit Cats produced by Christopher Cat, the owner of the tavern near Temple Bar in London where the club first met.

The product was developed by Rowntree's creative and productive marketing division headed by George Harris (1896-1958), the great grandson of Joseph Rowntree and the company's chairman during the pre-World War II period. Harris was obviously a man who recognised the potential of a good idea: In his period as chairman, the company also developed Black Magic (1933), Dairy Box (1936), and Smarties (1937) and during the War Kit Kat was portrayed as a valuable wartime food, with advertising describing the brand as 'What active people need.'

For most of its life Kit Kat has appeared in a red and white wrapper. It did, however, change to a blue wrapper in 1945 when shortages of milk after the war led to it being produced with a plain chocolate covering. This was withdrawn in 1947 when the standard milk chocolate Kit Kat was re-introduced.

Kit Kat first appeared on television in 1957 with the now famous slogan 'Have a break, have a Kit Kat.' The campaign and the slogan – which is still used today – proved so popular that sales increased by 25%.

In 1963 the first Kit Kat multipack – a six pack of two-finger Kit Kats – was produced and after only five years accounted for over 20% of total sales. Sales also increased dramatically in the

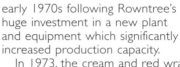

What active people need

Active people carry with them a block of concentrated staying-power—Chocolate Crisp. This chocolate block produces a slow rise of blood-sugar, and is therefore absorbed more slowly into the system, and keeps you satisfied longer. There's actually two hours of endurance capacity in every block of Chocolate Crisp.

If Chocolate Crisp is out of stock don't blame the shopkeeper. He does his best to get it, and we do our best to keep a fair supply all over the country with the materials available.

The biggest little meal in Britain 2½ᴰ

early 1970s following Rowntree's huge investment in a new plant and equipment which significantly increased production capacity.

In 1973, the cream and red wrapper was replaced by a new bright red and white wrapper. In 1986 Kit Kat became the UK's leading confectionery brand – a position it still holds today.

The name 'Nestlé' now appears on the wrapper in place of Rowntree following Nestlé's acquisition of Rowntree in 1988. The extremely high price paid was due to the strength of the total Rowntree brand and, not least, the pre-eminence of Kit Kat.

In 1994 Nestlé invested a massive £28 million in its fifth Kit Kat factory on the site, and £6 million worth of the product is manufactured each day.

Product

Kit Kat is a moulded wafer bar consisting of three layers of crisp wafer biscuit with a praline filling. The bar is covered in milk chocolate and shaped into four fingers (which not only makes it more interesting but means there is more chocolate on the bar).

Kit Kat owes its success to the fact that it is in the unusual position of existing both on the sweet counter of a local newsagent (as a four finger bar) and in the supermarket as a biscuit (in the two finger format). This means that Kit Kat is both the number one confectionery brand in the UK and the number one biscuit brand.

Kit Kat is sold through many retail outlets including the licence trade and garage forecourts. Through a series of different packs, Kit Kat is able to serve different customer needs. The two finger bar provides an impulse purchase for children and a multipack of two finger Kit Kat biscuits caters for a planned teatime snack. The four finger bar provides an impulse snack purchase for all ages and seasonal packs of each are produced both at Christmas and Easter.

Recent Developments

Kit Kat redesigned its logo in 1997, altering the lettering to give it a 3D appearance at the same

time as retaining the famous red oval. Multipacks were also updated, incorporating a metalised film for extra freshness.

Kit Kat's success has been a combination of sticking to the tried and tested and formula of classic milk chocolate, wafer and praline while invigorating the market new and exciting variants every so often.

In 1996 the first nationally available flavour variant of the brand was launched, Kit Kat Orange – a promotional line so well received that it was re-introduced two years later. The slogan for the advert, which featured a slice of orange peel adorned with the Kit Kat logo, was 'Have a break. Peel a Kit Kat', mirroring the brand's famous slogan.

Shortly after this, special 'temperature change' packs were launched. Racks for these Kit Kats were designed to encourage consumers to start eating the product straight from the fridge. This promotion aimed to flatten out the dip in total chocolate sales during the summer. Printed with inks that react to the temperature change, ice crystals and a blue halo appear round the logo when the packs are put in the fridge.

In 1998 a limited edition Five Finger Kit Kat was launched that offered a 'free fifth finger'. Not only did this offer 25% extra free, but it successfully reinforced a key brand property – a Kit Kat finger.

In April 1999 the single-finger giant version of Kit Kat was launched – Kit Kat ChunKy. This was the first new permanent format of Kit Kat since the launch of the two-finger biscuit version in 1951. Supported by £2 million of advertising, the launch was dubbed Nestlé's most successful launch of the decade with over 200 million Kit Kat ChunKys sold within the year.

The good news for Nestlé was that most ChunKy purchasers were relatively new to the brand rather than simply switching from four-finger to ChunKy. Kit Kat ChunKy is designed to appeal especially to teenagers not only because of its more substantial form, but because it is perfect for eating with one hand, on the move.

The flow-wrap metalised film packaging with tear-strip enhances the convenience.

Promotion

Consistency has been key to Kit Kat's advertising success. 98% of adults can complete the line 'Have a break' which has been used regularly to fuel sales ever since the 1950s.

Kit Kat has always used a combination of different media to advertise the product which in recent years has been supplemented by on-pack promotions.

Star of the advertisements during the 1950s was Kitty the Kat who emphasised the 'rich full cream milk' quality of the brand. Production improvements from the mid 1950s ensured that Kit Kat was always crisp and to reinforce the point, the kitten was depicted responding to the snap of a Kit Kat being eaten.

More recent campaigns included five new television films aired in March 1999 that amounted to the biggest re-vamp of Kit Kat advertising for twenty years.

The famous 'Have a break' slogan was still prominent in the adverts which illustrated the need for a break rather than the break itself. For example, the first three adverts showed a beetle struggling to roll a ball of mud, a moth repeatedly singeing itself on a light-bulb and a cartoon secretary gossiping. Later ads featured Loch Ness monster spotting and a baby trying to blow out trick candles.

The Kit Kat humour is still very much in evidence, but in a subtler, new way since the ads keep the viewer guessing about which brand they are for right up to the end frame,

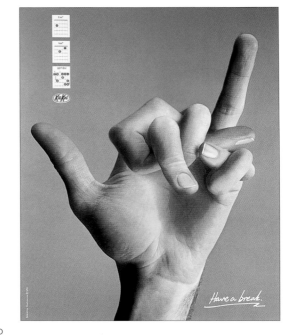

Have a break.

intensifying their impact.

September 1999 saw two more new commercials, the first of which featured a pair of cowboys who kept trying – and failing – to kill each other and, the second of which portrayed the frustrations of a Scrabble game. Both are based on the refreshed 'Have a break' theme.

Two ads for Kit Kat ChunKy were launched in March 1999 as part of a wider £12 million advertising campaign for Kit Kat. The 'Have a Big Break' slogan emphasised the ChunKy characteristics of the new bar, and both ads, which are youthful in feel, featured young hopefuls (a basketball player and a waitress) getting their 'big break' and being catapulted towards fame and fortune.

Packaging has played an important role in the brand's promotion and the opening of Kit Kat's distinctive paper strap and silver foil has been successfully designed to add a sense of ritual to the consumption of the product. This has been created in part by the way that the product is unwrapped in television adverts.

Brand Values

Kit Kat is now firmly established as a Superbrand with universal appeal and is synonymous with 'having a break'. It is a traditional, well-loved brand but also one that, in recent times, has been seeking to rejuvenate its appeal and remain contemporary through initiatives such as the launch of Kit Kat ChunKy. Throughout, Kit Kat maintains a wry, witty, quirky outlook on life.

Have a break.

Nestlé
Have a break....Have a Kit Kat

Market

Facial tissues are commonly associated as essential allies in the war against a cold, but they were originally positioned as cold cream and make-up removers. These uses are still in practice, but there is a variety of other uses, hence the growth of the facial tissue market. This market is comprised of a variety of different sized boxes, pocket packs and flow packs. Kleenex® has proved to be the fastest-growing brand in this highly innovative sector since 1996. The facial tissue market is the third largest household product category after detergent and toilet tissue.

Achievements

Kleenex® is the world's most famous tissue and largely pioneered the disposable tissue market. As a consequence, since it first began

production in 1924 it has remained the number one brand. It is as popular now as it was with previous generations. Its famous pop-up package is a familiar presence in millions of households throughout the world. More people buy Kleenex® facial tissue than any other brand. In the UK the Kleenex® facial brand equity revolves heavily around the biggest Kleenex® brand, Kleenex® for Men. When consumers talk about Kleenex®, they invariably think about Kleenex® for Men products. Having been the brand leader for over 40 years, it is not surprising that this drives the image of Kleenex® facial tissues in the UK.

The Kleenex® tissue range has constantly stayed ahead of the market and has sustained a modern, warm and quality image but is matched with its solid reputation for reliability. Indeed the Kleenex® brand celebrated its 75th anniversary in the UK, in 2000.

In 1996 Kleenex® facial tissue was named as the fastest-growing brand in the UK (Source: ACNielsen) and is now in the top 40 of all grocery brands (Source: ACNielsen 1999). In February 2000 the Kleenex® market value share hit 49.6% which set the stage for an all-time record year for the Kleenex® facial tissue brand (Source: ACNielsen 2000).

History

It was wartime ingenuity that led to the development on the company's first consumer product, the cellulose wadding tissue, which replaced cotton in World War I military hospitals. This wadding, trademarked Cellucotton by Kimberly-Clark, was first developed in 1914 and became an essential medical item. It was used in wartime hospitals and first aid stations where it often stood as an ideal substitute for cotton surgical dressing when cotton was scarce. Army nurses adapted this wadding for menstrual uses and soon after, in 1920, Kimberly-Clark began producing Kotex® feminine pads for the public. This was followed by one of the world's best-known products, Kleenex® facial tissue.

Kleenex® tissue was first presented as a cold cream remover, in response to the rash of cosmetics and cold creams then launched in the market. Kleenex® tissue was positioned as a disposable substitute for facial towels.

In 1929, the patented familiar interfold method used in the Kleenex® tissue pop-up box was added to the range of Kleenex® tissues. At the same time, coloured tissues were introduced. Through extending choice to the consumer, Kleenex® tissue steadily gained users. However, it was still regarded somewhat as a luxury item. Its primary usage was divulged through a consumer test in 1930 which clearly demonstrated that over 60% of Kleenex® tissue consumers used the tissues as a disposable handkerchief. As a consequence, Kimberly-Clark swung the positioning of its product towards this section of the market, and pioneered its usage as a handy disposable tissue suited for any purpose, at any event, at any time, with tremendous assurance. Advertising enforced this usage and sales promptly soared.

Kleenex® tissue was unavailable for civilian use during World War II. However, production of the base product – the wadding – was continued and diverted into the war effort, adapted for industrial use such as insulation. Once the war was over, tissue production resumed and production facilities increased to meet growing demand. In 1967, Kimberly-Clark introduced Kleenex® Boutique tissues in a new attractive upright designer package, and a new brand closely associated with the Kleenex® trademark was born.

The trademark 'Kleenex' was adopted by Kimberly-Clark for its 'cold cream remover' back

A fresh clean KLEENEX* tissue every time

Wiper...Bib...1001 uses!

in 1924. It was originally promoted as a cleansing tissue and this is likely to be the origin of the brand name, inasmuch as it could be shortened to 'cleen'. The distinctive capital 'K' and 'ex' ending were probably derived from its predecessor 'Kotex', a fellow consumer product trademark in the Kimberly-Clark stable. The Kleenex trademark was first registered with the United States Patent Office in 1924 to cover 'absorbent pads or sheets for removing cold cream.' This mark has now been registered in over 150 countries.

The Kleenex® Boutique tissues sister-brand, introduced in 1967, also became a federally registered trademark, as did the 'quadrant design' adopted as a prominent feature of

Kleenex® tissue packaging in 1938, although it was not formally registered until 1965. This, in fact, has been one of the few Federal trademark registrations ever granted on overall packaging design. The interfold method that typifies the Kleenex® tissue pop-up box has also been patented.

Product

The basic ingredient of Kleenex® tissue is high quality cellulose fibres, which are obtained principally from wood pulp that is processed into creped wadding. To ensure a ready supply, Kimberly-Clark conducts a well-planned forest management and reforestation programme that ensures a supply of pulpwood for present and future needs. The ideal 'Kleenex' tissue fibre is derived from selected tree species, which include spruce, fir and some hardwoods. These thin wood fibres contribute to the desirable characteristics of softness, absorbency and strength in the Kleenex® tissue.

Throughout the manufacturing process, Kimberly-Clark looks for ways to reduce the amount of energy used per unit of production. In accordance with this policy, each of the company's mills in the US employs an energy manager to oversee energy efficiency measures. Kimberly-Clark now uses recycled materials in about half of its total European production.

Before Kleenex® tissues leave the mill, they are subjected to a series of quality and performance checks. These include test for softness, absorbency, strength, size and colour. Random samples are sent to Kimberly-Clark's Quality Assurance Laboratory to ensure there is a uniformity of manufacturing standard and product quality among all plants.

Kleenex® facial tissue products are re-launched on a regular basis and always feature real tangible product improvements; for example, developing a softer, thicker or stronger product.

In 1983 Kleenex® Travel tissues were launched in a flexible pack for out of home use. The next major innovation saw the introduction of the

first dry-to-the-touch lotion treated tissues in 1994 – Kleenex® ULTRA (later re-branded in 1996 as Kleenex® UltraSoft). Kleenex® UltraSoft grew rapidly to become the number two product behind Kleenex® for Men. Over 20% of buyers of Kleenex® UltraSoft at launch were new buyers to the facial tissue category, with 30% volume from increased category purchasing. This increased the value of the market by 25% in the year following the launch of Kleenex® UltraSoft.

Kleenex® did not change ownership as a result of the Kimberly-Clark/Scott merger in 1995, so product development continued unabated.

Recent Developments

Kimberly-Clark is the largest tissue manufacturer in the world and has been one of Fortune magazine's 'Most Admired' companies since 1983. In October 1996 Kleenex® UltraBalm tissues were launched. These were the first tissues to leave behind a unique balm, containing calendula, clinically proven as protective, to help prevent the nose from becoming red and sore. The launch of Kleenex® UltraBalm tissues resulted in Kleenex® facial tissues being named as the fastest-growing brand in the UK (Source: ACNielsen 1996). Kleenex® UltraBalm was re-branded as Kleenex® Balsam in 1998 and continues its rapid growth, reaching a record 11.9% value share in February 2000.

The facial tissue market has increased in value by over 52% since 1997, driven by the launch of Kleenex® UltraSoft in 1994 and Kleenex® Balsam in 1996. These brands created the 'super premium' sector, which now accounts for approximately one-quarter of the total category value.

Promotion

Kleenex® tissue has always been heavily promoted through magazine, newspaper, and television advertising. As Kleenex® facial tissue started life chiefly as a cold cream remover, magazine and newspaper advertising of the time associated the brand with famous Hollywood actors and actresses of the day. Initial advertising copy stated: 'Actresses, screen stars – whose complexions are always under scrutiny – use Kleenex®,

the sanitary, velvety-soft tissue to remove their make-up.' The Hollywood make-up studios formed a glamorous backdrop to the brand and hailed Kleenex® as the new 'scientific way to remove cold cream.' Soon after, advertisements for the Kleenex® brand began featuring endorsements from the famous Hollywood faces of the time – the likes of Helen Hayes, Ronald Colman, Gertrude Lawrence and Elsie Janis.

Of course the multitude of other useful purposes Kleenex® tissue could be used for soon became apparent. Advertising expanded to feature the everyday needs of the average consumer, focusing on moments in daily family lives when Kleenex® tissue became a virtual necessity. Over the last 28 years Kleenex® facial tissue has enjoyed a continuous advertising presence in most of these years and has enjoyed 100% share of voice, as it was the only company advertising facial tissues. Recent television advertisements featuring the 'three girls' are the most successful Kleenex® ads ever and rank in the top 5% of all UK advertisements for awareness and correct brand recall. The campaign has been running since 1991.

Radio advertising is used to highlight key promotional activities such as the Kleenex® Hayfever and Winter Survival Promotions. The former was launched in 1991 and so far has collected nine Institute of Sales Promotion Awards including the 'Grand Prix Award' for the best UK and European promotions in 1991. Kleenex® is also sponsoring the National Cold and Flu Monitor, which is released in a map format reflecting the cold and flu situation in the UK throughout the autumn and winter seasons.

Brand Values

Throughout the world, the Kleenex® brand name stands for quality and softness, hence the new Kleenex® motto – 'Softness is our Strength'. Kleenex® tissues can be used by all members of the family for everyday purposes or when suffering from heavy colds and flu.

® Registered trademark Kimberly-Clark Corporation

A World of Difference

Market

Long haul travellers have become an increasingly familiar sight at airport check-ins over the past ten years as the market has expanded. Long haul's share of the travel market grew from 14% to 18% between 1994 and 1999, to 5.7 million holidays and record spending of £4,275 million – an average of £750 per holiday (Source: Mintel).

The requirements of the sophisticated modern day long haul traveller have developed extensively over this period. The traditional package holiday has gradually been replaced by a more customer-focused, personalised service. Kuoni Travel UK caters predominantly for this discerning traveller with a unique, tailor-made service which has seen the company voted Best Long Haul Tour Operator by British Travel Agents every year between 1982-2000.

Achievements

For more than 30 years Kuoni has led the UK long haul tour operation market and consistently been the most successful specialist tour operator.

Kuoni Travel UK enjoyed a vintage year in 1999, winning the coveted Golden Globe award – voted by travel agents – for Britain's Best Long Haul Tour Operator for the eighteenth consecutive year. The readers of the Daily Telegraph also voted Kuoni Britain's Best Tour Operator and there have been numerous accolades for best performer to selected destinations including Malaysia, Sri Lanka, Thailand and the Maldives.

For the last two years Kuoni has won the World Travel Award for the World's Leading Tour Operator.

History

Kuoni Travel Ltd was founded by Alfred Kuoni in 1906. He had previously spent a number of years working abroad, during which time three of his brothers opened a freight forwarding agency in Zurich. On returning to Switzerland in 1905, he entered his brothers' trade and soon suggested the addition of a travel agency to the already prospering freight business. Encouraged by the initial success of his new venture into the travel field, Kuoni's next move was to expand into international tourism. This was the birth of Kuoni Travel Ltd and the start of its growth into one of the world's leading travel companies.

The high rental being asked for the travel agency's new premises at the prestigious Bahnhofplatz in Zurich deterred the other Kuoni brothers from participating in the expanding business. Alfred Kuoni decided to take on the entire risk himself and in 1912 opened 'Travel Agency Kuoni'. During the 1920s, the first branch offices in Switzerland were opened in such world famous resorts as St Moritz, Lucerne and Pontresina, as well as in Nice in the South of France.

After World War II, Kuoni Travel Ltd took a leap forward with a major international expansion programme under the management of Jack Boli. He joined Kuoni in 1945 and took over as President in 1967 until his retirement in 1988.

In 1965 Kuoni entered the UK market with the acquisition of Challis and Benson Ltd, a highly reputable travel agency in Bond Street which had been operating for more than 30 years. In its first year, the operation had a turnover of £0.5 million. Peter Diethelm, current chairman, transferred from Switzerland to London in 1966 and established the tour operating division which developed rapidly. Kuoni UK was soon to become the leading tour operator in long haul travel, specialising in holidays to East Africa, the Caribbean and the Far East.

In 1974 Kuoni UK took over its biggest competitor – Houlders World Holidays – and moved tour operations to new offices in Dorking previously operated by Houlders. This combined company became market leader for long haul holidays and has retained the position ever since.

In 1998 Kuoni UK acquired Travel Promotions Ltd operating under the name of Voyages Jules Verne. The new millennium saw Kuoni UK take a stake in TV Travel Shop, in order to distribute holidays via television and in readiness for interactive technology.

Today Kuoni UK, under the chairmanship of Peter Diethelm and Managing Directorship of Sue Biggs, employs more than 500 staff and has strengthened its position as the leading long haul tour operator in the country.

Product

The Tour Operation Strategic Business Unit (SBU), based in Dorking, has established the most successful long haul tour operation in the UK. With a refreshing new approach and the use of innovative technology, Kuoni has created a concept of 'tailor-made holidays at package tour prices' – and offers a degree of flexibility unmatched by other operators.

As ever, the enormous range of Kuoni worldwide products enables Kuoni UK to balance the changing popularity of various destinations and not even the well publicised 'millennium flop' stopped its operation from achieving a record turnover.

Kuoni UK decided some years ago to invest in specialist niche markets. The creation of Independent Business Units (IBUs) met with great success. As a result of continuous strong growth, the IBUs now represent a substantial part of the total Kuoni UK business.

Among the IBUs are Incentive Travel, Sport Abroad, Specialist Product, Trade Fairs, Student Travel and The Far East Travel Centre (FETC). All of these are successful independent business units with full autonomy for product and marketing, but benefiting from the financial strength and central infrastructure of the Kuoni Group.

Recent Developments

Specialist travel company Voyages Jules Verne, acquired in 1998, is one of the latest additions to Kuoni UK. Voyages Jules Verne sells directly via the internet and traditional media and offers a wide range of specialist interest quality holidays.

In 1999 Kuoni UK secured the US tour

operator Intrav, resulting in its enlargement to SBU United Kingdom (UK) and North America. The Missouri-based company offers deluxe travel adventures around the globe, including cruises. Intrav's subsidiary, Clipper Cruise Line, operates four vessels and was named one of the ten top cruise lines in the world for four consecutive years between 1995 and 1998.

The recently acquired holding in the British television station TV Travel Shop is an important new building block in the worldwide e-commerce strategy of the Kuoni Group. It is designed to make the company a front runner in the new interactive distribution channels. TV Travel Shop markets leisure travel packages and associated products such as travel insurance and car rentals.

Promotion

Kuoni's experience within the travel market has ensured personal requirements are at the forefront of every promotion, appealing to different groups of consumers. As the UK's leading long haul tour operator, Kuoni quickly grasped that in order to maintain this market position, adressing the needs of the clients was imperative.

Dedicated specialist brochures are a direct response to these needs, featuring extensive itineraries which are also good value for money. Among them, the flagship Kuoni Worldwide brochure boasts more than 58 exotic countries offering thousands of holidays to choose from. Tropical Sun is committed to offering the most competitive prices on the best value itineraries to more than twenty destinations around the globe – strengthening the Kuoni brand very successfully in the three star category.

More recently, the World Class brochure has been launched by Kuoni, offering an exciting new collection of luxury holidays. Drawing on the most appealing international five star hotels, World Class aims to stretch the Kuoni brand even further upmarket than Kuoni Worldwide.

The strength of the Kuoni brand ensures Kuoni Travel UK does not have to rely on extensive television and radio campaigns. 'Dream holiday, think Kuoni', the instantly recognisable Kuoni globe, and the strapline 'World of Difference', all represent the attributes which are associated with quality and attention to detail.

The success of direct mail supports this strategic direction and Kuoni employs a number of initiatives. The Kuoni World Magazine is distributed to 250,000 clients three times a year covering topics of direct consumer interest. Leading newspapers including The Times and The Saturday Telegraph are key tools for reaching millions of prospective clients on a daily basis. Furthermore a very successful poster campaign was initiated on the London Underground and a successful radio campaign on Classic FM. In close association, the trade publications 'Travel Weekly' and 'TTG' (Travel Trade Gazette) are used to ensure the travel industry is kept informed of current promotions and developments within the product range.

Kuoni UK boasts the most comprehensive trade training operation in the country, Longhaul College. Around 5,000 travel agents are invited in-house each year to grasp the essential skills which are imperative in such a competitive market. In addition, 2000 selected agents are invited on 'Educationals' each year which allow trade and employees to experience Kuoni destinations first-hand. The trade is also offered self study manuals, personalised agency training, open houses and roadshows.

The internal training programme at Kuoni House is recognised as the most comprehensive in the trade. It forms part of company's culture to ensure staff are well rehearsed in procedure and product knowledge. An extensive training programme is offered to all new staff, while ongoing refresher courses are also run covering a number of key areas.

Brand Values

Kuoni stands for reliability, value for money, fairness in business and quality of services and products.

Through leadership, motivation and best use of technology, Kuoni aims to provide a quality product for its clients by offering tailor-made holidays at package prices. 'Dream holiday, think Kuoni' captures the ingredients which have made Kuoni Travel UK the leading long haul tour operator for the last two decades.

2001 Worldwide Out Now!

A World of Difference

Things you didn't know about Kuoni

In 1984 Kuoni became the first travel organisation to operate a series of chartered Concorde flights to the Caribbean.

Kuoni operated the first commercial round-the-world charter by Concorde in 1987 and introduced the first ever charter series to the Maldives in 1986 and Luxor in 1987.

In 1988 Kuoni successfully launched the KUDOS Viewdata Reservations System for travel agents. This was the first system which offered travel agents a considerable degree of flexibility.

Kuoni launched its own website in 1999 at www.kuoni.co.uk and was the first tour operator in the UK to offer online holiday bookings.

Market

There are over 26 million licensed cars on UK roads of which 77% are more than three years old. This average age is expected to lengthen, which will lead to an increase in the value of the UK aftermarket. It is a market currently worth more than £12.2 billon a year and is fuelled by legislation and the distress nature of purchases.

With more than 5,000 fast fit, independent garages, franchised dealers and auto accessory specialists, the market has never been more competitive. The Kwik-Fit brand guarantees consistency and provides an easy choice in a world in which there is more choice for motorists with less time than ever before.

Recognising the need to adapt to an increasingly fragmented and marketing literate audience, the Kwik-Fit Group now provides an expanded range of products and services that includes; tyres, exhausts, brakes, batteries, suspension, lubrication, servicing, vehicle glass repair and replacement, and motor insurance.

Achievements

Founded in 1971 in Edinburgh, Kwik-Fit has grown to become one of the world's leading automotive parts repair and replacement specialists. As market leader, the Kwik-Fit brand is distinctive, well known, trusted and respected. For nearly 30 years, Kwik-Fit has invested continuously in the brand and recent research has confirmed that spontaneous brand awareness is tracking above 90%. Despite fierce competition, Kwik-Fit has remained the dominant force in a market sector created by its founder and current Chairman and Chief Executive, Sir Tom Farmer CBE.

Within the industry, Kwik-Fit has set new standards for customer care. A nine-point Code of Practice remains the cornerstone of its operations. Kwik-Fit's aim of 100% customer delight is shared by over 10,000 people that now work for the Kwik-Fit Group from more than 2,300 service points covering the UK, Eire, Holland, Belgium, France, Germany, Spain, Switzerland and Poland. Over nine million motorists a year benefit from the services that Kwik-Fit provides, from Inverness to Barcelona, from Aberystwyth to Warsaw.

A recognised 'Investor in People', Kwik-Fit has also achieved the ISO9002 quality standard, demonstrating its total commitment to delivering the best customer service. More than 30 awards in recent years prove it, including 'Best Fast Fit' and 'Best UK Tyre Service Company' from Fleet News and the Institute of Transport Management.

More recently, the brand has become multi-faceted and has been able to successfully enter new markets and pursue its 'showroom to scrapyard' vision. This has included the launch of Kwik-Fit Insurance Services and a mobile vehicle servicing company called Kwik-Fit Hometune.

History

The automotive industry was transformed when Sir Tom Farmer established Kwik-Fit. It was founded on a very simple but, at the time, revolutionary idea: that the most important person in the organisation is the customer.

The first centre was opened in McDonald Road, Edinburgh in 1971. Rapid growth followed and this attracted the attention of a small listed conglomerate, GA Robinson. Kwik-Fit was amalgamated into the group, but the advent of the three day week caused major problems for most of GA Robinson's constituent companies. Sir Tom seized the opportunity, acquired a bigger stake in the Group, sold everything except the tyre centres and changed the company name to Kwik-Fit. As a newly created stock exchange listed company, one of the UK's most exciting specialist retail success stories had begun.

In 1979 with 52 centres, Kwik-Fit acquired Euro Exhaust Centres giving Kwik-Fit a total of 136 centres. This was followed in 1980 by the purchase of Firestone's 180 centres for £3.2 million. Described as the 'deal of the decade', 82 centres were re-sold to Dunlop for £3.25 million. With more than 200 centres nationally, Kwik-Fit entered the 1980s as a successful business that had developed and dominated its own niche market.

Kwik-Fit Fleet was formed in 1986 to serve the specialist needs of the company car driver. This service was enhanced further through Kwik-Fit Mobile (now the UK's largest mobile tyre fitting company), the launch of the Business Drive Card for fleets of less than 25 vehicles, and the Kwik-Fit Tyre Management Programme, enabling fleet customers to outsource their vehicle tyre maintenance for a negotiated fee per vehicle.

The Group's activities were expanded in 1995 to include Kwik-Fit Insurance Services. Offering branded motor insurance on behalf of a panel of leading insurance companies, all policyholders benefit from free membership of the Autosave Club. This provides preferential discounts across the Kwik-Fit Group.

In 1998, Kwik-Fit acquired Hometune Motoring Services. Providing mobile engine tuning and servicing expertise from more than 100 vehicles, it helped the Group move closer

to its goal of operating from 2,000 service points by the year 2000.

This goal was secured in 1999 when Kwik-Fit completed the acquisition of 400 Speedy Centres and 160 Pit Stop Centres. Covering France, Belgium, Spain, Switzerland and Germany, it gave the Kwik-Fit Group one of the most extensive European networks in the automotive repair business.

The Group's 'showroom to scrapyard' vision came closer still in 1999 when Kwik-Fit was acquired by The Ford Motor Company for £1 billion plus. This was quickly followed by Kwik-Fit's acquisition of Silver Shield Windscreens, a leading mobile automotive glass repair and replacement specialist.

The Kwik-Fit Group's new goal is to operate from 5,000 service points by 2005.

Product

Operating on a 'drive-in-while-you wait' basis, Kwik-Fit has developed a product range and expertise in areas that cover motorists' essential needs. A culture of continuous improvement has enabled Kwik-Fit to create a fast, efficient, friendly experience backed by quality, choice and value for money.

Convenient, accessible and well-presented centres are located close to where people live, work or shop. Quality parts with market leading guarantees are supplied by the world's leading manufacturers direct to centres based on a just-in-time stock replenishment system. Comprehensive stocks and automatic re-ordering from suppliers means that Kwik-Fit can meet the demands of almost every motorist immediately.

It is Kwik-Fit people who make the difference. It is their commitment and enthusiasm to deliver a first class service that has helped to drive the business forward. In turn, they are supported and trained to be the best in the industry. Through four training centres in the UK, Holland and France and a purpose built, hi-tech, multi-media Training Academy in Tannochside outside Glasgow, Kwik-Fit people can work towards nationally recognised qualifications which complement Kwik-Fit's bespoke training programmes.

THE BEST
BACKS IN
THE GAME.

www.kwik-fit.com

Measuring performance is critical if the goal of 100% Customer Delight is to be achieved. Kwik-Fit encourages all customers to comment on the standards of service they receive. A free telephone helpline and a reply paid questionnaire are available to every customer and from its Customer Survey Unit, more than 6,000 customers are contacted a day, within 72 hours of their visit to a Kwik-Fit centre. With this information Kwik-Fit is able to identify ways in which it can improve its service further. Contacting more than one million customers a year, this survey is the largest continuous research programme in the industry. And, in a recent survey, Kwik-Fit was acknowledged as the best firm in the UK at managing relationships with customers (Source: Round 2000).

You can't get better.
Kwik-Fit ///

Recent Developments

For motorists looking for an unusual size of tyre, there is Kwik-Fit Dial-a-Tyre. Using a freephone number, motorists can place their order and have it fitted at home, office or local Kwik-Fit centre. For customers who require brake repairs, further peace of mind is enjoyed as a result of Kwik-Fit's recently launched Lifetime Guarantee on brake pads and shoes.

Kwik-Fit has also introduced a number of innovations designed to make its products and services even more accessible and easy to use. Its online motorist centre at www.kwik-fit.com enables motorists to view the current offers, look up product and service information, find their nearest centre, buy motor insurance and arrange bookings for MOTs and vehicle servicing. With further developments in the pipeline, this will become an increasingly important medium for the Kwik-Fit Group.

Promotion

Successfully building a £1 billion brand whilst delivering immediate sales results is an achievement few can claim. Three factors have contributed to this success: an unrelenting passion and focus on delighting every customer; people programmes that have trained, supported and enabled all Kwik-Fit people to share in the success; and continuous and integrated marketing activity.

Above-the-line activity has been the mainstay of Kwik-Fit's promotional plans. In 1984, the 'Kwik-Fit fitter' commercials first appeared on television. Featuring the famous dancing Kwik-Fit fitters and catchy music jingle, they helped to make Kwik-Fit the household name it is today. At the same time, the advertising line 'You can't get better than a Kwik-Fit fitter' was introduced and first appeared on the back of the instantly recognisable blue overalls.

The advertising idea was updated in 1999. Research confirmed the importance of retaining the now famous strapline and the Kwik-Fit fitter as the brand spokesperson. This was achieved in a new advertising idea based around that great British institution, the soap opera. The new strategy involves the motoring public in a Kwik-Fit soap opera. It is based around a typical centre team with storylines that promote key products and services in a way that allows people to get to know the characters, their humour and their 'can do' attitude.

Using a combination of different media, the advertising strategy recognises the need to think nationally and act locally. Using television, national, regional and local press, Kwik-Fit continues to build trust and confidence in a contemporary brand in all communications.

Brand Values

Delivered across all media, Kwik-Fit has consistently promoted its convenient, friendly, helpful, fast, affordable and professional values. By using the famous Kwik-Fit fitter to reinforce this, the proposition 'you can't get better than a Kwik-fit fitter' has become synonymous with quality, service and value.

Community based sponsorships supporting youth development and business enterprise, also help to reinforce the Group's young, dynamic, forward thinking culture.

Things you didn't know about Kwik-Fit

Kwik-Fit sells one in three exhausts in the UK.

The Group was founded 30 years ago by Sir Tom Farmer CBE, the Kwik-Fit Group's present Chairman and Chief Executive.

The first Kwik-Fit centre opened in McDonald Road, Edinburgh in 1971.

If all the tyres sold by Kwik-Fit in a year were stacked on top of each other, they would be 130 times higher than Mount Everest.

Kwik-Fit solves a motorist's problem every two seconds.

Kwik-Fit aims to operate from 5,000 service points by 2005.

L'ORÉAL PARIS

Market

The health and beauty industry is a mature market which has evolved over the past 100 years. However, the industry is still in a state of growth, between 1993 and 1999 it grew by 36% (Source: Taylor Nelson Sofres Superpanel). The UK health and beauty market was valued at £4.7 billion in 1999.

In the twenty-first century, the cosmetics industry is not solely for the benefit of young women. The market has grown significantly and now encompasses products aimed at many varying sections of the population including children, teenagers, men and older women in the 55-74 age bracket. In 2000 it was estimated that there were over 6.8 million women aged in this group in the UK, representing 19% of the total population. In recent years older women have become keen to maintain their youthfulness for as long as possible. The skin care market has driven this desire amongst women, developing a multitude of creams aimed at reducing the signs of ageing. In recent years it has become much more acceptable for men to take care of their hair and skin with a resulting upsurge in the number of products available.

The UK male grooming sector is also in a state of growth and in 1999 was recorded as being worth £862 million (Source: Mintel).

Achievements

L'Oréal Paris is the signature brand of the L'Oréal Group. The group in the UK also consists of well known beauty brands such as Lancôme, Helena Rubinstein, Laboratoires Garnier, Maybelline and fragrance brands such as Armani, Cacharel and Ralph Lauren.

The L'Oréal Group is one of the five biggest companies quoted on the Paris Stock Exchange with its consolidated sales for the first half of 2000 totalling €6.15 billion.

The L'Oréal brand has evolved enormously in recent years and has filed 2000 patents and almost 40,000 international extensions between 1990 and 2000. Research and development is key to the brand's growth and indeed drives innovation and product performance within the industry. The L'Oréal Group employs nearly 2,400 people in its research laboratories worldwide and spends 3% of its entire turnover on research – a figure which has reached £1.2 billion over the last decade.

As part of its research programme, The L'Oréal Group combines the skills of chemists, physicists, biologists, doctors and mathematicians. In addition it has research units based in British hospitals and universities. L'Oréal also invests in dermatological research.

L'Oréal is the global leader in hair colourants. In the skin care category, L'Oréal Plénitude recorded its highest growth rate in 1999, strengthening its profile as a luxury product for a young market and strengthening its distribution through self-service outlets.

History

In 1907 Eugène Schueller, a young French chemist, developed the first synthetic hair dye, and he named his brand of hair colourants

Auréole. He continued to develop further dyes, formulating and manufacturing his own products, which he then sold to Parisian hair salons.

In 1909 Schueller registered his company as the Société Française de Teintures Inoffensives pour Cheveux – which was later renamed L'Oréal. From this early stage, research and innovation were key factors in the development of Schueller's business. By 1920 he was employing three chemists and by 1950 L'Oréal had 100 chemists. In 1984 L'Oréal had 1000 chemists worldwide.

The distribution of L'Oréal products was also carefully considered and grew rapidly. By 1912 L'Oréal products were available in Holland, Austria and Italy, closely followed by expansion into the US, South America, Russia and the Far East. In 1936 sunscreen was introduced to the L'Oréal Group's range. In the UK, the 1960s saw the launch of L'Oréal Paris Elnett hairspray, a product that is still strong and celebrates its 40th anniversary in 2001. Recital, a permanent

hair colourant was launched in the 1970s followed by Elvive Freestyle Mousse, the first ever hair styling mousse, in 1983. Studio Line was launched in 1985 encompassing a complete range of styling products and Plénitude was introduced in 1988. When the product was being promoted, emphasis was placed on how it had been technologically developed to offer a method of reducing the signs of ageing. Elvive gained a patent as the product contained a duplicate formulation of the natural hair ceramide. Ceramide R, as it became known, had the necessary properties to make hair stronger and thicker, and the launch took place in 1997. Le Grand Curl was the first mass-market curling mascara and was launched in 1999. L'Oréal Kids, also launched in 1999, was the first range of shampoos, conditioners and styling products manufactured by L'Oréal Paris for children. Line Eraser, a deep action moisturiser formulated with retinol to reduce the depth of wrinkles, was launched in the same year.

Product

Through the diversity of its sub-brands, L'Oréal Paris ensures that its products can be targeted at the maximum number of consumers possible. Distributed over a wide range of retail outlets worldwide in five different categories: hair colourants, hair styling, hair care, skin care and cosmetics. Ranges within these sectors have been developed to maximise the use of developing technologies and to enhance new segments of the market such as the growing male grooming area and products for children. In the UK, L'Oréal Paris is number one in the

hair colourants market with a 30.2% share and number two in the styling products sector with a 18% share. It is also number two in the shampoo and conditioner sector with 16.8% of the market (Source: IRI year-to-date August 13th 2000) and fifth in the cosmetics market with the L'Oréal Paris estimate of 8% of the market.

Recent Developments

L'Oréal Paris has its roots in product development. Among the new products launched in 2000 were Longitude, L'Oréal Paris's first lengthening and separating mascara, and Plénitude Revitalift Slim skin care, the first face sculpting lotion developed to refine facial

contours and enhance features with ParElastyl and Caffeine. Studio Line Special FX is a range of professional quality hair styling products and Color Fitness is a new range of home hair colourants specifically for young men between the ages of 25-44 years. For the older consumer, Grey Chic is a new range of home colourants for women with predominantly grey hair and is designed to enhance their grey rather than hide it. And new Plénitude Age Perfect skin care has been designed for women of 55 plus. Age Perfect benefits from the patented technology called Dermo-Peptide™, designed to improve skin firmness.

Promotion

The L'Oréal Group has had a strong history in its promotional activity. It commissioned promotional posters from graphic artists such as Coupot and Savignac, when advertising was still in its infancy. In 1933, Schueller created and launched a magazine called Votre Beauté, which was devoted to women and their wellbeing. In 1937, Schueller took part in a popular French radio programme which launched the 'Clean Children' campaign. In 1947 L'Oréal produced their first television advert and during the 1950s L'Oréal not only continued this activity but was one of the first brands to be advertised in cinemas with a commercial for Ambre Solaire. In 1953 L'Oréal won an advertising Oscar for its work.

In recent years, The L'Oréal Paris brand has established a recognised advertising image using the strapline 'Because I'm Worth It' which has been developed for use in the advertising of its children's products with 'Because they're worth

it too'. In a recent survey conducted amongst almost 1000 women, 83% were able to recall the 'Because I'm Worth It' advertising strapline.

L'Oréal Paris has chosen stars such as Andie MacDowell, Gong Li, Milla Jovovich, Jennifer Lopez and Virginie Lédoyen, as well as Laetitia Casta, Claudia Schiffer, Dayle Haddon, Vanessa Williams and Diana Hayden as spokespeople for the brand.

In 1998 through to 2000 L'Oréal Paris has been the Official Partner of the International Film Festival held in Cannes. This sponsorship reinforces the connection made in the mind of the consumer between L'Oréal and the glamorous film industry.

The brand is one of the most frequently advertised in the market, spending in excess of £35 million in the media in 1999. Within the UK, L'Oréal Paris ranks as number one in the money it spends on its health and beauty brands.

Brand Values

L'Oréal Paris aims to encapsulate a sense of Parisian glamour and sophistication through the brand. In addition to being truly international, it prides itself on the use of scientific technology in the development of new products. L'Oréal Paris aims to guarantee satisfaction for both its customers and distributors by ensuring total quality control of products and their availability for immediate delivery. L'Oréal Paris sees its customers as being people who care more about the way they look and are prepared to pay more to achieve the best possible results.

Things you didn't know about
L'Oréal

- L'Oréal does not test any of its products on animals. It invests heavily in alternatives to animal testing. The company developed a synthetic skin called Episkin® which reacts like human skin and upon which new ingredients and products can be tested.

- The L'Oréal Group is present in 150 countries worldwide, employs 42,000 people, has 500 brands and 2000 products.

- 85 L'Oréal products are sold per second throughout the world.

- L'Oréal patents more breakthrough ingredients and molecules for use in cosmetics ingredients than any other cosmetics manufacturer (2000 patents and almost 40,000 international extensions in the last ten years).

- Elnett Hairspray is still a firm favourite with leading hairstylists around the world. The product celebrates its 40th birthday in 2001.

Market

The UK car market was 2.198 million units in 1999, down slightly by 2.2% from 1998's 2.247 million but reasonably stable in the healthy economy of the late 1990s. Industry sources estimate that the market will remain at around this level for the next few years.

The 4x4 market in the UK rose dramatically through the 1990s to 110,000 units in both 1998 and 1999, or 5% of the total industry volume (Source: TIV. This includes around 110,000 light utility/commercial 4x4s not included in the car TIV figures.) This is up from 46,000 at the start of the decade (2.3% of TIV) and reflects a growing trend out of normal 4x2 saloons and estates and into 4x4 products to pursue outdoor activities, for towing, or simply for the secure and safe feeling they provide to owners and their families. The UK is now the world's third largest 4x4 market behind the US and Japan.

Achievements

Land Rover is one of the most famous car brands in the world – having originated and being manufactured in the UK but recognised worldwide as the four wheel drive vehicle for individuals, companies and military forces alike. Indeed, in some parts of the world, a Land Rover was the first car that people had ever seen.

Now in its 52nd year, Land Rover has created two unique sectors in the car market. With the original Land Rover (now Defender), it developed the market for a 'go anywhere' utility vehicle suitable for use in construction, forestry and agriculture – the original 'farmer's friend'.

The second innovation was in 1970 with the launch of Range Rover. This original bridge between a car and a Land Rover rapidly developed the market for upmarket four wheel drive vehicles and today Range Rover is still arguably the world's only true luxury 4x4.

In 1999 Land Rover sold a record 178,000 units worldwide, double the 90,000 unit volume of only five years previous. Central to this increase was the addition of a new smaller model, Freelander, and the latest generation of the Discovery. In the UK sales reached almost 40,000 in 1999, a 35% share of all 4x4 sales and 1.75% of all car sales in the UK – all this from a manufacturer that makes only 4x4s.

In Interbrand and CitiBank's 1999 UK brands survey, Land Rover appeared in tenth position – the only automotive brand in the top ten, reflecting the fact that the Land Rover brand is an enormous asset. In June 2000 Ford Motor Company made this value tangible by paying BMW $3 billion to acquire the Land Rover business.

History

Land Rover was created after World War II as the directors of the Rover car company sought to develop new products to assist in the business's recovery and expansion. At the time the government was encouraging the motor industry to manufacture products for export, and the Wilks brothers, Maurice and Spencer, the Engineering and Managing Directors

respectively, hit on the idea of manufacturing a light four wheel drive utility vehicle. It would use many existing Rover car components but with a separate chassis, permanent four wheel drive, dual range transmission and simple bodywork made from aluminium to get around the problem of steel rationing.

Launched at the Amsterdam Motor Show in April 1948, the Land Rover, as it was named, quickly became a huge success and production rapidly increased as the 'stop gap' model ended up being produced in greater numbers than the Rover cars. The original open topped utility vehicle featured a centre steering wheel, but this was changed as additional models were added. Longer wheel bases, new engines and different styles, including station wagon versions, were launched and by 1966 500,000 Land Rovers had been built.

By the mid 1960s Land Rover were also pursuing ideas to bridge the gap between cars and Land Rovers and in June 1970 the Range Rover was launched. It was fitted with Rover's 3.5 litre V8 petrol engine and long travel coil springs in place of the Land Rover's conventional leaf springs. It offered comfortable, high performance, on-road motoring and quickly established a following, setting the trend towards more luxurious vehicles in this market sector.

1989 saw the introduction of the Land Rover Discovery, Land Rover's response to the growing number of Japanese four wheel drives now being bought for leisure usage. It was a great success, immediately becoming the UK's best selling 4x4. The latest addition to the family, Freelander, was launched in 1997.

In 1978 Land Rover Limited was established as a separate autonomous subsidiary company within the nationalised British Leyland conglomerate. In 1982 Land Rover took over the whole of the Solihull site in the West Midlands when Rover car production moved to Cowley, Oxfordshire.

By the mid 1980s the British government was anxious to complete the privatisation of British Leyland. In 1986 it proposed to sell Land Rover to the American General Motors Group but this had to be abandoned in the face of massive public and parliamentary protests.

In 1988 British Aerospace bought the company, by then a closely integrated part of the Rover Group. When BMW bought the Rover Group from BAe in 1994, Land Rover was recognised as its main interest, regarded as 'the Jewel in the crown' of the Rover Group. Ford subsequently paid BMW $3 billion for Land Rover in June 2000. Land Rover joined Ford's Premier Automotive Group of prestige brands including Jaguar, Aston Martin and Volvo. The vehicles are sold in 160 countries worldwide and Land Rover is the sole manufacturer in the world to produce only four wheel drive products.

Product

The Land Rover brand is a cluster of vehicle experiences, appealing to individuals in quite separate areas of the 4x4 market. It offers a choice of products which are uniquely fit for their purpose – a multi-dimensional brand with conscious concept differentiation and communication focus.

The icon product is Defender, an off-road vehicle system of pure function, delivering extreme capability. It is trusted implicitly to deliver in the world's toughest conditions.

The brand's flagship is Range Rover. Peerless in its integration of comfort and capability, Range Rover combines everything you need from a vehicle that epitomises tough luxury.

Central to the brand is Discovery, a multi-faceted product that combines great design and new technology in a way that creates enjoyment for families and individuals alike.

The brand's latest addition is Freelander, attracting a whole new group of customers to the brand and to the Land Rover experience. It is a modern 4x4, meeting modern demands of four wheel drive leisure vehicles. Freelander was the best selling 4x4 in the UK and the whole of Europe in 1999.

Land Rover has been responsible for a number of significant innovations in four wheel drive technology, as the company continues to lead the market in off-road capability and to further develop its products on road handling and performance. Electronic air suspension, four channel ABS, twin airbags, four wheel Electronic Traction Control (ETC), Hill Descent Control (HDC) and Active Cornering Enhancement (ACE) are all firsts which Land Rover has introduced into the four wheel drive sector or into the car market as a whole.

Recent Developments

The new Freelander was launched in November 1997 to huge expectation and acclaim. It was awarded the 'What Car?' Car of the Year Award, the first 4x4 product ever to do so, and quickly

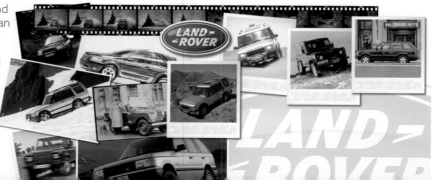

Originally Land Rover was promoted as 'the original go-anywhere vehicle'. The advertising copy in the 1950s stated that the Land Rover was as 'comfortable as a car, tough as a tank'. (As anyone who's sat in an early Land Rover will confirm, this doesn't say much for the comfort of cars in those days).

achieved benchmark status for the sector. Included in its specification was Hill Descent Control (HDC), a revolutionary set-up using the ABS system to control steep downhill descents to a limit of 5.6 mph. In September 2000 the Freelander range was further developed to include additional features such as a more powerful 2.5 litre V6 engine, a new common rail 2.0 litre diesel engine and availability of an automatic transmission with steptronic mode.

At the end of 1998 the Series II Discovery was launched, featuring an all new five cylinder 2.5 litre diesel engine and a number of new and unique features including rear forward facing seats and three point belts for every passenger.

Nowadays the line 'The Best 4x4xFar' has become synonymous with all aspects of Land Rover. The line was first coined in 1985 in a television commercial that showed a Defender winching itself up a dam to demonstrate that 'nothing gets in the way of a Land Rover'. This line has been used consistently ever since as an ad sign-off line which embodies everything Land Rover stands for.

Through the 1990s Land Rover, with Discovery and latterly with Freelander, has become much more of a mainstream car brand. Television advertising has featured more extensively including the award-winning Discovery launch ad, 'Followers', and the recent WCRS Freelander 'Born Free' commercial, winner of the gold medal at the British TV Advertising Awards and the Golden Lion at the Cannes International Advertising Festival.

Meanwhile Defender continues to develop. The introduction of the same five cylinder 2.5 litre direct injection diesel as Discovery further added to Defender's capability, while the addition of a One Ten Double Cab version early in 2000 gave it new competitiveness in a growing area of the 4x4 utility market.

There have also been extensive developments in the retail environment. The Land Rover dealer network, one of the strongest in the industry, has invested over £120 million since 1997 in new or expanded facilities. This, in part, was needed to cope with the increased volumes which Freelander has created but also to create a unique Land Rover retail experience. These Land Rover centres feature extensive planting and natural materials to 'bring the outdoors in', and include dramatic vehicle display areas and rock features. Many also incorporate off-road demonstration areas or courses which provide an exciting addition to the sales process. Land Rover has the only dedicated four wheel drive retail network in the UK.

Long-standing relationship marketing partners, Craik Jones, have worked with Land Rover for ten years and their work on the brand has received many DMA and international awards. The direct customer contact programme has been a valuable feature of Land Rover promotion and continues to be at the forefront of the communication strategy.

Another key promotional tool is the Driving Experience, a world renowned school of off-road driving based at the company's Solihull factory. Here at the 'Jungle Track', owners and prospects can be taught differing levels of off-road instruction on a purpose built off-road facility.

As the brand has continued to develop, its reach has been extended to encompass 'Land Rover Gear', a range of clothing and merchandise sold in dealerships and selected high street stores and 'Land Rover Adventures', top quality, individually designed trips involving Land Rover driving in locations as diverse as the Alps, Belize, Jordan or Colorado.

a long-standing, unique combination of emotional dimensions to the brand which, when added to rational factors such as 4x4 engineering, capability, heritage and so on, create a powerful, distinctive personality appealing to both the heads and the hearts of customers. These values are inherent in everything Land Rover does, from designing a product right through to the customer experience at a Land Rover Centre.

Land Rover plans to progressively develop the theme of 'Life's Greatest Outdoor Adventure'. Focusing on elements such as the retail experience, staff knowledge and passion, communications materials and the driving experience as well as the product expression, this is intended to create an integrated, intense experience which will highlight the difference of Land Rover and draw more and more customers to the brand.

Brand Values

Land Rover has used the expression 'The Best 4x4xFar' for over fifteen years and this succinctly summarises the brand position. Many Land Rover customers recognise in this statement all they feel about their vehicles and the brand.

Land Rover is associated with authenticity, supremacy, adventure and guts –

lastminute.com

Market

Since the website's launch in October 1998, lastminute.com has been one of the pioneers of e-commerce in the UK. The subsequent scale and speed of growth in the online market since then has been phenomenal – when the site launched, research company BMRB estimated that only 7.5 million people in the UK had accessed the internet in the previous six months; by May 2000 the number of regular internet users exceeded nineteen million. In an atmosphere of intense media scrutiny hundreds of internet start-ups and established 'bricks-and-mortar' brands have been vying for the attention and business of consumers. It is in this environment that the development of the lastminute.com brand should be viewed: to put the brand in context, when the last edition of this book was published in 1998, the lastminute.com website didn't even exist.

Achievements

lastminute.com aims to provide a global market place for last minute transactions in every product and service category, and since launching has experienced growth on a staggering scale. In the UK, the brand has established itself as one of the most visited and most recognised of all e-commerce companies. In June 2000 the site generated in excess of 30 million page impressions and a community of over 2.1 million users had registered to receive the lastminute.com weekly email Newsletter.

According to independent research published in April 2000, lastminute.com is the most recognised of all e-commerce brands among consumers in London, and the second most recognised nationwide. To demonstrate the speed with which this has been achieved, overall brand awareness increased from 22% to 46% in just four months between December 1999 and April 2000.

As the number of customers has grown, so too has the number of suppliers who provide last minute products and services for the site. lastminute.com now has individual relationships with over 3,400 key suppliers, including international scheduled airlines, hotels, package tour operators, theatre, sports and entertainment promoters, restaurants, specialty service providers and gift suppliers, both in the UK and internationally.

The company has mirrored this success with successful site launches in France, Germany and Sweden. International expansion remains a fundamental part of the lastminute.com business model, as technological developments are replicated and new suppliers in each market can sell their last minute goods and services to a global audience.

History

lastminute.com was founded by Brent Hoberman and Martha Lane Fox in 1998, based on the idea of matching last minute supply and demand using the power of the internet. They

began with a business plan devised around a kitchen table, moved on to two desks in a cramped office in Portobello and, as the staff grew several further moves followed until the lastminute.com website was launched in the UK in October of that year. By the end of March 1999 over 90,000 people had registered with the site and over 200 suppliers were offering their products and services through the site. Since then the business has grown at an astonishing rate – by June 2000 the number of subscribers had increased to 2.1 million and the total value of purchases made from the site exceeded £9.6 million.

Local versions of the web site launched in France, Germany and Sweden in September, October and December 1999 respectively, and joint venture agreements were signed for operations in Australia in March and South Africa in May 2000.

The company undertook an Initial Public Offering in March 2000 and is now listed on the London Stock Exchange and NASDAQ. The IPO raised funds for future international expansion, technological developments and investment in staff, marketing and infrastructure, and was the most talked about offering of all the UK start-ups that went public in 2000.

Product

lastminute.com aims to become the global marketplace for last minute goods and services, and there is no limit to the range of products that can be sold via the site – the service covers anything you can do or buy at the last minute. The inventory on the site is currently broken down into five sub categories: travel (including flights, package holidays and hotels), entertainments (tickets for everything from stand-up to opera), gifts (from the chance to commission a portrait to adopt an otter), restaurants (reservations at the most exclusive tables at top London and Parisian restaurants) and auctions (bids for everything from cars to charity galas).

What constitutes 'the last minute' to purchase a product or service can vary enormously depending on the product and the customer. While two weeks in advance may be perceived by traditionalists as short notice to book a long-haul flight or expensive holiday, two hours or even less may be normal for purchasing theatre tickets or making a restaurant booking. The lastminute.com service includes lots of facilities for the truly last minute customer – airline tickets can be picked up at the airport, the customer's flat can be cleaned while they're away, and it can even be arranged for fresh milk to be in the fridge upon their return.

There are also lots of instances when an individual may require a last minute solution or inspiration which may not necessarily mean distressed inventory for the supplier – a birthday present or romantic gift can be sold via lastminute.com all year round. By providing inspiration and solutions for users across the country (and across the world), lastminute.com is also able to supply new markets and new customers for product suppliers – from transcontinental hotel groups to tiny bespoke gift manufacturers.

Shopping and browsing at lastminute.com is different from exploring other e-commerce site. More than 40% of visitors to the site visit at least twice a week – they come to be amused, entertained and inspired. In providing a content rich environment and developing a host of personalisation and community based features to attract and retain customers, lastminute.com remains a unique destination for e-commerce.

Recent Developments

Alongside the development of a new version of the website with significant consumer benefits including personalisation and enhanced search facilities, there has been a significant investment in new technologies to provide the lastminute.com service via multiple platforms, including WAP enabled mobile telephones, Palm and other PDA devices and Interactive Digital television. The marketplace for last minute goods and services is uniquely suited to the opportunities afforded by mobile internet access – while consumers are unlikely to want to purchase a holiday or arrange a mortgage on their mobile phone, avoiding queues to get a restaurant table or finding tickets to a play just around the corner will become commonplace transactions to make from a phone or personal organiser.

This commitment to extending distribution of the service is mirrored by a number of significant distribution deals and strategic

available as internet access becomes more and more prevalent.

As the number of users, customers and distribution channels increases, there is a parallel growth in the number of product suppliers, creating a virtuous circle to the benefit of both parties. The unique opportunities afforded by the internet make it easier to match last minute supply and demand – for example using auctions to maximise revenue on everything from airline seats to mobile phones. Technology allows the process to develop even further, as real time dynamic pricing, reverse auctions, co-operative buying and other new business models emerge to take advantage of the net.

The scalability of the lastminute.com business model allows for rapid expansion into new markets, with localised versions of the site available in Germany, France and Sweden at time of writing and forthcoming launches in Spain, Italy, Benelux plus joint ventures in South Africa and Australia all imminent. The unique advantage of locally sourced supply providing content for each of the local sites is already in evidence on the UK site, where Parisian restaurants and Spanish hotels are available for easy booking by UK consumers.

Promotion

lastminute.com is promoted with an integrated combination of online marketing – attracting users to the site from other places on the internet – and offline marketing – advertisements and promotions in the 'real' world.

Central to the promotion of the site is the lastminute.com Newsletter, which is delivered via email to all registered subscribers (2.1 million at time of writing) each week. The newsletter alerts subscribers to the best of the offers on the site as well as special promotions, competitions and deals, but is much more than just a list of offers – it reflects the character of the site the brand, and is a unique marketing tool.

Online marketing includes a whole range of distribution channels and partnership arrangements, from placing content on key websites, providing a dynamic, constantly updated content feed of the latest offers from lastminute.com direct to other sites, and also banner ads on these partner sites.

In the UK, offline marketing to date has centred on a strong outdoor presence based on media on the Underground and buses in London, supported with advertising and promotions in radio and national press. Media choices have been based on speaking to people such as commuters and central London office workers when they are most receptive to the suggestion of doing something 'lastminute.com'. Creative executions like the poster line: 'Surprise the girl in your life. Take her sister to Paris.' sum up the spontaneity and wit of the lastminute.com brand that is reflected on the site and in the Newsletter.

As the lastminute.com service is available across multiple technology platforms, so the marketing of the brand has extended to utilise the opportunities this affords. During Euro2000 a specially-made football game for the Palm Pilot was developed as a viral marketing tool, distributed via download from the website, by email and also via infra-red beaming between Palm users. This was the first time that the principle of viral marketing has been applied to new digital platforms, and is a field in which lastminute.com will continue to pioneer and invest with new and as yet undiscovered technologies.

Brand Values

The brand is best summed up by the company's mission statement: 'lastminute.com wants to encourage spontaneous, romantic and sometimes adventurous behaviour by offering people the chance to live their dreams at unbeatable prices'.

In addition lastminute.com aims to provide easy and convenient solutions and inspirational ideas, and be the first place to look for something to do at the last minute.

partnerships lastminute.com has developed across all European markets. These include some of the biggest and best established telecoms and internet service providers, and ensure that the company remains at the forefront of new developments in technology and is easily

Market

The UK traditional toy market (excluding video games) was worth £1.7 billion in 1999 and has remained around this level for a number of years. The construction toy sector, which is valued at just over £100 million, is growing at around 2–5% each year. LEGO, for example, the leading construction brand, has

developed the LEGO MINDSTORMS range of multimedia construction sets and the LEGO Company acquired the UK licence for all Star Wars construction sets in 1999.

Companies are having to develop added value products to encourage parents to upgrade and spend more on toys for their children. Licensed merchandise will remain key to the industry's success.

Achievements

The LEGO Company, the world's fourth largest toy company, has been providing fun for children in the UK for over 60 years. LEGO products are sold in more than 130 countries. The LEGO brand is among the top five children's brands worldwide and an estimated 400 million children and adults all over the world play or have played with LEGO bricks. Every year children spend almost five billion hours playing with LEGO toys.

During the past 50 years over 320 billion LEGO bricks have been sold all over the world – equivalent to every member of the world's six billion population owning 52 LEGO bricks.

The LEGO Company is the only European manufacturer among the world's ten biggest toy companies. LEGO toys are the most widely owned toys in the UK, with 68% of children having LEGO products in their home and 27% of children saying LEGO products are their favourite toys (Source: Youth TGI survey of 7–10 year olds, BMRB 1999).

Over the years LEGO products have evolved from wooden toys to the LEGO brick, and have now developed towards intelligent robot systems, using technological progress to develop products that will continue to stimulate children's imagination and

creativity in the twenty first century.

The LEGO brick was recently described by Fortune, the international business magazine as having had a decisive effect on twentieth century people's lives. The British Association of Toy Retailers (BATR) has also honoured the LEGO brick with the Toy of the Century award.

History

The family-owned LEGO Company was founded in Billund, Denmark by a carpenter called Ole Kirk Christiansen, grandfather of current president and CEO Kjeld Kirk Kristiansen. (The surnames are spelt differently due to a mistake made on the birth certificate of Ole Kirk Christiansen).

Ole Kirk opened a carpentry shop in 1916, building houses and making furniture for the region's farmers. In 1932 he began making wooden toys, including buses, animal pull toys and piggy banks. Denmark had plunged into a depression, but Ole Kirk believed that while parents would make do without new furniture, they would still want to provide play opportunities for their children.

The LEGO Company produced its first plastic toys, including baby rattles and toy tractors, in 1947. In 1949, Ole Kirk introduced Automatic Binding Bricks – interlocking plastic blocks which were the forerunners of today's LEGO bricks.

During a 1954 trip to a toy fair, Ole Kirk's son, Godtfred, met a toy buyer who complained that no company offered a comprehensive toy system. In response Godtfred began to develop the LEGO System of Play.

Sales improved dramatically in 1958 when the company introduced a combinable brick. Two eight-stud bricks could now be joined in 24 ways. Three bricks could be combined in 1,060 ways. Children could build tall structures of practically any shape. By the end of the 1950s, LEGO bricks had become the most popular toy in Europe.

The LEGO Company introduced LEGO® DUPLO® pre-school toys in 1969 and the LEGO TECHNIC® advanced building line in 1977, expanding the LEGO System of Play from toddlers to teens. The introduction in 1995 of LEGO® PRIMO® (now called LEGO® BABY) expanded the LEGO System of Play to babies. The company continues to enhance the range, introducing new sets each year. In 1998, LEGO® MINDSTORMS™ robotics products and LEGO Media™ games were launched.

Today, the LEGO range includes more than 2,000 elements in more than 700 sets. The LEGO Company now covers six continents with 9,000 employees. The company continues to observe the motto adopted in the 1930s by Ole Kirk Christiansen: 'Only the best is good enough.'

In 1998 the Next Generation Forum was founded as a co-initiative between the House of Mandag Morgen and the LEGO Company to promote children's creativity, development and learning. The Next Generation Forum's experts recognise the twenty first century as the age of creativity and imagination. According to Professor Mitchel Resnick, LEGO Professor at the Massachusetts Institute of Technology in the USA: "Success in tomorrow's society will not be primarily based on information or knowledge, but on creativity."

Product

The classic LEGO brick stud-and-tube coupling system was developed more than 40 years ago. The system offered almost unlimited potential for combining LEGO bricks, affording children endless scope for exploring their creative universe. The interlocking plastic blocks filled a huge gap in the toy market by providing children with a system of play, rather than just individual toys.

In 1963, Godtfred Kirk Christiansen formulated ten characteristics for The LEGO Company's play materials which remain virtually unchanged today. Firstly, to provide unlimited play possibilities of LEGO toys suitable for girls as well as boys. To produce products that provoke enthusiasm in children of all ages and products

suitable for play all year around. He also maintained that LEGO toys should provide stimulating and absorbing play with endless hours of play, developing childrens' imagination and creativity. In addition each new product should be topical and have multiple play value. It is also of great importance that LEGO leads the way in safety and quality.

LEGO play materials include the following product lines: LEGO BABY, LEGO DUPLO, LEGO SCALA, LEGO Belville, LEGO SYSTEM, LEGO TECHNIC and LEGO MINDSTORMS. These product ranges are designed for children and young people of different ages and at different developmental stages. LEGO BABY, for example, develops the senses and motor abilities of children from birth to 24 months, while LEGO MINDSTORMS develops the understanding of complex concepts among children aged twelve and over. Children can play with LEGO products on their own or with others.

The LEGO Company has also developed an educational division called LEGO Dacta Learning Concepts. LEGO Dacta Learning Concepts encourage students to use their creativity and natural curiosity through hands-on experience. These concepts include teacher and student guides that balance teaching and learning according to the official curriculum.

The LEGO Company has also developed LEGOLAND Parks. These family theme parks, designed primarily for children aged 2–12, offer an entertaining world based around LEGO bricks. There are LEGOLAND Parks at Billund in Denmark and Carlsbad in the US, as well as Windsor in the UK. A fourth park, LEGOLAND Deutschland, is due to open at Günzburg in southern Germany in 2003. Around five million people visit LEGOLAND Parks each year. The ventures help raise the awareness and image of the brand, so boosting sales.

The LEGO Company has also developed a number of licensed spin-off products including LEGO Wear (collections of high-quality, colourful and practical children's wear,) as well as towels, shampoo, jigsaw puzzles, bags, bed linen, LEGO Time watches (which can be assembled from a range of different components to suit the wearer's mood), books, music, video, software and film products for children.

Recent Developments

While the classic LEGO brick is still the best-known symbol of the LEGO brand, there is more to the Company than bricks. LEGO has become synonymous with an integrated universe of experiences contributing to fun and play. New business categories – including software, clothes, learning materials and family attractions – have been added in recent years. The LEGO Company is also actively

involved in the world agenda on Lifelong Learning, and is working to strengthen its position both through its intensive, research-based product-development programme and through widening the scope of the LEGO brand.

LEGO Studios is a current example of an innovative new product which breaks the LEGO mould. It enables children aged 8–16 to bring to life the imaginative adventures in their LEGO worlds. They first build their 'story' and then capture the action on a PC movie camera. Using a professional but child-friendly software editing system, children can edit their footage adding music and sound effects. They can then play back their movies and even email their masterpieces to relatives and friends.

Another recent innovation is LEGO MINDSTORMS, which allows children to make their LEGO creations come alive. The MINDSTORMS Robotics Invention System has featured in the Guinness Book of Records as the most advanced toy robot currently available in the world. With traditional LEGO bricks, a child can build a LEGO creature that, for example, looks like a rabbit. Now, with LEGO MINDSTORMS, they can build a creature that actually acts like a rabbit, wandering around the room, reacting to things it 'sees' or bumps into. As children build and explore, they gain an understanding of important scientific and engineering concepts, involving sensing, feedback, and control. With the addition of the Vision Command accessory kit, children can use the most up-to-date technology to allow each robot to respond to what it sees. A PC digital camera can be quickly built into place, acting as the eye of the robot, reacting to colour, motion and light.

In 1999 the first LEGO-branded megastore opened at the Bluewater Shopping Centre in Kent.

Promotion

The LEGO Company uses shows and events, such as the Motor Show in the UK, to support its brand image and product expression. Creative competitions underline the LEGO brand's ability to stimulate creativity and the LEGO product's appealing three-dimensional nature.

Public relations also communicates the LEGO brand's unique values, look and feel. Direct marketing and websites provide more detailed information about the brand and help build a community among those who share a passion for LEGO products.

Pack inserts have also been used to cross-promote sub-brands, ensuring LEGO products grow with the child. The LEGO brand is clear and instantly recognisable in shops, particularly since the introduction of the new

LEGO 'homesites'. These are dedicated sections of selected retail outlets which are branded consistently across the UK.

LEGO continues to use television advertising throughout the year. It also featured in The Sunday Times and Channel 4 'Top 100 Ads Ever' poll in May 2000 with the Tommy Cooper 'Kipper' ad.

Brand Values

The LEGO Company has a set of 'fundamental beliefs', namely: children are our role models. They are curious, creative and imaginative and embrace discovery and wonder. They are natural learners; these are precious qualities that should be nurtured and stimulated throughout life. Lifelong creativity, imagination and learning are stimulated by playful activities that encourage hands-on and minds-on creation, fun, togetherness and the sharing of ideas. People who are curious, creative and imaginative – who have a childlike urge to learn – are the best equipped to thrive in a challenging world and to build our common future.

The company's mission statement is 'to nurture the child in each of us'. It does this as the world leader in providing quality products and experiences that stimulate creativity, imagination, fun and learning.

LEGO has been referred to as a universal language. You can put children from Africa, Asia, America and Europe in a room with LEGO bricks and they'll play happily together for hours regardless of age, sex or language. The LEGO Company also pioneered the concept of creative learning – the principle of developing children's knowledge and skills by nurturing their natural curiosity and desire to learn about the world around them. The LEGO Company still leads the field in creative learning through its innovative fun toys.

Things you didn't know about **LEGO**

Children around the world spend five billion hours every year playing with LEGO bricks.

There are 102,981,500 different ways of combining six eight-stud bricks of the same colour.

On average children use eighteen units when creating the bracelet for the LEGO Time Cruiser Watch. The units can be combined in 137,439,233,092 different ways.

320 billion LEGO elements have been moulded since 1949.

In 1999 The LEGO Company manufactured 311 million tyres making the LEGO Company the biggest tyre manufacturer in the world.

Market

Levi jeans were first manufactured for the gold miners of California in the 1850s. Since then jeans and denim clothing in general have become essential clothing items worldwide. Suitable for all occasions from working on a building site to clubbing it till dawn, jeans have become the one item of clothing almost everyone is guaranteed to own.

In the UK the jeans market has fluctuated throughout the 1990s as fashion trends have come and gone. However, a recent surge in the popularity of denim for the Millennium looks set to boost the market for the coming years.

Achievements

Levi Strauss & Co is the world's largest apparel manufacturer. It was the first company to develop denim as work and fashion wear and remains the best known denim brand.

Levi's jeans are synonymous with its title – the Originals. It has become a fashion classic for generation after generation; from the 501®'s look of James Dean in the 1950s, to the Engineered style of DJs, the Dreem Teem for the year 2000.

Levi's enduring success is due to its superb product quality, combined with one of the most powerful and persuasive advertising campaigns of all time. All the campaigns from the 'shrink-to-fit' Nick Kamen advert to the 'twisted attraction' Engineered promotion have served to push Levi's to the forefront of pop-culture consciousness. The brand has also remained young and dynamic with a policy of consistent renewal and diversification.

History

Levi Strauss began his career as a tailor during the Californian gold rush of the 1850s. A Bavarian immigrant, he arrived in San Francisco in 1853 hoping to open a dry food store like his brother. He had bales of canvas which he hoped to sell to the miners as tent material to make enough money to open his store. However, all the miners were interested in was gold and they didn't much care how they lived. Instead, they pointed out, they would have preferred some hard-wearing trousers for the tough work down the mines.

Levi Strauss saw this gap in the market and seized his opportunity at once, manufacturing canvas overalls for the mineworkers. His operation was such a success that he was able to open a store in 1856 called Levi Strauss & Co making his new brand of clothing from a tough dyed indigo cotton fabric from serge de Nimes. This was soon shortened to denim.

Over the next twenty years his company became more and more successful. In 1873 he and Nevada tailor Jacob Lewis patented the process of putting rivets in the overalls for strength and Levi's jeans were born. Levi Strauss continued to trade in and around California and was soon making luxury wear for city-dwellers as well as his main consumer base of miners, railroad workers and cowboys. His company was a family firm that remained under centralised control even when the business expanded throughout the USA and

began exporting overseas.

When Levi Strauss died in 1902 he was succeeded by his four nephews. They inherited a thriving company which was wholesaling a wide range of dried goods and manufacturing sturdy work clothes including the waist overalls that we know today as jeans.

The charmed life of Levi Strauss & Co continued even throughout the Depression when jeans were increasingly seen as affordable, desirable items of clothing. This led to the company's popularity spreading to the East Coast from its stronghold in the West.

In the 1940s the company abandoned the wholesaling of dry goods, determined to concentrate entirely on making its clothing. Spurred on by the post World War II baby boom and the growing popularity of jeans, especially among younger consumers, it created a national sales force. The US army also aided expansion to Europe when they introduced the Europeans to denim and demand soon outstripped supply with Levi's becoming a status symbol.

As the 1950s loomed, youth culture exploded with jeans tightly bound in with the identity of the new teenage generation. The company began offering double-knee jeans for boys, jeans with zippers for people who wanted an alternative to the original button fly of the 501®s and fashionable lighter blue jeans. Rock bands and famous actors sported jeans as fashion statements and increasingly, as a statement against conventional dressing and its matching lifestyle. This extended into the decades beyond when flared and then drainpipe jeans became the rage, with how you wore, not if you wore denim becoming the issue of the time.

During the 1960s the company introduced more products such as White Levi's jeans and Sta-Prest slacks as well as a new clothing division for women. Levi's also established an international division to market its jeans in Europe.

The 1970s and 1980s saw an attempt to

diversify into other products such as running gear. However, this was not a success and the company decided to refocus on its core products re-launching the original 501® jeans. These jeans, based on the original 1850s prototype and named after the warehouse lot number 501® to which the first serge de Nimes fabric was imported, featured the famous button fly and soon forged an unmistakeable, classic identity. Levi's 501® jeans have continued to grow in popularity, assuming cult status and generating strong worldwide sales.

Product

Levi's jeans were first manufactured from canvas and later from serge de Nimes imported from Europe. Today only one factory in the US manufactures Levi's denim material. The process remains a fiercely guarded secret. This denim is rigorously tested using machines that can wreak a lifetime's havoc to the denim in a few short hours, plus three washes to test for shrinkage.

Each pair of Levi 501®s is produced from 51 different pieces of fabric and undergoes 37 sewing operations, using six types of thread. All stress points are riveted by copper-plated steel, stamped LS & Co SF.

During 2000 Levi's made further developments to its total product offer. The RED TAB® collection was developed to include five distinct ranges. The core range being RED TAB® Basics which consists of two finish-focused ranges, RED TAB® Clean Jeans and RED TAB® Home Laundry, while the ALL-DUTY™ and STA-PREST® ranges aim to push a fresh direction and add seasonality to the brand.

RED TAB® jeans received a fresh approach through strong fabric and finish innovation and dark denim remains a key focus. RED TAB® Clean Jean were developed in collaboration with DuPont® and Levi Strauss & Co to create the combination of denim with Coolmax®. The result is a material with breathability, moisture transportation and quick drying properties combined with the 501®.

To drive the 'worn-in' look, Home Laundry introduced two finishes – Light Greaser and Dark Greaser. Light Greaser focuses on the 501®, and features rips and repairs to emphasise

customisation. Dark Greaser focuses on fabrication and showcases worn in dark indigo.

The ALL-DUTY™ range was designed to offer style and performance and is constructed from innovative hard-wearing fabrics.

The STA-PREST range saw the introduction of new fits and fabrics aiming to create a tough, edgier look. The range has expanded to include a greater selection of fits as well as other elements such as black denim and knitwear.

Recent Developments

During the 1990s the fortunes of the denim market continued to rise and fall. Sales reached a plateau in 1994 and 1995 but since then sales of denim jeans have steadily dropped to an estimated 33 million units in 1999. By the late 1990s it was all too apparent that the brand was slipping and needed to be put back on track. Since the 1960s success had been based on the brand's association with youth culture; during the 1990s this association began to lose

some of its vitality. While in the 1980s Levi's were seen as 'cool, youthful, innovative and sexy', market research revealed that this was no longer the case by the late 1990s.

Brand managers realised that they needed to revitalise perception of the brand. They saw that they needed to stop looking at wholesale merchandising and instead refocus their attention on the consumer. There has since been a concentrated effort by the brand managers to deliver the image of Levi's both to consumers and to retailers, as well as ensuring high sales volumes and achieving retailers' financial goals.

With this in mind Levi's launched Engineered Jeans for the year 2000 in a completely new shade of indigo blue, ergonomically designed to follow the contours of the human body. In addition, new features designed to benefit the wearer were incorporated, from lower slanting back pockets for easier access to a bigger watch

pocket. To complete the overall product offer, jackets and a range of tops were also made available in unisex and girl fits.

Promotion

From the beginning the Levi Strauss & Co brand has been marketed with immense success and innovation. Levi Strauss himself was a brilliant marketeer and the company has continued in his footsteps, most notably with the 501® jeans campaign.

Coordinated by Bartle Bogle Hegarty, the relaunch of the original jeans in 1985 spearheaded a mood that harked back to the 1950s heyday of America. A series of television commercials, offering witty storylines backed by classic soundtracks, soon re-established 501®s as the jeans to be seen in. In twelve months after the official relaunch of Levi's 501® jeans sales rose by 800% and sales doubled again the year after.

The launch of the Engineered jeans in spring/summer of 2000 was aimed at reversing the downward turn of denim sales in the late 1990s. It was the most significant launch for Levi's since the re-launch of 501®s. The campaign intended to create huge endorsement, media interest and potential consumer demand for Levi's Engineered. The advertisements appeared on television, in 'cool' youth magazines and newspapers and were endorsed by Radio One DJs, the Dreem Teem, once again showing Levi's flair for capitalising upon the latest trends.

It succeeded in obtaining massive interest from the media, with features appearing in The Observer, The Sunday Telegraph, Vogue, The Face and Melody Maker. Product placement was also a huge success with R&B talent Craig David wearing the Engineered jacket on Top of the Pops. Festival favourites Travis appeared in The Face magazine wearing items from the Engineered range. Billie Piper's dancers also wore the full Engineered ensemble when they performed on Saturday morning's CD:UK.

In addition to the headlining television commercials and poster advertising, Levi's has proved active in ensuring below-the-line promotional activities through in store posters, interactive computers and videos, as well as extensive and acclaimed work on the internet. Advertising continues to build on the focused, style-conscious message behind the Levi Strauss brand.

Brand Values

Levi's jeans are the prevailing fashion icon – not just for this generation but for all generations. Over the last 145 years denimwear has become present everywhere, valued for its hard-wearing, comfortable, multi-purpose qualities. It is equally suitable for home, work and going out.

Over the years Levi Strauss has stood the test of time to remain at the forefront of consumer consciousness, holding off the onslaught of copy-cat brands and cheaper makes. This is because Levi jeans are the symbol of a James Dean type rebellious youth expressed in clothes. The Levi's brand stands for individuality, attitude and style. It is a brand apart from other brands in that it owns the emotional heartland of this category.

Things you didn't know about Levi's®

The number 501® was an arbitrary lot number assigned to the jeans.

A typical pair of Levi's jeans takes about 1.3 yards of denim, 213 yards of thread, five rivets, five buttons and one Red Tab.

Levi Strauss & Co uses close to 1.2 million miles of thread annually for jean production. That amount would wrap 50.2 times around the world.

There are 37 separate sewing and four finishing operations involved in making one pair of Levi's 501® jeans.

Rivets were added to Levi's 501® jeans in 1873 because miners complained that their pockets ripped under the weight of gold nuggets. Today, reinforced stitching has replaced the back pocket rivets.

Levi's 501® jeans are part of the permanent collection at the Smithsonian Institution. They were first donated in 1964 by Walter Haas Snr.

Levi Strauss & Co's first jeans were made shrink-to-fit. In the early days, gold miners just put on their new jeans, submerged themselves in a water trough and left them on to dry.

LEXUS

Market

UK new car registrations rose steadily throughout most of the 1990s from 1.6 million in 1992 to 2.25 million in 1998, with a slight decline to 2.2 million in 1999.

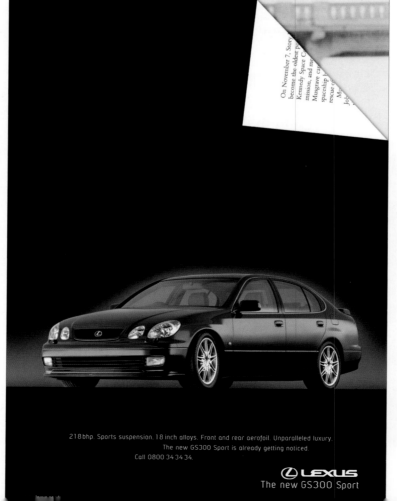

Your car can say a lot about you.
Or you can speak for yourself.

LS400
LEXUS
Call 0800 34 34 34.

Sales in 2000 remained reasonably strong despite difficult trading conditions. The market has proved turbulent, with high levels of consumer uncertainty generated by price differences between Britain and the rest of Europe. These have been largely due to the strength of sterling against the euro and different national taxation regimes.

Lately the competitiveness of the market has been fuelled by the emergence of internet car companies importing vehicles to exploit the exchange rate differentials.

Business buyers dominate the UK market and account for around 75% of purchases. Concerns about pollution and traffic have led the government to propose significant increases in the personal tax burden on company car drivers, based on list prices and carbon dioxide emissions of vehicles. This could significantly affect the premium sector of the car market.

Despite the difficulties, the premium car sector is still buoyant, albeit fiercely contested. Prestige car sales account for around 8.9% of total car sales. The premium market is traditionally associated with European manufacturers, in particular the long-established German brands.

Achievements

The concept of the Lexus brand was developed in the 1980s by the Toyota Motor Corporation to compete with the then-dominant European premium brands in the US market. Toyota's objective was to set new standards in terms of both product and service. Since its launch in the US, Lexus has become a key brand in the luxury car sector.

The success of Lexus in the US created a solid platform from which to tackle the European market. Consumers in Europe tend to be more brand conscious than their US counterparts and many consider brand image above the quality and equipment level of the vehicle itself. In this respect, without a long-established pedigree, the European market was a tougher one to crack.

But Lexus has succeeded and is now the fastest growing premium car brand in the world. The company increased its penetration of the UK premium market by 165% during the first half of 2000 against the same period in 1999. This growth is set to continue with the introduction of several new models which will tap into unexplored niche sectors.

Lexus celebrated its tenth anniversary in the

UK in July 2000. During this time it has competed with some of the world's most recognised brands and carved a reputation for balancing luxury with comfort and performance. Research shows Lexus enjoys exceptional levels of customer satisfaction.

Lexus has succeeded against the historic dominance of the premium car sector by European manufacturers. Where other Japanese manufacturers have tried and failed as prestige contenders, Lexus is the only manufacturer to make the breakthrough.

History

The concept of creating a luxury car to challenge the best in the world was originally conceived in 1983 at a meeting chaired by Eiji Toyoda, Chairman of Toyota Motor Corporation. A team of designers, engineers and technicians was assembled and over a few years built 450 running prototypes. By September 1986, a ten

month testing and evaluation programme began in America, resulting in further modifications. In 1987 the Lexus logo was unveiled at the Los Angeles Auto Show and by 1988 the process of nominating 80 franchises in the US was well under way.

May 1989 saw the first production of LS400 roll off the assembly line and by September the vehicles were on sale to the public. During that first month 2919 units were sold. Following the launch, Lexus has subsequently won JD Power awards in the US for customer satisfaction seven times, and has also won the Vehicle Dependability study every year it has been eligible.

Lexus was launched in Europe in 1990 with the LS400. For the next three years the brand reputation was established on this one model, positioned at the top end of the premium market. During this time, Lexus dealers ran their sales operations from within existing Toyota showrooms. With just the one model offered, it would not have been viable to build separate, dedicated Lexus showrooms.

While this was the only feasible business approach, the task of establishing the Lexus standalone brand was not made any easier with a facility being shared with the Toyota brand. While Toyota is a well respected brand in its own right it is aimed at a different consumer. Nonetheless, a new brand in luxury and comfort was established, offering, in keeping with the Lexus reputation every conceivable option as standard.

In 1993, the model line up doubled with the introduction of the GS300 executive saloon. This was received with great acclaim by the motoring press and continued Lexus' penetration of the market. Four generations of LS400 and two of GS300 have been

218bhp. Sports suspension. 18 inch alloys. Front and rear aerofoil. Unparalleled luxury.
The new GS300 Sport is already getting noticed.
Call 0800 34 34 34.

LEXUS
The new GS300 Sport

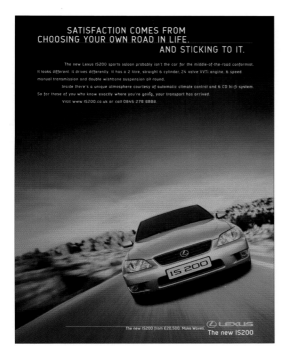

introduced. However, Lexus remained a two-model line-up until May 1999, with the introduction of the IS200 sports saloon. The launch was a milestone in raising awareness of the Lexus brand, bringing it within reach of a whole new segment of the premium market.

Since then, the expansion of the model range has accelerated. In 2000 Lexus brought three new vehicles to the British market: a new flagship saloon the LS430 which replaced the LS400; the high-performance GS430 and the long-awaited sports activity 4WD the RX300, the best-selling luxury 4WD in the US since its launch in 1998.

Further launches in 2001 include a hard-topped convertible sports coupe, the SC430 and additions to the IS range, including the high-performance IS300.

Expansion of the model range has been accompanied by development of the dealer network. Once trading from a corner of Toyota showrooms, dealers are now building state of the art dedicated Lexus Centres, which have been designed to transform the car retail environment.

Product

The Lexus range prides itself on high standards of build quality and ride, attention to detail, industry-leading security levels and what Lexus calls a 'complete' equipment specification. This is based on its belief that what competitors call options, Lexus makes standard.

The LS remains the flagship of the brand. When first launched, it established Lexus as a serious contender in the luxury market and raised the standard by which luxury vehicles are judged across performance, comfort and build quality.

Before designing the LS430, Lexus designers studied luxury and craftsmanship from outside the automotive world in locations such as five star hotels and first class airline cabins. They even observed jewellery designers, watchmakers and guitar makers at work.

The reputation for excellence has been reinforced by the rest of the Lexus range which, despite being more compact, is built and equipped to a similar generous standard.

Lexus aims to appeal to successful, discerning and confident individuals. The cars are designed to deliver the experience of luxury instead of merely being a symbol of status and wealth. The focus is on engineering detail and intelligent use of technology, rather than technology for technology's sake.

Recent Developments

1999 was a landmark year for Lexus. Having established the brand, the time was right to concentrate on separating Lexus from parent company Toyota and position it as a luxury brand in its own right. The process of brand separation duly began, with the design of a dedicated retail environment.

Research was conducted nationally to establish exactly what consumers felt about the car buying experience. It confirmed that people – especially women – disliked, even dreaded, buying cars because of the way they were treated. Many also saw the retail environment as emotionally and physically stressful.

Lexus' goal was to transform consumers' perception of buying cars and regard the process as a positive and enjoyable experience. Architects and designers once again took their cues from outside the industry. The result is an environment that is entirely different from the traditional car showroom. Every aspect is designed to optimise a customer's sense of comfort, well-being and space.

The first dedicated Lexus Centre in Europe was built in Bristol and opened in the autumn of 1999. The process has continued with twenty new centres open, and the remainder completed in 2001 to form a complete network of centres across the country.

Customer response to the new environment has been overwhelmingly positive and new Lexus Centres have already been responsible for a disproportionate percentage of both new and used vehicle sales. The environment has also had a beneficial effect on staff working in the new centres, with greater levels of motivation and pride. This is reflected in their dealings with customers and is critical in helping Lexus build and maintain its very strong reputation.

Promotion

Lexus has taken an integrated approach to promoting its brand and reinforced its brand building advertising campaigns through direct marketing, CRM, direct response advertising and internet/new media.

Saatchi & Saatchi London coordinate Lexus's advertising campaigns. In the years following its launch in the UK, television advertising was used to raise awareness of Lexus. The initial campaign was a series of top-and-tail advertisements, which teased drivers to assert their individuality by daring to break away from the stereotype of driving a German premium car.

Television and press campaigns have used the line 'It's the feeling

inside' which captures everything Lexus wants to say about its products, reflecting the brand positioning of contemporary luxury. Lexus defines luxury in the contemporary sense as a personal experience and a state of mind, rather than the traditional sense of conspicuous opulence.

The creative direction of television and press advertising reinforces the experience of being removed from the hurly-burly of modern life to 'the third space' of calm and inner tranquillity. 'It's the feeling inside' relates to the physical and emotional benefits of being in a Lexus, while building an involvement between the driver and the car. In execution, the national advertising tends to focus on the overall driving and ownership, rather than simply the car's features and benefits.

Direct response campaigns are used to complement national press advertising; whilst CRM programmes build relations with those responding to campaigns. Driving a Lexus can be the most captivating way to win customers and the most recent campaigns have invited readers to participate in driving events where they can experience it for themselves.

The internet plays a large part in marketing and Lexus was the first car brand to put its entire network on-line for new and used cars in 1996. Today the internet is a core part of an integrated contact strategy that channels all consumer communication through a sophisticated Lexus Contact Centre, handling both prospect and customer relationship marketing.

Brand Values

The brand positioning of contemporary luxury is supported by just two core brand values: integrity and intelligence.

Free from the constraints of heritage, Lexus has no rules to follow and as a brand it has the freedom to keep challenging the norms and redefining the standards. In doing so it has a unique platform to differentiate between itself and rival brands.

LURPAK®

SINCE 1901

Market

The UK is a nation of butter lovers and consumers purchase more than £220 million pounds worth of it every year. Enough butter is sold annually to spread over four billion slices of toast, butter two billion sandwiches or melt over two and a half billion jacket potatoes.

Despite our love of butter, deciding what to spread on our bread is far from easy.

Every time we visit the supermarket we are faced with an array of choices. As well as butters there are margarines, 'butter-like' spreads, low fat spreads and even cholesterol-lowering spreads — the list goes on.

Despite all these alternatives, most consumers regularly vote with their taste buds and choose butter — and in particular Lurpak.

Butter is now more convenient than ever, too. Thanks to the introduction of 'spreadables', such as Lurpak Spreadable, consumers can spread it straight from the fridge.

The success of spreadables has introduced a new wave of shoppers to butter, as it is particularly popular amongst younger consumers. Traditionally, core butter consumers have tended to be aged 45 and over, but the average buyer of spreadables is typically under 30. Given this trend, butter's long term future appears to be secure.

History

Lurpak was founded in 1901, which makes it one of the most authentic butter brands in the world.

At the beginning of the last century, when Lurpak first began arriving from Denmark, the individual packs that we are familiar with today were unheard of. Instead it was shipped from Denmark in wooden barrels the size of beer kegs.

Back then, your local shopkeeper would slice you a piece of butter from a large slab and wrap

It's the Danish dairyman's way with cream that gives Lurpak butter its lovely delicate taste

it in greaseproof paper.

It was not until 1957 that the first individual packs of Lurpak went on sale. These convenient 250g sized blocks were packed in silver foil and this silver packaging theme continues today.

Whether from the barrel, wrapped in silver foil or packed in a handy tub, one thing has remained constant on all Lurpak packaging formats — the famous Lurmark horns. These are the Danish Dairy Federation's highest seal of approval and testament to the fact that Lurpak is churned from the finest creams. The Danish Dairy Federation's seal of approval — the Lurmark — can be seen on every pack of Lurpak butter. The symbol consists of four lurs, wind instruments that date back to 800 BC.

Achievements

Lurpak is sold in more than 100 countries worldwide and is the UK's favourite butter brand with yearly sales in excess of £100 million.

In 2000, Lurpak beat off stiff competition from the world's best butters to take a gold

medal at the Cheese and Butter World Championships in Wisconsin, US. Run every two years, the awards recognise quality and excellence in dairy production and more than 1,000 products from seventeen countries took part.

Lurpak Spreadable has also recently been on the winner's rostrum and scooped the 'Brand Development of the Year' award at the prestigious Marketing Society awards. The judges commended the product as an excellent example of successfully extending an existing brand into new markets.

Lurpak Spreadable is worth £53 million in yearly sales and more than two and a half million packs are sold in the UK every week.

Lurpak is now the UK's favourite butter brand, taking the number one spot from Anchor butter in 1998, which was a landmark achievement for the brand.

Since then, the Lurpak brand has gone from strength to strength and now accounts for a third of all butter sold in the UK. Lurpak's biggest fans are the Scots. In Scotland it outsells its nearest competitor — Flora — by two packs to one.

Product

Lurpak's famous silver packaging is designed to catch your eye in the supermarket.

The butter boasts a natural, subtle taste and aims to bring out the flavour of other foods. Its taste is not only popular with the public but with many of today's celebrity chefs who use Lurpak in their cooking.

Traditional Lurpak block butter comes in both slightly salted and unsalted. It is packed in 125g, 250g and 500g blocks and foil wrapped for freshness.

With the arrival of Lurpak Spreadable, Lurpak now aims to be more convenient than ever. Lurpak Spreadable is available in a slightly salted variety, packaged in handy, resealable 250g, 500g and 1kg tubs.

The colour of Lurpak changes subtly throughout the year, depending on the season. In summer, the grass eaten by cows contains a high

concentration of the pigment beta-carotene and Lurpak consequently has a vivid yellow colour. In winter, when lush, green grass is thinner on the ground, it is paler in colour.

Recent Developments

The introduction of Lurpak Spreadable in 1997 changed the butter market for good. It followed research highlighting that many consumers found traditional block butter hard to spread. The research also indicated that consumers found foil wrappers inconvenient, due to their tendency to become greasy and messy.

Lurpak Spreadable became an immediate hit with consumers and additional production facilities had to be hurriedly built to meet demand. The product's popularity also led to its launch in 1kg tubs.

Lurpak Spreadable's recipe for success has been simple. It offers the taste of Lurpak but with the added convenience of spreading straight from the fridge and is perfect for people with busy lives.

Lurpak bid farewell to the 1990s and marked the millennium with a vibrant new packaging design. The new look features a bold blue wave that rolls continuously down the aisle when Lurpak is displayed in supermarkets.

Promotion

Lurpak's marketing has always been simple and consistent, focusing on its taste and quality. It is

an approach that has paid dividends.

The star of Lurpak's television advertising is Douglas the Butterman. Created by Aardman animations in 1985, Douglas has been the leading light in Lurpak's television ads, ably supported by the instantly recognisable voice of Penelope Keith.

The first Douglas ad was aired in 1986 and sixteen commercials have been produced over the years. The theme of the adverts is a perennial favourite. Douglas is seen romancing Penelope with his lovable charm, while infuriating her by fooling around with his prized trombone.

Douglas's appearances are not just confined to the small screen. An eight-foot high Douglas regularly visits schools, fun days and shows, as well as helping out with Lurpak product sampling exercises.

Douglas also features in on-pack giveaways. This included the biggest ever on-pack promotion for a butter – a recent limited edition Douglas butter dish with packs of Lurpak. More than 800,000 special edition butter dish packs were sold in just three weeks of the promotion.

The packs proved so popular that shoppers were seen trying to buy them off each other at twice the price they were being sold for in the shops.

If you hail a cab in London, look out for one of the four official Lurpak taxis. Decked out in the distinctive Lurpak silver packaging, they look like huge packs of Lurpak on wheels.

Douglas also has a head for heights and is the proud owner of two huge hot air balloons. The traditional Lurpak balloon stands at over 90 feet tall, but towering above that is the Douglas hot air balloon at 130 feet. It features Douglas seated aboard two huge packs of Lurpak butter. The balloons attend shows throughout the summer and have visited schools across the country.

The Douglas hot air balloon was stolen from Wandsworth Common in London in June 2000. Thankfully, it was safely recovered after a £1,000 reward and a free year's supply of Lurpak were offered for its return.

Douglas is such a brand icon that he has his own range of merchandise for fans to buy as well. The Douglas Collection includes aprons, tea towels, socks and lunch boxes.

Brand Values

The Lurpak brand values are centered around the product being premium quality, natural and authentic. Lurpak's quality is also projected through its distinctive silver packaging.

Its brand values are firmly established in the minds of consumers and are just as

relevant today as they were 100 years ago. The fundamentals of the brand have remained unchanged, which is one of the main reasons for Lurpak's continued success.

Ask Lurpak fans what they think of the brand and they may tell you that it's the best butter money can buy. If you probe deeper, they may explain why – made from only the finest ingredients with a 'distinctive, delicate taste'.

Because of the popularity of the Lurpak television advertising campaign, some fans may also be able to recount what high-jinx Douglas gets up to in their favourite advert. They may even liken Douglas to Ernie Wise, explaining that he has got the comic's magical way about him and that same twinkle in his eye.

Things you didn't know about Lurpak

Douglas the Butterman has his own fan club with more than 100,000 members.

Douglas the Butterman was created by Aardman animations, the company behind the television stars Wallace & Gromit and the blockbuster movie Chicken Run.

The Douglas the Butterman hot air balloon consists of Douglas perched on top of two huge packs of Lurpak butter. Each of the enormous packs could contain 2,250 tonnes of butter – enough for 1,000 million pieces of toast.

Lurpak Spreadable outsells its nearest competitor – Anchor Spreadable – in the UK by two packs to one.

If all the packs of Lurpak sold in the UK in a typical year were placed end to end, they would stretch from London to Copenhagen and back thirteen times.

MARKS & SPENCER

Market

The retail sector has become increasingly competitive with companies striving to increase market share by price-cutting and with the growing possibilities for customers to shop on the internet. Some well-established names have been forced out of the market, some new names using new technology have entered, but many have found trading conditions tough.

Marks & Spencer has gone through a period of business restructuring in response to these conditions. Profits have fallen from the heights of the 1990s but steps have been taken to stabilise the downturn and create a strong platform for future growth.

Marks & Spencer has a 13.7% share of the UK clothing market, 3% of the market for home products, and 3.7% for food.

Achievements

The Marks & Spencer brand has a long-established reputation for quality and service. Despite the toughening market conditions, it has been able to fight back by reasserting the power of its brand. A renewed focus on the customer has been at the heart of a major restructuring accomplished with minimal disruption.

Marks & Spencer currently operates a total of 691 stores worldwide, with a sales area in the UK alone of twelve million square feet in 297 stores. It remains a profitable business despite setbacks in recent years, and employs 75,000 people. In 1999/2000, group turnover was £8.2 billion, with pre-tax profits of £557million.

The company has a continuing reputation for innovation. Twelve of its product innovations achieved Millennium Products status, more than for any other company. One of these, 'Secret Support' – a unique hidden 'liner' that eliminates the need to wear a bra under garments – won the Queen's Award for Innovation.

Marks & Spencer has always taken its duties seriously as a corporate citizen, pioneering activities in areas such as the environment, equal opportunities, ethical trading and community involvement. The new millennium presented a particular opportunity, driven by the wish to mark this special occasion with a special approach. The 'Children's Promise' was the answer, an imaginative idea for people to donate their last hour of pay from the old millennium to improve the future for the children of the next. Children's Promise raised over £18 million for children's charities in the UK, with staff leading the way in fundraising. It became one of the largest-ever non-governmental programmes of support.

History

Marks & Spencer was founded by a young Russian refugee, Michael Marks, who arrived in the north east of England in the early 1880s. He started out selling haberdashery from a tray in the villages close to the industrial centre of Leeds. However, he had ambitious plans and borrowed £5 from a local wholesaler Isaac Dewhurst to enable him to buy fresh stock and set up a stall in Leeds market. His first advertising slogan was straight to the point.

It stated: 'Don't ask the price – it's a penny.' This helped Michael Marks get around the problem of his poor English.

Less than ten years on, Michael Marks was operating a chain of stalls across the north east. He formed a partnership with Tom Spencer, a cashier at the IJ Dewhurst wholesale company, which accelerated the growth of the business.

The family's involvement in the company continued when Michael's son, Simon Marks, was named as a director in 1911 and became chairman during World War I. During this period

the Marks & Spencer penny price point disappeared. In 1917 Simon Marks was joined on the board by his friend and brother-in-law Israel Sieff. Together they were to chart the next stage in Marks & Spencer's history. Both became chairman of the company at different stages, and were later granted peerages.

During the 1920s, the company introduced the revolutionary practice of buying stock direct from manufacturers, thereby forming long-lasting, close relationships with suppliers, many of which have continued into the present day. Many of the ground rules which have been key to the company's success were initiated at this time by Marks and Sieff.

In 1928 the company registered the St Michael trademark which distinguished all Marks & Spencer goods. The introduction of retail branding reassured consumers that Marks & Spencer products had a specific quality guarantee. The company grew at a rapid rate, opening its flagship Marble Arch store in Oxford Street, London, in 1930.

One of the aims of Marks & Spencer was to take care of its staff

as well as its customers. It set up an in-company Welfare Department in the early 1930s. After World War II – during which over a hundred stores were damaged – the company underwent a period of rapid expansion.

In 1975 it opened its first European store on Boulevard Haussmann in Paris. In the UK, further expansion in the 1980s led to the opening of the first Marks & Spencer edge-of-town store at the Metro Centre, Gateshead. The establishment of St Michael Financial Services led to the launch of the Marks & Spencer Chargecard in 1985 and by 1988, Marks & Spencer Financial Services had moved into the black, one year earlier than forecast.

Product

Marks & Spencer remains famous for its underwear and is a clear market leader in this product area for men and women.

The key to Marks & Spencer's clothing has been a commitment to selling high quality at competitive prices. In keeping with the principles of its founders, stylish clothes which have been influenced by leading fashion designers are sold at prices affordable to everyone. In 2000 Marks & Spencer introduced the Autograph Designer Collection, a lifestyle range aimed at women and men who want to buy designer clothing at reasonable prices. Leading fashion designers – such as Betty Jackson, Julien Macdonald and Katherine Hamnett – have created clothes exclusive to Marks & Spencer.

In 2000 Marks & Spencer completed the most comprehensive survey ever of size and fit. The purpose was to assess ways in which people's

sizes and shapes had changed since the previous survey a decade earlier. The survey produced clear evidence that the 'average' woman is now a size 14. Marks & Spencer has reacted to the research and changed its fit to accommodate and enhance the modern woman's figure.

Marks & Spencer's women clothes are available in sizes 8-22, with some styles available up to size 30.

The size survey has been extended to clothes for men and children, and the results will flow through into the design and point of sale for these clothes. The company has strong positions established in these areas – for example, one in four men's suits sold in the UK is from Marks & Spencer.

Marks & Spencer, though, is about much more than clothes. Its food ranges are recognised as introducing new, adventurous cuisines from around the world to customers whose taste buds have been educated by increased travel and dining out. Chinese, Indian and Italian ranges are constantly developed, and a new 'Fusion' range has brought Pacific Rim cookery to UK homes.

pay, including credit and debit cards.

Recent Developments

The growth of the internet and e-commerce has started to make big changes in the way all retailers operate. Marks & Spencer launched online shopping at the end of 1999, having run earlier trials and established its website as one of the UK's most popular destinations (five million page impressions per month). Online shopping becomes a natural development from Marks & Spencer's success in direct selling. To build on the skills and product innovation within the company, Marks & Spencer Ventures was set up in 1999. The intention is to spot, invest in and develop initiatives which bring additional benefits to customers. One of Marks & Spencer Ventures' first deals was to enter into a strategic partnership with the digital media and communications group Talkcast Corporation.

In the stores themselves there have been

the St Michael Promise – a commitment to achieving leading standards in all its dealings. St Michael (long described as 'the brand name of Marks & Spencer') became an endorsement of the main brand, now clearly and proudly seen as Marks & Spencer. The approach can now be seen in new-look stores: packaging, carrier bags, point of sale material – everything that affects the internal and external perception of the brand.

This repositioning was the background to a new advertising campaign by Marks & Spencer in autumn 2000. Although the company has not been a big advertiser over the years, a renewed focus on the customer and a commitment to marketing disciplines has led to a noticeably more dynamic and engaging advertising style.

Brand Values

The repositioning work built on Marks & Spencer's long-established values goes back to the times of Simon Marks and Israel Sieff. The same commitment to leading standards continues in all relationships with customers, employees, shareholders, suppliers and communities. Previously summed up as 'quality, service and value', the principles underlie the company's behaviour and form the backbone of its image. Marks & Spencer is a brand that people trust to guarantee high quality, excellent service and affordable prices.

Other product ranges include toiletries and cosmetics, gifts items and stationery, and there is a growing collection of home products from furniture to frying pans. Marks & Spencer is the most popular choice for wedding gifts.

Financial Services continues to grow, using the strength of the Marks & Spencer brand,

many new developments, including the opening of a new 200,000 square foot superstore in Manchester. Built to replace the store destroyed by an IRA bomb, the new store features a customer lounge, a play area for children, a personal shopping suite and a commission-free Bureau de Change.

Promotion

With the increasing competition in the market, technological developments and simply the passing of time, the Marks & Spencer brand has recently gone through a process of necessary questioning and refreshment. Following a programme of research and creative work, the Marks & Spencer brand has re-emerged with a clearer purpose and a sharper presentation. Part of this shift in emphasis has been the need to find a new role for St Michael, the company's trademark since 1928.

The new visual approach to the Marks & Spencer brand began to appear in 2000, featuring a revised logotype, colour and

with products ranging from loans to insurance to pensions to unit trusts and ISAs. The Marks & Spencer Chargecard remains the most used in-store card in the UK, but customers are now offered a comprehensive range of ways to

Market

As a nation it is clear that the UK has always had a sweet tooth. This was proven in 1999 when sales of chocolate in the UK topped £3.8 billion, with on average six confectionery purchases a second. Much of this was due to the number one selling chocolate bar, the MARS bar (Source: IRI infoscan).

Chocolate confectionery meets a variety of consumer needs in terms of delivering satisfaction in beating hunger, light snacking and indulgence. The past few decades have seen the confectionery market change from a 'special treat' to holding an important place in everyday life and consumer usage has developed with categories such as; eat now, take home, family sharing and gifts.

The market continues to grow despite recent developments in other snack and food products. This clearly demonstrates the enduring quality of the MARS bar and other brand variants in the eyes of the consumer. The diversity of formats and pack sizes means that there is a MARS for a range of consumers and continuing product development ensures that MARS keeps pace with changing consumer needs.

The MARS bar has been one of the UK's favourite since its launch in 1932 and in 2000 over three million MARS bars were made every day in the Mars factory in Slough.

The Mars chocolate range has grown over the years and the Slough factory now produces over 200,000 tonnes of product per annum. Along with the MARS bar, Mars Confectionery boasts an additional five to today's top ten chocolate single bars – all of which were developed following the success of the MARS bar.

Achievements

By far the MARS bar's biggest achievement in the UK is that it has remained the best selling chocolate bar ever since its launch.

In 1999 the MARS bar had UK sales of more than £140 million (Source: IRI infoscan) and global sales of nearly two billion bars.

The original factory in Slough has grown from hand-producing MARS bars in 1932 to producing sweets which are sold all over the world.

History

When the MARS bar was launched to the British public, it was a chocolate recipe not seen before in the UK. At that time most chocolate was produced as simple solid blocks. The MARS bar however combined for the first time layers of nougat, caramel and thick milk chocolate.

In May 1932, a young American, Forrest E Mars arrived in the UK with a recipe for a new chocolate bar – the MARS bar. He rented a small factory in Slough and registered the new company as Mars Confections Ltd.

In June of that year, the now famous MARS bar trademark was registered and within months the factory was fully operational.

The first MARS bar was made by hand on August Bank Holiday Monday 1932. By December, just four months after opening, there were over one hundred people working for Mars Confectionery. The first year saw over two million MARS bars made in Slough.

The first MARS bar sold for 2d and the current price of 29p is roughly the same in real terms. In fact an article in the Financial Times in 1981 entitled 'How MARS Bar Defeats Inflation' described the bar as 'a currency of our time'. Since then some have used the MARS bar as an indicator of the true value of the pound. It has also been used for price comparisons by organisations ranging from investment companies to the British Antique Collectors Club.

During World War II production was maintained and MARS bars were supplied to the Allied armed forces. Wartime rationing meant that Mars Confectionery had to make moderate changes to the recipe. Concerned about customers' views on this, Mars commissioned a survey in the early 1940s and was delighted that the general public was more than happy with the MARS bar.

The survey also revealed that people cut their MARS bar into little pieces to make it last longer. This lead to the introduction of the MARS FUN SIZE bars.

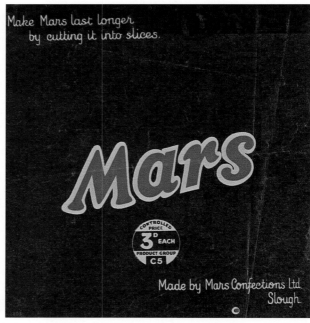

In 1941 there was a shortage of gold ink for wrappers and thus the gold disappeared temporarily from the logo.

In the late 1940s Mars introduced the first 'self-service display', making confectionery more accessible, thus unlocking the 'impulse' market. However, rationing was still in effect in the UK in the early 1950s. By 1953 the end of rationing was officially announced and one man was so delighted that he announced to the world that he would eat a MARS bar 'morning, noon and night', which he did – until his wartime supply dried up.

1953 was also Coronation year and the MARS bar was ready. Mars was the only confectioner to back advertising space to coincide with the big day. These ads gave the MARS bar a massive 50% increase in sales which, for the first time, passed the £10 million mark.

Product

Over the years, to complement the original bar, various additions have been developed. In 1972 the MARS FUN SIZE was introduced and in 1985 came the MARS KING SIZE, with the MARS Snack Size following in 1988.

In the late 1980s Mars introduced MARS bar flavoured milk drinks and ice cream. The MARS bar is included in the Celebrations range of boxed chocolates, which includes other miniature Mars Confectionery chocolates, such as SNICKERS and BOUNTY bars.

In addition, the MARS Bar Easter egg is produced on a seasonal basis and is one of the ten most popular Easter Eggs on the market. Limited edition bars have also become a regular addition to the MARS range, such as MARS Dark & Gold, first introduced for eight weeks from August 1999. The dark chocolate MARS bar was targeted towards women, it was an indulgent twist on the original MARS bar.

Recent Developments

In the autumn of 2000 Mars launched 5 Little Ones as an elegant variant on the MARS bar aimed at the female market and in response to research into how women like to eat MARS. The bar has been a huge success, enabling women to enjoy a taste of their confectionery and keep the rest for later.

The hugely popular MARS KING SIZE also saw a change at the end of 2000, relaunching as MARS Big One. MARS were the first to introduce the King Size concept and, as ever driving the market, responded to changing consumer attitudes. MARS Big One and MARS 5 Little Ones develop the MARS range for the future.

Promotion

MARS bar first advertised in print in the late 1930s in an advertisement, which reflected its nutritional values. Slogans included 'Packed with Nourishment', 'MARS for Energy' and 'Grand Food – Grand Flavour'.

By 1945 Mars introduced the slogan 'MARS are Marvellous' with a shift in emphasis to the taste.

When commercial television arrived in 1955, Mars was one of the first companies to take advantage of the new medium. Petula Clark, Bob Monkhouse and Richard Murdoch took part in the 'Stars Love MARS' advertisements.

In 1959 came the use of the now world famous slogan 'A MARS a Day, Helps You Work, Rest and Play'. At the time the Account Manager at Mars' advertising agency was Formula One racing commentator, Murray Walker and he is often credited with inventing this strapline. However it was actually penned by a team of copywriters and has since become an anthem worldwide.

1969 saw the first colour MARS bar commercial and in 1973 the introduction of a 'jingle' to go with the MARS advertising slogans. But throughout, it was the family values and 'wholesome goodness' of the MARS ingredients that were the focus in the advertising campaigns.

In the 1980s however, there was a shift from family values to the bar's values. The 'Biggest MARS bar ever' campaign ran with the 69 gram Jubilee bar, and advertising made announcements, such as 'In any job, whatever its size, you'll find the Biggest MARS Bar ever comes in handy'. This slowly moved into the 'Everyday' theme with mainstream advertising.

In the 1990s Mars recognised the 'me' generation was well established and developed a 'harder' edge.

One of the most successful promotional campaigns

produced by Mars was the 1999 'MARS – Make It Happen' campaign. Making 140 dreams come true for winning consumers and generating £4 million of media coverage, this on-pack promotion generated high levels of consumer awareness of the MARS bar.

The MARS bar has also had major associations with various sporting events over the years, including The London Marathon (1984-1988) the Olympics in 1992 and the Football World Cup in 1994.

But it is the performance of the bar itself which is MARS' greatest reward, with celebrities like Martine McCutcheon, Carol Vorderman and Lisa from Steps publicly announcing their praise of the product. Today the MARS bar is still the UK's number one selling single chocolate bar.

Brand Values

The MARS bar has always been built around two vital elements: quality and value for money, which is as important to the product today as it was in 1932.

Things you didn't know about MARS bar

The MARS bar is available in over 100 countries in the world.

The energy consumption of a flying bumblebee is equivalent to the amount of energy found in 120 MARS bars.

It would take the Slough factory only 4.5 days to produce sufficient MARS bars to stretch end to end from Lands End to John O'Groats.

One year's production would provide every man, woman and child in China with a MARS bar.

Market

The alcoholic mixables category saw a 13% rise in volume between 1995-1999 (Source: Mintel 1999). This market divides into wine-based and spirit-based products and it may also be broken down into modern (relatively new) and traditional classifications. The modern group includes Southern Comfort, Malibu, Archers and other schnapps, and Taboo, while the traditional group encompasses vermouths and bitters, brands such as Martini, Cinzano and Campari.

The UK vermouth market is effectively led by one brand, Martini, with Cinzano and supermarkets' own-label vermouth products also in the market. In the UK the Extra Dry style is the lead variant with Bianco and Rosso having a lesser share, in contrast to continental Europe.

Achievements

Following the peak sales years of the 1970s and the beginning of the wine boom, Martini began to lose volume to own label vermouth, wine and new entrants into the mixable category. However, in recent years brand volume has been successfully stabilised at over 11.2 million bottles a year, marking the beginnings of a return to popularity of this light, versatile drink. New and modern ways of drinking Martini, such as Rosso and cranberry or Bianco and orange, have begun to be sampled extensively using the silver Martini Taste Dome, and the brand has returned to strong share and volume growth in the key supermarket sector.

History

The Martini recipe is a variation of a potion first created in 460 BC by Hippocrates, who was inspired by soaking wild flowers in the highly sugared Greek wine of his native island Kos. Vermouth began to gain popularity throughout Europe as early as the reign of Louis XIV, whose court embraced the drink with a passion. Its modern association with Italy began in 1786 when the ruling Court of Savoy adopted the local tipple as the 'court aperitif'. From then, the vermouth trade in Italy became firmly established, with Torino, the area where Martini was first produced, at its centre.

Martini & Rossi, as we recognise it, first appeared in 1863 but the foundations of the Martini & Rossi company were actually laid in 1847, when a new venture was launched, producing and selling alcoholic drinks. It was in 1863, when one Alessandro Martini – along with herbalist and wine maker Luigi Rossi – took over the firm, that the brand acquired the Martini name which would soon become world famous.

Over the next decade, the company won a host of accolades at international exhibitions and within fifteen years Martini was being toasted in all the right places. The company promoted its award-winning product by featuring medals on its famous brand's label, on which several European royal families allowed their coats of arms to be displayed.

The company's partners decided to concentrate on exporting their products and in 1867 the first one hundred cases of vermouth were shipped to New York. By 1890, 300,000 cases a year were being exported.

In the twentieth century Martini & Rossi's network expanded, with subsidiary companies all over the world. Martini & Rossi had become and still remains one of the world's first truly international brands.

For the next 70 years the business remained in the family and was run by the grandsons and great grandsons of Luigi Rossi who were responsible for ensuring the brand lived on through the fighting, occupation and rationing of World War II.

By the 1960s, Martini had taken its place as a brand belonging to a world to which everyone aspired. In 1993, Martini & Rossi merged

Martini Art Gallery
M. Dudovich 1918

with another great family company to form Bacardi-Martini.

Product

Vermouth is an ancient drink, thousands of years old, made by infusing wine and herbs. In the case of Martini, the recipe is known only to a handful of people, and contains over 80 different aromatic herbs and spices. These are carefully blended and distilled before being added to the wine.

There are three variations of the Martini product. The original, produced since 1863 is Martini Rosso, characterised by its amber-brown colour and bitter sweet qualities. Martini Extra Dry was introduced on New Year's Day 1900 – a straw coloured drink invented to compete with drier French vermouth. Next in line was Martini Bianco, introduced in the 1910s. It is sweeter, has the taste of vanilla and is the most aromatic of the three variations.

Recent Developments

Martini has been making the most of being a brand with heritage in a modern world – it has diversified its products and moved into new segments, reducing the dependence on vermouth.

Martini Citro was launched in 1997, targeting 20-40 year old men and women. It is a young, sophisticated brand in the mould of Martini's vermouth products but more accessible to a youth audience, higher in alcohol content and with a refreshing citrus taste.

Not forgetting the core brand, in 1997 the Martini label, a design classic itself, was revised to differentiate itself from its many imitators. As well as a few alterations to the label which highlight the brand's place in history, the bottle shape was altered with a more oval shape, squarer shoulders and a shorter neck. This change meant plant technology had to be completely upgraded, but it was worthwhile, giving a contemporary, revitalised feel to the product.

Promotion

Martini's founding fathers seemed to have grasped the notion of marketing their product a long time before we traditionally think that advertising began.

As well as promoting the brand's credentials on its label, Martini & Rossi embraced poster advertising, engaging skilful artists to design the images that began to cover Italian city walls early in the twentieth century. Many famous artists such as Andy Warhol have designed for Martini. This method of promoting Martini soon spread to other countries, continued for many decades, and was commemorated in 2000 with a special series of labels which feature one of six classic Martini posters.

In the late 1960s, Martini began its long association with the world of motor racing. Team sponsorships with Porsche, Brabham,

Lotus, Lancia and Alfa Romeo followed, cementing the drink's image as one of sophisticated, international jetset glamour. This has continued for more than a quarter of a century and since 1999 Martini has been allied with Ford competing in the World Rally Championships.

But it is not only for poster advertising and motorsports that Martini is famous. In the 1970s, an unashamedly glamorous decade, Martini launched its famous 'Anytime, Anyplace, Anywhere' television campaign. Reflecting Martini's earlier understanding of how to build a global brand, the campaign was one of the first to regard the global market as a single place, with consistent international advertising.

So successful was the campaign, that a total of 54 commercials were made. Each featured stunning locations and focused on the glamour of skiing, powerboats, motor racing and hot air ballooning. Beautiful cocktail waitresses would glide by with silver salvers in hand, chinking glasses of Martini, reminding audiences it was the drink you could have wherever you were.

In the 1990s, Martini advertising took a different and equally individual line culminating in the famous 'Beautiful People' campaign. This was successful in raising the Martini profile, with its tightly integrated PR campaign putting Martini on the front pages of many national newspapers.

In continental Europe, the distinctive and award-winning Martini Man campaign in black and white also raised awareness and has marked the pan-European Martini come back. More recently in the UK there has been a return to the softer, more leisurely Martini 1970s style of advertising. To the delight of many, the 'Anytime, Anyplace, Anywhere' music is once more hitting our screens.

Without a doubt, the world's most famous Martini drinker is James 'shaken not stirred' Bond, and for an eighteen week, highly-publicised

season of Bond films shown on ITV in 1999, Martini was the sponsor.

This was followed by a £1.3 million television advertising campaign. Other activity undertaken to promote the brand includes the Bacardi-Martini Grand Prix, an international competition for bartenders, organised in collaboration with the International Bartenders' Association. It began in Italy in 1966, and sees male and female bartenders from all over the world compete against each other for four coveted prizes. Martini has also launched In the Mood, a lifestyle magazine mailed directly to consumers, with ideas for food and drink, health and beauty, and of course, ideas for serving Martini.

Brand Values

Martini is a truly international brand, with an impeccable heritage. It is chic and stylish, while remaining a classic brand, consumed by generations of sophisticates and still remaining accessible to those who merely aspire to such a lifestyle. It exemplifies the Italian 'Gioia di Vivere' – enjoyment of life.

Things you didn't know about Martini

- As well as being a glamorous brand, Martini's social and business credentials are very strong. In 1872, the company built its own connection with the main Turin-Genoa railway to speed its goods far and wide, and it also had a policy of housing its employees.

- Since 1925, the Martini label has featured a figure of a woman symbolising fame (who replaced Mercury, the god of merchants and the figure of Victory).

- Although the exact recipe is a secret, when sipping Martini you are enjoying ingredients such as the roots of rhubarb, the flowers of rose, lavender and cloves, lemon and orange rind, juniper berries and cinnamon bark, to name but a few.

- Bacardi-Martini owns The Martini Museum which gives information about wine-making and its history. Located in Torino, it celebrates wine-making through the ages and includes drinking vessels from Roman times and is one of the biggest wine museums in the world.

- In February 2000, Seattle hosted the second International Martini Classic Challenge, in which bartenders compete to mix the finest Martini cocktail.

- The artwork which has adorned the Martini label, as well as its advertising, is rated so highly, that it has been the subject of exhibitions in Italy and beyond.

Market

When McDonald's was launched in the UK in the mid 1970s, the path for quick service restaurants was already well established, with national favourites like fish and chip restaurants, paving the way for new international imports.

Since then, the quick service restaurant market has sustained dynamic growth. With the introduction of leading international chains such as KFC, Burger King, Wimpy and Pizza Hut increasing customer choice and making this a highly competitive market place.

Despite the increases in competitive pressure however, the McDonald's brand is still growing and few others can match it for the power and ubiquity embodied in its familiar Golden Arches.

Achievements

McDonald's is the world's largest and fastest growing food service organisation, with more than 26,000 restaurants in 119 countries serving food and drink to nearly 43 million customers daily. In the UK McDonald's operates over 1060 restaurants that generate a combined annual turnover of more than £1 billion. This success has not gone without recognition.

In 1996, McDonald's was rated the world's greatest brand in a publication by 'Interbrand'. The in-depth study looked at the strength and potential of many worldwide brands, but concluded that "Nothing compares with McDonald's for the power of a branding idea, the skill of its execution, and the longevity and width of its appeal." The study also pointed out that despite having its roots in the US, McDonald's has become an accepted citizen of the world. Certainly this acceptance has been felt in the UK.

In 1999, Campaign magazine voted McDonald's 'Advertiser of the Year.' The award was in recognition of the consistent quality of McDonald's advertising in the UK.

1999 was also the year that saw the brand's popularity with its UK consumers dramatically demonstrated in a two for the price of one Big Mac offer. The promotion was timed to celebrate the company's 25th anniversary in the UK, but nobody could have predicted how successful it would be when, at its height, eight times the usual number of Big Macs were sold due to the massive public demand.

INVESTOR IN PEOPLE

Customer satisfaction is also dependent on well trained, motivated staff and McDonald's is committed to the development of all of its employees, at every level of the organisation. Training is a continuous process, and employees attend courses in the restaurants as well as at the company's six Management Training Centres.

When they complete their initial training, all employees are eligible to receive an independently validated Basic Certificate in Food Hygiene, and successful completion of the Management Training programme can lead to a Diploma in Restaurant Management – a nationally recognised qualification accredited by Nottingham Trent University.

McDonald's commitment to the development of its employees was nationally recognised in 1998 when the company achieved the Investor in People accreditation, awarded to the UK's leading employers.

History

The McDonald's story began in 1954 in San Bernadino, California, where a salesman called Ray Kroc was supplying milkshake multi-mixers to a drive-in restaurant run by two brothers, Dick and Mac McDonald. After calculating that the restaurant – which served 15 cent hamburgers with fries and a shake every fifteen seconds – must be selling over 2,000 milkshakes a month, Kroc saw the massive potential of the brothers' thriving business and decided to get involved. On 15th April 1955 Kroc became the McDonald brothers' first franchisee when he opened his own McDonald's restaurant in Des Plaines, a suburb just north of Chicago.

Rapid growth followed: McDonald's served more than 100 million hamburgers within its first three years of trading and in 1959, the 100th McDonald's restaurant was opened. In 1961 Kroc paid $2.7 million to buy out the McDonald brothers' interest and in 1963 the billionth McDonald's hamburger was served live on prime-time television.

The brand proved equally popular outside the US. McDonald's had successfully established markets in Canada, Japan, Australia and Germany by the time the Golden Arches made their debut appearance in the UK in 1974 in Woolwich, south east London. By 1988, worldwide sales had topped $16 billion and today McDonald's is represented on all five continents from Beijing to the Arctic Circle.

Product

McDonald's has evolved into an international, multi-billion dollar quick service restaurant industry. Hamburgers and fries remain the mainstay of its business but central to the brand's success has been a menu that constantly evolves and expands to meet the needs of changing consumer lifestyles and eating habits.

A prime example of this is the Filet-O-Fish which was conceived by Lou Groen, a Cincinnati-based franchisee whose restaurant operated in a predominantly Catholic area. After noticing that trade was slow on Fridays, Groen concluded that this was because Friday is a day of abstention from red meat for many Catholics and he set out to develop a fish-based product to meet the needs of the local community. The Filet-O-Fish was launched in 1963 and has since become a mainstay on many McDonald's international menus.

In 1968, another franchisee – Jim Deligatti from Pittsburgh – was responsible for the creation of the Big Mac, which is the best known and most successful McDonald's menu item ever. Nine years later, Deligatti developed the McDonald's breakfast menu – a move that would change the breakfast habits of millions of Americans in the years that followed.

This spirit of innovation has played an important part in the growth of the company which continuously seeks to improve the consumer perceived quality and convenience of the McDonald's experience. A major breakthrough came in 1975 with an idea that sprang from the need to solve a local sales problem: when servicemen from a nearby Army base in Sierra Vista, Arizona, were forbidden to leave their cars in military fatigues, the first drive-thru restaurant was opened. The concept was an immediate success, and today, drive-thru accounts for more than half of McDonald's business in many of its international markets.

McDonald's is committed to providing its customers with food of the highest quality. This is achieved by using the best raw ingredients, sourced from approved local suppliers and ensuring that food is prepared to a consistently high standard. The menu is continually reviewed and enhanced to ensure that it meets – and wherever possible exceeds – expectations. In the UK, the McDonald's menu

includes beef, chicken, fish and vegetarian products, a full range of desserts, shakes and hot and cold drinks. To help customers make informed decisions about their diet, McDonald's was the first quick service restaurant to publish a complete ingredient listing and detailed nutritional analysis of all its products.

Recent Developments

Two of the most successful innovations from McDonald's have been its Extra Value Meals and its Happy Meals.

Extra Value Meals offer customers a hamburger, drink and fries sold together at a fixed money saving price. The meal offering combines variety in the choice of food as it incorporates current promotions, ease of purchase and above all excellent value for money.

Similarly, McDonald's Happy Meal boxes offer parents a simple and appealing package, with a smaller portioned meal served in a fun box with a toy. The unique alliance that McDonald's has with Disney means it is able to combine the popularity of its food with all the magic of Disney.

It is innovations like these that have been instrumental in building the McDonald's family business and establishing the brand's ownership of value within the quick service restaurant sector.

In 1999 the 1000th UK McDonald's opened in the Dome at Greenwich. As the Official Community Sponsor of the New Millennium Experience, McDonald's investment created the 'Our Town Story' programme, which invited children from every local education authority (approximately 21,000) to tell their story in the form of a show performed live at the Dome in the specially designed Our Town Story theatre.

Promotion

McDonald's has always recognised the key role of marketing in the brand-building process. Advertising is certainly not the only cause of McDonald's success but the two are inseparable.

As Ray Kroc put it: "There's something just as basic to our success as the hamburger. That something is marketing McDonald's style. It's bigger than any person or product bearing the McDonald's name." To this day, a fixed proportion of restaurant sales is reinvested into advertising and sales promotion in every market in which McDonald's operates.

In the UK, high profile brand advertising has been instrumental in building a powerful emotional relationship between McDonald's and its customers. The fundamental warmth and humanity it has demonstrated in its communication remains unmatched by its competitors.

One of the strongest relationships that McDonald's has managed to build in the UK has been through football, the nation's favourite sport. Through a combination of the high-profile sponsorship of professional events and also the work it has done on a grassroots level, McDonald's has linked the brand with sport in a way none of its competitors can rival. McDonald's uses its association with such prestigious global events to reinforce its international brand stature, whilst its television advertising in the UK uses national heroes such as Alan Shearer, to endorse its association with the game on a local level.

McDonald's continuously displays a rare ability to act like a retailer while thinking like a brand; delivering sales for the immediate present, while building and protecting its long-term brand reputation.

In 1999, McDonald's successfully demonstrated its ability to do this by offering a series of themed new menu items, based on foods from around the world, such as Italian, Indian and Chinese. Each promotion was supported with heavy weight above the line advertising that communicated the theme of each promotion with a McDonald's twist, presenting the products from a very British perspective.

The Curry and Spice promotion parodied the old Pearl and Dean cinema commercials for local curry houses, and the Chinese promotion parodied the dubbed Kung Fu films of the 1970s, with classic speeded up fight scenes. The commercials served to strengthen the position of McDonald's as part of the fabric of British culture.

In 2000 McDonald's launched the McFlurry in the UK (whipped dairy ice cream with a choice of Cadbury's Dairy Milk, Crunchie or Smarties pieces mixed in). This type of innovation in its regular menu ensures incremental sales for McDonald's.

committed to local restaurant marketing. This commitment is an enduring testimony to Ray Kroc who subscribed passionately to the belief that McDonald's should contribute to the communities which it serves. Local activity takes many different forms, ranging from free coffee mornings for senior citizens to fund-raising work

with local schools, youth groups and hospitals.

In 1989 Ronald McDonald Children's Charities was established in the UK. The charity has raised more than £10 million to date and makes grants to charities which benefit children with special needs, as well as providing support to the families of sick children through Ronald McDonald Houses and Family Rooms which provide accommodation for parents of children who are in hospital.

Brand Values

Ray Kroc developed his brand vision for McDonald's around a simple but effective consumer-driven premise: quality, service, cleanliness and value (QSC&V). These values remain the cornerstone of the brand and as a result, McDonald's has become known as a trustworthy brand that places the customer at the centre of its world.

The key to the company's success has been its capacity to touch universal consumer needs with such consistency that the essence of the brand has always been relevant to the local culture.

In addition to national advertising and promotional campaigns, McDonald's is strongly

MONOPOLY

Market

It is heartening to know, particularly for those technophobes among us, that the traditional toy market is holding its own against the computer games industry. UK traditional toys and games, which is part of the leisure and entertainment market have sales remaining steady at £1.7 billion, which equates to about £160 per child per year, in spite of the growth of sales of video games and software by between 10% and 40% per year. UK board games have sales of about £170 million, of which Monopoly has the biggest share of a highly competitive market – its closest rivals presently are Scrabble and Trivial Pursuit. These games have become classics but their sales are often affected by new products such as Who Wants to Be a Millionaire.

The continued success of Monopoly, which was invented in 1933, is testimony to its universal appeal. Monopoly is now marketed and distributed by Hasbro Inc, one of the world's leading children and family entertainment companies whose product portfolio includes famous brand names such as Action Man, Cluedo and Mr Potato Head to name but a few.

Children grow up and toy fashions come and go, but few games have stood the test of time as Monopoly has. Nevertheless, traditional toy makers are using electronic technology to breathe new life into long-standing brands and increase consumer choice. Hasbro launched Handheld Electronic Monopoly in 1999 and has recently launched a new CD-Rom version of the game.

The UK Leisure and Entertainment market is estimated to be worth around £102 billion in 2000/2001 – about the same size as the total household food and alcohol markets put together. So while toy manufacturers have huge opportunities, the winners in what is a highly competitive market will be those who capture children's imaginations and realise their dreams, giving them the opportunity to play with toys better than they ever hoped for.

Achievements

Monopoly remains the most famous and best-selling boardgame in the world. For more than

65 years over 500 million players from around the globe have played Monopoly. Over 200 million sets of the game have been sold worldwide, and in Britain over twenty million sets have been sold since 1935 – that is over 640 million houses and over £302,800,000,000 in Monopoly money. Half a million Monopoly sets are sold in the UK each year.

Monopoly is licensed or sold in 80 countries and is published in 26 languages, including Croatian. The game had a strong following in Cuba until Fidel Castro took power and ordered all sets to be destroyed. In 1989 the first Russian Monopoly was produced, and the Russian version was first played in the UK by Sir Edward Heath. Many famous people play Monopoly, including the Queen, Frank Bruno and Richard Branson.

A set made by Alfred Dunhill that included gold and silver houses and hotels sold for £20,000, and a $1 million gold and precious stones set was produced in 1988 by jewellery designer Sidney Mobell of San Francisco. A chocolate version has also been available for £500.

Playing Monopoly is not just restricted to terra firma. Monopoly fanatics feel compelled to indulge their passion in the most extraordinary places, including baths, lifts, underground, underwater and on balance beams. The game has also been played extra-terrestrially – during a space mission by American astronauts.

Monopoly has achieved cult status, with fans vying to beat various records. To date, the record for the longest game played in a lift is sixteen days, in a bath 99 hours, and the record for the longest antigravitational game, played on a ceiling, is 36 hours. The current world record for the longest game ever is 1,680 hours, or 70 days of continuous play.

History

In 1933, as America struggled to emerge from the Depression, Charles Darrow decided to invent a new board game to play with his friends and, he hoped, make himself some money. For the board he used a piece of oilcloth

that had been a table covering, and he made the houses and hotels from scraps of wooden moulding. The cards and title deeds were all handwritten and the original tokens were reputedly from his wife's charm bracelet.

Demand for the game grew and Darrow increased his daily output to six sets by contracting the board production out to a printer friend. He soon contracted out the entire printing and packaging, and began selling to department stores, John Wanamaker in Philadelphia being the first to put the game on sale in 1934. When orders started to arrive in wholesale quantities he offered to sell the concept to Parker Brothers, the world's largest games manufacturer. Initially the company turned down Monopoly on the grounds that it was too long and complicated and contained 52 fundamental playing errors. Darrow decided to market the game on his own, and when Parker Brothers heard of its phenomenal success in 1935 they reconsidered and bought the rights.

Sales rocketed, and the company was shortly producing 20,000 sets a week. Sales have continued to rise ever since.

In 1935 John Waddingtons Ltd took over UK production of Monopoly, first 'translating' it into English. The Atlantic City place names were replaced by London landmarks, the railroads became stations, dollars became pounds, and the cards were changed accordingly. Marjory Phillips, who was secretary to the head of Waddingtons, Victor Watson, settled the final list of place names, and the only pub on the board, the Angel, Islington, is reputedly where she had lunch on the day of her Monopoly game tour.

Waddingtons continued to manufacture Monopoly, apart from a brief halt in its commercial production during World War II. Even then, the game played a significant part. The War Office commissioned Waddingtons to produce games which, 'if properly used, would help prisoners of war'. Waddingtons set up a secret department, manned by a few of its most trusted staff, and made Monopoly game sets with silk maps inserted into the boards showing escape routes from the particular prison to which each game was to be sent. A tiny compass and files were inserted into the other side of the board, and the Monopoly money was replaced by money of the country for which the game was destined.

Monopoly has changed very little over the years. In 1972 there were minor tweaks to the design – the tokens increased in size, for instance. In the 1970s a braille edition was introduced for the visually impaired.

In 1989 the game was relaunched to include the original character, Mr Monopoly who was on the box lid and board. The same year it was produced in Russian, and plans were laid for the ultimate capitalist game to be manufactured in the country that had once banned it.

In 1995 Monopoly celebrated its 60th birthday with a star-studded party and charity auction at London's Park Lane Hotel, and released a commemorative limited edition to mark the event.

In 1996 Hasbro created its first movie based

an edible chocolate version and a Monopoly calculator to work out your most complicated deals.

Recent Developments

In 2000 Hasbro launched Pokémon Monopoly, featuring the most popular Pokémon characters and a Coronation Street Monopoly to commemorate the soap's 40th anniversary. The streets in the traditional game have become house numbers in Coronation Street, with Mayfair becoming the Rover's Return pub. The stations have been replaced by icons of the show, including Bet Lynch's earrings, Hilda Ogden's ducks and Ena Sharples's hairnet. In 2000 Hasbro also launched a dedicated website – Monopoly.co.uk – to keep Monopoly fans updated with all the latest news. Further specialist editions of Monopoly are also in the pipeline.

collector's edition – Star Wars Monopoly.

Ahead of the 1998 World Cup Finals in France, a Monopoly World Cup edition was introduced with football stadiums instead of the traditional hotels. Eight specially commissioned metal playing pieces were produced – a football, a boot, a whistle, a set of goals, a cap, a drink, a burger and the World Cup trophy.

And in 1999 Monopoly linked up with the world's most famous football club to produce Manchester United Monopoly, featuring Sir Alex Ferguson and his treble winners trying their hand at the property market. A new handheld version of Monopoly was also launched in that year.

Product

Monopoly is the most famous board game in the world. There cannot be many people who do not recognise the origin of that familiar command: 'Go straight to jail. Do not pass go. Do not collect £200.' There are currently over twenty Monopoly games available in the UK including Junior Monopoly, a game designed for younger children with a fairground theme, Travel Monopoly, two football Monopolies – Premier League and Manchester Utd, Star Wars Episode 1 and twelve regional Monopolies based on the streets of major UK and Irish cities. There is also

Promotion

Monopoly is advertised on television to children of eight and over, as well as in the women's press. PR and PR events are also an important part of the marketing mix, and the National, European and World Monopoly championships are the best examples. The Monopoly World Championship is staged every four years and brings together the world's best Monopoly wheeler-dealers to decide who is the ultimate Monopoly Millionaire. The winner takes

home the Championship title, and the same amount of money as there is in a Monopoly set – £15,140.

In 1996 the World Championships in Monte Carlo attracted the elite from 36 countries and over forty countries participated in the 2000 contest in Toronto.

Brand Values

In 2000, its 65th year, Monopoly was still the best-selling board game in the world, underlining its position as 'everyone's favourite boardgame'. It carries associations of traditional family-oriented fun, and is relevant to everyone, both young and old, around the world.

The essence of the game is about making deals and taking risks with the ultimate goal of 'owning it all'. Winning, success and status are the rewards, combined with sharing a fun time with family or friends when children can compete on the same level as adults. It plays to the fantasy of wealth and success that everyone can indulge in.

Things you didn't know about
Monopoly

- A special Monopoly set was made for the underwater Monopoly marathon attempts at a cost of $15,000. It disintegrated after the last record-breaking attempt – a 1,080 hour marathon.

- Charles Darrow, the inventor of Monopoly, retired at the age of 46, a millionaire. He became a world traveller and collector of orchid species.

- The total amount of money in a standard Monopoly game is £15,140.

- The most frequently landed-on squares are Bow Street, Vine Street and Marlborough Street.

- In 1978 the Neiman Marcus Christmas catalogue offered a chocolate version of the game, priced at £500.

- The 1988 UK Monopoly Championship took place at the London Stock Exchange and the 1991 final of the UK championships was held at the Bank of England, where it was played with real money.

- The 1999/2000 European champion is MP and television personality Gyles Brandreth.

- The 1999 UK championship was won by Jeff Collins, a Monopoly novice from Northern Ireland, who went on to represent the UK at the world championships in October 2000.

- In 2000 Monopoly was voted 'Game of the Century' by the British Association of Toy Retailers.

Market

The UK ambient packaged cake market is currently valued at £1.2 billion. Despite a fall in consumption at teatime, the traditional mealtime for cake, the market has been experiencing 3% annual growth over recent years. The growth is driven mainly by new snacking and lunch box opportunities which reflect the evolution of UK eating habits from formal family mealtimes to grazing – smaller, less formal meals – and eating outside the home. The challenge for manufacturers within today's market is to maintain the place of cakes on the nation's everyday menu despite changing consumer needs and lifestyles.

Out of all UK households, 96% are buyers of cake, and 50% buy Mr Kipling cakes. The average annual spend on cake per capita is £28.40. Mr Kipling has a 10.9% value share of the cake market, making it the biggest branded player by some distance.

Achievements

Mr Kipling has been a fundamental driver in the development of ambient packaged cake in the UK. Launched in 1967 in London and southern regions, the brand became fully national by 1970. By 1976, Mr Kipling was a brand leader and it has retained its leadership position ever since.

Within one year of going national, there was 89% awareness of the brand, and over the following 30 years, Mr Kipling has been the only consistent advertiser in the ambient cake market, contributing significantly to the creation of a brand with a powerful and long-standing reputation. Mr Kipling is synonymous with cake, and remains the benchmark for quality and innovation in the ambient cake marketplace.

The Mr Kipling range currently includes 38 lines of cake. In addition to this, there are over fifteen seasonal products and limited editions launched every year which bring variety and refreshment to the brand, reflecting the constant drive for innovation.

History

From its infancy Mr Kipling capitalised upon a totally integrated marketing proposition, that was generated as a result of a close alliance between the food manufacturer Rank Hovis McDougall (RHM) and the advertising agency J Walter Thompson (JWT). Whilst RHM recognised the market potential, JWT developed a brand identity which aimed to capture consumers' hearts as well as their stomachs.

In 1965, RHM began work on a brand new range of cake completely different from existing product offerings. It had conducted research among 6,000 housewives which revealed a distinct lack of choice within the packaged cake market. Of the limited range available, the research indicated that most were seen as dull and unappetising, with packaging that did little to enhance the overall impression.

Having identified a gap in the market, RHM set about filling it. Several RHM bakeries were involved in the process of creating the unique new range. The programme was allied to the

installation of new and modern plants in the bakeries, for the concept demanded not just expertise in the manufacture of the cakes, but also that they should be delivered in the best and most colourful packaging the market had ever seen.

By 1967, the total cake market was worth £150 million and average annual spend per head was £3. Although cake was as popular as ever, traditional corner shops and village bakeries were in decline, with supermarkets and grocery stores accounting for an ever-increasing percentage of packaged goods sales. The market was ready, therefore, for a new range of packaged cake products which carried the same stamp of quality, integrity and expertise that local bakers had provided, but in a more modern and convenient format.

Meanwhile, advertising agency JWT had been working hard to craft an identity for the products which would both distinguish them and familiarise them with the consumer. It was felt that they should be thought of as being made by a person, a specialist, and so in May 1967 the concept of Mr Kipling was born.

The initial range of twenty Mr Kipling products was based on the traditional baker's shop, and packed in colourful, premium boxes with handles for carrying home. The image of the handled box became the familiar Mr Kipling logo and acted as a mark of expertise on a range including Chocolate, Apricot and Florida Jam Sponges, Cherry Genoa, Butter Cake, Ginger Cake, Chocolate Jaffas, Seville Layer Cake, Nutty Slices, Chocolate Fudge Gateaux, Swiss Rolls, Lemon Meringue Tarts and Pecan Cake. All of these have played an important role in the range over the past 30 years. Others that performed exceptionally in the initial research were Manor-House Cake, French Fancies, Jam Tarts, Battenburg and Almond Slices, and these remain firm favourites in the Mr Kipling range today.

Product

It has always been the Mr Kipling strategy to produce cakes that cannot be bettered by the competition. Prior to the launch of Mr Kipling, small cakes accounted for 30% of all cakes – including tarts, iced cakes, cream cakes and slices – yet there was an almost complete absence of good packaged small cakes in the market. The Mr Kipling concept of a master baker whose local business was small enough to personalise his cakes was reinforced by concentrating the range on small cakes. These had the dual advantage of being easier to use whilst being harder to replicate at home. This meant that Mr Kipling established a position

traditionally held by the small local baker.

Despite the growth of the brand to a £130 million business, Mr Kipling remains true to its original proposition. The cakes are all made of the highest quality ingredients, boxed in attractive, convenient packaging, and distributed to stores far and wide by a dedicated field sales force. The unmistakable Mr Kipling vans can still be spotted delivering cakes to stores across the UK, and although the salesmen's uniforms have evolved somewhat from their original chocolate-brown and white striped blazers, their commitment to the local, personalised brand values of Mr Kipling products remains unfaltering.

Recent Developments

In response to the growing consumer tendency to snack and eat on the move, Mr Kipling launched a selection of individually wrapped cakes in 2000. The range of Flapjacks, Caramel Shortcakes, Muffin Bars and Cake Bites are the first products to be available under the Cake2Go brand, with more Mr Kipling favourites and new products to follow in the future.

Continuing its drive for innovation, Mr Kipling has launched several new products recently, including Cherry and Coconut Flapjackers and Butterfly Cakes. Limited editions of Orange and Lemon Battenburgs, Summer Fondant Fancies and Chocolate and Orange Cake Bars have also had great success.

As the range has expanded to include over 60 products annually, so the packaging has evolved to remain at the forefront of convenience and freshness.

Several of the cakes are twin-wrapped inside their boxes for extra freshness, and the new boxes have been designed to enable easier opening and sharing.

The year 2000 was a significant milestone in the life of Mr Kipling, with considerable development underway in terms of brand identity, packaging and advertising communication. 2001 sees a major relaunch of the brand.

Promotion

Advertising and promotion for the Mr Kipling brand has been planned as a totally integrated concept ever since its launch. The original objective of expressing the personality of the brand not only through the products themselves, but through the brand name, packaging, pricing, advertising, display and merchandising, still remains today.

Television was chosen as the primary launch medium, partly for its impact and immediacy, and partly for its ability to express the warmth and friendliness of the Mr Kipling character. Television has continued as the major medium for the brand over the past 33 years, and the phrase 'Exceedingly good cakes' has become one of best known and most frequently quoted slogans in advertising.

Although Mr Kipling himself is a fictitious character, he has generated affection amongst consumers as a kindly old gentleman, very British, respectable and proper, with a dry sense of humour and twinkle in his eye. Most importantly, he is recognised as a master baker and craftsman.

In recent years the television campaign has evolved, reflecting the changing nature of the brand and bringing it more up to date. The modernisation of the Mr Kipling brand continues in 2001, and although the medium for future promotion will continue to be mostly television, the other elements of the marketing mix, from PR to branded delivery vans and tailor-made uniforms, will continue to have equal importance in communicating the Mr Kipling story.

In February 1999 Mr Kipling became involved in its first major non-television promotion as one of the key sponsors of the Comic Relief charity. A special cake was produced featuring the Comic Relief red nose symbol, with 5p from every pack being donated directly to the Comic Relief fund. In the summer of 2000 the Mr Kipling Strawberry Sundae was featured at the Wimbledon Tennis Championships, and a figure in a giant Strawberry Sundae costume could be seen sampling the product outside the grounds of the All England Lawn Tennis Club.

Brand Values

Mr Kipling cakes have a high quality appearance, with a light and moist texture crafted by traditional methods to modern standards. They contain superlative quality ingredients and the right total recipe. This translates into a concept whose basic appeal is adult self-indulgence, a

treat rather than a food, which generates a feeling of happiness from a brand that is warm, friendly and personable. The brand values have evolved to reflect a product that can be eaten any time, any place, with modern, convenient packaging to appeal to today's consumer.

Things you didn't know about
Mr Kipling

More than 64 million Mr Kipling apple pies are sold per year.

In 1999, Mr Kipling made nearly 36 million Mini Battenburg cakes.

One in every two households in the UK consumes Mr Kipling cakes.

Mr Kipling cakes are exported to America, Australia, New Zealand, Europe, Canada and the Middle East.

Nationwide

Market

Before the financial deregulation of the 1980s, UK banks had a stranglehold on the supply of many personal financial services. After this point a diverse range of institutions entered this market. Building societies expanded their basic product offering to encapsulate personal banking and indeed several made the conversion to bank status, continuing consolidation through mergers and acquisitions. Other new entrants included supermarkets, insurance companies and online banks — all factors which have transformed the market and customers' expectations.

Nationwide is the largest building society in the world, and its commitment to remaining owned by its members rather than shareholders ensures its distinction from profit-driven high street banks. Nationwide remains at the forefront — not just as the UK's fourth largest mortgage lender and ninth largest retail banking, saving and lending organisation by asset size, but as a socially responsible organisation that prides itself in taking a leading position as consumer champion.

Achievements

One of Nationwide's proudest achievements is the £1 billion returned to its members between 1996-2000 in the form of better rates and products — clear evidence of the benefit of being a building society. But Nationwide has many other accolades and achievements to celebrate, and its trophy cabinet is a tribute to the benefits mutuality can bring. In 2000 alone the Society won twenty top awards for its excellent value and service, technological innovation, and employee focus. On the product side, it earned recognition with a raft of mortgage awards, topped by Your Mortgage magazine's special recognition as 'Lender of the Decade', as well as awards for its current account, online banking service, and internet website. Meanwhile, its savings, banking and mortgage products continue to appear consistently in the Best Buy tables in the national press, with Which? magazine highlighting its current account and travel insurance cover.

In 1987 Nationwide revolutionised the banking experience when it launched FlexAccount — the first full service current account to pay interest. The supporting television and press campaign won international acclaim. In 1999 the CashCard FlexAccount was introduced, giving people who do not have access to full banking facilities the opportunity to benefit from services such

as standing orders, Direct Debits and cash machine withdrawals. In 2000, the full service FlexAccount was named 'Best Overall Current Account' by Personal Finance Magazine.

Nationwide's achievements are not all product-oriented. It is a leader in the field of technological innovation with the world's first trial of a speech verification system, the world's most advanced self-service multi-media information system, and cash machines that recognise iris patterns in the eye as an alternative to PIN numbers.

In 1993 Nationwide became the first major building society to achieve the Investor In People award at the first attempt and is now the first financial services organisation to receive this accreditation three times. Nationwide aims to become a world leader in terms of employee care and its efforts are rewarded by the enthusiasm and imagination with which employees enter into the spirit of serving the community through charitable activities and fund-raising events.

Since 1994 Nationwide employees and members have raised nearly £2 million for Macmillan Cancer Relief, which is Nationwide's flagship charity. It has also established community-spirited initiatives such as the Nationwide Awards for Voluntary Endeavour, which recognise the efforts of individuals and groups in all parts of the country, and more recently the Local Heritage Initiative in conjunction with the Countryside Agency and the Heritage Lottery Fund.

History

Nationwide is the product of more than a hundred mergers, most significantly between the Nationwide and the Anglia Building Societies in 1987. Its history goes as far back as 1848, when a small assembly of men in the back of

LENDER OF THE DECADE

NATIONWIDE BUILDING SOCIETY

a tailor's shop in Northampton set about achieving their vision: 'to improve the social, to promote the moral and exalt the political condition of the unenfranchised millions'. So the Northampton Town and Country

Freehold Land Society was born in response to the shortage of housing in the area. Over time the society evolved into the Anglia Building Society.

Similarly in 1883, the committee of the Guild of Co-operators met in Londonto form the Southern Co-operative Permanent Building Society — a society that would make loans to enable co-operative retail societies to buy their own premises and individual members to buy their own houses. When the Co-operative Permanent Building Society withdrew from the Co-operative Union in 1970 a new identity was needed and the name 'Nationwide' was adopted.

Under the Nationwide name the society expanded rapidly, becoming a household name and fulfilling its ambitious growth plans by joining forces with the Anglia Building Society in 1987.

The resulting society boasted a larger branch network than any other building society and was set to change the face of retail banking. Ten years later, Nationwide had become the 'World's No.1 Building Society'. Despite its size and modernity, the Nationwide of today still holds true to the principles of its founding members of yesteryear.

Product

By having member, not shareholder, satisfaction as its focus, Nationwide is able to give customers better long-term benefits through its extensive product range. Nationwide offers a complete range of value-for-money products and services to meet financial needs at every life stage. Comprising more than just mortgages, its range now includes savings accounts, banking services, pensions, personal loans, credit cards and insurance for the home, car, travel, health, life and mortgage payments.

Core mortgage and savings products constantly evolve to meet consumer demand and product development at Nationwide means innovation and choice for the consumer. The Nationwide mortgage range now offers a wide choice of discounted, fixed rate, base rate tracker and cashback mortgages. Although extensive, the range remains simple and is underpinned by Nationwide's commitment to long term good value for members, which means a market-leading Standard Variable Rate and no hidden fees.

The key development on the savings side has been the recent launch of e-Savings, which is accessed through the internet and gives Nationwide current account holders the opportunity to earn a higher rate of interest. Another notable success was the introduction of Nationwide's instant access cash Individual Savings Account (ISA), which was consistently recognised as a 'best buy' in the national press, leading to the opening of some 840,000 accounts in its first year.

Recent Developments

Nationwide positions itself at the cutting edge of technological innovation, making the future of banking available to customers today. In 1997, years in advance of today's internet banks, it became the first UK financial services organisation

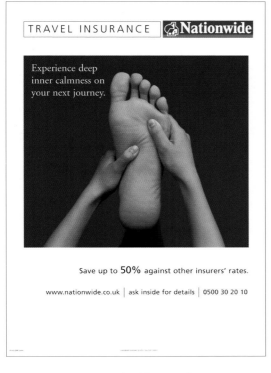

to launch an internet banking service – now recognised as one of the best. Where Nationwide differs from the new entrants and most of its competitors is that cheaper access channels such as the internet are not introduced to replace the one-to-one experience of using a branch, but to complement it.

Nationwide soon followed up this development by becoming an internet service provider – the first financial organisation to make access to the internet itself available to its members. It was also the first to develop a website, www.nationwide.co.uk, making use of interactive features including a mortgage calculator, a savings calculator, a house price calculator, a branch and cash machine finder facility, and the FootballNOW! area. In line with its policy of making products and services accessible to all, Nationwide has begun to install internet terminals for customer use in its branches, making it easy for everyone to access its award-winning website and internet banking service.

Nationwide has a track record in bringing innovations to the mass market and has been monitoring potential areas of interactive television, mobile phones, speech recognition/verification and electronic signatures. It is leading the traditional providers within the financial services industry by developing an integrated set of financial services products over the internet.

Promotion

Its position as a building society has not held Nationwide back in terms of its promotional style. In an evolutionary process, the underlying values of a mutual organisation were constantly re-framed to keep message relevant to the contemporary audience.

In 1992 the use of stop frame animation and a catchy signature tune became Nationwide's most memorable award-winning television campaign. Originally demonstrating accessibility and mass market appeal, this successful formula was updated and applied again in 1998.

Nationwide's style had been firmly established as innovative and human – displaying a personality that set it apart from traditional financial services providers. The same personality was translated into a new style for the 2000 television, outdoor and press campaign featuring relaxation techniques, which used understated visual humour to convey the message 'Relax – it's Nationwide.'

Creative innovation has also been reflected in Nationwide's press and branch promotions, direct mail, and even in its choice of media – which has included ATM screens and singing bus shelters. Successful campaigns have included a current account promotion portraying revolutionary demands on behalf of consumers, and mortgage campaigns using fast-moving consumer goods, such as shampoos and coffee, to portray the blend of ingredients to be found in Nationwide mortgage products and a 'sale' to convey the competitive pricing proposition.

Nationwide's commitment to the principle of accessibility led it to choose football sponsorship to raise awareness of the brand by reaching many millions of football supporters. In the spirit of all-inclusiveness, Nationwide is currently the biggest sponsor of football in the UK at all levels from grass roots to the national team.

In the context of evolving promotional activities and style, Nationwide has ensured that its logo is robust enough to represent the brand in the twenty first century as effectively as it has done in the past. In 2000 the logo was updated to incorporate a striking red underline – ensuring maximum impact, strength and modernity whilst retaining the values traditionally associated with the brand.

However, the true image of Nationwide – as perceived by the media, its members and the general public – rests on good value products and member-focused service. It is this that ensures Nationwide always stands out from the competition.

Brand Values

Long-term value, trust, fairness, honesty, openness, innovation, and true member focus drive the decision-making process within Nationwide. It has devoted more than 150 years to putting members first, and its roots still remain firmly in the local communities it serves. In the new era of internet account management, one-stop-shops and automation within which financial service providers compete, these are values that underpin all Nationwide's activities.

Nationwide's position as consumer champion is clearly demonstrated by its leading role in the campaign against cash machine charges proposed by banks, resulting in victory for consumers. Its commitment to free access for all means its own cash machine network is under continuous and imaginative expansion, and alternative access channels are constantly evaluated with a view to development for the benefit of the consumer. But its commitment to branch service remains strong, and Nationwide is opening new branches and refurbishing old ones at a time when former societies are closing theirs.

Nationwide's fulfilment of its brand values means it is now perceived by financial journalists as the UK's most trustworthy financial service organisation (Source: MORI survey) and it appears to have cultivated a confidence among the nation's young and old who trust it to provide competitive rates and professional customer support.

John Huet

Market

Sportswear has been a thriving market in recent years. From the moment training shoes began to be seen on the streets in the 1970s, the sports share of the total footwear market has expanded steadily, reaching 21.5% in 1998. UK sports footwear sales in 1998 were £1.05 billion, and the figure is set to top £1.20 billion by 2002 (Source: Mintel 1998). Footwear accounted for an estimated 30% of the consumer sports goods market in 1998, with a further 52% accounted for by clothing, and equipment (18%) making up the balance.

Globally this is a market in which brand is all-important, dominated by 'the big three' – Nike, Reebok and adidas. These companies have succeeded in evolving their products into lifestyle icons for millions of consumers across the world. In emerging markets 'the big three' brands are aspired to as symbols of modern sophistication, but they remain equally desirable in the US, Western Europe and other highly developed countries.

Achievements

Nike's growth has been phenomenal. Globally it is a $9 billion company and the largest in its market, having started as recently as 1971. Europe has been the star region for Nike recently, with revenues growing by 23% annually from 1996 to 2000. Britain is Nike's second-biggest market and Nike is the UK market leader, despite being a company with American origins in a country which is obsessive about football. Possibly Nike's greatest achievement in the UK has been to bring a new dynamism to football marketing.

History

The roots of Nike are on a running track at the University of Oregon, which is where the two founders met. Bill Bowerman was the track and field coach there, and during his tenure Oregon produced no fewer than 33 Olympians. He was so determined to help his athletes excel that he made shoes for them by hand in his spare time. Phil Knight was one of his runners. Together they founded Blue Ribbon Sports, the company that became Nike. Initially they each put up $500 to buy some Japanese

sports shoes which Knight sold at high school track events out of the back of a car. Their first major athlete endorser was Steve Prefontaine, holder of every US record from 2,000 to 10,000 metres.

The Nike name made its debut in the 1972 Olympic Trials. The company grew steadily until it held half of the booming US running footwear market by 1979. In that year Nike introduced AIR technology. It became number one in the US sports shoe market in 1981. The company grew rapidly as its basketball business took off and expansion took place in other areas such as tennis and baseball, spearheaded by high-profile athletes such as John McEnroe.

The mid 1980s were awkward times. The company had to overhaul much of its infrastructure and failed to take advantage of the aerobics boom. However it emerged stronger and more competitive. One reason for this was Nike's relationship with a young basketball star called Michael Jordan. His first signature shoe, the Air Jordan, was banned by US basketball authorities and became so prized that an unofficial secondary market developed with prices well above retail. 1987 was a momentous year in which 'Visible Air' was introduced for the first time, seen in a ground-breaking commercial set to the Beatles' song 'Revolution', which somehow caught the spirit of mass enthusiasm for playing sport and being physical. In that year Nike also introduced the first Cross-Trainers, multi-functional shoes for people with multiple sporting interests.

In order to be a truly global company, however, Nike recognised that most of the rest of the world was in love with football, a sport which wasn't particularly popular in the US. Nike's early football products lacked a real advantage, but as they steadily

improved, supported by great athletes and good advertising, Nike became a dynamic major brand in football. In the UK the company's profile was boosted by its association with football stars such as Ian Wright and Eric Cantona. During the 1990s UK sales grew by 600% and in 1999 London got its own Niketown – a superstore dedicated exclusively to Nike products.

Another important development, reflecting the fact that Nike is an athletic brand rather than a youth brand, was the company's expansion into golf. Nike began to work with Tiger Woods in 1996 and he won the US Masters by twelve strokes the following year.

Product

Since Nike was set up by someone who made shoes in his garage and someone else who ran in them, it is not surprising that product is important. The product goal is simple – to enhance athletic performance. That simple goal has led to some impressive innovations.

The first highlight was the Waffle outsole. Inspired by his wife's waffles, Bill Bowerman poured rubber into a waffle iron. The resulting outsole was durable, light, well-cushioned, and had good traction. It was initially known as the Moon Shoe for its unique footprint.

In 1980 Nike AIR arrived, courtesy of a former NASA engineer called Frank Rudy. His idea of using pressurised gas to cushion impact was pitched to a few shoe companies, but only Nike took it up. Shoes with air-filled urethane bags were tried out by Phil Knight and his staff on training runs. Initial scepticism soon evaporated as they realised that here was something that not only felt good, but really worked in preventing injury.

More recently, to obtain maximum performance, Nike shoes have used materials ranging from Kevlar to recycled old shoes manufactured in anything from silver mesh to shiny gold.

In clothing, one of Nike's technological advantages has been the FIT system, a four-fabric layering system that can cope with heat, cold, snow, wind, and copious amounts of sweat. People who have worn it rarely go back to cotton.

Nike equipment has also introduced innovations with real practical value. The Triax running watch gave runners numbers they could read and buttons they could find, in an asymmetrical format that sat better on the wrist.

Recent Developments

Tiger Woods started using the new Tour Accuracy golf ball, and shortly afterwards picked up Open championships on both sides of the Atlantic to become the youngest-ever winner of the Grand Slam.

Nike launched a division to make gear such as the Personal Sport Audio, which uses digital technology to create a no-skip, small-scale personal audio player ideal for sport.

Other significant product developments include Nike Shox. Nike Shox is regarded as the biggest technological development in footwear since AIR, described by the company as being 'like having springs in your feet'.

And anyone watching the Premiership in 2001 will see Nike's Geo Merlin ball in action – a faster and more accurate football.

Promotion

Nike is famous for its advertising as well as its athletes. They are the twin pillars of Nike promotion. The company does not hire athletes simply as mobile posters. They are the brand as much as products, advertising, or the people who work at Nike. The Nike personality has received contributions from such diverse characters as Ian Botham, Marion Jones, Steve Ovett, Seb Coe, Ronaldo, Sonia O'Sullivan, and the England rugby team. In this way a multi-faceted brand has been created. Instead of presenting one consistent, manicured proposition, Nike has over time delivered a wide variety of messages and exposed a number of different aspects of its personality. This is true to the athletic experience, and keeps the brand fresh.

Nike's advertising has been as diverse as its athletes. Much of it has featured top names, but not all. One of the commercials that launched 'Just Do It' featured an elderly runner in his 80s with false teeth. Ordinary athletes, people who might not even describe themselves as athletes, have found direct inspiration from Nike advertising. Nike adverts have featured celebrities as diverse as Dennis Hopper, Spike Lee and Bugs Bunny. A famous basketball star, Penny Hardaway, was given a puppet as an alter ego. The Brazilian football team was famously let loose in an airport during the 1998 World Cup.

Much Nike advertising appears to have been created without reference to marketing textbooks or batteries of research data. It frequently lacks an explicit product message, even a consistent endline, and has encompassed a wide variety of different advertising ideas. But the resulting 'post-advertising' has certainly struck a chord with a generation highly attuned to the tricks of the marketing trade.

In the UK, Nike has run advertising developed for a variety of intended markets, from London only, right through to global campaigns. Highlights have included some famously provocative posters, the 'Parklife' commercial celebrating the world of Sunday League football and the transformation of a Tube station into a tennis court for Wimbledon 1997. A year later, after England's traumatic exit from the World Cup, the company caught the mood of a shell-shocked nation with its 'Condolence' television advertisement.

Brand Values

For a company which has such a strongly defined personality, it may be surprising that there is no single list of brand values that is given to new employees and used to judge all marketing activity. Things do get written down, but fundamentally the Nike values are passed on through an oral tradition. And they are company values as much as brand values. The Nike brand comes over as risk-taking, competitive, irreverent and overwhelmingly consumed by sport. This is reflected in the people who work for the company.

NIVEA

Market

The market for skin care products is huge, diverse and ever-changing. Clear, healthy-looking skin is prized the world over, and women in particular are willing to invest time and money in products that promise to maximise its beauty potential. The sales figures speak for themselves: £215 million was spent on facial skin care products in the UK in 1999, while the sun care market is worth a staggering £111 million. General skin care, a sector that includes body moisturising formulas and hand lotions, was worth £91 million, and lip care £22 million. Interestingly, men are becoming more important to the market: sales of male facial skin care products witnessed growth of 209% in 1999, reaching a substantial £3.9 million (Source: IRI 2000).

The market is being driven by technology. Consumers are eager to try new, advanced formulas while demand for the next great innovation places enormous pressure on those companies active in this sector. Manufacturers at every level must maintain a frenetic programme of new product development in order to keep up with their competitors. The self-select skin care market is dominated by a small number of large brands, as only those manufacturers with significant research budgets can hope to compete in such a technology-focused arena. Foremost among these is Beiersdorf, manufacturer of NIVEA: the largest skin care brand in the world.

Achievements

The NIVEA brand now has a significant presence in over 160 countries, with its core business in Europe. In the UK its general skin care sales reached £23 million in 1999: accounting for around one quarter of the £91 million general skin care market. Its performance in other sub-categories is also impressive. It can claim a 16% share of the sun care category, 10% of the lip care market, 10% of the facial skin care sector and 69% of the male facial skin care market (Source: IRI 2000).

While these sales figures measure the commercial success of the NIVEA brand, they also represent a triumph in awareness penetration: the NIVEA name is synonymous with quality skin care on a global level. Its strong heritage as a brand that heals, soothes and nurtures the skin has generated unprecedented levels of trust among the world's consumers.

This solid foundation has allowed Beiersdorf to extend the brand's reach into all areas of skin care, from anti-ageing facial moisturisers to lip balms, hand lotions, sun care, body moisturisers and skin care for men.

As part of a wide and diverse portfolio, each product is developed by pioneering cosmetic scientists responsible for many major breakthroughs in skin care technology.

When NIVEA Creme was introduced nearly 90 years ago, it was already making skin care history as the first stable oil-in-water emulsion, and comparable groundbreaking innovations continue to this day. For instance, the importance of co-enzyme Q10 as a topical anti-ageing skin care ingredient was discovered by Beiersdorf scientists in 1998. The company successfully harnessed this vital substance and preserved its energy-giving properties in a delivery-system that works in harmony with the skin for the topical management of fine lines and wrinkles.

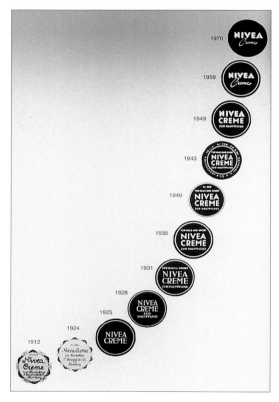

History

When Dr Oscar Troplowitz, medical researcher and owner of the Beiersdorf Company, decided to apply technology developed for making medical ointments to a new kind of cosmetic cream, he could scarcely have imagined that his work would still be world famous nearly a century later. The year was 1911, the place Hamburg, and a new emulsifier called Eucerit had caught the attention of a dermatologist called Professor Paul Gerson Unna, who happened to be Dr Troplowitz's scientific advisor.

Eucerit was an oil-in-water emulsion which encouraged the skin to repair itself, making it an ideal base for emollient ointments. However, Eucerit was special also because it was so stable, and this stability allowed medical ointments to be pre-packaged and stored. This had significant implications for first-aid medical treatment, but it also meant that cosmetic skin care formulas could be packaged, shipped and marketed on a global scale.

With Eucerit's creator Dr Isaac Lifschütz, the three men conceived, developed and marketed NIVEA Creme, a blend of Eucerit, glycerine, citric acid, rose oil and lily of the valley. Dr Troplowitz was so impressed with the pure whiteness of the formula, an indication of its fundamental stability, that he named it after the Latin word for snow white.

NIVEA Creme quickly gained a reputation for effective skin care and proved so successful that by the end of the decade a variety of soap and powder products had been launched under the NIVEA name. It also quickly became a global brand, reaching the UK and US in 1922, and South America in 1926 – a remarkable achievement given the turbulence and austerity in Europe and elsewhere during these years.

While NIVEA Creme's reputation as a soothing, healing skin moisturiser was consolidated over the next five decades, it was the 1970s that saw NIVEA make consistent moves to extend its product portfolio into other areas of skin care. This trend continued in line with both scientific discoveries and consumer demand, so that now the NIVEA brand is one of the most recognised and trusted skin care propositions in the world.

Product

The NIVEA brand name is now familiar on a wide range of skin care platforms. It enjoys a strong emotional heritage, as many people first encounter the soothing properties and distinctive fragrance of NIVEA Creme in childhood.

While NIVEA Creme remains the brand's signature product, a wide portfolio of sub-brands address specific skin care needs, and fortifies its reputation as the brand that cares for the whole family's skin.

NIVEA Creme works with the epidermis to minimise moisture loss, replenish lost or missing lipids, and replace the skin's natural protective barrier. It is ideal for soothing the dry stages of eczema, dermatitis and psoriasis, as well as the maintenance of everyday dry skin and the treatment of minor sunburn and nappy rash. In 1997 the NIVEA Creme proposition was adapted for younger consumers with the launch of NIVEA Soft.

NIVEA Visage is a complete facial skin care range offering cleansing, moisturising and anti-ageing formulas for women of all ages. The portfolio includes light Moisturising Fluid suitable for younger, oilier skins, and the Anti-Wrinkle Q10 Repair range for epidermal age management. The most recent innovation is NIVEA Visage Soft Facial Cleansing Wipes: disposable moisturising cleansing tissues that address the time-conscious skin care consumer.

NIVEA Sun provides exceptional sun protection for the whole family, and is committed to promoting the vital sun care message that protection must start as early in life as possible. A range of high-factor sunscreens provides ultimate protection from UV damage, while special sub-ranges meet the sun care requirements of skin with special needs, such as sensitive or compromised skin and that of children.

Because healthy skin is a top-to-toe concern, NIVEA Body is well-placed to deliver its skin care expertise below the neckline too. The current NIVEA Body range includes a spray-on moisturiser: a fast, convenient oil-in-water emulsion that can be applied quickly, spreads evenly over the skin, and is instantly absorbed to restore vital moisture to the epidermis.

For anti-ageing body care, NIVEA Body Firming Lotion with Q10 utilises Beiersdorf's coenzyme Q10 technology to help restore smoothness and elasticity all over the body and deliver long-lasting moisture where needed.

The NIVEA Hand range comprises caring, nourishing formulas that utilise similar technology originally developed for facial and body skin care, to ensure that hands stay soft, supple and young-looking.

There are four formulas in the NIVEA Lip Care range. Each contains advanced microspheres of skin-similar lipids small enough to slip between the epidermal lip cells to deliver superconditioning moisture. Sunscreens, vitamins and natural oils help protect, moisturise and repair vulnerable skin on the lips.

Recent Developments

NIVEA for Men was introduced in 1998 and has been credited with founding the market for male-specific skin care formulas. The range offers a choice of facial moisturisers and a cleansing range that includes blackhead removal strips, as well as shaving-oriented toiletries. An on-going promotional campaign is substantially growing the market year-on-year.

Facial cleansing has long been a problematic sector for skin care manufacturers as so many women reject it as too time-consuming. NIVEA's answer was a range of disposable emollient facial wipes that are effective enough to remove even water-proof eye make-up, yet gentle and moisturising enough to leave skin soft, smooth and comfortable.

Anti-ageing formulas are currently driving the whole skin care market, and Beiersdorf is at the forefront with NIVEA's Q10 technology. First introduced in 1998, the NIVEA Visage Anti-Wrinkle Q10 Repair range broke new ground in anti-ageing skin care technology, and the subsequent

innovations introduced around its Q10 proposition indicate that it will continue to be a major factor in the anti-ageing skin care market. Beiersdorf has also launched Q10 hand creme, body lotion and after sun formulas.

As life becomes more and more hectic, so consumers demand time-saving products. Because the time-factor was a barrier to many consumers using sun care products, Beiersdorf developed a range of Sun Protection Sprays: light, quickly absorbed SPF formulas that allow time-conscious consumers to literally spray and go. The range subsequently proved particularly popular with men and teenagers. Following the success of NIVEA's Sun Sprays, 1999 also saw the launch of a NIVEA Body Spray, formulated to encourage more women to invest in body moisturising.

Promotion

NIVEA has a strong advertising heritage, with campaigns as far back as 1920 focusing on many of the benefits and values the brand still stands for today. An integrated multi-media campaign is key to success in the skin care sector, and NIVEA benefits from television, radio, print, direct mail, sampling and ambient advertising in line with new product development and seasonal demand.

For NIVEA, promotion goes hand in hand with education, and many campaigns have been devised to communicate key messages that reinforce the association of healthy skin with general fitness and wellbeing. Joint promotions with breakfast cereals and mineral water manufacturers, as well as the David Lloyd chain of fitness centres proved mutually beneficial for all concerned, while NIVEA's school sun care campaigns are renowned for communicating in a fun and motivating way the necessity of protecting children's skin from the sun. Through its strong promotional heritage NIVEA is credited

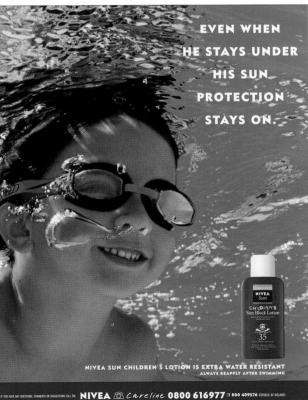

with kick-starting a number of problematic skin care submarkets, including body care and skin care for men, in which the company invested substantial amounts of its promotional budgets in basic consumer education.

While this may prove costly in the short term, long-term investment in the skin care sector serves to consolidate NIVEA's position as a leading skin care manufacturer and a source of valuable advice that inspires consumer trust and loyalty.

Brand Values

'NIVEA cares for your skin', the current strapline, is key to the complex emotional values associated with the NIVEA brand, values that have changed little since it was established nearly 100 years ago. Promotional visuals focus on health and wellbeing, the family, positivity, harmony and serenity. It is reflected and reinforced by the specific shade of blue that identifies the brand, its clean and pure imagery, light and calming fragrance and consistent delivery of its claims.

Family values are important to NIVEA's brand profile, as generations of consumers trust the brand to care for their children's skin as well as their own. While this strong family heritage is important to its continued success, appealing to younger, more fashion-conscious consumers is a key consideration too. By blending dynamic product innovation with stylish, contemporary imagery, the brand has effectively remained as relevant to today's teens and twenty-somethings as to their parents' generation.

Things you didn't know about NIVEA

The typography of the NIVEA® logo was specially created for the brand and is used internationally to identify it.

The signature shade of blue was specially mixed, and is known as: Ivocart NIVEA Blue B 65711.

Every five seconds someone in the world purchases a pot of NIVEA Visage Anti-Wrinkle Q10 Repair Creme.

According to ACNielsen data, the number of NIVEA Creme pots ever sold is equivalent to every single person who has ever lived.

NOKIA

Market

There's probably no faster growing market at the moment than mobile communications. At the last count – guaranteed to be out of date by the time you read this – there were 450 million mobile phone users in the world. By the end of 2002, that number is predicted to reach one billion. It is estimated that of the 275 million phones sold in 1999, 78.5 million were Nokia units, making it the world's largest mobile phone manufacturer.

Over the next few years, the telecommunications industry will face a period of massive change as we alter the way we communicate and work. This new era will be called the Mobile Information Society as a number of new technological innovations become readily available. These are: Wireless Application Protocol (WAP), Symbian, Bluetooth and Wireless Imaging.

WAP puts the internet into consumers' pockets, it offers customers access to many text based services available on the internet such as news, banking, weather reports, entertainment guides and share prices. WAP access is already available on many mobile phones – and the type of services available are growing all the time. Nokia offers WAP on its Nokia 6210, Nokia 7110 and Nokia 9110i Communicator handsets.

Symbian is a joint venture between Nokia and other companies to develop a new operating system for mobile information devices. Bluetooth is a short-range radio interface that enables interconnectivity between different types of electronic devices like mobile phones, digital cameras and PCs. Wireless Imaging will allow voice and visual content to be exchanged between terminals.

In addition, the arrival of third generation (3G) mobile communications allows for increases in the size and type of data which can be sent over the telecommunications networks.

Achievements

In 1998, Nokia became the world's leading supplier of mobile phones. The company has also been credited with making the mobile phone a mass-market item.

However, this milestone was no more than the end result of nearly a decade of achievement under the guidance of Jorma Ollila, Nokia's chairman and CEO.

Nokia was one of the first manufacturers to recognise that mobiles would become more than an expensive toy and be regarded as essential business and consumer accessories.

If there is one technical achievement that stands out for Nokia, it was being first into GSM. By developing the GSM technology (leading digital standard for mobile phones) and predicting that GSM would generate huge demand for handsets and networks, Nokia were in a prime position when digital mobile phones took off, whilst many competitors were still making analogue handsets.

History

Nokia was founded in 1865 by Fredrik Idestam. In those days it was a wood pulp mill on the banks of a river in Tampere, Finland, but Idestam soon moved it to a new position where a town slowly grew up around it. The town was given the name it still holds today – Nokia.

Initially, the company manufactured paper and card, but the business changed as it joined forces with the Finnish Rubber Company. It took the Nokia name and the company then became known for making galoshes.

In the 1920s Nokia took over the Finnish Cable Works in Helsinki. This saw the start of the industrial conglomerate that survived until the 1990s, with the three companies making anything from rubber tyres and cables to boats and raincoats. They formally merged in 1967 to form the Nokia Corporation. Nokia Plastics began operations in the early 1970s and in 1982 the group acquired Finnish Chemicals.

At the beginning of the 1980s, Nokia strengthened its position in the telecommunications and consumer electronic markets by acquiring Mobira, Salora, Telenokia and Luxor of Sweden.

In 1984 its Mobira Talkman was the world's first transportable phone (complete with a 22lb

charging box the size of a suitcase). In 1987 it launched the Cityman, the first hand-held mobile phone (about the same size as a loaf of bread).

Since the beginning of the 1990s Nokia has concentrated on its core business – telecommunications.

Product

Today, Nokia is made up of two groups: Nokia Networks and Nokia Mobile Phones. It also has a separate Nokia Ventures Organisation. By the end of 1999, Nokia had sales to over 130 countries, research and development in fourteen countries and production in eleven.

Nokia is best known for its mobile phones, selling one in four of all the phones purchased around the world in 1999. Beautifully styled products combined with cutting edge technology are extremely important to Nokia (in 1999 alone, it launched eighteen new models). It makes some of the smallest and sleekest handsets on the market like the super-small Nokia 8890, the stylish Nokia 8210 and the immensely popular Nokia 3310. Nokia was also the first manufacturer to launch a fully WAP-enabled phone – the Nokia 7110 in 1999, as well as the Nokia 9110 Communicator – a combined phone, fax, e-mail, web browser and personal organiser.

NOKIA
CONNECTING PEOPLE

Sound quality like this is music to your ears: improved reception, wide range with a built-in antenna.

As well as making mobile phones, Nokia is a leading supplier of data, video and voice network solutions. In addition, it is a world-leading supplier of mobile and fixed access solutions, as well as broadband and IP network solutions. It also supplies digital multimedia terminals for digital television and interactive services via satellite, cable and terrestrial networks.

Recent Developments

In February 2000, Nokia Ventures expanded its operations into Europe by opening a headquarters in London. This highlights the importance of the growing wireless internet sector in Europe and Nokia's leading role in developing it. Formed in 1998, Nokia Ventures invests in the internet, wireless, e-commerce and new media ventures. To date, it has invested in around fifteen start-up companies, such as eVoice, Pogo.com and FusionOne.

Promotion

Nokia Mobile Phones focuses on its 'Connecting People' message. Its advertising campaigns, highlight the technical advances of its phones, and portray the products as lifestyle accessories as well as cutting edge phones.

As well as television, Nokia makes imaginative use of other media. In 1999,

the company struck a high profile product placement deal to have its phones featured in the hit Keanu Reeves film, The Matrix.

In 2000 Nokia handsets were featured in the re-make of the seventies classic, Charlie's Angels starring Cameron Diaz, Drew Barrymore and Lucy Liu. The Angels – as the world's most stylish crime fighters – use Nokia's most fashionable mobile phones to help outwit their adversaries.

The Nokia 8210 is the mobile for the fashion conscious individual who wants a phone that looks good and performs

well. For customers determined to be at the forefront of fashion, new Xpress-on™ covers for the handset are introduced regularly. The Nokia 8210 is supported by stylish press and outdoor advertisements that feature trendy, colourful characters, using the individual Nokia 8210 handset covers to suit them.

Since 1997 Nokia has held the title of 'Official Mobile Phone of London Fashion Week', a sponsorship which reinforces the company's style and fashion credentials. Nokia runs a fashion-byte text message news service which keeps the media and the public in the 'fashion-know' with updates on catwalk trends and party gossip. The Nokia Designer Collection, unveiled at each new Fashion Week season, is a showcase of the hottest British design talent around. Designers ranging from Jasper Conran, to Louis Vuitton to Agent Provocature have all contributed to the one-off exclusive handset designs that are auctioned in aid of London Lighthouse.

In October 2000, Nokia launched a unique, Europe-wide multimedia game that ran simultaneously across eighteen countries. Nokia Game was played out in a variety of media – from television, radio and the press, to the internet, voicemail, email and SMS – throughout November 2000. Anyone owning a mobile phone with SMS functionality (regardless of brand) and access to the internet could register for Nokia Game, which was free to play and challenged players' endurance, wit, intelligence and dexterity. Over half a million people throughout Europe subscribed to play Nokia Game in 2000.

Brand Values

According to a survey in 2000 by Interbrand, Nokia is now the fifth most valuable brand in the world. The company's overriding concern is to deliver what the brand promises. Its core brand values are: Human Technology, Enduring Quality, Individuality and Freedom.

Fundamentally, Nokia develops mobile devices that support people's different lifestyles – rather than just fulfilling a communications need. Its aim is to combine user-friendliness with style and innovative technology.

Things you didn't know about
Nokia

For 100 years of its history, Nokia had nothing to do with telecommunications. Its core business was making paper and rubber.

Mikhail Gorbachev was televised making a call on the first true mobile phone, the Nokia Cityman, in 1989. The phone became known as 'The Gorba'.

Nokia phones played a key role in the plot of The Matrix, starring Keanu Reeves. So good was his Nokia – he could communicate with beings from another world.

Nokia is the Official Mobile Phone of London Fashion Week.

95% of Finns aged 18-21 have a mobile phone. Most don't install a landline when they leave home.

Nokia's research shows that people who are annoyed by mobile phone users in public are actually irritated because they can only hear half the conversation, not because of the noise.

NUROFEN®

Market

Market research indicates that people today are more interested in maintaining their own health than ever before. Recent years have seen a trend towards self-medication, with sales of over-the-counter (OTC) medicines reaching £1.69 billion in the UK alone (Source: Mintel, 1999). Worth in excess of £300 million (Source: ACNielsen, 1999), the size of the UK's painkiller market indicates that relief from pain rates highly in our healthcare priorities. As we continue to seek to prevent everyday ailments from interfering with the pace of modern life, the pain relief market is poised for further growth.

Within the market, today's consumers are more likely to buy a repertoire of products to suit different types of pain. A vast range of modern analgesics is now available OTC, differentiated not only by their active ingredients but also by their formats. Ibuprofen continues to be the primary driver of growth in the analgesics market, however paracetamol and aspirin remain popular. Industry innovation is continuing to provide more targeted and effective solutions, while the recent explosion of information on health matters and an increased awareness of safety amongst consumers has led to greater confidence in self-medication.

Achievements

Nurofen was the first brand of its kind in the UK, creating the OTC market's Ibuprofen sector and dominating it ever since. It is currently sold in 43 countries worldwide, and is the number one selling analgesic brand in the UK.

Since its launch in 1983, Nurofen has been instrumental in building the pharmacy analgesics category. Changes in legislation during the 1990s saw the brand extend its distribution into the grocery healthcare market, and its impact in this sector has proved equally phenomenal. Recent product launches and distribution gains have increased Nurofen's share of the adult analgesics market in UK grocery to around 23% – higher than that of any other brand (Source: ACNeilsen, Aug 2000).

History

Nurofen is one of the healthcare brands managed by Crookes Healthcare Ltd, the UK subsidiary of Boots Healthcare International. The Boots Company, whose healthcare heritage spans over 120 years, developed Nurofen's active ingredient Ibuprofen in the 1960s. Initially a prescription only product, Ibuprofen quickly established a worldwide reputation. In 1983, approval was given to switch Ibuprofen from a prescription only medicine to being available OTC, based upon its excellent efficacy and tolerability record. Nurofen was subsequently launched as a multi-indication analgesic across Europe.

Nurofen went on to establish itself as a leading OTC brand, maximising its market position by ongoing product innovation. Indeed, Nurofen Plus proved to be one of the UK's most successful OTC launches of the year when it came to market during the 1990s. In 1996, the regulatory status of Ibuprofen (200mg) changed from 'Pharmacy only,' leading to Nurofen Tablets being awarded 'GSL' (General Sales List) status. This allowed the brand to extend distribution beyond its pharmacy heartland into supermarkets and other convenience channels. It is now possible for consumers to buy Nurofen products from a variety of outlets, including vending machines, garage forecourts and even over the internet.

The growth of the Own Label proposition during the 1990s saw many consumers moving from branded goods to retailers' own lines, including own label healthcare products. By continuing to provide solutions to consumers' needs and by demonstrating its relevance to its target audience, Nurofen has proved sufficiently powerful to repel threats from both low priced own label products and strongly promoted branded competitors. Nurofen is now the UK's number one selling analgesics brand, continuing to grow in both market share and reputation.

Product

Since the launch of Nurofen Tablets in 1983, the brand has evolved into a portfolio of ten UK variants. The range encompasses not only adult oral painkillers, but also topical, cold and flu, and paediatric pain relief products.

The familiar sugar-coated tablet was joined in 1995 by an easy-to-swallow torpedo-shaped format: Nurofen Caplets. More recently, two further GSL-licensed oral formats have been added to the range: innovative Nurofen Liquid Capsules, and dissolve-in-the-mouth Nurofen Meltlets.

Nurofen's remaining adult oral products are designed to deliver specific types of pain relief, and are available only from pharmacies. Powerful Nurofen Plus provides relief for stronger pain through the dual action of Ibuprofen and codeine. Nurofen Advance is rapidly absorbed by the body to target pain fast, while Nurofen Long Lasting uses sustained release capsules to provide up to twelve hours of pain relief.

Nurofen extended its expertise into other sectors of the adult pain relief market in the 1990s with the launches of Nurofen Cold & Flu and Nurofen Muscular Pain Relief Gel. In the paediatrics market, Nurofen for Children Sugar Free (launched in 1998) is continuing to build both its reputation and brand share.

Recent Developments

The last two years have witnessed a variety of innovative new product launches from Nurofen. Launched in 1999, Nurofen Liquid Capsules were the first gelatin capsules of their kind in the UK. Absorbed more quickly by the body than ordinary tablets, the format has already acquired a loyal consumer following.

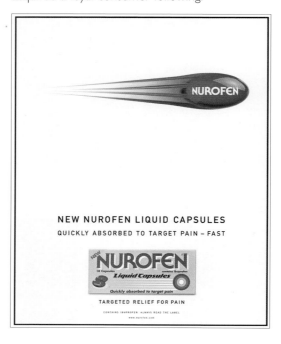

NEW NUROFEN LIQUID CAPSULES
QUICKLY ABSORBED TO TARGET PAIN – FAST

TARGETED RELIEF FOR PAIN

In April 2000 Nurofen grew the analgesics market further with the launch of Nurofen Meltlets, a revolutionary new kind of tablet which dissolves in the mouth. Since they can be taken without water, Nurofen Meltlets can be taken anywhere, providing convenient pain relief for people on the go – as well as for those who have difficulty in swallowing conventional tablets.

Promotion

Nurofen's familiar target logo, symbolising its ability to target pain, has been a consistent feature of its advertising since its launch in 1983. Indeed, reinforcing Nurofen's targeted strength remains a pillar of the brand's advertising strategy. Today, its phenomenal growth and expansion into 43 countries worldwide have given Nurofen a wider stage for its brand communications. It is therefore no surprise that like many other Superbrands, the dominant objective of Nurofen's advertising strategy is to create a global

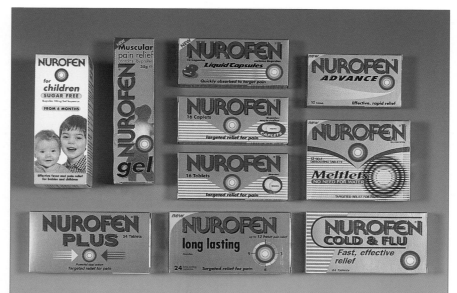

brand which acts in a consistent way.

Throughout the brand's history Nurofen has used television as a promotional vehicle in the UK and other key markets. In addition to the numerous commercials designed to raise awareness of new launches, broad brand-building campaigns have been used to promote Nurofen's values and establish its relevance to its target audience. The recent 'Bodymaps' brand creative proved to be one of the analgesics industry's most successful campaigns to date. Featuring a Nurofen target travelling through the pathways of the body to the site of pain, the advert reinforces Nurofen's efficacy credentials and visually communicates 'Targeted Relief from Pain' to consumers.

In recent years, many of Nurofen's promotional activities have been focused around its new product launches. The launch of Nurofen Liquid Capsules in 1999 was supported by attention-grabbing colour advertisements in daily press, followed by bursts of awareness-building television activity. For its launch in 2000, Nurofen Meltlets used novel tactical marketing techniques

to draw attention to the new product's convenience proposition. A poster campaign featuring the slogan 'H_2NO' appeared nationwide, with smaller plaques proclaiming 'Nurofen Meltlets - No Water? No Problem' positioned above mock 'Not Drinking Water' signs at taps. Accompanied by a new television execution and a variety of point of sale materials, Nurofen Meltlets proved to be one of the UK's biggest pain relief market launches to date.

Nurofen has also experimented with more innovative consumer media in recent years. It was the first analgesic in the UK to use backlit pharmacy signs, depicting the familiar Green Cross and with the Nurofen target and strapline 'Targeted Relief for Pain'. The Nurofen global website, which provides information on products and pain relief, was launched in 1998 (www.nurofen.com) with satellite sites providing regional information. The brand also sponsors an impartial internet site providing information and advice on pain and remedies (www.painforum.com), and has engaged

in partnerships with online health portals.

In addition to its consumer marketing, Nurofen has continued to support its pharmacy and health professional heritage. Its ongoing UK pharmacy program – Nurofen Pharmacy Solutions – provides an accredited pain training programme for pharmacy assistants. Similarly, the brand has worked with external organisations such as the charity Backcare to promote better pain management. The brand has also brought its expertise on pain relief to various industry events including Dental 2000 and the British Pharmaceutical Conference 2000, where Crookes Healthcare was one of the key sponsors.

Brand Values

Nurofen has a brand heritage which delivers substantial consumer trust. It is regarded by consumers, healthcare professionals and retailers as an effective product with considerable experience in the OTC market. Nurofen's expertise and continued new product development have allowed it to achieve its 'number one selling analgesic brand' status in the market, and helped it to accumulate a valuable loyal-user group. An innovative brand with a clear focus on providing people around the globe effective relief from pain, it continues to attract consumers and healthcare recommenders worldwide.

Nurofen, Nurofen Caplets, Nurofen for Children Sugar Free, Nurofen Long Lasting and Nurofen Liquid Capsules contain Ibuprofen. Always read the label.

OLYMPUS

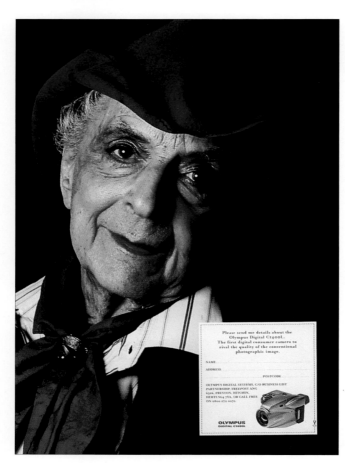

Market

People have always felt the desire to capture images of events or moments that might otherwise be forgotten. As technology evolves, the number of means by which these images can be captured has escalated, and the number of manufacturers offering ways of doing so has also increased. Currently there are nineteen brands, offering 800 models in total, controlling over 90% of the market.

The market has matured and technology has accelerated to the stage where any unique product feature remains unique only for the time it takes another manufacturer to copy it. The ranges of products offered by manufacturers are becoming increasingly hard to differentiate in terms of features, price and retail environment.

Amid this crowded market environment, Olympus has succeeded in commanding either first or second place in the compact camera market every year since 1983. The company has enjoyed market leadership in 35mm cameras since 1996 and is acknowledged as the global leader in digital photography.

Achievements

It is an achievement for any brand to maintain a clear and differentiated brand position in a homogenised market, but Olympus has always managed to retain its reputation for creativity and beautiful imagery.

With the introduction of the Trip camera, Olympus firmly established itself in the hearts of consumers. And by intelligent, innovative use of advertising, sponsorship and PR, it has injected an extra element of glamour, ensuring that share

of mind is greater than share of voice. Two recent television advertisements for Olympus generated £0.5 million and £0.25 million worth of PR coverage respectively.

There is no denying the impact that professional endorsement has had on the brand. Professional photographers have to perform and are only as good as their last picture. If the camera used were not up to scratch, it would be discarded very quickly. The fact that many of the world's top photographers continue to use Olympus speaks volumes.

History

Since 1919, Olympus Optical Co Ltd has pioneered optical technology. The company maintains excellence not just in cameras and binoculars but also in medical and scientific products such as endoscopes and microscopes.

Olympus has long been a brand leader in the camera market. The company was best known for the Trip 35, the first easy-to-use quality point-and-shoot camera, backed by strong advertising featuring the legendary photographer David Bailey. This used the strategy of endorsement to convince the public that compacts were not only easy to use but also delivered quality. This firm foundation in the compact camera market, together with a series of technological firsts and innovative products, spurred the continued success of Olympus over the years.

The early 1990s saw a dramatic change sweep across the camera market, and it was a change for the worse. The market had been hit hard by the recession, declining by 30% between 1989 and 1994. Making matters even more difficult was the fact that the market was saturated with 50 brands and 750 products and a 94% penetration of homes. The result was that cameras were no longer considered to be an exciting, stylish buy. Instead they were seen more in terms of their functional benefits rather than their emotional appeal.

By the mid 1990s, however, the tide had begun to turn. New research suggested that although the market was mature, the youth audience presented

an untapped opportunity. These were consumers who saw brands as an important statement of their identity, and who were open to the Olympus values of quality and style.

Hence the introduction of the Champagne Gold Mju Zoom 105. A design classic, this camera was sold in Terence Conran stores and used by stylish celebrities such as Paul Smith. It breathed new life into the market, and 1997 saw Olympus return to number one in the 35mm compact market.

The next challenge was the arrival of APS. The manufacturers' consortium supported this new format with large marketing budgets, and the traditional Olympus heartland – 35mm compacts – was under threat.

But again Olympus rose to the challenge with the i Zoom range, backed by advertisements featuring the actress Joan Collins. The commercials were an outstanding success, resulting in consumers walking into retail stores and requesting the 'Joan Collins camera'.

The current challenge for Olympus is ensuring the best product range and the best creative work to maintain the company's reputation for style and quality as the digital revolution takes hold.

Product

Style is at the heart of the Olympus brand and this is reflected in everything from advertising to product design. The highly successful Mju camera, the European camera of the year in 1997, was exhibited in London's Design Museum. Its small, sleek style is now being transferred to the digital camera range.

The Olympus Trip cameras were made famous for their ease of use, bringing photography to the mass consumer. Olympus are again pioneering this philosophy by ensuring that all Olympus Digital cameras are not only stylish but also easy to use.

The company's core competence at the cutting edge of technology means that all Olympus cameras have exellent lens systems. As every photographer knows, it doesn't matter which film, shutter speed or aperture are chosen – if the lens isn't good enough then the pictures won't be either. This is true of all Olympus cameras and was communicated as the core benefit in a recent television campaign with Joan

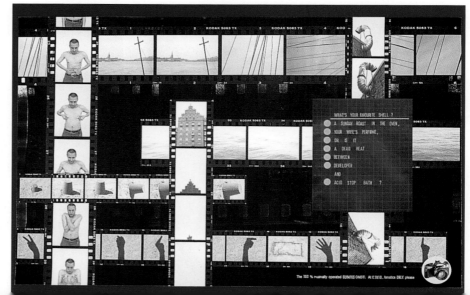

Promotion

The Olympus brand is characterised by consumer friendliness, style and quality. These three qualities have been used to build the brand in a consistent and focused communications strategy spanning 23 years.

The first Olympus television campaign began in 1977 featuring the professional photographer David Bailey. The message was that anyone could use an Olympus camera with professional results, and the advert used a style that was humorous and friendly. Olympus and Bailey produced a total of ten television advertisements in fourteen years, establishing the Olympus Trip as a household name which is still front of mind today, fifteen years after the camera was withdrawn from the market.

1991 saw the advent of a new era in style with the introduction of the Mju camera. Marketing strategies focused on the chic nature of the camera, employing fashion icons such as Naomi Campbell in press and television advertisements.

In 1997 Olympus launched its first APS cameras. Joan Collins featured in a television campaign that won Gold from among 11,000 entries at the European Marketing Effectiveness Awards. The campaign built on the central elements of style and ease of use by concentrating on the core competence of the product – the lens. In the advert, Collins became a stalker who pursued a photographer because his Olympus camera picked up every line and wrinkle.

Collins, featuring the strapline 'so sharp it hurts.'

With digital cameras the lens is even more important as it has to shed light on pixels that measure just microns across. The excellence of Olympus lenses has ensured superior picture quality in its digital range and with the phenomenal growth of this medium continuing, Olympus is in an extremely strong position as it enters this exciting new era in photography.

Recent Developments

It was not so long ago that some observers were predicting the demise of the camera. It was said that stills photography would fall behind in the rush to embrace the new video technology. What has happened, however, is that the camera market has continued to demonstrate powerful growth, with the market for digital cameras strongly boosted by the demand for personal

computers into which digital images can be scanned.

The rate of growth in the digital camera market has seen product life cycles grow ever shorter amid intense competitive pressure. Olympus has responded with continued innovation, developing new generations of high-quality cameras which drive the marketplace.

Optics of the highest quality have been incorporated into a new consumer product called 'Eye-Trek'. Although only the size of a pair of sunglasses, Eye-Trek presents video and television films impressively large, as if the viewer were watching a 52" screen from a few footsteps away.

A six month full page advertising campaign was launched in 1999 within key lifestyle publications to promote the style and quality of Olympus Digital Cameras. Realising that digital cameras involve a much more complex buying process than their less expensive film-based counterparts, Olympus focused on third party product reviews for below-the-line promotions.

Brand Values

Olympus cameras are associated the world over with the core brand values of style, glamour, quality and ease of use. Olympus is perceived as a highly desirable and stylish camera brand in the eyes of consumers, generated through years of groundbreaking creative work and professional endorsement.

The company's reputation for style is based on the smooth, sleek design of its cameras, whilst the glamour has been emphasised by linking the brand to fashion models, showbusiness stars and celebrity events. For example, Olympus organises an exhibition in which celebrities use Olympus cameras to take pictures which are then auctioned for charity. This has become an established feature of the London arts and fashion scene.

The company recognises that the most important part of any camera is the quality of the lens. Olympus makes the finest optics in the world and this is a key part of its communications approach. This is reflected in the television campaign featuring the 'so sharp it hurts' strapline.

Ease of use has been a critically important element of the brand ever since the first David Bailey commercial in 1976 promoting the Olympus Trip camera. In fact, the company has always been synonymous with high quality cameras that are easy to use. This value is true for all its products, including the Microscope and Diagnostic range.

one 2 one

Pay as you go phones you'll want to be seen with.

Matthias Clamer

More 2 Say

Pay as you go phones you won't want to hide

one 2 one
www.one2one.co.uk

Tim Simmons

Market

Arguably one of the most competitive and fast-changing sectors in the UK, the mobile phone market continues to grow and develop in a dynamic fashion. Over 60% of UK households have at least one mobile phone (Source: Total Research February 2000) rising to around 70% by the end of 2000. An increasing number are also abandoning landline telephony in favour of the flexibility and accessibility that mobile solutions offer.

With the introduction of new applications to suit a wide range of consumer and business needs, the market is expected to grow even more considerably. Gone are the days of the focus being purely on voice traffic. Key Note research predicts that over the next three years the sector will grow to be worth £16 billion. This takes into account the anticipated take-up of new technologies such as WAP (Wireless Application Protocol) and GPRS (General Packet Radio Service) that will enable the mobile internet to become a reality.

Since mobile phones first began appearing in the early 1990s, they have changed from being seen as a business tool and a yuppie accessory, to a vital way of staying in touch for many parts of the population. Research shows that for first time more mobiles are now owned by women than men, but 41% of women who own mobile phones have received them as a gift, mainly from either their partner

or parents. The youth market also has an incredibly high take up of mobile phones; penetration is estimated at 95% in the 16-24 age band, clearly reflecting the phenomenal impact the industry has had on the country.

Achievements

A world without mobile phones seems hard to remember now, but as recently as 1994 One 2 One had only 65,000 subscribers. Indeed it took four years for One 2 One to reach the million customer mark. Now over a million new connections are regularly achieved by the network in a standard three-month trading period.

The One 2 One brand is a real innovator, and behind numerous 'firsts' in the UK market. One 2 One was the first operator to offer free calling time and also a standard, free voicemail service for subscribers. Moreover, it remains the only network to offer voicemail services without charging customers. In 1997 it became the first to offer digital pre-paid mobile phones, and this section of the market now accounts for 73% of One 2 One's customers, with over five million sold in total since then. In a wider context, pre-pay phones account for 90% market growth. Recently One 2 One became the first operator to allow overseas roaming for prepaid customers, evidence of its continuing focus on developing and improving services to customers.

History

Initially a south east-based network, the brand launched as Mercury One 2 One in 1993 with a service confined to the area within the M25. Then in 1996, with the One 2 One name firmly established with consumers, the Mercury name was withdrawn to actively compete with the other national networks. By December 1997, the One 2 One network covered 97% of the population. A month later, its one-millionth customer was signed to the network. A special business tariff, Precept, with EFR – enhanced digital sound was launched in 1998, for high level users. This technology was offered to all One 2 One customers a year later. In August 1999, One 2 One was bought in its entirety for £8.4 billion by Deutsche Telekom, Europe's largest telecommunications company.

Product

The One 2 One mobile phone network is the backbone of its service. This now covers over 98% of Great Britain's population, with 53 million people living in the coverage area. One 2 One has international roaming agreements with 198 networks, allowing customers to recieve service

manchester airport choose **one 2 one**

welcome 2 coverage in 64 countries

Telekom was completed, the brand has announced a £600 million investment in enhancing the quality and depth of its network. One 2 One currently has the greatest capacity per customer of any network – it handles over 235 million calls every week. £300 million has been invested in customer services over the last two years to make the brand synonymous with a first rate offering not just in the mobile industry but nation-wide across all sectors.

In 2000, One 2 One was named as one of the successful bidders for a third generation (3G) licence but the brand is currently active in developing a range of services that will be of benefit to customers now and in the near future. Coupled with WAP (Wireless Application Protocol), GPRS (General Packet Radio Service) is a key element of this new range of services.

in 91 countries on five continents. Over £2 billion has been invested in this network so far, but each working day another £2 million is spent improving it further.

Customers are able to choose a wide range of tariffs for both post and pre-pay propositions. The aim is to offer a service that suits all types of users. Features offered on these packages include free Voicemail, SMS text messaging and a host of technological innovations that are continuing to make One 2 One the communications hub of many people's lives.

Recent Developments

In November 1999, One 2 One launched a 50/50 joint venture with Virgin establishing Virgin Mobile, which challenged the way mobile phones were retailed in the UK. The pre-paid packages were sold through Virgin Megastores, and other high street retailers, allowing access to mobile phones for people who might have previously been excluded.

Since the sale of One 2 One to Deutsche

September 2000 saw the start of GPRS trials in the south east of England. Referring to high speed packet data technology, the introduction of GPRS improves the end-user experience of mobile data transmission by making it possible and cost effective to remain constantly connected, as well as to send and receive data at much higher speeds than today.

Promotion

Integral to the growth and awareness of the brand has been its high profile and award-winning advertising campaigns. Back in October 1996, One 2 One first asked 'Who would you most like to have a One 2 One with?' From Kate Moss to Vic Reeves, John McCarthy to Trevor Bayliss, famous and not-so-famous faces were invited to answer that very pertinent question.

August 1999 saw the introduction of a new campaign called 'Welcome 2 your world.' With a new look and feel, it combined the emotional benefits of having a One 2 One with the rational advantages of high capacity mobile

communication. Campaign executions have focused on Vinnie Jones, Michael Parkinson and Zoë Ball. Memorably the Zoë Ball advert also starred friends and family, including Naked Chef star, Jamie Oliver and Zoë's famous father, Johnny Ball.

Sponsorship is a crucial element of the promotion of One 2 One. It is one of ten associate sponsors of the Football Association and is the preferred mobile phone supplier of the England football team, which means One 2 One branding is seen at all of England's international games. Coupled with this is the sponsorship of the FA Charity Shield.

Since 1997, One 2 One has been a sponsor of Everton Football Club in the Premier League as well as Rotherham United Football Club in the National League Division Two. Both these sponsorships are signs of how the brand has moved away from its south east-based roots.

Affinity deals and strategic alliances also play an important role in ongoing One 2 One marketing activity. In 1999 One 2 One kicked off its biggest ever promotional programme when it tied-in with the world's biggest brand, Coca-Cola to offer Coca-Cola branded mobile phones, connected to the One 2 One pay as you go service, from an on-pack token collect scheme.

Brand Values

Branding has successfully differentiated One 2 One from its competitors. Research has shown that customers perceive the network as having human and emotional characteristics. The name automatically suggests intimacy of communicating one to one and the brand has always stood out as appealing to those who like to talk. In the mobile phone network market, One 2 One stands out as a brand with an especially strong youth appeal and a high perception of value.

With the key theme of 'Welcome 2 your world' the brand is positioned as being the central communication cog in the busy lifestyles of today's customers. And with the introduction of new technologies this will play an even bigger role in attracting and keeping customers.

Things you didn't know about
One 2 One

Each year, the One 2 One network handles close to ten billion calls.

The storyline for Zoë Ball's 'Welcome 2 your world' One 2 One advert was actually based on the television presenter's real life – even featuring the name of her first sweetheart, Dave Johnson, whom she imagines marrying in the ad.

In 1999, One 2 One ran an advertising campaign which actually positioned mobile phone handsets as fashion items, and compared choosing a pay as you go phone package to buying a pair of trainers.

To ensure service levels are maintained consistently, One 2 One makes over half a million test calls every year.

One 2 One has a dedicated seven-strong in-house team liaising with local planners, communities and individuals over the expansion of its network and health and safety issues over phone masts and mobile phone use.

During the Euro 2000 football championships, each member of the England squad, as well as management, received a special edition Ericsson T28 handset bearing the Three Lions crest, to promote the One 2 One international roaming service.

OXO MAKES IT RICH & BEEFY

Market

Despite press reports about the demise of the family meal, a survey conducted by Mintel suggests that they are exaggerated.

Although eating patterns have shifted, with individual family members eating at different times and TV dinners being commonplace more than half of fathers and mothers think that it is still important to have at least one family meal a day (Source: NOP/Mintel).

Mothers in particular are very likely to insist that main meals in their household be eaten at the table, with six in ten doing so. Half of all mothers, whatever the age of their children, say the whole family eats the same meal (Source: NOP/Mintel).

The slight down-turn in traditional family meals has hit the stock cube market. The market is suffering the effects of younger consumers, who are cooking less traditional meals in which stock is not commonly used. A further general decline in culinary skills means that young consumers do not know how to use stock in these less traditional meals.

The stock cube market is worth over £65 million and Oxo cubes account for 54.2% of it. Oxo cubes did not have any significant competition until the launches of Bovril and Knorr cubes in the 1970s but they are still the market leader.

Achievements

Oxo cubes are the UK's largest stock cube brand. Some 75% of UK households have Oxo cubes in their cupboard and over two million Oxo

cubes are used everyday. Since its creation Oxo has been endorsed by a wide range of diverse characters such as Florence Nightingale, the second Duke of Wellington and Captain Scott of the Antarctic, who took a supply of Oxo on his South Pole mission.

History

Oxo was originally launched in 1847 as a fluid beef concentrate dietary supplement for invalids and explorers, under the name 'Liebig's Meat Extract'. It was created by the chemist Justus Liebig, the son of a German paint and colour manufacturer. The product was so successful that doctors started writing to Liebig asking for the extract, but he found it increasingly difficult to meet this escalating demand. To combat the problem he decided to take advantage of the huge surplus of meat in South America where cattle were slain purely for their hides, then discarded. In 1861 a young engineer called George Christian Giebert read of Liebig's work and wrote to him suggesting that they should meet to discuss a manufacturing plant in Uruguay. A factory was built in the South American country in a town called Fray Bentos. The product was by now called Extractum Carnis Liebig.

Liebig's Extract first came to England in 1865 and was marketed throughout the country as being 'invaluable not only in the sick room but also in the kitchen'. Liebig's Extract became Oxo in 1899. Surprisingly, nobody knows exactly how the name came about. One unsubstantiated legend is that while a crate of the extract was at the docks a keen docker chalked O-X-O on the side to distinguish it from other cargo. Oxo was

Be sure to send OXO

registered as a trademark in 1899 everywhere in Europe though not until June 1900 in the UK.

In the early 1900s there was a certain amount of anxiety about the quality of the product, caused by the unappetising sediment left in the bottom of the cup or bowl. Chemists were set to work on the problem and they came up

with the idea of selling Oxo in capsules. Liebig's chief chemist was given absolute control to pursue a 'penny product' and by mean of feeding beef essence and beef fibrine into a Swiss cube-making machine the Oxo cube was born.

The poor took the cube to their hearts and their stomachs, making a meal of it with a hunk of bread. There were no major changes to the product until the launch of the Golden Oxo (later called Chicken Oxo) in the 1960s, to coincide with Oxo's Golden Jubilee, and in 1968 the parent company merged with Brooke Bond.

Oxo was one of the first to advertise on television in the 1950s and thanks to highly successful, long-running campaigns starring the likes of 'Katie' and the 'Oxo family', the brand has continued to stay close to the hearts of the British public.

Product

The product has come a long way from its creation as a dietary supplement for invalids and explorers, from its initial liquid format to being foil-wrapped in the well known cube format.

As well as being available in the distinctive original beef flavour, Oxo cubes are now also available in chicken, vegetable and lamb flavours. In more recent years the company extended its range of products when it launched a range of Oxo gravy granules, available in beef, chicken, onion and vegetable flavours.

Today, all Oxo cubes are produced at the company's factory in Worksop.

The Oxo family presented the real ups and downs of family life. The children shouted and squabbled and the parents rowed and sometimes were not even on speaking terms at all. They would, however, occasionally share a sexy memory or two over the supper table. After the popular family had spent almost two highly successful decades on the nation's television screens, the lead up to the Millennium saw Oxo adopt a new advertising approach. The new advertisements portray families of the new millennium. These adverts give clear instructions on how and why to use an Oxo cube when preparing a mince meal. The voiceover explains how, adding Oxo will add depth to such a meal. The households featured in the ads give the impression of being genuine. The style of the new adverts is a complete departure from the previous advertisements, establishing a more contemporary and functional image for Oxo whilst maintaining the emotional 'warmth' and 'care' associated with previous Oxo campaigns.

Recent Developments

Oxo celebrated its 100th birthday in 1999 and to mark the occasion it underwent a major packaging redesign and a new television campaign. The new adverts focused on modern mince meals in different family environments reflecting 'families of the new millennium'. Recent promotions, in conjunction with mince, have helped younger consumers learn how to use Oxo cubes through recipes attached to packets of meat. The new pack design uses the Oxo logo in a fun, modern way. In addition to this eye-catching design element, simple instructions with usage suggestions can be found on the packs. Oxo has launched a website that contains the history of the product and provides modern recipe ideas (www.oxo.co.uk).

Promotion

As soon as Oxo was introduced to the UK market in the early 1900s it was advertised in a number of women's magazines.

In 1902 the first Oxo promotional gift was given away, this being a baby's rattle with a handle that spelled Oxo, offered in exchange for one bottle wrapper.

Oxo made itself synonymous with health, strength and endurance by the simple device of sponsoring athletics events such as the London to Brighton walk. The company was not only an official caterer to the 1908 London Olympics, supplying the runners in the marathon with drinks of Oxo to sustain them, but also managed to persuade the entire British team of athletes to recommend the product. By the mid 1950s the television commercial had arrived. One of the

first television adverts for the product starred the popular glove puppet Sooty. As the 1950s drew to a close, Oxo created one of the most successful characters ever to appear in a television commercial – 'Katie'. By the dawn of the early 1960s she was established as believable, attractive and interesting. Her trials and tribulations became so real to the nation that people wrote to her in their thousands. The advert was so famous that it became part of the fabric of the social life of the 1960s and 1970s.

Some eighteen years after her television debut, Oxo felt that Katie had become rather dated. Her 'Gives a meal man appeal' slogan stayed but the new symbol of the product was a pair of fingers doing the 'Oxo crumble' which was used in poster campaigns.

The first famous on screen face to replace Katie was Dennis Waterman of the 'Sweeney' fame. Despite the popularity of these new advertisements, the ghost of Katie lingered. She was finally reincarnated with the introduction of Lynda Bellingham and the 'Oxo family'.

Brand Values

Oxo's brand values haven't really changed since its introduction in 1899.

Oxo has always stood for nutrition, flavour, and nurturing in the consumers minds. Its quirky name and instantly recognisable packaging have given Oxo a fun and wholesome brand identity. It is a familiar, trusted brand that conjures up images of bringing families together at the dinner table. The heritage of the brand is also endearing, with much of its early advertising merchandise highly sought after by collectors today.

PENTAX

Market

The camera market around the world is booming. Increasing numbers of amateur photographers are taking advantage of ever more sophisticated yet reasonably-priced cameras. In addition, demand from professional photographers is also growing, not least because of the burgeoning glossy magazine market.

The total UK camera market size is 3.4 million cameras worth £263 million a year. The zoom compact accounts for some 27% of its value and the single lens reflex (SLR) around 20%. Pentax has shaped today's camera market. It invented the first 35mm zoom compact camera and is still the brand leader in this sector.

The SLR and the zoom compact are two of the most popular categories of cameras on the market. Pentax now has 20% of the SLR market and 24% of the zoom compact market, which means that one in every four zoom compact cameras sold is a Pentax.

Advanced Photo System (APS) cameras and digital cameras are being embraced enthusiastically by consumers and are taking a growing share of the market. New offerings from Pentax are exploiting this sector.

Pentax continues to increase its share of the camera market generally. But while the name Pentax is synonymous with high-quality cameras, it also covers a vast range of other products from optical measuring instruments to spectacle lenses and synthetic tooth roots and bones. The brand name is so strong that many believe it is the name of the parent company. But it was the Asahi Optical Company of Japan which created and registered the brand name Pentax in the late 1950s, intending it to be used for photographic cameras. Asahi Optical was the first manufacturer to incorporate a pentaprism viewfinder and reflex mirror system into a camera, and the word Pentax is derived from a combination of the words pentaprism and reflex. The company expanded into other areas and Pentax now produces CAD/CAM systems, surveying instruments, closed circuit television (CCTV) lenses, industrial instruments, electrovisual instruments, medical video and fibreoptic endoscopes.

The company performs strongly in all areas of its business. For example, the Ophthalmic division is steadily building on its strong brand name in the diverse and highly competitive ophthalmic marketplace. Key to its success is the strong relationships it has developed with high street brand names such as Boots.

The CCTV, Surveying and Medical divisions have developed a strong brand presence in each of their markets and are achieving consistently high sales in a difficult and dynamic marketplace.

Achievements

The Asahi Optical Company has demonstrated its pioneering spirit ever since it was founded in 1919. The company has married design innovation with technical breakthroughs in all areas of the photographic market, and over the years has been first to market with an array of products. These range from the instant return mirror in 1954 to the world's first auto focus

SLR with built-in flash (the SFX) in 1987 and the introduction of the world's thinnest, lightest resin lens for spectacles in 1992.

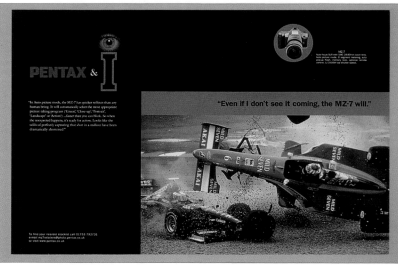

Launching the auto focus SLR in 1981 – the Pentax ME-F – was one of the company's biggest breakthroughs. Today nine out of ten SLRs are auto focus. Then, in 1996, Pentax took the market by storm with a new SLR, the MZ-5, which promptly won the two most prestigious European Camera of the Year awards. Its successor, the MZ-5N, launched a year later, won Camera of the Year 1998 and SLR Camera of the Year 1998 with Amateur Photographer magazine. The MZ-10 and MZ-50 have followed, building a complete range of compact, technically advanced SLR cameras.

Another major landmark was Pentax's launch in 1986 of the first zoom compact (the Zoom 70). Within four years it had produced five million units. Today one camera in four sold in the UK is a zoom compact and Pentax still leads the field in innovation and design. For example, the longest zoom compact currently available is the Pentax Espio 200. Pentax zoom compact cameras have been awarded European Compact Camera of the Year three times and in 1994

total production hit the ten million mark. Pentax's sustained success is supported by a brand reputation that consumers trust.

History

Asahi Optical Company was established in Japan in 1919 as a producer of spectacle lenses. In 1923 it started making lenses for motion picture projectors and in 1931 it produced the first still camera lens. In 1948 it began manufacturing prism binoculars, and launched the Asahiflex in 1951, the first Japanese 35mm SLR. The instant return mirror was introduced in 1954, and in 1957 the first Asahi camera to carry the name Pentax appeared.

In 1967 the Pentax Gallery, Japan's first camera museum, opened in Tokyo and in 1970 the company listed on the Tokyo Stock Exchange.

In 1979 Pentax UK was established with headquarters at South Harrow in Middlesex. The UK subsidiary quickly achieved new sales records with the ME Super Camera and the Auto 110, the world's first single lens reflex camera using the miniature 110 film format.

The early 1980s saw the number of SLR cameras produced hit the ten million mark and Asahi Optical entered the video market. Further expansion saw the introduction of the synthetic tooth root Apaceram and the company enter the compact camera market with the Pentax PC35AF. In 1985 the company produced Japan's first synthetic bone filler, Apatite.

The Pentax Zoom 70 was voted 'European Compact Camera of the Year' in 1987, and in the same year, the company entered the electronic endoscope market. At the end of the decade and the beginning of the next, Asahi developed the digital still camera with recording facility and the Z-10 single lens reflex with 'intelligent' power zooming.

Pentax UK began distributing CCTV lenses in 1980 and rapidly established itself as number one in the UK market. Major clients include the police, the government, local councils, railways,

airports, schools, hospitals, banks and many large corporations.

Pentax UK's Surveying Division was set up in 1982 to supply surveying instruments to the construction industry. The Medical Division was established two years later, selling a range of fibre optic endoscopes to the National Health Service. In 1988 the Ophthalmic Division was established, focusing on producing thin, light and clear spectacle lenses which enhance the wearer's appearance and improve comfort while maintaining good vision.

Product

Pentax has products in most areas of the photographic market. Its wide range of 35mm zoom compact cameras is particularly successful, but SLRs, both auto focus and manual focus, have also become very popular again. It is possible to buy one of the Pentax range of non-zoom compact cameras for less than £50, while at the other end of the scale there are professional medium format SLRs in 6x7 and 6x4.5 formats. The relatively new Advanced Photographic System (APS) is represented in the Pentax range with the stylish ultra-compact 'Efina' cameras and the company also produces a number of different digital cameras.

Pentax cameras are distributed through four main channels. Independent camera shops sell mainly high-ticket SLR and zoom compact cameras. The multiples offer lower-priced products which appeal to the less technically minded. Pentax also sells cameras to the premium and incentive markets, and through duty free outlets.

Using high quality optical components, produced to the same exacting standards, Pentax binoculars enjoy a reputation similar to that of cameras.

Pentax CCTV lenses are used on the Docklands Light Railway, the Jubilee Line Extension, the railway network for the new Hong Kong airport, Old Trafford, the Royal Festival Hall, and in over 100 city and town

centres. People think of CCTV lenses primarily as a security tool but they can also analyse images. So, for example, they have been used on production lines for quality control and in remote underwater vehicles for inspecting the legs of oil rigs.

Endoscopes, which use the latest developments in fibre optics, are vital in medical diagnosis. Pentax is at the leading edge of development in endoscopy and has recently developed an ultrasound scope for specialist use.

Pentax UK's Ophthalmic Division offers customers a range of high quality and attractive lenses and frames. These include the world's thinnest lens which is around 45% thinner than standard resin lenses.

Recent Developments

In November 1999 Pentax launched the Efina T. The stylish compact stainless steel camera, which has been described as 'the ultimate fashion accessory', is the latest addition to the range of Advanced Photographic System (APS) cameras. Shortly afterwards came the Espio 120Mi, the newest 35mm zoom compact. Its scratch-resistant aluminium body and zoom lens are incorporated in one of the world's smallest zoom compacts. In September 2000 Pentax launched two new digital cameras.

Pentax now has a strong worldwide presence on the internet. As people travel more frequently and farther afield, the internet affords them immediate access to the company and its products.

Promotion

Public relations play an important role in the Pentax marketing mix. PR campaigns over many years have consistently gained wide coverage on television, radio and in the national and consumer press. The company used PR very successfully to promote its sponsorship of the BT Global Challenge Round the World Yacht Race in 1996-1997. Pentax regards PR as vital for informing consumers of its key brand and product messages.

In 1998, an advertising campaign provided a radical departure from Pentax's previous activities. Building on the message 'Pentax is right for me' (whether in business or at leisure), the 'Pentax & I' campaign was launched at all levels, both above and below-the-line, across all

areas of the business. Strong photographic images support the campaign, which featured heavily in a variety of media and promotional activities.

The advertising campaign was underpinned by a very successful range of small-space advertisements in the national press based around key events, including the wedding of Prince Edward and Sophie Rhys-Jones, the Chelsea Flower Show, Wimbledon Tennis Championships and Euro 2000. More recently, the company won a major coup with its small-space advert which appeared directly under a full page picture of the Queen Mother in the Daily Express in July 2000. The picture was taken by Norman Hartnell on her 95th birthday.

Brand Values

The Pentax brand enjoys a reputation for excellent product innovation and quality engineering. Pentax understands the importance of introducing excellent and relevant products for the consumer in order to maintain a strong brand image that is memorable, sustainable and different. The brand's core values are built on its optical expertise, and 'seeing' is at the heart of the Pentax brand and products.

Pentax works hard to ensure that its customers are confident that the company understands their needs and that its products, while technologically advanced, are easy to use and therefore suit their requirements, whether for business or leisure.

MY PENTAX
GIVES ME PERFECT PICTURES
EVEN WITHOUT FILM.

PENTAX BINOCULARS

Market

The global soft drinks industry is one of the most vibrant and hotly-contested of all markets, with around 800 million product servings being sold every day. In the US, consumers drink almost 55 gallons of carbonated soft drinks per year, making soft drinks by far the country's most consumed beverage. In Europe, that number is closer to twelve gallons of soft drinks per person each year, but the figure is growing steadily as soft drinks become an increasingly important feature of the beverage industry.

In the UK, colas represent the largest component of the carbonated soft drinks sector by a considerable margin. Cola sales expanded by 49% in volume terms between 1993 and 1998 to reach an estimated 2,607 million litres (Source: Mintel 1999). Value has lagged behind volume, however, rising by only 41% over the same period to £2.89 billion. This reflects the introduction of higher-quality own-label supermarket colas, and new branded products, together with aggressive promotional activity on the part of the brand leaders.

Achievements

When it comes to Pepsi, the statistics speak for themselves. Nearly one out of every four soft drinks sold worldwide is a Pepsi product,

totalling more than 200 million servings every day. In 1999, Pepsi's parent company, PepsiCo Inc, recorded sales of over $20 billion, and was the number one contributor of sales growth and net profits to US retailers. Headquartered in Purchase, New York, the Pepsi-Cola Company is the global beverage division of PepsiCo Inc.

The power of PepsiCo lies in the strength of Pepsi and its other global brands. These include Frito-Lay, the world's most successful snack food company, and Tropicana, the US leader in chilled juices.

Pepsi-Cola beverages can be found in every corner of the globe and in more than 195 countries. Key Pepsi-Cola international markets include Brazil, China, India, Saudi Arabia, the UK, Germany and Scandinavia. The company also has established operations in the emerging markets of the Czech Republic, Hungary, Poland, Slovakia and Russia – where Pepsi was the first US consumer product to be marketed.

From humble beginnings at the turn of the twentieth century, Pepsi survived two bankruptcies to grow into the world's second-largest beverage company. Today, the Pepsi globe icon is one of the most recognised logos in the world.

History

The Pepsi story started in 1886 when a North Carolina pharmacist, Caleb Bradham, developed a digestive aid made from carbonated water, sugar, vanilla and rare oils. Locals affectionately called his concoction 'Brad's Drink'. In 1898, Bradham renamed his refreshing, energising beverage Pepsi-Cola, and soon afterwards the Pepsi-Cola Company was born. The brand fared well until World War I, when sugar rationing, supply shortages and lack of transportation led to the company's first bankruptcy in the early 1920s. New ownership subsequently injected fresh life into the brand – with a little help from Prohibition – only to see it fall into bankruptcy for a second time during the Great Depression. At this point Charles Guth stepped forward. The president of Loft Industries, a candy and fountain store chain, Guth purchased a majority

stake in Pepsi in 1931 and put it on fountains throughout the Loft chain. One of Guth's greatest obstacles was the high price of bottles. To avoid this problem, he purchased a number of used twelve ounce beer bottles – twice the size of regular soft drink bottles – and filled them with Pepsi. The larger bottles sold for 10 cents, which was twice the price of six ounce soft drinks at the time. Sales failed to improve, so Guth decided to slash the price to five cents but keep Pepsi in twelve ounce bottles, a cut price strategy that was to remain in place for two decades.

Further investment allied to strong marketing carried the brand through World War II and into the 1950s, which is when Pepsi truly became part of the American way of life. It was at this time that Pepsi developed a distinctive 'swirl' bottle and a new advertising campaign, 'Be Sociable, Have a Pepsi.' This was a sign of things to come: the first Pepsi campaign to focus on young people. From there, the stage was set for another advertising breakthrough. A new generation of post-war baby boomers, uncommitted to the values of the past, were heading into the future with a conviction that what lay ahead was better than what lay behind.

Pepsi sensed that attitude and captured its spirit with a name that has stood the test of time – The Pepsi Generation. This is the theme that has linked the promotion of the brand across the decades to the present day. In 1998, Pepsi celebrated its 100th anniversary and unveiled a fresh new look. The new logo – a three-dimensional globe against an ice blue background – unified the brand's graphic identification around the world and marked a new look for the new millennium.

Product

The Pepsi-Cola Company continually strives to be a 'total beverage' company, producing and marketing quality brand-name products that consumers prefer. The Pepsi-Cola Company's

brands in the US include Pepsi, Diet Pepsi, Pepsi ONE, Wild Cherry Pepsi, Mountain Dew, Slice, Mug, Aquafina, All Sport Body Quencher and FruitWorks. The company also makes and markets ready-to-drink iced teas and coffees via joint ventures with Lipton and Starbucks. Major products sold internationally by Pepsi include Pepsi Max, Mirinda and Seven-Up.

Product excellence is Pepsi's recipe for growth and the single greatest reason for its success around the world. The recipe for the product itself is a closely guarded secret. But the Pepsi system is open for all to see. The system starts with the finest ingredients available – kola nuts, vanilla beans, flavour oils, citrus, sweeteners and the purest waters around.

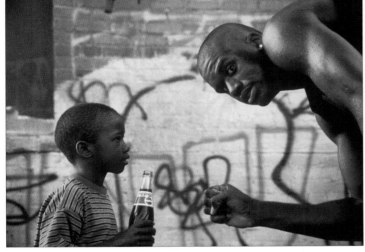

Then Pepsi uses the best technology available and all the care it can muster to blend the ingredients. During the 100 plus years Pepsi has been making soft drinks, the company has also created its own exacting production and quality standards, monitored with constant testing to guarantee quality and consistency in its products.

Finally, Pepsi has its own local distribution system. This is designed to make sure that the product tastes just as fresh at home as it was when it was sealed at the plant.

Recent Developments

For the first time since 1983, Pepsi has brought back the 'Pepsi Challenge' – its most compelling promotional campaign ever. Consumers throughout the US are invited to take the Challenge and taste the difference for themselves. Though the look has been updated, the essence of the Pepsi Challenge is unchanged. It is a blind, side-by-side taste competition between Pepsi and its largest competitor. As an added twist, the new Pepsi Challenge also includes Pepsi ONE, the company's one-calorie cola.

Heralding the return of the Challenge are television commercials with US baseball stars Sammy Sosa and Ken Griffey Jr as well as advertisements featuring ordinary people who have taken the Challenge and switched to Pepsi. Consumers interested in more details about the Pepsi Challenge, including how to conduct the taste test in their homes, are being invited to log on to www.pepsi.com.

Promotion

Staying on the leading edge of advertising and consumer promotions is a hallmark of the Pepsi-Cola Company. In fact, the company is recognised worldwide as a leader in advertising, marketing, sales and promotional support. This is demonstrated by the outstanding success of the Pepsi Challenge campaign, born in the mid 1970s.

The Pepsi Challenge was based on consumer tests which showed that more people preferred the taste of Pepsi to that of the largest brand of cola, and soon the Challenge made its way into television advertising. By 1976, Pepsi became the single largest-selling soft drink brand in American supermarkets, and by the time the 1980s dawned, Pepsi was the number one brand in take-home sales.

By the middle of the 1980s, the success of the Pepsi Challenge had become clear.

The company's biggest rival abandoned its century-old recipe in favour of a new product formulated to taste more like Pepsi. However, consumers quickly rejected the new offering, and in short order it was reintroduced under a new name.

Throughout the 1980s into the 1990s, a long list of superstars lent their magic to Pepsi including Michael Jackson, Tina Turner, Michael J Fox, Ray Charles, Cindy Crawford and the Spice Girls. Pepsi also pioneered the concept of freshness dating, providing consumers with an easy-to-read 'best by' date that has since become an industry-wide practice.

The 2000 advertising campaign, called 'Ask For More', leverages Pepsi's key equities of humour, humanity and music and captures the passionate feelings offered by the Pepsi experience. The message is clear: teenagers who want the most out of life should choose Pepsi.

Brand Values

The Pepsi brand is all about taste, choice and a feeling of optimism and youthful exuberance. These qualities come through in all Pepsi advertising, and are reflected in the development of Pepsi's 'Ask for More' campaign, which combines the core values of fun, creativity and daring. Pepsi has always tried to be a little younger, a little more hip and a little more relevant to teenagers than its competitors have managed to be.

Market

The drinking of bottled natural mineral water is a way of life for millions of UK consumers. More than 1000 million litres of mineral water were sold in 1999, making it the fastest growing sector of the soft drinks market.

Once dismissed as a fad or short-term fashion, bottled water is riding on the tide of the big consumer swing to all things natural. Today many people prefer to drink water that is wholesome and drinkable in its natural state rather than water that is chemically treated to make it safe to drink.

With lifestyles changing as rapidly as shopping patterns, drinking mineral water 'on the move' has become a habit among children and adults. And for the health conscious, young and trendy sector, a bottle of water is seen as a conspicuous fashion accessory. The market for natural mineral water continues to grow significantly, every year. It is a fiercely competitive market and Perrier continues to lead this market not only because of its position in the market, but most importantly by its enormous influence. Over 35% of UK households now drink mineral water and the influence of young people is immense. There is a whole generation now who have

been brought up to go to the fridge rather than the tap for a glass of water.

Still water sales, which began to overtake those of sparkling water in 1990, now account for around two thirds of the market. Still water is very often drunk as a substitute for tap water and has become something of a commodity. Sparkling water, on the other hand, is seen as a drink in its own right. Its growth depends on strong brand development playing an active and creative role in the market place. The sparkling water brands tend to have memorable and cool advertising.

Achievements

Perrier built the UK natural mineral water market virtually single-handed. It has invested more in the market than any other brand and is currently exported to over 120 countries. It is fitting, then, that in a fiercely competitive marketplace Perrier remains the best-selling sparkling mineral water brand in the UK. It is the bottled water most often asked for by name, and is found at more social and sporting occasions, including Wimbledon, Henley, Ascot and Oxbridge balls, than any other brand. The famous green bottle, instantly recognisable to consumers all round the world, has changed little since it was first produced almost 100 years ago. Its powerful brand presence, characterised by style, wit and quality, sets it apart from its competitors, and is reinforced by its distinctive and witty advertising – 'OUT OF THE H₂ORDINARY' – and by its creative approach to promotional activity.

Perrier has almost 20% of the branded sparkling mineral water sector in terms of value, a figure which rises to over 30% at times of celebration such as Christmas. Perrier sells twice as much sparkling mineral water (bottles) through grocers than any other brand in the UK, and enjoys wide distribution in restaurants, pubs, clubs and hotels.

Perrier has a long tradition of setting trends in the UK bottled water market. It was the first to introduce sparkling mineral water in 330ml cans for instance, and the first to launch a flavoured water, Perrier with a Twist.

In 1998 Perrier was appointed official mineral water to the Wimbledon Lawn Tennis Championships and continues to enjoy this status.

Perrier Pick of the Fringe Comedy Awards which were launched in 1981, are now established as 'the Oscars of alternative comedy'. The Perrier Awards have launched great comedians like Frank Skinner, Steve Coogan and Jenny Eclair who have gone on to find fame and fortune on television, radio and the big screen.

In 1998 Perrier introduced the Perrier Young Jazz Awards, now recognised as the premier competition for young jazz musicians in the UK. Success in the Awards has opened doors for all the winners. In 2000 the Perrier Young Jazz Award Winners' CD produced by Jazz FM resulted in excellent reviews by the national, regional and music press and this led to radio, television and club appearances for the Perrier winners.

History

In 2004 Perrier will celebrate its centenary, but the water has been around for a lot longer than 100 years.

In 218 BC Hannibal discovered an effervescent Spring in the Vistrenque Plain at Vergeze in France. The Spring was conveniently situated just 200 metres from a road built between Italy and Spain by the Romans. The Spring's reputation soon began to spread, and before long people travelled great distances to drink 'the bubbling waters' and to enjoy the Roman baths which were served by the Vergeze Spring. Sadly the fall of the Roman Empire led to a fall in the use of the bubbling waters, and the Spring faded into obscurity. Only the locals continued to use the water and to have faith in its health-giving properties.

But in 1863 Napoleon III ordered that the water should be bottled and sold 'for the good of France' and Vergeze was developed into a spa resort. Disaster struck in 1869 when the site was gutted by fire, and it was only through the interest of an Englishman, St John Harmsworth, that the Perrier brand came about at all.

Harmsworth went to Vergeze to recuperate after a motor car accident in 1903. A Doctor Perrier introduced Harmsworth to the bubbling spring and suggested he should drink the water as the local people had great faith in its revitalising qualities, Harmsworth drank the water and immediately recognised its commercial potential. He bought the spring, intending to bottle and market the water, but before he could start production he needed a name for it and to create striking packaging for it. He decided to name the water Perrier in honour of the doctor and to base the now famous French green bottle on the Indian clubs

bubbling waters. It springs from a source in the Vistrenque Plain near Vergeze in Southern France, where a volcanic eruption thousands of years ago resulted in this unique water with natural bubbles. The water is of very high quality. It is a refreshing and enjoyable drink and an excellent mixer. Perrier with a Twist, a refreshing blend of Perrier with a dash of lemon, has proved particularly popular among young people.

Recent Developments
For the first time in its 100 year history, Perrier extended its range in 2000 to include a new 50cl bottle designed especially for restaurants, cafés, clubs and bars. Tall and elegant in the traditional Perrier green glass, it is the perfect size for the table. The 50cl size is already well known in Europe and has proved the most popular format in the burgeoning restaurant sector. Special machinery and tooling had to be introduced into the bottling plant at Vergeze to achieve the tactile shape for which the brand is famous.

Promotion
Perrier's hugely successful 'Eau' campaign, which teased the consumer with its subtle play on words, ran for over ten years. Equally witty and stylish was the 'Pour' campaign, launched in October 1997, with executions including 'Pour la vie', 'Ready to pour' and 'Pour le moment'.

In 2000 the theme focused round the summer season. The 'head swirling' advertising campaign kicked off with 'OUT OF THE H$_2$ORDINARY', launched to celebrate the Wimbledon Lawn Tennis Championships.

Later in the year to promote the new 50cl bottle Perrier ran a £500,000 campaign which included advertorials in leading magazines. A great success during 2000 was Perrier's sponsoring of the Champagne Bar at the Restaurant Show which took place in London's Olympia Exhibition Centre. The promotion included Perrier branded glasses specially created for the new 50cl Perrier bottle by French designer Martin Szekely.

Brand Values
Perrier is invigorating, healthy, stylish and French. Marketing aims to sustain the brand's star status in the soft drink sector year after year. Its name, packaging and advertising are all instantly recognisable. It attracts enormous goodwill and commands universal respect. And it has become the natural choice of those influential people who determine fashion it its widest sense.

he used for exercising.

Harmsworth was a visionary and he identified a significant marketing opportunity for Perrier among the military and civil service expatriate community in the far-flung outposts of the British Empire. Local water was often contaminated and quality water was in short supply. Perrier provided an ideal alternative and was a great mixer with whisky.

The British loved it. Perrier was even favoured by royalty, receiving Royal Warrants from both Edward VII and George V. In 1907 Dr Wilson Hake PhD FIC FCS of the Westminster Hospital School of Medicine, who visited the spring at Vergeze, reported that Perrier was of 'remarkable organic purity'.

Harmsworth's marketing initiative proved successful. Perrier was advertised as 'the Champagne of table waters' and could be found in high-class establishments across the world – except in France. It was easier to find Perrier in Singapore than Paris. By 1922 six million bottles of Perrier were being produced every year and when Harmsworth died in 1933 the figure had risen to eighteen million.

Perrier returned to French hands in the late 1940s when a French company, Société Source Perrier bought the brand. It built a new bottling plant at Vergeze which increased production to over 130 million bottles a year. The product became increasingly Francocentric, with only 20% exported abroad.

Until the 1970s Perrier was not marketed seriously in the UK and in 1972 only half a million bottles a year were sold. But interest in French mineral water developed again when a

subsidiary company, Aqualac (Spring Waters) opened in London. Spurred on by the brand's high profile advertising, the British renewed their love affair with Perrier. By 1986 over 77 million bottles were being sold in the UK every year. The parent company was acquired by Nestlé in 1993 and renamed Perrier Vittel Groupe Nestlé to reflect its expertise in both sparkling and still waters.

Today the company markets Perrier in all five continents. It owns 56 bottled water brands, but Perrier remains the flagship brand and the most international.

Product
Perrier is one of the world's few naturally

Persil

Market

Every day seventeen million washes are carried out in the UK – that is five loads per week for the average UK household. With annual sales in the UK of 320 million packs of detergent to facilitate this number of washes, the laundry market is worth more than £900 million per year.

The laundry detergents market in the UK is one of the most competitive in Europe, and successful products rely on continuous innovation to maintain their competitive advantage. There are four distinct product areas within this market: biological products for tough cleaning, non-biological products for people with concerns about their family's skin, colour care products which help keep coloured items looking vibrant and new, and special care products for delicate fabrics such as silk and wool.

The detergent market can also be split into three product formats: powders, liquids and tablets. Powders still account for 55% of the market, but Persil Tablets, which were introduced only in May 1998, have already claimed an 18% share, and their share continues to grow. Responding to consumers' desire for convenience when buying everything – including detergent – Lever has led the way in simplifying the detergents market. Most brands now offer just one powder, one liquid and one tablet.

Persil is the UK's number one laundry brand with a 26% share of the market. Lever's other laundry brand, Surf, is the fastest growing brand, fighting for share against Procter & Gamble's Ariel, Daz, Bold and Fairy.

Achievements

Persil was the foremost brand in this competitive market for almost the whole of the twentieth century and as the new millennium finds its feet, it remains the UK's number one detergent brand. In Interbrand's Biggest Brands 2000 report, Persil was rated as the fifth biggest brand in the UK with sales of £235 million. Its place in the country's cupboards has been maintained by continuous innovation of the brand throughout its 91 year history. Persil has always been at the leading edge of new technology and is consequently seen as both reliable – by virtue of its heritage and product performance – and innovative.

The first ever laundry tablet was launched by Lever in May 1998 under the Persil Performance and Persil Non-Biological brands. The success of tablets can be measured by the 30% growth in the Persil brand that resulted. Aside from meeting the need for a more convenient format which makes washing less of a chore, tablets also injected fresh growth and dynamism into a mature category. The success of Persil Tablets was recognised by Information Resources, which voted it the Most Successful New Grocery Product of 1998.

History

Persil was launched in 1909, as the 'Amazing Oxygen Washer'. Originally developed by two Stuttgart professors – Professor Hermann Gessler and Dr Hermann Bauer, the brand was owned by Crosfield until 1919, when it was acquired by Lever Brothers.

Before the launch of Persil, soap bars were used to wash clothes. Persil was introduced as a soap-based powder which was combined with an oxygen bleaching agent to remove staining in the wash. Persil functioned rather differently from the traditional bar soaps – it had to be stirred into a paste before being added to the water. The brand was therefore advertised as soap powder that would do away with the dolly rub, the washboard and the labour of rubbing clothes. Persil made the washing process much easier, simplifying it to 'soaking, boiling and rinsing'. Initially, the conservative housewife was a little reluctant to desert her established cleaning methods. However, Persil's convenience and the whitening power that it offered combined to gradually win over British housewives.

The 1950s saw the next dramatic change in clothes washing habits, brought about by the introduction of the first reasonably priced washing machine to the UK. As machines became more and more sophisticated, a low lather washing powder was required to prevent excess foam interfering with the spin drying and rinsing process or causing overflowing. At the same time, other trends were affecting people's requirements for washing powders – coloured fabrics were becoming more common, synthetic fibres were replacing natural fibres, and before

long high temperature washing was superseded by the low-temperature wash.

Persil responded to these changes with a continuous programme of product innovation and improvement. In 1968, once the early twin-tub machines had given way to the more advanced automatic front-loading drum

machines, Persil launched Persil Automatic. The name identified the newly-created detergent technology with the new machine technology.

Persil has always been in step with people's changing lifestyles: for example, Persil made its detergents biodegradable well ahead of legislation. During the 1980s stain removal was enhanced with the energy-efficient ingredients such as enzymes and offered greater convenience with the launch of detergent liquids.

All these innovations mirrored technological development in washing machines, the change in washing load and an increased concern about the environment. Indeed, environmental concerns were further alleviated with Persil's exciting and revolutionary innovation of 1998 – laundry tablets. Unit dosing minimised product wastage previously caused by consumers using too much powder, thus addressing environmental concerns about washing and washing powders.

Product

The name Persil is derived from two of the product's original ingredients – perborate and silicate, both registered in 1906. Persil prides itself on being able to meet any type of washing needs by always having a product in the Persil range to suit.

Within each of the three product formats – powders, liquids and tablets – Persil has a range of different formulations. Persil Performance, used most widely, is a biological product containing enzymes formulated for tough cleaning to help break down stubborn stains at low temperatures. The 2-Layer Persil

Performance Tablets also contain a Whiteguard ingredient that helps to prevent colours running into each other. People with concerns about their family's skin often prefer Persil Non-Biological which is formulated without enzymes. Persil also has a range of products specifically developed for coloured clothes – Persil Colour Care. This does not contain any bleach or optical brighteners and so helps to keep coloured items looking vibrant and new. Finally, Persil Silk and Wool is a new product, introduced in 1999, containing neither enzymes nor bleach making it ideal for use on delicate fabrics.

Recent Developments

Persil Tablets, introduced in May 1998, was the most exciting innovation in the laundry market for some time. Tablets offer a far more convenient washing product which makes doing washing less of a chore, being simpler to use, less messy and less wasteful than any previous detergent on the market. The success of Persil Tablets encouraged the launch of tablets across the whole laundry detergent category. Tablets now have nearly 25% of the laundry detergent market. This is indicative of the enthusiastic reception given to tablets by consumers and retailers alike.

Lever has also recently led the way in simplifying the detergents market, responding to consumer desire for an easier experience when shopping for laundry products. As a result, Persil no longer produce concentrated powders or concentrated liquids.

Meanwhile Lever keeps up the improvement of the Persil brand's performance, exploiting all relevant technological advances to the full. New production processes of the 1990s allowed new ingredients to be included in Persil. Every component of the powder was therefore improved: a new active system; a new builder; a more effective enzyme system; a new perfume and a new bleaching system. Efficiency and improved stain removal were also further increased with the introduction of the polymer-based Stain Release System™ to all Persil variants, except Silk & Wool.

In 2000, new enzymes were added to Persil in an anti-ageing campaign for clothes. The enzymes help to delay the onset of the bobbles that form on clothes when they have been washed a lot, and keep clothes looking new for longer.

Promotion

Persil has always taken a progressive approach to advertising. It was the first detergent to be advertised in the press in 1910 and was also the first detergent to be advertised on television in 1955. Persil was also the first washing powder to show a man doing the washing in a television advertisement. Persil has taken numerous approaches in its advertising campaigns across the years.

During World War II, it emphasised the whitening benefit of the brand, often through comparison with inferior brands, using the slogan 'Persil washes whiter'. This style of advertising was perpetuated into the 'TV age'. And it worked. The consistency of the message and familiar packaging built a huge brand loyalty that has been sustained over many decades.

Into the twenty-first century, Persil still makes effective use of a whole range of marketing communications – television, press, outdoor poster campaigns and radio. The success of Persil Tablets can be partially attributed to the new style of 'to the point', 'tongue in cheek' advertising which accompanied the launch.

Other successful campaigns include the Persil Original Non-Biological Roadshow based on the concept of skincare. A ten foot fibreglass model of a female named Feel-icity, with touch screens highlighting problem skin areas, travelled the country's shopping centres in July 2000.

Persil has also recently been leading the trend towards new media, showing that Persil is not simply a traditional brand. Persil Non-Biological has been advertised with an interactive television advertisement and Persil Performance has been advertised extensively on the web. Persil itself launched a website – www.persil.co.uk – focusing on clothes care advice and tips to complement the current Careline service.

As a company, Lever has always had a strong social conscience and cause related marketing has become popular within the business. In 1999, Persil ran a successful campaign with Comic Relief. Special Red Nose packs were produced and for every pack sold, Lever donated money to Comic Relief. Furthermore a roadshow was held in Sainsbury's top 50 stores and a Go Red Information pack was produced which suggested red-themed fund-raising ideas. As a result of this activity, Persil raised over £260,000 for Comic Relief, simultaneously seeing a 25% uplift in sales.

Brand Values

Historically, Persil has been regarded as a trusted family brand with a strong heritage. The launch of Persil Tablets in 1998 also attracted younger people to the Persil brand, creating a brand with a contemporary, progressive feel whilst retaining its family values.

Persil is primarily a caring brand – helping the family and their clothes stay clean. Consistent research and new product innovation has helped Persil maintain the nation's trust and uphold its caring image.

The brand produces variants to suit everybody's needs and had a Careline set up in 1993 to help people understand how the brand can help them. The Careline also helps Lever understand the people using the brand and assess what they want and expect from Persil. This in turn reinforces Persil's image as a caring and trusted brand.

He must be sensitive. Everything he wears is irritating.

Persil Non-Bio for sensitive types.
www.loveyourskin.co.uk

Keep your clothes looking young, if nothing else.

Market

Whoever declared that 'lunch is for wimps' may have been stretching the point, but in an increasingly competitive and pressurised work environment lunch breaks are getting shorter. A recent report found that the British worker spends on average just 32 minutes on lunch. These days, employees are more likely to pop out and grab a sandwich to eat at their desk than sink a couple of pints and a plate of shepherd's pie at the pub. It is difficult to say whether the growing range of retail outlets selling ready made or made-to-order sandwiches is catering for this trend or contributing to it, but over the past fifteen years the great British sandwich has made a glorious comeback.

Gone are the days of soggy white bread and plastic ham wrapped in sweaty clingfilm. The range of bread – from French to focaccia, pitta to ciabatta – is almost as wide and exotic as the fillings: roasted vegetables, mozzarella, crayfish – you name it. Twenty first century sandwiches aren't just delicious, nutritious and convenient, they are fashionable too. The UK sandwich market is the most highly developed in the world. It has grown from £1 billion in 1990 to around £3.5 billion, and in 1999 accounted for 1.9 billion sandwiches (Source: Mintel).

Much of this success is down to Pret A Manger which, since it was established in 1986, has revolutionised the market. From the outset the company has used fresh and natural ingredients in its sandwiches, which are served promptly by friendly and helpful staff in a clean modern environment at affordable prices. The concept has been copied by others, but Pret's relentless innovation, attention to detail and good quality service have kept it ahead.

Achievements

Pret A Manger has grown from a single shop in London's Victoria in 1986 to a chain with over 100 outlets. The number of shops has doubled over the past three years and there are now Pret A Mangers in major cities and provincial centres throughout the UK and at major visitor destinations, including Heathrow Airport and the Earls Court and Olympia Exhibition Centres. In July 2000 Pret ventured overseas, opening its first international outlet in the heart of Manhattan's financial district, a few steps from the New York Stock Exchange.

Pret has a strong reputation for customer service and care, and invests heavily in recruitment and training to develop teams of effective and motivated employees. Only 4-5% of applicants are successful, and those who are taken on go through an intensive ongoing training plan. However, staff are encouraged to develop their own personalities and are not constrained by prescriptive customer service training. Employees are constantly incentivised to offer excellent service. A mystery shopper system, for instance, gives staff in any shop the chance to share a team bonus every week.

Pret's innovative recruitment and incentive programmes have won awards and attracted the attention of many major corporations. The company has also won a host of awards over the years for the quality of its food and service. In the first six months of 2000 alone it received the British Sandwich Industry Award 2000, the Egon Ronay Award for Best Airport Catering, the IPD Recruitment Excellence Awards, and was a finalist in the UK Retailer of the Year competition.

In 2000 founders Julian Metcalfe and Sinclair Beecham were acclaimed as 'legends in their own lunchtime' and were awarded MBEs in recognition of their contribution to the food service industry.

History

In 1986 Julian Metcalfe and Sinclair Beecham quit their City jobs and opened the first Pret A Manger on Victoria Street in London with a £17,500 bank loan. They were fed up with having to endure long queues to buy mediocre lunches and were convinced that they were not the only ones who wanted to buy fresh, healthy food quickly at lunchtime. They built a kitchen in the basement of the shop and bought fresh produce in the food markets early every morning.

The company built its reputation on being 'passionate about food', and aimed from the start to sell fresh, delicious food that was affordable and served fast. Sandwiches were made throughout the day using fresh ingredients, containing none of the artificial additives, preservatives or chemicals which were common in other fast foods.

The concept took off and within a year the shop was serving more than 7,000 customers a week. Today over 100 shops employ more than 2,500 staff and turnover more than £100 million. Pret hopes to expand the chain to around 200 outlets by 2005.

The new Chief Executive, Andrew Rolfe, joined Pret in 1998 but 40 year old Metcalfe and 41 year old Beecham remain very involved in the company. Metcalfe is the creative force behind Pret's food, environment and service development and Beecham is the business developer who is currently spearheading the company's international expansion.

Product

Pret A Manger is a fast food retailer, selling sandwiches, snacks and drinks made with natural, chemical-free ingredients served promptly by

friendly, energetic people in a clean, modern environment.

The company's approach is summed up in its strapline 'Passionate About Food'. It pays painstaking attention to the way it both creates and produces food, from sourcing the right ingredients through to selling products at their best to customers who are in a rush. There is no central production kitchen: everything is produced fresh and by hand throughout the day in each shop's kitchen. For example, each shop bakes baguettes and croissants and toasts almonds and pinenuts for sandwich fillings every day. Anything left unsold at the end of the day is offered to charities for the homeless: Crisis FareShare in the UK and City Harvest in New York.

The core product range comprises twenty different granary sandwiches, four baguettes and five tortilla wraps. But Pret is constantly searching for new ingredients and recipes. The pickle recipe has changed fifteen times in five years, for example. The Pret mission statement, displayed prominently in each shop, states that Pret creates handmade natural food avoiding the chemicals, additives and preservatives commonly found in much prepared and fast food. All Pret food, whether a special fish sushi or the traditional egg and cress sandwich, freshly pressed carrot juice or the indulgent chocolate brownie, complies with these principles.

Pret's innovations extend beyond sandwiches. It was the first retailer to put sushi on to the high street, among the first to make all products GM-free and the first to use organic milk. And its enthusiastic, friendly and efficient staff give it a strong competitive edge. Pret's service standards require that it should take no longer than 90 seconds for customers to buy their lunch. Even a cappuccino will be freshly made and served within 60 seconds.

At the heart of Pret's success is a single-minded focus on delivering great food and great service to customers. Customers' views are actively solicited, via comment cards in the shops, by printing the partners' telephone numbers on every piece of packaging and through the website www.pret.com.

Recent Developments

Pret is constantly refreshing its range of food. Customers might visit the shop three or four times a week so there is a constant stream of product improvements and new developments to offer variety and sustain interest. A new sandwich, baguette or wrap is introduced nearly every week,

and new cakes, juices, sushis, smoothies and desserts appear regularly. In the first six months of 2000 Pret introduced or upgraded over 50 items on its menu.

It recently replaced the traditional plastic sandwich box with the revolutionary Pretbox, a cardboard box designed to last only as long as the sandwich. The development is part of its commitment to move towards more environmentally friendly packaging. The message on the box reads: 'The Pretbox goes soggy. Just like a good sandwich it has a very short life. No preservatives, no distribution depots and no 'sell-by' dates.'

Pret opened 26 new shops in 2000. In addition to the first international outlet in Manhattan, it opened five shops in the Earls Court and Olympia Exhibition Centres in London, and has also expanded into Scotland.

Promotion

Pret A Manger has used neither conventional advertising nor promotion to communicate the fact that it is 'passionate about food'. Its reputation has grown through word of mouth recommendations from customers and through press endorsement. The products and service inspire strong advocates.

The look and feel of the shops is distinctive: stainless steel interiors and bright colours give a sense of vibrancy and create an expectation of cleanliness and pace. Customers experience the 'passion' through the quality of the food, the attitude and service of the staff and the messages on the packaging and the walls of the shops. The mission statement is displayed prominently in every outlet, and the walls are adorned with 'Pret Passion Facts' – a selection of stories about the lengths Pret goes to find the right ingredients and suppliers to guarantee delicious fresh products.

The packaging carries messages such as: 'We don't mind the fact that natural food goes off quickly. We don't want to extend the shelf life of our food. We don't like sell-by dates. At the end of each day we offer all our unsold sandwiches to Crisis FareShare to help feed the homeless.'

Metcalfe and Beecham's attitude to food, service and staff is central to the values and personality of Pret A Manger. Metcalfe, who has been brand spokesman from the outset, has been described as 'larger than life' because of

the passion with which he expounds the company's values. It is his single-minded dedication that has driven the brand.

But Pret does carry out small-scale tactical promotions. For example, as part of its advertising-free launch in Scotland, it delivered free sandwiches to offices around Glasgow. This is done for most new shop openings. Pret is very confident about its food and believes that the most effective marketing is for people to taste the difference themselves.

Brand Values

Though Pret has never carried out conventional brand or product advertising, customers have a strong clear image of the brand personality and style. The components of this are cosmopolitan, young, discerning, principled, obsessive, conscientious and passionate. The personality and style are underpinned by Pret's core values: passion (enthusiasm and belief, a love of life and others), integrity (honesty, principled with the courage of their convictions), uncompromising (striving for perfection, driven yet respectful of others and approachable), seize the day (enjoy it, you never get it back, be fresh in everything, imagine you have the shelf-life of a Super Club).

The brand values are reflected in Pret's culture, service, people and products. For example, the Pret chocolate brownie has been improved 33 times, it took three years to perfect the new sandwich box, and the founders' telephone numbers appear on every piece of Pret packaging.

My name is Dawn, I'm the General Manager of Pret at Goswell Road.

My team and I meet every morning. We will discuss the points you've raised... the good, the bad and the ugly. If we can deal with it ourselves we will. If we can't, I will forward your card to Julian Metcalfe at the office. I know he will do what he can.

Either way, thanks.

Things you didn't know about Pret A Manger

Placing change directly into a customer's hand is compulsory at Pret A Manger. Research shows that a customer who has been touched by a shop assistant leaves with a better impression of their experience.

There are regular 'buddy days' where even the most senior executives including Metcalfe, Beecham and Chief Executive Andrew Rolfe make sandwiches and serve behind the counter so they can talk to staff and customers.

Any member of staff mentioned by name in a letter from a customer for good service gets a silver star made exclusively by Tiffany.

Each morning every member of staff receives a freshly laundered shirt, which is collected by Pret at the end of the day and dry-cleaned.

Sinclair and Beecham bought the name for £100 from a shut-down shop in Hampstead which they drove past the week before they opened.

The quest for perfection means the mixture for the Fruit and Oat Slices is stirred by hand with a four-foot oar.

Pret developed the revolutionary Pretbox — sandwich packaging designed to last only as long as its contents.

PSION

Market

The mobile computing and wireless communication market is exploding. Miniaturisation means that palm-top size computers are now as powerful as cumbersome desktops used to be just a few years ago. What is more, the arrival of broadband wireless telecommunications (3G and GPRS) technologies, means that mobile devices can be used for much more than personal computing alone. Internet access and data delivery at broadband speeds are set to transform the mobile communications market and the Psion brand is at centre stage.

In the emerging age of mobile internet, increasing numbers of people will depend on personal, wireless access to the internet wherever they are. There are expected to be one billion mobile devices in the world by 2003 (Source: Gartner) and 41 million internet users in the UK by 2005. Mobile internet will empower people in their work and personal lives, with information, communications, services and entertainment. Psion is in a position to shape and lead the mobile internet age by delivering distinctive mobile internet solutions and devices to people and organisations.

Achievements

With revenues of £160 million and a market capitalisation of more than £3 billion, Psion plc is recognised as one of the few companies worldwide to be pioneering convergence between computing and communications technologies. With a particular focus on mobile internet and network access devices and services, Psion's strengths are enhanced through partnerships with some of the world's leading technology companies such as IBM, Sun Microsystems, Vodafone Airtouch, Lotus, Citrix and Oracle.

The company has become a major exporter

and commercial success. It has grown at a rate of over 35% per year since it was formed. In 1997, Management Today and WM Mercer rated it as the London Stock Exchange's leading company for total shareholder returns and, in 1996 and 1997, it received the Exporter of the Year and Innovation in Export awards. It has also won four Queen's Awards for Export and Technological Achievement.

The latest Series 5mx handheld computer has been acknowledged as delivering unprecedented computer power combined with cutting edge design. The Series 5mx was rewarded when the Design Council picked it as a 'Millennium Product', representing the best of British innovation and design. Psion Computers' product range has won numerous other

international awards, including Comdex Asia Best Hardware award by Byte Magazine (US), Editor's Choice Award of Distinction, the Golden Globe and the Design Business Association's Best Consumer Design and Grand Prix awards.

Psion has blossomed from a twinkle in the eye of David Potter, founder and Chairman, in 1980 into one of the UK's most successful high-tech stars. Nor are its boundaries limited to the UK shores alone: Psion's current distribution tentacles extend to over 51 countries in the world, with over 50% of its turnover generated in continental Europe.

History

The company was founded in 1980, when it originally concentrated on software development for the Spectrum and the Commodore, early computer gaming consoles. Some of the programs were extraordinarily successful, Flight Simulator for example, selling over one million copies. The revenue from this initial foray into the world of computing was to help finance the next major development for the company.

1984 was the first real turning point for Psion, with the invention of the world's first electronic organiser. The idea for the Psion Organiser emerged at a lunch in London in 1982 where Potter and Development Director Charles Davies were furiously scribbling on napkins. At the end of the lunch, they began to wonder if there could be a better portable medium to capture thoughts and ideas when on the move. After that conversation, they went back to work and two years later the Psion Organiser was born. In developing the Organiser, Psion pioneered the use of groundbreaking production methods and the device was based on Psion's own 8-bit operating system. But key to Psion's success was the excellent marketing for the Organiser, so much so that it achieved the ultimate accolade of the company becoming synonymous with the product category, in a similar vein to Kodak, Xerox or Hoover.

Despite the challenges, sales of the Organiser were high particularly with corporations and in 1987 Psion launched the Organiser II. Sales soared, and, in 1989, anticipating the convergence of communication technologies,

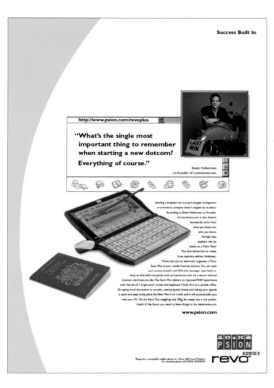

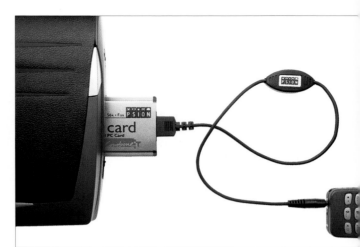

Psion launched its Psion Dacom arm to specialise in portable data communications.

During the late 1980s, Psion invested to develop a new generation of 16-bit machines, including the Series 3, the HC and Workabout ranges. Soon the Series 3a was the world leader in palmtop computing and Psion Dacom was leading the European PC Card modem market. By 1996, the company's turnover exceeded £124 million and it had sales subsidiaries in the US, Holland and Germany, as well as sales to over 45 countries.

In 1997, Psion unveiled the EPOC operating system, a new 32-bit software platform that took over 100 man-years to complete. This was designed to provide a platform for the next generation of handheld devices that Psion predicted would integrate mobile computing and cellular communications. The first product based on EPOC was the Series 5, launched in 1997 to huge acclaim.

June 1998 was another significant landmark in the history of Psion. In a groundbreaking deal, it managed to persuade some of the fiercest rivals in the mobile phone industry to link up with Psion in a joint venture to establish EPOC as the standard platform for future mobile devices. The joint venture called Symbian, consists of Psion (28%), Nokia (21%), Motorola (21%), Ericsson (21%) and Panasonic (9%).

Like all good ideas, the rationale behind the company was simple. Licensees of the technology would pay between $5-$10 per unit depending upon the type of device produced. With industry analysts predicting an explosion in mobile phone sales of up to one billion units by 2003, the opportunities for Symbian are substantial. So far, apart from the shareholders, other significant licensees to sign up to Symbian include Qualcomm, Sony and Philips.

Product

Psion comprises four principal operating divisions all based in the UK. Psion Computers is the market leader in enterprise and consumer mobile internet and computing solutions. The range includes products like the Psion Revo and, Series 5mx and Series 7, as well as a wide range of peripherals and software applications.

Psion Connect Ltd (formerly Psion Dacom) designs, manufactures and markets a number of mobile communications and connectivity products. The company recently received the highest level of recognition available to British firms in the form of the Queens Award for Enterprise 2000.

Psion Enterprise Computing focuses on the growing global demand for commercial and industrial handheld computing and network access products. Psion Enterprise's product range includes the Psion netBook, Workabout, HC and Organiser brands.

In early 2000, Psion introduced its InfoMedia Division. Psion InfoMedia focuses on product development, design and market understanding to develop a new range of groundbreaking appliances for mobile environments. Wavefinder, its first product, facilitates digital radio by automatically detecting digital radio signals and allowing content to be broadcast and received over a PC.

Recent Developments

Psion's commitment to exploring opportunities in mobile internet services and in wireless internet for mobile enterprise applications led to a number of key investments for the company in 1999/2000.

Firstly, Psion acquired Fonedata Ltd, one of the UK's leading WAP portals and corporate WAP and SMS services companies. It also acquired a 7.4% stake in RadioScape Ltd, a London-based software house specialising in digital radio technology. RadioScape develops software components for digital radio, and its technology forms part of Wavefinder.

Psion also agreed to acquire a 3.2% stake in WIDCOMM Inc, a privately owned San Diego, California-based wireless networking company and an emerging leader in Bluetooth technology. Furthermore, Psion signed an agreement to take a circa 3% stake in Quicknet Technologies, the US-based specialist in low-density internet telephony products.

Finally, Psion and United News and Media plc have created a joint venture company to target the rapidly growing market for enriched mobile internet services across all device platforms. The company, Trivanti Ltd, will work in partnership with a range of mobile technology companies and media businesses to develop and market wireless internet services for business-to-business and business-to-consumer users.

Promotion

'The customer is king' could well be the motto of Psion's global marketing. From registration, each customer begins a journey which the company hopes will last a lifetime. Psion believes in regular communication with its users through a number of highly customised vehicles, such as online magazines, tailor-made e-communications and interactive web demonstrations in each individual market. It also actively encourages the communication to be two-way, seeking feedback on product improvements, design ideas and user experiences.

Advertising spend is targeted specifically at vertical market segments rather than at simple brand enhancement, while Psion's merchandising is designed to reflect the warm experience of becoming a member of the Psion family. Detail is everything, from the out-of-box experience right through to the after sales service. Sponsorships too are chosen to emphasise the Psion values of innovation, creativity and design, as are corporate exhibitions such as CeBIT in Hanover and Comdex in Las Vegas. Messages are kept consistent across the different sales regions, but taking into account local input and considerations. Psion's marketing is supplemented by a powerful public relations programme, ranked by Presswatch in the UK fourth out of 1600 international companies in terms of favourable coverage.

Psion's advertising in the business and consumer press targets corporate users of personal computing devices during their work and leisure hours. Advertisements for products like the Psion Revo organiser show a range of people benefiting from having access to the internet and to email while on the move. The advertising headline 'E-mail anywhere' fits Psion's aim to be at the centre of the mobile internet revolution.

Brand Values

Psion is one of the leading brands in the emerging age of the mobile internet. It is dedicated to providing innovative solutions addressing real customer needs. Psion aims to shape and lead the mobile internet age by delivering distinctive mobile internet solutions and devices to people and organisations.

The internet has moved to centre stage in the digital revolution whilst the frontier in communications technology has moved from fixed line to digital wireless systems. Psion is positioned at the heart of these developments in mobile data, mobile internet and software systems for cellular wireless systems. Psion's core purpose is to take advantage of the investment and market opportunities presented by its pivotal position in these fast growing markets.

Things you didn't know about
Psion

The PSION initials stand for 'Potters Scientific Investments or Nothing'.

Psion's first offices were above an estate agents in North London.

Psion is a pioneer in the new Bluetooth wireless technology arena and will supply Dell and Compaq with their Bluetooth products.

Psion won the Best Hardware Award at Comdex, Las Vegas for its newest organiser, the Psion Revo.

Psion has a secret division for new product development codenamed 'the Nursery'.

Alfred Yaghobzadeh, a French journalist, had his life saved by his Psion when reporting in Chechnia. His Psion deflected shrapnel from a bomb away from slicing a major artery. Remarkably, his Psion still worked afterwards.

Famous people who use Psion include Jonathan Ross, Terry Waite, Kylie Minogue, Cher, Madonna and Rolf Harris.

Market

Quality Street competes in what is known as the 'twistwrap' market alongside brands such as Roses, Celebrations and Heroes. This is a very competitive market that is constantly growing and evolving as manufacturers seek to find ways of making the product appeal to an increasing range of consumers of all ages.

Quality Street has always been a versatile brand and has become known as the ideal gift or seasonal product to share with friends. Recently however, the brand's success has been rooted in its ability to expand its potential by establishing itself as a year-round product to be enjoyed in all sorts of different situations, rather than simply at Christmas time.

Achievements

Quality Street is the world's top-selling boxed chocolate brand. UK sales in 1999 amounted to £89 million, which makes Quality Street the third best selling chocolate in the country. Export sales of Quality Street rose from just over 4000 tones in 1989 to over 9000 tons in the late 1990s.

History

The world's first toffee factory was built in Halifax by one Lord Mackintosh in 1898. After his death in 1920 his son, Lord Mackintosh Jr took over the family business, moving it, when the factory burnt down ten years later, to an old carpet factory called Albion Mills. It was here, in 1936, that Quality Street was born.

The name Quality Street was inspired by

a play by J M Barrie, author of Peter Pan, and the characters that until recently still appeared on the box were inspired by the two principle characters, Phoebe Throssel and Valentine Brown. The brand immediately distinguished itself from other competitors with the groundbreaking decision to mix chocolates and toffees. When it was launched in 1936, a box of Quality Street cost two shillings (10p), which is equivalent to £3.69 today.

Quality Street continued to be manufactured during World War II, but was made with a reduced number of sweets due to rationing and the only formats on the market were the 1/2 lb carton and 5lb tin. However the relative excess of the post war period saw a huge expansion of the Quality Street range and a steady increase in sales that gradually made it into a trusted fixture of family life. Until the 1970s, Quality Street had a completely different sales profile in the UK. Most bulk sales were from 'weigh out' sales over the counter from 5lb tins which were returned to Halifax when empty, washed and filled again for resale.

Quality Street is now exported to over 50 different countries and one of the brand's sustained strengths has been its ability to appeal to people the world over. For example, the range used to contain many more toffees, with two main types being manufactured. While one was of a normal consistency, the other was boiled much harder so that after being shipped to warm climates like South Africa, it would be in a perfect state to eat.

Despite focusing on the need to become a year-round product, Quality Street is perhaps best known and loved as a seasonal family product and nearly 70% of annual Quality Street sales take place in the last third of the year.

Product

Quality Street consists of twelve sweets each of which is very different and has its own packaging and distinct brand identity. Combining milk and dark chocolate with hard and soft toffees, soft fruit centres, pralines and nuts, the brand caters for varying tastes inside a single box.

The sweets are wrapped in brightly coloured shiny wrappers and have been marketed since the brand's inception as a delightful fun-filled box to share with family and friends.

After the purple-wrapped hazelnut in caramel, the most popular Quality Street sweets are the caramel cup, noisette triangle, hazelnut éclair and the toffee finger.

Quality Street has become a well known brand all over the world and almost half of the Quality Street made in the UK is exported to 50 countries worldwide, including Cyprus, Iceland, Paraguay, Gambia, Peru, Japan and Bolivia. Quality Street is particularly popular

in the Middle East and Iran is supplied Quality Street through Dubai, where the packs are loaded onto dows and sent across the gulf. The brand is also very popular in Iceland because its tin format is often given as a gift for trawlermen and sailors since it can be kept fresh on board ship for several months.

Recent Developments

In 2000, Quality Street launched a new-look pack and advertising campaign to revitilise the brand. The re-launch was designed to appeal to a younger generation of consumers and aimed at 25-44 year olds to encourage people to re-think the role of Quality Street, as well as triggering all year round sales rather than

By the end of the night Abigail realised that she had nothing in common with Carl except their unusual dislike for the purple ones.

Quality Moments with Quality Street

primarily at Christmas. The traditional bow and the Major and Miss figures have been replaced by new packaging that emphasises what the product is all about – the sweets inside.

The traditional ribbon and bow design with its associations of gift-giving has been replaced by a bold and fresh design focusing on the core asset of the brand: its iconic sweets. Two modern packaging formats – a 900g and a 2kg cone – injected a sense of newness and excitement into the seasonal fixtures offering great potential for re-use after the sweets have been eaten. The new range includes boxes and novel cones designed specifically for informal sharing and produced from an unusual semi-opaque plastic material which lends a distinct and contemporary feel to the brand.

A new impulse bag retailing at 99p, was also introduced. This aimed to expand the possibilities of Quality Street in the mind of consumers, offering an indulgent impulse buy for established Quality Street lovers.

Every Quality Street consumer has a favourite Quality Street sweet. After identifying the most popular sweets within the Quality Street spectrum, the number of sweets in the Quality Street assortment was reduced from fifteen to twelve, thus offering more 'favourites' per pack. This element of the re-launch cost £1 million as the most popular sweets are also the more expensive to produce.

With the UK's favourite flavour combination in mind, Quality Street devised the new orange chocolate crunch which was launched and added to the selection in 2000. Significant improvements have also been made to the texture and flavour of fudge and strawberry cream sweets.

Promotion

The arrival of television in every home brought with it many famous and successful Quality Street adverts. The product was promoted by the Quality Street gang in the 1960s and the slogan 'all the fun of the share' ran throughout the 1970s.

One feature of Quality Street campaigns over the years has been the strategic use of well-known and loved songs. The 'Magic Moments' campaign starred Mr Johnson, the lollipop lady, the dawdling schoolboy and the businessman whose briefcase always sprang a surprise. The campaign featured a song that was co-written by Burt Bacharach and Hald David and was immediately recogniseable since it had topped the hit parade for US crooner Perry Como for two months in 1958.

In 1998 a colourful new television advert hit the screen featuring the memorable Nat King Cole song 'On the Street Where you Live' and focused on people whose lives are intertwined with their favourite Quality Street sweet.

The 're-launch' of Quality Street in 2000 was backed up by a television advertising campaign that started in September and was followed up in the vital run-up to Christmas. Representing a major departure from the cosy feel of the Magic Moments adverts of the 1990s, the adverts are modern in feel with an alternative sense of humour.

The overall theme of the new media and PR was the idea of 'Quality Moments' as exemplified by a 'National Quality Moments Day' on October 22nd 2000. This idea focuses on celebrating the numerous and often impromptu special occasions in people's lives that happen every day, whether it is a glass of wine on a Friday night or a night in with friends watching a video.

Quality Street launched an intense consumer communications drive. The introduction of the first ever 'National Quality Moments Day', as well as sponsorship of the Friday night ITV movie and a print and television advertising campaign all combined to raise the profile of Quality Street at the same time as changing and expanding people's perceptions of the brand.

Four press executions were also tailored to hit publications such as FHM and New Woman, targeting a wider collection of more diverse consumers.

Brand Values

Quality Street is loved worldwide and is perceived as lively, involving and generous. The brand's popularity stems from its inherent warmth and shareability and its unique variety of indulgent easily recognisable sweets.

It is the aim of Quality Street that when a pack is opened, young and old alike instantly dive in, searching for their favourite – whether the toffee penny or the green triangle. The appeal of Quality Street is the wide variety of sweets and chocolates on offer, most of which have become as well known in their own right as a branded chocolate bar.

Things you didn't know about
Quality Street

Almost four million Quality Street sweets are manufactured every day at the Nestlé Rowntree factory in Halifax, West Yorkshire.

Laid end to end, a week's production of Quality Street would stretch from Halifax to London and back.

Despite being sold in over 50 different countries, the purple-wrapped hazelnut in caramel sweet remains the favourite the world over.

In 1998 11,500 tonnes of Quality Street were sold.

Over 20,000 sweets are made per minute on the different production lines. Roughly 270 packs of Quality Street are packed per minute and 18 x 20 ton tankers of chocolate are used weekly.

RAC

Market

It is a fact of life that cars break down. Most drivers will find themselves let down by their vehicle at some time or other. New cars may be becoming increasingly reliable from a mechanical standpoint, but the incidence of simple faults such as flat batteries and flat tyres remains stubbornly high, supplemented with a whole host of modern electronic-related incidents. For most of us, the answer to these problems is to call for assistance from a breakdown recovery organisation. There are 27.5 million cars on the road in the UK and 30.6 million licensed drivers. Of these some 75% have membership of a motoring breakdown organisation, either individually or as part of a corporate scheme. RAC's share of the total market is about 30%.

Achievements

RAC has been meeting the needs of the motorist since the beginning of motoring itself. The core of RAC's offering has been its roadside breakdown service and this is the main benefit now enjoyed by the organisation's 6.5 million motorists – two million individuals and 4.5 million corporate members. Currently, half of all new subscribers to breakdown services join RAC and additionally RAC cover is included in the purchase of new cars from several leading manufacturers: over 60% of new cars carry motorists with RAC cover.

In 1986 RAC revolutionised its provision of breakdown recovery with the introduction of CARS – Computer Aided Rescue Service. This prompted a massive surge in the organisation's fortunes. In five years, RAC membership doubled and profits trebled to outstrip its competitors by far. These days RAC patrols reach over 80% of breakdowns in under an hour. The use of leading edge technology, including sophisticated diagnostic equipment and a complete library of technical data accessed within seconds via CD Rom, enables 1,300 expert RAC patrols to fix over 80% of breakdowns at the roadside and get members back on the move quickly and safely.

RAC has also developed a host of additional services which are available both to members and non-members alike, so that the organisation can now claim to offer the broadest range of services completely dedicated to the needs of motorists.

To maintain the tradition of RAC as a campaigning body on behalf of the motorist, RAC Foundation has been established – an independent body to take on the role of protecting the interest of the motorist.

History

The modern RAC has its roots in the Royal Automobile Club, the UK's oldest and most influential motoring organisation, which was established in 1897. In the early days of motoring, most drivers joined the RAC, which became the arbiter of matters relating to cars and driving. It promoted and enhanced the new 'motoring movement' by teaching driving, issuing road maps, approving garages and hotels, organising insurance and eventually establishing Road Patrols to help its members. These became the forerunners of the breakdown service for which it is best known today.

The RAC carried great prestige and authority and it became the governing body of motorsport, set standards and advised governments. Its palatial Edwardian clubhouse in Pall Mall was 'the Vatican of motordom' and its word was law on everything from automobile etiquette to engineering refinement. For at least the first 25 years of the RAC's existence, its history was virtually synonymous with the history of motoring in the UK.

However, complacency and lack of vigorous leadership saw RAC's fortunes, if not its respectability, decline over time to crisis point in the 1970s, mirroring the woes of the domestic motor industry.

A renaissance in the 1980s and 1990s saw the RAC's motoring services revolutionised, becoming the most technologically advanced in the world, setting new standards of service which its competitors struggled to match, and attracting an enormous increase in membership.

In 1998, the full members of the RAC voted to sell the motoring services division, and in June 1999 it was purchased by Lex Service plc – the leading business and motoring services organisation. RAC Motoring Services is no longer related in any way to the Royal Automobile Club (still based in Pall Mall). RAC's core product remains breakdown assistance, but this is now just one aspect of an

organisation that has the ability to offer a true 'cradle-to-grave' service to the motorist.

Product

RAC's vision is to be the first-choice provider of individual motoring solutions for both the consumer and business marketplace.

RAC provides an outstanding range of services to motorists, including roadside assistance, traffic information, driving tuition, servicing and repair, car financing and insurance, as well as hotel and travel services.

RAC is at the forefront of the development of in-car telematics with RTT, a joint venture with Trafficmaster, providing traffic and travel information using communications and satellite location technology. The award-winning RAC website provides online services to members and the general public, from live traffic news, journey times and booking hotels to vehicle examinations and advice on the car.

RAC members benefit from a comprehensive range of motoring services including legal advice and enjoy discounts on a wide range of products

and services, the scope of which has grown as a result of integration with Lex Service plc.

RAC also supplies bespoke solutions to corporate customers including the leading passenger car, truck and motorcycle manufacturers, contract hire and leasing companies and insurance companies. In addition to breakdown and recovery, the services offered to business customers include accident management, warranties, driver training, risk management and journey management.

Customers travelling at home and abroad have access to services including European breakdown assistance, travel insurance, travel accessories, route planning and hotel and holiday reservations.

Fully qualified engineers conduct vehicle examinations for individual motorists, manufacturers and garages. A search into the vehicle's background is undertaken through a direct online computer link with the specialist information providers.

RAC's driving school, BSM, is the world's largest driver training company and the only national driving school to have a high street presence with over 100 centres. BSM is at the forefront of training technology, having invested early in driving simulators and computerised theory training.

Recent Developments

New developments in the range of products and services offered by RAC are constantly being explored.

In partnership with Lex Service's 140 Autocentres, RAC is now providing servicing, repairs and MOT testing for all makes of car. In October 1999, RAC launched Red, a pay-as-you-go service. Members pay only £1 per month subscription, and incur additional fees only in the event of a breakdown.

The whole identity of the brand has been thoroughly overhauled in recent years, bringing the organisation's image up to date and shedding the last of the Royal Automobile Club associations. The most visible expression of this is the distinctive orange livery of RAC's fleet of breakdown vehicles, which provides both a striking new image and a practical safety feature.

RAC has taken up the tradition of publishing the annual Report on Motoring, which for the previous eleven years Lex Service plc had produced. These have provided a consistent source of fact and reason amidst the heat of transport debates and RAC is proud to maintain those standards.

Despite the rapid expansion in the range of products and services it offers, RAC remains dedicated to motoring and motorists. All developments and opportunities are focused in this area, with no expansion into non-motoring ventures. This commitment makes RAC unique amongst its motoring breakdown competitors, who have either expanded beyond the core of motoring services or moved into breakdown cover from a non-motoring base.

Promotion

RAC has a considerable history as a television advertiser, with campaigns that have for the most part focused on roadside breakdown, perhaps most memorably with the 'New Knights of the Road' imagery.

The decision to adopt the new positioning – 'Individual Motoring Solutions' – prompted a new advertising approach and the appointment of a new Agency, WCRS, in March 2000.

The new advertising campaign was developed specifically to broaden perceptions and understanding of RAC beyond its traditional role as a breakdown organisation. A selection of specific product and service messages was to be featured, each highlighting a key benefit that RAC can offer, which would combine to build a better awareness and appreciation of the extent of RAC's capabilities and relevance to all motorists, not just its members.

Five commercials were aired in June 2000 and ran for three months. They included the new strap line: 'A to B – we RAC to it' which was developed to communicate the sentiment of RAC's new vision and positioning. It is used consistently throughout all communications, internal and external, as an encapsulation of RAC's new aspirations.

Brand Values

In 1997, RAC was repositioned as a 'mobility' organisation. However, this was reviewed following the purchase by Lex Service plc. In light of the new opportunities presented by the takeover and following an extensive programme of research, 'Individual Motoring Solutions' was developed as a phrase to describe the present and future role of RAC. This has become the central brand positioning statement to differentiate the organisation within the broader motoring market it has entered.

RAC has a powerful set of imagery and values attached to it by consumers, but not all of these are relevant to the new positioning the brand was looking to adopt. Too many were rooted in the past and the old, traditional RAC. Nevertheless, there were some inherent strengths in the way the RAC was perceived, which provided a platform for the development of new values.

The research project enabled clarification of the differentiating values that together define a strong and distinctive personality for RAC. These were split into functional, product-related, solutions-based values of flexibility, practicality and willingness as well as emotional, service-related, individual-based values of responsibility, individuality and honesty.

These brand values have been adopted in its organisational values which in turn dictate RAC behaviours. All individuals within the organisation are thus given a direct line of sight into the brand, helping them to understand their role in delivering the RAC experience.

Market

Robinsons operates in one of the most competitive arenas – the UK soft drinks market. It is one of the largest retail markets in the UK and in competing for consumers' 'share of throat' must stave off competition from everything from water to carbonated soft drinks, fruit juices, other squashes and even tea and coffee.

Recent growth in the soft drinks market demonstrates the importance of soft drinks to consumers in today's society, even given their changing demands and lifestyle. 1999 saw sales reach nearly £8 billion, up 11.4% on the year before (Source: Canadean), reinforcing its position as one of the most important categories in the UK. However, there is still considerable potential for further growth. Consumers in the UK drink on average 173 litres of soft drinks each per year, compared to 202 litres in the rest of Western Europe and an astonishing 400 litres in the US. That equates to over one litre per day for every man, woman and child in the country.

Achievements

Robinsons sits like a giant in its own sector of the soft drinks market – squashes, where in value terms it accounts for 38.6% of this £681 million sector. This in turn equates to a 41.2% volume share (Source: ACNielsen), making it the UK's biggest squash brand in value terms and the fourth largest 'take home' soft drinks brand in the country (Source: ACNielsen).

By 2000 it had the distinction of being the UK's twelfth largest grocery brand, purchased by one in every two households (Source: ACNielsen). Robinsons now produces over 200 million litres of undiluted squash every year – the equivalent of over four billion glasses of Robinsons squash when diluted.

History

Robinsons traces its history back to 1823 when barley vendors Robinson and Bellville first opened for business, selling Matthias Robinsons patent barley powder. Then, thirsty customers would add boiling water to make a barley drink that was credited as a cure for fever and kidney complaints. The brand soon acquired a powerful relationship with mothers and children as one of the leading infant foods of its time.

In 1862 the firm merged with Keen and Son, a century-old mustard business, from whom

the expression 'keen as mustard' is derived. 41 years later, in 1903, J&J Colman of Norwich, which was destined to eventually evolve into the global soap giant Reckitt and Colman, acquired the company.

Robinsons' best known product, Barley Water, was not invented for another 31 years – and even then it was only by chance. A Colman's medical representative, Eric Smedley Hodgson was attending The Wimbledon Tennis Championships in the summer of 1934 when he decided to make up a refreshing drink to be served in the men's dressing rooms. It was made from Robinson's patent barley, fresh lemon juice, ice and sugar. The drink was an instant success and over 250 gallons were consumed during that year's tournament alone.

Following that, Robinsons launched its first bottled Lemon Barley Water the next year, priced at one shilling and nine old pence (the equivalent of 9p today). It was followed by Lemon Barley Crystals in 1936. Lime Barley Water was launched in 1937 and two years later an orange flavour was introduced.

The 1960s was a decade of hectic development and innovation for the Robinsons brand. It entered the fruit squash sector with Lemon Squash in 1960. In 1961 a grapefruit flavour was launched and three years later the first carbonated drinks bearing the Robinsons name were unveiled. Low calorie Orange and Lemon drinks were launched in 1965 and in 1966. These were re-launched under the name Robinsons Special R in 1984.

Following that, in 1995, Fruit & Barley was launched, initially in four flavours, summer fruits, blackcurrant, peach and orange.

1997 saw the launch of Robinsons Fruit and Barley Ready to Drink. This was re-branded Fruit Break in 1999 and is aimed at adults for immediate consumption whilst out and about. In 1998 Robinsons launched

High Juice, a premium squash containing 50% fruit juice, which is aimed at the adult consumer. 1999 also demonstrated that Robinsons is at the forefront when it comes to innovation, when five different vitamins were added to the Original and Special R ranges. Barley Water, the oldest brand in the Robinsons portfolio, was re-launched in 2000 with a new flavour added to the range, Orange and Cranberry.

An important addition to the Robinsons portfolio came in 2000 with the launch of Fruit Shoot, a fruit drink with added vitamins in a sports bottle pack. Fruit Shoot is aimed at active children and is the first fruit drink on the UK market with a 'push/pull' sports cap. Fruit Shoot aims to maintain Robinsons' position as a contemporary brand which is relevant to the tastes of modern children.

Product

Today the Robinsons portfolio consists of seven distinct sub brands covering different usage occasions and drinkers. Brands targeted at the family are mainly for consumption in the home and include Robinsons Original, containing the juice of the whole fruit with the added benefits of vitamins, Robinsons Special R, a no added sugar whole fruit squash also with the added benefits of vitamins, and Robinsons Fruit and Barley, a juice drink with barley flour and no added sugar.

Brands aimed at adults include High Juice, a premium squash containing 50% fruit juice and aimed at adults primarily for in home consumption. It also has no added sugar variants. Barley Water is the oldest of the Robinsons brands. It is aimed at adults as the drying qualities of the barley it contains makes it ideal for the adult palate. Fruit Break is a no added sugar low calorie still fruit drink aimed at adults for when they are out and about.

Fruit Shoot is the newest brand in the Robinsons stable and is aimed at active children. It too is available in both regular and no added sugar variants.

Recent Developments

In 1995 the brand was acquired by the soft drinks company Britvic Soft Drinks Ltd, a division of Bass plc. The sale by Colman, which had owned it for 94 years, made perfect sense in the competitive modern business environment which has seen firms concentrating more and more on their core competencies. Britvic already owns leading soft drinks brands such as Tango and R Whites Lemonade and has the UK franchise to produce and market Pepsi and 7Up. They were therefore ideally placed to ensure that Robinsons maintained its leading position in the squash sector.

Britvic embarked on a massive brand development programme aimed at exploiting the Robinsons consumer franchise to the full and extend the brand further into growth areas. Advertising spends increased and many new products were launched, thus ensuring Robinsons market leading position at the helm of the squash category.

Promotion

Key to the success of Robinsons has been its ability to communicate with each of its audiences in turn, namely adults, parents, and children. There are many examples of advertising campaigns where the brand talks directly to each of these audiences.

Robinsons has also reinforced its long standing association with the Wimbledon Tennis Championships — after all, it was here that Robinsons Barley Water, the oldest brand

in the range, was invented. This has allowed it to stress its healthy and refreshing credentials and has underlined its associations with Britishness and summer.

Although Robinsons was originally confined to the men's changing room, once bottled, it was displayed on court. It was in 1935 that advertising started to use the character 'Old Hethers' – a genial club steward who was deeply concerned for the well being of the players, as evidenced by the fact that he served them Robinsons. Old Hethers became the mainstay of press advertising throughout the 1930s and 1940s.

In the 1970s, Old Hethers was replaced by a new butler known as Robinson, who appeared in television commercials. By then the Wimbledon Tennis Championships had become the subject matter of nearly all of Robinsons advertising on television and in the press. Often they employed tennis stars themselves to feature in the advertising, as in the 1993 and 1994 campaigns with Pat Cash.

In 1998, the successful 'Feed their Imagination' television campaign was aired for the first time. It supports the family brands and in particular Robinsons Fruit & Barley, by implying that parents can play a role in nurturing their children by giving them Robinsons Fruit & Barley. This is communicated by a series of scenes portraying the innocence, creativity and wholesomeness in the way children look at the world, the end line being 'Feed their Imagination'.

In later years, Robinsons developed a successful ongoing promotional link with Disney. The initiatives, which appealed directly to children, started in 1998 when the brand linked up with Disney's 'Mulan'. In 1999 this continued with a promotion based around 'A Bug's Life'. This followed with huge promotional campaigns around the films 'Tarzan' and in early 2000, 'Toy Story 2'. In autumn 2000 the brand supported the release of the Disney film 'Dinosaur' with on-pack promotions featuring two characters from the film. All of the promotions based on the link with Disney have also been supported with heavyweight television advertising.

The launch of Fruit Shoot in summer 2000 was supported with a television advertising

campaign which depicts individual children demonstrating remarkable maturity at crucial moments in active situations. This develops the idea behind the brand as being for kids who are becoming 'little adults', embracing the new challenges of an active life in asserting their new-found independence.

Robinsons also has ongoing advertising communication aimed at adults. This is primarily based around the idea of re-hydration and that fact that it is recommended that we drink at least eight glasses of water a day in order to stay healthy. The campaign goes on to suggest that the water could be made more interesting by simply adding some Robinsons High Juice to a glass.

Brand Values

Like all powerful brands Robinsons has a finely balanced combination of physical and emotional attributes.

The brand's foundations were laid in 1934 when Barley Water was first mixed at the Wimbledon Tennis Championships. The combination of lemon, sugar and barley makes it an ideal thirst quenching drink, which explained its rapid success at the Championships. That success in turn allowed the brand to add layers of association drawn from the Championships: principally notions of straightforward healthy outdoor pleasures and a quintessential Englishness.

The product's unique taste made it popular with children, which in turn led to new product developments such as Robinsons Original and Special R. As one generation grew up, it in turn served Robinsons to its children and so on. As a consequence of this, the brand has been embedded deep in the national psyche as a timeless symbol of maternal indulgence and caring.

Market

Pottery and ceramics are a strong indicator of the art and lifestyle of a given age. Indeed archaeologists rely on shards of pottery fragments to establish the level of sophistication of past civilisations.

Today's consumers are more demanding and discerning than ever before.

The rise in home entertainment has been matched by the introduction of contemporary, functional tableware. At the other end of the spectrum however, the decrease in traditional family meals and rise in solo eating, TV dinners and convenience foods has seen the companies extend their casual tableware ranges.

Withstanding market fragmentation, ceramic giftware has enjoyed considerable growth – gift-giving, home decoration and investment being the main motivations. Despite the introduction of many alternative forms of gifts, the ceramic form is sought after as offering true qualities of heritage, traditional craftsmanship and real long-lasting value for money.

The key markets worldwide for premium ceramic tableware and giftware are the UK and Continental Europe, North America, Asia Pacific and Australasia. In total the global market is estimated to be worth over £1.5 billion.

Achievements

Royal Doulton plc is one of the world's largest manufacturers and distributors in the premium ceramic tableware and giftware market. Its illustrious brand names include Minton, Royal Albert and the core Royal Doulton brand.

With almost 200 years of heritage, Royal Doulton is a thriving global organisation, with around £200 million annual turnover, employing around 6000 people across its UK production houses and numerous distribution operations worldwide. Approximately half of Royal Doulton's sales are generated overseas.

Royal Doulton is a market leader within the ceramics and chinaware markets, around 40% of all English bone china being produced by Royal Doulton as well as almost half of the UK's ceramic sculptures.

The company's Hotel and Airline division is also the world's largest supplier of bone china to the international airlines industry. Indicative of its continuing favour, the division holds major contracts to supply chinaware to British Airways Club World and Club Europe.

Contracts are held also for Emirates and South African Airlines. All three airlines are noted for their high quality in-flight service, and Royal Doulton – aware of the need for brand differentiation – prides itself on creating contemporary ranges for each of its clients which, through the use of shape and surface designs, are uniquely distinctive.

In total, Royal Doulton produces a range of 30,000 different items across a broad range of product groups. As well as the company having provided Royal Doulton devotees with their treasured collection pieces, its Royal Albert design 'Old Country Roses' has become the world's best selling bone china tableware pattern, with over 150 million pieces having been sold since its introduction in 1962.

History

Royal Doulton has been producing ceramics and tableware for almost 200 years. As far back as 1815 the company founder, John Doulton, began producing practical and decorative stoneware from a small pottery in Lambeth, south London.

His son, Henry Doulton, built up the business, relocating it sixty years later to Stoke-on-Trent. By 1901 the quality of Doulton's tableware had caught the eye of King Edward VII, who permitted the company to prefix its name with 'Royal' and the company was awarded the Royal Warrant.

As Royal Doulton, the company expanded its production facilities and by the 1930s was involved in the manufacture of figurines and giftware.

Royal Doulton was awarded the Queen's Award for Technical Achievement in 1966, for its contribution to china manufacture – the first china manufacturer to be honoured with this award.

During the 1960s and 1970s Royal Doulton discarded its drainpipe production interests and acquired Minton, which had begun china

production in 1793, and Webb Corbett, a crystal manufacturer.

In 1972, Royal Doulton was bought by Pearson and merged with Allied English Potteries. The move introduced a number of key brands, including Royal Albert, founded in 1896, and also Lawley's retail chain of china and glass giftware.

In 1993, Royal Doulton was demerged from Pearson and became a publicly quoted company listed on the London Stock Exchange.

Product

Each of Royal Doulton's principal brands – Royal Doulton, Minton and Royal Albert – enjoys a long association of royal patronage, and holds at least one Royal warrant. They are also trademark registered.

When drawing up new product design, Royal Doulton designers study the market, analyse consumer research and often refer to their own museum and archives for inspiration.

The Royal Doulton Archives, located at the Sir Henry Doulton Gallery, the museum of Royal Doulton in Burslem, Stoke-on-Trent, house a variety of material dating from 1815 to the present day. Contents include Royal Doulton Pattern Books containing over 10,000 hand-painted water-colours illustrating the talent of artists employed over the years by the Burslem Art Studio.

Apart from providing an invaluable historical record of decorative ceramic styles – from the exquisitely gilded and delicately hand-painted cabinet and tableware of the Victorian and Edwardian era to the bright and bold angular design of the 1930s Art Deco – this collection is an inspirational source for Royal Doulton's current Design Studio.

Today, Royal Doulton provides a wide range of domestic tableware manufactured in bone china and fine china the brand is also featured in an extensive range of crystal stemware and giftware.

Royal Doulton lists amongst its products an extensive giftware range, character jugs, china flowers and an array of collectable figurines often known as the Royal Doulton 'pretty ladies'. Some of the figurines are inspired by history and literature, for example the figure of Heathcliffe and Cathy from 'Wuthering Heights'.

For the junior members of the household, Royal Doulton also produces nurseryware, and many of these ranges are of interest to adult collectors. Its most popular collection is 'Bunnykins', while 'Brambly Hedge' giftware; the Disney collections such as 'Winnie the Pooh' have also excited and sustained much interest.

Royal Albert, which traces its origins back to 1896, has become an internationally recognised brand, offering domestic tableware and gift items. Equally famous, with an illustrious heritage, dating back to its inception in 1793, is the Minton range, best known for its most popular pattern Haddon Hall, which is particularly favoured by the Japanese market. Minton is also renowned for its intricate gold patterns, where one plate can cost £5,000. These, however, are unique works of art, many of which are purchased as heirlooms. The artists at Minton also undertake special commissions.

Royal Doulton has a manufacturing capacity of around 500,000 pieces per week. Its tableware production factories are considered amongst the most advanced in the world – a tribute to the research and development department based at Baddeley Green, Stoke-on-Trent. In addition, the company runs around 3,000 tests per week to ensure that the highest possible quality of manufacture is maintained. Royal Doulton is noted for its high standard of working practices and technology which is heralded as being amongst the most advanced and professional in the entire international china industry.

As the corporate ambition is to generate 50% of its sales overseas, an extensive distribution chain is required to oversee global sales and marketing. The company currently operates in over 80 different markets and has distribution companies in the US, Canada, Australia and Japan.

Recent Developments
Royal Doulton is undergoing an important period of change in its long history as it implements a brand master-vision as a first step in repositioning the company's brands. Clarity for the position of the Royal Doulton and Royal Albert brands within the tableware and collectables marketplace has been key to the review.

The Royal Doulton brand has been segmented into five categories – Classics, Archives, FUSiON, Café and Studio – and identities have been created for each of the sub-brands, together with a new Royal Doulton brand logo. New global merchandising systems, in-store environments, point of sale and trade and exhibition design have all been identified as key to the repositioning.

Of course, despite significant changes in

new product sectors, has achieved considerable success, not least the launch of 'Doulton' luxury perfume, created by Patricia Bilodeau, Senior Perfumer at Dragoco. Other categories inspired by the company's rich heritage and design include an extensive collection of decorative fabrics and furniture sold in the US market as well as teas, textiles and ties in Japan.

In the UK licensed products include, kitchen textiles, Flemish tapestries and throws, stationery, children/baby gifts and accessories.

centred on the communication and effective introduction of the recent significant changes.

Royal Doulton's immediate goal is to become more global, offering greater consumer relevance through a diversity of products and an extension of its offering in contemporary creations.

At grass roots level, Royal Doulton continues to employ a variety of traditional promotional techniques ranging from trade fairs, in-store promotions, seasonal magazine and selected press advertising including supplements in bridal and lifestyle magazines.

There is also a strong and effective public relations campaign in place, which is reviewed annually.

Added to this, the visitor centre which was opened at the Royal Doulton factory, Nile Street, Burslem in 1996, is very popular. Open seven days a week, it features the world's largest public display of Royal Doulton figures, numbering over 1,500. Visitors are able to tour the factory during the week, although bookings have to be made in advance.

As an acknowledged leader in china tableware, Royal Doulton is working to maintain its unique position at the cutting edge of product development. Through building on its investments in areas such as Indonesia, Royal Doulton can maintain close control of its production and marketing throughout the world, making the most of its high brand recognition.

Brand Values
Around the globe, Royal Doulton is valued for its sense of heritage and Englishness. As one of the oldest and best-recognised chinaware brands in the world, Royal Doulton has earned itself a reputation for excellence, quality and distinctiveness of design – values which it intends to build on in order to take the brand forward in the new millennium.

Prized by collectors the world over, Royal Doulton has an international reach extending way beyond its English roots and product. To sustain its position, Royal Doulton's emphasis for future brand growth centres on its ability to focus on people, to understand its consumer base fully and then to produce products which suit individual tastes and needs.

Royal Doulton identifies its core brand values as integrity, innovation, creativity, craftsmanship and decorative skills.

direction, Royal Doulton has continued to do what it does best – produce top quality chinaware collections. The new ranges of casual diningware are stylish, functional and user friendly, suited to all modern appliances including dishwashers, microwaves, ovens and freezers.

The Licensing Division, created in the mid 1990s to propel the Royal Doulton brand into

Promotion
Central to Royal Doulton's promotional and marketing activity have been the re-positioning and rationalisation of the brand and the communication of same. The introduction of everything from new logos to in-store promotional material and branded fixtures have demanded that the focus of activity be

Royal Mail

Market

Royal Mail operates in a marketplace which is undergoing massive change. Alternative media, such as fax, email and mobile phones, have created significant competition in the letter and packet delivery sector.

Developments in e-commerce in recent years have also changed the distribution market, and Royal Mail has been quick to identify and take advantage of new areas such as trusted third party security (ViaCode).

Further external factors – globalisation, technology developments, the advent of the regulator and European cross-border mail liberalisation – are shaping the marketplace and demanding that Royal Mail adapts to meet the changing needs of current and future customers.

As well as Royal Mail's core market in the UK, it also has an international customer base. As one of Europe's largest carriers of international mail and the second biggest worldwide, Royal Mail despatches mail on 1400 scheduled flights every week to over 280 postal gateways worldwide. This ensures the fastest and most efficient transmission of important international business mail.

Achievements

Much of Royal Mail's focus in recent years has been on developing customer understanding of the unique benefits of mail in relation to other forms of communication.

The 'I Saw This and Thought of You' campaign developed this theme in the social market by showing how the mail can be complementary to the wide mix of new technologies, e.g. sending a pay-as-you-go phone card in the post to a loved one, highlighting the emotional impact of receiving it in the mail. Campaign awareness proved very successful, consistently achieving above 80% for the target audience (females aged 25-54). It has also won an Advertising Planning Group Silver Medal award.

For business customers this is also reflected in campaigns which focus on direct marketing opportunities and customer contact strategies. The call to action from television and poster executions was to www.royalmail.com, where a wealth of information is available on how to use the mail effectively as a business tool. This approach not only dramatically increased visits to the site, but it also enabled Royal Mail to capture valuable data on customers and identify potential sales opportunities to be followed up by the sales force.

Awards can also be a key measure of success for marketing activity. In 1999 Royal Mail's Special Delivery re-launch campaign won the 'Business Services integrated campaign of the year' award at the IPA Business Ad Awards. This paid tribute to the successful multi-agency approach that was taken to re-launch Royal Mail's flagship priority services product.

History

Royal Mail is one of the most trusted brands in the UK. It is a valuable asset which has evolved and grown since 1635 when the service of accepting and handling mail by the Royal Posts

we **swear**

specialdelivery next day by 12 noon*

www.royalmail.co.uk

YOU HAVE OUR WORD

Royal Mail

*Monday to Friday

was opened to the public by Charles 1. This royal proclamation and the establishment of the General Post Office in 1660 began the crucial social change which put the Post Office at the centre of the community and heralded a communications revolution.

Letters were originally collected from households and handed to the local postmaster. Occasionally he would arrange onward delivery, but this was not granted to all until Queen Victoria's Jubilee Declaration in 1897. This face-to-face contact began the relationship for which Royal Mail is well known today.

The awareness of Royal Mail grew considerably once the Mail Coach service was introduced in 1784, launching a national postal network. New postal routes were opened and mail volumes increased dramatically with the introduction of the uniform postage rate in 1840. Around the same time mail carriages began to use the words 'Royal Mail' for the first time alongside the Royal Cypher.

The term 'Royal Mail' is steeped in history and has been in use since the sixteenth century, but The Post Office established Royal Mail as a business only in 1986 with its own identity following three years later. The Cruciform logo now used includes the royal crowns – St. Edward's for England and Wales, St. James's for Scotland.

Stamps, postmen and postwomen, vans and postboxes continue to symbolise the Royal Mail brand. Its heritage provides a solid foundation for people's beliefs and expectations about the business which continues to bring people together.

Product

Royal Mail's core offering centres around a range of physical distribution products for both consumers and businesses, as well as an increasing portfolio of electronic and internet solutions. Currently Royal Mail handles twenty billion items each year.

As part of the Post Office's universal service, a first class letter can be sent anywhere within the UK and arrive at its destination the following day (except Sundays). Alternative forms of communications may be cheaper as well as quicker through electronic media, but the mail still offers emotional and tangible benefits for both sender and receiver.

Mail is also increasingly used as part of the business communication mix to attract customers and nurture business relationships as well as strengthening a brand. A range of services are available (including Mailsort and Presstream) to business customers and significant savings can be made on standard postal rates depending on how the customer pre-sorts mailings. Despite the advent of fax, telephone and internet, direct mail volumes have trebled over the last ten years and in 1999 represented 12% of all advertising revenues.

Royal Mail is also establishing itself in areas outside its core postal business. ViaCode from Royal Mail is the first commercially independent Trusted Third Party service enabling secure electronic commerce. Internet development is significantly changing the way in which business is and will be done. However, it is not a secure medium and 71% of large UK businesses will not send confidential or sensitive information via the internet (Source: NOP Business Internet Survey wave three). ViaCode provides this security. The move into this market supports the core brand attribute of 'trust', whereby Royal Mail acts as the trusted party which confirms user identities to ensure secure transfer of electronic information.

Royal Mail has also continued to develop unique and thought-provoking special edition stamps. The years 1999 and 2000 saw the

release of the Millennium Collection celebrating under twelve monthly themes, 1000 years of British achievements, and Britain's national millennium projects which look to the future under twelve monthly themes. In the very competitive collectables market, stamp collecting continues to be very popular across all age groups.

In addition to these core services, Royal Mail still offers a free service for Petitions to both the Queen and Parliament. Also, recognising Royal Mail's role in the community, the 'Royal Mail Postbus' has become a vital part of rural life providing a free local transport service.

Recent Developments

In common with all industries, the distribution market has been significantly affected by the opportunities represented by e-commerce. Royal Mail has been quick to seize upon these opportunities and develop a presence in this marketplace, particularly in terms of the ViaCode service offered.

Royal Mail is also working closely with a number of online businesses, most notably Amazon.co.uk, for whom Royal Mail is the contracted delivery arm. Online retailers face the challenge of creating a real brand in an e-world and this is where Royal Mail can add value to its brand experience by becoming the

above-the-line, direct mail, PR and sponsorship of major events such as the DMA/Royal Mail Awards.

Supporting the core brand value of 'innovation', Royal Mail is always looking to develop new products and services which meet the ever-changing needs of the customers. One such example is the introduction of self-adhesive stamps that use glue specially developed for Royal Mail. Also, to support a cross-media relationship management programme, a proactive e-marketing strategy has been successfully used to email registered customers with a 'Business Update' service.

Front line employees effectively act as ambassadors of the Royal Mail brand and therefore uniforms are a key element of the physical representation of the brand. A new uniform has been designed to meet the very different needs of the varying roles of operational employees. Working together with a work-wear design company, the new uniform takes account of the extreme outdoor conditions delivery staff can encounter, as well as ensuring all health and safety standards are met.

Royal Mail has also recognised the importance of enabling its visually and hearing-impaired customers to have the same access to information as other customers. A dedicated Textphone service has been introduced in all Royal Mail Customer Service Centres allowing hearing-impaired customers to interact with staff. Also, Royal Mail provides a service for visually-impaired social customers where all printed communications are made available in an alternative large type format available by calling any Customer Service Centre.

Promotion

Much of the continued growth in mail volumes is attributed to a carefully planned and well executed marketing communications strategy.

Even though the Royal Mail brand is one of the most well known in the UK, it does not rely on this alone to ensure continued growth. Good marketing communications help strengthen the brand and enable the reinforcement of the core brand value of 'caring'.

generated as a result of advertising.

Recognising the importance of new media, Royal Mail continues to develop its online presence (www.royalmail.com) in line with customer needs. The site has consistently received industry recognition as a well designed and customer focused site.

Working together with Rufus Leonard, one of Royal Mail's new media agencies, the site provides online information about products and services, but also provides interactive services. 'Postcode Finder' allows customers to type in an address which then displays the relevant postcode. 'Track and Trace' enables customers to follow the delivery trail of items they have posted using Special Delivery. The unique reference number of the item can be typed in, and within seconds the status of the item is displayed.

Increasingly the website is being used as an effective campaign support vehicle, driving customers directly to the site in response to a promotional message, whether it be in a piece of direct mail or in a television commercial. The site will continue to be a key component in Royal Mail's marketing communications strategy.

Brand Values

The Royal Mail brand touches many people with different feelings and beliefs in their hearts and minds about what the brand stands for.

Brand positioning is focused on fostering relationships between senders and receivers. This is reflected in the brand vision statement, 'Bringing people closer together in relationships they value'. Supporting this are three core brand values of reliability, innovation and caring, which help shape positioning to enable Royal Mail to become customers' first choice.

To be a strong brand in customers' eyes, it is recognised that Royal Mail employees are the living embodiment of the customer experience. Therefore they must also engage with the brand and this is a key element of the brand strategy.

You press all the right ones

WHAT WOULD YOU SEND?

trusted carrier for online customer orders.

Developments in internet capability have also been key elements of the delivery of the brand experience. This was demonstrated internally with the launch of 'Ben', an online brand and project management system which provides brand information, visual identity guidelines and a project workflow system that enables project managers and agencies to interact electronically.

Keen to develop its mail media ownership, Royal Mail has set up a centre of excellence to ensure all direct mail activity to customers is high-quality and 'on-brand'. To gain credibility in the business world, an integrated marketing strategy has been developed, encompassing

Probably the most well known advertising is the long running and highly successful 'I saw this and thought of you' campaign which was developed with Royal Mail's above-the-line agency, Bates UK. The campaign uses television, cinema and poster executions and has been running since December 1996. The campaign plays on the idea that actions speak louder than words, which epitomises the philosophy behind the whole campaign: that you can send tangible objects in the post to convey a powerful emotional message.

The campaign consistently received high recall figures and has been directly responsible for an increase in social and business mail volumes

Things you didn't know about
Royal Mail

Royal Mail handles over 77 million letters, cards and packages every day. New records for mail volumes were set over Christmas 1999, with more than 2.5 billion cards, letters and packets handled by Royal Mail in the four weeks up to Christmas Day.

Royal Mail employs 169,000 people and has a transport fleet of 29,000 vehicles covering all of the UK's 25 million addresses.

Over 4,500 redundant Royal Mail bicycles are donated every year to Africa for children to use to get to school, and adults to work.

Royal Mail has the world's most advanced sorting equipment which has reduced the time for processing a letter from 90 minutes four years ago to 90 seconds today.

Sainsbury's

making life taste better

Market

The £73 billion UK supermarket sector is an intensely competitive arena where only the very fittest survive. Sainsbury's market is characterised by extreme price sensitivity and sharply escalating consumer expectations on quality, choice and value.

Powerful new entrants from the US and Europe, the growth in new 'convenience' store formats, diversification into internet shopping and non-traditional supermarket offers such as financial services have further raised the stakes for all players in this market.

Because food products are uniquely close to people's hearts and consumers spend a relatively large proportion of their shopping time buying food, their interaction with supermarket brands is particularly 'immersive'. Trustees of premier brands such as Sainsbury's have certain responsibilities to meet their customers' rising expectations by offering experiences of the brand that are consistently engaging and positive. Good design, great packaging and constant innovation are just part of the job in this market – real success is founded on delivering the product quality and outstanding service that is at the heart of Sainsbury's brand promise 'Making Life Taste Better' for its customers.

Achievements

Over the last 130 years, Sainsbury's has pioneered many of the most significant breakthroughs in quality, convenience and value for UK food shoppers. Sainsbury's can boast an impressive list of 'firsts', including the introduction of the first Supermarket in 1950 and the first own brand range as early as 1903.

As well as championing customer choice in the 1960s with such novelties as avocados and self-service wine departments, the company was also the first supermarket to offer banking services, the first to introduce debit card payment, and the first to set up an internet service. Other recent innovations include being the first of the big four supermarkets to eliminate GM ingredients from its own brand products and pioneering new partnerships with UK farmers to support a move to more organic produce.

Sainsbury's can claim to have invented the modern supermarket in the UK and has frequently led the way in meeting and exceeding consumer expectations.

History

John James and Mary Ann Sainsbury opened their first shop in 1869 in London's Drury Lane selling milk, eggs and 'the best butter in the world'. The family business quickly expanded into the suburbs. By 1890 Sainsbury's stores already had a recognisable house style with decorative tiled walls, mosaic floors and marble-topped counters to provide a uniquely cool and hygienic shopping environment.

As the business grew, the founders' six sons became more involved and the eldest, John Benjamin, became a full partner in 1915. Although the company was incorporated in 1922 it remained a family business until flotation in 1973. For four generations, the Sainsbury family's commitment to the founder's core values has been a crucial factor in shaping the modern company's brand personality.

Sainsbury's introduced its first grocery departments in 1920, increasing the range of own brand products. After rapid expansion in the 1930s the company suffered through World War II when rationing led to a 50% decline in sales volume. The company's response to the difficult post war years was typically radical and innovative. The first self-service store was opened in June 1950 in Croydon. Now widely regarded as the UK's first modern supermarket, this large store set new standards with a dazzling range of fresh products on display and helped establish Sainsbury's as the UK's leading supermarket brand for many years to come.

The 1960s and 1970s saw further expansion of the supermarket concept. By 1970 over half of Sainsbury's 255 shops offered self-service and new lines of high quality goods were added including own brand packaged groceries and fresh meat; the choice of products offered increased more than threefold during the 1960s and 1970s. The continuing success of the Sainsbury's formula culminated in the company's flotation on the stock market in 1973. It was the biggest and most successful flotation the City had ever seen. The mid 1970s saw a period of astonishing success as Sainsbury's opened its first large edge of town stores and consolidated its position as the UK's leading grocer.

The last twenty years have seen intense competition among all the major supermarket chains, and the battle for supremacy has been characterised by Sainsbury's competitors playing catch up and with some success. The company's response has been to launch a stream of new initiatives that are aimed at delivering the Sainsbury's promise – 'making life taste better' for all.

Product

Sainsbury's today has over 420 supermarkets throughout the UK, including a range of formats to serve different shopping needs while delivering the same consistent high quality product range. These include Sainsbury's larger format out of town stores, city centre stores – 'Sainsbury's Central' – aimed at shoppers and workers, with a good range of fresh sandwiches, sushi and salads as well as a complete choice of prepared meals. The smaller 'Sainsbury's Local' format is a neighbourhood store with its own small bakery, coffee bar and ready meals on offer. Meanwhile the larger stores encompass the full range of traditional supermarket products and more, with the very largest on a par with continental hypermarkets selling toys, clothes and electrical items.

Over 55% of Sainsbury's sales are made up of own-brand products, including national

bestsellers such as the Be Good to Yourself and Economy ranges.

Sainsbury's own label food is a major brand in its own right, outselling all other supermarkets in this field and consistently outperforming big name brands in taste tests.

The offer of various stores change according to size and locations and larger stores now offer a full range of meat and fish counters, pharmacies, coffee shops and petrol stations. Sainsbury's customer loyalty scheme, the Reward Card, has over fourteen million members who enjoy benefits such as special interest clubs like Drinks Club, 0 to 5 Club and Pet Club as well as interactive terminals in store which dispense discount vouchers. Sainsbury's Magazine, a joint venture with Delia Smith's company, has become the UK's bestselling food magazine.

In 2000 Sainsbury's successfully relaunched its internet shopping home delivery service, 'Sainsbury's to You', which offers customers an easy-to-use website coupled with a fast and accurate delivery service.

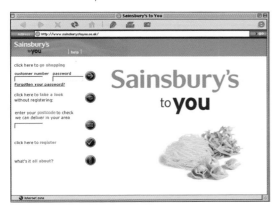

Sainsbury's Bank, a joint venture with Bank of Scotland, has been a successful diversification of the brand that has created new added value benefits for Sainsbury's customers. The award winning Fresh Banking operation now offers a full portfolio of banking services including instant access savings accounts, bonds, ISAs, loans, car finance, insurance and credit cards.

Recent Developments

Sainsbury's works constantly to improve the range and quality of its products and services to ensure that the company continues to deliver the brand's promise 'Making Life Taste Better' for consumers. The recent return to the company of Sir Peter Davis as CEO signals a new commitment to make Sainsbury's special again by focusing on the brand's strengths – in particular its association with better food.

Central to Sainsbury's brand strategy is a commitment to make continuous improvements to the products it sells. The company has been pioneering the move to increase its organic range since 1986 and has over 900 organic products on sale – more than any other supermarket. Sainsbury's is also pushing for international verifiable standards of organic farming and is working closely with farmers to help them through the transition. Today

Sainsbury's sells over 50% of all UK organic production of milk, eggs, strawberries, pork and chicken and is guaranteeing volume and pricing levels to organic farmers for up to five years.

Sainsbury's has been quick to remove GM ingredients from own brand products, and through the integrated crop management (ICM) initiative is working with farmers to reduce the use of pesticides, encourage biodiversity and give a stronger emphasis to naturally farmed products. Promoting healthier foods through initiatives such as the Be Good to Yourself, Food to Go ranges and new salad bars are more examples of how the company aims to meet customers' escalating expectations.

Recent years have seen substantial new investment in stores, with particular emphasis on modernising existing sites with a bright new design idiom and extending the ranges in individual stores. Added value attractions include Starbucks coffee shops, kids' shops, Wellbeing centres, pharmacies, health and beauty offers, sushi, and water ('O' to go). Like other leading retailers, Sainsbury's believes that adding features that make shopping a more enjoyable and motivating experience for consumers will extend the appeal of the brand and aid the success of the business.

Service is another major focus for the business and various enhancements in training offer customers ever higher levels of service and satisfaction.

Recent initiatives include extra staff on duty to help with fetching, packing and carrying products for customers, fast track checkouts, an order and collect service, and more product sampling. Training is given extra priority as a high level of staff commitment is central to Sainsbury's quality drive.

E-commerce is a key element of Sainsbury's improved service offer. The 'Sainsbury's to You' internet shopping offer is backed by Europe's largest picking centre. The company has also formed partnerships with leading international retailers such as Sears and Carrefour in a new global internet-based system, GlobalNetXchange, which helps reduce costs and increase buying efficiencies.

Promotion

In the hyper-competitive world of supermarkets, high profile marketing is essential to reinforce and advance brand equity. Sainsbury's has invested heavily over the years in promotional campaigns. The 'famous recipe' campaign made use of high profile celebrities to show how to make delicious dishes from Sainsbury's ingredients. Dawn French, Selina Scott, Catherine Zeta-Jones, Nick Berry and Dennis Healey are just a few of the celebrities who have been recruited to lend their strong public recognition to Sainsbury's offer of a reliable and inspirational shopping experience.

In 2000 Sainsbury's promotion drive, the 'Making Life Taste Better' campaign, dramatised

the role that good food plays in adding quality to people's lives. Star TV chef, Jamie Oliver, is the latest face of Sainsbury's and can be seen demonstrating how to make easy dishes, sampling food on the delicatessen counter and visiting farmers who supply the company. In addition Jamie is working closely with Sainsbury's to develop new product ranges to create a stronger identification for the company with the appeal of his personality and skills as a chef.

Sainsbury's sees its Reward Card loyalty club as another key element of the company's promotional strategy. The range of benefits and offers on the Reward Card has been extended to include discounts in restaurants and shops that are outside of the Sainsbury's group. The core message of great food and good value every day is at the heart of every Sainsbury's promotion drive. Buy one get one free offers, extra reward points, and swaps for benefits such as air miles are core elements of the overall 'value' message.

Brand Values

Sainsbury's is committed to six core brand values:- Higher Standards, Great Value, More New Ideas, Wider Choice, Easier Shopping, and Respect and Thanks. These reflect the way that its corporate culture relates to customers and colleagues.

The concept of value above all is what the Sainsbury's brand means to consumers and is the foundation of the company's continuing success. The 'Making Life Taste Better' positioning expresses these values by emphasising that as well as selling food, Sainsbury's is about experiencing the pleasures of eating delicious fresh food and enjoying the benefits of healthy eating. This reflects the fact that food is central to people's lives and Sainsbury's can provide the food, the shopping environment, the new ideas and the service that really can improve the quality of our lives. That's a big commitment for a brand to make but one that the company clearly believes it can deliver.

SCOTTISH WIDOWS

Market

As governments in the UK and elsewhere admit that the state alone cannot guarantee people a secure and comfortable old age, the savings and investments market is booming. The UK life and pensions market is already the third largest in the world (after the US and Japan) and in Europe, the market is expected to double in size over the next ten years.

Pressure on companies in the market is also increasing: consumers are more knowledgeable and demanding; the industry is consolidating and the government is in the middle of the greatest regulatory shake up in half a century.

These are exciting times, in which brand value is, if anything, yet more important than ever before. The name 'Scottish Widows' might not be the first name a brand-consultancy would suggest for a financial services company, nor perhaps would a woman in a black cloak be the focus-group choice for a corporate icon. But together they have delivered an enviable reputation for this Edinburgh-based life company, including the highest brand-recognition in its sector.

Achievements

Founded in 1815 as Scotland's first mutual life office, Scottish Widows has gone from strength to strength becoming, the UK's second largest provider of pensions, life and investment products.

The company's investment arm, Scottish Widows Investment Partnership, manages over £90 billion of client funds, making it Scotland's biggest investment manager and one of the largest in Europe. The company has a well-established multi-channel sales capability, distributing its products through Independent Financial Advisers, Direct Marketing and – via Lloyds TSB, the UK's largest bank branch network.

A strong brand may help sales, but without well-made products and excellent customer service, even the best brand would not last long. Scottish Widows is proud to have won the 5-Star Award for service from Financial Adviser in 1996, 1997, 1998, 1999 and again in 2000. In addition, it has also won significant recent awards from Money Management, Money Marketing and Standard & Poor's, recognising the high standards of the company.

History

On 25 March 1812, at the height of the Napoleonic Wars, a number of eminent Scotsmen crunched their way through the snow along Edinburgh's High Street. They were heading for the warmth of the Royal Exchange Coffee Rooms and a meeting to consider the prospectus for 'a general fund for securing provision to widows, sisters and other females'. These were relatives of deceased clergymen, schoolmasters and the like; the fund was designed as a safety net should they be left poverty-stricken, as was all too common at that time. However, these gentlemen envisaged one vital difference between their idea and other established funds. Theirs would extend its benefits throughout the UK.

The Scottish Widows' Fund and Equitable Assurance Society opened for business in 1815, at the home of its first manager, William Wotherspoon. From its earliest days, Scottish Widows seemed to have the secret of profitable growth. In September 1821, the Society had funds of £20,000; by 1831, it stood at well over £250,000; and in 1845, it exceeded £1,700,000.

In 1924, the Daily Telegraph commented that "the chief characteristic of the Scottish Widows' Fund for more than a century has been uniformity of excellence. From time to time other life offices have had streaks of brilliance lasting for a few years and have fallen back in to mediocrity, but for a sustained level of quality the Scottish Widows' Fund stands supreme".

A continuous, if quiet, tradition of value for money, good returns and care for the customer transformed itself into a powerful brand with the launch in 1986 of 'The Scottish Widow' – a landmark in advertising which powerfully conveyed the company's core qualities: strength, trust, reliability, integrity and confidence.

In March, 2000, Scottish Widows demutualised and joined the Lloyds TSB Group of companies, absorbing Lloyds TSB's previous life, pensions and investment businesses and relinquishing its mutual status to become Scottish Widows plc. The challenge Scottish Widows now faces, as the company moves into the top league, is to continue 'Looking Good for Your Money', as its advertising strapline proclaims.

Product

Scottish Widows' ultimate product is financial security; the company packages strong, dependable investment performance into flexible products to meet customers' changing needs at every stage of life.

The three major areas of business are protection, savings and investment. Protection products include life assurance, critical illness and mortgage cover, while savings cover regular savings plans and the new Individual Savings Account (ISA). In addition, Scottish Widows Bank offers a variety of deposit and mortgage products, while Scottish Widows International addresses the market for offshore investment. Scottish Widows was also among the first to offer ISAs and term-assurance products through www.scottishwidows.co.uk.

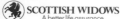

Recent Developments

Joining the Lloyds TSB Group was both a recognition of Scottish Widows' achievements so far and an opportunity to extend them into new areas. The company is developing plans to bring its product offering, not just to existing Lloyds TSB customers, but to the wider European market; the investment business, too, is establishing itself as a global brand, with a significant US, European and Far Eastern presence.

Promotion

The strength of the Scottish Widows brand is based on a radical marketing decision taken in 1986: to create a living logo. Scottish Widows management saw that their business was about to change fundamentally. It was to move from a stable, conservative industry – where word of mouth recommendation and advice were the principal source of new customers – into a consumer-driven marketplace where strong brand recognition would be essential.

Until the mid 1980s, the Scottish Widow was well known among professionals (such as solicitors, bankers and accountants) and by word of mouth. But at that time, there were over 30 competing companies in the market, six of which had the word 'Scottish' in their name. In addition, widows, in general, do not immediately suggest positive associations in most people's minds.

The first brand image produced by Scottish Widows was an emblematic device based on Sir John Steel's sculpture 'Cornucopia – The Horn of Plenty'.

This was followed with a graphic by the Edinburgh illustrator, Walter Crane. The slogan integrated with the emblem was 'Fronte Capillata Est Occasia Calva' – Take Time by the Forelock. Later, the shift was made to a stylised Pegasus. These emblems, although successfully providing a consistent image across corporate literature and signage, did not encapsulate the spirit of the company. How best could Scottish Widows build brand awareness while conveying the idea that it was 'good with your money', in every aspect of financial management?

The solution was to create an icon that countered all the negative values associated with the word 'widow' by presenting them as positives: young, confident, assured, professional and sophisticated. The impact of the first television commercial featuring this modern Widow, 'Looking Good', was immediate. Name awareness, which had hovered around 30%, shot up to 86% within six weeks of the launch of the campaign – and stayed there.

A new corporate logo was also developed for the company. The emblem selected was stylish, clean and incorporating the name of the company, instantly recognisable.

After two years, Milward Brown, declared Scottish Widows "the most successful insurance advertising ever monitored"; and a comparison of the advertising spend of top financial brands showed that Scottish Widows' awareness levels easily beat those of brands with much higher advertising budgets.

The first Widow, chosen after a long and careful selection process, was Debbie Barrymore, daughter of the actor Roger Moore. Debbie appeared in several television commercials – 'Birthday Party' in 1990 which marked the 175th Anniversary of the company, and in 1992, 'Venture Out' was set in a gentleman's club. In 1994, the model Amanda Lamb succeeded Debbie Barrymore. Amanda's first commercial was 'The Maze', shot on location at Ross and Wye and Gloucestershire in 1994. This was followed by 'Lights' in 1997, 'Boardroom' in 1998 and more recently, 'In the Black' in 1999. The choice of director was equally important: David Bailey, one of the world's best-known photographers, struck the ideal balance of style and essential humanity. It is a balance which all subsequent advertising and promotion has been careful to maintain.

The Scottish Widow also leads the company's print and poster presence. Careful use of her expression and gesture, combined with effective headline and copywriting, has allowed this living icon to express even the most complex aspects of financial services in a way the public responds to – and remembers.

The imagery of the Widow has been carefully guarded and controlled since her introduction in 1986. In 1999, the guidelines which safeguard her use, ('An Expression of our Brand') were entered in the New York Festival's Advertising and Design Awards, and won a prestigious bronze medal.

Brand Values

As a long-term savings and investment company, Scottish Widows is asking for people's trust, often over an entire lifetime. That trust is hard to obtain and easy to lose. For this reason, the brand values expressed in the company's advertising must genuinely be the values of the company itself; any conflict between expectation and experience loses customer confidence.

Market research reveals that the values people associate with the Scottish Widows brand are indeed those the company hopes to project: quality, expertise, trust, security and value for money. The Widow embodies those values in a way, which is both enduring and contemporary. It is a powerful proposition; one, which Scottish Widows, is taking into the global marketplace.

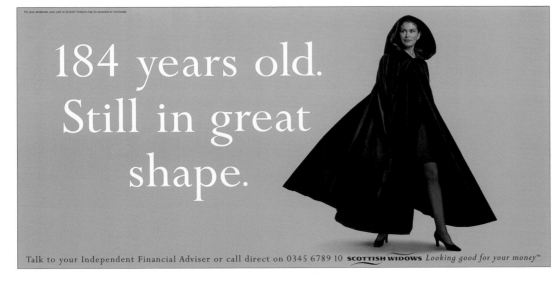

184 years old.
Still in great shape.

Talk to your Independent Financial Adviser or call direct on 0345 6789 10 SCOTTISH WIDOWS *Looking good for your money*™

SEGA

Market

All those parents who throw up their hands in despair when the only thing their children want to do is play video games have Sony, Sega and Nintendo to thank. These three titans continue to dominate the video games market, and their success over the past decade or more has generated huge customer loyalty which has made them apparently unassailable by the competition. Love them or loathe them, in just a few short years, Sega's Sonic the Hedgehog and the fabulous Lara Croft have emerged from obscurity to become household names.

Kate,
Naomi,
Linda,
Lara.

The Dreamcast beauty
treatment, as used by Lara Croft.

Lara Croft

Dreamcast.

TOMB RAIDER THE LAST REVELATION

The first stage of the video game console revolution focused on building up the market and establishing primitive hardware. The second stage saw the arrival of the Sega Mega Drive and the Sony PlayStation. But the market is in transition again: existing consoles are reaching the end of their natural life and new generation (NG) consoles are taking over. Sega was first off the blocks, launching its Dreamcast console in 1999, followed in 2000 by Sony's PlayStation 2. This third stage is characterised by a shift towards a home entertainment package which offers convergence of the console with television.

The NG consoles compete not just with each other, but with PCs too, so they pose a severe challenge to PC gaming. Sony remains the number one in the market, but Sega has repositioned itself as the console for the gaming enthusiast, being the first to provide online link-ups and multiplayer games. And now, with Microsoft entering the sector, the market landscape is changing yet again.

Achievements

Sega sold 100,000 Dreamcast consoles in the UK in the first month after its release in October 1999. A year later, more than one million Dreamcasts had been sold in Europe. Dreamcast was the first non-PC gaming system to offer internet access, exploiting the rapid growth in internet users in the UK. The Dreamcast was the first 128-bit machine to be launched by the major manufacturers, included a free modem and free internet access, allowing users to email, chat online, browse the web and play games online. By April 2001 more than 200 Dreamcast games were available.

Dreamcast was launched to huge acclaim. It was praised in particular for taking very expensive top-end PC technology and bringing it down to an affordable level. The launch price of the console was £199, and this was cut to £149 six months later.

Business Week magazine called Dreamcast one of the 'hot products of 1999' and TIME Digital hailed it 'Machine of the Year'.

History

Sega of America, based in San Francisco, was established in 1986 as the wholly-owned subsidiary of Sega Enterprises Ltd of Japan, and Sega Europe was set up a year later. But the company's history goes back more than 40 years.

Sega was founded in Japan in 1951 by an American, David Rosen, as Services Games Company which developed amusement-type games. In 1956 Rosen started importing mechanical coin-operated games which were popular on US military bases in Japan. During the early days Rosen learnt a lesson that still guides Sega – better technology plus great gameplay wins the market.

In 1965 Rosen started making his own coin-operated games and began stamping SEGA – short for Service Games – on them. Rosen adopted the name for the company.

Rosen sold Sega to Gulf & Western Industries, but continued as CEO, and revenues hit $214 million in 1982. By 1983 Sega had several firsts under its belt, including the first laser disc game, Sega Astron Belt, the first 3D video game, SubRoc-3D, and Sega's first consumer video game console, SG-1000.

Soon afterwards the market all but

collapsed, but Sega clung on. Rosen and some Japanese investors bought the Japanese assets for $38 million, and the Japanese entrepreneur Hayao Nakayama became chief executive. Rosen ran the US subsidiary. From that moment, the company vowed not to stick with one concept too long, realising that each generation of technology has a life and a death.

In 1986 Sega Enterprises was listed on the Tokyo Stock Exchange and Sega of America and Sega Europe were established to adapt and market video game products to rapidly expanding American and European markets. In the late 1980s Sega Enterprises introduced a line of highly successful video games, making it the world's second largest producer of video games and propelling it to international fame. In 1990 the company had a full listing on the Tokyo Stock Exchange.

At the same time Sega aimed its products at a slightly older market than its main competitor, Nintendo, and released the world's first 16-bit console, the Sega Mega Drive. Sega quickly became recognised by its fast-paced in-your-face marketing and advertising, and achieved cult status alongside Nike and Levi's among American youth. Sega Genesis became the video console of choice in the early 1990s and remained an important platform until 1997.

In the same year Sega released Sonic the Hedgehog, who soon appeared on pencil cases, socks, comics and pillow cases, and even got his own television series.

In 1995 SegaSoft was formed through a joint venture between Sega of America and CSK Corporation to create interactive content.

In 1995 the company also concentrated on making high quality games for its popular Sega Saturn 32-bit console. With more than 250 games in its library and an installed base of over seven million worldwide and 1.7 million in the US, Sega was dedicated to producing quality games at competitive prices. It also released the Sega Saturn Net Link, a peripheral which allowed users to surf the web and play games with other users on the network.

In 1996 Sega, MCA and the

DreamWorks creative team, which included Stephen Spielberg, joined forces as Sega GameWorks to create family-oriented entertainment centres, with the aim of expanding the gaming market.

Sega launched its new 128-bit machine, the Dreamcast – the ultimate gaming machine – in Japan in 1998 and in the UK a year later. The most powerful games console to date, Dreamcast put Sega in a competitive position to win back market share over Sony and Nintendo.

Product

Sega's Dreamcast is the most powerful games console ever created. It is fifteen times more powerful than a Sony PlayStation, ten times more powerful than a Nintendo 64, and has four times the graphics processing power of the fastest Pentium II processor. Dreamcast was also the first console to utilise hand-held gaming through its Visual Memory System (VMS), a multi-function unit that plugs into the Dreamcast controller. The VMS allows players to swap saved games, play VMS-specific games, or play head-to-head with friends by connecting two VMSs together.

Sega launched a range of games for the Dreamcast, including Sonic Adventure, the first truly 3D outing for Sega's blue-haired trainer-wearing hedgehog mascot. The company aims to provide the ultimate gaming experience. By the end of 2000 there were more than 200 Sega Dreamcast games in the library. Shen Mue, which features hundreds of speaking characters, 3D worlds with thousands of rooms and motion-captured movements, has been hailed as the most realistic game ever designed.

Dreamcast was also the first console to provide internet capability, offering free unlimited pan-European internet access from its launch. Users can chat online, email, browse the web and play online games.

Recent Developments

In May 2000 Sega Europe set up Dreamarena Ltd, a wholly owned subsidiary, to develop the online activities of the company's online portal Dreamarena. At the same time it launched Europe's first online console game ChuChu Rocket, the fast and furious puzzle that allows players to compete with up to three others. Other multi-player online games followed.

Sega has also launched a range of peripherals for Dreamcast, including items that will enhance online multiplayer gaming via SegaNet, the only high-speed online console gaming network and internet service provider (ISP). It launched a range of new colours for Sega Dreamcast controllers and VMUs, an ethernet card for broadband gameplay, an MP3 player for downloading music, a zip drive for storage space, an attachable microphone for interactive games, and an internet-oriented digital camera.

Sega and Motorola have agreed to develop a mobile phone based on the Dreamcast games console, and this is forecast to be a major player in the wireless entertainment sector. Sega is developing a games programming interface – as well as games – for Motorola's next generation phones, which will be able to display images in real time.

Sega continues to work on broadband technology to allow faster gaming and downloading of games.

Promotion

Sega uses national television campaigns to promote its products, backed by substantial budgets which allow prime-time advertising. But cinema is also important, as it reaches a key demographic audience. Most of the massive budget for the launch of Dreamcast went on cinema advertising, but there were also competitions in the national press to win consoles and games, along with free tickets to major sporting events.

In June 2000 Sega launched a £5 million pan-European advertising campaign, encompassing television, print, poster and ambient media, to highlight the arrival of online gaming with ChuChu Rocket. The bold decision to give away a copy of the world's first online console game paid huge dividends – Dreamarena, Dreamcast's internet portal, was swamped with over 100,000 users during the first two weeks after ChuChu Rocket was launched. Anticipating such a response Sega set up the European ChuChu Rocket Challenge when the game was launched. Gamers from all over Europe participated in the online event, the winner bagging a trip to the NASA Space Centre in Florida.

The television campaign took a light-hearted look at European rivalry. In one scenario the French challenged the 'roastbeefs' and the Germans bragged about their economy. Their European neighbours took up the challenges, and everyone united online. The campaign was aired during the Euro 2000 football championship, exploiting the huge audiences for the televised matches, and included prime slots within the half-time advertising breaks of the England games and France v Holland.

Sega also sponsored the 2000 MTV Video Music Awards, which played to an audience of 12-24 year-olds. It also does large-scale consumer promotions at events such as the music tour Ozzfest, and the ACG indoor

Snowboarding Exhibition.

Sega also sponsors Arsenal football club: Dreamcast is emblazoned on home shirts, Sega on away shirts.

Brand Values

Sega is recognised as the industry leader in interactive entertainment experiences and is the only company that offers those both inside and outside the home. Its reputation is built on state of the art technology and great gameplay, and it supports this by fast-paced in-your-face marketing and advertising. The company aims to provide the ultimate gaming experience, with its flagship Dreamcast console being the ultimate gaming machine.

Things you didn't know about Sega

The Dreamcast console took more money on its first day than the film Star Wars.

The game Shenmue is probably the most expensive game ever made, at $60 million.

There is a celebrity and sport star seeding programme for Dreamcast, which has appeared in movies, at music events and on the hottest shows – including South Park and The Simpsons.

Sega has games developed not only by its own software house, but also by a number of other companies, including Microsoft, Fox and Acclaim.

Market

Customers are more demanding than ever – they want value for money, they require service as well as products and expect the total buying relationship to be a great experience. Increasingly, customers will buy from companies that have values they can respect.

Life for the cash-rich time-poor early twenty first century consumer revolves round the car: whether for work, shopping or leisure, the car is the quickest and most convenient mode of transport. Both the number of cars on the road and the number of miles driven continue to rise.

The potential increase in fuel volumes from this increased usage is partly offset by improvements in fuel efficiencies. Consumers might be paying more for their petrol at the pump, but the oil companies are seeing little of it: a big slice goes in tax to the Government. Dwindling revenues from fuel has prompted the oil companies to look to other product areas and to reduce their cost base.

There has been a consolidation of some global players over recent years; Total took over Belgian Petrofina, BP and Amoco merged, and Exxon got together with Mobil.

Another key feature of the marketplace is the growth in non-conventional competition, such as supermarkets.

Achievements

The Shell name and Pecten are among the most recognised names and symbols in the world. Shell uses the same logo, colours and brand the world over, and is one of the few companies which has an instantly recognisable graphic symbol as its logo. The Pecten is as familiar to global consumers as the Coca-Cola swirl or the McDonald's golden arches – the result of over 100 years investment in the brand and continued delivery against customer needs and expectations.

Research continues to show that Shell is the most popular petrol brand among motorists and, with 45,000 sites across the world Shell is the largest single branded network in the industry.

Shell does more than most companies in its field to safeguard the environment and local communities, investing around £60 million per year in these types of project.

Research conducted at the end of the 1990s showed that little was known about Shell's long-held business principles or its commitment to sustainable development. It was perceived to be aloof, indifferent and arrogant. Shell decided to open a dialogue with the world, and its report, 'Profits and Principles – does there have to be a choice?', was the first of an annual series of investigations into Shell companies' economic, environmental and social performance. The third report, 'How do we stand?', was published more recently. The reports have become widely acknowledged as best practice in the field of corporate reporting. The reports invite stakeholder feedback through the 'Tell Shell' campaign, much of which, both positive and negative, is also published.

Shell continues to innovate within and beyond its traditional businesses in order to anticipate the future needs of its customers. It demonstrated its commitment to sustainable development when it set up the Shell Renewables business in 1997, for example, recognising modern customers' different expectations of a traditional oil company.

History

Shell's origins go back to 1833, when Marcus Samuel opened a small shop in London's East End dealing in antiques, curios and oriental sea shells. His trade in shells – a fashionable item in Victorian households – became so profitable that he set up regular shipments from the Far East. Before long this had turned into a general import/export business.

The connection with oil was established in 1890, when Marcus Samuel Jr visited the Black Sea coast where Russian oil was exported to Asia. Samuel started exporting kerosene to the Far East, sending the world's first oil tanker through the Suez Canal. Samuel remembered his father's original business when he branded the kerosene 'Shell'.

In 1897, Samuel elevated the status of the Shell name, calling his enterprise the Shell Transport and Trading Company. A Pecten seashell emblem was chosen to give the name visual emphasis.

In 1907, Shell Transport and Trading merged with a Dutch rival Royal Dutch Petroleum, which was also active in the Far East, and formed the group of companies we still call Shell today. Rapid growth followed, leading to the development of an international network of oil exploration and production facilities. As with many other petroleum companies, the new motor car age literally fuelled growth for decades to come.

By the late 1950s, oil had

become the world's major energy resource. Supply and demand both boomed, and during this period Shell supplied almost one seventh of the world's oil products. During the 1960s, there was a similar boom in the market for natural gas, leading to the exploration for and production of natural gas in the North Sea. Shell was a major player in these early years of North Sea operations and even more so when large oil fields were also discovered there in the early 1970s.

The years ahead saw North Sea exploration and production become a major focus for Shell. Shell has been a leader in developing the UK's oil and gas reserves for over 30 years. Since North Sea production began in the 1960s, Shell has invested over £10 billion locating and producing oil and gas. The development of the Brent oil field, the biggest discovery in the UK sector of the North Sea, is acknowledged to be one of the greatest ever technical feats of British private enterprise. At this time, Shell also started diversifying into a new growth area – producing chemicals from petroleum products. Over the next twenty years, its chemical product range grew enormously, being manufactured in 30 locations around the world.

Product

Shell sells fuel and oil to motorists through a network of 45,000 petrol stations worldwide. Shell's fuels and lubricants are tested and developed with Ferrari, with which it has a well-established technology relationship. Shell's fuel and lubricants powered Ferrari to success in both the 2000 Formula One Drivers and Constructors Championships.

The Shell Helix brand of lubricants is being revitalised to ensure that customers do not view it simply as 'another motor oil' – from another faceless oil company. It offers better protection because it is being developed in the extreme conditions of Formula One, which delivers a credible 'reason to believe' in the superior protection of Shell Helix. Customers will have already started noticing large Shell Helix logos around Formula One race circuits. On the basis of customer knowledge, the packaging has been modernised and revitalised for the existing family of Shell Helix motor oils – red (Standard), yellow (Super), blue (Plus) and Silver (Ultra). As well as being redesigned front and back for a fresher look and feel with more 'personality' in the logo, each has a grid-system label on the back which explains what the oil is intended for in a transparent and meaningful way.

Shell pioneered forecourt retailing, and now boasts 3,600 Select forecourt shops, offering a wide range of quality products and services. It is one of the largest sandwich retailers in the UK, selling over thirteen million sandwiches a year. The stores rapidly became retail outlets in their own right: 16% of customers arrive on foot, and more than 25% of customers who drive to a Select shop do not buy fuel.

Shell operates a customer loyalty scheme, SMART, which currently has four million members. The SMART card can also be used with various third parties, such as cinemas and hotels. The Euroshell card system offers motorists and transport companies the most comprehensive charge card service for fuels, lubricants and service in Europe. For transport companies Shell offer a European wide fuel and performance monitoring system using advance wireless technology.

WISH UPON A STAR   OR MAKE A DREAM COME TRUE?

Recent Developments

ATMs are now available on 250 of Shell's forecourts in a deal with Abbey National, as well as conventional offers such as car washes and vacuuming facilities, forming part of the forecourt offer.

Shell is embracing the internet as a communication medium and new sales channel. It has set up a European journey planner (www.shellgeostar.com), which offers comprehensive route planning and travel assistance to customers throughout Europe.

Shell has also pioneered solar powered sites, transponders for easy payment, and screens on pumps for information and pre-ordering, for example.

Promotion

Shell owes the fact that its Pecten logo is one of the most famous brand symbols in the world to a great tradition of advertising. The famous 'You can be sure of Shell' strap line dates back to 1932.

More recently, Shell's marketing has focused on a different message. In 1999, it embarked on a ground-breaking corporate communications campaign, based around television, print, new media advertising and public relations. The aim of the global 'Profits and Principles' marketing programme was to communicate Shell's new open, socially accountable structure to the world.

The television advertising, devised by J Walter Thompson, featured real Shell employees talking about their jobs and their work to protect the environment. Print ads in the campaign pose questions demonstrating Shell's desire to stimulate debate about business, the environment and society. Questions like, 'Exploit… or Explore?', 'Cloud the issue… or clear the air?' and 'Wish upon a star… or make a dream come true?' formed the basis of the campaign. This campaign won The Business Week Award for Excellence in Corporate Advertising.

The advertising is backed up by imaginative new media work which sees Shell constantly inviting discussion and seeking feedback on its performance. Its website (www.shell.com) is a forum for debate and includes links to environmental pressure groups like Greenpeace.

Making Shell distinct demands a visual identity that is different from the rest. It is difficult to see how current competitor communications' differ significantly from those of Shell. Petrol retailers show happy motorists filling up at service stations, all of which feel much alike apart from their colours and names. Lubricant advertisements show pistons pumping or engines being soothed by clear, sun-yellow, poured nectar. Customers find it hard to distinguish between the brands in

the industry, because none have a distinctive visual territory to call their own.

Building on the relationship with Ferrari motor racing that dates back to 1950, many of Shell's ads use Ferrari and Formula One to promote products such as Shell Helix motor oil. The theme, Waves of Change using the sea as a branding idea, is proving a useful context for conversation with stakeholders, and a means of establishing unique territory for Shell. It is new, innovative and, research has shown, is credible when linked with Shell. Shell's origins are the sea, which is powerful, vast (both broad and deep), has associations with change and renewal, is both calming and stormy and as a metaphor, offers a range of emotions and visual ideas.

In the area of sponsorship, Ferrari and Shell recently signed a deal to extend their successful Formula One partnership for another five years. The relationship also covers the close technological co-operation between the two companies, which has been an important factor in their relationship.

Brand Values

Shell's 'One Brand' initiative is based on a philosophy and vision which reflects the brand's new positioning as an energy company committed to sustainable development. Recent communications from Shell show a company that cares about its customers and the world in which we live and demonstrates how Shell innovates to help build a better future.

Shell is committed to carrying out its business operations efficiently, responsibly and profitably. In order to achieve this Shell will search for innovative energy solutions with the intent of improving the wellbeing of the planet and its people. Shell companies, therefore, are committed to contribute to sustainable development.

Market

Over the last decade the media market has been transformed by new technology. First it was the arrival of satellite television services, then the internet and now digital television. During this revolution, a handful of analogue television channels have been replaced by a new multichannel television world where a vast content is providing the British viewer with an unprecedented amount of choice. It is amazing to think that around ten years ago we could choose between only four terrestrial television channels.

All this has made the media market increasingly complex and fragmented, allowing content owners to target ever smaller niche audiences and creating red-hot competition amongst media owners and content owners.

As the company that started the non-terrestrial television revolution in 1989, Sky is in a unique position to be at the forefront of these sweeping changes. In the race to be master of the digital television world, the stakes are high. To date, of the UK's 21 million households that have televisions, 20% also have digital television, a figure which is projected to reach 53% by 2003 and 75% by 2008 (Source: The Henley Centre). By 2010, the Government hopes all UK homes will have digital television so that it can switch off the analogue television signal for good.

Every broadcaster is working hard to reconfigure its services into a multichannel offering, as well as developing new services to harness the opportunities for interactive viewing, e-commerce, video on demand and television via the internet. Furthermore, services will be available across a wide variety of platforms, ranging from digital satellite to cable and broadband phone lines such as ADSL. As such, the number of competitors in the market is getting larger and larger, including not only the likes of the BBC and ITV, but also ONdigital, NTL, Telewest, Kingston Communications and BT.

Achievements

Sky will always be remembered as the brand that began the UK's television revolution. It introduced the concept of choice to UK viewers, doubling the number of channels on offer when it launched its satellite broadcasting service in 1989.

Over a decade later, Sky is a media phenomenon. Almost one in three UK households subscribes to Sky channels, attracted by a compelling range of content. Sky One attracts higher ratings than any other non-terrestrial general entertainment channel. Sky News wins plaudits for the breadth and depth of its coverage – its reputation peaking during

the Kosovo crisis – and its movie channels show an unrivalled diversity of motion pictures.

One of Sky's greatest achievements has been in its sports coverage, especially football. Its astute acquisition of FA Premier League live soccer coverage was a masterstroke, injecting unprecedented revenues into the English game. In the process, Sky has not only transformed television soccer coverage, but also helped to make the Premier League a star-studded stage for some of the world's best footballers.

More recently, Sky has overseen one of the world's most successful launches of a new digital television service. The 1998 launch was the UK's first digital television platform, offering over 200 channels. It was the fastest digital television launch in Europe, attracting 2.6 million customers in its first fourteen months. The technical excellence of its new digital platform was recognised by the Royal Television Society in 1999, when it awarded Sky digital the Judges' Award for Technical Innovation. It was also awarded a Computerworld Smithsonian Laureate Medal for its pioneering role in the launch of digital and interactive television.

History

Rupert Murdoch launched Sky Television's Direct-To-Home service in the UK in 1989. Broadcasting via the Astra satellite, Sky initially comprised a four-channel network. The early days were not easy as a market used to only four terrestrial television channels was slow to wake up to the virtues of the new satellite service. As the new venture reported losses of £2 million per week in its first year, many observers said it had little chance of success.

However, it made steady progress, signing up one million UK homes by 1990 and launching Sky Movies, the UK's first encrypted channel. A rival satellite operation – British Satellite Broadcasting – had launched, but then merged with Sky to form British Sky Broadcasting. The nine channels of the two new partners were streamlined in 1991 into a five channel network comprising: Sky Movies, The Movie Channel, Sky Sports, Sky One and Sky News.

In 1992, BSkyB made a landmark deal – securing exclusive rights to live FA Premier League football coverage. This radically changed

the face of football television coverage and also revolutionised the Premier League itself, which benefited from the increased revenue. Movies were the other cornerstone of its offering, the importance of which was reflected in 1994 when Sky announced a £13 million investment in British films.

By 1995 BSkyB boasted a package offering 24 channels including Sky Sports 2, the Disney Channel and the History Channel. This wide-ranging offering helped it notch up over five million subscribers and in 1996 it renewed its deal for exclusive live coverage of Premier League football until the end of the 2000/2001 season.

By this point, BSkyB had helped establish non-terrestrial television as a major force in the UK, with satellite and cable achieving a 10.8% share of the total UK viewing audience, a figure which surpassed BBC2 and Channel 4 for the first time. It continued to innovate with new services, pioneering pay-per-view in the UK with the coverage of Frank Bruno's defence of the World Heavyweight Championship in 1996.

In 1998 Sky entered an important new stage of its development, launching Sky digital. Initially offering 140 channels, the service attracted over 100,000 subscribers in the first 30 days. Using highly innovative new technology – developed in a £100 million investment – Sky digital opened the door for interactive television for the first time in the UK.

Product

Today, Sky offers viewers the widest range of general entertainment, movies, sports, documentary, music and specialist channels.

The cornerstone brands of Sky's offering are Sky One, Sky News, Sky Sports, Sky Premier, Sky MovieMax, Sky Cinema and Sky Box Office. The general entertainment channel, Sky One, attracts a huge following with a mix of original programming as well as hit series like ER and Friends. Millions of pounds are invested in original programming via Sky's television production division, Sky Productions.

Sky digital now has a seven strong line up of sports channels comprising Sky Sports 1, 2, and 3, as well as Sky Sports Extra, Sky Sports.comTV, MUTV and British Eurosport. Together, they cover a host of sports, ranging from Premier League football to golf, cricket and rugby league.

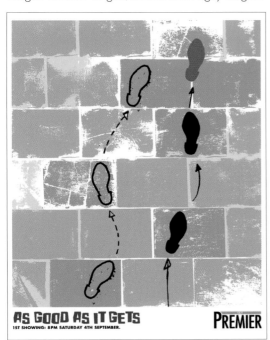

As Good As It Gets
1ST SHOWING: 8PM SATURDAY 4TH SEPTEMBER.   **PREMIER**

Sky Premier is the entertainment channel showing movies and original programming. It also carries authoritative programmes on the film industry, presented by gurus such as Barry Norman. Sky MovieMax is the home of high-action escapist entertainment featuring stars like Jean Claude Van Damme and Bruce Willis, while Sky Cinema is devoted to cinema classics. Sky Box Office brings customers the very latest movie releases as well as exclusive live concerts and sporting events. Some of the movies carried on these channels are made by Sky itself via its new feature film production division, Sky Pictures.

Sky digital provides an exciting platform for this product line to be radically expanded. It offers 200 channels, catering for every taste. Movie buffs can select from thirteen movie 'screens', sports fans have a choice of seven channels, there are fifteen news and documentary channels, eight for children, as well as eighteen non-subscription channels.

Recent Developments

Sky recently underlined its commitment to the UK film industry by launching Sky Pictures – a feature film production division. Dedicated to commissioning, financing and producing a wide range of movies, Sky Pictures is committed to producing up to twelve feature films per year. Films to emerge from the Sky Pictures stable so far include Saving Grace, starring the Oscar-nominated Brenda Blethyn, which scored a lucrative distribution deal at the Sundance Film Festival.

With the launch of Sky digital, Sky paved the way for the introduction of interactive services. In 1999 it launched two new interactive services, Sky Sports Extra and Open.... the interactive channel.

Open.... allows Sky digital customers to shop, bank, play games and send and receive e-mail via their television sets. This, the first fully-fledged interactive television service in the UK, has been a massive success and is attracting hosts of new users and content providers.

In July 2000, BSkyB reached an agreement to increase its stake in Open.... to 80% (subject to regulatory approval). Open.... has become the largest television e-commerce platform in the UK with access to over nine million people in four million homes.

Sky Sports Extra is a new interactive sports channel. It allows digital customers to choose how they want to watch sport, enabling them to choose their own action replays and highlights, camera angles and additional statistics. The technology went live for the first time during a match between Arsenal and Manchester United in August 1999. The service is being improved all the time, providing more camera angles and extending to other sports such as cricket, tennis and international rugby. The opportunities digital technology offers for enhanced television such as this are boundless and Sky has already begun to apply this technology to other parts of its product range, with the launch of Sky News Active, a world first in television news, which puts the viewer in control, giving them a wider choice – at the touch of a button – of how and when they view their news and what they can see.

Sky's investment in new media has led to its website, sky.com, becoming a focal point of its activities. The site carries a huge amount of information about Sky's product and services. As broadband connection speeds increase the functionality of the internet, sky.com will become a crucial platform for Sky to bring the benefits of television and the internet closer together.

Promotion

Advertising has always been used to drive the digital television marketplace and Sky's share within it. Campaigns focus on educating the general public about the benefits of digital television. Across a year advertising will feature the general digital benefits as well as key programming highlights and launches of new services.

One of Sky's biggest ad campaigns of recent years was its launch of Sky digital in 1998. Based on the premise of how people should expect more from their television than the

A digital vision for **busy people**

Nowadays, people don't just watch TV, they use it too. Digital satellite viewers have the chance to do their shopping by TV, as well as sending and receiving e-mails, and even banking from the comfort of their homes.

For information on Sky's free minidish and digibox offer call now on
08702 40 40 80
or visit your nearest electrical retailer.
You pay for installation.

sky

a digital vision for everyone

sky.com

You do not need to subscribe to Sky digital to get a free minidish and digibox.

limited choice and non-interactivity of analogue television, the campaign positioned Sky digital as a brave new dawn in broadcasting. Old televisions were seen leaping off a cliff as the new world of Sky digital arrived.

More recently Sky launched its animated campaign based on the tagline, 'A digital vision for everyone'. Fronted by a character who takes the viewer through the world of Sky, the ads show the breadth of Sky's activities and showcase the benefits of digital television.

Sport has always been central to Sky's service offering. Each summer sees a major advertising campaign to launch the start of the FA Carling Premiership. From the 'Football is our religion' campaign to the most recent 'Let the power of sport into your life' campaign, Sky has always championed its unparalleled passion for Sport.

Brand Values

Sky has always been an innovator and its brand is infused with embracing technology to break the boundaries of television. It did so with the introduction of satellite television, with the launch of digital and with the introduction of the UK's first interactive services. As such, innovation and challenging convention lie at the heart of its brand.

Recently, Sky has defined its brand as providing 'A digital vision for everyone'. This is based on bringing the extraordinary benefits of digital television to everyone, using Sky's best traditions of invention, creativity and ground-breaking ideas. But most of all, Sky's brand is about entertainment. It wants to inform, entertain and delight its customers using the best that digital entertainment and technology can provide.

Market

The drinks market is constantly evolving, with product innovation, as well as brand strength, at the heart of its growth. Doubtless, the root of success of SMIRNOFF® vodka is the consistently high standard of classic vodka that its owner has produced over the years. However, as the market has evolved, so has the SMIRNOFF brand. With a growing range of flavoured vodkas and pre-mixed cocktails that perfectly tap into the lucrative ready to drink sector, SMIRNOFF is successfully supplying the constant demand for new products that will target the younger, style-conscious adult drinker.

White spirits are better suited as summer refreshers rather than winter warmers. However, unlike many other alcoholic beverages, the white spirits market is not adversely affected by seasonality. Sales within the white spirits market are not limited to the summer season alone, but are equally included in the general upsurge in alcohol consumption over the festive season which sees around 22% of annual volume sales being made in the Christmas period (Source: Mintel 2000).

Vodka is a drink that appeals to young adult drinkers, partly because of its versatile character. It has benefited from its lack of association with, or limitation to, any one particular mixer, meaning that the different possibilities of consumption are multiplied.

Achievements

In 1877, the Smirnov vodka company in Moscow was awarded the right to use three Russian State coats of arms and in 1886 became Purveyor to the Imperial Russian Court. Between 1874 and 1897 it won numerous awards for quality and variety at international exhibitions.

By the end of the nineteenth century, the SMIRNOFF vodka brand was generating the equivalent of nearly $20 million a year in revenues.

Since 1975, vodka – led by SMIRNOFF – has outranked bourbon as the US's most popular spirit. In 1978, SMIRNOFF became the number one spirit brand in the US, its largest market (Source: SMIRNOFF Impact Newsletter). Although overtaken by Bacardi it has remained a strong second ever since and is growing more rapidly than Bacardi on a worldwide basis.

SMIRNOFF is now the largest premium international vodka brand in the world, selling more than three times than its nearest competitor, Absolut (Source: ACNielsen).

History

The Smirnov family is believed to have made their start in Moscow's wine and vodka business during the early 1800s. But it was in 1864, following the abolition of serfdom after the Napoleonic wars, that Piotr Arsenyevitch Smirnov founded his own vodka distillery near the Chugunny Bridge, achieving rapid success on a national and international scale. By the time Smirnov died in 1898, his company employed over 1,500 people, produced over 4,000,000 cases of wines, spirits and liqueurs and was generating the equivalent of $20 million a year in revenues, making the Smirvov family one of the richest in Russia.

Disaster struck with the Russian Revolution which saw the confiscation by the Bolsheviks of all private industries in Moscow including the Smirnov distillery. One of Piotr's sons, Vladimir, was determined to carry on the family

business and fled Russia for Paris where he was cut off from his roots and fortune. Adopting the French version of his family name – 'SMIRNOFF', Vladimir then began his struggle to make a success of the business in Europe.

SMIRNOFF vodka was brought to America after a meeting between Vladimir and Rudolph Kunett, a representative from the Helena Rubenstein cosmetics company who was on business in Paris. Vladimir granted Kunett the exclusive rights and licence to all Smirnoff alcoholic beverages in the US, Canada and Mexico, and on September 21st 1933, Ste Pierre Smirnoff Fils of New York was incorporated, transplanting the exiled vodka brand to the New World.

But when US production of SMIRNOFF vodka began in March 1934, business was not as good as Kunett had anticipated. First year sales reached 1,200 cases and by 1937 that figure had reached only a little over 4,000 cases. By 1938, when business was so bad that he could not afford the $1500 mandatory sales licence, he contacted John Martin, president of Heublein, asking them to act as an agent for SMIRNOFF vodka.

By 1941, Heublein's sales of SMIRNOFF had reached 22,115 cases a year. Although this was a dramatic improvement on previous figures, the real turning point came when the product began to be marketed as 'white whisky', with 'no taste, no smell'.

This concept seemed to appeal to consumers who did not care for the traditional characteristics of whisky and discovered that vodka could be mixed with pretty much anything. This, combined with heavy national promotion by SMIRNOFF of cocktails like the Moscow Mule, resulted in a rapid escalation of SMIRNOFF sales.

In the 1950s Heublein purchased the remaining worldwide rights to the Polish Smirnoff company from Tatiana Smirnoff, Vladimir's widow and heir. W&A Gilbey Ltd of England was then commissioned to manufacture and sell, on a royalty basis, SMIRNOFF vodka in the UK, Canada, Australia, New Zealand, and South Africa. Heublein bought the French Smirnoff company, the last independent Smirnoff producer, on May 12th 1954, therefore securing the world rights to the brand and making SMIRNOFF into the truly global company that it is today.

Product

The SMIRNOFF brand owner uses only the highest quality raw materials in its production process. The process includes a triple distillation, a filtration process that lasts a minimum of eight hours and 47 individual

quality control checks. It is this process that has set SMIRNOFF apart from other vodkas, securing and sustaining customer confidence in the consistent premium quality of SMIRNOFF vodka.

SMIRNOFF 'Red' is the world's leading international premium vodka and second best selling spirits brand. However, SMIRNOFF has developed many variations on the vodka theme, thus ensuring that it is leading, rather than merely keeping up with, the competitive pace of the drinks market.

SMIRNOFF 'Black Label' is distilled using the traditional methods of Tsarist Russia. Made in a copper pot at a very slow pace, it is then passed through Siberian silver birch charcoal to a strength no lower than 40% ABV, thus preserving the natural flavour of the original grain spirit.

Recent Developments

SMIRNOFF flavours were launched in March 1998 into the off trade, and currently have a growing distribution in the on trade. Flavours include Twisted (citrus), Bloody (hot spice and pepper), Creamed (vanilla and burnt spice) and Black'n'Blue (natural berry flavours) a selection of flavours that are daring, innovative and new,

yet packaged in a way that is reassuringly 'SMIRNOFF'.

Flavoured vodkas have been available for a long time but until recently were confined to specialist outlets and aimed at very small niche markets. The introduction of a varied range of flavoured vodkas by the Smirnoff brand owner has brought it into the mainstream, putting SMIRNOFF on to supermarket shelves, and exposing all vodka drinkers to the concept in a way that entices them to experiment.

This innovation has created another facet of the premium sector and has stimulated interest in the market since shot drinking, driven by the 'big night out' occasion, has increasingly become an integral part of drinkers' repertoire. 61% of young adult consumers drink shots monthly and 41% weekly (Source: Cardinal Research 1999). Since shots supplement regular drinks they

therefore drive incremental sales and tapping into this market has enabled SMIRNOFF to stay ahead of the game.

Smirnoff Ice – a blend of pure SMIRNOFF 'Red' vodka with the classic taste of lemon – was launched in July 1999 in the UK as part of an ongoing strategy to broaden the SMIRNOFF footprint and to lead the brand into more drinking occasions.

Promotion

Since the 1950s, SMIRNOFF has been renowned for its ingenious and highly evocative advertising campaigns. In 1952, the 'it leaves you breathless' slogan was coined and made a splash when it appeared in an advertisement in Life magazine. The 'driest of the dry' campaign, launched in 1953, was a series of distinctive surrealistic executions that ran for over twelve years that established and encapsulated – rather unleashed – the spirited atmosphere surrounding the SMIRNOFF brand. The surrealistic adverts were mingled with high profile 'celebrity ads' which saw characters like Woody Allen, Zsa Zsa Gabor, Marcel Marceau, Groucho Marx and Buster Keaton endorsing Smirnoff – albeit in the guise of a seemingly endless variety of drink concoctions – as their spirit du choix.

The 'effect is shattering' campaign which followed used lines like 'Accountancy was my life until I discovered Smirnoff.' It was this campaign that firmly established the personality of the SMIRNOFF drinker as individual, relaxed, rebellious and mysterious. SMIRNOFF advertising ever since has talked the distinctly unconventional and imaginative language of its target consumer.

The 'Pure Thrill' campaign was the first truly global spirits advertising campaign. The campaign, which was a huge success, consisted of a series of conventional images that were distorted – transformed into something slightly different – as a result of being viewed through the lens of a SMIRNOFF bottle. The campaign was developed across a global network of agencies and its various executions have since won over 50 advertising awards including the coveted Cannes Golden Lion award. The recent 'No Imperfections' campaign continues SMIRNOFF's tradition of innovative and creative advertising.

Brand Values

The SMIRNOFF brand's huge international success is in part due to values that can be successfully described and translated into any language. Whether warming up a frosty Moscow night or cooling down a steamy Tennessee evening, the brand essence of SMIRNOFF is that of stimulating sociability.

The core brand values of SMIRNOFF are freedom, originality and versatility. This has been conveyed and endured through a series of hugely successful advertising campaigns and built on the foundation of consistency and quality that was implemented by Piotr Smirnov when he first devised what has evolved to become known internationally as SMIRNOFF vodka.

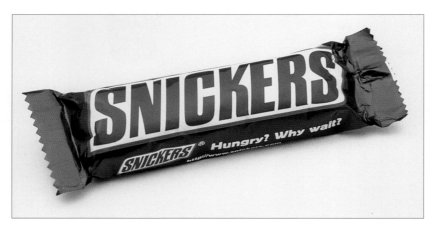

Market

The British like confectionery, in fact six pieces are bought every second in the UK, making them one of the greatest consumers of confectionery in the world. UK sales were worth £5.7 billion in 1999 (Source: IRI, Mars Internal Sources, BCCCA) with sales at least twice the size of other impulse categories.

In particular, consumption of chocolate confectionery is high in the UK, ahead of the US and France with British consumers eating over £10,000 worth of chocolate every minute (Source: Mintel 2000). One of the reasons for chocolate's popularity is that its format fits modern lifestyles, being an ideal snack when on the move or sitting in front of the television or the cinema screen.

Impulse is a big factor in the chocolate confectionery market, and high-profile advertising plays a significant role in driving sales.

According to Mars, some 60% of chocolate sales are to satisfy an impulse or immediate need whilst around 40% of market value is attributable to products purchased for later consumption. These include gifts and chocolate bought to eat at home. Seasonal promotions at Easter, Christmas and occasions such as Valentine's Day help to add value in a relatively static market.

Chocolate manufacturers have extended their brands to the ice-cream market too, and demand for branded lines such as TWIX, MARS and SNICKERS is also high. Ice-cream multi-packs are particularly popular, reflecting the growth of more flexible individual foods which can be served to meet the particular tastes of the household.

SNICKERS is one of Mars Confectionery's flagship filled bars and one of the UK's best selling confectionery products (Source: Consumer Sales Value 1999) SNICKERS is the clear leader in the peanut bar category.

The chocolate confectionery market is one of the most heavily promoted. In the year to June

1998 advertising expenditure totalled nearly £98 million (Source: Mintel), and most of this was spent on countlines and chocolate bars. Annual advertising expenditure of over £2 million on a brand is not unusual in this market, and reflects the fact that television advertising reaches a mass market audience.

Achievements

Since it was first launched in the US in 1930, SNICKERS has become the biggest selling chocolate bar in the US and one of the most popular in the world. SNICKERS is now worth over £87 million (Source: Consumer Sales Value 2000/Company Despatches) in the UK.

In 2000, SNICKERS was awarded a bronze in the British Television Awards, Programme Titles Sponsorship category for its sponsorship of ITV's On The Ball football programme.

SNICKERS has established a pledge to the NSPCC Full Stop Campaign that will see a minimum of £40,000 donated to the charity following sales of multipacks of special promotional bars and packs of FUN SIZE.

History

SNICKERS was first manufactured in the US in 1930 and was launched in the UK as MARATHON in 1967. In 1990, the name changed to SNICKERS. Mars Confectionery has successfully developed its confectionery portfolio through brand extensions, and SNICKERS exemplifies this strategy. In 1968 MARATHON FUN SIZE was launched, 1987 saw the first SNICKERS Multipack, followed by the SNICKERS ice cream in 1990 and the SNICKERS KING SIZE the

following year. The variety of SNICKERS formats are designed to broaden the brands appeal.

Product

SNICKERS is ideal to satisfy hunger whilst on the move. It combines nougat, caramel and peanuts and is covered in milk chocolate. SNICKERS is sold everywhere from corner shops to supermarkets, service stations to sports centres.

Recent Developments

Long associated with football related initiatives such as World Cup sponsorship, SNICKERS is building on these major sponsorship activities through fan as opposed to game-orientated initiatives. At the same time, SNICKERS continues to support grass roots football and following its successful SNICKERS Midnite League™ initiative, has created a Europe-wide under-fourteens street soccer initiative called SNICKERS StreetZONE™.

SNICKERS Midnite League™ was a very successful under-fifteens five-a-side football initiative that ran over three years, featuring parallel tournaments for boys and girls in cities across Britain. The tournament captured the imagination of the footballing world with Sky Television broadcasting reports from the different leagues each week, along with the national finals that took place at Bisham Abbey, the training ground of the England football squad.

The latest grass root initiative that took place Summer 2000 was SNICKERS StreetZONE™. StreetZONE is different to conventional football in that it is played with a smaller ball on a hard surface. Goal posts are piles of coats and bags and each team has six members, including a floating goalie. The game lasts 40 minutes with no half-time break.

The finals of SNICKERS StreetZONE™ took place in Amsterdam's Dam Square to coincide with the finals of the 2000 European Championships. Teams from across the Continent took part including the UK, Hungary, France, Poland, Germany and Russia. The UK team, selected at regional football festivals, was led and coached by Premier League

football manager Alan Curbishley.

In 1998, ITV introduced a flagship Saturday lunchtime football programme – On The Ball – hosted by Gabby Yorath and Barry Venison. This saw SNICKERS entry into broadcast sponsorship with specially commissioned fan films, starring real football fans with their own individual idiosyncrasies, broadcast to show SNICKERS' passion for the game.

SNICKERS association with On The Ball extended onto the internet and the SNICKERS sponsored On The Ball website during the 1999-2000 season generated 13,000 hits each week.

Promotion

Much of SNICKERS communication is geared towards the 16-24 year old hungry young male. SNICKERS uses many forms of advertising and sponsorship, including television and radio, on-pack promotions, poster sites, bus stops, television programmes and the internet. Indeed, it was one of the first big brands to use the internet in 1996 with its Euro 96 website.

Peanuts have played an important part in SNICKERS communications. For example, in

1968, the slogan was 'It keeps you going, going, going with peanut power' and in 1975 'Comes up peanuts slice after slice'. As SNICKERS' positioning in the market has evolved, the benefits of peanuts in satisfying hunger has played an increasing role. Building on both the hunger and football themes, SNICKERS bars were marketed under the strapline 'Tackles your hunger in a big way' during Euro 96.

More recently, SNICKERS' desire to become the world's favourite street eat and on the move hunger satisfier, has led to the 'Hungry? Why wait?' campaigns designed to show that if you are not going anywhere for a while, you should grab a SNICKERS bar.

SNICKERS has helped maintain its appeal through a series of on-pack offers designed to attract consumers to this impulse buy. Past examples of successful offers include a medal competition (1972), a giant jackpot competition (1977), American National Football League (1988), JVC and adidas Predator instant wins (1996), World Cup tickets (1998) and Sports results pagers (2000).

2000 culminated in the 'Grab Wembley Glory' on-pack promotion with the company offering SNICKERS eaters the opportunity to win pieces of the hallowed turf from the Wembley pitch. 300 pieces of turf were up for grabs, together with 'hot spots' which had seen significant action over Wembley's 77 year history.

MARATHON became SNICKERS in 1990 under the slogan 'All that's changed is the name.' Bringing the UK brand name into line with the rest of the world has allowed SNICKERS to fully become a global brand and to take part in worldwide sponsorship initiatives.

Sport – and humour – has played a big role in SNICKERS communication, from the long distance runner looking to satisfy his hunger in the 1970s, to the football fan not going anywhere for a while in 2000.

SNICKERS long association with football is an excellent match for its target market of hungry 16-24 year old males. As the official sponsor of both the 1994 and 1998 World Cup tournaments and official snackfood of Euro 96, SNICKERS has positioned itself at the heart of the game, which has benefited its sales performance. In 1996 UK sales increased by 10% due to the sponsorship of Euro 96 (Source: Consumer Sales Value).

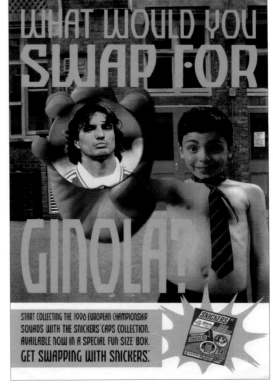

Brand Values

Amongst young men, SNICKERS aims to be the world's greatest street eat. This is optimised by the phrase 'Hungry? Grab a SNICKERS.'

SONY

Market

Television, video and sophisticated audio equipment have over the last decade become an integral part of our lives rather than a luxury.

However, the world is in the midst of a revolution which will blur the divisions between electronics, telecommunications, computers and the entertainment industry. New media will offer consumers the benefits of interactivity, multimedia and online services.

Sony's core electronics market is one of the most competitive in the business. Its biggest sector is the consumer electronics market, of which it has a 21% share. Datamonitor predicts that 79% of Europeans will be 'interactive' by 2004, using an increasingly wide range of devices.

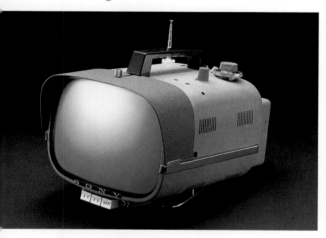

Achievements

1996 marked Sony's 50th anniversary and the Japanese consumer electronics giant had plenty to celebrate. In addition, 1998 marked the 30th anniversary of Sony's presence in the UK. The company has been at the cutting edge of technology since it was founded by Akio Morita and Masaru Ibuka in 1946 and has had a major impact on the way in which we live our lives. Few companies are better-placed to drive the digital age into homes and businesses around the world over the next 50 years and beyond.

Sony has developed a wide range of products which have now become part of the mainstream. It invented the first Japanese magnetic tape and tape recorder in 1950; the first successful transistor radio in 1955; the world's first all-transistor television set in 1960; the world's first colour video-cassette recorder in 1971; the Walkman personal stereo in 1979, which has now sold over 200 million units and has become a way of life for a generation; the compact disc; the first 8mm Camcorder; the MiniDisc in 1992; and the launch of the DVD in 1998. Sony is entering one of the most exciting eras in multimedia technology. One example of the popularity of Sony's products is the success of the PlayStation. Since its launch in December 1994, PlayStation has become the world's leading home game console. By the end of March 2000, cumulative production shipments worldwide had reached approximately 73 million units.

Sony is not just a market leader in consumer electronics – through research and development,

it has made considerable inroads into the world of professional broadcasting, telecommunications, PC technology and now, the internet. Its increasingly high profile as an entertainment company through its divisions, Sony Music Entertainment Group and Sony Pictures Entertainment Group, is set to consolidate the international recognition it enjoys.

Sony is also one of the most respected companies worldwide. Its ability to innovate and its constant drive for self-improvement earned Sony worldwide sales of $63 billion in 1999. The company now employs 189,700 staff.

The key to the success of the brand is how it meets the challenges of change. For over fifty years Sony has led the market in terms of innovation and this is the challenge for the next fifty years. Products will no longer be developed with just hardware in mind. The convergence of technologies – PC, telecommunications, consumer electronics, entertainment and PC software is now a reality.

History

Sony was born out of the chaos in Japan at the end of the World War II. Fired with a vision for a new future and with an abundance of talent and marketing skill – but with a market capitalisation of the equivalent of £850, 20 employees and no machinery – Akio Morita and Masaru Ibuka founded Tokyo Tsushin Kogyo (Tokyo Telecommunications Engineering Corporation), in 1946.

Their declared aim was to: "Avoid the problems which befall large corporations while we create and introduce technologies which large corporations cannot match." They believed that the reconstruction of Japan depended on the development of dynamic technologies. By developing innovative high-tech electronics products, Sony was able to expand its

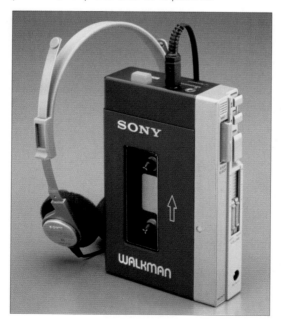

operations outside Japan into the US, Europe, Asia and other regions. Sony's most famous product – and one which created a whole sector was the Walkman personal stereo. The prototype Sony Walkman was produced in 1978. At that time, engineers at Sony had been developing a stereo cassette recorder based on the compact Pressman (TCM-10) cassette recorder but it had proved difficult to install recording and play-back mechanisms in such a small unit. Undeterred, Sony set about finding a solution and produced a system equipped with a play-back only mechanism, and such high quality sound reproduction that the product was simply begging to be marketed. Its chief attraction was its size – used with a set of lightweight headphones it could be used anywhere. The name Walkman was chosen because it reflected the product's debt to the Pressman technology and because Walkman summed up the sense of mobility which characterised the product.

At first, the Walkman was poorly received by retailers. Eight out of ten Sony dealers were convinced that a cassette player without a recording mechanism had no real future. However, its compact size and excellent sound quality attracted consumers. During 1980, the Walkman was hailed as one of the most popular new fashion products and young consumers adopted it as an essential part of their lifestyles. In its first two years on the market, Sony sold 1.5 million Walkman units.

Fierce competition from rival products, spurred Sony to research and develop improved products to ensure that it continued to lead the market. The WM-20 model, often called the 'Super Walkman', was engineered to the same size as a cassette-tape case. Walkman sales have topped 200 million units worldwide and it has become the single best selling consumer electronics product ever produced.

Product

Sony operates in the electronics and entertainment markets. It manufactures video equipment including digital video and still cameras; televisions (announcing the first ever completely flat television screen in 1997 and launching Integrated Digital televisions onto the UK market in 1999); audio equipment, specifically supporting MiniDisc as a replacement for the cassette tape; CD-Rom drives and computer monitors and much more. Sony has always been involved in the development and production of recording media.

This precipitated Sony's acquisition of CBS Records in 1988, and Columbia Pictures Entertainment in 1989, which today form Sony Music Entertainment and Sony Pictures Entertainment. Sony Music Entertainment has produced a string of best-selling albums from artists such as Michael Jackson, Mariah Carey, Sade, Pink Floyd and Oasis.

The Picture Group has achieved almost a 19% market share in the US box office, propelled by a number of hit films which have included Big Daddy, Stuart Little and Blue Streak.

Sony Pictures Entertainment also holds a stake in STAR TV's music service, Channel·V, and is a partner in the German music channel Viva and the Latin American pay-TV channel HBO Olé and satellite service HBO Asia. The company also operates satellite channels in India and Latin America under the name Sony Entertainment Television.

The fruits of Sony's research is not only limited to the enjoyment of the average consumer. Sony's professional product range is used for a variety of applications by broadcast stations, production houses, educational organisations, research facilities, and medical institutions.

Recent Developments

Sony continues to be at the forefront of new product development. The Sony MiniDisc, launched in 1992, is pegged to be the replacement for the compact cassette. With a diameter of just 6.4cm, MiniDiscs are available in two formats – pre-recorded and recordable blanks.

In March 2000 Sony's PlayStation2 was launched in Japan, which spurred growth in Japan's DVD-Video software market. PlayStation2 possesses impressive image rendering capabilities and has the ability to play DVD-Video software, whilst also being compatible with previous PlayStation titles. Following its success in Japan, Playstation2 was launched in Europe and North America in November 2000.

Sony has also taken advantage of the PC boom, manufacturing electronic components such as chips and pick-ups, and began to market VAIO, its own Sony-branded PC in 1998. The company says that its long term strategy is to bring its expertise in the home entertainment market to the less innovative PC market. Its intention is to be perceived increasingly as an IT brand as well as a consumer electronics brand.

Sony is also a leading player in the fast growing DVD industry. DVD is a single layer disc holding more than seven times as much information as a CD and can contain a full-length feature film plus additional features. This format for carrying audio and visual information gives home cinema experience true substance.

2000 has been one of the most exciting years in the world of technology with the digital age meaning that products in the home will be able to be networked together. The launch of the Memory Stick, which is the size of a piece of chewing gum, promises to be Sony's universal medium to make convergence a reality. Sony is moving towards fulfilling its president Nobuyuki Idei's strategy of building new products for 'digital dream kids', the next generation of consumers in a digital future.

Promotion

Marketing is not just a function for Sony – it is a cornerstone of the company's business philosophy. As much attention is paid to innovation in marketing as it is within the development of Sony's new products. This strategy has helped keep the Sony brand at the top of its markets for over 50 years.

In the digital network era, Sony's brand has embraced a new direction, summed up by the message of 'Go Create', not only in terms of the focus of its advertising strategy, but as the introduction of a dramatic new philosophy which it brings to the company as a whole. This embodies how Sony's products are at the forefront of technological change, opening up new possibilities at work, home and play. Sony and its products aim to invite and inspire people to do more and explore these new possibilities in their lives. Emphasis is also being placed on the adoption of a vertical rather than horizontal structure within the organisation. This is particularly relevant in today's digital environment where product development is seeing ever increasing convergence between traditional product categories. Sony believe that the re-education of its traditional channels is the link to delivering the 'Go Create' concept to its end customers.

In the UK, Sony invests around £40 million per year in the marketing support of its brands, using a mixture of television, cinema, specialist and consumer magazines and public relations. It tends to employ a localised strategy for individual international markets, but passes everything through a centralised marketing committee to ensure consistency of look and feel.

It is a heavy user of television advertising, running dramatic campaigns such as 'Armchair', which showed a man in an armchair freefalling from an aeroplane.

In 1999 Sony launched a 'Power of Television' commercial to raise awareness in the UK of the possibilities of the digital television future. This was broadcast on television and in cinema and is typical of Sony's strategy to promote not only its own products but the television industry as a whole.

Sony doesn't just rely on brilliantly executed advertising campaigns to secure public attention. Back in the 1980s, slick PR strategy ensured the Walkman was launched in a blaze of publicity. Sony was canny in its pre-launch marketing, encouraging famous Japanese singers and young Sony employees to sport Walkmans while out and about, exciting both media attention and curious glances from the general public. By the time the Walkman was officially rolled out, Japan was in a state of high excitement. Within three months, the entire stock of 30,000 units had been sold. Production couldn't match demand.

In a world where technology is moving forward at a phenomenal rate, Sony puts its full marketing muscle behind explaining the benefits and range of products available to the public today, whilst continually searching for ways of doing things others don't.

Brand Values

Sony signifies innovation, state of the art technology, superior quality and durability. It pursues a policy of continuous improvement – known in Japanese as 'kaizen' – reflected in its considerable investment in research and development. Sony continues to strengthen its leading position in the markets in which it operates through strengthening its product range and developing for the future.

Get inside the music.
Sony Super Audio CD.

go create
SONY

Things you didn't know about Sony

In 1986, Walkman was included in the Oxford English Dictionary.

Before the Walkman became a worldwide brand name, it was introduced under a variety of names, including 'Soundabout' in the US, 'Stowaway' in the UK and 'Freestyle' in Australia.

Sony created the TC-50 tape recorder used in the historic Apollo 10 space flight.

After its debut in March 2000, Playstation2 console production shipments reached two million units in less than three months.

Amidst initial concerns that the Walkman would flop because it didn't feature a recording mechanism, Akio Morita had such faith in the product he declared: "If it doesn't sell well, I'll resign as Chairman."

Sony's first product was a rice cooker.

Market

Sugar is one of the world's most important food commodities, a staple feature of human diets across the globe. It is believed that sugar cane originated in Polynesia around 3,000 years ago, but it was not until 1099 that the product reached the UK, courtesy of the Crusaders. In the fifteenth century it was known as white gold because of its value.

Today the UK consumes more than a third of a million tonnes of packet sugar each year, worth £201 million. Granulated sugar accounts for 87% of all sugar sold. Caster (6%), icing (6%) and demerara

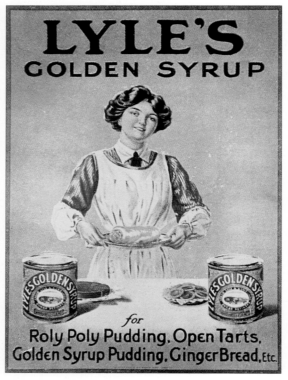

(2.4%) are the other main products, with brown sugar, preserving and jam-making sugar and sugar cubes making up the total.

Achievements

Tate & Lyle is a global company with a turnover of £4.1 billion and businesses in Europe, the Americas, Africa and Asia. Each year its 20,000 employees produce eleven million tonnes of carbohydrates, including sugar and molasses, for both home and industrial use.

The company is Europe's largest cane sugar refiner and imports 1.2 million tonnes of raw sugar from the tropics every year. Refining is carried out at the 23-acre Tate & Lyle plant at Silvertown on the River Thames in London, the biggest sugar cane refinery in the world.

Tate & Lyle also owns the famous Lyle's Golden Syrup brand, commanding 75% of the £20 million syrup and treacle market in the UK.

History

When people speak of sugar, they tend to think of Tate & Lyle. It was Sir Henry Tate, towards the end of the nineteenth century, who created the sugar cube, whilst Sir Abram Lyle invented golden syrup. The two men ran separate companies during their lifetimes, but the businesses merged in 1921 to create what would become one of the strongest brand names in the world.

Tate's invention of the sugar cube was to have far-reaching implications for the sugar industry. The new product offered immense convenience compared with the alternative that existed at the time, typically a 1.5 foot tall 'sugar loaf'. Tate also became a generous philanthropist, perhaps best known for his endowment of the Tate Gallery in London, built in 1897.

Marketing and branding have always been integral to Tate & Lyle. Indeed, it was smart marketing which saw off the threat of nationalisation after

World War II. The post-war Labour government sought to nationalise strategic industries, including sugar, but Tate & Lyle fought back with a strong advertising campaign including posters and press features. The company finally won the propaganda battle through the clever use of slogans on Tate & Lyle bags of sugar.

Between the 1960s and the 1980s, Tate & Lyle and Lyle's Golden Syrup continued development. In 1969 Tate & Lyle launched its first flavoured dessert sauces, followed by Crunchy Toppings to accompany these sauces. Breakfast Orange flavoured powdered drinks also appeared at this time.

In the early 1980s, Mint Choc Chip and Butterscotch easy-pouring sauces were launched under the Lyle brand for cooking and desserts. These evolved into the Tate & Lyle TOPS dessert topping range of the 1990s, which is still sold in Maple, Toffee, Strawberry and Chocolate flavours today.

Also under the Lyle brand, in addition to the 1lb and 2lb tins of Lyle's Golden Syrup, came Lyle's Black Treacle in a can and Lyle's Pouring Syrup – a slightly thinner golden syrup in a clear bottle.

Innovative product development has continued to keep Tate & Lyle at the forefront of the worldwide sugar and syrup industry, and today it is far and away the UK's best-known sugar brand with 97% consumer awareness.

Product

Tate & Lyle produces an extremely wide range of sugar products. Granulated sugar is used in virtually every UK household in a wide variety of ways, the largest usage being in hot drinks and on breakfast cereals.

The company also offers a vast variety of sugars for home baking use. Caster Sugar is best suited for general homebaking and cooking, as it

dissolves more quickly than granulated. Caster exhibits finer crystals than granulated due to a slight variation in the refining process.

Icing Sugar is made by grinding granulated to a powder and blending it with anti-caking agents to avoid lumpiness. It is used to create icing, fondants and meringues.

Demerara Sugar is traditionally used as a rich flavour in coffee and for creating crunchy toppings for puddings such as crumbles.

Brown Sugar possesses a higher proportion of molasses, creating a moist appearance and distinctive aroma. These add flavour and colour to cooking. Jam and Preserving Sugars, as their names suggest, are used to make tangy fruit preserves.

Tate & Lyle produces a number of other consumer and catering products, including brown sugar crystals, plain and rough-cut sugar cubes (demerara and white), and sugar for the UK's many drink vending machines.

Originally a by-product of the sugar refining process, Lyle's Golden Syrup is used in many sweet and savoury recipes, as well as being a dip or spread. Lyle's Black Treacle is made from a combination of molasses and syrups.

Recent Developments

As the UK market evolves, Tate & Lyle has kept pace and created products and packaging to suit the varying needs of the modern cook. Every cooking eventuality is catered for, from making jam and meringues to icing wedding cakes and baking Christmas puddings. In 1999 Tate & Lyle introduced Fondant Icing, offering sugarcraft enthusiasts and cake decorators an easy-to-use product made by simply adding water.

In 2000 the company took the sugar market one step further, with the introduction of its first range of organic sugars – Granulated, Caster and Demerara. These products are approved by the Soil Association.

Also in 2000 came the launch of Shake and Pour, a sugar dispenser designed to make life simpler for cooks of all ages and abilities. Filled with Tate & Lyle Granulated cane sugar, it is ideal for storing as well as dispensing sugar, and has a clever dual-purpose flip-top lid through which the sugar can be shaken or poured as required.

The seal of approval of Le Cordon Bleu culinary academy, the world's leading cookery school, has been awarded to Tate & Lyle's range of light and dark brown soft sugars.

A further accolade has come from the National Federation of Women's Institutes, which has endorsed Tate & Lyle Jam and Tate & Lyle Preserving Sugars.

Promotion

Tate & Lyle's successful 'Smile, it's Tate & Lyle' advertising campaign, fronted by celebrity chef Gary Rhodes, has won critical acclaim for creating a brand positioning for cane sugar versus other sugars. The chef starred in three mouthwatering television commercials for Bread & Butter Pudding, Cane Sugar and Syrup Pudding, and Lyle's Golden Syrup. These have been supported by classic recipes on pack, door drop leaflets, press advertising and an exclusive 'Classic British Cuisine' booklet with recipes by Gary Rhodes, used in on-pack competitions and to gain media recommendation.

Tracking studies have shown that over seven million housewives saw the commercials more than ten times, raising the awareness of Tate & Lyle to a new high of 97%. Over recent years, the endorsement of Gary Rhodes has been

used across the marketing mix from point of sale, to on-pack, through PR and into homebaking relationship marketing with both adults and children.

An example is the Tate & Lyle Cooks' Club, which was launched in 1995 and now has over 100,000 members. The club provides help to consumers in the kitchen, offering an opportunity to discover 'Rhodes to Successful Cooking.' Club members receive four full-colour magazines each year with ideas for seasonal recipes, competitions and special offers, as well as information from Tate & Lyle.

The involvement of Gary Rhodes has helped to bring the Tate & Lyle brand to a new generation of cooks, not least children. Under the 'Kids In The Kitchen' banner, Tate & Lyle has produced recipe booklets, promotional tools, and most recently the Lyle's Junior Cooks' Club with the mascot Lyle the Lion.

Brand Values

Tate & Lyle has very strong brand values which focus on its heritage, the quality of its cane products and their consistent reliability. Over 40% of sugar consumed in the UK is derived from cane, and Tate & Lyle is the leading cane sugar brand. Cane sugar is regarded by many expert cooks to be the professionals' choice. One of the differences between cane and beet sugar, for example, is that cane sugar performs better in certain applications. Beet sugar has a tendency to foam more when boiled, which can make it less suitable for jam making.

Tate & Lyle is a trusted brand which has stood the test of time and is considered by many to be the leader in its field. Despite its long and illustrious history, Tate & Lyle is contemporary and has stayed in touch with cooking trends. Its work with Gary Rhodes and its new product introductions have enabled it to appeal to a new and modern audience.

Things you didn't know about
Tate & Lyle

Tate & Lyle is helping to maintain the UK's arts heritage as a major donor to the Tate Gallery.

Long before it was fashionable to go green, Tate & Lyle was producing and selling fully recyclable and environmentally friendly bags for its sugar.

Scott of the Antarctic took cans of Lyle's Golden Syrup on his expeditions. Years later these were found intact, buried in the snow.

Sugar has many uses apart from cooking and baking. Adding a cube of sugar to a vase prolongs the life of the flowers. Adding a sugar cube to a tin of biscuits keeps them fresh.

TESCO
Every little helps.

Market

The UK grocery retail sector is among the most competitive in the world. It is dominated by a core of four brands, Tesco, Sainsbury's, Asda and Safeway, which battle fiercely for market share and customer loyalty. Tesco is the UK's leading retailer with a 15.8% share of the market (Source: Institute of Grocery Distribution 2000).

International mergers, including the arrival of Wal-Mart through its acquisition of Asda in 1999 and the growth of the internet have shaped the UK retail market in recent years. Tesco actively leads the way, not only by continuing to widen the gap between itself and competitors' share of the market, but also by being the world's largest online grocer.

Achievements

Tesco has come a long way since its 'pile it high, sell it cheap' image of the 1970s. It pioneered the development of superstores and in the 1980s began investing heavily in the format. By 1986, its turnover was £3.5 billion and operating profit was £145 million.

These developments led to Tesco becoming the market leader in 1995, (Source: Audits Great Britain – AGB). Success has continued into 2000 with the highest market share, greatest customer loyalty at 40% (Source: AGB) and highest ever market penetration of 48% in a twelve week period (Source: AGB). Tesco's turnover has now reached £20.6 billion, with an operating profit of over £1 billion and the average weekly spend in stores of £19.76 (Source: AGB).

In 1997, the company won 'Retailer of the Year' award and was voted the UK's 'Most Parent-Friendly Supermarket' by Great Ormond Street Hospital's 'Tommy's Campaign' award scheme. Tesco is also well respected in the business community, winning Management Today's 'Most Admired Company' award again in 1999, the same year that it was voted to have Britain's favourite advertising in the National TV Awards.

The highly successful Tesco Computers for Schools scheme reached its ninth year in 2000. Since 1992, the scheme has helped to equip schools with over £54.5 million worth of computing equipment. This includes 38,700 state of the art computers – equivalent to one for every school in the country and 263,000 additional items of computer related equipment.

History

Tesco was founded by Jack Cohen in 1919. After serving in the Royal Flying Corps during World War I, 21 year old Cohen invested his serviceman's gratuity of £30 in NAAFI surplus groceries to sell from a stall in the East End of London.

Cohen went on to trade successfully in a number of London markets and also started selling wholesale goods to market traders. By the late 1920s he had switched his attention from market stalls to open fronted shops on the high street and in 1929 the name Tesco first appeared above a lock-up shop in Edgware, North London. Cohen began to expand his business empire and by 1939 there were 100 branches of Tesco. After the war, the company floated on the Stock Exchange with a share price of fifteen shillings and Cohen began to acquire a string of other companies.

In 1960, Tesco began selling clothing and household goods and by 1968 it opened the UK's first superstore in Crawley, Sussex selling both food and non-food products. Throughout the decade it also introduced 'Green Shield Stamps' which consumers could collect and redeem against a range of household goods. These were replaced in 1977 by a price cutting campaign called 'Checkout at Tesco'.

In 1982, Tesco celebrated its 50th anniversary as a private limited company and raised £500,000 for charity. In the same year it introduced the first computerised checkouts. A year later Tesco changed its name to Tesco plc and in 1985 a rights issue was launched to raise £145 million for a superstore development program. This was followed by a £500 million investment program to build 29 new stores which provided 10,000 new jobs.

However, there was a fundamental weakness in the company – the Tesco brand itself. Consumer research showed that rival Sainsbury's had a better image than Tesco on quality, value for money, reputation and customer service and that its traditional strength – price – was being eroded. The brand's main problem was that consumers didn't know what Tesco stood for: superstores or old high street stores, low prices or quality, food stores or 'home and wear'. There was no overall identity to pull the diverse images of Tesco

together. The company set about transforming the brand in order to improve the total offer and strengthen customer loyalty. A range of marketing and service initiatives was employed, including long running and popular advertising campaigns, new store formats and continuous development of the width and depth of the total product range.

Product

Tesco now has over 650 stores throughout Britain and continues its overseas expansion including 76 in Ireland, 42 in Hungary, 35 in Poland and eighteen in the Czech Republic and Slovakia, as well as 22 stores in Thailand and two in South Korea and Taiwan.

The launch of Tesco Metro stores in 1992 and Tesco Express stores in 1994 took supermarketing into a new era by focusing on convenience and fresh food. Consumers see Metro stores as upmarket, stylish and modern.

Tesco's aim was now to offer a diverse range of premium, exotic and luxury foods as well as Tesco's more traditional value for money items, in order to cater for a wide variety of tastes and budgets. Tesco launched the first economy, own-label range within the sector, with their 'Value Range'. This was followed by other targeted ranges such as the Finest range, and an organic food range. The number of lines in the organic range is now well over 700. In addition to these very focused ranges, the company is continuously expanding its total range and now has

over 20,000 lines on offer. In addition, it has expanded its fresh food counters and an increasing number of stores offer fish, hot chicken, salad and delicatessen counters. The non-food product range has expanded to include clothing, stationery, books, videos, CDs and computer software. Tesco now accounts for 3% of the non-food retail market.

The first Tesco Extra store was opened in Pitsea in 1997. The larger store format allows Tesco to offer this wider range of products as well as non-food items such as electricals, sportswear, designer clothing, computers and luggage. Popular special offers, including great price reductions on such items, have been aptly named WIGIGs 'When it's gone, it's gone'.

Great improvements were also made in customer service, including a commitment to its 'One in Front' queue policy, no quibble guarantees and baby changing facilities as well as additional in-store services such as opticians, photoprocessing and Pharmacy.

Tesco Clubcard was launched in 1995 and was the first national loyalty card in the grocery sector. The number of Clubcard holders has increased to fourteen million. Every quarter, Tesco mails seven million Clubcard members a magazine, of which there are five different editions tailored to different customer lifestages, and reward vouchers tailored to shopping preferences. In 1999 Tesco Clubcard used over 80,000 targeted variations in communications and to date over £1 billion worth of reward vouchers have been given to customers. The Clubcard has been developed to enable customers to redeem their points for airfares, theatre tickets and other entertainment. Tesco Personal Finance was launched in 1997 in a joint venture with The Royal Bank of Scotland and now offers ten financial products including Clubcard Plus, loans, savings accounts and Visa cards. It has 1.5 million customers and attracted 750,000 new customers in 1999.

Recent Developments

Tesco initially offered customers the added flexibility and convenience of home delivery in 1993 with the launch of their Wine Mail Order. This service has expanded over the years and now products such as the Baby and Toddler Catalogue, Tesco Personal Finance, and a choice

of one million books plus 300,000 CDs, DVDs and videos is offered for sale online. Tesco has led the revolution in online shopping through the internet and continues to expand so it is now the world's largest online grocery retailer, with a choice of over 25,000 food products and sales of £125 million. By September 2000, 90% of the UK population were able to access the site www.tesco.com, which currently receives 1.5 million 'hits' per week and has 2,500 new customers signing up every day.

Tesco became the official Millennium Education Sponsor, sponsoring the Learning Zone of the Millennium Dome in Greenwich, London. In addition, Tesco is investing heavily in Tesco 'SchoolNet 2000', one of the world's biggest school internet projects, which so far has involved over 16,800 schools in the UK.

Promotion

Communication by Tesco is inevitably multifaceted through a combination of television, press, in-store and direct marketing. Advertising has made a significant contribution to changing brand perceptions, by bringing the improvements and innovations Tesco offers to the attention of the public.

Tesco's 'Quest for Quality' advertising campaign ran from 1990-1992. It starred Dudley Moore as the Tesco buyer who scoured the world in pursuit of an elusive flock of French free-range chickens, discovering en route other surprisingly high quality products to add to the Tesco range. The campaign adopted a deliberately (and, at the time, highly unusual) lighthearted approach in order to present the changes at Tesco in a way that would build a more positive brand identity. The campaign made a strong impact, peaking at 89% awareness (Source: BJM Tracking).

In 1992, a strategy review suggested a new direction focusing on a new shopping deal: 'quality + price AND service = value'. Tesco needed to adapt to new market realities shaped by the recession, the success of discounters and the improvement of its rivals' advertising campaigns. Tesco understood that shopping is so much more than the products you buy and realised that none of its competitors was making serious attempts to improve the whole experience of shopping. Tesco capitalised on this by launching 114 new initiatives and ran an advertising campaign under the umbrella positioning of 'Every Little Helps' to demonstrate that whilst not everything in life goes perfectly, Tesco was doing its best to make at least one aspect – doing the shopping – a little easier. Between 1993-1995, Tesco ran twenty executions, each one focusing on a different initiative including Mother and Baby changing facilities, Tesco Clubcard and the removal of sweets from the checkouts. Awareness peaked at 64% and attracted new shoppers, helping to secure market leadership.

By 1995, the advertising needed a change. Britain had come out of the recession and Tesco could afford to mirror the public's increased confidence. Instead of focusing on

Tesco's attitude to its customers, Tesco turned the tables and concentrated on consumers' attitudes to Tesco.

The new campaign centered on the 'mother of all shoppers', Dotty Turnbull, played by Prunella Scales and her long-suffering daughter, Kate, played by Jane Horrocks. Dotty regards each of Tesco's initiatives as an opportunity to put the store to the test and in doing so allows the staff to shine. Even though the campaign is in its sixth year, and even after 33 commercials, it is still the most likeable in the retail sector and the humour and simple messages have obviously struck a chord with the public. Despite Tesco's relatively low media spend versus its competitors, it has regular prompted recall scores of 90%, its highest awareness levels ever, thereby making Tesco one of the most efficient advertisers in its category. The Dotty campaign is flexible and has enabled Tesco to communicate service, quality and value for money initiatives.

By remaining true to its 'Every Little Helps' philosophy, Tesco successfully communicated its commitment to offering low prices without damaging its service and quality image.

Brand Values

Once known for its 'pile it high, sell it cheap' approach, Tesco still has a reputation for value for money but the brand is now also highly regarded for the standard of its customer service and the quality and breadth of its product range.

Market

As a nation of tea-drinkers, the British population has a particularly strong bond with Tetley. An astonishing 1016 cups of tea are consumed per person per year in the UK, creating a retail tea market worth £540 million. Tea is by far the most popular hot drink, with only 548 cups of coffee consumed per person per year.

However, leading brands like Tetley are competing in a market where overall tea consumption is slowly falling. The old image of the traditional British 'cuppa' is giving way to a more modern environment of 'repertoire drinking' with consumers drinking more coffee and soft drinks. The growing popularity of coffee bars and a new 'cappuccino culture' is putting tea under particular pressure, especially as coffee is available in a wider variety of locations.

However, the sector's leading brands are continuously innovating to bring new products to market, keeping the thirst for tea alive. We are also drinking different types of tea, such as fruit and herbal infusions.

So, despite coffee's advance, we still drink more tea than any other nation – 100,000 tonnes per year. Nearly 20% of this volume is Tetley tea, making it a brand that has become synonymous with our national drink. Tetley is a giant amongst consumer brands, being one of the biggest food and drink brands in the UK.

Achievements

Tetley is the second biggest tea bag brand worldwide, with sales in a number of key markets across the globe. Tetley is one of the leading brands in both the UK and Canada, is a well established major brand within both the USA and Australian tea markets, and has a developing presence in France, Poland and Russia.

Despite its traditional image, innovation is particularly important in the tea industry and Tetley has established a reputation for being at the very forefront of new developments in the sector. For example, in 1953, it was the first to introduce teabags into the UK market and, in 1989, it introduced the round bag. This was the result of extensive research and development and it helped grow Tetley's share by approximately 30%, achieving brand leadership.

In 1997, it continued its record of innovation with the launch of the drawstring bag, in the UK, giving consumers the chance to squeeze every last drop of flavour into their cup. The Tetley Group has around 1100 employees worldwide and currently has manufacturing sites in the UK, Australia and the US and one, together with a joint venture partner, Tata Tea Limited, in India.

History

Tea was first publicly sold in Britain by Thomas Garway in the middle of the seventeenth century. 150 years later, Joseph and Edward Tetley started to sell it in the Yorkshire Moors, peddling it from the back of the pack horse along with other provisions such as salt. Soon, they were doing well enough to set themselves up as tea merchants, establishing Tetley Brothers in Huddersfield.

In 1856, the brothers moved the business to London, setting up in Callum Street, which in those days was very close to the centre of the world tea trade, Mincing Lane. However, the brothers soon parted company and Joseph was left to run the business alone, changing the name to 'Joseph Tetley and Company, Wholesale Tea Dealers'.

Interestingly, the company's earliest success was in the US, distributing packet tea through an agreement with an American agent, Wright & Graham. This partnership established Tetley as a major trade name in America more effectively than had been so far achieved in Britain, and also led to the partnership becoming a world force in packet tea distribution. In 1913, Wright & Graham became Tetley Tea Incorporated.

Having introduced the tea bag to the US 33 years earlier, Tetley brought it to the UK only in 1953. In 1954, the Stock Exchange Gazette reported: "Joseph Tetley is particularly well-known for the introduction of tea in small bags for immediate use in the pot."

The company stayed loyal to its invention during a period of tumultuous market change as the retail market began to be dominated by large multiples and strong, national brands began to take centre stage. With the tea bag giving it a clear point of differentiation, Tetley was in a good position to ride the storm.

Tetley has continued with its innovative approach ever since, launching round tea bags in 1989 and drawstring bags in 1997.

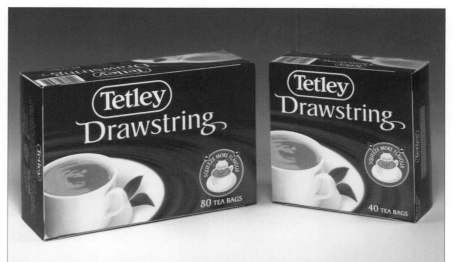

Product

Tetley tea bags are blended and packed at the company's factory in Eaglescliffe, Teeside, one of the world's largest tea-packing facilities. It produces approximately 200 million Tetley tea bags every week, blending tea from over twenty different estates around the world.

As well as the core Tetley tea brand, the company also makes Tetley Decaffeinated, launched in January 1997. This now accounts for 23% of the decaffeinated sector (Source: ACNielsen May 2000) and is the fastest-growing decaffeinated tea brand.

Recent Developments

Tetley has continued its emphasis on innovation, with the launch of a new 'soft pack' format, replacing cartons with a more compact, resealable bag. In 1999, it also reacted quickly to a growth area in the tea market – the rising popularity of speciality teas – with the launch of Jade Garden, a new brand of green tea.

In March 2000, the Tetley Group was acquired by Tata Tea Ltd, a division of the Tata Group. Tata Tea shares Tetley's 'passion for tea'. Originally a tea estates company, since 1983 Tata Tea has transformed itself to a 'tea bush to tea cup' company and is now one of the best known tea brands in India. It currently has a 21% share of the Indian branded teas market – making it the nation's number two in tea. Tata Tea has 54 tea estates, ten tea blending and packaging factories and employs around 59,000 people.

Also in 2000, Tetley became a sponsor of the British Olympic Team for Sydney 2000 Games. This tie-up was part of Tetley's Sydney 2000 campaign, in which the company offered 'free sports stuff' to schools. Participating schools collected tokens from Tetley packs, which could be redeemed against a range of over 2000 items of sports equipment. The campaign was supported by the Olympic silver medallist Roger Black.

Promotion

Since 1973, the face of Tetley has been the Tetley Tea Folk, the brown-capped, white-coated band of characters led by Gaffer. Having starred in a string of animated commercials, the tea folk have become some of the best-known and loved promotional characters in the UK. Tag lines such as, 'That's better, that's Tetley', are among advertising's most famous. Many people still fondly remember ads such as 'Lovely Day' and 'Keep me Warm'.

During the 1990s, Tetley broadened the role of the Tea Folk, using ads which showed them outside of the factory in new situations. For example, the recent 'Only Tetley Will Do' campaign showed the Gaffer out on a date.

But there is much more to Tetley's promotional strategy than advertising alone. The competitive tea market demands innovative promotional solutions and Tetley has done some interesting work. Throughout the 1990s, it ran a series of high perceived-value promotions, offering free in and on-pack goods like Tetley Tea Folk houses, Disney merchandise and a particularly successful promotion offering free Roald Dahl books. Often, these popular promotions were supported by advertising campaigns.

Since the late 1990s there has been more of a focus on value for money, leading to a shift in promotional strategy to price-led tactics like multi-buy packs. Tetley has also directed more effort towards cause-related marketing, an example being its 'Free Sports Stuff for Schools' programme. The Tea Folk were also called into action to help support this campaign, with Sydney featuring in three advertising executions, trying his hand at various sports in the Olympic arena.

Tetley also runs significant PR activity, using large costumed characters of the Tea Folk giving out tea in public places and from the Tetley Bus, which embarks on promotional tours around the country. Collectable merchandise has always been an important activity and Tetley still makes character-based items available on-pack, in special offers and from the internet. Consumers can buy merchandise directly from the www.teafolk.com website, which in addition provides information and amusing profiles of each of the Tetley Tea folk – Head Gaffer, Sydney, Teana, Clarence and Oliver.

Only Tetley will do. Tetley

Brand Values

Tetley brand values are epitomised in the Tea Folk themselves, who are perceived as warm, caring, down to earth tea experts who can be trusted by the consumer to do the right thing. They help to reinforce the message that Tetley knows and cares more about tea than any rival brand.

Things you didn't know about Tetley

Tetley was the first to introduce the tea bag into the UK and the US. When the tea bag was introduced to Britain in 1953, it had already been in the US for 33 years.

One of the biggest problems for Tetley when introducing the tea bag was finding a type of bag tissue that did not taint the tea. In 1964, this was achieved and tea bag sales rose from 450 tonnes in 1960 to 5,000 tonnes in 1968.

Gaffer's tea shop was opened in Manchester in 1998, offering customers a wide range of Tetley teas plus the chance to buy Tea Folk items.

Tetley tea folk merchandise is incredibly popular. One in five UK homes is estimated to have a Tea Folk item and, in 1991, a Tetley cookie jar changed hands for £200.

The Tea folk commercials have appeared round the world – Gaffer's Yorkshire accent has been translated into Polish and Maltese.

The Tetley drawstring bag is the preferred tea bag in all UK McDonald's restaurants.

Market

In 1999 the total toiletries and cosmetics market was worth £4.43 billion, with four market sectors reaching sales of more than £500 million: haircare, skincare, cosmetics and oral hygiene, with the highest rates of growth being in the wet shaving products and haircare products sectors (Source: Mintel 2000).

However, as sales continue to boom, so does criticism of the industry's sophisticated marketing approach. The opinion is growing that the majority of the mainstream cosmetics industry is selling a fantasy of beauty likely to wreck the self-esteem of anyone who doesn't fit into such a narrow definition. Similarly, many unscrupulous and cleverly-worded claims are being made as to the anti-ageing properties of certain products.

The Body Shop is leading the calls for a change in approach, promoting instead an honest, alternative concept of 'beauty' which is based on diversity and personal freedom, the philosophy of which is 'love your body – just the way it is'.

HEMP REVIVAL FOR SKIN SURVIVAL

◯ THE BODY SHOP

This unconventional approach represents the brand's main point of difference in an extremely congested market. The Body Shop 1999/2000 worldwide retail sales totalled £634.6 million. For a company that positions itself so firmly in opposition to the prevailing attitudes of the majority of the cosmetics industry, this is a truly impressive achievement.

Achievements

The Body Shop has spent the last 25 years proving it is possible both to have an ethical approach to business and be successful; that profit with principles is a viable proposition.

The Body Shop has a unique ethical approach, and the resulting products have not only created

a new cosmetics category, but also a new way of doing business.

As a cosmetics retailer with a high street profile, as well as being home to a range of innovative products, The Body Shop is uniquely positioned to campaign on those issues with which it aligns itself as a brand. The Body Shop prides itself in creating opportunities for its customers to get involved with a variety of local, national and worldwide issues, and the brand counts the success of these campaigns as integral to its success as a company.

There have been plenty of success stories. Four million customers gave their support when The Body Shop teamed up with Amnesty International for the 'Make Your Mark' campaign to highlight human rights breaches around the world – the repercussions of which resulted in eight of the twelve imprisoned human rights defenders accrediting The Body Shop campaign as being instrumental in their release.

Similarly, The Body Shop campaigned tirelessly on the issue of animal rights for over a decade, and the British government banned the testing of cosmetics on animals in November 1998. It represented a great step forward, but the company is still fighting on for a worldwide ban.

These campaigns would not be possible without the solid background provided by the success of The Body Shop products. It is estimated that in 1998 and 1999, The Body Shop sold a product every 0.4 seconds with over 80 million customers transactions through stores worldwide.

As with all pioneers, The Body Shop has inevitably spawned a plethora of imitators. Its use of natural ingredients in product development has been widely copied, and its stance against animal testing has been assumed by larger multinational cosmetics brands.

But The Body Shop continues to be respected for its principles and authenticity. Indeed, in 1999 The Body Shop brand was voted the second most responsible company in the UK in the Citizens Brand survey undertaken by the Futures Foundation and the Consumers Association. In 1998 a Financial Times survey of international Chief Executives ranked The Body Shop as the 27th most respected company in the world.

History

In 1976 in Brighton, Anita Roddick opened the first The Body Shop store. It was a fresh approach, retailing home-made, naturally-inspired products that used minimal packaging, refillable containers, and did not test on animals.

Since its inception, The Body Shop has pioneered new paradigms of beauty, retail and business. The Body Shop brand was an undisputed revolutionary and brand leader. In terms of its product, it created the market for natural products. It created a new model of experience and consumer relationship. Shrewd targeting brought it all to the masses while retaining its aspirational nature; it became the first mass market beauty and body care brand.

The power of the brand at the time of its launch resided in its relevance for the consumer and to the birth of 'green' culture generally. It was a brand that was plugged into what was happening in the world at large.

The first overseas franchise opened in 1978. Franchising allowed for rapid growth and international expansion as hundreds of entrepreneurs worldwide bought into Roddick's vision. In 1984 the company was floated on the stock exchange and in 1988 The Body Shop brand was launched in the USA. Throughout the 1990s it continued to expand throughout the world. It now has more than 1700 shops in over 49 countries.

Product

The Body Shop created a niche market sector for naturally inspired skin and hair products. It retains its leading position in this sector by a unique approach in which principles frame business practices, which in turn shapes the products.

For The Body Shop, researching new product ranges takes place all over the world, often gaining inspiration from diverse cultures and the wisdom of ancient civilisations. Its Ayurvedic range, introduced in 2000, is a prime example based on a holistic Indian system over 2500 years old. Similarly, The Body Shop interest in the health of the mind, body and spirit led it to develop product lines based around holistic theories of total wellbeing. The Body Shop was selling aromatherapeutic products years before its major high street competitors.

As a pioneering company, The Body Shop is still unafraid to break new ground with its choice of ingredients in its products. The hemp range is a perfect example of this approach, hemp being an incredibly versatile ingredient which makes a great moisturiser. However, the ingredient's distant relation to the drug cannabis was picked up by the press, which helped to ensure that the launch was an even greater success than anticipated.

Its visionary, holistic approach to product

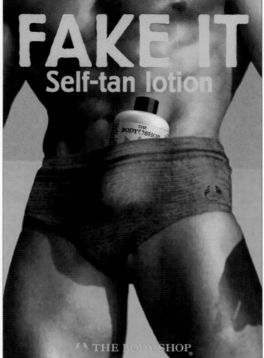

ranges helps The Body Shop reinforce its alternative to the conventional beauty – and youth-obsessed cosmetics industry.

Still retaining its trademark emphasis on naturally inspired products using traditionally-influenced recipes, The Body Shop has, since the 1980s, also developed a Community Trade programme that aims to create sustainable trading relationships with disadvantaged communities around the world. The goal is to help build livelihoods and to explore trade-based approaches to supporting sustainable development by sourcing ingredients and accessories from socially and economically marginalised producer communities.

Through this programme The Body Shop sources natural materials for inclusion in some of its best-selling products, from the cocoa butter used in Cocoa Butter Hand & Body Lotion to babassu oil used in White Musk Body Lotion, as well as accessory items including massagers from India and baskets from Bangladesh.

The Body Shop trades with over 35 Community Trade suppliers in 23 countries and these relationships demonstrate the company's attitude towards responsible global trading.

Recent Developments

The year 2000 saw the launch of The Body Shop Human Rights Award, the largest award of its kind. It recognises the outstanding achievements of grassroots groups and organisations working for human rights around the world. The first award aimed to raise awareness of poverty and social exclusion by focusing on child labour and its role in restricting the opportunities for children to receive an education.

The company also recently joined forces with Friends of the Earth in calling for a five year freeze on genetic engineering and patenting in food and farming. Establishing close links with certain charities and non-government organisations in order to add weight to its various campaigns has been a feature of The Body Shop's strategy ever since it linked up with Greenpeace in 1985.

In 1999 The Body Shop embarked on an ambitious scheme to redesign the environment of its stores. The result is a redefinition and reinterpretation of the retail environment, ensuring that the company retains its well established position within the industry.

The Body Shop also continues to develop and produce innovative new skin and hair care products and passionately supports a wide range of charities and campaigns with commitment that has become its trademark.

Promotion

Despite having chosen not to rely on external advertising, billboards, television or newspaper advertising, The Body Shop has enough promotional expertise to retain a strong presence in the market.

Having Anita Roddick OBE as the public face of the company has been of tremendous benefit; indeed, the perception of the company as 'approachable, outspoken and radical' is due in no small part to the influence of The Body Shop founder and co-chairperson.

The Body Shop's dual positioning on product and campaigns led to essential exposure which has reinforced The Body Shop brand.

The stores themselves remain the most effective promotional devices that The Body Shop relies upon. The distinctive green and gold livery and logo are instantly recognisable and the franchise system ensured significant expansion and encouraged a huge presence, first in the UK and now worldwide.

Promotionally, the stores rely upon window displays and posters, the themes of which are continued in-store. This vital advertising is characterised by verbal wit, a striking colourful visual presence, and an eccentric sense of fun, skilfully rendered by the award-winning design team. Promotions change frequently and may vary from product promotions to campaigns to seasonal celebrations; they all successfully convey the passion and vitality of the brand.

Brand Values

Brand values are the very foundation of The Body Shop. In a sense, everything it does, be it a new product range, or a new campaign, springs from its deeply held set of beliefs.

The Body Shop believes that business can and should act as a force

for positive change and it has never been afraid to use its position to challenge the really big issues. As a business, it is dedicated to the pursuit of social and environmental change.

Its core values include a belief in the importance of self-esteem, especially amongst women. The Body Shop believes that it is immoral to try constantly to make women feel dissatisfied with their bodies, or to deceive a customer by making unrealistic miracle claims for a product.

The Body Shop passionately campaigns for the protection of the environment through its reuse, refill and recycle schemes. Its involvement with human and civil rights campaigns is well known, as is its stance against animal testing within the cosmetics and toiletries industry.

The Body Shop was the first public company in the UK to use a process of annual social auditing to monitor performance and ensure that practice is living up to the needs and expectations of its stakeholders.

The Body Shop has a continuing commitment to ethical procedures that encourages empowerment and raises awareness, giving the customer the opportunity to make a real difference.

Things you didn't know about The Body Shop

The logo of The Body Shop was designed for just £25, back in 1976.

The Body Shop employs approximately 13,000 people worldwide.

The Body Shop Direct, a home selling programme, provides a livelihood for over 2,000 consultants.

In November 1998, The Body Shop was the first UK company to be accredited to the Humane Cosmetics Standard for its steadfast opposition to animal testing.

The Body Shop operates in 49 countries with over 1,700 outlets spanning 25 languages and twelve time zones.

The Big Issue paper started life as a project of The Body Shop Foundation, a charity set up by The Body Shop.

The first products sold at the first branch of The Body Shop were packaged in a Boston Round bottle. The company still uses this distinctive bottle shape today.

THE NATIONAL LOTTERY®

Market

The launch of The National Lottery in November 1994 signified a radical transformation in the nature and size of the UK gaming industry. Overnight, gaming was transformed into a part of everyday life for a large proportion of the population. The lottery was positioned as a 'harmless flutter' which could be enjoyed by all adults in the UK.

The National Lottery has undoubtedly had an impact on other areas of the gaming market. Whilst it has taken market share away from its competitors, including bingo and pools operators, it has also been instrumental in increasing the size of the gaming market as a whole. The UK gaming market is worth £26 billion and the National Lottery accounts for around 20% of this market.

Achievements

The National Lottery has been a massive success. The National Lottery Online game (the technical term for the Saturday and Wednesday draws), Thunderball and Instants, have become an integral part of everyday life. They have drastically altered people's perceptions of gaming and created a new and powerful structure for raising money for good causes around the country.

It took only eighteen months after the launch for Camelot to establish the world's most efficient lottery and the UK's biggest consumer brand with sales by March 1998 totalling more than £13 billion. The Henley Centre concluded after just fourteen weeks that The National Lottery represented 'the most dramatic product launch in British history'.

The lottery quickly became a national institution with more than 60% of the country playing regularly. It is estimated that more than 90% of the UK adult population has played at least once. By the end of its first week, the National Lottery had raised £12 million for the five 'good causes' chosen by Parliament – Sports, Arts, Heritage, Charities and the Millennium.

In just five years The National Lottery has grown to become a national institution. From its expanding portfolio of games including Instants, Thunderball and Big Draw 2000, The National

Lottery has made a significant contribution to the future of British society through the money raised for the good causes.

Further achievements include being voted 'Brand of the Year' in 1995 by The Marketing Society for the launch of The National Lottery and being ranked as the most efficient lottery in the world for four consecutive years by the La Fleur's World Efficiency Study.

History

In March 1992 the government proposed the creation of a UK National Lottery. The aim was to provide designated 'good causes' in the UK with a huge injection of funds. With this objective in mind, the government put the operation of the UK lottery out to tender. Eight organisations applied and in May 1994, after a lengthy review of all applications, the government announced that Camelot Group plc had won the tender and would run the lottery for its initial seven year license. Camelot had committed to raise £9 billion for good causes, a commitment achieved in October 2000 and subsequently increased to £10.5 billion.

Camelot Group plc was a consortium set up by five separate companies – Cadbury-Schweppes, De La Rue, GTECH, Racal Electronics and ICL. Each company brought important expertise to the successful running of The National Lottery.

Winning the license was only the first step in what was to be a very long road. The newly formed company had just 24 weeks to set up the lottery from scratch and would be fined £1 million a day for any delay.

Camelot faced three major hurdles to launch the lottery: technical requirements, establishing a retailer network, and a communications strategy. Camelot created the largest communications network in the UK, equivalent to the four biggest high street banks combined. The network was capable of processing up to 400,000 transactions per minute, while its software

equated to 200 person years of software development time.

Retailers needed to have terminals installed. More than 10,000 retailers were selected by Camelot to have terminals installed in their premises. These included multiple and independent retailers, forecourt operators, off licenses and post offices.

By launch, at least 93% of the UK adult population lived or worked within two miles of a lottery outlet. Each of the 10,000 retailers needed trained operators and this required 80,000 individuals to be trained between September and October 1994. Camelot set up ten regional centres to train retailers and act as payment centres for major winners.

Getting the communications and education right at launch was essential: the public had to understand and believe in the brand and be inspired to purchase National Lottery tickets. The National Lottery was launched with the now famous advertising campaign featuring the slogan 'It Could Be You' and the 'Hand of Good Fortune' acting as the random hand of luck.

Product

The National Lottery Game remains the largest component of The National Lottery portfolio. Players can win from £10 to £7 million or more. Twice weekly, the lottery balls are drawn randomly on the BBC produced National Lottery Show. The first show attracted more than 22 million viewers.

If no one wins the draw jackpot, it rolls over to the next consecutive draw up to a maximum of three times. If there is no jackpot winner on the fourth rollover draw, the jackpot is shared between players who have matched five numbers plus the bonus ball. The jackpot has rolled over many times, including five double rollovers but there had never been a triple rollover at the time of writing.

From time to time the jackpot is boosted to increase player interest. These 'Superdraws' are often themed: for example, the 'Christmas Superdraw' in 1997 had a guaranteed minimum jackpot of £25 million, while the 'Building Superdraws' in April 2000 offered a series of jackpots that increased from £10 million to £15 million and to £20 million.

National Lottery Instants was launched in March 1995 and became the biggest impulse brand in the UK. It consists of a variety of themed cards, with different prize levels and odds of winning. Players simply scratch off the latex play area to find out if they have won from £1 up to £100,000.

A second National Lottery Game draw was launched on Wednesdays in 1997. The first eight weeks saw total sales rise by 28%, with weekly sales of around £28 million.

Recent Developments

Thunderball, a new online game, was launched in 1999. This was designed to play a complementary role in the Online portfolio by offering a smaller fixed top prize (£250,000) and also better odds of winning a prize.

It aimed to provide a very different playing experience, revolving around the last ball to be drawn (the Thunderball) and holding players in the game for longer. Thunderball's launch was highly successful with the first draw taking sales of £6.4 million, nearly £2 million above budget. The game has achieved weekly sales of more than £4.7 million, making it the second largest little lottery game of its type in the world.

By October 2000 Thunderball had achieved total sales of £321 million, contributed over £98 million to good causes and paid out more than £170 million in prizes to over seventeen million lucky winners.

National Lottery Big Draw 2000 was launched as a special draw to mark the celebration of the new millennium. The game involved two draws and both had a strong link to the millennium through the selection of special years.

National Lottery Big Draw 2000 was an enormous success. The predicted sales target of £75 million was surpassed at £80.6 million. Big Draw 2000 created more millionaires in one night (eighteen) than any other lottery in the world and was an event played by more than sixteen million adults. It also raised £22.3 million for good causes in one night. With the launch of Big Draw 2001 in December 2000, this game looks set to become an annual event.

The next online game, Lottery Extra, was launched in November 2000. Lottery Extra is a jackpot only game which means that if no one wins, the jackpot will continue to grow until it reaches £50 million, thus giving players an extra chance to win it big.

Camelot has emphasised the importance of new

media in its marketing mix by investing in an internet site – www.national-lottery.co.uk which provides an important source of information for all aspects of National Lottery games.

Promotion

Few advertising campaigns of the 1990s will be remembered as well as the 'It Could Be You' campaign. The 'Hand of Good Fortune' image conveyed the central idea that chance was the motivating factor behind the lottery.

The launch saw a marketing campaign on an unprecedented scale with more than £39 million spent on television, radio, press, poster, point-of-sale and direct mail packs. By November 1994 approximately 40 million adults had seen the commercial at least thirteen times. The direct mail push was the largest recorded and sent to 21.8 million homes.

The launch of The National Lottery was a resounding success. Marketing magazine concluded: "The National Lottery took the country by storm in 1995 – it is by far the leading brand in both Adwatch of the year tables – the highest total recall during the year and the highest single awareness figure recorded."

Professor Barwise, Director of the Centre of Marketing at the London Business School, who led an independent audit looking at the lottery, concluded: "The launch of The National Lottery has been a clear marketing success. I believe this has not been a matter of mere good luck, but instead reflects the high quality of marketing analysis and planning in the successful application."

Four years after its successful launch, it was time to refresh the brand. In the past the advertising had largely focused on the prospect of winning with the strapline, 'It could be you.' However, after four years fewer and fewer people believed 'it could be them' and it was time to update this famous campaign.

Advertising needed to inject a renewed sense of enthusiasm, optimism and enjoyment about playing the main National Lottery Game, whilst also delivering a sustainable product truth. A change in direction from focusing on the probability of winning to the more realistic possibility of winning was heralded by the new slogan, 'Maybe, just Maybe.'

The launch of the new advertising campaign in November 1998 saw more than just a change in the slogan. It coincided with television advertising which for the first time featured some of the beneficiaries of the good cause funds. The advertising aimed to challenge the widespread misconceptions about how lottery money was spent and to encourage the general public to reassess its value to the betterment of the nation.

National Lottery advertising has not, however,

been confined to the flagship twice-weekly draws and the good causes which they benefit. It has also supported new product development including the launch of Thunderball in 1999. This game was given its own distinct identity through a campaign focusing on the excitement of playing an online game that offers a better chance of winning. This was brought to life through the dramatisation of the big red Thunderball.

Instants also returned to television screens with a vox pop campaign featuring National Lottery retailers recounting stories of customer wins and the message 'Anyone can win in an Instant.'

Brand Values

The National Lottery has become part of British daily life and the brand is trusted, as well as respected by many. The random elements of the online game – where lives can be transformed by winning – gives the brand a magical quality. The National Lottery makes dreams come true.

The Instants brand is light hearted. It provides the opportunity for people to have a break from everyday life and have fun – instantly.

> *What's your lottery dream?*

Market

Printed publications such as newspapers and magazines are some of the few information sources that one can take where and when one likes. Newspapers remain the longest standing and most effective medium through which the topics and stories of the day are reported and discussed. As a main source of daily news and information, newspapers have an unrivalled ability to drive brand loyalty and pass their brand values on to their reader. A British newspaper thus plays a virtually unique role in our daily lives, and as a result it has a place in the heart of the population that is unmatched by European counterparts.

Around thirteen million newspapers are sold in the UK every day, making it a highly competitive and dynamic market.

In the UK newspapers are generally grouped into three segments – tabloids, the mid-market and broadsheets. Unlike other European countries there are no daily all-sport newspapers. The tabloid sector comprises three daily and three Sunday titles. They represent the popular end of the market, being smaller in format and highly entertaining in style. They are characterised by their attention-grabbing red logos along with bold, punchy headlines, concise articles and a

strong focus on celebrity and human interest.

The tabloid titles include two renowned titles, The Sun and The Mirror who are long term rivals. The continued fading of The Mirror has meant that The Sun's closest competitor is now the mid-market Daily Mail. Characterised by its middle-England positioning, the Daily Mail has profited in recent years from the changing mood and social make-up of Britain. This has left The Sun as the pre-eminent voice piece of working-class Britain. Long-associated with its committed support of the Conservative party under Thatcher, the title has in fact continually shifted its political support to represent the interests of its readers. Thus in 1997, The Sun urged its readers to vote for the Labour party and Tony Blair.

Achievements

The Sun has now been the biggest selling daily newspaper in Britain for 30 years with a daily readership of 9.6 million. The impact and influence that it has had on the British people is therefore highly significant. Renowned for its ability to capture and reflect the mood of the nation, its famous front pages have entered British folklore. 'Gotcha!', 'Freddy Star Ate My Hamster', 'Paddy Pantsdown', 'Up Yours Delors' and 'Is this the most dangerous man in Britain?' amongst others have set the agenda, entertained the population and taken their rightful place in history. The Sun has also become famous for its determination to reward its readers beyond all others. To this end, it paved the way with the first cheap channel-ferry crossings, the first massively-discounted holiday flights and a continuous succession of tickets, offers and prizes that no other newspaper has matched. So successful has The Sun been in these offers that it has actually become the biggest booker of short-break holidays in Britain and became the first newspaper ever to give away a £1 million prize.

History

The modern Sun was born in 1969, but its pedigree dates back to 1911 when trade unions produced a strike sheet called the Daily Herald. By 1933, it had become the world's biggest selling newspaper with a circulation of two million copies per day.

However, by the 1960s the Daily Herald was in serious difficulties. Its columns were filled with nothing but dry trade union reports and readers deserted it in droves.

In 1964 its owners, the International Publishing Corporation (IPC), decided to kill off the Herald and launch a new paper, The Sun, aimed at the affluent young as well as graduates emerging from red-brick universities and technology colleges.

The target circulation was two million but by the middle of 1969 sales had slumped to around eight hundred thousand and the paper was losing money rapidly.

In July 1969, IPC began negotiations with Rupert Murdoch and sold the title for just £600,000.

The new look Sun was launched as the newspaper we know today with the promise

of being a fresh and lively campaigning paper. It took the country by storm, with the very first issue selling more than a million copies. Within a year, sales had doubled, and after four years the circulation reached three million.

In 1970 the first topless Page Three Girl appeared causing massive controversy, and in 1983 the most famous Page Three Girl of all, Samantha Fox, made her first appearance.

In 1986 the Sun moved to Wapping with the other News International titles in a move that instantly broke the dangerous stranglehold that the trade unions had on the national press. By 1990, massive investment in new print processes enabled The Sun to shake up the market again with higher quality print, full-colour reproduction and various extra supplements and pull-outs. Most noticeable of these was the launch in 1996 of the first free TV listings, that again re-shaped not only the tabloid market but the paid-for TV

listings market itself. Through all of this, The Sun has long established itself as the premier source for news, celebrity gossip and sport.

Product

The Sun newspaper has questioned, challenged and demanded reactions for the last 30 years and has established itself as a leader of the mood and opinions of the British public. In a world dominated by increasingly sophisticated media spin PR and clever marketing, The Sun can always be relied on to give a firm opinion. The result is that many people will have different reactions to The Sun on different days – whether that be laughter, tears, outrage or pride – but few can ever ignore it.

This is crucial, because The Sun gives the ordinary person's point of view. It continues to report on the issues important to the nation in an uncomplicated manner using language to which millions of people in Britain can quickly relate. It also shares the humour and wit that characterises the best of British. The result is a newspaper read by the Prime Minister and Chief Executives, but most importantly by millions of ordinary men and women in Britain. The Sun therefore continues to be the people's paper and the voice of the people that no-one in authority can ignore.

The breadth of The Sun's news and sports coverage is one of its great strengths, ranging from Del Piero, the world-famous Italian footballer, to Del Trotter, the equally famous Peckham trader. The paper also prides itself on

getting those who are actually making the news to be columnists. Thus Sir Alex Ferguson, Delia Smith and Jeremy Clarkson are all examples of those to be found in the newspaper, giving the inside track and expert opinion on a wide spectrum of issues. Bizarre, with Dominic Mohan, also excels in its role as the premier source of exclusive celebrity news and gossip.

Promotion

The Sun has long believed in the power of word of mouth and personal recommendation as its strongest form of promotion. Supported by carefully selected sales promotions and reader-offers to keep the brand very much at the front of the consumers' minds, The Sun has developed a level of brand awareness and strength of brand personality almost without precedent. Few have not heard of The Sun or cannot recount one of its amusing stories or headlines. The key to the brand's success also lies in its ability to bring its equities of humour, passion and entertainment to bear on all the most relevant situations of the day. Thus if there is a major new craze or development, The Sun can be guaranteed to be amongst the first to provide an associated offer, presented in the unique approach of The Sun.

Recent Developments

The Sun has achieved some great extra successes in recent times. It celebrated recognition of Richard Pelham as Sports Photographer of the Year at the British Press Awards in 2000, and also took the Front Page

of the Year award for its front cover on the day following the Solar Eclipse in 1999.

It also won the Hugh Cudlipp award for the book 'Hold Ye Front Page' – a history book written in the style of The Sun that has achieved phenomenal popularity throughout the country.

Brand Values

The Sun is a brand that represents the values and concerns of the British public. Over the past twenty years its activity has made it an icon of contemporary British culture.

It is emotive, passionate and humorous. It entertains and informs but always remains uncomplicated and down to earth. The result is an extraordinary brand that brings millions of people together through shared reactions and emotions.

In an increasingly fragmented world The Sun aims to be a focal point around which people unite: an enduring point of daily reference.

Things you didn't know about The Sun

There is a 30% higher chance of Sun readers being white van drivers than the population average.

Every year The Sun uses more than 80 million kilometres of paper – enough to go to the moon and back many times – but a huge amount is now recycled.

The Sun's first lotto game in March 1988 entered the Guinness Book of Records for the largest number of entrants in a newspaper competition – over 4.3 million.

The Sun has been used as a model by the Foreign Office and the Department of Social Security to help their staff phrase issues clearly and concisely.

The first few editions of the modern Sun in 1970, set in 'hot metal' type, were limited by a shortage of the letter 'E'. Any headline could therefore only use the letter twice.

Timberland ® 🌲 ®

Boots Shoes Clothes Gear

Market

For a long time now, the trend in everyday fashion has been towards more casual dress. Even the working uniform of the suit is beginning to give way to a more casual look. And, the rising profile of sport in our lives is also having an effect on the way we dress. All in all, sports clothing and footwear sales reached £3.65 billion in the UK in 1999, accounting for nearly 15% of all clothes and shoe sales (Source: KeyNote).

Timberland is well positioned to benefit from all of these trends. Its mixture of 'outdoorsy casual' wear and more specialist sports gear means it has its feet planted firmly in both camps.

In the clothing and footwear market, brands are king. In fact, there are few sectors where they are more influential. The importance of branding has led to increasing crossover of clothing manufacturers into footwear and vice-versa. As a result, Timberland, which started out making footwear, has expanded into apparel. Changes in retail are also affecting the market. Footwear is being sold by a wider range of outlets, including department stores, fashion retailers, sports and outdoor shops, as well as traditional high street shoe shops. For example,

fashion multiples such as Next and River Island as well as Marks & Spencer are now major shoe retailers. Mail order is another important channel, especially as catalogues targeting more affluent consumers are becoming more widespread.

The growth of the sector is being further stimulated by increased levels of advertising and promotion, especially in the new, highly successful men's glossy magazines such as FHM, GQ and Esquire.

Achievements

Timberland has won several accolades over the years. For example, in 1994, it was hailed as 'premier brand' in the outdoor market by the Wall Street Journal.

However, its biggest achievement was in defining a new category of footwear. Its sand-coloured Classic Boot is a fashion icon which has inspired innumerable imitators. As with any brand that creates a new category, Timberland has the kudos of being the 'genuine article' in this area of footwear. This has inevitably boosted the reputation of its brand and helped it establish credibility across its wider clothing and footwear range.

Timberland can also take credit for a revolutionary technology that would change the footwear industry forever. In 1965, it introduced an injection-moulding technique which meant that boots and shoes could be produced with soles fused to the uppers without stitching, making them waterproof.

Timberland has also made important strides in the area of ethical business. Its culture and brand identity are grounded in the belief that 'doing well' and 'doing good' are not contradictory. Timberland's partnership with city year, a US based organisation aimed at encouraging young people from diverse backgrounds to participate in their community, has become a valuble part of Timberland's strategy. In 1989 Timberland donated 50 pairs of work boots to City Year initiating the start of a long term relationship that continues to flourish to this day.

Timberland has invested over $1 million in the project and set up its community action programmes for employees, called Path of Service. This allows each full-time member of staff across the world paid leave to work on voluntary projects in and around their local community. In 1997 Timberland pledged 40,000 hours to America's Promise and increased paid community service time for employees to 40 hours per year.

History

Timberland can trace its origins back to 1952, to New England in the US. That was the year that Nathan Swartz bought a 50% interest in the Abingdon Shoe Company, a Massachusetts-based outfit manufacturing 'own label' shoes for leading US footwear brands.

By 1955, Swartz had bought the

remaining interest in the business and was joined by his two sons. Swartz and sons made their first boots under the 'Timberland' name in 1973. Thanks to the revolutionary injection moulding technique they had introduced eight years earlier, they were guaranteed waterproof and were an instant hit. As its leather boots and shoes appeared on the market, the brand became well-known and in 1978 the business changed its name to The Timberland Company.

In 1980 Timberland footwear was launched in Italy, its first foray into the international market. In 1986, the first Timberland store opened in Newport, Rhode Island, in the eastern US. Two years later, Timberland introduced the HydroTech boat shoe as well as their first men's sportswear collection. Timberland came to the UK in the 1980s through distributor partnerships, but a subsidiary of the business was set up in 1989.

In 1991, Jeffrey Swartz, the grandson of founder Nathan, was named as Chief Operating Officer. Timberland began trading on the New York stock exchange under the symbol TBL and in the following year became the founding national sponsor of City Year, making its first $1 million investment.

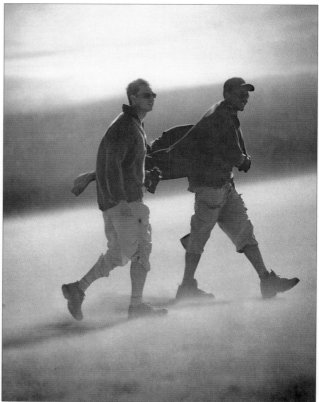

In 1996 a new line of women's dress casual footwear was introduced, as was a multi-purpose outdoor line of performance footwear. Kids' footwear was also launched and new licencing agreements signed for gloves, travel gear, eyewear and socks. In 1998 Jeffrey Swartz became Timberland's president and in the same year revenues hit $862.2 million.

Product

Since the development and launch of the classic boot in 1973, Timberland has built its reputation of delivering long lasting, hard wearing product. Its success in footwear continues to be driven by a diverse product portfolio, focused on meeting the distinct needs of Timberland's key consumer segments. With a focus on innovation, value and distinction, Timberland's footwear delivered its third consecutive year of double-digit worldwide unit shipment increases in 1999.

Timberland clothing continues to be an integral part of Timberland's evolution as a global lifestyle brand. In the UK, Timberland has developed a profitable and well-established men's apparel business.

Timberland focuses its experience and forte in footwear and clothing, with the aim of ensuring that the brand encompasses a total lifestyle and has licensee agreements with reputable manufacturers of accessories. This range has increased over the years, with the introduction of watches, luggage and back packs, children's clothing and eyewear.

Recent Developments

1999 marked the introduction of the Timberland PRO™ Series and Mountain Athletics™ by Timberland, new endorsed brands reaching new consumers.

The Timberland PRO™ Series is a line of footwear designed for the professional tradesperson. In 1999, the Timberland PRO™ Series was distributed through reputable outlets that reach blue-collar workers. Timberland plans to further expand distribution in 2001 and strengthen awareness of Timberland PRO™ products through marketing and promotional activities directed at point-of-sale and retailer catalogues to capitalise on the work consumer's shopping behaviour.

Mountain Athletics™ by Timberland, an aggressive and rugged new outdoor athletic brand, was introduced in 1999. The company has had similar success with Mountain Athletics™ by Timberland, with a range of performance products, designed to meet the needs of outdoor athletes. The Mountain Athletics™ brand gained retail placement in speciality sports and athletic outlets and is rapidly building a consumer following worldwide.

Promotion

Timberland promotes the brand through an integrated product offering, based on: 'Boots, Shoes, Clothes and Gear' that equip people to make a difference in their world. Advertising is centralised through the US Corporate Head Office, and subsidiaries and distributors worldwide ensure that it reaches each individual market's target consumer. Recent campaigns have included the highly successful 'Our Boots Work' campaign, which focuses on the Classic Boot.

The 'Boots, Shoes, Clothes and Gear' creative platform is designed to support the notion that the 'journey outside' is a metaphor for the 'journey within'. The ads capture real people experiencing a 'Timberland moment' – an outdoor experience that connects on a deeper, more emotional level.

The Mountain Athletics range is promoted using a separate ad campaign, entitled 'Go there'. Positioned to reflect the balance between the performance of the product and the sense of spirit gained from taking part in mountain athletic sports, the campaign encapsulates the spirit of the brand.

Brand Values

Ever since Timberland developed the first guaranteed waterproof boot, the company has been committed to quality, durability, authenticity, value and performance, and to delivering the experience of 'the great outdoors' to its customers. The central pillar of Timberland's long term strategy is to provide value and innovation to consumers throughout its entire product offering. Applying this formula to all the company's activities has enabled Timberland to move beyond being a source of great footwear to become an integrated lifestyle brand.

Market

The market in which the Virgin brand operates is diverse and far reaching, from insurance and music industries to soft drinks and travel. Above all Virgin prides itself on getting people the best deal and offering better value and service than its competitors. Virgin is unique in that it has no one major rival as it operates in so many sectors. Divisions and investments of Virgin Group include amongst others: Virgin Retail, Virgin Travel, Voyager Investments, Virgin Hotels, Virgin Entertainment Group, Virgin Direct, Virgin Rail and Virgin Express.

Achievements

The Group's interests, which are now operating in 27 countries, include retailing, the internet, book and software publishing, travel, hotels, telecommunications and financial services. Virgin is one of the UK's largest groups and achieved organic growth from sales turnover in 1983 of £50 million to more than £3 billion in 1999. Virgin retail has 94 stores in the UK and Ireland and a further 54 stores trading across the US, Europe and Asia. In the US, Virgin has one of the most successful e-tailer sites with Virgin Megastore online at virginmega.com. V2 records, a record company set up after the sale of Virgin Records to help promote new bands, has had phenomenal success with its signings. Acts including the Stereophonics, Madasun and Moby are all signed to the label and in 1999 V2 was the only single record label to achieve two nominations for the Mercury Music Prize.

History

Richard Branson started his first business with the launch of Student magazine in 1968. The first Virgin business was a small mail order record retailer established in 1970. Virgin Records was set up in 1972 by Branson and his cousin, Simon Draper, neither of whom knew much about the music business at that time. It grew to become the largest independent UK record company and the sixth largest record company in the world, signing such acts as Mike Oldfield, Culture Club and the Sex Pistols along the way.

Branson sold the company to Thorn EMI in 1992 to free funds for his investment into his now very successful Virgin Atlantic venture. As Virgin Music became increasingly successful, it started to diversify. In 1983, it began to distribute films and videos through Virgin Vision and Virgin Games, a computer games software publisher, was launched. The group's combined pre-tax profit climbed to £2 million on a turnover of just under £50 million. In 1984 it took what was perhaps its biggest gamble when it launched Virgin Atlantic, offering a higher level of service at competitive prices.

Virgin Holidays was introduced shortly afterwards. By 1989 the airline announced pre-tax profits of £10 million and has continued to expand and add further routes. Two years later Virgin Retail Group and WH Smith announced a joint venture to develop the Virgin Megastore business in the UK and open stores in Spain, the Netherlands, Australia and the US. By 1994, Virgin Retail had acquired the Our Price chain in the UK and Ireland and became the UK's largest music retailer.

Branson then decided to take on the financial services sector and provide consumers with no-nonsense financial packages, cutting out sales people and their commission.

In 1996 Virgin acquired Euro Belgian Airlines, renamed it Virgin Express and began to operate a low cost, no frills service to a number of European cities. The V2 music label and music publishing company was launched and Virgin Net was set up to enable users to get the most out of the internet. Also in this year Virgin Bride opened its doors for business and the Virgin Group was awarded the Cross Country trains passenger rail franchise. A year later Virgin Vie, a cosmetics and beauty care company, opened its first four stores. This later became known as Virgin Cosmetics.

Product

Virgin Atlantic Airways and Virgin Express (which operates from its Brussels base to many European cities) are both elements of Virgin's airline business and were founded on the idea that people would fly more often if it were more affordable. The notion was correct and they have succeeded.

Virgin Retail prides itself on making a customer's visit to its stores an 'experience', whether by the use of one of the many interactive listening stations, by playing the latest Dreamcast or Playstation game, enjoying a cup of coffee in one of the cafés, e-mailing a friend from the in-store internet terminals or even seeing a band play live in-store. In the US, Virgin Retail operates one of the most successful e-tailer sites with Virgin Megastore online at www.virginmega.com. Building on this success, Virgin rolled out the first genuine global offering on the internet with the launch of sites in the UK, Europe and Japan in 2000. Virgin Retail has also launched the Virgin JamCast service, www.virginjamcast.com, a web service that broadcasts digital music files directly to the customer's PC.

V2 Music Group had a very successful 2000 with its signings receiving several nominations for awards such as the Mercury Music Prize, the Q Awards and two Grammy nominations for Moby. The group specialises in new and upcoming artists who have no previous back catalogue. V2 is the only independent company to have set up offices in all the key international music markets offering exclusive priority to all V2 signings, in contrast to the majors who also market and distribute many subsidiary labels.

In the financial sector, Virgin Direct offers customers investment and insurance products that do not involve the payment of commission to salesmen or middlemen. As one would expect with Virgin, the service doesn't stop once the product has been bought; regular statements are issued and the service can be accessed at

any time over the phone or via the internet. Since its launch in 1995, Virgin Direct has attracted well over 200,000 customers and has gross sales of £2.3 billion. The Virgin One account, launched in 1998, offers a whole new way of banking, combining customers' mortgages with their current accounts.

Launched in 1996, Virgin Net, is now the UK number one entertainment as well as leisure service online. A joint venture between Virgin and NTL, Virgin Net provides entertainment and leisure content and services, and is consistently placed in the top ten most visited UK sites. Virgin Net has built its business on a reputation for innovation through attention to online customer needs. It offers its customers, reliable fast access to the internet and a host of additional value added online services including, five email addresses per user, integrated web search facilities and internet support at competitively priced rates. Looking forward, Virgin Net has teamed up with a number of leading UK companies for high-profile content and access deals, including Yahoo! (UK and Ireland), Twentieth Century Fox and Microsoft. New content and communications services are being introduced each month, while Virgin Net's entertainment and leisure content will continue to appear across new and emerging online platforms throughout the world, including mobile phones and interactive television.

Virginbiz.net evolved out of the need for businesses to harness the sales power of the internet. It helps small business owners who want to develop their own web presence, by providing services to help them develop, maintain and attract visitors to their website. The service also helps small business owners manage their current businesses more effectively through the internet. Within the Virginbiz.net channels small business owners get access to legal, financial, human resource and marketing information. This service is already very popular, with the number of users doubling every month since its launch.

Launched in 1991, Virgin Publishing has grown to become one of the major forces in British publishing, producing about two hundred new books each year and with an active back-list of around 500 titles. Virgin Publishing has built its reputation as a niche publisher of books on popular culture, particularly music, film, television and sport and also as an opportunist publisher in strong genres such as true crime and erotica. In recent years Virgin Publishing has broadened

its output to include a wide range of general titles aimed at mainstream bookshops and a back-list programme of Virgin-branded popular reference titles and travel guides.

Brand promotions using airships and balloons have really taken off in the last few years. Virgin Airship and Balloon Company is the world's leading operator of airships and hot air balloons. A full service agency approach provides direct brand exposure, television and newspaper coverage and all the associated corporate hospitality, retail support and sales promotion opportunities.

The Group also has operations including Virgin Active, a 'life-centre' which offers members a total lifestyle package with twenty clubs planned throughout the UK and Virgin Bride which offers a fresh approach to the big day.

Recent Developments

Apart from moving further into the world of online services across many services, Virgin has also recently moved into the energy market. Virgin Energy, launched July 2000, is an internet based gas and electricity supplier offering unrivalled customer service and a unique price guarantee. The online company, a joint venture between Virgin and London Electricity, will provide gas and electricity to homes in England, Scotland and Wales. The price guarantee, an industry first, means that if after the first year the customer hasn't saved money, Virgin Energy will refund the difference plus 20% of that difference. So the customer simply can't lose. The company will also reward households for being energy efficient. If customers can reduce their energy consumption, year on year they can claim £1 for every 1% saved.

Virgin Mobile is a 50:50 joint venture with One 2 One which launched in November 1999 and has become the fastest growing mobile phone company in history. It offers customers a simple, single tariff, with no line rental, monthly charges or hidden catches — they simply pay for the calls they make. Virgin Mobile also offers customers an ever-expanding range of Virgin Xtras, services which give discounts on shopping, a range of special offers, and a world of information and advice at the touch of a button. Virgin Mobile launched in Australia in November 2000. This is its second global joint venture in the sector.

In September 2000 V.SHOP was launched with a total of 100 stores opened in the last quarter of 2000. The aim was to be the first ever internet to high street retail offer in the UK, combining old economy retailing with new.

Promotion

One of the results of Richard Branson's products, and indeed the man himself, is that Virgin don't need to spend vast amounts on advertising. Word of mouth and the quality of the Virgin portfolio is almost enough to sell a Virgin product on its own. Virgin Cola is a good example of where PR has been used to its full potential: a ground breaking promotional giveaway ran in The Sun newspaper, with Virgin

offering a stake in the fortunes of the company. The promotion gained over £2 million worth of in-depth exposure both in terms of in-paper support and The Sun's television advertising.

Virgin Cola has recently launched a loyalty scheme called i-can which introduces consumers to the world of Virgin at vastly reduced costs. An estimated total of £15 million will be discounted off a host of products across the Virgin Group in the scheme's first year.

Virgin Mobile was launched in November 1999 with a high profile press and television campaign following a taster campaign prior to launch. Features of the Virgin Mobile service include having only one tariff with no line rental and no fixed-term contact.

By November 2000 Virgin Mobile had attracted 500,000 customers, with mobile phone users being encouraged by television ads to 'get divorced' from their old networks and switch to Virgin Mobile. Additions to the Virgin mobile offer since launch have included the first MP3 phone in April 2000.

Brand Values

The Virgin brand is famous the world over. The signature logo tells customers that something is a Virgin business, with all the associations and aspirations that conveys. In a sense the Virgin logo is seen as Richard Branson's personal signature. The brand name embodies value for money, quality, service, fun and innovation. Each new Virgin product comes with a promise to deliver these values.

Things you didn't know about
Virgin

The Virgin logo was first drawn on the back of a napkin by graphic designer Trevor Key.

In one week, 175,000 people walk through the Oxford Street Virgin Megastore, buying 55,000 items.

2000 saw the introduction of the world's only airship passenger operation. The Las Vegas Lightship operates nightly flights down the fabulous Vegas Strip.

Virgin Bride was the idea of an air stewardess on Virgin Atlantic.

Through Virgin Active's club, Club Active, you can learn to drive a 40 tonne tank or go trekking in Nambia.

Virgin is comprised of over 200 companies worldwide, employing around 30,000 people.

virgın atlantıc

Market

At the beginning of the new millennium, the international airline industry is a highly profitable and increasingly competitive market. A difficult period during the recession of the early 1990s, marked by a general consumer reluctance to book long haul holidays, gave way to a period of slow growth as consumer confidence returned. Since 1994 there has been a 46% volume growth in the long haul market (Source: Mintel 1999).

Coupled with this, the new millennium paved the way for a period of increased growth in the airline industry as new markets in the Pacific Rim, India and China began to open up for trade. Transatlantic and European routes also remain hugely important markets for airlines to operate in, particularly in the field of business travel.

In order to survive and compete, it is vital that airline companies evolve constantly, focusing on capturing the market with an ever-improving range of services.

Achievements

Since its launch in 1984, Virgin Atlantic has been notable for being one of the most forward-thinking companies within the market. As a result, it quickly became the UK's second largest long haul airline and the first to succeed in breaking British Airways' monopoly on transatlantic routes with a 25% market share.

Right from its launch, Virgin Atlantic set new standards for customer care by introducing a number of innovative products and ideas that other airlines strived to emulate. The airline quickly became renowned for its consideration of all passenger needs, both in-flight and at the airline's airport facilities. Virgin Atlantic's own in-flight surveys revealed that 91% of passengers in Upper Class would fly with Virgin Atlantic again and would recommend the service to others.

Since 1984 Virgin Atlantic has won countless prestigious annual awards. In 1999 alone it won 'Best Business Airline' at The Guardian and Observer Travel Awards, 'Best Longhaul Airline', 'Best Transatlantic Airline', and 'Best European Airline' at the Official Airline Guides awards. It has been voted 'Best Transatlantic Airline' nine times by Travel Weekly readers and 'Airline of the Year' four times by the readers of Executive Travel. Its Upper Class service has been voted 'Best Business Class' eight times by Executive Travel and seven times by the readers of Business Traveller Holiday. In additon, Which? voted Virgin Atlantic the best British airline for the second time in 1997.

The result of this success is that in 1998/1999 the Virgin Travel Group had a staggering turnover of £1067 million and carried 3.6 million passengers – a far cry from the 125 thousand passengers carried by the company in 1984.

History

In the early 1980s, transportation – rather than customer care – was the top priority of the airline industry. When Virgin Atlantic burst on to the scene offering not only better service and lower costs for passengers but a commitment to put the customer first, the effects were radical.

The company was set up in 1984 when an Anglo-American lawyer, Randolph Fields, approached Richard Branson – the young and unorthodox chairman of the Virgin Group – with an idea for a new airline that would fly between the UK and the US. Better known at the time as the leading light in the world of pop and rock music, Branson was enthusiastic about the opportunity to diversify. His characteristic energy and enthusiasm meant that within three months the airline began to lease its planes and June 22nd 1984 marked Virgin's inaugural flight from London to Newark.

Virgin Atlantic pioneered a string of industry 'firsts'. Abandoning the traditional three tier structure used by other airlines, they were the first airline to offer just two flight classes: Economy (a choice of Premium Economy and Economy) and Upper Class, a first class service at a business class fare. Other 'firsts' included individual television screens for all passengers, on-board automatic defibrillators, child safety seats and staff trained to handle cardiac problems. Virgin Atlantic's Upper Class was the first to offer a dedicated sleeping cabin for business class passengers and a sleeper service with flexible meal options.

From the outset, Virgin Atlantic's mission was to provide the highest possible level of service for all classes of air travellers at excellent value for money. Very soon, the airline's transatlantic routes expanded to Miami (1985), Orlando (1986), New York JFK (1989), Los Angeles (1990), and Boston (1991). This was followed by flights to Tokyo, Athens, Hong Kong,

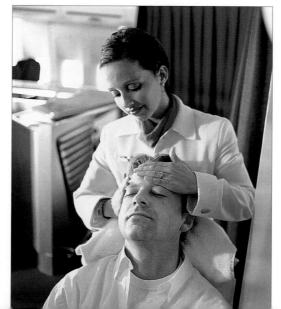

San Francisco, Washington, Johannesburg and Antigua, and the formation of the Asia Pacific Partnership with Malaysia Airlines and Ansett Australia.

In 1998, the company commenced a new codeshare agreement with Continental Airlines that, with the sale of seats on Continental's Gatwick-Newark services, enabled Virgin to offer its passengers the flexibility of six London-New York flights daily.

Virgin Atlantic's sustained success lies in the fact that despite huge growth and a solid reputation, the service still remains customer driven with a continued emphasis on value for money, quality, fun and innovation.

Product

Virgin Travel Group consists of Virgin Atlantic, Virgin Holidays – which has become one of the largest transatlantic tour operators – Virgin Aviation Services and Virgin Sun, a European and Mediterranean holiday operation.

The principal subsidiary, Virgin Atlantic Airways Ltd, is based at Heathrow, Gatwick and Manchester and carries over three million passengers a year. Virgin Atlantic operates departure lounges at Heathrow – the flagship Clubhouse – in addition to lounges at Gatwick, New York (JFK and Newark), Boston, Washington and Johannesburg and provides lounge facilities at each of its gateways.

Virgin's Upper Class is marketed as a first class service at a business class fare and therefore competes with other carriers' business class products. Since its launch in 1984 it has won every major award in the travel industry and changed the face of business travel. Upper Class passengers are supplied with a chauffeur-driven car – both outbound and returning – to their final destination, a first class baggage allowance, separate check-in plus a 'Drive-Thru' check-in service at Heathrow, Gatwick and Newark.

Once onboard, passengers can spread out in a 60 inch seat pitch, drink in the onboard bar and lounge, and enjoy the services of an inflight beauty therapist. Virgin Flying Club – previously Virgin Freeway – is one of the most generous frequent flyer programmes available and was the first to offer air miles for travel in all classes. Designed with the aim of building passenger loyalty, the scheme is offered on three levels: red, silver and gold. Miles and rewards can also be earned with Virgin's partner airlines and by American Express Card members.

Virgin Atlantic was the first airline to recognise the different needs of economy travellers. Premium Economy is aimed at cost conscious business travelers and offers facilities and service more comparable to a traditional short haul business class with separate check-in, a separate cabin on board, and comfortable seating with 38 inch seat pitch. For the price of a fully flexible ticket, passengers also have priority meal service, duty-free and baggage handling, complimentary pre-take-off drinks and newspapers.

Virgin Atlantic Economy service focuses on maximum value for money and was the first to provide every passenger with a seat-back television screen broadcasting Virgin's own inflight entertainment system, Arcadia, with a selection of up to 45 channels of movies, comedy, news, music and drama, as well as Nintendo and classic PC games. Passengers also receive free drinks, an amenity kit including a non-disposable headset, complimentary drinks and a menu with the choice of three entrees with meals.

The safety, comfort and entertainment of children in all classes has been catered for with an 'unaccompanied minors programme', baby changing facilities on all aircraft, special meals and snack boxes for kids and a dedicated children's visual channel.

Recent Developments

In recent years, Virgin Atlantic has extended its network of routes around the world and captured market share from the leading players in the industry.

In 1995, a partnership agreement was signed with Malaysia Airlines to provide a double daily scheduled service from London to Kuala Lumpur and a daily service onward to Australia.

All aircraft delivered since 1997 are fitted with state of the art Matsushita Avionic Systems IFE, offering an increase of screen size in all classes, and an increased range of video and audio channels.

In 1999 Virgin Atlantic transformed its Upper Class products and services in a £37 million re-launch. The focus of the launch was a new seat that transforms into a full length bed which became the signature piece for Virgin Atlantic's Upper Class service. The seat can be for dining, reading and reclining to a flat-out sleeping position without taking up any more room on the aeroplane.

Other features include the ability to power laptops, with power leads available on board covering 80% of different laptops. Other added service elements were expanded bar facilities and a totally flexible meal service.

At the end of 1999, Richard Branson signed an agreement to sell a 49% stake of Virgin Atlantic to Singapore Airlines for £600.25 million.

Also in 1999, Virgin Atlantic launched the first

ever direct service from London to Shanghai as well as services to Chicago and Cape Town. In the same year the airline signed a code share agreement with Air India to operate services between London and Delhi, implemented in July 2000, the year that also saw the first ever scheduled service between London and Las Vegas. August 2000 saw the introduction of 'Virgin Blue', a flight running between Brisbane and Sydney.

In May 2000 Virgin Atlantic signed a deal to be the first airline to introduce the latest onboard tele-medicine equipment and in July, they became the first airline to enable passengers to receive calls via their mobile number whilst in flight. Branded 'Earth Calling', the service has been developed by BT and

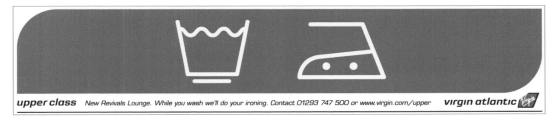

allows passengers to charge their air-to-ground calls to their GSM account.

Promotion

The greatest and most well known advertisement for Virgin is Richard Branson himself. Branson is often perceived as the consumer's hero, an entrepreneur operating in a style all of his own, with Virgin's brand values emanating from his personality. At the same time he is one of Britain's most admired businessmen, and his daredevil antics, such as ballooning across the Atlantic, have given the Virgin brand additional publicity. Branson also keeps a shrewd eye on promotional opportunities: for example, when he heard of British Airways' decision to remove the Union Jack from their plane exteriors, he capitalised on the change by introducing the Union Jack on to Virgin planes.

Virgin Atlantic has proved an astute advertiser over the years. Its logo is highlighted on all its goods and services and is a highly protected

property. Virgin Atlantic has implemented an integrated media strategy to promote its brands, including television, newspapers, posters, promotions, direct mail and the internet, often to wide acclaim. The 'Grim Reaper' ad, for example, won numerous marketing awards and creative accolades including a Golden Lion in the Travel Transport and Tourism category at the Cannes International Advertising Festival; a Silver in the British TV Advertising Awards, a Solis award for Travel & Air Transport TV at the International Tourism & Leisure Festival and was also the winner in the Travel category in the London International Advertising Awards. In 1999 it won The Guardian newspaper Recruitment Award for Best Commercial Advert and Best Written Advert.

A selection of strip advertisements emphasising Virgin Atlantic's Upper Class services and comfortable facilities have featured in the UK press and have also won several leading marketing awards. In 1997 Virgin Atlantic countered BA's and Sainsbury's half price flights promotion by taking full page ads in the national press over a four day period with a less restricted offer. It resulted in over £3 million worth of bookings. The company also ran a 'route network' outdoor ad campaign utilising posters and the side of London taxis in one month bursts per quarter over twelve months which boosted awareness of routes flown by Virgin by up to 19%.

Brand Values

Virgin Atlantic strives to provide the best possible service at the best possible value. It is a distinctive, fun-loving and innovative brand which is admired for its intelligence and integrity. Judging from the results of a poll conducted by the research agency NOP, the public also associates it with friendliness and high quality.

We cover more countries than any other network.

Market

The use of mobile phones has grown dramatically in recent years, already over one in two people own a mobile. Mobile communications is growing faster than the internet. Between 1999 and 2000 market penetration rose from 26% to 54% in the UK, where there are now over 30 million mobile phone customers. Prepaid products have driven the recent growth in the mobile market, and the developments in wireless technology which allow internet access have

driven the market further. The mobile phone is no longer just a means of talking: it is a way of accessing a whole raft of information. As such it has become a valuable addition to today's lifestyle.

Achievements

It took just fifteen years, eight months and one week to connect the ten millionth customer to the Vodafone network in the UK. It took the company nine years to reach its first million customers and another five years to reach five million. Then, in twenty months, to autumn 2000, it doubled its customer base. Around six million of its customers are on Pay as you Talk, Vodafone's prepaid product.

Since it was established in 1985 Vodafone has connected an average of 1,748 customers a day, with the last million customers being connected in under four months – the equivalent of 8,300 customers a day, or one customer every ten seconds.

In 2000 Vodafone reached two more major milestones: on one day in August a record six million text messages were sent on the Vodafone network, and 50 million voice calls a day were made.

On the Vodafone network mobile phones are sold in 12,000 retail outlets, including almost 300 of its own retail stores. It has 267 network roaming agreements in 121 countries. Vodafone has maintained its clear leadership in a highly competitive marketplace with a market share of 29.4%, which is 4% ahead of its nearest rival.

In its most recent survey OFTEL, the telecommunications regulatory body, found that Vodafone UK was top out of all of the networks for customer satisfaction. Vodafone achieved a customer satisfaction rating of 97% – three percent higher than their nearest rival.

Vodafone was the first company in the UK to launch a cellular telephone network. It led the development of, and is still the market leader in, the prepaid mobile phone service which has led to such explosive growth in UK and European markets. It pioneered international roaming and led the field in developing new and innovative information services, such as sports results, traffic reports and City financial news accessible through mobile phones.

Vodafone's global strategy embraces voice, information, video, m-commerce (mobile commerce) and other data services. It focuses on satisfying individual needs, as technology makes it possible to

deliver an ever-wider and more comprehensive range of personalised services.

It has increased its geographic reach by winning new licences and securing strategic mergers and acquisitions and the Vodafone network now covers 99% of the UK population.

Vodafone Group plc is the world's largest mobile telecommunications company, Europe's largest company, and one of the top ten companies in the world. By April 2000 it was providing mobile communication services to over 53 million customers in 25 countries.

History

Vodafone was formed originally as Racal Telecom to bid for a UK cellular licence and the right to compete with BT in mobile services. The licence was granted in April 1983 and the service opened on January 1st 1985 with a call made from London's Trafalgar Square to Newbury and the service was launched by Ernie Wise of Morecambe and Wise fame. In 1991 Vodafone demerged from Racal Electronics, and on June 30th 1999 merged with AirTouch Communications, a leading US-based international mobile business. On September 21st 1999 agreement was reached with Bell Atlantic to create a US wireless joint venture composed of the company's US wireless assets, leading to the formation of a new company, Verizon, in April 2000.

In March 2000 Vodafone AirTouch acquired with German company Mannesmann and it was agreed at the AGM in July that the company's name would return to Vodafone Group plc to help create one of the top ten companies in the world.

YOU ARE HERE
Weather updates through your handset. From Vodafone.

CUS10MERS

Vodafone is the first UK network to have 10 million customers. So, to all the service providers, mobile phone specialists and distributors who have helped us to reach this milestone, a million thanks. Or should that be 10 million?

In the UK the principal business of Vodafone AirTouch is the operation of digital cellular radio networks. Vodafone is one of four UK network operators, the others being BTCellnet, Orange and One 2 One. Vodafone supplies products and services to independent outlets and has its own wholly owned distribution channels and over 300 retail stores in the UK. Through Vodafone's data services, the company also has a record of successful technical innovation in the areas of messaging, wireless data applications and information services.

Product

Vodafone UK develops and operates the Group's UK network and makes air time available to service providers. The company's 300 retail stores in prime high street locations throughout the UK offer a comprehensive range of contract and Pay as you Talk packages to customers. It also has specialist centres aimed at local businesses and occupies 54% market share, leading position among corporate accounts. A 24 hour online shopping service for customers was launched in 1998.

Vodafone a leader in the field of wireless data, provides customised solutions to corporates and small businesses. Working with third parties it drives forward new technologies and business applications.

Vodafone also operates a UK paging network which markets a wide range of paging products and services. It prides itself on the coverage and reliability of its network and on its extensive range of state of the art hardware.

Vizzavi provides a vast array of information based content such as entertainment and voice activation. In the near future customers will be able to benefit from location based services and m-commerce.

Recent Developments

In December 1999 Vodafone launched its internet portal in the UK as part of its move to provide mobile phone users with access to a range of internet-based services. These include text alerts direct to your mobile phone – reminders, horoscopes, weather and in July 2000 the company launched Vizzavi, a Joint Venture with Vivendi. This new multi-access internet service enables users to access the internet from their PC or directly through their mobile phone and will in the future allow access through television.

Furthermore, in September 2000 Vodafone updated its Pay as you Talk service with Pay as you Talk Smartstep – a prepay product which carries no service charge, and incorporates a discount based on daily usage. After the first three minutes everyday customers pay 5p per minute thereafter.

Promotion

Vodafone's 1999/2000 advertising campaign focused on Pay as you Talk allcalls and Pay as you Talk Smartstep. The campaign built on the previous year's and was designed to raise awareness and educate existing and potential customers about the benefits of paying upfront. The tone of voice used in the campaign was straightforward, clear, simple and accessible, using the likable and trustworthy Hamish character who appeared in previous campaigns.

The first ad, 'Twister', used the proposition 'With Pay as you Talk you're in control of your mobile phone.' Hamish was on a surreal looking prairie landscape when a mobile was whipped out of his hand by a twister – meant to signify worries about mobile phone costs spiralling out of control. Hamish later held a Pay as you Talk phone and was completely in control, even when in the eye of the twister, while all around him was chaos. Viewers were made to feel that Pay as you Talk was the most straightforward way to have a mobile phone and that it let you stay in control.

The second ad demonstrated the range of stylish phones available with Pay as you Talk, and again used the Hamish character. The campaign ran on television, outdoor poster sites and in style magazines.

Target audiences for the advertising included high call making 20-34 year olds with active social lives and disposable incomes; 18-21 year old students concerned about costs and

mothers in their role as present buyers.

Recent brand advertising for Vodafone has led with the headline 'You are here', with the key proposition being: 'You are now truly mobile. Let the world come to you.' In the era of the mobile internet, this new campaign embodies Vodafone's vision: become a global mobile leader in terms of profit, customer service and value, making mobile networks the 'nervous system' of the networked economy and spanning three major developed markets – Europe, US and Japan.

The campaign focused on how Vodafone can deliver sports, news, weather, traffic updates and cinema listings direct to customers' mobile phones. In press and outdoor advertising the company employed an arrow device to indicate that Vodafone can bring all this information to customers, wherever they are.

Vodafone helps build awareness of its brand throughout the UK and further afield through its sponsorship of Manchester United FC, the England cricket team and major horse racing events, such as the Derby and the Oaks.

Brand Values

Vodafone's 'can do' approach makes life easier for its customers. It is helpful – human, personal, approachable clear, authentic, down to earth and reassuring. Powerful – relaxed but authoritative, confident, credible and accountable. Resourceful – right here, right now, practical and contemporary.

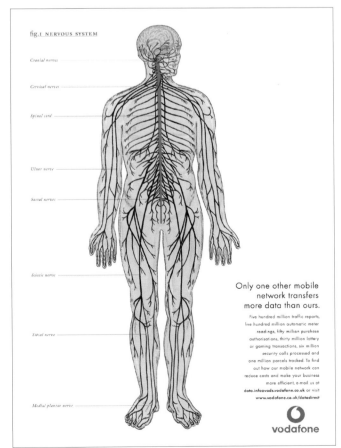

fig.1 NERVOUS SYSTEM

Cranial nerves
Cervical nerves
Spinal cord
Ulnar nerve
Sacral nerves
Sciatic nerve
Tibial nerve
Medial plantar nerve

Only one other mobile network transfers more data than ours.

Five hundred million traffic reports, five hundred million automatic meter readings, fifty million purchase authorisations, thirty million lottery or gaming transactions, six million security calls processed and one million parcels tracked. To find out how our mobile network can reduce costs and make your business more efficient, e-mail us at data.info@vods.vodafone.co.uk or visit www.vodafone.co.uk/datadirect

Market

Sausages are a well-loved staple of the British diet. Today half of British households serve up sausages for a meal every week. An amazing 300 million kilogrammes of sausages are eaten every year. And England's schoolchildren eat 12,756 km worth of sausages per annum (Source: Wall's).

Sausages are still a strong favourite for the barbecue, and their enduring popularity as a breakfast staple has been boosted by sandwich bars and fast food outlets offering an early morning snack for workers and shoppers keen to grab a bite on the hoof.

But sausages are also becoming more sophisticated, with new speciality sausages in a variety of flavours expanding the category on supermarket shelves. However, for today's consumer convenience is king, so products that can be simply lifted off the shelf in pre-packed portions are growing more and more popular.

The sausage market is worth some £300.8 million (Source: TNS April 2000) and continues to grow in value.

Achievements

Wall's is the second biggest brand in the sausage market, behind its sister brand Richmond, with a 6.7% value share (Source: TNS April 2000). Both brands are owned by Kerry Foods. Wall's is also the best loved and most well known brand within the sausages market.

Established over 200 years ago, Wall's is a respected and trusted brand and has had royal warrants since 1812. By the early twentieth century demand for Thomas Wall & Sons' products was such that Wall's opened its first factory in Battersea, London. Since then, driven by an ever-increasing demand for its products, the Wall's name has grown into a huge franchise, spanning not only meat products but other pastry and snack products as well as frozen foods manufactured in sites across the UK.

In November 1994 Kerry Foods purchased the Wall's business. The company has invested heavily in new machinery, equipment and logistics at its factory in Hyde, Manchester, helping to ensure continuing success for the brand.

Investment in the Wall's brand increased by more than 300% between 1994 and 2000, from £2 million per year to £7.5 million, and is expected to grow year-on-year.

Dedication to producing high quality products and new product development are of paramount importance to Wall's and the brand continues to keep up with current trends and consumer demands. For example, Wall's Lean Recipe 95% Fat Free, launched in 1999, provides a healthy alternative for those who love bangers but worry about their waistline. The sausages outperformed their low fat competitors in blind taste tests.

In 1998 Wall's launched into the bacon market, and already has a 2.87% share (in terms of volume) of the pre-packed bacon market, worth £445 million (Source: TNS March 2000). The Wall's bacon range has grown in value by 372% since it was launched and listed by the major multiples including Tesco and Sainsbury's,

it is now one of the best performing bacon products. The brand has also helped to generate interest in the sector as a whole by its innovative 'peel and seal' packaging.

Wall's ability to consistently provide people with what they want has helped it remain 'The Nation's Favourite'.

Since its launch in 1999, Wall's revamped website, www.bangers.co.uk, has won a number of awards including the London International Advertising New Media Award, the Food and Beverage Advertising Award for New Media – Savoury Division, and a New Media award from FAB Grand Prix. In addition, the brand featured in Checkout's Top 100 Grocery Brands for 1999.

History

Sausages were first introduced to Britain by the Romans. The word sausage is derived from the Latin 'salsicius', meaning 'salted', and was a general description for preserved meats. The original 'salsicius' was probably a dried sausage which would keep fresh in the hot Italian climate.

The sausage developed over the centuries and each county in the UK had its own particular way of flavouring the local sausage. Cheshire used caraway and coriander, for example, while Staffordshire preferred marjoram, pimento and thyme. One of the oldest types of sausage, still popular in Scotland and the North of England,

is the black pudding, made using hog's blood.

Sausages earned the nickname 'bangers' during World War II because of their large water content which makes them explode when fried.

Thomas Wall's father, Richard, opened his sausage and pie business in St James's Market, London, in 1786. He quickly earned a reputation as a pork butcher, and word of his superb quality cuts of meat and delicious pork sausages soon reached the royal household. In 1812 Richard Wall received his first Royal Appointment as 'Pork Butcher to the Prince of Wales'.

By 1834, Wall's commitment to quality was legendary. The business moved to larger premises at 113 Jermyn Street and the company continued to flourish under Thomas and his sons who ran the business with such dedication that a series of other royal appointments followed.

At the turn of the century the Wall brothers realised they would have to expand further to keep pace with demand. They built a new factory in south London and began to advertise for the first time. In 1920 the family sold the company for £120,000 to Mac Fisheries, which later became part of Unilever. It continued to thrive up to and during World War II, when sausages were one of the few foods never to be rationed.

In the 1950s Wall's were quick to spot the potential of television advertising. Since Kerry Foods acquired the brand in 1994, innovative product development and marketing has helped sustain its popularity.

In the face of competition from other brands over the past fifteen years, Wall's has constantly striven to improve the flavour, taste and value for money of its sausages, investing heavily in sausage machines and refrigerated vehicles.

Product

Wall's has a wide range of sausages to suit all tastes. There are ten different types of fresh and frozen sausages, including the Lean Recipe 95%

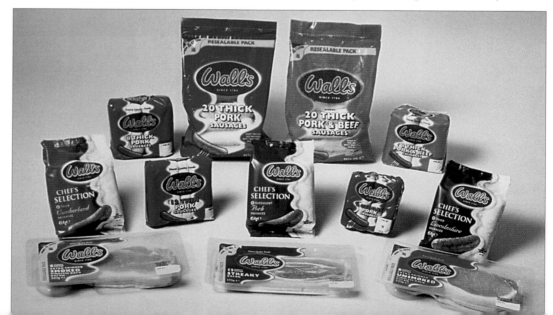

Fat Free, Wall's microwaveable Instants, and a premium range, Chef's Selection.

The Chef's Selection comprises Pork, Lincolnshire and Cumberland sausages, each in distinctive parchment-wrapped 454g packs of eight. Wall's Lean Recipe 95% Fat Free uses a unique blend of ingredients to deliver the taste and texture expectations of a traditional full-fat sausage, with just one sixth of the fat content. Other fresh and frozen sausages include pork, beef, skinless, thick and thin variants.

While many may think sausages are fattening, a Wall's thick pork sausage actually contains 35% fewer calories than a typical bar of milk chocolate. Sausages also contain a high proportion of protein – typically 11.1g per 100g.

Recent Developments

Wall's has continually introduced new variants to support the brand and keep it relevant to today's lifestyles. For example, it has met the growing demand for healthier foods by launching lower fat products across a range of categories. Wall's Lean Recipe 95% Fat Free, launched in 1999, was a complete reformulation of its existing healthier option to deliver better taste and succulence, with one sixth of the fat content of traditional sausages. Low fat sausages already account for £11 million annual sales in the fresh sausage market. Wall's Lean Recipe has a 14.3% share of this sector and grew 74% in 2000 (Source: TNS June 2000).

Wall's also demonstrated its commitment to meeting consumers' needs with the launch in 1999 of the first ever 'peel and seal' packs for bacon and frozen sausages. These allow the meat to be resealed in its own airtight plastic container after opening, doing away with the frantic search for clingfilm.

In September 2000 Wall's launched its Instants range – pre-cooked microwaveable bacon and sausages. Ready in under a minute, Instants cater for today's hectic lifestyles. Quick, easy and convenient, Instants also do away with dirty pans, which

research indicates is a major turn-off among infrequent sausage buyers. Instants have allowed Wall's to capitalise on the microwaveable snacks market, which has grown by 14% in value since 1998.

Wall's recently launched a major marketing offensive in Scotland, where familiarity with the Wall's brand indicated a massive untapped opportunity.

Promotion

Wall's kick-started the new millennium with a major relaunch that heralded a new era for the brand. The marketing drive included a £6 million ad campaign by McCann-Erikson and extensive PR activity, with the new creative theme being 'simple pleasures'.

Wall's television ads have traditionally featured

the dog that could say 'sausages' which has helped to make sausages synonymous with Wall's. The new ads were also humorous, and showed Wall's sausages as an irresistible indulgence. The relaunch included a striking new logo and parchment packaging which brought the Wall's image up-to-date and helped the brand stand out better on supermarket shelves.

Wall's Euro 2000 on-pack promotion was highly successful and supported the brand's relaunch across the entire range of sausage and bacon. The promotion offered customers a fun, blow-up football referee when they collected two tokens from the wide range of participating Wall's products. The promotion was covered in the national newspapers and on radio, and the blow-up referee seen among the crowds at Euro 2000 games also received significant television coverage.

The Wall's 'Break Teaser' promotion on Carlton television – the first of its kind to be broadcast in the London area – was a competition that ran on eitherside of the ad breaks during Euro 2000. To the distinctive sound of a sizzling frying pan viewers were asked: 'When your mind turns to sausages who do you think of?'. The answer came in a Wall's commercial in the middle of the ad break, and viewers who called a hotline could win a family holiday to Florida. The competition attracted more than 40,000 responses, outstripping all expectations by generating nearly four times more calls than predicted.

The campaign has helped to prompt spontaneous purchases by reminding people of what a tasty everyday indulgence sausages are.

Brand Values

Wall's sausages have become a popular family meal that can be trusted to provide quality and taste. Consumers associate the Wall's product with Britishness, quality, family, safety and comfort, and the brand evokes warm, secure feelings. Wall's aims to capitalise on this strong heritage by positioning Wall's as a 'simple pleasure' – an extravagance that you can have every day.

Brand Guardians

ANCHOR

JASPAL CHADA
Strategy Manager, Core Business
Jaspal Chada has worked for New Zealand Milk (UK) Ltd for three years. Prior to this, Jaspal held senior marketing positions at Trebor Bassett for ten years, managing its core mint portfolio and family ranges, including Bags and 'Pick 'n' Mix' Confectionery. Jaspal is married with one child and enjoys competitive sports including hockey and golf.

SIMON TUCKEY
Managing Director
Simon Tuckey joined New Zealand Milk (UK) Ltd as Managing Director in February 2000. Prior to his current appointment, Simon worked for United Biscuits for over twenty years, which included four years in Japan as Managing Director – Japan and South Asia, and Managing Director – Asia based in Hong Kong. Simon is married with two children and he is a keen sportsman.

Andrex®

ALLISTER FROST
Marketing Manager
Allister Frost is a graduate of European Management from the École Supérieure de Commerce Marseille. He joined Kimberly-Clark in 1993, and has since held brand management roles for Kleenex® Facial Tissues, Huggies® Pull-Ups® Training Pants and Kotex® products. He was appointed as Marketing Manager for Andrex® products and Chief Puppy Handler in 2000.

SOPHIE WOODFORD
Brand Manager
Sophie Woodford, Andrex® Brand Manager, joined Kimberly-Clark as a Graduate Trainee in 1996, having gained a degree in Business Studies and Marketing from Newcastle Business School. She worked on Kleenex® Facial Tissues across Europe, before becoming Head Puppy Walker and Brand Manager of Andrex® in 1999.

AOL

KEITH HAWKINS
Group Head of Marketing, AOL UK
Keith worked as a marketing consultant for AOL Europe before joining permanently in August 1999. Responsible for all AOL's marketing in the UK, which encompasses the three brands AOL, CompuServe and Netscape Online. Keith's successful consumer marketing career has included working at Seagram as a Senior Brand Manager and The Mirror Group as Marketing Manager, after starting his career at Procter & Gamble.

KAREN THOMSON
Managing Director, AOL UK
Executive Vice President,
AOL Europe
Karen is responsible for the management and marketing of the Company's three UK brands AOL, CompuServe and Netscape Online. Karen previously served as Executive Vice President of Marketing for AOL Europe and as Marketing Director for AOL UK since its launch in January 1996. Widely viewed within the internet industry as one of the top marketing professionals, Thomson was responsible for bringing 'Connie the online genie,' to the UK's TV-watching consumers.

Ask Jeeves

ADRIAN COX
Vice President Marketing
Ask Jeeves UK

Adrian Cox joined Ask Jeeves UK in April 2000 and is responsible for all elements of brand, consumer and B2B marketing, advertising, PR, promotions, direct mail, market research and loyalty programmes. He brings to the business twenty years of experience working for FMCG companies such as St Ivel Group and Cadbury, where he was Head of Marketing for eight years and looked after all its major chocolate brands, as well as the launch of Twirl, Time Out and Boost. Adrian is a qualified mountaineering instructor and pilot and lives in Gloucestershire with his wife and three children.

Avis

LUKE MEDLEY
Managing Director, Avis UK

Previously, Medley was Managing Director of Avis Australia and President of the Australian Customer Service Association. Medley joined Avis Australia as National Franchise Manager in 1983 and established the franchise divisions for Australia and New Zealand. In 1987 he was appointed National Sales and Marketing Director for Australasia and in 1989 moved to the US to become Southern Regional Manager with responsibility for five states. In 1993 he was appointed Operations Manager for the Mid West based in Chicago. He returned to Australia in 1995 and was appointed Managing Director. Under his leadership Avis Australia has won State and national Australian Customer Service Awards.

BBC

HELEN KELLIE
Head of Marketing Strategy,
Marketing & Communications

After graduating from Oxford, Helen began her career in consumer goods marketing at Reckitt and Colman. In the ten years Helen spent there, she was responsible for the marketing of a range of diverse products in the UK and around the globe such as Lemsip, Disprin, Lysol and Harpic. From 1994 to 1998 Helen was Global Category Manager for the household cleaner business in New York. From August 1998, Helen was European Category Director for two household categories in Paris.
Helen joined the BBC in January 2000 as Head of Brand Strategy and in the recent restructure she has been promoted to Head of Marketing Strategy across all the BBC business.

Branston

DAVID GLIK
Category Marketing Director,
Nestlé Food Division

David joined Nestlé UK Ltd in 1986. During this time he spent four years working internationally, in Australia, on the development of Nestlé global coffee brands and then returned to the UK to take on the role of Marketing Manager, Food Division. In 1994 David left Nestlé to take on the role of Marketing Manager at Coca-Cola and subsequently moved to Kimberly-Clark as European Marketing Director.
David returned to Nestlé UK in 1998, as Category Marketing Director for the Food Division working across key brands including Branston, Buitoni, Sarson's and Sun-Pat.

Classic FM

ROGER LEWIS
Managing Director &
Programme Controller
Roger Lewis was appointed to his present position and as a Board Director of Classic FM's parent company, GWR Group plc in 1998. Immediately prior to this he spent eight years in the record industry as a Managing Director at EMI Records and President of the Decca Record Company. He began his radio career in 1981 at Radio Tees, followed by Capital Radio and then the BBC where he became Head of the Radio 1 music department.

GILES PEARMAN
Brand Controller
Giles started his marketing career in 1989 at Birds Eye Wall's where he managed Unilever's impulse ice cream brands like Magnum, Cornetto and Solero. His interest in radio was nurtured during a two year sabbatical in the Philippines where he broadcast a show on a national commercial radio station before being appointed Classic FM Brand Controller in the Spring of 1999.

CNN

TONY MADDOX
Vice President & Managing
Editor, Europe
Tony Maddox has played an integral part in the development of CNN's editorial output to include pan-European and localised content for use on all platforms, overseeing more than 50 hours a week of original programming, reflecting CNN's core brand values.

NIGEL PRITCHARD
Head of Press, Europe,
Middle East & Africa
Nigel Pritchard has been instrumental in reflecting CNN's evolution from a single television network into a multi-platform brand, making its core values of objectivity, accuracy and speed the central message for a global audience.

Coca-Cola

TOM LONG
President, Coca-Cola Great Britain & Ireland Division
Tom Long most recently served as Vice President and Director of Strategic Marketing, before his promotion in February 2000 to President, Coca-Cola Great Britain & Ireland Division. He has a background in advertising, sales, and brand management and an MBA from the Harvard Business School.

CHARLOTTE OADES
Marketing Director, Coca-Cola Great Britain & Ireland Division
Charlotte Oades joined Coca-Cola Great Britain in 1986 and in 1991 she moved to Coca-Cola USA and was appointed Global Director, Brand Marketing, Sprite in 1995.
From 1998, Charlotte served as Marketing Director South Pacific Division and in 2000 was appointed Marketing Director, Coca-Cola Great Britain & Ireland Division.

Coutts

CAROLINE MOSS
Head of Marketing & Strategy at Coutts Group, Internationally
Caroline oversees the strategy and marketing of a number of brands within the Coutts Group portfolio, including Coutts and Co in the UK, and Coutts International private banking in Switzerland, Miami, Asia and Middle East. She began her career in 1987 at NatWest USA in New York having completed a Bachelor of Science in Economics. Additional responsibilities include e-commerce, sales management and internal communications.

SARAH WILLIAMS
Head of Brand Management for Coutts Internationally
Sarah has over thirteen years experience of working with financial brands such as Prudential and NatWest. She has an MA in Design and Communications from St Martin's where her dissertation explored how the principles of packaging design could be applied to multi media formats. Her prime focus is on corporate identity, brand management and design.

Direct Line

MILES RUSSELL
Head of Corporate Affairs
Miles Russell became Head of Corporate Affairs in July 2000, having previously been the Group's Public Affairs and Strategy Manager. Miles is responsible for the day to day running of the press office, all consumer PR, Public Affairs and internal communications.

JIM WALLACE
Marketing Director
Jim Wallace joined the Direct Line Group in March 1999. Previously he was Sales and Marketing Director for Privilege insurance, the specialist insurer, now part of the Direct Line Group. Prior to this, Jim was Sales and Marketing Director for Car Care Plan, Europe's leading vehicle warranty company.

Dr. Martens

DAN GYVES
Advertising, New Media & Marketing Manager

Dan joined AirWair Ltd in 1997 after graduating from Plymouth University in Design Technology and Business. During his three years Dan has worked across all areas of the business to finally settle in the marketing department, where he currently undertakes the brands international advertising and new media strategy.

Dulux

PHIL KENT
Marketing Controller

Phil's brand building and marketing expertise have helped make the Dulux brand the resounding success that it is today. Phil's career started at Rowntree plc in Sales and Customer Marketing. Phil was a Marketing Manager at Grand Metropolitan. In 1996 he moved to United Biscuits as Head of Marketing on Phileas Fogg where he re-launched the brand with an innovative structural pack design. In 1999 Phil was appointed Marketing Controller for ICI Dulux.

Duracell

STEPHEN TENNANT
Business Unit Director

Stephen is responsible for the Duracell UK business. Ten years with the company, he has witnessed many changes since joining as Business Development Manager. Initially involved with sales, Stephen set up the Trade Marketing Department which quickly grew to encompass Consumer Marketing, Category Management and Market Research. As Chairman of the British Battery Manufacturers' Association (BBMA) Stephen has a unique insight into the battery business. Of Duracell's Superbrand status he says "Duracell successfully cuts through to consumers and ensures clear messages of superior product quality and performance are consistently presented and understood."

easyJet

MIKE COOPER
Commercial Director
Mike joined easyJet in Spring 2000 with the task of managing all aspects of the easyJet brand towards its flotation in the last quarter of 2000 and in the brave new world of life as a plc.
Mike's career is grounded in brand management, he spent nine years at ICI including the position of Marketing Manager for the Dulux brand.

TOBY NICOL
Head of Communications
Toby joined easyJet in late-1999 from Charles Barker BSMG Worldwide where he gained big brand and aviation experience, with a brief to maintain and build the easyJet brand. As head of communications for the airline, Toby is responsible for all aspects of media, government relations and campaigning.

Ericsson

ALEX RODRIGUES
Marketing Director of Ericsson Consumer Products, UK
Alex joined Ericsson Ltd in 1995 as Marketing Manager, having been an Account Director on the Ericsson account at Bates Advertising and, before then, worked in media sales at Haymarket Publications on Management Today. Rodrigues is constantly seeking ways to keep one step ahead in the fast pace, ever-changing telecommunications trading environment.

KEITH WESTCOTT
Managing Director, Ericsson UK
Keith joined Ericsson in April 1992 and in this period introduced the first mobile phones from Ericsson into the UK and has developed to date a business positioning Ericsson as one of the top three manufacturers and suppliers of mobile phones and accessories within the UK marketplace.
Keith is married with two children, both boys, aged four and six.

Evian

DAVID GRAHAM
Marketing Director
David Graham joined Groupe Danone in 1988, creating and implementing international strategies and identifying key marketing opportunities. Following a three year commercial assignment in the US, he recently returned to London as Director of Marketing for Evian and helped spearhead dramatic sales growth during 2000.

CORINNA ORTNER
Managing Director
Corinna Ortner joined Groupe Danone in 1989 and held several positions in the Dairy sector in Germany. In 1995 she was promoted to Marketing Director where she was also responsible for the very successful German launch of Actimel. Her move in May 1999 brought her to the UK, to take on the exciting role of Managing Director, Danone Waters (UK & Ireland) Ltd.

First Direct

PETER SIMPSON
Commercial Director

Peter Simpson is an original founder of First Direct. He has been intimately involved with the organisation since its inception and became Commercial Director in 1991. An Economics graduate from Cambridge, Peter has worked for Midland Bank, (HSBC since 1999) throughout his working life. He takes pride in seeing his vision for First Direct being transformed into reality on the basis of a strong and differentiated brand, underscored by its unique service culture. Leading edge customer dialogue techniques are central to his marketing philosophy. Peter is 51, lives in West Yorkshire and describes First Direct as his hobby, and doing jigsaws as his real work.

Ford

JOHN W MENDEL
Director, Marketing

Mendel was appointed Director of Marketing (Ford of Britain) in June 1999. He was previously Manager, Franchise and Business Development for Lincoln Mercury US. Mendel began his career with Ford US operations in 1976, and has held numerous sales and marketing positions within Ford, Lincoln Mercury and Ford Customer Service. He was appointed Major Markets/Dealer Advertising Manager for Ford in Dearborn MI in 1990, and Regional Operations Manager for Ford in Chicago in 1992. He served as Regional Manager for Ford's San Francisco and Los Angeles California operations from 1993 through 1998. Mendel has degrees in Business and Economics and an MBA from Duke University.

Gillette

ANNE-MARIE CHAMBERLAIN
Senior Brand Manager,
Blades & Razors
Born in France, Anne-Marie has worked in marketing for nine years, and with Gillette in the UK for five years working on Female Shaving, Right Guard and Natrel Plus. She also has a year and a half of experience in Category Management, and her latest position has been in charge of Male and Female Blades and Razors.

JACKIE JORDAN
Business Unit Director
for Grooming
Jackie joined Gillette in 1996 as Senior Brand Manager on Male Blades & Razors. Shortly after, she acquired additional responsibility for Female Shaving and in 1998 was responsible for the UK launch of Mach3. Jackie has been Business Unit Director for Grooming, responsible for Blades, Razors and Toiletries since March 1999.

Goldfish

SUSAN BROOKS
Head of Brands

DAVID OLIVER
Brand Communications Manager

HMV

BRIAN McLAUGHLIN
Chief Operating Officer,
HMV Media Group
Brian McLaughlin joined HMV in 1968 and was rapidly promoted to become Operations Director in 1980 and Managing Director of HMV UK in 1987. In 1996 he took on responsibility for HMV Europe, and in January 2001 was promoted to the key position of Chief Operating Officer for HMV Media Group plc.

JOHN TAYLOR
Marketing Director, HMV Europe
John Taylor joined HMV as Marketing Director in April 1997 having previously been with Virgin Retail. As Marketing Director, he has ultimate responsibility for HMV's advertising and in-store merchandising, local marketing, press and PR and third party promotions. As brand guardian, John seeks to ensure the consistent application of the HMV trademark.

Hotmail

JUDY GIBBONS
Director, MSN UK
As the UK Director of MSN, Microsoft's internet portal, Judy is one of the most powerful women in Britain's internet industry. Since joining Microsoft in 1995, she has developed MSN in the UK from launch until now when it has become the UK's favourite web destination (Source: MMXI Europe At Home Panel June 2000).

SHEREEN MEHARG
Marketing Manager, MSN UK
Shereen is responsible for the marketing and promotion of MSN's core communication products, including Hotmail and MSN Messenger Service. Working with on- and off-line advertising, direct marketing, media buying and public relations agencies, her remit is to drive Hotmail registrations, MSN Messenger Service downloads and adoption of other communication and personal information management tools.

Hovis

PETER BAKER
Managing Director

Peter Baker, Managing Director of British Bakeries, took up this position in May 1996 after six years in charge of Rank Hovis Ltd's milling business, first as Managing Director of Rank Hovis and later of RHM Cereals Division. Peter is Chairman of the Federation of Bakeries, past president of the National Association of British and Irish Millers and of the Bakers Benevolent Society Appeal. He is also a member of the Food and Drink Federation's Food Policy and Resources Committee. Recent brand achievements include launching Hovis Crusty bread, which created a whole new market sector, and diversifying into the prepared sandwiches market.

Interflora

HELENA BISSETT
Head of Marketing
Helena Bissett is responsible for marketing at the UK's largest floral relay brand. Having a genuine passion for the brand and a clear commitment to shaping and implementing a new direction, Helena is responsible for marketing Interflora to the consumer within the context of the new Millennium.

JONATHAN SMITH
Brand Marketing Manager
As Interflora's Brand Marketing Manager, Jonathan Smith is responsible for the development of through-the-line marketing activity surrounding the Interflora brand and relay service. Currently working on above-the-line press and outdoor campaigns, point of sale development and consumer promotions, Jonathan's background is consumer brands marketing across sectors, including soft drinks and media.

Kleenex®

LORNA BRUCE
Brand Manager
Lorna joined Kimberly-Clark in 1997, after graduating from St Andrews University with a BSc Hons in Physiology. Since joining the company she has progressed through the Graduate training scheme, gaining experience in Sales, Regional and European Marketing. Now she is a member of the Kleenex® brand team and is responsible for the day-to-day running of the brand.

JOHN WATERS
Marketing Manager
John joined Kimberly-Clark in 1977 after graduating from Nottingham University. He has held various roles including thirteen years in Sales and National Accounts. For most of the last ten years he has worked in marketing, responsible for the Kleenex® brand in the UK and Eire.

Kuoni

SUE BIGGS
Managing Director
Sue Biggs has been with Kuoni UK for eighteen years. She became Managing Director in October 1999, having previously been Deputy Managing Director. She is responsible for the company's £350 plus million turnover incorporating Kuoni and Voyages Jules Verne, which have a combined staff of over 500.

PETER DIETHELM
Executive Chairman, UK &
North America
Peter Diethelm joined Kuoni in 1963 as a tour leader, moving to London in 1966 to set up a long haul tours programme. In 1974 he became Managing Director until October 1999 when he became Executive Chairman of the new enlarged division of the UK and North America. Kuoni Group turnover worldwide is approximately $3 billion.

Kwik-Fit

SIR TOM FARMER CBE, KCSG
Chairman and Chief Executive
Sir Tom Farmer is the founder of Kwik-Fit.
He started his first business, Tyres and Accessory Supplies in 1964 in Buccleuch Street, Edinburgh. In 1971, he opened the first Kwik-Fit centre, also in Edinburgh. For almost 30 years, Sir Tom has led the expansion and development of the Kwik-Fit brand.

PETER HOLMES
Group Director of Marketing
Peter Holmes joined Kwik-Fit in 1983. Responsible for developing and launching the now famous Kwik-Fit fitter campaign, he has been an integral part of the rapid expansion of the Kwik-Fit Group. He now directs the marketing operations across nine Group companies, covering seven European countries.

Land Rover

JOHN EDWARDS
Director, Global Marketing
John, 38, was appointed as Director of Global Marketing on the day Ford Motor Company formally acquired Land Rover from the BMW Group. Previously, John was Managing Director of Mini/MG UK, a new division with the BMW Group established to manage sales, marketing and distribution of Mini and MG vehicles in the UK. John has also held positions in Brand Management, Product Planning and Customer Research. John graduated in Sports Science before studying marketing. He now lives near Stratford-upon-Avon with his family.

COLIN GREEN
Marketing Director, Land Rover UK
Colin, 43, is a 'Veteran' of over 21 years with Land Rover. He has been in his current role since June 1st 1999 and prior to that had two years as a Regional Business Manager. From 1994-1997 he was Land Rover's first Brand Director and other previous roles include Brand and Product Marketing and Product Planning on the original Discovery project. Colin studied Economics at Bradford University and lives in Coventry with his wife Sandra and his two children.

lastminute.com

BRENT HOBERMAN
Joint Founder & CEO
Before setting up lastminute.com, Brent was formerly General Manager, Head of Business Development and a founding member of QXL, a leading online auction business. Prior to this he worked in business development at LineOne (the UK internet service provider now owned by BT, News International and United News & Media). Brent holds a MA from Oxford University.

MARTHA LANE FOX
Joint Founder & CEO
Martha co-founded lastminute.com with Brent Hoberman in April 1998. Formerly Head of Network Development at Carlton, Martha worked on all applications for emergency digital technologies. Prior to this she was an associate at Spectrum Strategy Consultants working on projects in Asia and in the US. She holds a MA from Oxford University.

LEGO

KJELD KIRK KRISTIANSEN
President & CEO
Kjeld Kirk Kristiansen was born in 1947 and is the grandson of founder Ole Kirk Christiansen. He has a close personal association with LEGO's values and their dynamic development. Kristiansen has achieved a high profile for the LEGO Company and its products on the world map and in the universe of children.

POUL PLOUGHMANN
Executive Vice President & COO
Poul Plougmann is responsible for the day-to-day operations of the LEGO Company as well as Chairman of the Operations Team. Furthermore, Plougmann is head of Global Business Support, Global Brand Development and Strategic Development Support.

Lexus

DAVID BRIMSON
General Manager, Lexus Marketing
Brimson started his career in the motor industry with Rover Cars in 1988. Joining Toyota in 1995 as Marketing Communications Manager for Toyota and Lexus brands. Appointed as Toyota Regional General Manager in 1996 before moving to the newly established Lexus management team as General Manager of Marketing.

STUART McCULLOUGH
Lexus Director
Joined Lexus in 1998 after setting up and running a prestige car retailer operation for Lind. Prior to that he spent twelve years with Volkswagen Audi Group where he gained experience in many key areas of the automotive business including product planning, marketing and used car management.

Lurpak

SIMON EYLES
Marketing Controller for Butter, Spreads & Margarines, Arla Foods
Simon Eyles has worked with the Lurpak brand since he joined Arla Foods, overseeing the development and spectacular success of Lurpak Spreadable. He has progressed from Brand Manager to Senior Brand Manager and is now Marketing Controller for all of Arla Foods' Butters, Spreads and Margarines in the UK.

FREDE JUULSEN
Marketing Director, Arla Foods
With a degree in dairy science, as well as sales and marketing, Arla Foods UK Marketing Director Frede Juulsen has held a range of managerial positions, starting in R&D before moving to Trade Marketing and Exports and has worked as Business Unit Manager both in the UK and Denmark.

Marks & Spencer

ALAN J McWALTER
Non-Executive Director, Marks & Spencer Ventures
Alan McWalter is Director responsible for Marketing, Marks & Spencer Direct and e-commerce. He is also a Non-Executive Director of Marks & Spencer Financial Services. Alan was previously with Kingfisher, where he was Marketing Director at Woolworths (1994-1999) and Marketing and Development Director at Comet (1991-1994).

LUC VANDEVELDE
Chairman, Marks & Spencer
Luc Vandevelde, aged 49, joined Marks & Spencer on 28th February 2000 as full time Executive Chairman focusing on the strategic development of the group with the Chief Executive. Previously he was Chairman of Promodès, which he built into an international retailer with operations across Europe, Asia and South America.

Martini

MAURICE DOYLE
Marketing Director, Bacardi-Martini
Doyle has worked across Bacardi-Martini's wide product portfolio, which currently comprises eighteen brands including Bacardi rum, the world's number one spirit brand, since 1992. He was responsible for developing and launching Bacardi Breezer, the most successful UK spirits launch (in volume terms) to date.

CAROLINE HERBERT
Marketing Manager, Bacardi-Martini
Caroline joined Martini in 1988 to work on its still and sparkling wine ranges as well as Noilly Prat and Cadbury's Cream Liqueur. In more recent years she has been responsible for Martini vermouth and for the launch of Martini Citro and has successfully stemmed the severe volume decline on Martini vermouth and is now busy positioning the brand for future greatness.

Nationwide

STEVE CLODE
Divisional Director, Marketing
After completing post-graduate studies in finance, Steve held a number of senior marketing roles in major UK financial institutions. In 1996 he joined Nationwide and was appointed Divisional Director of Marketing in 1999. He has overall responsibility for product development and management, pricing, marketing communications, direct marketing, sponsorship and market research.

DR B E DAVIS CBE, BSc, PhD, FRSA, CIMgt
Chief Executive
Brian Davis joined Nationwide in 1986 as General Manager with responsibility for technology, having previously worked in the oil industry. He was appointed Operations Director in 1989 and then Chief Executive in 1994. He was Chairman of the Building Societies Association for two consecutive terms between 1996 and 1998.

Nike

ROD CONNORS
Marketing Director
Rod started his marketing career with Unilever where he spent twelve years in various marketing positions working on brands as diverse as Lynx Deodorant, Mentadent toothpaste and Faberge fragrances. Three years were spent in Milan, Italy helping to establish Unilever's global dental innovation centre, before returning to the UK to help lead Elida Faberge's Global Deodorant and Fragrance business. Rod joined Nike as Marketing Director, UK in February 2000.

JACK GOLD
Head of Brand Communications
Jack has spent his advertising career at Saatchi & Saatchi UK and then at Team One in Los Angeles. In 1997 as European Advertising Manager he was responsible for The '98 World Cup, the Alpha Launch and Football Training campaigns. In September 1999 Jack moved back to London as Head of Brand Communications for Nike UK as well as select European assignments within the football and running categories. Jack plays golf and supports Aston Villa whenever he has a spare moment.

NIVEA

NORBERT KRAPP
Corporate Vice President, International Brand Management, Skincare Beiersdorf AG, Hamburg

"To work for NIVEA is a challenging marketing experience. In the last 30 years we have extended the brand and at the same time we have kept the core of the brand 'NIVEA Creme' young. Today NIVEA is by far the largest skincare brand in the world."

Nokia

ALISON BROLLS
Head of Marketing, Nokia Mobile Phones UK & Ireland
Alison is responsible for the marketing and promotion of Nokia Mobile Phones. Working with on- and off-line advertising, direct marketing, media buying and public relations agencies, her role is to increase sales and awareness of Nokia handsets and the company's communications services.

PHIL BROWN
Managing Director, Nokia Mobile Phones UK & Ireland
Phil was appointed as Managing Director, Nokia Mobile Phones UK & Ireland in June 1999, after joining Nokia in 1991 as a Marketing Manager. He is responsible for maintaining Nokia's market positioning as the leading mobile phone manufacturer in the UK and Ireland.
This includes driving further growth and innovation in the UK and Irish markets as the industry moves towards the next generation of mobile phones.

Nurofen

AMANDA JENKINS
Head of Marketing for Analgesics, Boots Healthcare International
Amanda is responsible for the Nurofen brand globally. Prior to this she held a number of marketing roles in Crookes Healthcare (Boots Healthcare International's UK subsidiary) and most recently the role of Marketing Director. Before joining Boots, Amanda held marketing positions in Smith & Nephew and Barclays Bank as well as a market research role at ACNielsen.

SIMON MERRITT
Director of Marketing (Healthcare), Crookes Healthcare
Simon has been with Crookes Healthcare (Boots Healthcare International's UK subsidiary) since 1999, moving from an international strategic role within BHI to focus on the UK market. Prior to working in the OTC arena, Simon spent ten years with Reckitt & Coleman, working in a variety of local and international marketing positions.

Olympus

BEN COCHRANE
Marketing Co-ordinator
With a Marketing Degree, CIM diploma and two years marketing experience under his belt, Ben now works as Marketing Co-ordinator for Olympus. Covering all divisions, Ben drives the brand forward through trade marketing, POS, packaging, sales promotions and exhibition management.

SARA CUBITT
Head of Marketing Communications
A small team of marketers combining creativity with strategy act as brand ambassadors for the whole mix. Sara Cubitt oversees the marketing communications for the wide-reaching portfolio. Six years at Olympus, preceded by four years of running the press office for an air display team (which included a 1940's bi-plane wingwalking role – a windy, yet effective hangover cure) and prior to that, a job in ad sales and a job as a customer services advisor, bring a melting pot of experience across the whole 'marcomms' mix.

Pentax

DAVID COWPERTHWAITE
Marketing & Operations Director
David joined Pentax in 1979 as Assistant Product Manager, responsible for new product development. In 1981 David was appointed Manager, having completed research development of new product areas. David became General Marketing Manager in 1986. In 1992 David was appointed Marketing Director and Member of Board of Directors for Pentax UK Ltd. He was appointed to his present position in 1997. He is responsible for the company's corporate and brand image, marketing direction and day-to-day operations.

BRIAN LIGHT
Director & General Manager, Photographic Division
Brian Light joined Pentax as an Area Sales Executive in 1982. He was promoted to the position of Sales Manager for the Photographic division in 1986. In 1992 Brian was appointed Sales Director and Member of Board of Directors for Pentax UK Ltd, and in 1997 was appointed to his current position of Director and General Manager of the Photographic division, where he is responsible for the divisions sales and marketing.

Perrier

SCOTT SLOAN
Managing Director, Perrier Vittel UK

Scott Sloan was appointed Managing Director of Perrier Vittel UK Ltd in December 2000. He came to London from Paris where he has been Global Project Director for the Nestlé Pure Life Brand. Prior to this, he spent four years as Marketing Manager with the bottled water division of Nestlé Japan Limited based in Tokyo. During 2000, for the first time in its 100 year history, Perrier introduced a 50cl bottle made especially for restaurants, cafes, clubs and bars.

Persil

ANNA CREED
Brand Manager, Lever Brothers
Anna was born and educated in Sheffield before going on to read Combined Science at Leicester University. She worked with Nestlé Rowntree for three years in Brand Development, working on well-known brands such as Quality Street and Matchmakers. Anna then worked at Colgate Palmolive on Soft and Gentle and Palmolive before becoming Brand Manager at Lever Brothers where she has been working for the last eighteen months on Persil and Surf.

ALISON CULPIN
Senior Brand Development Manager
Alison Culpin studied at Cambridge where she attained a BA Hons Natural Sciences. She has been with Lever Brothers since 1994, initially working on brands such as Surf and Comfort before moving on to become Customer Business Manager and then National Category Strategy Manager for Household Cleaners. Alison has been the Persil UK Senior Brand Development Manager since December 1999.

Pret A Manger

SINCLAIR BEECHAM
Co-founder
Sinclair (41) graduated from the Polytechnic of Central London in 1983 after studying Urban Estate Management, where he met Julian Metcalfe. In 1986 he teamed up with his partner Julian Metcalfe and opened the first Pret A Manger in Victoria. Pret now has over 100 shops and employs more than 2500 people with a turnover of more than £100 million. Sinclair has spearheaded the company's launch in New York. Pret remains a private company. Sinclair lives in New York and London and his interests include flying and running.

JULIAN METCALFE
Co-founder
Julian (40) also graduated from the Polytechnic of Central London in 1983 after studying Urban Estate Management. In 1986 he teamed up with his graduate friend Sinclair Beecham and opened the first Pret A Manger in Victoria in 1986. By 1993 Pret had fifteen London shops. Julian remains integrally involved with the day to day running of the business.
Julian is married and lives in London and Oxfordshire. He has three children. His interests include flying, boating and diving.

Psion

DAVID LEVIN
CEO
David Levin is Psion plc's Chief Executive Officer. David joined Psion in February 1999 from Euromoney Publications plc, where he had been Chief Operating Officer. Prior to that he worked for Bain & Co focusing on acquisition, integration and strategy. David also worked for Apax Partners & Co as an Associate Director until 1994. Since 1999 David has been responsible for defining Psion's vision and developing a strategy across all divisions of the company.

ALASDAIR SETON-MARDSEN
International Marketing Director
Alasdair Seton-Marsden is responsible for global marketing for Psion handheld computers, and for the Branding and Corporate Identity across the Psion Group. Alasdair joined Psion in 1999, bringing with him a broad range of experience in both B2C to B2B marketing. His previous roles have included Account Director at branding consultants Enterprise IG (WPP), founder of the first New Media unit at Saatchi & Saatchi plc and Marketing Communications Manager at Microsoft UK.

RAC

KEN LEE
Marketing Director
44 year old Ken Lee has been RAC's Group Marketing Director since 1999. As such he is custodian of the RAC brand, overseeing all internal and external communication. With a strong sales and marketing background, most recently with Hyundai Car (UK) Ltd, Ken has already successfully established RAC's new brand proposition of individual motoring solutions. In his spare time, Ken enjoys his sports boat and keeping fit.

GRAEME POTTS
Managing Director
Graeme took up his post in 1999 after sixteen years with leading motor retailer Reg Vardy plc. A past President of the National Franchised Dealers Association, 43 year old Graeme is a well-known advocate for higher standards of professionalism within the motor industry. When not working, Graeme's interests include football, cricket, and current affairs. He is an Evangelical Christian and a lay preacher.

Robinsons

TONY GOTTS
Factory Manager
Tony Gotts is the Factory Manager at Britvic Soft Drinks' production site in Norwich, which employs 248 people. Tony is responsible for the factory, which produces all of the Robinsons range, including Robinsons Original, Special R, High Juice, Barley Water, Fruit and Barley, Fruit Break and the recently launched Fruit Shoot.

ANDREW MARSDEN
Category Director
Andrew is responsible for brand marketing, category planning, innovation, consumer insight and consumer care. He began his career with Unilever before joining Freudenberg in 1992. Andrew then joined Groupe Danone as Marketing Director, HP Foods. Andrew was appointed Marketing Director of Britvic in 1997.

Royal Doulton

MIKE BOZMAN
Director for Global
Marketing & Design
Key brand champion, Mike Bozman joined Royal Doulton in 1998 following a career in fashion oriented brand marketing. In 1999, he was appointed Director for Global Marketing and Design when he instigated a review of the company's brand focus and retail presentation and its design thinking. Concentration centred on the Royal Doulton brand, followed by Royal Albert and Minton, resulting in new invigorated brand personalities relevant to twenty-first century consumers.

WAYNE NUTBEEN
Chief Operating Officer
Chief Operating Officer since January 2000, Wayne Nutbeen joined Royal Doulton in 1996 as Managing Director of Royal Doulton Australia. In 1999, he became president of Royal Doulton's North American business, and shortly afterwards was appointed to the Board as Director of Sales and International Markets. In his earlier career, he worked with leading brand names including Lladro, Lalique, Baccarat and Waterford Wedgwood.

Royal Mail

RICHARD DYKES
Group Managing Director
Mail Services
A member of the Post Office Executive Board, Richard has overall profit accountability for Royal Mail. He joined The Post Office in 1986, becoming Managing Director of Post Office Counters Ltd in 1992. Richard's previous experience includes policy-making in Government and heading the Unemployment Benefit Service.

SARAH LARVOR
Head of Branding
Sarah has worked for the Business for nine years, principally in business strategy and strategic communications, before taking up her current role last year. As Head of Branding, she has ultimate responsibility for all the branded Royal Mail activity, almost 50 rostered agencies, and in development and deployment of the brand strategy.

Sainsbury's

ANDREW GROUND
Director of Brand Marketing
Prior to his current position, Andrew was the Senior Manager in Brand Development, where he created the new brand identity and managed national advertising. He worked for two years in LEK Partnership doing strategy consultancy for major corporations. He began his career at Procter & Gamble, working in Brand Management on skin and hair care. He studied History and Law at Cambridge where he was President of the Union. He is Councillor in Fulham and Governor of a local school.

SARA WELLER
Marketing Director
Sara joined Sainsbury's in 2000 having previously held the position of Marketing Director at Abbey National. Sara's career began with thirteen and a half years at Mars Confectionery, joining as a sales-person and progressing to Sales Manager before moving to Personnel Manager and then the marketing department. In the marketing department she held several positions, both UK and European. Sara is 39, married with two children, Sophie seven and Adam four and has a degree from Oxford University in Chemistry.

Scottish Widows

DAVID GRAHAM
Director, Network & Brand
Development Director
David Graham joined Scottish Widows in 1965. After fulfilling several major roles within Marketing, in 1986, David became responsible for product development, product design, literature design and advertising. In this role, he was a key player in the introduction of the current Scottish Widows corporate logo and the 'Scottish Widow'. In 1998, David was appointed Chief Executive of Tesco Life, returning to Scottish Widows in March 2000 to take up his current role.

KEVIN SIME
Head of Advertising
Kevin Sime joined Scottish Widows in 1975. He joined Marketing in 1987 (just six weeks before the Black Monday Crash). Between 1989 and 1995, he headed Unit Trust Marketing, then was given the position of Product Marketing Manager for Life and Unit Trust products, with International Products being added three years later. In April 2000, Kevin was appointed Head of Advertising dealing with all advertising for the Scottish Widows group, including Brand Management.

Sega

J F CECILLON
Chief Executive Officer,
Sega Europe
Cecillon was appointed to his current role in November 1998. Managing the Sega teams across the UK, Spain, France and Germany, Cecillon's principle brief has been to add a new dynamic to the European Leisure Industry with Dreamcast. Before joining Sega Europe, Cecillon held executive positions in France and the UK at EMI Group and Polygram Records.

KAZUTOSHI MIYAKE
Chief Operating Officer,
Sega Europe
After graduating from Osaka University of Foreign Studies, Miyake-San joined Nissho Iwai Corp. where he worked for twenty years, reaching the position of Senior Manager of its Automotive Division for Europe. He joined Sega Enterprises Ltd in 1993 and moved to Sega Europe in March 1994. He holds the fourth Dan Black belt in Karate.

Shell

VENETIA HOWES
Global Brands Strategy Manager
Venetia Howes has recently taken up responsibility for the Shell brand and its strategic development. Her previous career has given her direct experience of many of the consumer, business-to-business and corporate activities in which the Shell brand is used, including time in the chemicals, marine and commercial oil products businesses. Prior to her current role, she was the Marketing Manager for Shell's global aviation business.

RAOUL PINNEL
Global Head of Brands
& Communictions
Raoul Pinnell developed an early interest in business whilst at school, Bradfield College, leaving to pursue Business Studies, subsequently followed by a post-graduate Diploma in Marketing. Following seventeen years with Nestle, five years at Prudential and three years at NatWest. Shell International appointed him to the post of Global Head of Brands & Communications in 1997.

Sky

JON FLORSHEIM
Managing Director of Open....
Jon joined British Sky Broadcasting in April 1994 as Marketing Director, Direct To Home, working with retailers nationwide to increase dish sales. Jon has responsibility for the Sky Brand and Advertising, Channels and Product Marketing, Customer Marketing and Loyalty, all Subscription Sales Channels, Commercial Marketing and New Product Development. Jon has recently been promoted to Managing Director of Open......

SCOTT N MENNEER
Marketing Director
In 1996 Scott joined British Sky Broadcasting as a Marketing Manager and as Brand Director in 1998 was jointly responsible for the consumer launch of digital television to the UK. Scott currently runs brand development, advertising, media planning and buying and research across all of Sky's channels and platforms (satellite TV and New Media applications such as online and WAP).

Tesco

Titles and positions held vary from Chief Executive to Customer Assistant, but the responsibility for understanding and promoting the Tesco brand is shared by all staff.
'We all believe that in order to win our customers' lifetime loyalty, we must try harder than any other and treat people how we like to be treated'.

Tetley

NIGEL HOLLAND
GB Marketing Director
Nigel joined Tetley in January 1998 as Marketing Controller, having gained marketing experience in organisations such as Boots Healthcare International, Kraft Jacobs Suchard and Scottish & Newcastle Breweries. In November 1999, he was promoted to Marketing Director, with responsibility for marketing the Tetley product range in the UK and Ireland.

JOHN NICHOLAS
Commercial Director
John joined Tetley within marketing in 1986 following marketing roles with Mars and RHM Foods. He became Director of Marketing of the GB business in 1993, and in March 2000 joined the Tetley Group board as Commercial Director, with responsibility for the commercial operation and performance of all Tetley businesses worldwide (except the US).

The Body Shop

PATRICK P GOURNAY
Chief Executive Officer
Patrick Gournay was appointed as Chief Executive Officer in July 1998, having previously worked for 26 years with Groupe Danone in a number of key roles in Europe and the US. His vision and leadership have already been reflected in the improving performance of The Body Shop International plc.

ANITA L RODDICK OBE
Founder and Co-Chair
Anita Roddick opened the first branch of The Body Shop in Brighton in 1976. The public face of The Body Shop, she is the creative inspiration behind the Company's style and image, and remains an inspiration to women in business. Anita was awarded an OBE in 1988.

The National Lottery

IAN MILLIGAN
Director of Sales & Marketing
Ian joined Camelot in 1998. He directs a team of 25, ensuring that the brand remains popular and exciting, whilst achieving average weekly sales of over £95 million. Ian's portfolio includes online games, Instants and New Product Development. Ian has previously worked with Smith & Nephew, Reckitt & Colman and Kellogg's during his sixteen-year career.

DIANNE THOMPSON
Chief Executive Officer
In a career spanning 25 years, Dianne has worked in marketing for ICI Paints and Sterling Roncraft. She was a lecturer at Manchester Polytechnic for seven years whilst founding and running her own advertising agency. Dianne was Managing Director for Sanvik Saws and Tools and moved on to become Director of Marketing for Woolworths. She then spent three years turning the Ratner business into a profit generator. Dianne now heads up a team of 420 at Camelot and is responsible for sales, marketing, player services and 36,000 retailers.

Vodafone

PAUL DONOVAN
Managing Director –
Commercial

On 1st October 1999, Paul Donovan was appointed Managing Director – Commercial of Vodafone UK. Previous to this, Paul was with Cable & Wireless from 1995, first as Sales & Marketing Director and then subsequently Commercial Director for One 2 One. In 1998 he moved as Chief Commercial Officer for Cable & Wireless Optus in Australia, with responsibility for all commercial aspects of the Optus cellular, fixed line, internet and pay TV businesses. Paul joined the telecommunications sector in 1993 at BT as Head of Business Marketing and subsequently as Director for Online Services for Business.

Wall's

RUTH TOBBELL
Marketing Director, Kerry Foods

Ruth is responsible for market leading Richmond, Wall's and Mattessons brands, Ruth is currently heading up a programme of ambitious growth driven by heavy investment and innovation. Following graduate training with The Boots Company Ltd, she joined Johnson & Johnson as Product Manager and then moved through the marketing ranks at SmithKline Beecham and SC Johnson Wax. There she became European Brand Manager and later gained sales experience as National Account Manager responsible for J Sainsbury.

Directory

Abbey National
Abbey National plc
Abbey House
201 Grafton Gate East
Milton Keynes
MK9 1AN

adidas
adidas UK Ltd
PO Box 39
Pepper Road
Hazel Grove
Stockport
Cheshire
SK7 5SD

Alfa Romeo
Alfa Romeo (GB)
266 Bath Road
Slough
Berkshire
SL1 4HJ

American Airlines
American Airlines Inc
23-59 Staines Road
Hounslow
Middlesex
TW3 3HD

American Express
American Express Europe Ltd
Portland House
Stag Place
London
SW1E 5BZ

ANCHOR
New Zealand Milk Ltd
Frankland Road
Blagrove
Swindon
Wiltshire
SN5 8YP

Andrex®
Kimberly-Clark Ltd
1 Tower View
Kings Hill
West Malling
Kent
ME19 4HA

AOL
AOL
80 Hammersmith Road
London
W14 8UD

Ask Jeeves
Ask Jeeves UK Ltd
53 Parker Street
London
WC2B 5PC

Avis
Avis Rent a Car
Trident House
Station Road
Hayes
Middlesex
UB3 4DJ

BBC
BBC Marketing & Communications
Room 207
Brock House
19 Langham Street
London
W1N 5RB

Birds Eye
Birds Eye Wall's Ltd
Station Avenue
Walton on Thames
Surrey
KT12 1NT

Black & Decker
Black & Decker
210 Bath Road
Slough
Berkshire
SL1 3YD

Blu-Tack
Bostik Findley Limited
Ulverscroft Road
Leicester
LE4 6BW

Branston
Nestlé UK Ltd
St George's House
Park Lane
Croydon
Surrey
CR9 1NR

BT
BT
BT Centre
81 Newgate Street
London
EC1A 7AJ

Channel 4
Channel Four Television Corporation
124 Horseferry Rd
London
SW1P 2TX

Classic FM
Classic FM plc
Classic House
7 Swallow Place
Oxford Circus
London
W1B 2AG

Club Med
Club Mediterranee
Kennedy House
115 Hammersmith Rd
London
W14 0QH

CNN
CNN
CNN House
19-22 Rathbone Place
London
W1P 1DF

Coca-Cola
Coca-Cola Great Britain & Ireland
1 Queen Caroline Street
Hammersmith
London
W6 9HQ

Coutts
Coutts & Co
440 Strand
London
WC2R 0QS

Direct Line
Direct Line Group Ltd
Direct Line House
3 Edridge Rd
Croydon
CR9 1AG

Dr. Martens
AirWair UK Ltd
Nene Park
Station Road
Irthingborough
Northamptonshire
NN9 5QG

Dulux
ICI Paints
ICI Paints Division
Wexham Road
Slough
Berkshire
SL2 5DS

Duracell
Gillette Group UK Ltd
Great West Road
Isleworth
Middlesex
TW7 5NP

easyJet
easyJet
easyLand
London Luton Airport
LU2 9LS

Ericsson
Ericsson Ltd
Telecommunications Centre
Ericsson Way
Burgess Hill
West Sussex
RH15 9UB

Eurostar
Eurostar Group Limited
Eurostar House
Waterloo Station
London
SE1 8SE

Evian
Danone Waters (UK & Ireland) Ltd
4 Hillgate Place
London
SW12 9ER

First Direct
First Direct
40 Wakefield Road
Leeds
West Yorkshire
LS98 1FD

Flora
Van den Bergh Foods Ltd
Brooke House
Manor Royal
Crawley
West Sussex
RH10 2RQ

Ford
Ford Motor Company Ltd
Central Office
Eagle Way
Warley
Brentwood
CM13 3BW

Gillette
Gillette UK Ltd
Great West Road
Isleworth
Middlesex
TW7 5NP

Goldfish
Goldfish Group Marketing
17 London Road
Staines
Middlesex
TW18 4AE

Gordon's®
UDV UK Ltd
Templefields House
Riverway
Harlow
Essex
CM20 2EA

Häagen Dazs
Pillsbury UK Ltd
Harman House
1 George Street
Uxbridge
Middlesex
UB8 1QQ

Heinz
H J Heinz Company Limited
South Building
Hayes Park
Hayes
Middlesex
UB4 8AL

HMV
HMV UK Ltd
Film House
142 Wardour Street
London
W1V 4LN

Hotmail
MSN UK
Microsoft Campus
Thames Valley Park
Reading
RG6 1WG

Hovis
British Bakeries
King Edward House
King Edward Court
PO Box 527
Windsor
Berkshire
SL4 1TJ

HSBC
HSBC Holding plc
10 Lower Thames Street
London
EC3R 6AE

IKEA
IKEA UK Ltd
255 North Circular Road
London
NW10 0JQ

Interflora
Interflora [FTDA] BU Ltd
Interflora House
Sleaford
Lincolnshire
NG34 7TB

Kellogg's Corn Flakes
Kellogg Marketing and Sales
Company (UK) Limited
The Kellogg Building
Talbot Road
Manchester
M16 0PU

Kit Kat
Nestlé UK Ltd
York
YO91 1XY

Kleenex®
Kimberly-Clark Ltd
1 Tower View
Kings Hill
West Malling
Kent
ME19 4HA

Kuoni
Kuoni Travel Ltd
Kuoni House
Deepdene Avenue
Dorking
Surrey
RH5 4AZ

Kwik-Fit
Kwik-Fit Holdings
17 Corstorphine Rd
Edinburgh
EH12 6DD

L'Oréal
L'Oreal UK Ltd
255 Hammersmith Road
London
W6 8AZ

Land Rover

Land Rover
Banbury Road
Liththorne
Warwick
CVB5 0RG

lastminute.com

lastminute.com
4 Buckingham Gate
Victoria
London
SW1E 6JP

LEGO

LEGO UK Ltd
33 Bath Rd
Berkshire
SL1 3UF

Levi's®

Levi Strauss UK Ltd
1 Little Marlborough Street
London
W1V 1HB

Lexus

Lexus [GB] Ltd
The Quadrangle
Redhill
Surrey
RH1 1PX

Lurpak

Arla Foods plc
87 Kirkstall Road
Leeds
LS3 1JE

Marks & Spencer

Marks & Spencer plc
Michael House
Baker Street
London
W1V 8EP

MARS bar

Mars Confectionery UK Ltd
Dundee Road
Slough
Berkshire
SL1 4JX

Martini

Bacardi-Martini Ltd
West Bay Road
Southampton
Hampshire
SO15 1DT

McDonald's

McDonald's Restaurants
  Head Office Ltd
11-59 High Road
East Finchley
London
N2 8AW

Monopoly

Hasbro UK Ltd
2 Roundwood Avenue
Stockley Park
Uxbridge
Middlesex
UB11 1AZ

Mr Kipling

Manor Bakeries
3rd Floor
Minton Place
Victoria Street
Windsor
Berkshire
SL4 1EG

Nationwide

Nationwide Building Society
Nationwide House
Pipers Way
Swindon
SN38 1NW

Nike

Nike UK Ltd
1 Victory Way
Doxford International Business Park
Sunderland
SR3 3XF

NIVEA

Beiersdorf UK Ltd
PO Box 3261
Alum Rock Road
Birmingham
B8 3DW

Nokia

Nokia Mobile Phones
Headland House
The Chord Business Park
London Road
Godmanchester
Cambridgeshire
PE18 8NX

Nurofen

Crookes Healthcare Ltd
PO Box 57
Central Park
Lenton Lane
Nottingham
NG7 2LJ

Olympus
Olympus Optical Co UK Ltd
2-8 Honduras St
London
EC1Y 0TX

One 2 One
One 2 One Personal
  Communications Ltd
Maxwell Road
Imperial Place
Borehamwood
Herdfordshire
WD6 1EA

Oxo
Van Den Bergh Foods Ltd
Brooke House
Manor Royal
Crawley
West Sussex
RH10 2RQ

Pentax
Pentax UK Ltd
Pentax House
Heron Drive
Langley
Slough
SL3 8PN

Pepsi
Pepsico International Ltd
63 Kew Road
Richmond
Surrey
TW9 2QL

Perrier
Perrier Vittel (UK) Ltd
Trinity Court
Church Street
Rickmansworth
Hertfordshire
WD3 1LD

Persil
Lever Brothers Ltd
Lever House
3 St James's Road
Kingston-Upon-Thames
Surrey
KT1 2BA

Pret A Manger
Pret A Manger
16 Palace Street
London
SW1E 5PT

Psion
Psion Computers plc
Alexander House
85 Frampton Street
London
W1M 1LA

Quality Street
Nestlé UK Ltd
York
YO91 1XY

RAC
RAC Motoring Services
RAC House
1 Forest Road
Feltham
TW13 7RR

Robinsons
Britvic Soft Drinks Ltd
Britvic House
Broomfield Road
Chelmsford
Essex
CM1 1TU

Royal Doulton
Royal Doulton plc
Minton House
London Road
Stoke on Trent
Staffordshire
ST4 7QD

Royal Mail
The Post Office
Gavrelle House
2-14 Bunhill Row
London
EC1Y 8HQ

Sainsbury's
Sainsbury's
Stamford House
Stamford Street
London
SE1 9LL

Scottish Widows
Scottish Widows
PO Box 12757
67 Morrison Street
Edinburgh
EH3 8YF

Sega
Sega Europe Ltd
266-270 Gunnersbury Avenue
London
W4 5QB

Shell
Shell International Petroleum
  Company Ltd
OMM/3 Shell Centre
London
SE1 7NA

Sky
British Sky Broadcasting Ltd
Grant Way
Isleworth
Middlesex
TW7 5QD

SMIRNOFF
UDV UK
Templefields House
River Way
Harlow
Essex
CM20 2EA

SNICKERS
Mars Confectionery UK Ltd
Dundee Road
Slough
Berkshire
SL1 4JX

Sony
Sony United Kingdom Ltd
The Heights
Brooklands
Weybridge
Surrey
KT13 0XW

Tate & Lyle
Tate & Lyle Sugars
Thames Refinery
Factory Road
London
E16 2EW

Tesco
Tesco Stores Ltd
Tesco House
PO Box 18
Delamare Rd
Cheshunt
Hertfordshire
EN8 9SL

Tetley
Tetley GB Ltd
325 Oldfield Lane North
Greenford
Middlesex
UB6 0AZ

The Body Shop
The Body Shop International plc
Watersmead
Little Hampton
West Sussex
BN17 6LS

The National Lottery
Camelot Group plc
Tolpits Lane
Watford
Hertfordshire
WD1 8RN

The Sun
News International Newspapers plc
1 Virginia Street
London
E98 1XY

Timberland
Timberland UK Ltd
River Park Avenue
Staines
Middlesex
TW18 3EN

Virgin
Virgin Management Ltd
120 Campden Hill Road
London
W8 7AR

Virgin Atlantic
Virgin Atlantic Airways Ltd
Crawley Business Quarter
Manor Royal
Crawley
West Sussex
RH10 2NU

Vodafone
Vodafone Group Services Ltd
The Courtyard
2-4 London Road
Newbury, Berkshire
RG14 1JX

Wall's
Kerry Foods Limited
Thorpe Lea Manor
Thorpe Lea Road
Egham
Surrey
TW20 8HY

© Infratest Burke

Research

**Research conducted by
Infratest Burke, September 1998**

The Power of Superbrands

Powerful brands represent the heartbeat of successful businesses; be they products or services or even football clubs. Everyday companies deliver value through their brands, and successful companies deliver exceptional value through Superbrands.

Infratest Burke set out to explore the complex relationships that consumers have with their brands. This report provides some further insights into the complex issues of brand loyalty, brand values, brand recognition and the brands that defined the close of the Millennium in Britain.

Methology and Sample

Infratest Burke interviewed a nationally representative sample of 869 adults 18+.

Interviews were conducted face-to-face in 30 cities across Britain in the first week of September 1998. Sample composition was as follows:

SEX:
Male   50%
Female   50%

AGE:
18-34   39%
35-54   38%
55+   23%

SOCIAL GRADE:
ABC1   44%
C2DE   56%

Respondents were assigned into three groups to evaluate the different issues of brand loyalty, values, recognition and durability.

Brand Loyalty: Some Conclusions

The strength of a consumer's relationship to a brand is perhaps best reflected by their degree of loyalty to it. Such loyalty is evident in various aspects of purchasing behaviour; not merely the intention to continue purchasing, but also, for example, reactions to the brand's absence in-store and loyalty under price pressure. Consumers were questioned about six grocery categories: mineral water, crisps, chocolate wafers, ice cream, baked beans and digestive biscuits.

Perhaps the ultimate measure is how Superbrand loyalty holds up under price competition. Consumers were asked how much Own Label would need to reduce price to get them to brand switch. Between 40-60% of respondents, depending on category claimed they wouldn't switch at any price. Of those who might be prepared to switch, on average, respondents would need Own Label to cut their prices in half to generate a change in behaviour. Against such a background, it's hardly surprising that retailers are investing as much into building brand values for their own brand, as in developing price cutting strategies. When it comes to Superbrands it seems a case of if you can't beat them, join them.

In four of the six categories a single

BRAND LOYALTY: ICE CREAM

BRANDS BOUGHT IN THE LAST 6 MONTHS

	TOTAL
BASE: ALL	(134)
	%
SUPERMARKET'S OWN BRAND	38
WALL'S BLUE RIBBON	25
HÄAGEN DAZS	16
NONE	30

FUTURE BUYING HABITS

	HÄAGEN DAZS	WALL'S	OWN LABEL
BASE: ALL BUYING PAST 6 MONTHS	(22)	(34)	(51)
	%	%	%
ALWAYS BUY THIS BRAND, UNLIKELY TO BUY ANYTHING ELSE	46	35	18
MIGHT CARRY ON WITH THIS BRAND, MIGHT START BUYING SOMETHING ELSE	50	59	80
UNLIKELY TO BUY THIS BRAND MUCH IN THE FUTURE	-	3	2
DON'T KNOW	4	3	-

REACTION IF BRAND UNAVAILABLE

	HÄAGEN DAZS	WALL'S	OWN LABEL
BASE: ALL BUYING PAST 6 MONTHS	(22)	(34)	(51)
	%	%	%
ABSOLUTELY FURIOUS	-	-	2
REALLY ANNOYED	5	-	2
A LITTLE IRRITATED	18	12	12
SLIGHTLY PUT OUT	36	24	41
WOULDN'T CARE AT ALL	41	65	43

ACTION IF BRAND UNAVAILABLE

	HÄAGEN DAZS	WALL'S	OWN LABEL
BASE: ALL BUYING PAST 6 MONTHS	(22)	(34)	(51)
	%	%	%
BUY ANOTHER BRAND	46	82	71
WOULDN'T BUY CATEGORY AT ALL THAT DAY	14	3	26
WOULD GO SOMEWHERE ELSE TO GET THE BRAND	41	12	4

BRAND LOYALTY: BAKED BEANS

BRANDS BOUGHT IN THE LAST 6 MONTHS

	TOTAL
BASE: ALL	(134)
	%
HEINZ	54
SUPERMARKET'S OWN BRAND	40
HP	14
CROSSE & BLACKWELL	5
NONE	12

FUTURE BUYING HABITS

	HEINZ	HP	OWN LABEL
BASE: ALL BUYING PAST 6 MONTHS	(72)	(19)	(54)
	%	%	%
ALWAYS BUY THIS BRAND, UNLIKELY TO BUY ANYTHING ELSE	63	37	33
MIGHT CARRY ON WITH THIS BRAND, MIGHT START BUYING SOMETHING ELSE	38	63	67
UNLIKELY TO BUY THIS BRAND MUCH IN THE FUTURE	-	-	-

REACTION IF BRAND UNAVAILABLE

	HEINZ	HP	OWN LABEL
BASE: ALL BUYING PAST 6 MONTHS	(72)	(19)	(54)
	%	%	%
ABSOLUTELY FURIOUS	3	-	-
REALLY ANNOYED	8	5	4
A LITTLE IRRITATED	17	21	2
SLIGHTLY PUT OUT	31	26	33
WOULDN'T CARE AT ALL	42	47	61

ACTION IF BRAND UNAVAILABLE

	HEINZ	HP	OWN LABEL
BASE: ALL BUYING PAST 6 MONTHS	(72)	(19)	(54)
	%	%	%
BUY ANOTHER BRAND	50	74	74
WOULDN'T BUY CATEGORY AT ALL THAT DAY	28	5	13
WOULD GO SOMEWHERE ELSE TO GET THE BRAND	22	21	13

BRAND LOYALTY: DIGESTIVE BISCUITS

BRANDS BOUGHT IN THE LAST 6 MONTHS

	TOTAL
BASE: ALL	(134)
	%
McVITIE'S	59
SUPERMARKET'S OWN BRAND	32
HOVIS	5
BURTON'S	2

FUTURE BUYING HABITS

	McVITIE'S	OWN LABEL
BASE: ALL BUYING PAST 6 MONTHS	(79)	(43)
	%	%
ALWAYS BUY THIS BRAND AND, UNLIKELY TO BUY ANYTHING ELSE	40	33
MIGHT CARRY ON WITH THIS BRAND, MIGHT START BUYING SOMETHING ELSE	60	65
UNLIKELY TO BUY THIS BRAND MUCH IN THE FUTURE	-	-

REACTION IF BRAND UNAVAILABLE

	McVITIE'S	OWN LABEL
BASE: ALL BUYING PAST 6 MONTHS	(79)	(43)
	%	%
ABSOLUTELY FURIOUS	4	2
REALLY ANNOYED	4	2
A LITTLE IRRITATED	13	2
SLIGHTLY PUT OUT	32	30
WOULDN'T CARE AT ALL	48	61

ACTION IF BRAND UNAVAILABLE

	McVITIE'S	OWN LABEL
BASE: ALL BUYING PAST 6 MONTHS	(79)	(43)
	%	%
BUY ANOTHER BRAND	58	65
WOULDN'T BUY CATEGORY AT ALL THAT DAY	24	26
WOULD GO SOMEWHERE ELSE TO GET THE BRAND	18	7

BRAND LOYALTY: CRISPS

BRANDS BOUGHT IN THE LAST 6 MONTHS

	TOTAL
BASE: ALL	(136)
	%
WALKERS	78
SUPERMARKET'S OWN BRAND	32
GOLDEN WONDER	24
KP	10
NONE	12

FUTURE BUYING HABITS

	WALKERS	GOLDEN WONDER	KP	OWN LABEL
BASE: ALL BUYING PAST 6 MONTHS	(103)	(32)	(13)	(43)
	%	%	%	%
ALWAYS BUY THIS BRAND, UNLIKELY				
TO BUY ANYTHING ELSE	40	22	8	21
MIGHT CARRY ON WITH THIS BRAND,				
MIGHT START BUYING SOMETHING ELSE	60	78	92	79
UNLIKELY TO BUY THIS BRAND MUCH				
IN THE FUTURE	-	-	-	-

REACTION IF BRAND UNAVAILABLE

	WALKERS	GOLDEN WONDER	KP	OWN LABEL
BASE: ALL BUYING PAST 6 MONTHS	(100)	(32)	(13)	(43)
	%	%	%	%
ABSOLUTELY FURIOUS	5	-	-	-
REALLY ANNOYED	8	3	-	5
A LITTLE IRRITATED	15	22	15	9
SLIGHTLY PUT OUT	33	31	23	33
WOULDN'T CARE AT ALL	40	44	62	54

ACTION IF BRAND UNAVAILABLE

	WALKERS	GOLDEN WONDER	KP	OWN LABEL
BASE: ALL BUYING PAST 6 MONTHS	(103)	(32)	(3)	(43)
	%	%	%	%
BUY ANOTHER BRAND	65	88	92	91
WOULDN'T BUY CATEGORY AT ALL				
THAT DAY	8	3	8	9
WOULD GO SOMEWHERE ELSE TO				
GET THE BRAND	27	9	-	-

BRAND LOYALTY: MINERAL WATER

BRANDS BOUGHT IN THE LAST 6 MONTHS

	TOTAL
BASE: ALL BUYING PAST 6 MONTHS	(136)
	%
HIGHLAND SPRING	31
SUPERMARKET'S OWN BRAND	18
BUXTON	17
PERRIER	14

FUTURE BUYING HABITS

	PERRIER	BUXTON	HIGHLAND SPRING	OWN LABEL
BASE: ALL BUYING PAST 6 MONTHS	(19)	(22)	(42)	(24)
	%	%	%	%
ALWAYS BUY THIS BRAND, UNLIKELY				
TO BUY ANYTHING ELSE	11	26	17	13
MIGHT CARRY ON WITH THIS BRAND,				
MIGHT START BUYING SOMETHING ELSE	89	70	81	87
UNLIKELY TO BUY THIS BRAND MUCH				
IN THE FUTURE	-	4	2	-

REACTION IF BRAND UNAVAILABLE

	PERRIER	BUXTON	HIGHLAND SPRING	OWN LABEL
BASE: ALL BUYING PAST 6 MONTHS	(19)	(22)	(42)	(24)
	%	%	%	%
ABSOLUTELY FURIOUS	-	-	-	-
REALLY ANNOYED	5	4	5	-
A LITTLE IRRITATED	11	9	5	4
SLIGHTLY PUT OUT	37	35	24	38
WOULDN'T CARE AT ALL	47	52	67	58

ACTION IF BRAND UNAVAILABLE

	PERRIER	BUXTON	HIGHLAND SPRING	OWN LABEL
BASE: ALL BUYING PAST 6 MONTHS	(19)	(22)	(42)	(24)
	%	%	%	%
BUY ANOTHER BRAND	68	78	83	71
WOULDN'T BUY CATEGORY AT				
ALL THAT DAY	5	9	7	21
WOULD GO SOMEWHERE ELSE TO				
GET THE BRAND	26	13	10	8

BRAND LOYALTY: CHOCOLATE WAFERS

BRANDS BOUGHT IN THE LAST 6 MONTHS

	TOTAL
BASE: ALL	(136)
	%
KIT KAT	70
TIME OUT	23
SUPERMARKET'S OWN BRAND	17
TUNNOCK'S	15
NONE	18

FUTURE BUYING HABITS

	KIT KAT	TIME OUT	TUNNOCKS	OWN LABEL
BASE: ALL BUYING PAST 6 MONTHS	(95)	(31)	(20)	(23)
	%	%	%	%
ALWAYS BUY THIS BRAND, UNLIKELY				
TO BUY ANYTHING ELSE	36	19	35	9
MIGHT CARRY ON WITH THIS BRAND,				
MIGHT START BUYING SOMETHING ELSE	62	81	65	87
UNLIKELY TO BUY THIS BRAND				
MUCH IN THE FUTURE	2	-	-	4

REACTION IF BRAND UNAVAILABLE

	KIT KAT	TIME OUT	TUNNOCKS	OWN LABEL
BASE: ALL BUYING PAST 6 MONTHS	(95)	(31)	(20)	(23)
	%	%	%	%
ABSOLUTELY FURIOUS	2	3	-	-
REALLY ANNOYED	3	3	5	4
A LITTLE IRRITATED	11	3	30	4
SLIGHTLY PUT OUT	31	39	25	7
WOULDN'T CARE AT ALL	54	52	40	74

ACTION IF BRAND UNAVAILABLE

	KIT KAT	TIME OUT	TUNNOCKS	OWN LABEL
BASE: ALL BUYING PAST 6 MONTHS	(95)	(31)	(20)	(23)
	%	%	%	%
BUY ANOTHER BRAND	62	71	70	74
WOULDN'T BUY CATEGORY AT ALL				
THAT DAY	15	19	10	22
WOULD GO SOMEWHERE ELSE TO				
GET THE BRAND	23	10	20	4

Superbrand dominates current purchasing; Walkers Crisps, Kit Kat, Heinz Baked Beans and McVitie's Digestives. Yet a brand can exhibit the characteristics of Superbrand loyalty without necessarily dominating purchasing. Häagen Dazs ice cream is a good example. As a premium brand it may not have the strongest penetration, but still creates strong feelings of loyalty among its buyer base.

While current purchasing delivers shareholder results today, what is the long-term prognosis? In five of the six categories considered, consumers provide a strong signal that they will stick to their Superbrand. In all these five categories the level of long-term Superbrand loyalty is significantly greater than for either

other brands or Own Label. The strongest response is for Heinz Baked Beans, where nearly two thirds of the current franchise claim they 'will always buy this brand' and are 'unlikely to buy anything else'.

Lack of availability of Superbrands can elicit strong feelings. On average, between 15 to 30% of consumers, depending on the category, claim they would either be irritated, angry or even furious if their Superbrand were not available in-store. Heinz Baked Beans and Walkers Crisps generate the most concern regarding absence. Five times as many consumers claim they would be upset if Heinz Baked Beans were not in stock than the Supermarket Own Label equivalent, while 5% of consumers claim they would be

absolutely furious if Walkers Crisps were unavailable. But how does this bad feeling translate into behaviour? A significant number of consumers claim they would rather do without or go hunting in another store, than opt for another brand. The strongest example of this is Häagen Dazs, where more than half the brand's buyers (55%) claim they would not make do with another brand. All the Superbrands evaluated perform better than either the tertiary brands or the Supermarket Own Label brands evaluated in the category. For a Superbrand owner the low likelihood of brand switching is strong protection in the battle to maintain high distribution; a vital pre-requisite for strong sales.

BRAND LOYALTY

PRICE REDUCTION REQUIRED OF OWN LABEL TO SWITCH FROM SUPERBRAND

	HÄAGEN DAZS	HEINZ	McVITIE'S	PERRIER	WALKERS	KIT KAT
BASE: ALL BUYING PAST 6 MONTHS	(22)	(72)	(79)	(19)	(103)	(95)
WOULDN'T SWITCH AT ANY PRICE (%)	41	60	41	32	42	34
MEAN PRICE CHANGE (PENCE)	77	14	27	37	13	11
TYPICAL OWN LABEL PRICE (PENCE)	200	23	55	59	19	20

BASE	LABOUR PARTY		ROYAL FAMILY		MARKS & SPENCER		VIRGIN		CONSERVATIVE PARTY		AMERICAN EXPRESS	
	1998	1996	1998	1996	1998	1996	1998	1996	1998	1996	1998	1996
Reliability	5.6	5.0	5.1	5.2	7.2	7.4	6.5	7.0	3.9	4.2	5.8	6.2
Trustworthy	5.4	5.0	5.2	5.2	7.3	7.5	6.6	7.1	3.7	4.0	6.0	6.4
Caring	5.5	5.3	4.7	5.5	6.5	7.0	6.1	6.7	3.7	3.7	5.3	5.9
Exciting	4.1	4.4	3.6	4.3	4.8	5.1	5.8	6.5	2.7	3.0	4.1	5.0
Modern/up to date	6.1	5.4	4.1	4.6	6.3	6.5	7.5	7.7	3.7	5.0	6.3	6.3
Irritating	5.5	5.4	5.6	5.9	3.4	4.0	3.3	3.7	6.8	6.9	4.3	4.1
Intelligent	6.1	5.5	5.4	5.6	6.8	6.9	7.4	7.3	4.7	5.4	6.4	6.2

(Mean Scores : 10 point scale)

SUPERBRAND VALUES

	LABOUR PARTY	ROYAL FAMILY	MARKS & SPENCER	VIRGIN	CONSERVATIVE PARTY	AMERICAN EXPRESS	HEINEKEN	MOTHERCARE	TAMPAX
BASE	148	148	148	148	148	148	148	148	148
Reliability	5.59	5.05	7.17	6.50	3.91	5.78	6.58	6.75	7.05
Trustworthy	5.36	5.18	7.25	6.56	3.74	6.03	6.30	7.01	7.01
Caring	5.49	4.74	6.52	6.14	3.68	5.29	5.24	7.07	6.40
Exciting	4.07	3.61	4.81	5.76	2.67	4.12	5.61	4.88	3.70
Modern/up to date	6.14	4.11	6.26	7.49	3.66	6.26	6.66	6.84	6.46
Irritating	5.47	5.61	3.40	3.26	6.80	4.25	3.66	3.30	4.16
Intelligent	6.12	5.41	6.83	7.41	4.73	6.43	6.26	6.79	6.25

	JEFFREY ARCHER	MONICA LEWINSKY	THE SPICE GIRLS	DR GEORGE CAREY	GLEN HODDLE	KEN LIVINGSTONE	PRESIDENT CLINTON
BASE	151	151	151	151	151	151	151
Reliability	5.00	3.27	4.01	6.65	5.33	5.27	4.03
Trustworthy	4.93	3.03	4.62	6.97	5.47	5.45	3.69
Caring	5.03	3.23	4.97	7.01	5.68	5.51	4.74
Exciting	3.53	3.31	5.05	3.08	3.71	3.79	4.36
Modern/up to date	4.72	5.73	8.30	4.24	5.79	5.01	6.43
Irritating	5.60	6.91	6.22	4.28	4.69	4.77	5.32
Intelligent	7.97	4.11	3.97	7.58	5.81	7.17	7.19

(Mean Scores : 10 point scale)

Brand Values: Some Conclusions

Consumers continue to rate their favourite brands much more strongly than either political parties or the Royal Family. A coalition government of Marks & Spencer, Mothercare and Virgin would knock even New Labour off its lofty pedestal. Mothercare joins Marks & Spencer as having the strongest brand values. While Marks & Spencer is seen as the most trustworthy and reliable, Mothercare is, not surprisingly, seen as most caring.

The Superbrands examined are successful in projecting their core brand values:

Marks & Spencer:
    Reliable, trustworthy, intelligent
Mothercare:
    Caring, trustworthy, modern and up-to-date
Virgin:
    Exciting, modern and up-to-date, intelligent
Tampax:
    Reliable, trustworthy, caring
Heineken:
    Exciting, modern and up-to-date
Amex:
    Intelligent, modern and up-to-date, trustworthy

As a brand, New Labour is clearly head and shoulders above the Conservative party. It is also the 'brand', including the Superbrands, that has shown the greatest improvement in perceived brand values since the last evaluation in 1996. While significant improvement in presentation has clearly improved brand image, can the same be said for its shift to the centre? Interestingly, Ken Livingstone, a hero of the hard left, scores higher for being trustworthy, caring and intelligent.

For the Tories the picture is increasingly grim, with their brand value profile appearing even worse than in 1996. The greatest decline is in perceptions of being modern and up-to-date. But perhaps there is at least some consolation for William Hague in the knowledge that his party is seen as more trustworthy than Bill Clinton and less irritating than Monica Lewinsky. Although they are also seen as less intelligent than Glen Hoddle!

One year on from the death of Diana Princess of Wales, 'the Firm' are still struggling to lift their image. An improved score from 1996 for trustworthiness will help to abate any lingering fears that the conspiracy theorists may be having an impact. However, perceptions of being caring still remain low. Having a better image profile than Jeffrey Archer is probably not much consolation, although being less irritating than the Spice Girls is a good start. But for the Royal Family the target image is perhaps that of George Carey, the Archbishop of Canterbury a 'brand' overflowing with caring, intelligence, trustworthiness and reliability.

Brand Recognition: Some Conclusions

Brand logos and symbols become part of the very personality of the brand. They are important visual cues to trigger brand imagery and values. For some Superbrands, such as the adidas three stripes, they pass into the realms of style iconography. In order to explore the power of such branding, twelve Superbrand logos were chosen and produced as visual symbols without the brand name. Consumers were asked if they recognised the symbols, and if they could name the brand they represented. As a point of reference what better logos of the New Labour government than the faces of its Cabinet Ministers? Twelve portraits were also shown to evaluate similar response.

More than half the sample claimed to recognise all twelve Superbrand logos, and can correctly name the brand they represented.

SUPERBRAND LOGO AWARENESS

	RECOGNISED	NAMED CORRECTLY
	%	%
McDONALD'S	95.0	89.3
BT	93.0	82.7
THE NATIONAL LOTTERY	89.3	82.3
MICHELIN	88.7	77.7
BMW	85.7	75.7
DIRECT LINE	85.3	73.7
FOSTER'S	79.3	62.0
AUDI	75.7	61.3
VISA	72.0	59.3
INTERFLORA	70.0	58.3
YELLOW PAGES	68.7	54.7
WILKINSON SWORD	55.0	46.3

CABINET MINISTERS AWARENESS

	RECOGNISED	NAMED CORRECTLY
	%	%
TONY BLAIR	98.7	93.3
ROBIN COOK	90.0	52.7
GORDON BROWN	70.3	39.0
MARGARET BECKETT	63.7	33.3
JACK STRAW	59.7	29.3
CLARE SHORT	58.7	28.0
FRANK DOBSON	43.0	17.3
GEORGE ROBERTSON	40.7	17.0
JACK CUNNINGHAM	40.0	13.7
DONALD DEWAR	39.3	11.0
ALISTAIR DARLING	32.3	8.3
ANN TAYLOR	26.7	8.0

Perhaps not surprisingly, the best-known logo was the golden arches of McDonald's, with nine in ten consumers able to correctly name the brand. High levels of identification were also evident for the National Lottery's hand (83%) and BT's piper (82%). The automotive industry also performed well, with strong identification of the yuppies favourite BMW logo (78%) and the ageing Michelin Man (76%).

As for New Labour, the cabinet clearly needs to pay some attention to its branding. Not surprisingly, Tony Blair achieved universal recognition; achieving the best name identification of all, including the Superbrands. Yet his colleagues in the Cabinet trail far behind in the identification stakes. The next highest is Robin Cook (53%); although whether his identification has more to do with the coverage of his private life in the tabloids than his work as Foreign Secretary is debatable. Limping home in third place (39%) is the Chancellor of the Exchequer, Gordon Brown. This means that all twelve Superbrands achieved higher levels of identification than did the Chancellor and the other nine members of the Cabinet included in the research.

That the public are more familiar with their favourite brands, than the men and women who lead them, says much about the power of Superbrands, and perhaps the quality of government. Some interesting inferences can perhaps be made. Does the fact that twice the number of consumers can identify the National Lottery than the Chancellor suggest they believe they have more chance of winning the jackpot than of him keeping us out of recession? More than five times as many know Direct Line than the new Social Security Secretary. Who do they trust more to look after them in difficult times? And more than four times as many correctly recognise the Michelin Man than Frank Dobson. Who would they prefer to run the Health Service? With five times as many recognising McDonald's than Jack Cunningham, he may be relieved to

leave the problems of BSE behind him.

Millennium Brands: Some Conclusions

With brands playing such a leading role in the lives of the British public, it seemed an appropriate time to ask what brands consumers felt should represent the close of the Millennium. Respondents were asked which brands they felt should be buried in a time capsule to represent Britain in the last ten years of the twentieth century. They were also asked which brands they felt people would still be buying in the year 2050.

The top twelve brands provide a fascinating reflection on the themes of Britain's daily life; aspiration, communication, food, drink, sport, fashion and money. While Camelot may receive some criticism in government circles, the impact of the National Lottery on British society cannot be denied. This most aspirational of brands was the leading choice for the time capsule.

With the vastly changed competitive environment for the telecommunications industry BT will no doubt be proud to be the second choice. And in 4th place the BBC reaffirms its position as the symbol of broadcasting in Britain.

The high-ticket strategy of global branding has been a clear success in Britain, as represented by McDonald's (3rd choice) and Coca-Cola (6th choice).

The massive investment in sport in recent years is best epitomised by the consumers' 5th choice: Manchester United - a football club that has now undoubtedly been transformed into a Superbrand. It is perhaps unsurprising that Sky wish to pay such a high price for such an important brand.

No self-respecting time capsule could be

without the most vital British product, a pair of Marks & Spencer knickers (7th choice). The top twelve list is completed by communication (Yellow Pages – 8th), booze (Bell's Whisky – 9th), money (Visa Card – 10th), food (Heinz – 11th) and leisure (adidas – 12th).

Superbrands Time Capsule buried at the entrance of the Business Design Centre, London